Lecture Notes in Artificial Intel

T0253658

Subseries of Lecture Notes in Computer Sci
Edited by J. G. Carbonell and J. Siekmann

Lecture Notes in Computer Science

Edited by G. Goos, J. Hartmanis, and J. van Leeuwen

Springer
Berlin
Heidelberg
New York
Barcelona
Hong Kong
London
Milan
Paris
Tokyo

Andrei Voronkov (Ed.)

Automated Deduction–CADE-18

18th International Conference on Automated Deduction
Copenhagen, Denmark, July 27-30, 2002
Proceedings

 Springer

Series Editors

Jaime G. Carbonell, Carnegie Mellon University, Pittsburgh, PA, USA
Jörg Siekmann, University of Saarland, Saarbrücken, Germany

Volume Editor

Andrei Voronkov
University of Manchester, Department of Computer Science
Oxford Rd, Manchester M13 9PL, UK
E-mail: voronkov@cs.man.ac.uk

Cataloging-in-Publication Data applied for

Die Deutsche Bibliothek - CIP-Einheitsaufnahme

Automated deduction : proceedings / CADE-18, 18th International Conference
on Automated Deduction, Copenhagen, Denmark, July 27 - 30, 2002. Andrei
Voronkov (ed.). - Berlin ; Heidelberg ; New York ; Barcelona ; Hong Kong ;
London ; Milan ; Paris ; Tokyo : Springer, 2002
   (Lecture notes in computer science ; Vol. 2392 : Lecture notes in
artificial intelligence)
   ISBN 3-540-43931-5

CR Subject Classification (1998): I.2.3, F.4.1. F.3, D.3

ISSN 0302-9743
ISBN 3-540-43931-5 Springer-Verlag Berlin Heidelberg New York

Springer-Verlag Berlin Heidelberg New York
a member of BertelsmannSpringer Science+Business Media GmbH

http://www.springer.de

© Springer-Verlag Berlin Heidelberg 2002
Printed in Germany

Typesetting: Camera-ready by author, data conversion by PTP-Berlin, Stefan Sossna e.K.
Printed on acid-free paper   SPIN: 10873510   06/3142   5 4 3 2 1 0

Preface
The First CADE in the Third Millennium

This volume contains the papers presented at the Eighteenth International Conference on Automated Deduction (CADE-18) held on July 27–30th, 2002, at the University of Copenhagen as part of the Federated Logic Conference (FLoC 2002). Despite a large number of deduction-related conferences springing into existence at the end of the last millennium, the CADE conferences continue to be the major forum for the presentation of new research in all aspects of automated deduction. CADE-18 was sponsored by the Association for Automated Reasoning, CADE Inc., the Department of Computer Science at Chalmers University, the Gesellschaft für Informatik, Safelogic AB, and the University of Koblenz-Landau.

There were 70 submissions, including 60 regular papers and 10 system descriptions. Each submission was reviewed by at least five program committee members and an electronic program committee meeting was held via the Internet. The committee decided to accept 27 regular papers and 9 system descriptions. One paper switched its category after refereeing, thus the total number of system descriptions in this volume is 10. In addition to the refereed papers, this volume contains an extended abstract of the CADE invited talk by Ian Horrocks, the joint CADE/CAV invited talk by Sharad Malik, and the joint CADE-TABLEAUX invited talk by Matthias Baaz. One more invited lecture was given by Daniel Jackson.

Not covered in these proceedings are several important CADE-18 events. Four workshops and three tutorials were offered. The automated theorem-proving system competition (CASC-18) was organized by Geoff Sutcliffe. The Herbrand award for distinguished contributions to automated deduction was presented to Mark Stickel, in recognition of his many important contributions to our discipline.

I would like to thank the many people who made CADE-18 possible. Having CADE as part of FLoC incurred an unusually large amount of work on conference chair Reiner Hähnle and the tutorial and workshop chair Mateja Jamnik. Their efficient work saved several weeks, if not months, of my time. I am also grateful to: the CADE-18 publicity chair Peter Baumgartner, the FLoC organizers Henning Makholm and Sebastian Skalberg, the CASC organizer Geoff Sutcliffe, my fellow CADE Trustees, and last, but by no means least to the members of the Computer Science Department at Manchester, in particular Sergio Tessaris, Konstantin Korovin, Daphne Tregear, and Adrian Cummings.

May 2002   Andrei Voronkov

Preface

The First CAiSE in the Third Millennium

Conference Organization

Chairs

Reiner Hähnle (conference chair)
Andrei Voronkov (program chair)
Mateja Jamnik (tutorial and workshop chair)
Peter Baumgartner (publicity chair)

Program Committee

Jürgen Avenhaus	Franz Baader
Leo Bachmair	David Basin
Peter Baumgartner	Christoph Benzmüller
Maria Paola Bonacina	Alan Bundy
Li Dafa	Anatoli Degtyarev
Gilles Dowek	Harald Ganzinger
Xiao-Shan Gao	Fausto Giunchiglia
Jean Goubault-Larrecq	John R. Harrison
Ryuzo Hasegawa	Tom Henzinger
Steffen Hoelldobler	Reiner Hähnle
Andrew Ireland	Mateja Jamnik
Deepak Kapur	Claude Kirchner
Christoph Kreitz	Kim Larsen
Alexander Leitsch	Maurizio Lenzerini
Alexander V. Lyaletski	Christopher Lynch
Zohar Manna	Ursula Martin
Fabio Massacci	William McCune
Tom Melham	Dale Miller
Ralf Moeller	Paliath Narendran
Ilkka Niemela	Robert Nieuwenhuis
Tobias Nipkow	Andreas Nonnengart
Leszek Pacholski	Lawrence C. Paulson
Frank Pfenning	David Plaisted
David J. Pym	Maarten de Rijke
John K. Slaney	Manfred Schmidt-Schauss
Peter H. Schmitt	Carsten Schürmann
Natarajan Shankar	Wayne Snyder
Geoff Sutcliffe	Moshe Vardi
Andrei Voronkov	Toby Walsh
Igor Walukiewicz	Christoph Weidenbach
Volker Weispfenning	

List of Referees

Wolfgang Ahrendt
Serge Autexier
Sebastian Bala
Kai Bruennler
Henry Chinaski
Ingo Dahn
Niklas Een
Amy Felty
Bertram Fronhoefer
Ulrich Furbach
Enrico Giunchiglia
Bernhard Gramlich
Thomas Hillenbrand
Jan Hladik
Tomi Janhunen
Kristofer Johannisson
Jaap Kamps
Felix Klaedtke
Michael Kohlhase
Miyuki Koshimura
Reinhold Letz
Rupak Majumdar
Maarten Marx
Oskar Miś
Wojciech Mostowski
Hans-Juergen Ohlbach
Jeff Pelletier
Silvio Ranise
Christophe Ringeissen
Georg Rock
Albert Rubio
Stefan Schlobach
Henny Sipma
Viorica Sofronie-Stokkermans
Lutz Strassburger
Cesare Tinelli
Valery Trifonov
Miroslav Velev
Uwe Waldmann
Claus-Peter Wirth
Hantao Zhang

Carlos Areces
Matthias Baaz
Stefan Berghofer
Marco Cadoli
Michael Colon
Eric Deplagne
Matt Fairtlough
Armin Fiedler
Hiroshi Fujita
Juergen Giesl
Isabelle Gnaedig
Keijo Heljanko
Pascal Hitzler
Ullrich Hustadt
Ranjit Jhala
Tommi Junttila
Emanuel Kieronski
Gerwin Klein
Boris Konev
Theodor Lettmann
Alexei Lisitsa
Matthias Mann
Andreas Meier
Marcin Młotkowski
Leonor Prensa Nieto
Sam Owre
Ganesh Ramesh
Julian Richardson
Jussi Rintanen
D.J. Rosenkrantz
Cesar Sanchez
Roberto Sebastiani
Rolf Socher
Frieder Stolzenburg
Armando Tacchella
Ashish Tiwari
Anni-Yasmin Turhan
Laurent Vigneron
Lida Wang
Ting Zhang

Table of Contents

Session 1. Description Logics and Semantic Web

Reasoning with Expressive Description Logics: Theory and Practice 1
Ian Horrocks

BDD-Based Decision Procedures for $\mathcal{K}$ 16
Guoqiang Pan, Ulrike Sattler, and Moshe Y. Vardi

Session 2. Proof-Carrying Code and Compiler Verification

Temporal Logic for Proof-Carrying Code 31
Andrew Bernard and Peter Lee

A Gradual Approach to a More Trustworthy, Yet Scalable,
Proof-Carrying Code 47
Robert R. Schneck and George C. Necula

Formal Verification of a Java Compiler in Isabelle 63
Martin Strecker

Session 3. Non-classical Logics

Embedding Lax Logic into Intuitionistic Logic 78
Uwe Egly

Combining Proof-Search and Counter-Model Construction for
Deciding Gödel-Dummett Logic 94
Dominique Larchey-Wendling

Connection-Based Proof Search in Propositional **BI** Logic 111
Didier Galmiche and Daniel Méry

Session 4. System Descriptions

DDDLIB: A Library for Solving Quantified Difference Inequalities 129
Jesper B. Møller

An LCF-Style Interface between HOL and First-Order Logic 134
Joe Hurd

System Description: The MathWeb Software Bus for Distributed
Mathematical Reasoning 139
Jürgen Zimmer and Michael Kohlhase

Proof Development with ΩMEGA 144
  Jörg Siekmann, Christoph Benzmüller, Vladimir Brezhnev,
  Lassaad Cheikhrouhou, Armin Fiedler, Andreas Franke,
  Helmut Horacek, Michael Kohlhase, Andreas Meier, Erica Melis,
  Markus Moschner, Immanuel Normann, Martin Pollet,
  Volker Sorge, Carsten Ullrich, Claus-Peter Wirth, and Jürgen Zimmer

LearnΩmatic: System Description 150
  Mateja Jamnik, Manfred Kerber, and Martin Pollet

HyLoRes 1.0: Direct Resolution for Hybrid Logics 156
  Carlos Areces and Juan Heguiabehere

Session 5. SAT

Testing Satisfiability of CNF Formulas by Computing a Stable Set
of Points 161
  Eugene Goldberg

A Note on Symmetry Heuristics in SEM 181
  Thierry Boy de la Tour

A SAT Based Approach for Solving Formulas over Boolean and
Linear Mathematical Propositions 195
  Gilles Audemard, Piergiorgio Bertoli, Alessandro Cimatti,
  Artur Kornilowicz, and Roberto Sebastiani

Session 6. Model Generation

Deductive Search for Errors in Free Data Type Specifications
Using Model Generation 211
  Wolfgang Ahrendt

Reasoning by Symmetry and Function Ordering in Finite Model
Generation 226
  Gilles Audemard and Belaid Benhamou

Algorithmic Aspects of Herbrand Models Represented by Ground
Atoms with Ground Equations 241
  Bernhard Gramlich and Reinhard Pichler

Session 7.

A New Clausal Class Decidable by Hyperresolution 260
  Lilia Georgieva, Ullrich Hustadt, and Renate A. Schmidt

Session 8. CASC

SPASS Version 2.0 275
*Christoph Weidenbach, Uwe Brahm, Thomas Hillenbrand, Enno Keen,
Christian Theobald, and Dalibor Topić*

System Description: GrAnDe 1.0 280
Stephan Schulz and Geoff Sutcliffe

The HR Program for Theorem Generation 285
Simon Colton

AutoBayes/CC – Combining Program Synthesis with Automatic Code
Certification – System Description – 290
Michael Whalen, Johann Schumann, and Bernd Fischer

CADE-CAV Invited Talk

The Quest for Efficient Boolean Satisfiability Solvers 295
Lintao Zhang and Sharad Malik

Session 9.

Recursive Path Orderings Can Be Context-Sensitive 314
Cristina Borralleras, Salvador Lucas, and Albert Rubio

Session 10. Combination of Decision Procedures

Shostak Light 332
Harald Ganzinger

Formal Verification of a Combination Decision Procedure 347
Jonathan Ford and Natarajan Shankar

Combining Multisets with Integers 363
Calogero G. Zarba

Session 11. Logical Frameworks

The Reflection Theorem: A Study in Meta-theoretic Reasoning 377
Lawrence C. Paulson

Faster Proof Checking in the Edinburgh Logical Framework 392
Aaron Stump and David L. Dill

Solving for Set Variables in Higher-Order Theorem Proving 408
Chad E. Brown

Session 12. Model Checking

The Complexity of the Graded μ-Calculus 423
Orna Kupferman, Ulrike Sattler, and Moshe Y. Vardi

Lazy Theorem Proving for Bounded Model Checking over Infinite
Domains 438
Leonardo de Moura, Harald Rueß, and Maria Sorea

Session 13. Equational Reasoning

Well-Foundedness Is Sufficient for Completeness of
Ordered Paramodulation 456
Miquel Bofill and Albert Rubio

Basic Syntactic Mutation 471
Christopher Lynch and Barbara Morawska

The Next WALDMEISTER Loop 486
Thomas Hillenbrand and Bernd Löchner

Session 14. Proof Theory

Focussing Proof-Net Construction as a Middleware Paradigm 501
Jean Marc Andreoli

Proof Analysis by Resolution 517
Matthias Baaz

Author Index

Author Index 533

Reasoning with Expressive Description Logics: Theory and Practice

Ian Horrocks

Department of Computer Science, University of Manchester
Oxford Road, Manchester M13 9PL, UK
horrocks@cs.man.ac.uk

Abstract. Description Logics are a family of class based knowledge representation formalisms characterised by the use of various constructors to build complex classes from simpler ones, and by an emphasis on the provision of sound, complete and (empirically) tractable reasoning services. They have a wide range of applications, but their use as ontology languages has been highlighted by the recent explosion of interest in the "Semantic Web", where ontologies are set to play a key role. DAML+OIL is a description logic based ontology language specifically designed for use on the web. The logical basis of the language means that reasoning services can be provided, both to support ontology design and to make DAML+OIL described web resources more accessible to automated processes.

1   Introduction

Description Logics (DLs) are a family of class (concept) based knowledge representation formalisms. They are characterised by the use of various constructors to build complex concepts from simpler ones, an emphasis on the decidability of key reasoning tasks, and by the provision of sound, complete and (empirically) tractable reasoning services.

Description logics have been used in a range of applications, e.g., configuration [43], and reasoning with database schemas and queries [15,13,37]. They are also widely used as a formal basis for ontology languages and to provide reasoning support for ontology design and deployment. This latter application has been highlighted by the recent explosion of interest in the "Semantic Web", where ontologies are set to play a key role [31].

The current web consists mainly of handwritten and machine generated HTML pages that are primarily intended for direct human processing (reading, browsing, form-filling, etc.). The aim of the so called Semantic Web is to make web resources (not just HTML pages, but a wide range of web accessible services) more readily accessible to automated processes by adding meta-data annotations that describe their content [7]. Ontologies will be used as a source of shared and precisely defined terms that can be used in such meta-data.

A. Voronkov (Ed.): CADE-18, LNAI 2392, pp. 1–15, 2002.

2 Ontologies and Ontology Languages

An ontology typically consists of a hierarchical description of important concepts (classes) in a domain, along with descriptions of the properties of each concept. The degree of formality employed in capturing these descriptions can be quite variable, ranging from natural language to logical formalisms, but increased formality and regularity clearly facilitates machine processing.

Examples of the use of ontologies on the Web could include:

– in e-commerce sites [40], where ontologies can facilitate machine-based communication between buyer and seller, enable vertical integration of markets (see, e.g., http://www.verticalnet.com/), and allow descriptions to be reused in different marketplaces;
– in search engines [41], where ontologies can help searching to go beyond the current keyword-based approach, and allow pages to be found that contain syntactically different, but semantically similar words/phrases (see, e.g., http://www.hotbot.com/);
– in web services [44], where ontologies can provide semantically richer service descriptions that can be more flexibly interpreted by intelligent agents.

2.1 Ontology Languages

The recognition of the key role that ontologies are likely to play in the future of the web has led to the extension of web markup languages in order to facilitate content description and the development of web based ontologies, e.g., XML Schema,[1] RDF[2] (Resource Description Framework), and RDF Schema [17]. RDF Schema (RDFS) in particular is recognisable as an ontology/knowledge representation language: it talks about classes and properties (binary relations), range and domain constraints (on properties), and subclass and subproperty (subsumption) relations.

RDFS is, however, a very primitive language (the above is an almost complete description of its functionality), and more expressive power would clearly be necessary/desirable in order to describe resources in sufficient detail. Moreover, such descriptions should be amenable to *automated reasoning* if they are to be used effectively by automated processes, e.g., to determine the semantic relationship between syntactically different terms.

A recognition of the limitations of RDFS led to the development of new web ontology languages, in particular OIL [20,21], a language developed by a group of (largely) European researchers, several of whom were members of the On-To-Knowledge consortium,[3] and DAML-ONT [26], a language developed in the DARPA Agent Markup Language (DAML) program.[4] These two languages were

---

[1] http://www.w3.org/XML/Schema/
[2] http://www.w3c.org/RDF/
[3] http://www.ontoknowledge.org/oil
[4] http://www.daml.org/

subsequently merged to produce DAML+OIL, which has recently been submitted to W3C,[5] and forms the basis of a proposed W3C web ontology language.[6]

2.2   DAML+OIL

DAML+OIL describes the structure of a domain in terms of *classes* and *properties*. A DAML+OIL ontology consists of a set of *axioms* that assert, e.g., subsumption relationships between classes or properties. Instances of classes (properties) are assumed to be RDF resources[7] (pairs of RDF resources). Asserting that a given resource (pair of resources) is an instance of a given DAML+OIL class (property) is left to RDF, a task for which it is well suited.

From a formal point of view, DAML+OIL can be seen to be equivalent to a very expressive description logic, with a DAML+OIL ontology corresponding to the Tbox, and RDF type and property assertions corresponding to the Abox. As in a DL, DAML+OIL classes can be names (URIs) or *expressions*, and a variety of *constructors* are provided for building class expressions, with the expressive power of the language being determined by the class (and property) constructors supported, and by the kinds of axiom supported.

Constructor	DL Syntax	Example
intersectionOf	$C_1 \sqcap \ldots \sqcap C_n$	Human $\sqcap$ Male
unionOf	$C_1 \sqcup \ldots \sqcup C_n$	Doctor $\sqcup$ Lawyer
complementOf	$\neg C$	$\neg$Male
oneOf	$\{x_1 \ldots x_n\}$	$\{$john, mary$\}$
toClass	$\forall P.C$	$\forall$hasChild.Doctor
hasClass	$\exists P.C$	$\exists$hasChild.Lawyer
hasValue	$\exists P.\{x\}$	$\exists$citizenOf.$\{$USA$\}$
minCardinalityQ	$\geqslant n P.C$	$\geqslant$2hasChild.Lawyer
maxCardinalityQ	$\leqslant n P.C$	$\leqslant$1hasChild.Male
cardinalityQ	$= n\, P.C$	$=1$ hasParent.Female

Fig. 1. DAML+OIL class constructors

Figure 1 summarises the constructors supported by DAML+OIL, where C (possibly subscripted) is a class, P is a property, x (possibly subscripted) is an individual and n is a non-negative integer. The standard DL syntax is used for compactness, as the RDF syntax is rather verbose. In the RDF syntax, for example, Human $\sqcap$ Male would be written as

---

[5] http://www.w3.org/Submission/2001/12/
[6] http://www.w3c.org/2001/sw/WebOnt/
[7] Everything describable by RDF is called a resource. A resource could be web accessible, e.g., a web page or part of a web page, but it could also be an object that is not directly accessible via the web, e.g., a person. Resources are named by URIs plus optional anchor ids. See http://www.w3.org/TR/1999/REC-rdf-syntax-19990222/ for more details.

```
<daml:Class>
  <daml:intersectionOf rdf:parseType="daml:collection">
    <daml:Class rdf:about="#Human"/>
    <daml:Class rdf:about="#Male"/>
  </daml:intersectionOf>
</daml:Class>
```

while $\geqslant$2hasChild.Lawyer would be written as

```
<daml:Restriction daml:minCardinalityQ="2">
  <daml:onProperty rdf:resource="#hasChild"/>
  <daml:hasClassQ rdf:resource="#Lawyer"/>
</daml:Restriction>
```

DAML+OIL also supports the use of XML Schema *datatypes* in class expressions. These can be so called primitive datatypes, such as strings, decimal or float, as well as more complex derived datatypes such as integer sub-ranges. Datatypes can be used instead of classes in toClass and hasClass constructs (e.g., hasClass age integer), and data values can be used in the hasValue construct (e.g., hasValue age (integer21)).

The meaning of the language is defined by a standard model-theoretic semantics.[8] The semantics is based on interpretations, where an interpretation consists of a domain of discourse and an interpretation function. The domain is divided into two disjoint sets, the "object domain" $\Delta_{\mathcal{O}}^{\mathcal{I}}$ and the "datatype domain" $\Delta_{D}^{\mathcal{I}}$. The interpretation function $\mathcal{I}$ maps classes into subsets of the object domain, individuals into elements of the object domain, datatypes into subsets of the datatype domain and data values into elements of the datatype domain. In addition, two disjoint sets of properties are distinguished: object properties and datatype properties. The interpretation function maps the former into subsets of $\Delta_{\mathcal{O}}^{\mathcal{I}} \times \Delta_{\mathcal{O}}^{\mathcal{I}}$ and the latter into subsets of $\Delta_{\mathcal{O}}^{\mathcal{I}} \times \Delta_{D}^{\mathcal{I}}$.

Figure 2 summarises the axioms supported by DAML+OIL, where C (possibly subscripted) is a class, P (possibly subscripted) is a property, P^- is the inverse of P, P^+ is the transitive closure of P, x (possibly subscripted) is an individual and $\top$ is an abbreviation for $A \sqcup \neg A$ for some class A. These axioms make it possible to assert subsumption or equivalence with respect to classes or properties, the disjointness of classes, the equivalence or non-equivalence of individuals, and various properties of properties.

A crucial feature of DAML+OIL is that subClassOf and sameClassAs axioms can be applied to arbitrary class expressions. This provides greatly increased expressive power with respect to standard frame-based languages where such axioms are invariably restricted to so called *definitions*, where the left hand side is an atomic name, there is only one such axiom per name, and there are no definitional cycles (the class on the right hand side of an axiom cannot refer, either directly or indirectly, to the class name on the left hand side).

---

[8] http://www.w3.org/TR/daml+oil-model

Axiom	DL Syntax	Example
subClassOf	$C_1 \sqsubseteq C_2$	Human $\sqsubseteq$ Animal $\sqcap$ Biped
sameClassAs	$C_1 \equiv C_2$	Man $\equiv$ Human $\sqcap$ Male
subPropertyOf	$P_1 \sqsubseteq P_2$	hasDaughter $\sqsubseteq$ hasChild
samePropertyAs	$P_1 \equiv P_2$	cost $\equiv$ price
disjointWith	$C_1 \sqsubseteq \neg C_2$	Male $\sqsubseteq \neg$Female
sameIndividualAs	$\{x_1\} \equiv \{x_2\}$	{President_Bush} $\equiv$ {G_W_Bush}
differentIndividualFrom	$\{x_1\} \sqsubseteq \neg\{x_2\}$	{john} $\sqsubseteq \neg${peter}
inverseOf	$P_1 \equiv P_2^-$	hasChild $\equiv$ hasParent$^-$
transitiveProperty	$P^+ \sqsubseteq P$	ancestor$^+ \sqsubseteq$ ancestor
uniqueProperty	$\top \sqsubseteq \leqslant 1P$	$\top \sqsubseteq \leqslant 1$hasMother
unambiguousProperty	$\top \sqsubseteq \leqslant 1P^-$	$\top \sqsubseteq \leqslant 1$isMotherOf$^-$

Fig. 2. DAML+OIL axioms

A consequence of the expressive power of DAML+OIL is that all of the class and individual axioms, as well as the uniqueProperty and unambiguousProperty axioms, can be reduced to subClassOf and sameClassAs axioms (as can be seen from the DL syntax). In fact sameClassAs could also be reduced to subClassOf, as a sameClassAs axiom $C \equiv D$ is trivially equivalent to a pair of subClassOf axioms $C \sqsubseteq D$ and $D \sqsubseteq C$. Moreover, the distinction between Tbox and Abox breaks down, as Abox assertions can be expressed using Tbox axioms. E.g., an assertion that an individual x is an instance of a class C (written $x \in C$) can be expressed as $\{x\} \sqsubseteq C$, and an assertion that a tuple $\langle x, y \rangle$ is an instance of a property P (written $\langle x, y \rangle \in P$) can be expressed as $\{x\} \sqsubseteq \exists P.\{y\}$.

As far as property axioms are concerned, it is possible to assert that a given property is unique (functional), unambiguous (inverse functional) or transitive (i.e., that its interpretation must be closed under composition). It is also possible to assign a name to the inverse of a property, thus allowing inverse properties to be used in class expressions. Transitive properties are preferred over transitive closure as this has been shown to facilitate the design of (efficient) algorithms [34].

As usual, an interpretation is called a model of an ontology $\mathcal{O}$ if it satisfies each of the axioms in $\mathcal{O}$. An ontology $\mathcal{O}$ is said to be satisfiable if it has a model, and a class C is said to be satisfiable w.r.t. $\mathcal{O}$ if there is a model of $\mathcal{O}$ in which the interpretation of C is non-empty.

3 Reasoning with Ontologies

As we have seen, DAML+OIL is equivalent to a very expressive description logic. More precisely, DAML+OIL is equivalent to the $\mathcal{SHIQ}$ DL [33] with the addition of existentially defined classes (i.e., the oneOf constructor) and *datatypes* (often called concrete domains in DLs [3]).[9] This equivalence allows DAML+OIL to exploit the considerable existing body of description logic research, e.g.:

- to define the semantics of the language and to understand its formal properties, in particular the decidability and complexity of key inference problems [19];
- as a source of sound and complete algorithms and optimised implementation techniques for deciding key inference problems [33,32];
- to use implemented DL systems in order to provide (partial) reasoning support [28,47,24].

Key inference problems (w.r.t. an ontology $\mathcal{O}$) include:

Consistency. Check if the knowledge is meaningful.
- Is $\mathcal{O}$ consistent? i.e., does there exists a model $\mathcal{I}$ of $\mathcal{O}$?
- Is C consistent? i.e., $C^{\mathcal{I}} \neq \emptyset$ in some model $\mathcal{I}$ of $\mathcal{O}$?

Subsumption. Structure knowledge and compute a taxonomy.
- $C \sqsubseteq D$ w.r.t. $\mathcal{O}$? i.e., does $C^{\mathcal{I}} \subseteq D^{\mathcal{I}}$ hold in all models $\mathcal{I}$ of $\mathcal{O}$?

Equivalence. Check if two classes denote same set of instances.
- $C \equiv D$ w.r.t. $\mathcal{O}$? i.e., does $C^{\mathcal{I}} = D^{\mathcal{I}}$ hold in all models $\mathcal{I}$ of $\mathcal{O}$?

Instantiation. Check if individual is an instance of a class.
- $i \in C$ w.r.t. $\mathcal{O}$? i.e., does $i^{\mathcal{I}} \in C^{\mathcal{I}}$ hold in all models $\mathcal{I}$ of $\mathcal{O}$?

Retrieval. Retrieve the set of individuals that instantiate a class.
- Retrieve the set of i s.t. $i \in C$ w.r.t. $\mathcal{O}$?

In DAML+OIL, all of the above problems are recucible to class consistency (satisfiability) w.r.t. an ontology. In particular, $C \sqsubseteq D$ w.r.t. $\mathcal{O}$ (written $C \sqsubseteq_{\mathcal{O}} D$) iff $D \sqcap \neg C$ is not consistent w.r.t. $\mathcal{O}$, and $i \in C$ w.r.t. $\mathcal{O}$ (written $i \in_{\mathcal{O}} C$) iff $\{i\} \sqcap \neg C$ is not consistent w.r.t. $\mathcal{O}$. Moreover, by using a rewriting technique called *internalisation*, satisfiability w.r.t. an ontology can be reduced to the problem of determining the satisfiability of a single concept [33].

Reasoning can be useful at many stages during the design, maintenance and deployment of ontologies.

- Reasoning can be used to support ontology design and to improve the quality of the resulting ontology. For example, class consistency and subsumption reasoning can be used to check for logically inconsistent classes and (possibly unexpected) implicit subsumption relationships [6]. This kind of support has been shown to be particularly important with large ontologies, which are often built and maintained over a long period by multiple authors. Other so-called "non-standard" reasoning tasks, such as approximation, matching, unification and computing least common subsumers could also be used to support "bottom up" ontology design, i.e., the identification and description of relevant classes from sets of example instances [11].

---

[9] Note that the DL oneOf constructor corresponds to the use of *nominals* in hybrid logics [8].

- Like information integration [16], ontology integration can also be supported by reasoning. For example, integration can be performed using inter-ontology assertions specifying relationships between classes and properties, with reasoning being used to compute the integrated hierarchy and to highlight any problems/inconsistencies. Unlike some other integration techniques (e.g., name reconciliation [42]), this method has the advantage of being non-intrusive with respect to the original ontologies.
- Reasoning with respect to deployed ontologies will enhance the power of "intelligent agents", allowing them to determine if a set of facts is consistent w.r.t. an ontology, to identify individuals that are implicitly members of a given class etc. A suitable service ontology could, for example, allow an agent seeking secure services to identify a service requiring a userid and password as a possible candidate.

3.1   Reasoning with Datatypes

DAML+OIL supports the use of XML Schema datatypes in class expressions. This is facilitated by maintaining a clean separation between instances of "object" classes (defined using the ontology language) and instances of datatypes (defined using the XML Schema type system). In particular, as mentioned in Section 2.2, it is assumed that that the domain of interpretation of object classes is disjoint from the domain of interpretation of datatypes, so that an instance of an object class (e.g., the individual "Italy") can never have the same interpretation as a value of a datatype (e.g., the integer 5). The set of object properties (which map individuals to individuals) is also assumed to be disjoint from the set of datatype properties (which map individuals to datatype values).

The disjointness of object and datatype domains and properties was motivated by both philosophical and pragmatic considerations:

- Datatypes are considered to be already sufficiently structured by the built-in predicates, and it is, therefore, not appropriate to form new classes of datatype values using the ontology language [27].
- The simplicity and compactness of the ontology language are not compromised: even enumerating all the XML Schema datatypes would add greatly to its complexity, while adding a logical theory for each datatype, even if it were possible, would lead to a language of monumental proportions.
- The semantic integrity of the language is not compromised—defining theories for all the XML Schema datatypes would be difficult or impossible without extending the language in directions whose semantics may be difficult to capture within the existing framework.
- The "implementability" of the language is not compromised—a *hybrid* reasoner can easily be implemented by combining a reasoner for the "object" language with one capable of deciding satisfiability questions with respect to conjunctions of (possibly negated) datatypes [32].

From a theoretical point of view, this design means that the ontology language can specify constraints on data values, but as data values can never be instances of object classes they cannot apply additional constraints to elements of the object domain. This allows the type system to be extended without having any impact on the ontology language, and vice versa. Similarly, the formal properties of hybrid reasoners are determined by those of the two components; in particular, the combined reasoner will be sound and complete if both components are sound and complete.

From a practical point of view, DAML+OIL implementations will probably choose to support only a subset of the available XML Schema datatypes (sound and complete reasoning may not be possible for all datatypes). For supported data types, they can either implement their own type checker/validater or rely on some external component. The job of a type checker/validater is simply to take zero or more (possibly negated) data values and one or more (possibly negated) datatypes, and determine if there exists an element of $\Delta_D^{\mathcal{I}}$ that is (not) equal to the interpretation of every one of the (negated) data values and (not) in the interpretation of every one of the (negated) data types.

3.2   Practical Reasoning Services

The concept satisfiability problem for expressive DLs is known to be of high complexity: at least PSPACE-complete, and rising to EXPTIME-complete for very expressive logics such as $\mathcal{SHIQ}$ [18]. Fortunately, the pathological cases that lead to such high *worst case* complexity are rather artificial, and rarely occur in practice [45,25,50,29]; by employing a wide range of optimisations, it has proved possible to implement systems that exhibit good *typical case* performance, and work well in realistic applications [2,12,29,24,48].

Most modern DL systems use *tableaux* algorithms to test concept satisfiability. These algorithms work by trying to construct (a tree representation of) a model of the concept, starting from an individual instance. Tableaux expansion rules decompose concept expressions, add new individuals (e.g., as required by $\exists R.C$ terms),[10] and merge existing individuals (e.g., as reqired by $\leqslant nR.C$ terms). Nondeterminism (e.g., resulting from the expansion of disjunctions) is dealt with by searching the various possible models. For an unsatisfiable concept, all possible expansions will lead to the discovery of an obvious contradiction known as a *clash* (e.g., an individual that must be an instance of both A and $\neg A$ for some concept A); for a satisfiable concept, a complete and clash-free model will be constructed [34].

Tableaux algorithms have many advantages. It is relatively easy to design provably sound, complete and terminating algorithms, and the basic technique can be extended to deal with a wide range of class and role constructors. Moreover, although many algorithms have a higher worst case complexity than that of the underlying problem, they are usually quite efficient at solving the relatively easy problems that are typical of realistic applications.

---

[10] Cycle detection techniques known as *blocking* may be required in order to guarantee termination.

Even in realistic applications, however, problems can occur that are much too hard to be solved by naive implementations of theoretical algorithms. Modern DL systems, therefore, include a wide range of optimisation techniques, the use of which has been shown to improve typical case performance by several orders of magnitude [30]. Key techniques include lazy unfolding, absorption and dependency directed backtracking.

Lazy Unfolding. In an ontology, or DL Tbox, large and complex concepts are seldom described monolithically, but are built up from a hierarchy of named concepts whose descriptions are less complex. The tableaux algorithm can take advantage of this structure by trying to find contradictions between concept names before adding expressions derived from Tbox axioms. This strategy is known as *lazy unfolding* [1,29].

The benefits of lazy unfolding can be maximised by lexically *normalising* and *naming* all concept expressions and, recursively, their sub-expressions. An expression C is normalised by rewriting it in a standard form (e.g., disjunctions are rewritten as negated conjunctions); it is named by substituting it with a new concept name A, and adding an axiom $A \equiv C$ to the Tbox. The normalisation step allows lexically equivalent expressions to be recognised and identically named, and can even detect syntactically "obvious" satisfiability and unsatisfiability.

Absorption. Not all axioms are amenable to lazy unfolding. In particular, so called *general concept incusions* (GCIs), axioms of the form $C \sqsubseteq D$ where C is non-atomic, must be dealt with by explicitly making every individual in the model an instance of $D \sqcup \neg C$. Large numbers of GCIs result in a very high degree of non-determinism and catastrophic performance degradation [29].

Absorption is another rewriting technique that tries to reduce the number of GCIs in the Tbox by absorbing them into axioms of the form $A \sqsubseteq C$, where A is a concept name. The basic idea is that an axiom of the form $A \sqcap D \sqsubseteq D'$ can be rewritten as $A \sqsubseteq D' \sqcup \neg D$ and absorbed into an existing $A \sqsubseteq C$ axiom to give $A \sqsubseteq C \sqcap (D' \sqcup \neg D)$ [38]. Although the disjunction is still present, lazy unfolding ensures that it is only applied to individuals that are already known to be instances of A.

Dependency Directed Backtracking. Inherent unsatisfiability concealed in sub-expressions can lead to large amounts of unproductive backtracking search known as thrashing. For example, expanding the expression $(C_1 \sqcup D_1) \sqcap \ldots \sqcap (C_n \sqcup D_n) \sqcap \exists R.(A \sqcap B) \sqcap \forall R.\neg A$ could lead to the fruitless exploration of 2^n possible expansions of $(C_1 \sqcup D_1) \sqcap \ldots \sqcap (C_n \sqcup D_n)$ before the inherent unsatisfiability of $\exists R.(A \sqcap B) \sqcap \forall R.\neg A$ is discovered. This problem is addressed by adapting a form of dependency directed backtracking called *backjumping*, which has been used in solving constraint satisfiability problems [5].

Backjumping works by labeling concepts with a dependency set indicating the non-deterministic expansion choices on which they depend. When a clash is discovered, the dependency sets of the clashing concepts can be used to identify the most recent non-deterministic expansion where an alternative choice might alleviate the cause of the clash. The algorithm can then jump back over intervening non-deterministic expansions *without* exploring any alternative choices. Similar techinques have been used in first order theorem provers, e.g., the "proof condensation" technique employed in the HARP theorem prover [46].

4   Research Challenges for DAML+OIL

Class consistency/subsumption reasoning in DAML+OIL is decidable (as it is contained in the C2 fragment of first order logic [22]), but many challenges remain for implementors of "practical" reasoning systems.

4.1   Individuals

The OIL language was designed so that it could be mapped to the $\mathcal{SHIQ}$ DL, thereby providing a implementation path for reasoning services. This mapping is made possible by a very weak treatment of individuals occurring in existentially defined classes, which are treated not as single elements but as the extensions of corresponding primitive classes. This is a well known technique for avoiding the reasoning problems that arise with existentially defined classes (such as classes defined using DAML+OIL's oneOf constructor) and is also used, e.g., in the CLASSIC knowledge representation system [9].

In contrast, DAML+OIL gives a standard semantics to such individuals, i.e., they are interpreted as single elements in the domain of discourse. This treatment of individuals is very powerful, and justifies intuitive inferences that would not be valid for OIL, e.g., that persons all of whose countries of residence are (oneOf) Italy are kinds of person that have at most one country of residence:

$$\text{Person} \sqcap \forall \text{residence}.\{\text{Italy}\} \sqsubseteq \leqslant 1\text{residence}$$

Unfortunately, the combination of such individuals with inverse properties is so powerful that it pushes the worst case complexity of the class consistency problem from ExpTime (for $\mathcal{SHIQ}$ /OIL) to NExpTime [32]. No "practical" decision procedure is currently known for this logic, and there is no implemented system that can provide sound and complete reasoning for the whole DAML+OIL language. In the absence of inverse properties, however, a tableaux algorithm has been devised [32], and in the absence of individuals (in existentially defined classes), DAML+OIL can exploit implemented DL systems via a translation into $\mathcal{SHIQ}$ (extended with datatypes) similar to the one used by OIL. It would, of course, also be possible to translate DAML+OIL ontologies into $\mathcal{SHIQ}$ using OIL's weak treatment of individuals,[11] but in this case reasoning with individuals would not be sound and complete with respect to the semantics of the language.

---

[11] This approach is taken by some existing applications, e.g., OilEd [6].

4.2   Scalability

Even without the **oneOf** constructor, class consistency reasoning is still a hard problem. Moreover, web ontologies can be expected to grow very large, and with deployed ontologies it may also be desirable to reason w.r.t. a large numbers of class/property instances.

There is good evidence of empirical tractability and scalability for implemented DL systems [29,23], but this is mostly w.r.t. logics that do not include inverse properties (e.g., $\mathcal{SHF}$ [12]). Adding inverse properties makes practical implementations more problematical as several important optimisation techniques become much less effective. Work is required in order to develop more highly optimised implementations supporting inverse properties, and to demonstrate that they can scale as well as $\mathcal{SHF}$ implementations. It is also unclear if existing techniques will be able to cope with large numbers of class/property instances [35].

Finally, it is an inevitable consequence of the high worst case complexity that some problems will be intractable, even for highly optimised implementations. It is conjectured that such problems rarely arise in practice, but the evidence for this conjecture is drawn from a relatively small number of applications, and it remains to be seen if a much wider range of web application domains will demonstrate similar characteristics.

4.3   New Reasoning Tasks

So far we have mainly discussed class consistency/subsumption reasoning, but this may not be the only reasoning problem that is of interest. Other tasks could include querying, explanation, and non-standard inferences such as approximation, matching, unification and computing least common subsumers. Querying in particular may be important in Semantic Web applications. Some work on query languages for description logics has already been done [49,14,36], and work is underway on the design of a DAML+OIL query language, but the computational properties of such a language, either theoretical or empirical, have yet to be determined.

Explanation may also be an important problem, e.g., to help an ontology designer to rectify problems identified by reasoning support, or to explain to a user why an application behaved in an unexpected manner, and as discussed in Section 3, non-standard inferences could be important, e.g., in "bottom-up" ontology design. Non-standard inferences are the subject of ongoing research [4, 11,39,10], but it is not clear if they can be extended to deal with languages as expressive as DAML+OIL.

5   Summary

Description Logics are a family of class based knowledge representation formalisms characterised by the use of various constructors to build complex classes

---

[12] $\mathcal{SHF}$ is equivalent to $\mathcal{SHIQ}$ without inverse properties and with only functional properties instead of qualified number restrictions [33].

from simpler ones, and by an emphasis on the provision of sound, complete and (empirically) tractable reasoning services. They have been used in a wide range of applications, but perhaps most notably (at least in recent times) in providing a formal basis and reasoning services for (web) ontology languages such as DAML+OIL.

What of the future? The development of the Semantic Web, and of web ontology languages, presents many opportunities and challenges for description logic research. Even for less expressive languages, acceptable performance can only be achieved by using a wide range of optimisation techniques. A "practical" (satisfiability/subsumption) algorithm for the full DAML+OIL language has yet to be developed, and it is not yet clear that sound and complete reasoners will be able to provide adequate performance for typical web applications. Finding answers to these questions is the subject of ongoing investigations.

Acknowledgements. I would like to acknowledge the contribution of all those involved in the development of DAML-ONT, OIL and DAML+OIL, amongst whom Dieter Fensel, Frank van Harmelen, Deborah McGuinness and Peter F. Patel-Schneider deserve particular mention. Important contributions were also made by members of Franz Baader's group at TU Dresden, in particular Ulrike Sattler and Stephan Tobies, and by members of the Information Management Group at the University of Manchester, in particular Sean Bechhofer, Carole Goble and Sergio Tessaris.

References

1. F. Baader, E. Franconi, B. Hollunder, B. Nebel, and H.-J. Profitlich. An empirical analysis of optimization techniques for terminological representation systems, or: Making KRIS get a move on. In *Proc. of the 3rd Int. Conf. on the Principles of Knowledge Representation and Reasoning (KR'92)*, pages 270–281, 1992.
2. F. Baader, E. Franconi, B. Hollunder, B. Nebel, and H.-J. Profitlich. An empirical analysis of optimization techniques for terminological representation systems or: Making KRIS get a move on. *Applied Artificial Intelligence. Special Issue on Knowledge Base Management*, 4:109–132, 1994.
3. F. Baader and P. Hanschke. A schema for integrating concrete domains into concept languages. In *Proc. of the 12th Int. Joint Conf. on Artificial Intelligence (IJCAI'91)*, pages 452–457, 1991.
4. F. Baader, R. Küsters, A. Borgida, and D. L. McGuinness. Matching in description logics. *J. of Logic and Computation*, 9(3):411–447, 1999.
5. A. B. Baker. *Intelligent Backtracking on Constraint Satisfaction Problems: Experimental and Theoretical Results*. PhD thesis, University of Oregon, 1995.
6. S. Bechhofer, I. Horrocks, C. Goble, and R. Stevens. OilEd: a reason-able ontology editor for the semantic web. In *Proc. of the Joint German/Austrian Conf. on Artificial Intelligence (KI 2001)*, number 2174 in Lecture Notes in Artificial Intelligence, pages 396–408. Springer-Verlag, 2001.
7. T. Berners-Lee. *Weaving the Web*. Harpur, San Francisco, 1999.
8. P. Blackburn and J. Seligman. Hybrid languages. *J. of Logic, Language and Information*, 4:251–272, 1995.

9. A. Borgida and P. F. Patel-Schneider. A semantics and complete algorithm for subsumption in the CLASSIC description logic. *J. of Artificial Intelligence Research*, 1:277–308, 1994.

10. S. Brandt, R. Küsters, and A.-Y. Turhan. Approximation and difference in description logics. In *Proc. of the 8th Int. Conf. on Principles of Knowledge Representation and Reasoning (KR'2002)*, pages 203–214, 2002.

11. S. Brandt and A.-Y. Turhan. Using non-standard inferences in description logics — what does it buy me? In *Proc. of KI-2001 Workshop on Applications of Description Logics (KIDLWS'01)*, volume 44 of *CEUR (http://ceur-ws.org/)*, 2001.

12. P. Bresciani, E. Franconi, and S. Tessaris. Implementing and testing expressive description logics: Preliminary report. In *Proc. of the 1995 Description Logic Workshop (DL'95)*, pages 131–139, 1995.

13. D. Calvanese, G. De Giacomo, and M. Lenzerini. On the decidability of query containment under constraints. In *Proc. of the 17th ACM SIGACT SIGMOD SIGART Symp. on Principles of Database Systems (PODS'98)*, pages 149–158, 1998.

14. D. Calvanese, G. De Giacomo, and M. Lenzerini. Answering queries using views in description logics. In *Proc. of the 1999 Description Logic Workshop (DL'99)*, pages 9–13. CEUR Electronic Workshop Proceedings, http://ceur-ws.org/Vol-22/, 1999.

15. D. Calvanese, G. De Giacomo, M. Lenzerini, D. Nardi, and R. Rosati. Description logic framework for information integration. In *Proc. of the 6th Int. Conf. on Principles of Knowledge Representation and Reasoning (KR'98)*, pages 2–13, 1998.

16. D. Calvanese, G. De Giacomo, M. Lenzerini, D. Nardi, and R. Rosati. Information integration: Conceptual modeling and reasoning support. In *Proc. of the 6th Int. Conf. on Cooperative Information Systems (CoopIS'98)*, pages 280–291, 1998.

17. S. Decker, F. van Harmelen, J. Broekstra, M. Erdmann, D. Fensel, I. Horrocks, M. Klein, and S. Melnik. The semantic web: The roles of XML and RDF. *IEEE Internet Computing*, 4(5), 2000.

18. F. M. Donini, M. Lenzerini, D. Nardi, and W. Nutt. The complexity of concept languages. In J. Allen, R. Fikes, and E. Sandewall, editors, *Proc. of the 2nd Int. Conf. on the Principles of Knowledge Representation and Reasoning (KR'91)*, pages 151–162. Morgan Kaufmann, Los Altos, 1991.

19. F. M. Donini, M. Lenzerini, D. Nardi, and W. Nutt. The complexity of concept languages. *Information and Computation*, 134:1–58, 1997.

20. D. Fensel, I. Horrocks, F. van Harmelen, S. Decker, M. Erdmann, and M. Klein. OIL in a nutshell. In R. Dieng, editor, *Proc. of the 12th European Workshop on Knowledge Acquisition, Modeling, and Management (EKAW'00)*, number 1937 in Lecture Notes in Artificial Intelligence, pages 1–16. Springer-Verlag, 2000.

21. D. Fensel, F. van Harmelen, I. Horrocks, D. L. McGuinness, and P. F. Patel-Schneider. OIL: An ontology infrastructure for the semantic web. *IEEE Intelligent Systems*, 16(2):38–45, 2001.

22. E. Grädel, M. Otto, and E. Rosen. Two-variable logic with counting is decidable. In *Proc. of the 12th IEEE Symp. on Logic in Computer Science (LICS'97)*, pages 306–317. IEEE Computer Society Press, 1997.

23. V. Haarslev and R. Möller. High performance reasoning with very large knowledge bases: A practical case study. In *Proc. of the 17th Int. Joint Conf. on Artificial Intelligence (IJCAI 2001)*, 2001.

24. V. Haarslev and R. Möller. RACER system description. In *Proc. of the Int. Joint Conf. on Automated Reasoning (IJCAR 2001)*, 2001.

25. J. Heinsohn, D. Kudenko, B. Nebel, and H.-J. Profitlich. An empirical analysis of terminological representation systems. *Artificial Intelligence*, 68:367–397, 1994.
26. J. Hendler and D. L. McGuinness. The darpa agent markup language". *IEEE Intelligent Systems*, 15(6):67–73, 2000.
27. B. Hollunder and F. Baader. Qualifying number restrictions in concept languages. In *Proc. of the 2nd Int. Conf. on the Principles of Knowledge Representation and Reasoning (KR'91)*, pages 335–346, 1991.
28. I. Horrocks. The FaCT system. In H. de Swart, editor, *Proc. of the 2nd Int. Conf. on Analytic Tableaux and Related Methods (TABLEAUX'98)*, volume 1397 of *Lecture Notes in Artificial Intelligence*, pages 307–312. Springer-Verlag, 1998.
29. I. Horrocks. Using an expressive description logic: FaCT or fiction? In *Proc. of the 6th Int. Conf. on Principles of Knowledge Representation and Reasoning (KR'98)*, pages 636–647, 1998.
30. I. Horrocks and P. F. Patel-Schneider. Optimizing description logic subsumption. *J. of Logic and Computation*, 9(3):267–293, 1999.
31. I. Horrocks, P. F. Patel-Schneider, and F. van Harmelen. Reviewing the design of DAML+OIL: An ontology language for the semantic web. In *Proc. of the 18th Nat. Conf. on Artificial Intelligence (AAAI 2002)*, 2002. To appear.
32. I. Horrocks and U. Sattler. Ontology reasoning in the $\mathcal{SHOQ}$(D) description logic. In *Proc. of the 17th Int. Joint Conf. on Artificial Intelligence (IJCAI 2001)*. Morgan Kaufmann, Los Altos, 2001.
33. I. Horrocks, U. Sattler, and S. Tobies. Practical reasoning for expressive description logics. In H. Ganzinger, D. McAllester, and A. Voronkov, editors, *Proc. of the 6th Int. Conf. on Logic for Programming and Automated Reasoning (LPAR'99)*, number 1705 in Lecture Notes in Artificial Intelligence, pages 161–180. Springer-Verlag, 1999.
34. I. Horrocks, U. Sattler, and S. Tobies. Practical reasoning for very expressive description logics. *J. of the Interest Group in Pure and Applied Logic*, 8(3):239–264, 2000.
35. I. Horrocks, U. Sattler, and S. Tobies. Reasoning with individuals for the description logic $\mathcal{SHIQ}$. In *Proc. of the 17th Int. Conf. on Automated Deduction (CADE 2000)*, number 1831 in Lecture Notes in Artificial Intelligence, pages 482–496. Springer-Verlag, 2000.
36. I. Horrocks and S. Tessaris. A conjunctive query language for description logic aboxes. In *Proc. of the 17th Nat. Conf. on Artificial Intelligence (AAAI 2000)*, pages 399–404, 2000.
37. I. Horrocks, S. Tessaris, U. Sattler, and S. Tobies. How to decide query containment under constraints using a description logic. In *Proc. of the 7th Int. Workshop on Knowledge Representation meets Databases (KRDB 2000)*. CEUR (http://ceur-ws.org/), 2000.
38. I. Horrocks and S. Tobies. Reasoning with axioms: Theory and practice. In *Proc. of the 7th Int. Conf. on Principles of Knowledge Representation and Reasoning (KR'2000)*, pages 285–296, 2000.
39. R. Küsters. *Non-Standard Inferences in Description Logics*, volume 2100 of *Lecture Notes in Artificial Intelligence*. Springer Verlag, 2001.
40. D. L. McGuinness. Ontological issues for knowledge-enhanced search. In *Proc. of FOIS*, Frontiers in Artificial Intelligence and Applications. IOS-press, 1998.
41. D. L. McGuinness. Ontologies for electronic commerce. In *Proc. of the AAAI '99 Artificial Intelligence for Electronic Commerce Workshop*, 1999.

42. D. L. McGuinness, R. Fikes, J. Rice, and S. Wilder. The Chimaera ontology environment. In *Proc. of the 17th Nat. Conf. on Artificial Intelligence (AAAI 2000)*, 2000.
43. D. L. McGuinness and J. R. Wright. An industrial strength description logic-based configuration platform. *IEEE Intelligent Systems*, pages 69–77, 1998.
44. S. McIlraith, T. Son, and H. Zeng. Semantic web services. *IEEE Intelligent Systems*, 16(2):46–53, March/April 2001.
45. B. Nebel. Terminological reasoning is inherently intractable. *Artificial Intelligence*, 43:235–249, 1990.
46. F. Oppacher and E. Suen. HARP: A tableau-based theorem prover. *J. of Automated Reasoning*, 4:69–100, 1988.
47. P. F. Patel-Schneider. DLP system description. In *Proc. of the 1998 Description Logic Workshop (DL'98)*, pages 87–89. CEUR Electronic Workshop Proceedings, http://ceur-ws.org/Vol-11/, 1998.
48. P. F. Patel-Schneider. DLP. In *Proc. of the 1999 Description Logic Workshop (DL'99)*, pages 9–13. CEUR Electronic Workshop Proceedings, http://ceur-ws.org/Vol-22/, 1999.
49. M.-C. Rousset. Backward reasoning in ABoxes for query answering. In *Proc. of the 1999 Description Logic Workshop (DL'99)*, pages 18–22. CEUR Electronic Workshop Proceedings, http://ceur-ws.org/Vol-22/, 1999.
50. P.-H. Speel, F. van Raalte, P. E. van der Vet, and N. J. I. Mars. Runtime and memory usage performance of description logics. In G. Ellis, R. A. Levinson, A. Fall, and V. Dahl, editors, *Knowledge Retrieval, Use and Storage for Efficiency: Proc. of the 1st Int. KRUSE Symposium*, pages 13–27, 1995.

BDD-Based Decision Procedures for $\mathcal{K}$

Guoqiang Pan[1⋆], Ulrike Sattler[2], and Moshe Y. Vardi[1⋆]

[1] Department of Computer Science, Rice University, Houston, TX
gqpan,vardi@cs.rice.edu
[2] Institut für Theoretische Informatik, TU Dresden, Germany
sattler@tcs.inf.tu-dresden.de

Abstract. We describe BDD-based decision procedures for $\mathcal{K}$. Our approach is inspired by the automata-theoretic approach, but we avoid explicit automata construction. Our algorithms compute the fixpoint of a set of types, which are sets of formulas satisfying some consistency conditions. We use BDDs to represent and manipulate such sets. Experimental results show that our algorithms are competitive with contemporary methods using benchmarks from TANCS 98 and TANCS 2000.

1 Introduction

In the last 20 years, modal logic has been applied to numerous areas of computer science, including artificial intelligence, program verification, hardware verification, database theory, and distributed computing. In this paper, we restrict our attention to the smallest normal modal logic $\mathcal{K}$ [14] and describe a new approach to decide the satisfiability of formulas in this logic. Since modal logic extends propositional logic, the study in modal satisfiability is deeply connected with that of propositional satisfiability. In the past, a variety of approaches to propositional satisfiability have been combined with various approaches to handle modal connectives and implemented successfully. For example, a tableau based decision procedure for $\mathcal{K}$ is presented in [18,14]. It is built on top of the propositional tableau construction procedure by forming a fully expanded propositional tableau and generating successor nodes "on demand". A similar method uses the Davis-Longemann-Loveland method as the propositional engine by treating all modal subformulas as propositions and, when a satisfying assignment is found, checking modal subformulas for the legality of this assignment [13,27]. Another approach to modal satisfiability, the inverse calculus for $\mathcal{K}$ [30] can be seen as a modalized version of propositional resolution. Non-propositional based methods take a different approach to the problem. It is well known that formulas in $\mathcal{K}$ can be translated to first order formulas via standard translation [28,21]. Recently, it has been shown that, by encoding the modal depth infomation into the translation, a first-order theorem prover can be used efficiently for deciding modal satisfiability [2]. The latter approach works nicely with a resolution-based first-order theorem prover, which can be used as a decision procedure for modal satisfiability by using appropriate resolution strategies [16]. Other approaches for modal

---

⋆ Supported in part by NSF grants CCR-9700061, CCR-9988322, IIS-9908435, IIS-9978135, and EIA-0086264, by BSF grant 9800096, and by a grant from the Intel Corporation.

A. Voronkov (Ed.): CADE-18, LNAI 2392, pp. 16–30, 2002.

satisfiability such as mosaics, type elimination, or automata-theoretic approaches are well-suited for proving exact upper complexity bounds, but are rarely used in actual implementations [5,14,29].

The algorithms presented here are inspired by the automata-theoretic approach for logics with the tree-model property [29]. In that approach one proceeds in two steps. First, an input formula is translated to a tree automaton that accepts all tree models of the formula. Second, the automaton is tested for non-emptiness, i.e., does it accept some tree. In our approach, we combine the two steps and apply the non-emptiness test without explicitly constructing the automaton. As was pointed out in [3], the inverse method described in [30] can also be viewed as an implementation of the automata-theoretic approach that avoids an explicit automata construction.

The logic $\mathcal{K}$ is simple enough for the automaton non-emptiness test to consist of a single fixpoint computation. This computation starts with a set of states and then repeatedly applies a monotone operator until a fixpoint is reached. In the automata that correspond to formulas, each state is a *type*, i.e., a set of formulas satisfying some consistency conditions. The algorithms presented here all start from some set of types, and then repeatedly apply a monotone operator until a fixpoint is reached: either they start with the set of *all* types and remove those types with "possibilities" $\Diamond \varphi$ for which no "witness" can be found, or they start with the set of types having no possibilities $\Diamond \varphi$, and add those types whose possibilities are witnessed by a type in the set. The two approaches, top-down and bottom-up, corresponds to the two ways in which non-emptiness can be tested for automata for $\mathcal{K}$: via a greatest fixpoint computation for automata on infinite trees or via a least fixpoint computation for automata on finite trees. The bottom-up approach is closely related to the inverse method described in [30], while the top-down approach is reminiscent of the "type-elimination" method developed for Propositional Dynamic Logic in [23].

The key idea underlying our implementation is that of representing sets of types and operating on them symbolically. Our implementation uses Binary Decision Diagrams (BDDs) [6]: BDDs are a compact representation of propositional formulas, and commonly used as a compact representation of states. One of their advantages is that they come with efficient operations for certain manipulations on BDDs. This paper consists of a viability study for our approach. To see whether it yields competitive algorithms, we used existing benchmarks of modal formulas, TANCS 98 [15] and TANCS 2000 [19], and we compared our algorithms with *SAT [27] and DLP [22]. A straightforward implementation of our approach did not yield a competitive algorithm, but an optimized implementation did yield a competitive algorithm (see Fig. 1) indicating the viability of our approach.

The paper is organized as follows. After introducing the modal logic $\mathcal{K}$ in Section 2, we present our algorithms and discuss how they can be implemented using BDD packages in Section 3. In Section 4, we discuss three optimizations that we applied, and compare in Section 5 the performance of our implementations with *SAT on formulas from TANCS 98 and TANCS 2000.

2 Preliminaries

In this section, we introduce the syntax and semantics of the modal logic $\mathcal{K}$, as well as types and how they can be used to encode a Kripke structure.

The set of $\mathcal{K}$ formulas is constructed from a set of propositional variables $\Phi = \{q_1, q_2, \dots\}$, and is the least set containing Φ and being closed under Boolean operators $\wedge$ and $\neg$ and the unary modality $\square$. As usual, we use other Boolean operators as abbreviations, and $\Diamond \varphi$ as an abbreviation for $\neg \square \neg \varphi$. The set of propositional variables used in a formula φ is denoted $AP(\varphi)$.

A formula in $\mathcal{K}$ is interpreted in a Kripke structure $K = \langle V, W, R, L \rangle$, where V is a set (containing Φ) of propositions, W is a set of possible worlds, $R \subseteq W \times W$ is the accessibility relation on worlds, and $L : W \to V \to \{0,1\}$ a labeling function for each state. The notion of a formula φ being *satisfied* in a world w of a Kripke structure K (written as $K, w \models q$) is inductively defined as follows:

- $K, w \models q$ for $q \in \Phi$ iff $L(w)(q) = 1$
- $K, w \models \varphi \wedge \psi$ iff $K, w \models \varphi$ and $K, w \models \psi$
- $K, w \models \neg \varphi$ iff $K, w \not\models \varphi$
- $K, w \models \square \varphi$ iff, for all w', if $(w, w') \in R$, then $K, w' \models \varphi$

The abbreviated operators can be defined as follows:

- $K, w \models \varphi \vee \psi$ iff $K, w \models \varphi$ or $K, w \models \psi$
- $K, w \models \Diamond \varphi$ iff there exists w' with $(w, w') \in R$ and $K, w' \models \varphi$.

A formula ψ is *satisfiable* if there exist K, w with $K, w \models \psi$. In this case, K is called a *model* of ψ.

To simplify the following considerations, we restrict our attention to formulas in a certain normal form. A formula ψ of $\mathcal{K}$ is said to be in *box normal form* (BNF) if all its subformulas are of the form $\varphi \wedge \varphi'$, $\varphi \vee \varphi'$, $\square \varphi$, $\neg \square \varphi$, q, or $\neg q$ where $q \in AP(\psi)$. All $\mathcal{K}$ formulas can be obviously converted into BNF by pushing negation inwards and, if not stated otherwise, we assume all formulas to be in BNF. The *closure* of a formula $cl(\psi)$ is defined as the smallest set such that, for all subformula φ of ψ, if φ is not $\neg \varphi'$, then $\{\varphi, \neg \varphi\} \subseteq cl(\psi)$.

Our algorithms will work on *types*, i.e., sets of (sub)formulas that are consistent w.r.t. the Boolean operators, and where (negated) box formulas are treated as atoms. A set $a \subseteq cl(\psi)$ of formulas is called a ψ-*type* (or simply a type if ψ is clear from the context) if it satisfies the following conditions:

- If $\varphi = \neg \varphi'$, then $\varphi \in a$ iff $\varphi' \notin a$.
- If $\varphi = \varphi' \wedge \varphi''$, then $\varphi \in a$ iff $\varphi' \in a$ and $\varphi'' \in a$.
- If $\varphi = \varphi' \vee \varphi''$, then $\varphi \in a$ iff $\varphi' \in a$ or $\varphi'' \in a$.

For a set A of types, we define the relation $\Delta \subseteq A \times A$ as follows:

$$\Delta(a, a') \text{ iff for all } \square \varphi' \in a, \text{ we have } \varphi' \in a'.$$

Given a set $A \subseteq 2^{cl(\psi)}$ of types, we can construct a Kripke structure K_A using the relation Δ as follows: $K_A = \langle AP(\psi), A, \Delta, L \rangle$ with $L(a)(q) = 1$ iff $q \in a$. Then we almost have that, for all $\varphi \in cl(\psi)$:

$$K, a \models \varphi \text{ iff } \varphi \in a. \tag{$*$}$$

The only reason why $(*)$ might be false is due to formulas of the form $\neg\Box\varphi \in a$: it might be the case that $\varphi \in b$ for all b with $\Delta(a, b)$, i.e., a negated box formula might not be "witnessed".

3 Our Algorithms

The two algorithms presented here take a certain "initial" set of types and apply repeatedly a monotone operator to it. If this application reaches a fixpoint, we can show that it yields a set of types where the above construction yields indeed a Kripke structure that satisfies the condition $(*)$, i.e., all negated box formulas are indeed "witnessed" by some $b \in A$. This Kripke structure is then a model of ψ iff $\psi \in a$ for some $a \in A$.

The first algorithm follows a "top-down" approach, i.e., it starts with the set $A \subseteq 2^{\text{cl}(\psi)}$ of all types, and the monotone operator removes those types containing negated box formulas which are not witnessed in the current set of types. Dually, the second, "bottom-up", approach starts with the set of types that do not contain negated box formulas, and then adds those types whose negated box formulas are witnessed in the current set of types.

Both algorithms follow the following scheme, in which X, X' are sets of types:

$X = Initial(\psi)$
repeat
    $X' \Leftarrow X$
    $X \Leftarrow Iterate(X')$
until $X = X'$
if exists $x \in X$ such that $\psi \in x$ **then return** "ψ is satisfiable"
else return "ψ is not satisfiable"
endif

Since this algorithm works on a fixed set of types and uses a monotone operator $Iterate(\cdot)$, it obviously terminates. In fact, we can show that it will terminate in $d + 1$ iterations, where d is the modal nesting depth of the input formula ψ. It remains to define $Initial(\psi)$ and $Iterate(\cdot)$.

3.1 Top-Down Approach

The top-down approach is closely related to the type elimination approach which is, in general, used for more complex modal logics, see, e.g., Section 6 of [14]. For the algorithm pursuing the top-down approach, the functions $Initial(\psi)$ and $Iterate(\cdot)$ are defined as follows:

- $Initial(\psi)$ is the set of *all* ψ-types.
- $Iterate(A) := A \setminus \text{bad}(A)$, where $\text{bad}(A)$ are the types in A that contain unwitnessed negated box formulas. More precisely,

$$\text{bad}(A) := \{a \in A \mid \text{there exists } \neg\Box\varphi \in a \text{ and, for all } b \in A \text{ with } \Delta(a, b),$$
$$\text{we have } \varphi \in b\}.$$

3.2   Bottom-Up Approach

As mentioned above, the algorithm pursuing the bottom-up approach starts with a small set of types (i.e., those without negated box formulas), and repeatedly adds those types whose negated box formulas are witnessed in the current set. More precisely, for the bottom-up approach, the functions $Initial(\psi)$ and $Iterate(\cdot)$ are defined as follows:

– $Initial(\psi)$ is the set of all those types that do not require any witnesses, i.e., they do not contain any negated box formula or, equivalently, they contain all positive box formulas in $cl(\psi)$:

$$Initial(\psi) := \{a \subseteq cl(\psi) \mid a \text{ is a type and } \Box\varphi \in a \text{ for each } \Box\varphi \in cl(\psi)\}.$$

– $Iterate(A) := A \cup supp(A)$, where $supp(A)$ is the set of those types whose negated box formulas are witnessed by types in A. More precisely,

$$supp(A) := \{a \subseteq cl(\psi) \mid a \text{ is a type and for all } \neg\Box\varphi \in a, \text{ there exists } b \in A \text{ with } \neg\varphi \in b \text{ and } \Delta(a,b)\}.$$

We say that a type in $supp(A)$ is *witnessed* by a type in A.

3.3   Implementations

We use Binary Decision Diagrams (BDDs) [6,1] to represent sets of types. BDDs, or more precisely, Reduced Ordered Binary Decision Diagrams (ROBDDs), are obtained from binary decision trees by following a fixed variable splitting order and by merging nodes that have identical child-diagrams. BDDs provide a canonical form of representation for Boolean functions. Experience has shown that BDDs provide a very compact representation for very large Boolean functions. Consequently, over the last decade, BDDs have had a dramatic impact in the areas of synthesis, testing, and verification of digital systems [4,7]

In this section, we describe how our two algorithms are implemented using BDDs. First, we define a *bit-vector representation* of types. Since types are complete in the sense that either a subformula or its negation must belong to a type, it is possible for a formula and its negation to be represented using a single BDD variable.

The representation of types $a \subseteq cl(\psi)$ as bit vectors is defined as follows: Since both formulas and their negations are in $cl(\psi)$, we define

$$cl_+(\psi) = \{\varphi_i \in cl(\psi) \mid \varphi_i \text{ is not of the form } \neg\varphi'\},$$
$$cl_-(\psi) = \{\neg\varphi \mid \varphi \in cl_+(\psi)\},$$

and use m for $|cl_+(\psi)| = |cl(\psi)|/2$. For $cl_+(\psi) = \{\varphi_1, \ldots \varphi_m\}$, a vector $a = \langle a_1, \ldots, a_m \rangle \in \{0,1\}^m$ represents a set[1] $a \subseteq cl(\psi)$ with of $\varphi_i \in a$ iff $a_i = 1$. A set of such bit vectors can obviously be represented using a BDD with m variables. It remains to "filter out" those bit vectors that represent types.

We define $Consistent_\psi$ as the characteristic predicate for types: $Consistent_\psi(a) = \bigwedge_{1 \le i \le m} Cons_i(a)$, where $Cons_i(a)$ is defined as follows:

---

[1] Please note that this set is not necessarily a type.

- if φ_i is neither of the form $\varphi' \wedge \varphi''$ nor $\varphi' \vee \varphi''$, then $Cons_i(\boldsymbol{a}) = \boldsymbol{1}$,
- if $\varphi_i = \varphi' \wedge \varphi''$, then $Cons_i(\boldsymbol{a}) = (a_i \wedge a' \wedge a'') \vee (\neg a_i \wedge (\neg a' \vee \neg a''))$,
- if $\varphi_i = \varphi' \vee \varphi''$, then $Cons_i(\boldsymbol{a}) = (a_i \wedge (a' \vee a'')) \vee (\neg a_i \wedge \neg a' \wedge \neg a'')$,

where $a' = a_\ell$ if $\varphi' = \varphi_\ell \in \mathsf{cl}_+(\psi)$, and $a' = \neg a_\ell$ if $\varphi' = \neg\varphi_\ell$ for $\varphi_\ell \in \mathsf{cl}_+(\psi)$ (and analogously for a''). From this, the implementation of $Initial$ is fairly straight forward: For the top-down algorithm,

$$Initial(\psi) := \{\boldsymbol{a} \in \{0,1\}^m \mid Consistent_\psi(\boldsymbol{a})\},$$

and for the bottom-up algorithm,

$$Initial(\psi) := \{\boldsymbol{a} \in \{0,1\}^m \mid Consistent_\psi(\boldsymbol{a}) \wedge \bigwedge_{\varphi_i = \Box\varphi'} a_i = 1\}.$$

In the following, we do not distinguish between a type and its representation as a bit vector $\boldsymbol{a}$. Next, to specify $\mathsf{bad}(\cdot)$ and $\mathsf{supp}(\cdot)$, we define auxiliary predicates:

- $\Diamond_{1,i}(\boldsymbol{x})$ is read as "$\boldsymbol{x}$ needs a witness for a diamond operator at position i" and is true iff $x_i = 0$ and $\varphi_i = \Box\varphi'$.
- $\Diamond_{2,i}(\boldsymbol{y})$ is read as "$\boldsymbol{y}$ is a witness for a negated box formula at position i" and is true iff $\varphi_i = \Box\varphi_j$ and $y_j = 0$ or $\varphi_i = \Box\neg\varphi_j$ and $y_j = 1$.
- $\Box_{1,i}(\boldsymbol{x})$ is read as "$\boldsymbol{x}$ requires support for a box operator at position i" and is true iff $x_i = 1$ and $\varphi_i = \Box\varphi'$.
- $\Box_{2,i}(\boldsymbol{y})$ is read as "$\boldsymbol{y}$ provides support for a box operator at position i" and is true iff $\varphi_i = \Box\varphi_j$ and $y_j = 1$ or $\varphi_i = \Box\neg\varphi_j$ and $y_j = 0$.

For a set A of types, we construct the BDD that represents the "maximal" accessibility relation Δ, i.e., a relation that includes all those pairs $(\boldsymbol{x}, \boldsymbol{y})$ such that $\boldsymbol{y}$ supports all of $\boldsymbol{x}$'s box formulas. For types $\boldsymbol{x}, \boldsymbol{y} \in \{0,1\}^m$, we define

$$\Delta(\boldsymbol{x}, \boldsymbol{y}) = \bigwedge_{1 \le i \le m} (\Box_{1,i}(\boldsymbol{x}) \to \Box_{2,i}(\boldsymbol{y})).$$

Given a set A of types, we write the corresponding characteristic function as χ_A. Both the top-down and the bottom-up algorithm can be defined using the predicates χ_A, Δ, $\Diamond_{j,i}$, and $\Box_{j,i}$.

The predicate bad is true on those types that contain a negated box formula $\varphi_i = \neg\Box\varphi_j$ that is not witnessed in the current set of types. The corresponding predicate for bit vectors χ_{bad_i} can then be written as follows:

$$\chi_{\mathsf{bad}_i(X)}(\boldsymbol{x}) = \Diamond_{1,i}(\boldsymbol{x}) \wedge \forall \boldsymbol{y} : ((\chi_X(\boldsymbol{y}) \wedge \Delta(\boldsymbol{x}, \boldsymbol{y})) \to \neg\Diamond_{2,i}(\boldsymbol{y})),$$

and thus $\mathsf{bad}(X)$ can be written as $\chi_{\mathsf{bad}(X)}(\boldsymbol{x}) = \bigvee_{1 \le i \le m} \chi_{\mathsf{bad}_i(X)}(\boldsymbol{x})$.

In our implementation, we compute the characteristic function $\chi_{\overline{\mathsf{bad}_i(X)}}$ of the complement of each $\mathsf{bad}_i(X)$ and use it in the implementation of the top-down and the bottom-up algorithm. It is easy to see that $\chi_{\overline{\mathsf{bad}_i(X)}}$ is equivalent to

$$\Diamond_{1,i}(\boldsymbol{x}) \to \exists \boldsymbol{y} : (\chi_X(\boldsymbol{y}) \wedge \Delta(x, y) \wedge \Diamond_{2,i}(\boldsymbol{y})).$$

For the top-down algorithm, the $Iterate$ function can be written as:

$$\chi_{X \setminus \mathsf{bad}(X)} := \chi_X(\boldsymbol{x}) \wedge \bigwedge_{1 \leq i \leq m} (\chi_{\overline{\mathsf{bad}_i(X)}}(\boldsymbol{x}))$$

For the bottom-up algorithm, additionally, we must take care of only adding those bit vectors representing types, and so the $Iterate$ function can be implemented as:

$$\chi_{X \cup \mathsf{supp}(X)} := \chi_X(\boldsymbol{x}) \vee (\chi_{Consistent_\psi}(\boldsymbol{x}) \wedge \bigwedge_{1 \leq i \leq m} (\chi_{\overline{\mathsf{bad}_i(X)}}(\boldsymbol{x}))$$

These functions can be written more succinctly using the pre-image function for the relation Δ:

$$\mathsf{preim}_\Delta(\chi_N)(\boldsymbol{x}) = \exists \boldsymbol{y} : \chi_N(\boldsymbol{y}) \wedge \Delta(\boldsymbol{x}, \boldsymbol{y}).$$

Using pre-images, we can rewrite $\chi_{\overline{\mathsf{bad}_i(X)}}$ as follows:

$$\chi_{\overline{\mathsf{bad}_i(X)}}(\boldsymbol{x}) = \diamondsuit_{1,i}(\boldsymbol{x}) \to \mathsf{preim}_\Delta(\chi_X(\boldsymbol{y}) \wedge \diamondsuit_{2,i}(\boldsymbol{y})).$$

Finally, the bottom-up algorithm is implemented as an iteration over the sets $\chi_{X \cup \mathsf{supp}(X)}$, and the top-down algorithm is implemented as iterations over $\chi_{X \setminus \mathsf{bad}(X)}$. Both stop when a fixpoint is reached. Then checking whether ψ is present in a type of this fixpoint is trivial.

The pre-image operation is a key operation in both the bottom-up and the top-down approaches. It is also known to be a key operation in symbolic model checking [7] and it has been the subject of extensive research (cf. [8,11,24,9]) since it can be a quite time and space consuming operation. Various optimizations can be applied to the pre-image computation to reduce the time and space requirements. A method of choice is that of *conjunctive partitioning* combined with *early quantification*. The idea is to avoid building a monolithic BDD for the relation Δ since this BDD can be quite large. Rather, we take advantage of the fact that Δ is defined as a conjunction of simple conditions. Thus, to compute the pre-image we have to evaluate a quantified Boolean formula of the form $(\exists y_1) \ldots (\exists y_n)(c_1 \wedge \ldots \wedge c_m)$, where the c_i's are Boolean formulas. Suppose, however, that a variable y_j does not occur in the clauses $c_{i+1}, \ldots, c_m$. Then the formula can be rewritten as

$$(\exists y_1) \ldots (\exists y_{j-1})(\exists y_{j+1}) \ldots (\exists y_n)((\exists y_j)(c_1 \wedge \ldots \wedge c_i) \wedge (c_{i+1} \wedge \ldots \wedge c_m)).$$

This enables us to apply existential quantification to smaller BDDs. Of course, there are many ways in which one can cluster and re-order the c_i's. We used the methodology developed in [24], called the "IWLS 95" methodology, to compute pre-images.

4   Optimizations

The decision procedures described above handles a formula in four steps. Firstly, the formula is converted into box normal form. Secondly, a set of bit vectors representing types is generated. Thirdly, this set is updated through a fixpoint process. Finally, the answer of the algorithm depends on a simple syntactic check of this fixpoint. In this section, we will describe three different optimization techniques, each related to a different step of the procedure.

4.1 Particles

In the approaches presented so far, we memorize and take care of redundant information: for example, a bit vector represents both a conjunction and the corresponding conjuncts, whereas the truth value of the former is determined by the truth value of the latter. Now we propose a representation where we only keep track of the "non-redundant" subformulas, which possibly reduces the size of the corresponding BDDs. To do so, it is convenient to work on formulas in a different normal form.

A $\mathcal{K}$ formula ψ is said to be in *negation normal form* (NNF) if all its subformulas are of the form $\varphi \wedge \varphi'$, $\varphi \vee \varphi'$, $\Box\varphi$, $\Diamond\varphi$, q, or $\neg q$ where $q \in AP(\psi)$. We write $NNF(\psi)$ for the NNF of ψ and sub(ψ) for the set of subformulas of $NNF(\psi)$. All $\mathcal{K}$ formulas can be converted into negation normal form by pushing negation inwards.

A set $p \subseteq$ sub(ψ) is a *full ψ-particle* if it satisfies the following conditions:

- If $\varphi = \neg\varphi'$, then $\varphi \in p$ implies $\varphi' \notin p$.
- If $\varphi = \varphi' \wedge \varphi''$, then $\varphi \in p$ implies $\varphi' \in p$ and $\varphi'' \in p$.
- If $\varphi = \varphi' \vee \varphi''$, then $\varphi \in p$ implies $\varphi' \in p$ or $\varphi'' \in p$.

Thus, in contrast to a type, a full particle may contain both φ' and φ'', but neither $\varphi' \wedge \varphi''$ nor $\varphi' \vee \varphi''$.

For particles, $\Delta(\cdot, \cdot)$ is defined as for types. From a set of particles P and the corresponding $\Delta(\cdot, \cdot)$, we can construct a Kripke structure K_P in the same way as from a set of types.

For the top-down approach, the auxiliary functions $Initial(\cdot)$ and $Iterate(\cdot)$ for full particles are defined as follows:

- $Initial(\psi)$ is the set of all full ψ-particles.
- $Iterate(P) = P - \mathsf{bad}(P)$, where $\mathsf{bad}(P)$ is the particles in P that contain unwitnessed diamond formulas, i.e.

$$\mathsf{bad}(P) = \{p \in P \mid \text{there exists } \Diamond\varphi \in p \text{ such that, for all } q \in P \\ \text{with } \Delta(p, q), \text{ we have } \varphi \notin q\}.$$

Analogously, these functions are defined for the bottom-up approach as follows:

- $Initial(\psi)$ is the set of full ψ-particle p that do not contain diamond formulas, i.e., $\Diamond\varphi \notin p$ for all $\Diamond\varphi \in$ sub(ψ).
- $Iterate(P) = P \cup \mathsf{supp}(P)$, where $\mathsf{supp}(P)$ is the set of witnessed particles, i.e., .

$$\mathsf{supp}(P) = \{p \subseteq \text{sub}(\psi) \mid p \text{ is a } \psi\text{-particle and, for all } \Diamond\varphi \in p, \\ \text{there exists } q \in P \text{ with } \varphi \in q \text{ and } \Delta(p, q)\}.$$

While encoding particle sets by BDDs may require more BDD variables, we still might see a reduction in BDD size because particles requires fewer constraints than types.[2] Besides a possible reduction in the size required to encode a bit-vector representation of particle sets, the particle-based approaches also can improve running time. We

---

[2] Of course, BDD size is always formula dependent. In our experiments, we observed that particle approaches gives BDD sizes between a small constant factor (i.e., 2-3) larger to orders of magnitudes smaller compared to type approaches.

can see that for each iteration, the number of pre-image operations a type based approach will need to do is equal to the total number of modal operators, while the corresponding number for particle based approaches is only equal to the number of diamond operators in the NNF form.

4.2   Lean Approaches

This optimization is also motivated by the idea to compress the size of the bit vector representing a type by omitting redundant information. To this purpose, we first define a set of "non-redundant" subformulas $\mathrm{atom}(\psi)$ as the set of those formulas in $\mathrm{cl}(\psi)$ that are neither conjunctions nor disjunctions, i.e., each φ is of the form $\Box\varphi'$, q, $\neg\Box\varphi'$, or $\neg q$. By the definition of types, each type $a \subseteq \mathrm{cl}(\psi)$ corresponds one-to-one to a *lean type* $a' := a \cap \mathrm{atom}(\psi)$. So storing types in lean form is equivalent to storing them in full form.

Analogously, we can define a lean representation for particles. First, we define the relevant subformulas $\mathrm{part}(\psi)$ as follows: For $\varphi \in \mathrm{sub}(\psi)$, if φ is $\Diamond\varphi'$, $\Box\varphi'$, q, or $\neg q$, then φ is in $\mathrm{part}(\psi)$. For a full particle $p \subseteq \mathrm{sub}(\psi)$, we define the corresponding *lean particle* p' as follows: $p' = p \cap \mathrm{part}(\psi)$. Because the (first) condition on particles is more relaxed than that of atoms, a lean particle does not correspond to a single full particle, but can represent several full particles. Although lean approaches can possibly reduce the size required for representing worlds, we have to pay for these savings since computing bad and supp using lean types and particles can be more complicated.

4.3   Level-Based Evaluation

As already mentioned, $\mathcal{K}$ has the finite-tree-model property, i.e., each satisfiable formula ψ of $\mathcal{K}$ has a finite tree model of depth bounded by the depth $md(\psi)$ of nested modal operators in ψ. Here, we take advantage of this property and, instead of representing a complete model using a set of particles or types, we represent each layer (i.e., all worlds being at the same distance from the root node) in the model using a separate set (for a level-based approach in the context of the first-order approach to $\mathcal{K}$, see [2]). Since only a subset of all subformulas appears in one layer, the representation can be more compact. We only present the optimization for the approach using (full) types. The particle approach and the lean approaches can be constructed analogously. For $0 \leq i \leq md(\psi)$, we write

$$\mathrm{cl}_i(\psi) := \{\varphi \in \mathrm{cl}(\psi) \mid \varphi \text{ occurs at modal depth } i \text{ in } \psi\},$$

and we adapt the definition of the possible accessibility relation Δ accordingly:

$$\Delta_i(a, a') \text{ iff } a \subseteq \mathrm{cl}_i, a' \subseteq \mathrm{cl}_{i+1}, \text{ and } \varphi' \in a' \text{ for all } \Box\varphi' \in a.$$

A sequence of sets of types $A = \langle A_0, A_1, \dots, A_d \rangle$ with $A_i \subseteq 2^{\mathrm{cl}_i(\psi)}$ can be converted into a tree Kripke structure

$$K_A = \langle AP(\psi), \bigcup_{0 \leq i \leq d} A_i, R, L \rangle$$

(where the worlds are the disjoint union of the A_i) as follows:

– For a world $a \in A_i$ and $q \in AP(\psi)$, we define $L(a)(q) = 1$ if $q \in a$, and $L(a)(q) = 0$ if $q \notin a$.
– For a pair of states a, a', $R(w, w') = 1$ iff, for some i, $a \in A_i$ and $a' \in A_{i+1}$ and $\Delta_i(a, a')$.

The algorithm for level-based evaluation works as follows, where X_i are sets of types/particles:

$d = md(\psi)$
$X_d = Initial_d(\psi)$
for $i = d - 1$ downto 0 **do**
    $X_i \Leftarrow Iterate(X_{i+1}, i)$
end for
if exists $x \in X_0$ such that $\psi \in x$ **then return** "ψ is satisfiable"
else return "ψ is not satisfiable"
endif

Please note that this algorithm works bottom-up in the sense that it starts with the leaves of a tree model *at the deepest level* and then move up the tree model towards the root, adding nodes that are "witnessed". In contrast, the bottom-up approach presented earlier can be said to start with *all* leaves of a tree model.

For the level based algorithm on types, the auxiliary functions are defined as follows:

– $Initial_i(\psi) = \{a \subseteq cl_i(\psi) \mid a \text{ is a type}\}$.
– $Iterate(A, i) = \{a \in Initial_i(\psi) \mid \text{ for all } \neg\Box\varphi \in a \text{ there exists } b \in A \text{ where } \neg\varphi \in b \text{ and } \Delta_i(a, b)\}$.

For A a set of types of formulas at level $i + 1$, $Iterate(A, i)$ represents all types of formulas at level i that are properly witnessed in A.

5   Results

We implemented the aforementioned algorithms in C++ using the CUDD 2.3.0 [25] package for BDDs. The parser for the languages used in the benchmark suites are taken with permission from *SAT [27]. In the following, we describe and compare the performance of the different algorithms. [3]

As benchmarks, we used both the $\mathcal{K}$ part of TANCS 98 [15] and portions of the MODAL PSPACE division of TANCS 2000 [19], and compared our implementation with *SAT [27] and portions with DLP [22]. [4] We compared the different algorithms with respect to the number of benchmark formulas whose satisfiability they can decide within a specific time frame. In contrast to compare solvers formula by formula, this approach gives a global view of their performance, and the risk of being drawn into

---

[3] All the tests run on a Pentium 4 1.7GHz with 512MB of RAM, running Linux kernel version 2.4.2. The solver is compiled with gcc 2.96.

[4] Our goal was to test the viability of our approach by comparing our algorithms to a known competitive modal satisfiability solver. Thus, we chose *SAT and DLP as a representative solvers. We return to this point in the conclusions.

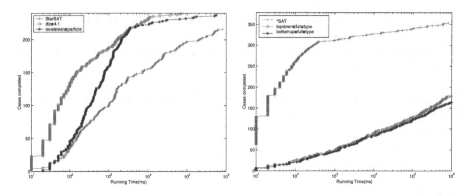

Fig. 1. Perf. on cnfSSS class of TANCS 2000   **Fig. 2.** Perf. on TANCS 98 (basic approaches)

too many details on how different solvers give preference to different formula classes is minimized [26,12].

The time out is set at 1000s and the space limit for BDDs is set at 384MB. For each test case, we plot the number of formulas decided versus the time limit. Thus, the solver with a higher curve is faster than one with a lower curve. The chart is scaled so the full scale is the total number of cases in the benchmark.

5.1   TANCS 2000

The portion of TANCS 2000 we used is the easy-medium part of the Modal QBF formulas in the MODAL PSPACE division. The problems are generated as QBF formulas of different density, and encoded into $\mathcal{K}$ with the Schmidt-Schauss-Smolka translation (cnfSSS). TANCS 2000 also provides formulas from other translation schemes, namely the Ladner translation and the Halpern and Moses translation. However, we restricted our attention to cnfSSS since both *SAT and our algorithms could only handle very small and separate parts of the other formulas, which made a comparison meaningless. We also present results for DLP, a highly optimized tableaux engine.

With the optimizations described in this paper, we are able to achieve performance comparable to other provers. The results can be found in Fig. 1, where the performance of the level-based lean-particle approach represents our best BDD-based approach. This approach uses all the optimizations presented in this paper, and turned out to perform best of all our BDD-based approaches. We can see that, although the BDD-based approach has a higher overhead, it scales more gracefully than *SAT for the formula class used in this test. We are still slower than DLP.

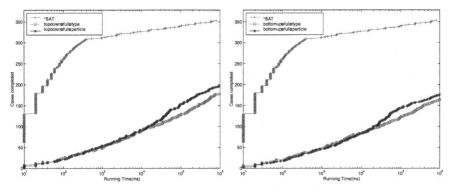

Fig. 3. Performance on TANCS 98 (particles vs. types)

5.2 TANCS 98

To analyze the usefulness of each optimization technique used, we run the algorithm with different optimization configurations on the $\mathcal{K}$ part of TANCS 98 benchmark suite[5] [15], a scalable benchmark which contains both provable and non-provable formulas.

The basic algorithms. To compare our approaches, we first run the basic algorithms on TANCS 98. The results are presented in Fig. 2. We can see that *SAT clearly outperforms our two basic algorithms. An explanation of this "weak" behavior of our approaches is that the intermediate results of the preimage operation are so large that the BDDs space constraint is usually reached. Top-down slightly outperforms bottom-up since bottom-up requires an extra conjunction per iteration step for the $Consistent$ predicate.

Optimizations. Now we compare the variants using types with their full particle-based variants. The results are presented in Fig. 3. We can see that, for TANCS 98, the particle approach slightly outperforms the type approach. Most of the improvements come from the use of negation normal form, which allows us to distinguish between diamonds and boxes, resulting in the reduction of the image operations needed.

Next, for types and particles, bottom-up and top-down, we compared the "full" approaches with their lean variants (see Fig. 4). Intuitively, the full variants trade a larger number of BDD variables in the representation of the transition relation for simpler consistency constraints. On TANCS 98, we can see that the lean approaches outperform in each combination their full variants. This shows that, as a general guideline, we should always attempt to reduce the number of BDD variables, since this results in smaller BDDs. Indeed, experience in symbolic model checking suggests that BDD size is typically the dominant factor when evaluating the performance of BDD-based algorithms [17].

---

[5] We did not use TANCS 2000 because unoptimized approaches time out on most of TANCS 2000 formulas, giving very little comparison between approaches.

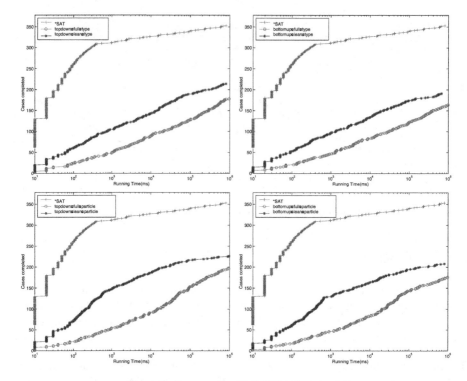

Fig. 4. Performance on TANCS 98 (lean vs. full)

Finally, we have compared the level-based approach with the top-down and the bottom-up approach. It turns out that the level-based approach outperforms both, and that, both for types and particles, the lean approach again outperforms the full one, see Fig. 5. The reason for this is that, by taking advantage of $\mathcal{K}$'s layered model property, we can split various space-consuming BDDs into smaller ones—depending on the modal depth of the corresponding subformulas. This minimizes space-outs and improves run time.

When compared with *SAT on the TANCS 98 benchmarks, all our approaches are still weaker than *SAT. Our implementation, however, is still open to a number of optimizations. In BDD-based symbolic model checking, it turned out that performance is extremely sensitive to the chosen order of BDD variables [7]. Moreover, there are different approaches to conjunctive partitioning [20]. So far, we did not optimize our implementation with respect to these aspects, and so we have yet to investigate the effect of problem-specific heuristics for variable ordering and conjunctive partitioning on the performance of our solver.

6   Conclusions

We have described various BDD-based decision procedures for $\mathcal{K}$. Our approach is inspired by the automata-theoretic approach, but we avoid explicit automata construction.

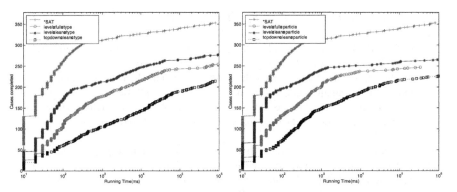

Fig. 5. Performance on TANCS 98 (level-based evaluation)

We explored a variety of optimization techniques and concluded that, in general, it is preferred to work with looser constraints; in general, we got the best performance with lean particles. We also showed that it is necessary to use a level-based approach to obtain a competitive implementation.

Our goal in this paper was not to develop the "fastest $\mathcal{K}$ solver", but rather to see whether the BDD-based approach is viable. From the competitiveness of our approach relative to *SAT on portions of the TANCS 2000 benchmark suite, we conclude that the BDD-based approach does deserve further study. In particular, we plan to study other optimizations strategies and also compare our approach to other modal satisfiability solvers.

References

1. H. R. Andersen. An introduction to binary decision diagrams. Technical report, Department of Information Technology, Technical University of Denmark, 1998.
2. C. Areces, R. Gennari, J. Heguiabehere, and M. de Rijke. Tree-based heuristics in modal theorem proving. In *Proceedings of the ECAI'2000*, 2000.
3. F. Baader and S. Tobies. The inverse method implements the automata approach for modal satisfiability. In *Proc. of IJCAR-01*, volume 2083 of *LNCS*. Springer Verlag, 2001.
4. I. Beer, S. Ben-David, D. Geist, R. Gewirtzman, and M. Yoeli. Methodology and system for practical formal verification of reactive hardware. In *Proc. of CAV-94*, volume 818 of *LNCS*, pages 182–193, 1994.
5. P. Blackburn, M. D. Rijke, Y. Venema, and M. D. Rijke. *Modal logic*. Cambridge University Press, 2001.
6. R. E. Bryant. Graph-based algorithms for boolean function manipulation. *IEEE Transactions on Computers*, Vol. C-35(8):677–691, August 1986.
7. J. Burch, E. Clarke, K. McMillan, D. Dill, and L. J. Hwang. Symbolic model checking: 10^{20} states and beyond. *Infomation and Computation*, 98(2):142–170, 1992.
8. J. R. Burch, E. M. Clarke, and D. E. Long. Symbolic model checking with partitioned transition relations. In *Int. Conf. on VLSI*, pages 49–58, 1991.
9. A. Cimatti, E. M. Clarke, F. Giunchiglia, and M. Roveri. NUSMV: A new symbolic model checker. *Int. Journal on Software Tools for Technology Transfer*, 2(4):410–425, 2000.

10. R. Dyckhoff, editor. *Proceedings of TABLEAUX 2000*, volume 1847 of *LNAI*. Springer Verlag, 2000.

11. D. Geist and H. Beer. Efficient model checking by automated ordering of transition relation partitions. In *Proc. of the sixth Int. Conf. on CAV*, pages 299–310, 1994.

12. E. Giunchiglia, M. Maratea, A. Tacchella, and D. Zambonin. Evaluating search heuristics and optimization techniques in propositional satisfiability. In *IJCAR*, pages 347–363, 2001.

13. F. Giunchiglia and R. Sebastiani. Building decision procedures for modal logics from propositional decision procedure - the case study of modal K(m). *Infomation and Computation*, 162:158–178, 2000.

14. J. Y. Halpern and Y. Moses. A guide to completeness and complexity for modal logics of knowledge and belief. *Artificial Intelligence*, 54:319–379, 1992.

15. A. Heuerding and S. Schwendimann. A benchmark method for the propositional modal logics K, KT, S4. Technical report, Universität Bern, Switzerland, 1996.

16. U. Hustadt and R. Schmidt. MSPASS: modal reasoning by translation and first order resolution. In Dyckhoff [10], pages 67–71.

17. G. Kamhi, L. Fix, and Z. Binyamini. Symbolic model checking visualization. In *Proc. of FMCAD'98*, volume 1522 of *LNCS*, pages 290–303. Springer Verlag, November 1998.

18. R. E. Ladner. The computational complexity of provability in systems of modal propositional logic. *SIAM J. Comput.*, 6(3):467–480, 1977.

19. F. Massacci and F. M. Donini. Design and results of TANCS-00. In Dyckhoff [10], pages 52–56.

20. I.-H. Moon, G. D. Hachtel, and F. Somenzi. Border-block trianglular form and conjunction schedule in image computation. In W. H. Jr. and S. Johnson, editors, *FMCAD2000*, volume 1954 of *LNCS*, pages 73–90. Springer Verlag, 2000.

21. H. Ohlbach, A. Nonnengart, M. de Rijke, and D. Gabbay. Encoding two-valued non-classical logics in classical logic. In J. Robinson and A. Voronkov, editors, *Handbook of Automated Reasoning*. Elsevier, 1999.

22. P. F. Patel-Schneider and I. Horrocks. DLP and FaCT. In *Proc. of TABLEAUX-99*, volume 1397 of *LNAI*, pages 19–23. Springer Verlag, 1999.

23. V. Pratt. A near-optimal method for reasoning about action. *Journal of Computer and System Sciences*, 20(2):231–254, 1980.

24. R. Ranjan, A. Aziz, R. Brayton, B. Plessier, and C. Pixley. Efficient BDD algorithms for FSM synthesis and verification. In *Proceedings of IEEE/ACM International Workshop on Logic Synthesis*, 1995.

25. F. Somenzi. CUDD: CU decision diagram package, 1998.

26. G. Sutcliffe and C. Suttner. Evaluating general purpose automated theorem proving systems. *Artificial intelligence*, 131:39–54, 2001.

27. A. Tacchella. *SAT system description. In *Collected Papers from the International Description Logics Workshop (DL'99)*. CEUR, 1999.

28. J. van Benthem. *Modal Logic and Classical Logic*. Bibliopolis, 1983.

29. M. Vardi. What makes modal logic so robustly decidable? In N. Immerman and P. Kolaitis, editors, *Descriptive Complexity and Finite Models*, pages 149–183. American Mathematical Society, 1997.

30. A. Voronkov. How to optimize proof-search in modal logics: new methods of proving redundancy criteria for sequent calculi. *Computational Logic*, 2(2):182–215, 2001.

Temporal Logic for Proof-Carrying Code

Andrew Bernard and Peter Lee*

School of Computer Science
Carnegie Mellon University
Pittsburgh, PA 15213 USA
(andrewb|petel)@cs.cmu.edu

Abstract. *Proof-carrying code* (PCC) is a framework for ensuring that
untrusted programs are safe to install and execute. When using PCC,
untrusted programs are required to contain a proof that allows the
program text to be checked efficiently for safe behavior. In this paper,
we lay the foundation for a potential engineering improvement to PCC.
Specifically, we present a practical approach to using temporal logic to
specify security policies in such a way that a PCC system can enforce
them.

Keywords. Proof-carrying code, temporal logic.

1 Introduction

Proof-carrying code [11] (PCC) is a framework for ensuring that untrusted programs are safe to install and execute. When using PCC, untrusted programs are
required to contain a proof that allows the program text to be checked efficiently
for safe behavior. PCC can check optimized object code, and a program checker
is relatively easy to implement. These advantages, among others, make PCC
an attractive scheme for enabling a network of computers to distribute software
safely. In this paper, we lay the foundation for a potential engineering improvement to PCC. Specifically, we present a practical approach to using temporal
logic to specify security policies in such a way that a PCC system can enforce
them. The PCC system would furthermore be "universal," in the sense of not
needing to be modified or extended for each new security policy, as long as each
such policy can be specified in temporal logic. This approach additionally enables us to replace a substantial portion of the program-checking software with
formal specifications, but at the cost of larger proofs.

A central component of a PCC program checker is the *security policy*, which
defines the precise notion of "safety" that the host system demands of all untrusted code. In the work cited above, a major portion of the security policy is
given by a verification-condition (VC) generator that in practice takes the form
of a manually constructed computer program (written, in this particular case, in
the C programming language). While this is an expedient approach that is also

---

* This work has been partially supported by the National Science Foundation under
grant CCR-0121633.

A. Voronkov (Ed.): CADE-18, LNAI 2392, pp. 31–46, 2002.

consistent with the desire to implement PCC as an operating system service, it does not necessarily lead to a trustworthy checker, nor does it permit easy adaptation of the checker to new security policies.

Using PCC, a *code producer* provides an untrusted program to a *code consumer*. A trusted *enforcement mechanism* checks the program against one or more security policies before it is allowed to run.

Until now, our PCC implementations have encoded security proofs in first-order logic, and the enforcement mechanism included a trusted VC generator that essentially encoded the security policy in a C implementation (*e.g.*, Necula [11]). We will argue here that *temporal logic* [8] has certain advantages over first-order logic for PCC. Using temporal logic, we can remake the VC generator as an *untrusted* component and thereby allow the security policy to be separated from the enforcement mechanism. This also provides the crucial advantage of reducing the amount of software in the trusted computing base, though as we shall see, this advantage comes at the cost of larger proofs. In this respect, our approach resembles *foundational PCC* [1], although, unlike foundational PCC, our code producer and consumer must agree on a shared notion of type safety.

A temporal logic is characterized by its temporal operators: they enable us to distinguish the different times at which a proposition is true. In this paper, we will identify time with the CPU clock and regard propositions as statements about machine states. For example, the proposition $\text{pc} = 0 \supset \bigcirc(\text{pc} = 1)$ asserts that "if the program counter is 0 now, then it will be 1 in the next state." We can also specify security policies in temporal logic. For example, the proposition $\Box(\text{pc} \geq 0 \wedge \text{pc} < 100)$ asserts that "the program counter is always between zero and 100," but we can also interpret this as the requirement "the program counter must always be between zero and 100"—a specification for a simple form of control-flow safety [7]. We will exploit this duality to reap a practical benefit.

For a PCC system based on first-order logic, the enforcement mechanism generates a proposition from the program and the security policy together—the security proof is a proof of this proposition. For temporal-logic PCC, the enforcement mechanism recognizes the program as a formal term, and the operational semantics of the host machine is encoded as a set of trusted inference rules. We can then encode the security policy directly—the security proof shows that the security policy is a consequence of running the program from a set of initial conditions. Notice that the security policy is independent of the enforcement mechanism, but we require no additional mechanism to interpret it.

We want to be confident that the security policy is correct: this confidence is difficult to obtain for a security policy in C code. In contrast, temporal logic has a clear semantics, and security policies are comparatively compact.

As we shall see, we can implement a simple enforcement mechanism for temporal-logic PCC at the cost of increasing proof sizes. This can be a favorable trade-off, because we are shifting work from a trusted component to an untrusted one. Initial experiments show that the size increase relative to a first-order proof is a small multiple of the code size.

The body of this paper lays a theoretical foundation for temporal-logic PCC. Section 2 outlines a first-order temporal logic that is suitable for PCC security proofs. Section 3 defines an abstract RISC processor for which our system is intended. Section 4 details how the machine semantics is encoded and why it is sound. Section 5 shows we can systematically obtain efficient temporal type-safety proofs from first-order type-safety proofs. Finally, in Section 6 we examine related work and suggest future improvements. Due to space limitations, we must omit many important details in this paper, but a complete development will be available as a technical report [2].

2 Temporal Logic

2.1 Syntax

The syntax of our logic (see Figure 1) is based on disjoint countably infinite sets of parameters and variables; a *parameter* a is always free in a proposition, whereas a *variable* x is normally bound.[1] This is a many-sorted logic, so each parameter or variable is annotated with an explicit type τ, of which there are countably many; types have no internal structure. We often omit type annotations when they can be inferred. Primitive functions and relations are named by a countable set of *constants* (f and R, respectively). Constants are also annotated with types: $\tau_1 \times \cdots \times \tau_k \to \tau$ is the annotation of a function from k parameters to a value of type τ, whereas $\tau_1 \times \cdots \times \tau_k \to o$ is the annotation of a relation on k parameters. Constant values c^τ are nullary functions, whereas constant propositions (*i.e.*, $\top$, $\bot$) are nullary relations. There is a binary equality relation for each type. This is a first-order logic, so functions and relations appear only as constants.

Times	$t ::= 0 \mid t_1 + 1$
Rigidities	$\rho ::= +_r \mid -_r$
Expressions	$e^\tau ::= a^\tau \mid x^\tau \mid f^{\tau_1 \times \cdots \times \tau_k \to \tau}(e_1^{\tau_1}, \ldots, e_k^{\tau_k})$
Propositions	$p ::= R^{\tau_1 \times \cdots \times \tau_k \to o}(e_1^{\tau_1}, \ldots, e_k^{\tau_k}) \mid p_1 \wedge p_2 \mid p_1 \vee p_2 \mid p_1 \supset p_2$
	$\mid \forall x^\tau{:}\rho.\ p_1 \mid \exists x^\tau{:}\rho.\ p_1 \mid \Box p_1 \mid \bigcirc p_1 \mid p_1 \mathcal{U} p_2$
Core Judgments	$J ::= t_1 \geq t_2 \mid e{:}\rho \mid p{:}\rho \mid p \,@\, t \mid p \,@\, [t_1, t_2)$
Contexts	$\Gamma ::= \cdot \mid \Gamma, J$

Fig. 1. Abstract Syntax (Temporal Logic)

Expressions e^τ are constructed from parameters, variables, and applications of constant functions; τ is the type of e. The simple type system for our logic is built into the syntax: ill-typed expressions are not well formed.

---

[1] The syntactic distinction between parameters and variables simplifies inference rules.

Following Manna and Pnueli [8], some expressions are *rigid*: it is syntactically evident that a rigid expression has the same value at all times. A *flexible* expression may (but need not) have different values at different times. For example, the constant 5 is rigid, whereas the stack pointer register is flexible. Variables also have rigidity: rigidities must match when a variable is instantiated. We declare the rigidity ρ of a variable when the variable is bound: $+_r$ denotes a rigid variable, whereas $-_r$ denotes a flexible variable. A rigid expression contains only rigid variables and parameters.

Propositions p include a selection of the usual connectives and quantifiers of first-order logic, plus the following temporal operators:

- $\Box p$ holds iff p holds at all future times.
- $\bigcirc p$ holds iff p holds at the next future time.
- $p_1 \, \mathcal{U} \, p_2$ holds iff p_2 holds at some future time, and p_1 holds until then.

A rigid proposition has only rigid parameters (bound variables may be flexible).

Some propositions are associated with a *time expression* t; we count time in unary notation: 0 denotes the earliest possible time (*e.g.*, the start of execution), and $t + 1$ denotes the time immediately following time t.

$[e_1/x] \, e$ is the usual *substitution* of expression e_1 for variable x in expression e. For substitution to be well formed, e_1 must have the same type as x, and e_1 must be closed (*i.e.*, it must not contain variables); e need not be closed. $[e/x] \, p$ is the usual extension, where e must be closed, but p need not be.

2.2 Semantics

We define a formal model for our temporal logic. Each expression is assigned the infinite sequence of values that the expression takes over time. A satisfaction relation determines whether a given proposition holds at a given time. This model is similar to the usual models of temporal logic.

Definitions. Val^τ is the set of values v^τ of type τ. A *sequence* π^τ is mapping from natural numbers (representing times) to values of type τ. An *environment* ϕ maps each parameter to a sequence of its type.

We assume an *interpretation function* $\mathcal{J}$ mapping each constant to its value, which may be a simple value (nullary functions), a total function (other functions), or a set of tuples (relations).

Valuation. A *valuation function* $\mathcal{V}$ assigns values to expressions (see the companion technical report). Thus, $\mathcal{V}(t)$ is the value of time expression t as a natural number. $\mathcal{V}_\phi$ evaluates expressions to sequences of the same type in the environment ϕ; e must be closed for $\mathcal{V}_\phi(e)$ to be well formed.

Satisfaction. A sequence is *rigid* if it has the same value at all times; the value of a rigid expression is always a rigid sequence, but the converse does not always hold. We write $\pi : +_r$ when π is rigid.

A *core judgment* J encodes a property of an environment. The *satisfaction* relation $\vDash$ defines when a core judgment holds for a particular environment (see Figure 2 for representative connectives: the complete definition can be found in the technical report); the judgment must be closed for satisfaction to be well formed. We informally describe each core judgment:

- $t_1 \geq t_2$ holds when t_1 denotes the same time as t_2 or a later time than t_2.
- $e : \rho$ holds when e denotes a sequence with rigidity ρ.
- $p : \rho$ holds when the truth/falsity of p has rigidity ρ.
- $p \, @ \, t$ holds when p is true at time t.
- $p \, @ \, [t_1, t_2)$ ("p is true over t_1 to t_2") holds when p is true at all times in the half-open interval $[t_1, t_2)$.

Thus, $\phi \vDash p \, @ \, t$ ("ϕ satisfies p at time t") holds if p is true of ϕ at time t.

$\phi \vDash R(e_1, \ldots, e_k) \, @ \, t$ iff $\langle \mathcal{V}_\phi(e_1)(\mathcal{V}(t)), \ldots, \mathcal{V}_\phi(e_k)(\mathcal{V}(t)) \rangle \in \mathcal{J}(R)$

$\phi \vDash p_1 \wedge p_2 \, @ \, t$ iff $\phi \vDash p_1 \, @ \, t$ and $\phi \vDash p_2 \, @ \, t$

$\phi \vDash \forall x^\tau : \rho. \, p \, @ \, t$ iff $\phi[a^\tau \mapsto \pi^\tau] \vDash [a^\tau / x^\tau] \, p \, @ \, t$ for some a^τ not appearing in p
                               and all π^τ such that $\pi^\tau : \rho$

$\phi \vDash p_1 \, \mathcal{U} \, p_2 \, @ \, t$ iff $\phi \vDash p_2 \, @ \, t_2$ for some t_2 such that $\phi \vDash t_2 \geq t$ and $\phi \vDash p_1 \, @ \, [t, t_2)$

$\phi \vDash p \, @ \, [t_1, t_2)$ iff $\phi \vDash p \, @ \, t$ for all t such that $\phi \vDash t \geq t_1$ and $\phi \vDash t_2 \geq t + 1$

Fig. 2. The Satisfaction Relation (Excerpt)

2.3   Proof System

The *provability relation* $\vdash$ asserts that there is a proof that a particular core judgment holds. Note that provability for rigidity is efficiently decidable.

A *context* Γ is a collection of hypothetical judgments that weaken provability. For example, $a :_r \vdash [a/x] \, p \, @ \, t$ asserts that it is provable that $[a/x] \, p$ holds at time t, assuming that a is rigid. An environment satisfies a context ($\phi \vDash \Gamma$) when it satisfies each judgment in the context (the context must be closed).

We present our proof system in the technical report; we only claim here that it is sound with respect to the semantics.

Proposition 1 (Soundness). $\phi \vDash J$ *if* $\phi \vDash \Gamma$ *and* $\Gamma \vdash J$

Proof. See the technical report.

3   Machine Model

We define an idealized RISC processor that will provide a foundation for the remainder of this paper. This processor operates on "words" of some fixed size (*e.g.* 32-bit numbers). There are a small number of general-purpose registers that each contain a single word, a word-sized program counter, and a memory register that contains a mapping from words to words. The processor executes a program that is simply a sequence of instructions. We assume that the program is in a separate memory and thereby protected from modification: we do not address self-modifying code in this paper.

3.1   Instruction Set

A *machine word* i is a value of type wd; Val^{wd} is an initial subrange of the natural numbers. Words are inherently unsigned, but negative numbers can be simulated by signed operators using a suitable convention (*e.g.*, two's complement). A *register token* r identifies a general-purpose register; each register token r_j is a value of type ureg. We designate a small, machine-dependent subset of the total functions from pairs of words to words as *executable operators eop* (type eop). A *conditional operator cop* (type cop) is a selected unary word relation. The exact set of operators is unimportant, as long as it includes modular addition.

We use a small RISC instruction set[2]; programs are instruction sequences:

$$\text{Instructions } I ::= r_1 \leftarrow i_1 \mid r_1 \leftarrow r_2 \mid r_1 \leftarrow r_2 \, eop_1 \, r_3$$
$$\mid \text{cond } cop_1 \, r_1, i_1 \mid r_1 \leftarrow \text{m}(r_2) \mid \text{m}(r_1) \leftarrow r_2$$

$$\text{Programs} \quad \Phi ::= \cdot \mid I; \, \Phi$$

An instruction I is a value of type inst, a program Φ is a value of type prog. For example, the following program replaces register r_0 with its own factorial:

$r_1 \leftarrow 1$	// r_1 is current counter
$r_2 \leftarrow 1$	// r_2 is current product
$r_3 \leftarrow 1$	// r_3 is always one
$r_4 \leftarrow r_1 \, \text{gtw} \, r_0$	// r_4 is nonzero iff $r_1 > r_0$
$\text{cond neq0w} \, r_4, 3$	// skip 3 when r_4 is nonzero
$r_2 \leftarrow r_2 \, \text{mulw} \, r_1$	// accumulate product
$r_1 \leftarrow r_1 \, \text{addw} \, r_3$	// increment counter
$\text{cond truew} \, r_0, -5$	// always skip back 5
$r_0 \leftarrow r_2$	// replace r_0
halt	

Our calling convention starts execution at the first instruction; halt is an abbreviation for cond truew $r_0, -1$. Program length ($|\Phi|$) and subscript (Φ_i) are defined in the obvious way.

We model a general-purpose register file as a single value of type mapu, mapping from register tokens to words. Memory is modeled by a total function from words to words (type mapw).

---

[2] The instruction set does not include procedure call instructions, but it is a simple matter to add an indirect jump instruction that will support the usual RISC calling conventions; this does not complicate the enforcement mechanism.

3.2   Syntax

We now specify how our machine model is incorporated into the logic.

The constants $0^{\tt wd}$, $1^{\tt wd}$, ... denote words; n is an arbitrary word constant. $\mathtt{selw}^{\mathtt{mapw} \times \mathtt{wd} \to \mathtt{wd}}$ (apply map) and $\mathtt{updw}^{\mathtt{mapw} \times \mathtt{wd} \times \mathtt{wd} \to \mathtt{mapw}}$ (update map) are function constants; for example, $\mathtt{updw}(\mathtt{m}, 3, 4)$ denotes the same map as $\mathtt{m}$, except that address 3 is mapped to 4. The constants $\mathtt{selu}^{\mathtt{mapu} \times \mathtt{ureg} \to \mathtt{wd}}$ (select register) and $\mathtt{updu}^{\mathtt{mapu} \times \mathtt{ureg} \times \mathtt{wd} \to \mathtt{mapu}}$ (update register) operate on register files. There are no operations yielding register tokens, just designated constants (c_r).

We associate a constant $c^{\tt eop}$ with each executable operator, and likewise with each conditional operator; $\mathtt{addw}^{\tt eop}$ denotes addition. $\mathtt{appe}^{\mathtt{eop} \times \mathtt{wd} \times \mathtt{wd} \to \mathtt{wd}}$ is a function constant that applies an executable operator, and $\mathtt{appc}^{\mathtt{cop} \times \mathtt{wd} \to o}$ is a relation constant that applies a conditional operator; we ordinarily elide these constants in the interest of readability and use infix notation for executable operators (*e.g.*, $e_1 \mathbin{\mathtt{addw}} e_2$ stands for $\mathtt{appe}(\mathtt{addw}, e_1, e_2)$). $\mathtt{compl}^{\mathtt{cop} \to \mathtt{cop}}$ is a function constant that complements a conditional operator (*e.g.*, $\mathtt{compl}(\mathtt{eq0w}) = \mathtt{neq0w}$).

Identifiers for the special-purpose registers are chosen from parameters; the interpretation of these parameters is constrained by the machine model. *Reg* is the set of all register parameters (note that these are *not* register tokens). pc (the program counter) is a parameter of type wd, u (the contents of the register file) is a parameter of type mapu, and m (the contents of memory) is a parameter of type mapw. Propositions can express properties of machine states: for example, $\mathtt{selu}(\mathtt{u}, \mathtt{r_0}) \neq 0^{\tt wd}$ asserts that general-purpose register $\mathtt{r_0}$ is not zero.

Our logic encompasses instructions and programs by means of constant functions. For example, $\mathtt{imv}^{\mathtt{ureg} \times \mathtt{ureg} \to \mathtt{inst}}$ constructs a move instruction from two register tokens, $\mathtt{len}^{\mathtt{prog} \to \mathtt{wd}}$ returns the length of a program, and $\mathtt{fetch}^{\mathtt{prog} \times \mathtt{wd} \to \mathtt{inst}}$ extracts a particular instruction from a program. The logic is coupled to a particular untrusted program by means of the constant $\mathtt{pm}^{\mathtt{prog}}$: $\mathcal{J}(\mathtt{pm})$ is the program whose first instruction is at address zero of the program memory.[3]

Intuitively, a value of type prog is "object code," and an expression of type prog is "assembly code." Instruction expressions enable us to model the operational semantics of our abstract machine directly in temporal logic (see Section 4) and are also useful for specifying security policies.

3.3   Semantics

Our operational semantics defines a set of executions for each program.

A *state s* maps each register to a value of its type; a state is simply a snapshot of the machine at a particular time. An *execution σ* is an infinite sequence of states representing the trace of a computation. Finite executions are represented by repeating the final state infinitely (this is the effect of the halt instruction).

---

[3] Because the program code is presumably ready to be run by the code consumer, we use pm as a "stand in" to avoid replicating the program inside the proof. Alternatively, the program code could be stored in the proof and extracted by the code consumer after proof checking (*i.e.*, "code-carrying proof").

We can turn an environment into an execution (see Section 2.2) by sampling each register at each time; $\phi|_{Reg}$ is the execution for environment ϕ:

$$\phi|_{Reg} = \sigma \text{ such that } \sigma_j = a \mapsto \phi(a)(j) \text{ for all } j \text{ and } a \in Reg$$

We call $\phi|_{Reg}$ the *erasure* of ϕ (*i.e.*, non-register parameters are "erased"). An execution σ *satisfies* a proposition p at time t ($\sigma \vDash p_@ t$) if all environments that erase to σ satisfy p at t. The *execution set* Σ_p of a proposition p is the set of executions that satisfy it at time zero ($\Sigma_p = \{\sigma \mid \sigma \vDash p_@ 0\}$). Given a security-property p, an execution σ does not violate security if and only if $\sigma \in \Sigma_p$. We discuss security properties further in Section 4.

We now specify a transition relation between states for any given program: $\Phi \triangleright s \to s'$ asserts that there is a valid transition from state s to state s' when executing program Φ (see Figure 3 for representative instructions: the complete definition can be found in the companion technical report). $i_1 \dotplus i_2$ abbreviates $\mathcal{J}(\mathtt{addw})(i_1, i_2)$ in this figure. The notation $\psi[v_1 \mapsto v_2]$ is the redefinition of the mapping ψ such that v_1 is mapped to v_2.

$\Phi \triangleright s \to s'$	
$\Phi_{s(\mathrm{pc})}$	s'
$r_1 \leftarrow r_2$	$s[\mathrm{pc} \mapsto s(\mathrm{pc}) \dotplus 1][\mathbf{u} \mapsto s(\mathbf{u})[r_1 \mapsto s(\mathbf{u})(r_2)]]$
$\mathrm{cond}\ cop\ r_1, i_1$	$\begin{cases} s[\mathrm{pc} \mapsto s(\mathrm{pc}) \dotplus 1 \dotplus i_1] & \text{if } s(\mathbf{u})(r_1) \in cop \\ s[\mathrm{pc} \mapsto s(\mathrm{pc}) \dotplus 1] & \text{if } s(\mathbf{u})(r_1) \notin cop \end{cases}$

Fig. 3. The Transition Relation (Excerpt)

The execution set of a program (*i.e.*, its possible behavior) comprises all executions with valid transitions ($\Sigma_\Phi = \{\sigma \mid \Phi \triangleright \sigma_j \to \sigma_{j+1} \text{ for all } j \geq 0\}$).

4   Enforcement

We now address the code consumer's principal concern: how do I tell if my system is secure when I execute an untrusted program?

Current PCC enforcement mechanisms are implemented in the C programming language and generate a *verification condition* (VC) that is true only if the program does not violate the security policy; an LF type checker establishes that the security proof is a correct proof of the VC.

For temporal-logic PCC, we provide a proof of $\vdash p_{\mathsf{sp}} @ 0$ instead of a proof of a VC. p_{sp} is a *security property* that must hold for the system to be secure. p_{sp} is specified by the code consumer directly; the definition of satisfaction can be used to verify that it has the intended meaning.

Contrast this approach with a first-order PCC system, in which the code producer proves a VC derived from the security property by a trusted analysis. In our system, the code producer proves the security property directly from a formal encoding of the abstract machine's transition relation. To show that our enforcement mechanism is sound, we need only show that the encoded transition relation is valid (see Section 4.2).

4.1 Encoding the Transition Relation

We provide one inference rule for each instruction type; Figure 4 specifies two such rules (see the companion technical report for the remaining rules).

In each rule, we identify the current-time values of the registers with the rigid variables xpc, xu, and xm. Then, for any program that contains an instruction of the appropriate type at the current program counter, we provide new values of the registers at the next time instant. Rigid variables name the previous-time values of the registers inside the $\bigcirc$ operator. In the case of rule trans_mv (move register), the program counter is incremented by one, and the general-purpose register r1 is assigned the value of r2 in the register file. In the case of rule trans_cond (conditional branch), a branch is taken if a conditional test succeeds; otherwise, the program counter is simply incremented; the other registers are unchanged by this instruction.

Note that the transition relation does not check that the program has proper control flow, unlike other implementations of PCC. We permit any control flow that has a valid security proof, but the security property will ordinarily require that the program counter stay within the program.

$$p_{\text{trans\_mv}} \equiv \forall \text{xpc} :+_r. \; \forall \text{xu} :+_r. \; \forall \text{xm} :+_r. \; \forall \text{r1} :+_r. \; \forall \text{r2} :+_r.$$
$$\text{xpc} = \text{pc} \wedge \text{xu} = \text{u} \wedge \text{xm} = \text{m} \supset \text{fetch}(\text{pm}, \text{pc}) = \text{imv}(\text{r1}, \text{r2})$$
$$\supset \bigcirc (\text{pc} = \text{xpc addw } 1 \wedge \text{u} = \text{updu}(\text{xu}, \text{r1}, \text{selu}(\text{xu}, \text{r2}))) \wedge \text{m} = \text{xm})$$

$$p_{\text{trans\_cond}} \equiv \forall \text{xpc} :+_r. \; \forall \text{xu} :+_r. \; \forall \text{xm} :+_r. \; \forall \text{cop1} :+_r. \; \forall \text{r1} :+_r. \; \forall \text{i1} :+_r.$$
$$\text{xpc} = \text{pc} \wedge \text{xu} = \text{u} \wedge \text{xm} = \text{m} \supset \text{fetch}(\text{pm}, \text{pc}) = \text{icond}(\text{cop1}, \text{r1}, \text{i1})$$
$$\supset \bigcirc \left(\begin{array}{l} (\text{cop1}(\text{selu}(\text{xu}, \text{r1}))) \supset \text{pc} = \text{xpc addw } 1 \text{ addw i1}) \\ \wedge((\text{comp1}(\text{cop1}))(\text{selu}(\text{xu}, \text{r1}))) \supset \text{pc} = \text{xpc addw } 1) \\ \wedge \text{u} = \text{xu} \wedge \text{m} = \text{xm} \end{array} \right)$$

$$\frac{}{\Gamma \vdash p_{\text{trans\_mv}} @ t} \; \text{trans\_mv} \qquad \frac{}{\Gamma \vdash p_{\text{trans\_cond}} @ t} \; \text{trans\_cond}$$

Fig. 4. Encoding the Transition Relation (Excerpt)

4.2 Soundness

To show that our enforcement mechanism is sound, we first show that the encoded transition relation is valid for any execution of the untrusted program:

Proposition 2 (Transition Soundness). $\phi \vDash p_{\text{trans\_}l} @ t$
for each $l \in \{\text{mvi}, \text{mv}, \text{eop}, \text{cond}, \text{load}, \text{store}\}$ *if* $\phi|_{Reg} \in \Sigma_{\mathcal{J}(\text{pm})}$

Proof. By the definition of the transition relation and the definitions of valuation and satisfaction (see the technical report for details).

Now, let p_{sp} be a security property. The following proposition establishes that the system is secure with respect to any program that has a security proof:

Proposition 3 (Enforcement Soundness). $\Sigma_{\mathcal{J}(\mathrm{pm})} \subseteq \Sigma_{p_{\mathsf{sp}}}$ *if* $\vdash p_{\mathsf{sp}} @ 0$

Proof.
for all $\sigma \in \Sigma_{\mathcal{J}(\mathrm{pm})}$
    for all ϕ such that $\phi|_{Reg} = \sigma$
        $\phi \vDash p_{\mathsf{sp}} @ 0$ Proposition 2 and Proposition 1
        $\sigma \vDash p_{\mathsf{sp}} @ 0$ Def. $\sigma \vDash p @ t$
        $\sigma \in \Sigma_{p_{\mathsf{sp}}}$ Def. Σ_p
                                                                          $\square$

Let $\Phi = \mathcal{J}(\mathrm{pm})$. The code producer provides a derivation of $\vdash p_{\mathsf{sp}} @ 0$ along with Φ; we use a trusted proof checker (*e.g*, Necula [14]) to verify its correctness. From Proposition 3, we conclude $\Sigma_{\Phi} \subseteq \Sigma_{p_{\mathsf{sp}}}$: no execution of Φ violates p_{sp}.

5   Certification

We now address the code producer's principal concern: how do I generate a security proof for my program such that it will satisfy the code consumer?

Of course, as a last resort, the code producer can always write proofs by hand, but this approach is feasible only for small programs. Practical systems for PCC rely on a certifying compiler [14] (a *certification mechanism*) to produce a security proof in the normal course of compiling a program. We would like to have temporal-logic certifying compilers.

Unfortunately, certification appears to be significantly harder than enforcement: existing certifying compilers [3,14,10] provide proofs of type safety only for relatively standard type systems. In this section, we restrict our attention to programs without procedure calls and provide an algorithm for transforming the output of a first-order PCC compiler into a temporal-logic proof of type safety. This limits our choice of security policies, but note that type safety is an essential starting point for any practical PCC system, and that type systems exist for many "expressive" security policies [18,5,4].

Our certification mechanism generates derivations of judgments of the form $\vdash \mathsf{pc} = 0 \wedge p_{\mathsf{pre}} \supset \Box p_{\mathsf{safe}} @ 0$, where p_{pre} and p_{safe} are assertions (*i.e.*, $p_{\mathsf{sp}} \equiv \mathsf{pc} = 0 \wedge p_{\mathsf{pre}} \supset \Box p_{\mathsf{safe}}$); an *assertion* is a proposition that contains no temporal operators. This class of security properties represents a slight generalization of the *invariance properties* [8], and includes all type safety properties. Intuitively, an invariance property requires us to prove that some assertion (*i.e.*, p_{safe}) holds at all times. We generalize this class by allowing the code producer to assume that the program counter is zero and that a precondition assertion (*i.e.*, p_{pre}) holds at the start of execution.

In addition to object code, existing certifying compilers for PCC produce a set of loop invariants and a proof of a first-order VC. A *loop invariant* is an assertion that holds at the head of each loop; a complete set of loop invariants ensures that the VC generator will terminate, even if the program does not. For temporal-logic PCC, we pass the object code, loop invariants, and first-order proof to an *ad hoc* proof generation algorithm that produces a temporal-logic security proof. The *ad hoc* proof generator mimics the operation of the VC generator; both are untrusted components in our system.

In order to obtain efficient temporal-logic proofs, we factor fixed sequences of inferences into derived rules that are introduced by the *prelude* of the proof. The prelude is identical for all programs compiled by the same compiler, and is thus a constant overhead. We call the temporal-logic component of the security proof a *proof skeleton*. The proof skeleton is constructed by the application of derived rules; the derivations of the derived rules (in the prelude) are first checked by the proof checker. The "leaves" of the original first-order proof are embedded in the temporal proof skeleton, after purely structural rules are stripped away.

5.1   VC Generation

We first adapt Necula's VC generator [11] to our machine model to fix the strategy of our proof generator (see the companion technical report for details).

For certifying control-flow safety and memory safety, p_{safe} is

$$\mathtt{neq0(len(pm)\,gtu\,pc)}$$
$$\wedge(\forall \mathtt{r1{:}+_r}.\ \forall \mathtt{r2{:}+_r}.\ \mathtt{fetch(pm,pc) = iload(r1,r2)} \supset \mathtt{saferd(m,selu(u,r2)))}$$
$$\wedge(\forall \mathtt{r1{:}+_r}.\ \forall \mathtt{r2{:}+_r}.\ \mathtt{fetch(pm,pc) = istore(r1,r2)}$$
$$\supset \mathtt{safewr(m,selu(u,r1),selu(u,r2)))}$$

We call this the *essential safety policy* [7]. It allows the program counter to range over the entire program. The constants $\mathtt{saferd}$ and $\mathtt{safewr}$ denote arbitrary relations that encode the memory safety policy [14]; the VC proves that these relations hold for each possible program state.

Let $VC_{p_{\mathsf{pre}},\mathcal{I}}$ be the VC for program $\mathcal{J}(\mathtt{pm})$, precondition p_{pre}, and loop invariants $\mathcal{I}$. The certifying compiler produces $\mathcal{I}$ along with a proof of $\vdash VC_{p_{\mathsf{pre}},\mathcal{I}} @ 0$.

5.2   Proof Generation

The proof generator extends first-order proofs to temporal invariance proofs by mimicking the operation of the VC generator in temporal logic. In effect, the proof skeleton is a trace of a particular run of the VC generator encoded in the language of temporal logic. The proof of control-flow safety is encoded in the proof skeleton itself; other properties are demonstrated by the first-order proof. Our proof generator is not a search algorithm: given a well-formed first-order proof, a temporal proof is always found in time directly proportional to the size of the VC. Note that because our enforcement mechanism does not depend on the VC generator, we are free to change VC generators at any time, even after the enforcement mechanism has been widely deployed.

It should not be surprising that we can reduce temporal invariance proofs to first-order proofs, because this is a well-known technique for verifying reactive systems [8]. However, instead of using the usual global invariance rule [8], we instead show that some loop invariant always recurs after a finite amount of time, and that the system is safe in the meantime: this is essentially the function of the VC generator. This property can be encoded easily enough by appealing to the "until" operator: $\Box(p_\mathcal{I} \supset p_\mathsf{safe} \wedge \bigcirc(p_\mathsf{safe}\, \mathcal{U}\, p_\mathcal{I}))$ where $p_\mathcal{I}$ is the disjunction of all loop invariants. If we combine this with a derivation of $\mathsf{pc} = 0 \wedge p_\mathsf{pre} \supset p_\mathsf{safe}\, \mathcal{U}\, p_\mathcal{I}$, we can derive p_sp through a constant number of temporal inferences.

We now realize two benefits: our safety proofs are considerably smaller than the equivalent global invariance proofs, and we obtain a correspondence with the VC generator that is close enough to embed a first-order proof directly. The reduction in proof size is brought about by specifying an invariant only for each loop head, rather than for each reachable instruction. Michael and Appel [9] achieve a similar reduction by factoring invariants using predicate transformers.

By realizing this strategy as an algorithm, we obtain the following result:

Proposition 4 (Relative Completeness). *There is an algorithm that derives*
$\vdash \mathsf{pc} = 0 \wedge p_\mathsf{pre} \supset \Box p_\mathsf{safe} @ 0$
from $\vdash VC_{p_\mathsf{pre}, \mathcal{I}} @ 0$, *where* p_safe *is the essential safety policy*

Proof. In the technical report, we specify an algorithm for deriving a temporal security proof from the proof of a corresponding first-order VC.

We have implemented a prototype proof generator for the abstract RISC processor as a logic program in the Twelf [15] meta-logical framework, along with a simulator for the enforcement mechanism. Small experiments based on a binary encoding of temporal logic suggest that the size of the temporal proof skeleton is less than five times the code size; this overhead is in addition to the first-order proof and the prelude. Though such proofs are relatively large by current standards [13], the experiments indicate that our approach is practical.

We are currently in the midst of implementing an experimental framework based on the SpecialJ certifying compiler for Java [3]. The SpecialJ compiler produces certified x86 executable code from Java class files; our new framework generates temporal-logic proofs from this certified code. When completed, this framework will allow us to obtain more comprehensive measurements of proofs sizes for Java programs. Initial results are so far consistent with the results of our earlier experiments.

6   Conclusion

The contributions of this research are threefold:

- A temporal-logic framework for PCC that is parameterized by formal security properties

- An enforcement mechanism for security properties that is simple to implement and easy to verify
- A certification mechanism for type safety that adapts existing certifying compilers to temporal logic

Our contributions are practical applications of proven techniques for program verification: our challenge lies principally in engineering efficient security proofs and in minimizing the complexity of the trusted enforcement mechanism.

Our approach offers these benefits:

- Temporal logic is a suitable specification language for security policies, including "expressive" [18,16] safety properties and liveness properties. Thus, we can specify security policies directly without a special interpreter, and without having to write any C code.
- Enforcement is simple—we minimize the amount of trusted code by moving the VC generator out of the code consumer. Soundness of the enforcement mechanism is a direct consequence of the abstract machine semantics.
- Enforcement is also flexible—the enforcement mechanism adapts to different VC generators as a matter of course. Additionally, it does not anticipate and thereby restrict control flow; an indirect jump, for example, can branch to any address that is proven safe.

These advantages come at a cost, however, because our security proofs require a temporal proof skeleton in addition to first-order security proofs; in practice, we expect the proof skeleton to grow linearly with the size of the program.

We should acknowledge that temporal logic is not a fundamental requirement of our approach: for example, temporal logic can be translated into first-order logic with explicit time parameters, and state transition relations can mimic temporal operators by transitive closure.[4] However, the choice of notation for PCC has practical consequences, because formalisms that are equivalent in a foundational sense may not enable equally compact security proofs. Temporal logic is well established as a specification language, but only further experiments will reveal whether it is a good notation for a PCC implementation.

6.1   Future Work

Our machine model does not have a procedure mechanism: we might adapt the procedure mechanism from Necula [14], but at the cost of additional trusted code and restrictions on control flow. It would be more satisfying to develop an untrusted mechanism based on new certification techniques, and thereby continue to use the same simple enforcement mechanism we have presented here. However, in order to prove the specification of a recursive procedure, we must be able to assume provisionally that the specification holds—thus, we may need fixed-point operators to encode the general case of mutually-recursive procedures.

---

[4] We conjecture, however, that an explicit representation of a state transition is needed to make the VC generator into an untrusted component.

We plan to adapt instrumentation techniques for security automata [16] to the certification problem. Security automata can specify all safety properties, and program transformations exist [6,18] that will guarantee in many cases that such properties hold. A security automaton that has been threaded through a program by instrumentation is known is an *inline reference monitor* (IRM). Adding an IRM transformation to our certification mechanism would considerably broaden the class of security properties that we can automatically certify.

Our enforcement mechanism can be extended to check self-modifying code by encoding the processor's instruction decoder as a formal relation. This is not fundamentally difficult, though it requires a substantial effort (see Appel and Felty [1], for example). PCC certification for self-modifying code, however, is still largely unexplored, and we would be incurring a significant cost for standard programs by requiring additional proofs of instruction decodings.

6.2   Related Work

We touch here only on work related to security policies for untrusted software. For a more comprehensive PCC bibliography, we refer the reader to Necula [14].

Necula and Lee [12] pioneered the use of PCC for resource bounds. Appel and Felty [1] argue that we should rely upon an encoding of the machine semantics in higher-order logic and derive an untrusted type system from it; the proof checker should be the only trusted component. Interesting safety properties can be specified by extending the machine model. In some respects, our work represents a less radical step in a similar direction: the enforcement mechanism disassembles the program, but does not to analyze its control flow or generate a VC.

The enforcement mechanism for *typed assembly language* (TAL) [10] is a type checker that does not accept unsafe programs; type annotations accompany program instructions. A TAL compiler translates a well-typed source program into a well-typed object program. Walker [18] developed a TAL based on security automata; this version of TAL is novel because, like our system, the security policy is separate from the enforcement mechanism. Additionally, Walker provides an IRM transformation for ensuring that the security policy is always satisfied. Crary and Weirich [5] developed a TAL that enforces resource bounds. Crary, Walker, and Morrisett [4] developed a TAL to enforce security policies based on a capability calculus; this calculus can ensure the safety of explicit deallocation.

Software fault isolation (SFI) [17] instruments a program so that it cannot violate a built-in memory safety policy. *Security automata SFI implementation* (SASI) is an SFI-based tool developed by Erlingsson and Schneider [6] for enforcing security policies encoded in a security-automata language.

Acknowledgements. We thank Frank Pfenning for his guidance during the development of our temporal logic. We also thank Fred B. Schneider, Bob Harper, and the anonymous referees for helpful comments on earlier drafts of this paper.

References

1. Andrew W. Appel and Amy P. Felty. A semantic model of types and machine instructions for proof-carrying code. In *Proceedings of the 27th ACM SIGPLAN-SIGACT Symposium on Principles of Programming Languages*, pages 243–253, Boston, MA, January 2000.
2. Andrew Bernard and Peter Lee. Temporal logic for proof-carrying code. Technical Report CMU-CS-02-130, Carnegie Mellon University, School of Computer Science, 2002. In preparation.
3. Christopher Colby, Peter Lee, George C. Necula, Fred Blau, Mark Plesko, and Kenneth Cline. A certifying compiler for Java. In *Proceedings of the ACM SIG-PLAN '00 conference on programming language design and implementation*, pages 95–107, Vancouver, BC Canada, June 2000.
4. Karl Crary, David Walker, and Greg Morrisett. Typed memory management in a calculus of capabilities. In *Proceedings of the 26th ACM SIGPLAN-SIGACT Symposium on Principles of Programming Languages*, pages 262–275, San Antonio, TX, January 1999.
5. Karl Crary and Stephnie Weirich. Resource bound certification. In *Proceedings of the 27th ACM SIGPLAN-SIGACT Symposium on Principles of Programming Languages*, pages 184–198, Boston, MA, January 2000.
6. Úlfar Erlingsson and Fred B. Schneider. IRM enforcement of Java stack inspection. In *RSP: 21th IEEE Computer Society Symposium on Research in Security and Privacy*, 2000.
7. Dexter Kozen. Efficient code certification. Technical Report TR98-1661, Cornell University, Computer Science Department, January 1998.
8. Zohar Manna and Amir Pnueli. *The Temporal Logic of Reactive and Concurrent Systems: Specification*. Springer Verlag, 1991.
9. Neophytos G. Michael and Andrew W. Appel. Machine instruction syntax and semantics in higher order logic. In *Proceedings of the 17th International Conference on Automated Deduction (CADE-17)*, June 2000.
10. Greg Morrisett, David Walker, Karl Crary, and Neal Glew. From system F to typed assembly language. In *Proceedings of the 25th ACM SIGPLAN-SIGACT Symposium on Principles of Programming Languages*, pages 85–97, San Diego, CA, January 1998.
11. George C. Necula. Proof-carrying code. In *Proceedings of the 24th ACM SIGPLAN-SIGACT Symposium on Principles of Programming Languages*, pages 106–119, Paris, France, January 1997.
12. George C. Necula and Peter Lee. Safe, untrusted agents using proof-carrying code. In *Mobile Agents and Security*, volume 1419 of *Lecture Notes in Computer Science*. Springer Verlag, 1998.
13. George C. Necula and S. P. Rahul. Oracle-based checking of untrusted software. In *Proceedings of the 28th ACM SIGPLAN-SIGACT Symposium on Principles of Programming Languages*, pages 142–154, London, UK, January 2001.
14. George Ciprian Necula. *Compiling with Proofs*. PhD thesis, Carnegie Mellon University, September 1998. Available as Technical Report CMU-CS-98-154.
15. Frank Pfenning and Carsten Schürmann. System description: Twelf — A meta-logical framework for deductive systems. In H. Ganzinger, editor, *Proceedings of the 16th International Conference on Automated Deduction (CADE-16)*, pages 202–206, Trento, Italy, July 1999. Springer-Verlag LNAI 1632.

16. Fred B. Schneider. Enforceable security policies. Technical Report TR99-1759, Cornell University, Computer Science Department, July 1999.
17. Robert Wahbe, Steven Lucco, Thomas E. Anderson, and Susan L. Graham. Efficient software-based fault isolation. In *Proceedings of the Fourteenth ACM Symposium on Operating Systems Principles*, pages 203–216, Asheville, NC, December 1993.
18. David Walker. A type system for expressive security policies. In *Proceedings of the 27th ACM SIGPLAN-SIGACT Symposium on Principles of Programming Languages*, pages 254–267, Boston, MA, January 2000.

A Gradual Approach to a More Trustworthy, Yet Scalable, Proof-Carrying Code

Robert R. Schneck[1] and George C. Necula[2],[*]

[1] Group in Logic and the Methodology of Science
University of California, Berkeley
schneck@math.berkeley.edu
[2] Department of Electrical Engineering and Computer Sciences
University of California, Berkeley
necula@cs.berkeley.edu

Abstract. Proof-carrying code (PCC) allows a code producer to associate to a program a machine-checkable proof of its safety. In the original approach to PCC, the safety policy includes proof rules which determine how various actions are to be proved safe. These proof rules have been considered part of the trusted code base (TCB) of the PCC system. We wish to remove the proof rules from the TCB by providing a formal proof of their soundness. This makes the PCC system more secure, by reducing the TCB; it also makes the system more flexible, by allowing code producers to provide their own safety-policy proof rules, if they can guarantee their soundness. Furthermore this security and flexibility are gained without any loss in the ability to handle large programs.

In this paper we discuss how to produce the necessary formal soundness theorem given a safety policy. As an application of the framework, we have used the Coq system to prove the soundness of the proof rules for a type-based safety policy for native machine code compiled from Java.

1 Introduction

Proof-carrying code (PCC) [7] is a technique that shifts the burden of certifying properties of a program or data from the consumer to the producer, with the main goal of keeping the consumer's trusted code base (TCB) as small and trustworthy as possible. However, in the existing implementations of proof-carrying code there seems to exist a tension between the minimality of the TCB and engineering considerations necessary for handling realistic safety policies and large programs.

---

[*] This research was supported in part by National Science Foundation Career Grant No. CCR-9875171, ITR Grants No. CCR-0085949 and No. CCR-0081588, gifts from AT&T Research and Microsoft Research, and a National Science Foundation Graduate Research Fellowship. The information presented here does not necessarily reflect the position or the policy of the Government and no official endorsement should be inferred.

A. Voronkov (Ed.): CADE-18, LNAI 2392, pp. 47–62, 2002.
© Springer-Verlag Berlin Heidelberg 2002

The system described by Necula [8] was engineered to scale to large programs (up to half a million lines of code) and to realistic safety policies (e.g. a type-safety policy for native machine code compiled from Java [3]) with a relatively modest investment (about two person-years).

The typical interaction taking place in this PCC system is depicted in Figure 1 as a negotiation between a code producer and a code consumer. Upon being presented with a code fragment, the code consumer uses a verification-condition generator (VCGen) which produces a set of verification conditions (VC), whose validity entails the safety of the code. The validity of the VC must be proved with respect to a set of proof rules that are provided (and trusted) by the code consumer. In the second stage, the code producer constructs a representation of a proof of the VC and presents that to the code consumer, who can now simply run a proof checker to satisfy itself that the VC is provable.

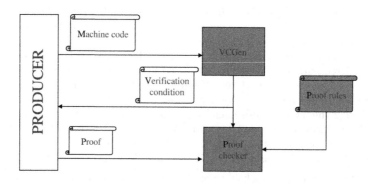

Fig. 1. The structure of a proof-carrying code system showing a "dialogue" between the code producer (on the left) and the code consumer (composed of the trusted elements shown shaded).

Thus, in addition to the proof checker, the TCB for this system includes a verification-condition generator (VCGen) and a list of proof rules, which together constitute the safety policy. Altogether the TCB requires about 15,000 to 25,000 lines of code, depending on configuration and underlying architecture. It is not inaccurate to describe this infrastructure as simple and small, and therefore easy to trust, at least when one considers possible alternatives such as trusting optimizing compilers.

However, it is reasonable to ask whether it is possible to create a working PCC where the TCB is smaller. We want to combine the low-cost and scalability benefits of the traditional implementation of PCC with the security of a reduced TCB. In particular, we observe that among the many lines of code that one must trust in a PCC implementation, most are independent of the safety policy. This category includes the proof checker and the VCGen (which essentially contains a machine-code decoder, and the handling of control-flow). These parts are shared between safety policies and change very rarely, which implicitly means that they are tested more extensively and thus are more trustworthy. On the other hand the proof rules of the safety policy change with every safety policy. In our experience these parts are more likely to contain errors. We consider it more cost-effective to focus heavy-weight tools such as theorem provers for the purpose of certifying policy-dependent extensions to PCC, while trusting the implementation of the core system.

We propose to remove the safety-policy proof rules from the TCB, by providing a framework in which the proof rules can be formally proven sound. This not only increases the security of the PCC system, but also its flexibility, as code producers would be able to supply their own safety policies, as long as the proof rules could be formally proven sound in our framework. One way to view this approach is as an attempt to extend the dialogue between the code producer and the code consumer to the level of the safety-policy rules: the code producer expresses the intention to install a new set of proof rules; the code consumer inspects the rules and replies with a soundness theorem which the code producer must prove. The question then is what is the counterpart of a VCGen for producing the soundness theorem for proof rules? And furthermore, what is the reference proof system against which the new rules are being judged?

This paper describes the prototype of a framework to take proof rules for a safety policy, and produce a formal theorem to guarantee that, relative to the still-trusted behavior of VCGen, the notion of safety given by the proof rules really does imply *memory safety*. Note that we do not show how to produce the formal *proof* of this theorem; in particular, although it is necessary to the feasibility of a PCC system that the safety proofs for programs can be automatically generated (e.g. by a certifying compiler), at this point the soundness proofs for safety policies still need to be interactively generated. Also note that our framework only ensures memory safety. Safety policies are often expected to handle more than memory safety: for instance, a type-safety policy will also enforce abstraction, or a safety policy may include other features such as instruction counting. Memory safety can be considered to play the role of a *safety meta-policy*: the system will not accept a new safety policy unless it can at least guarantee memory safety, regardless of what else it promises to do.

Using the specification language of the Coq system, we have implemented the framework in the case of typing rules for native machine code compiled from Java, providing the formal statement of the theorem that these rules guarantee memory safety. Moreover we have used the Coq proof system to produce a formal proof of this theorem.[1]

We begin with the development of our framework for how to take a safety policy and produce the statement of the necessary soundness theorem, using a

---

[1] Note that the handling of Java in PCC requires extensions to VCGen to handle e.g. dynamic dispatch and exceptions; our framework is concerned *only* with the proof rules of the safety policy, so our proof does not guarantee the soundness of these VCGen extensions. The soundness of VCGen extensions is the subject of our current research.

"toy" safety policy as a motivating example. Next we briefly consider the Java safety policy and our formal proof of the soundness of these proof rules. Finally we compare our work with other approaches for more secure proof-carrying code, and consider future directions for this research.

2   Stating Soundness for Safety Policies

Our intention, which is currently only partly realized, is to give an entirely modular framework which can take a description of a safety policy and produce the statement of the soundness theorem for the proof rules of the policy.

2.1   Safety Policies

First we must detail what constitutes a description of a safety policy. A safety policy comprises[2]

1. a list of proof rules;
2. trusted run-time support functions;
3. extensions to the VCGen mechanism.

The soundness theorem states only the soundness of the proof rules, so currently we require any extensions to VCGen to remain in the trusted code base.

The proof rules. Most importantly there is a formal description of the proof rules for the predicates `saferd` and `safewr`, which are used by VCGen as the proof obligations for memory reads and writes. The proof rules specify the meaning of these predicates—and thus the meaning of safety in the policy—by defining how they are to be proved. The proof rules may define various auxiliary types and predicates and the rules for them as well. For instance, a type-safety policy will typically define a (logical) type whose values are the various (computational) types of the type system considered, as well as a typing predicate with various rules; then the single rule for `safewr` will be that ($safewr$ E_1 E_2) is provable given a proof that E_1 is a pointer to a type T and E_2 is of type T.

As a motivating example, consider the following "toy" safety policy. The basic idea is that there is a type of "boxes". Boxes encode some kind of value if odd; for instance, they might encode integers in all but the least significant bit—however for our purposes we ignore the coding and simply allow anything odd to be a box. Boxes which are even are pointers to other boxes. The proof rules are as follows. The typing predicate is `ofType`; `ofmem` is intended to hold of well-typed memory states.

---

[2] Certain safety requirements are imposed by the core VCGen (e.g., each instruction is valid, each jump is within the code block); we will not consider these general requirements when looking at any particular safety policy.

box : type, ptr_box : type

$$\frac{(\text{odd } E)}{(\text{ofType } E \text{ box})} \qquad \frac{(\text{ofType } E \text{ ptr\_box}) \quad (\text{even } E)}{(\text{ofType } E \text{ box})}$$

$$\frac{(\text{ofType } E \text{ box}) \quad (\text{even } E)}{(\text{ofType } E \text{ ptr\_box})} \qquad \frac{(\text{ofType } E \text{ ptr\_box}) \quad (\text{ofmem } M)}{(\text{ofType } (\text{sel } M\ E) \text{ box})}$$

$$\frac{(\text{ofmem } M) \quad (\text{ofType } E_1 \text{ ptr\_box}) \quad (\text{ofType } E_2 \text{ box})}{(\text{ofmem } (\text{upd } M\ E_1\ E_2))}$$

$$\frac{(\text{ofType } E \text{ ptr\_box})}{(\text{saferd } E)} \qquad \frac{(\text{ofType } E_1 \text{ ptr\_box}) \quad (\text{ofType } E_2 \text{ box})}{(\text{safewr } E_1\ E_2)}$$

These rules exhibit that anything odd can be a box; that even pointers and even boxes coincide; that reading a pointer in a well-typed memory produces a box; and that well-typedness of memory is preserved by memory writes of the appropriate type. Finally there are the rules for **saferd** and **safewr** based on the pointer type.

Observe that the proof rules alone provide no instances of the form (ofType E ptr_box) or (ofmem M). Such hypotheses will arise instead from trusted functions.

Trusted run-time functions. A safety policy may also specify trusted run-time functions. Each function is given as executable code accompanied by a precondition and postcondition, given in terms of the predicates specified by the proof rules of the safety policy.

The trusted run-time functions affect our handling of the soundness of the proof rules because of the extra assumptions created by the postconditions. The semantics of the predicates occurring in the postconditions changes, as they may hold for reasons other than those given by the proof rules. Consider again our box safety policy. It provides a trusted function which allocates memory for a box. The postcondition of the function is that, for the returned memory address *RES*,

$$(\text{ofType } RES \text{ ptr\_box}).$$

This should not be taken to mean that this instance of **ofType** is provable using the proof rules: this is a new way of obtaining an instance of this predicate. Similarly, (ofmem M) holds for M the memory state after the most recent allocation.

When we try to prove soundness, we will need to consider the actual code of the allocation function as well. We will certainly want as an invariant that, whenever (ofType E ptr_box) is provable, then the memory at E has actually been allocated. As discussed in Section 2.2, the soundness theorem involves the execution of a hypothetical program on a certain abstract machine; we require encoding the trusted functions as state transitions on this machine.

VCGen extensions. A safety policy may provide extensions to VCGen. These extensions adjust the behavior of VCGen to handle situations expected by the safety policy. Examples include the handling of dynamic dispatch and exceptions in Java; another kind of example would be an instruction counter, which ensures (via emitted proof obligations) that a certain number of instructions intervene between two successive operations of a given type. Since our framework currently assumes the behavior of VCGen (and all extensions) is trusted, we can mostly ignore the exceptions in stating the soundness theorem.

However, an extension may change the meaning of a predicate from the proof rules by providing assumptions of that predicate based on static information obtained from the code. Essentially, new proof rules are added in a program-specific way. Instead of being formalized as an inductive type whose inductive constructors are the given proof rules, such a predicate needs to formalized as a parameter, where which instances hold is dependent on the particular program being considered. We call these predicates *trusted assumptions*. An example from the Java safety policy is the predicate `jifield`, where (`jifield` C *OFF* T) is intended to mean that class C has a field of type T at offset *OFF*.

The extension which collects the trusted assumptions may emit proof obligations about them. These are *consistency guarantees*. An example of this is that any field of a class needs to fit within the specified size of an instance of a class, so

$$(\forall C, \textit{OFF}, T)(\texttt{jifield}\ C\ \textit{OFF}\ T) \rightarrow (\textit{OFF} + 4) \leq (\texttt{size\_of\_instance}\ C)$$

(here, the type is assumed to require four spaces in memory). These consistency guarantees will typically be required in order to prove the soundness theorem. In fact, the extension will emit only the particular proof obligations for the particular instances of the assumptions which it creates; our meta-theorem will require the appropriate universal quantification to deal with the general case.

Finally, these extensions which collect static information may provide some assumptions from an initialization phase of the programs. In the Java policy the trusted assumptions include the locations of the the virtual-method tables and static members. So the soundness theorem must take into account that the assumed memory has in fact been allocated. To handle assumptions about the state of the memory before the program begins, we must specify a *start state* of the machine discussed in Section 2.2.

We collect here the various pieces of the safety policy which must be encoded in order to produce a statement of the soundness theorem:

1. the proof rules of the safety policy;
2. postconditions of trusted functions;
3. the trusted functions as state transitions;
4. trusted assumptions obtained about a given program;
5. consistency guarantees on the trusted assumptions; and
6. a start state.

In the current implementation of the PCC system, only the proof rules are encoded as an easily manipulable formal object (a file in LF format), such that it is easy to translate them into the formal language of the soundness theorem. In order to use our soundness approach as a modular framework where new safety policies can be introduced and one can easily construct the statement of the necessary soundness theorem, we must do more work to create an appropriate encoding of the necessary pieces of a safety policy.

2.2   The Reference Machine

The idea of the soundness theorem is to set up two abstract machines, modeled as state transition systems. The *reference* machine only allows memory reads and writes to memory which has in fact been allocated for the program; memory safety is guaranteed by run-time checks. The *auxiliary* machine only allows memory reads and writes when the appropriate instance of safe rd or safewr is provable, using the proof rules of the safety policy. Soundness then amounts to showing that, among states reachable from the start state of the safety policy, any auxiliary transition can be effected by reference transitions.

Because we trust the core capabilities of VCGen, we do not need to model executions on a real architecture: VCGen is responsible for correctly determining the semantics of real instructions. We can instead model executions in a very simple way, as long as its computational power is equivalent. We assume a type exp of expressions to be used for both memory addresses and values. We need exp to be equipped with arithmetic operations, but it seems irrelevant what exp really is; in our formal development we use the Coq built-in type of natural numbers. We also assume a type mem of memory states, together with operations upd, sel, and addr, corresponding to memory update, memory select, and the test of whether an address has been allocated, respectively.

$$E : \mathtt{exp}$$
$$M : \mathtt{mem}$$
$$(\mathtt{upd}\ M\ E_1\ E_2) : \mathtt{mem}$$
$$(\mathtt{sel}\ M\ E) : \mathtt{exp}$$
$$(\mathtt{addr}\ M\ E) : \mathtt{Prop}$$

To keep the memory model generic we make only the following assumptions about mem and these operations.

$$(\forall m : \mathtt{mem})(\forall a, e : \mathtt{exp})(\mathtt{addr}\ m\ a) \rightarrow$$
$$(\mathtt{sel}\ (\mathtt{upd}\ m\ a\ e)\ a) = e$$
$$(\forall m : \mathtt{mem})(\forall a_1, a_2, e : \mathtt{exp})(\mathtt{addr}\ m\ a_1) \rightarrow$$
$$\neg(a_1 = a_2) \rightarrow$$
$$(\mathtt{sel}\ (\mathtt{upd}\ m\ a_1\ e)\ a_2) = (\mathtt{sel}\ m\ a_2)$$
$$(\forall m : \mathtt{mem})(\forall a_1, a_2, e : \mathtt{exp})(\mathtt{addr}\ m\ a_1) \rightarrow$$
$$(\mathtt{addr}\ m\ a_2) \rightarrow$$
$$(\mathtt{addr}\ (\mathtt{upd}\ m\ a_1\ e)\ a_2)$$

(We assume here for ease of presentation that all values stored in memory have a uniform size of one word and so there is no danger of aliasing. In our actual formal development we require a slightly more complicated picture of memory.)

The machine state is a quadruple with two registers a and b of type exp, a memory of type mem, and a history, which is intended as a list of reads and writes performed. The history will allow us to use just the final state of a sequence of state transitions, to determine whether there was any violation of memory-safety over the whole sequence, rather than having to prove the safety of each individual transition.

$$s ::= (E_a, E_b, M, H)$$
$$H ::= \texttt{nil} \mid (\texttt{read\_inst } M\ E) :: H \mid (\texttt{write\_inst } M\ E_1\ E_2) :: H$$

Machine execution steps are modeled by a transition system on the machine state. Two features of the system should be noted. First, we ignore control flow. VCGen is responsible for collecting assumptions and emitting proof obligations in order to handle control flow; e.g. if a memory read occurs in a loop, the relevant proof obligation will be generalized to ensure the safety of the read in any particular iteration of the loop. For the purposes of the soundness theorem we will trust that VCGen does its job correctly, and so we are free to concentrate on straight-line code where all loops, branches, and function calls have been unfolded. Thus, in the example just mentioned, we will consider the particular proof obligation for each specific memory read in each iteration of the loop; because of the (here trusted) semantics of VCGen, each such proof obligation follows by instantiation from the general proof obligation actually emitted by VCGen.

Second, we allow a non-deterministic system. In essence, we work with a completely generic program rather than a specific program which dictates the next instruction at each step. We need only consider the safety of a given instruction in a given state.

The transitions includes a number of uninteresting register manipulations, as well as the memory operations: read, write, and allocate. Just as for the functions upd and sel for reading and writing memory, we define the function allocate axiomatically. For a state s and a natural number n, (allocate $n\ s$) = (a, b, m, h) is intended to be a new state where n previously unallocated words in memory, beginning at location a, have been allocated (and initialized to zero), and the memory is otherwise unaltered. If the memory of the old state s is m_s, the axioms defining this are:

$$(\forall k)(k < n) \to (\texttt{addr } m\ (a + k))$$
$$(\forall k)(k < n) \to \neg(\texttt{addr } m_s\ (a + k))$$
$$(\forall e : \texttt{exp})(\texttt{addr } m_s\ e) \to (\texttt{addr } m\ e)$$
$$(\forall e : \texttt{exp})(\texttt{sel } m\ e) = (\texttt{sel } m_s\ e)$$
$$(\forall k)(k < n) \to (\texttt{sel } m\ (a + k)) = 0$$

The reference machine transitions are as follows. The salient feature by which the reference machine encodes a policy of memory soundness is that the memory read and write transitions are allowed only on allocated memory.

$$(a, b, m, h) \rightarrow_{\texttt{ref}} (b, b, m, h)$$
$$(a, b, m, h) \rightarrow_{\texttt{ref}} (a, a, m, h)$$
$$(a, b, m, h) \rightarrow_{\texttt{ref}} (e, b, m, h) \qquad\qquad \text{for } e : \texttt{exp}$$
$$(a, b, m, h) \rightarrow_{\texttt{ref}} (a, e, m, h) \qquad\qquad \text{for } e : \texttt{exp}$$
$$(a, b, m, h) \rightarrow_{\texttt{ref}} (a + b, b, m, h)$$
$$(a, b, m, h) \rightarrow_{\texttt{ref}} ((\texttt{sel } m\ b), b, m, (\texttt{read\_inst } m\ b) :: h) \qquad \text{if } (\texttt{addr } m\ b)$$
$$(a, b, m, h) \rightarrow_{\texttt{ref}} (a, b, (\texttt{upd } m\ a\ b), (\texttt{write\_inst } m\ a\ b) :: h) \quad \text{if } (\texttt{addr } m\ a)$$
$$s \rightarrow_{\texttt{ref}} (\texttt{allocate } n\ s) \qquad\qquad \text{for } n \in \mathbb{N}$$

2.3   The Auxiliary Machine

Now we need to show how to create a machine which reflects a particular safety policy. On this *auxiliary machine*, memory accesses are controlled by the provability of appropriate instances of $\texttt{saferd}$ and $\texttt{safewr}$.

We have seen that certain hypotheses result from calls to the trusted functions rather than from the proof rules directly. To handle this, we define the states of the auxiliary machine by extending the machine state (a, b, m, h) with an additional *pseudo-state*; the pseudo-state encodes the information about which hypotheses are available as a result of calls to trusted functions. Consider again the box safety policy; in this instance, an appropriate pseudo-state consists of a list of allocated addresses, as well as the memory resulting from the most recent allocation. The auxiliary state for the box safety policy is thus given by:

$$s_{\texttt{aux}} ::= ((E_a, E_b, M, H), P)$$
$$A ::= \texttt{nil} \mid E :: A$$
$$P ::= (A, M)$$

Now we take each predicate introduced in the proof rules of the safety policy, including $\texttt{saferd}$ and $\texttt{safewr}$, and formalize it as an inductive type parameterized by the auxiliary state. The inductive constructors include all of the proof rules given (in which the state plays no role), as well as additional constructors for the postconditions of trusted functions, which examine the state to determine if the predicate holds in that state. In the example of the box safety policy, $\texttt{ofType}$ will be an inductive predicate taking a state, an expression, and a type, with constructors including

$$\frac{(\texttt{ofType } s\ E\ \texttt{box}) \quad (\texttt{even } E)}{(\texttt{ofType } s\ E\ \texttt{ptr\_box})}$$

and similar versions of all the other proof rules; ofType will also have an additional constructor (here, let A be the first component of the pseudo-state of s):

$$\frac{E \in A}{(\text{ofType } s\ E\ \text{ptr\_box})}$$

This constructor reflects that in states s where an address E has been provided by the trusted allocator function, the extra hypothesis (ofType $s\ E$ ptr_box) will be available. Similarly, ofmem will have an additional constructor such that (ofmem $s\ M$) holds when M is the second component of the pseudo-state of s.

Thus, the predicates from the proof rules are formalized as inductive types, in such a way that the postconditions of trusted functions are accounted for. In a safety policy with trusted assumptions, such assumptions are formalized as parameters: we assume there is such a predicate, without making any assumption on when the predicate holds. This reflects the fact that we consider a generic program; when the trusted assumptions hold is program-specific. The consistency guarantees, which restrict what combinations of trusted assumptions are possible for legal programs, are formalized as axioms.

Finally we can describe the auxiliary transitions. We include all the register manipulations, which do not alter the pseudo-state; memory read and memory write also do not change the pseudo-state, but are restricted to be allowed only when saferd or safewr hold in the appropriate state. We forbid the general allocation, since type-safety policies will typically define their own typed allocators; and we add transitions for each trusted function. Each trusted function will need to be encoded as a state transition on the machine state; we also require the appropriate change in the pseudo-state. For a trusted function f, where we consider f itself to take reference states to reference states, let f_{pseudo} be the corresponding operation taking the auxiliary state to the new pseudo-state.

$$((a, b, m, h), p) \rightarrow_{\text{aux}} ((b, b, m, h), p)$$
$$((a, b, m, h), p) \rightarrow_{\text{aux}} ((a, a, m, h), p)$$
$$((a, b, m, h), p) \rightarrow_{\text{aux}} ((e, b, m, h), p) \qquad \text{for } e : \text{exp}$$
$$((a, b, m, h), p) \rightarrow_{\text{aux}} ((a, e, m, h), p) \qquad \text{for } e : \text{exp}$$
$$((a, b, m, h), p) \rightarrow_{\text{aux}} ((a + b, b, m, h), p)$$
$$((a, b, m, h), p) \rightarrow_{\text{aux}} (((\text{sel } m\ b), b, m, (\text{read\_inst } m\ b) :: h), p)$$
$$\qquad\qquad\qquad\qquad \text{if } (\text{saferd } s\ m\ b)$$
$$((a, b, m, h), p) \rightarrow_{\text{aux}} ((a, b, (\text{upd } m\ a\ b), (\text{write\_inst } m\ a\ b) :: h), p)$$
$$\qquad\qquad\qquad\qquad \text{if } (\text{safewr } s\ m\ a\ b)$$
$$(s, p) \rightarrow_{\text{aux}} ((f\ s), (f_{\text{pseudo}}\ (s, p))) \qquad \text{for trusted function } f$$

In the example of the box safety policy, the trusted allocator function (call it alloc_box) corresponds to the machine transition

$$(\text{alloc\_box } s) = (\text{allocate } 1\ s).$$

The effect on the pseudo-state is to add the newly allocated space (i.e. the a register of the new machine state) to the list of allocated addresses, and to replace the last-allocated memory with the newly allocated memory. In other words, if $(\texttt{alloc\_box}\ s) = (a, b, m, h)$, then

$$(\texttt{alloc\_box}_{\text{pseudo}}\ (s, (addrs, last)) = (a :: addrs, m).$$

At this point in time, our handling of trusted functions is still at a prototype stage. It remains to be worked out, in the general case, exactly how to determine the appropriate pseudo-state, how the various functions alter the pseudo-state, and what the additional inductive constructors for the predicates must be.

2.4   Stating the Soundness Theorem

Now we can state the theorem which, for a given safety policy, will express soundness relative to memory safety. Let s_{start} refer to the start state of the safety policy.

Theorem 1. *There is a pseudo-state p_{start} such that the following holds: for any auxiliary state (s, p) reachable from $(s_{\text{start}}, p_{\text{start}})$, if $(s, p) \rightarrow_{\text{aux}} (s', p')$, then $s \rightarrow^*_{\text{ref}} s'$.*

In other words, the reference system can safely emulate the machine execution of any auxiliary transition. Because reads and writes are recorded in the machine history, all reads and writes allowed by the auxiliary transition would also be allowed in the reference system; in particular, if **saferd** or **safewr** is provable at a certain state, then the memory to be read or written has been allocated, so can, in fact, be safely read or written according to the reference system as well.

The idea of the general framework is that a code producer can provide a safety policy, appropriately encoded, and the code consumer will produce a formal statement of this theorem, together with all the necessary formal definitions corresponding to the reference and auxiliary machines, as well as the appropriate formalizations of the state-relativized proof rules. The code producer is then obligated to provide a formal proof of the theorem in order for the consumer to use the provided safety policy.

3   A Safety Policy for Java

We have applied the framework provided above to a PCC safety policy for Java, which is used for certifying that native machine code programs compiled from Java are indeed well-typed, according to the Java type system, and use properly various run-time mechanisms such as dynamic dispatch and exception handling. This policy is used in the system described in [3], and has been shown to scale to large programs. We want to be sure that it guarantees memory safety. As indicated we will not consider here the various extensions to VCGen (such as handling of dynamic dispatch), and prove only the soundness of the proof rules of the type system.

The soundness proof first requires generating the appropriate auxiliary machine, as was done with the "toy" safety policy above; then the reference and auxiliary machines are formalized in Coq, at which point it is easy to state the soundness theorem formally. Due to space limitations, here we can only very briefly introduce the general parameters of the safety policy and the soundness proof. The full Coq development, specifying the theorem as well as the proof, is available at http://www.math.berkeley.edu/~schneck/javacade/.

The proof rules of the safety policy introduce a set type along with constructors: jint, jbool, etc. for primitive types, (jarray T) for arrays of type T, (jinstof C) for instances of class (or interface) C. We also have types that do not correspond to source-level types but are instead necessary to describe implementation details: for instance, (jvirtab C) is the type of a virtual-method table for class C, and (jimplof SIG) is the type of implementations of functions with signature SIG.

The proof rules also define auxiliary predicates: (ofType E T) to express that E has type T; (ptr E ro T) and (ptr E rw T) to express that E is a (read-only or read-write, respectively) pointer to an element of type T; and (ofmem M) to express that the contents of the memory M is well-typed.

The Java safety policy provides certain trusted assumptions, declaring for each class provided either by the program or the trusted run-time system, the name of the class, the name of the superclass and that of the implemented interfaces, the layout of the class instances and that of the virtual-method table. There are consistency guarantees restricting these trusted assumptions; an example is that any field of a class needs to fit within the specified size of an instance of a class, so

$$(\forall C, OFF, T)(\texttt{jifield}\ C\ OFF\ T) \rightarrow (OFF + 4) \leq (\texttt{size\_of\_instance}\ C)$$

where (jifield C OFF T) is intended to mean that class C has a field of type T at offset OFF, and (size_of_instance C) is the memory space required to allocate an instance of class C.

The trusted assumptions include data from a trusted initialization phase of the program; for instance, the function (loc_of_virtab C) returns the location in memory where the virtual-method table for class C is allocated. The safety policy thus assumes a start state where the virtual-method tables and static class members have been allocated.

Finally, the safety policy specifies trusted allocation functions for objects, arrays, and primitive types. In the cases of objects and arrays, the functions also provide some very basic initialization, such as writing the location of the virtual-method table at the appropriate offset. The postcondition of an allocation for a type T is that the returned memory address RES satisfies (ofType RES T).

In order to formalize the auxiliary machine, we need an appropriate pseudo-state. In this case we use a *memory-type representation*, which is a list of memory addresses and associated types. The representation indicates which types have been allocated at which locations, and is used to produce the instances of ofType and ptr which follow from the postconditions of the allocations. The pseudo-state also includes the state of the memory after the most recent allocation, used to produce the correct instances of ofmem.

$$R ::= \texttt{nil} \mid (E, T) :: R$$
$$P ::= (R, M)$$

Then we can formalize ofType, ptr, and ofmem as mutually inductive predicates parameterized by the auxiliary state; as in the example of the box safety policy, the inductive constructors incorporate all the proof rules given by the safety policy (without considering the state parameter), as well as additional constructors to reflect which postconditions of the trusted allocators will be available. The predicates saferd and safewr are also specified inductively, with just one constructor each:[3]

$$(\texttt{ptr } s \; E \; RWFLAG \; T) \rightarrow (\texttt{saferd } s \; E)$$
$$(\texttt{ptr } s \; E_1 \; \texttt{rw} \; T) \rightarrow (\texttt{ofType } s \; E_2 \; T) \rightarrow (\texttt{safewr } s \; E_1 \; E_2)$$

In outline, the soundness proof runs as follows. We develop an invariant on (auxiliary system) states, such that the invariant implies that whenever the saferd or safewr predicates hold, the appropriate memory has in fact been allocated. From this it follows that on all states satisfying the invariant, auxiliary transitions can be emulated by reference transitions. Next we establish that all auxiliary transitions preserve the invariant, and we define the start state and show that it satisfies the invariant. This entails that all reachable states satisfy the invariant, and the proof is complete. For more information, see the Coq development at http://www.math.berkeley.edu/~schneck/javacade/.

4   Aspects of Formalization

For a formalization tool we use the Coq system [4]. Coq has two main advantages over other choices. One is that Coq produces a proof object (a lambda-term in a typed lambda-calculus) for all proven theorems. This is vital for any PCC application, because the proof-checker is part of the trusted base, and so it is important not to require the full power of a complicated theorem prover just to check that a proof is correct. When the framework is sufficiently generalized to allow code producers to submit their own safety-policies, these proof objects will also be submitted, as the guarantees that the submitted policies ensure memory safety.

The second main advantage of Coq, and the one that makes it particularly suited to this application, is its strong handling of inductively defined types and predicates. The soundness proof requires defining typing predicates inductively,

---

[3] This is slightly simplified; the actual formal development has to take into account that the various types require different sizes in memory.

as derivations via inference rules, and then making arguments such as induction over the structure of the derivation, or inversion based on the form of the typing predicate (i.e., noting which inference rules allow a result of the given form, and then arguing that the hypotheses of one of those rules must hold). All of this is extremely easy in Coq.

There is, of course, some tension between these two advantages: Coq is far from a minimal formalism, having a rich type system (including inductive types as a primitive notion), and this makes its proof checker more complicated. It seems to us that Coq strikes the appropriate balance.

Coq's automation facility was quite useful. It uses a Prolog-like technique to try to prove the goal from the hypotheses and user-supplied hints. Unfortunately, only goal-directed hints are accepted; it many cases it would have been helpful to have a hint of the form, "if there is a hypothesis of a certain inductively defined predicate, proceed by performing inversion on that hypothesis". Also, reasoning based on equality seemed tricky to automatize. For these reasons, there were many steps of the proof that would be considered obvious in an informal presentation, but were not comfortably handled automatically by Coq. A large amount of the work of formalization was exploring the limits of automation.

5   Comparison with Foundational Proof-Carrying Code

Appel, Felty, and others have introduced a variant PCC framework which they call *foundational proof-carrying code* (FPCC) [2,1]. Instead of having a trusted VCGen to generate the theorem whose proof guarantees safety, foundational PCC defines, in some foundational logic, the semantics of machine instructions and when instructions are considered safe. The safety theorem is then directly expressible in the logic: simply that when the integers which compose the program are loaded into memory and the machine's program counter is set to the beginning of the program, the machine will never reach a state of attempting an unsafe instruction.

FPCC certainly requires a very small set of trusted components. One must still trust a proof checker, of course. There must indeed be code which, analogous to VCGen, looks at a program and produces the theorem, a proof of which witnesses the safety of the given program; however this code must do very little more than correctly produce the list of integers which constitutes the given program. The decoding of those integers into machine instructions is given as a set of logical definitions, rather than as a program which performs the decoding. (It is unclear whether it is actually *easier* to trust that a large set of logical definitions correctly specifies the decoding, than to trust a program which does the decoding; however it is surely not *harder* to trust.) Finally, one must trust logical axioms which encode the semantics of the machine instructions and the safety policy: both the effect of executing the instruction on the machine state, and what conditions must hold for the execution of a given instruction to be considered safe.

In general, it seems that a paradigm essentially similar to VCGen will be used to construct the FPCC proof of safety [6]. That is to say, the integers which constitute the program will be decoded into a list of machine language instructions; local invariants will be constructed for various points in the program in such a way that whenever an invariant holds, progress can be made in the execution of the program, and any other local invariant next reached will still hold; and finally, the local invariant corresponding to the initial state of the program is proven. In VCGen-based PCC, this initial invariant *is* the theorem that guarantees safety, and its proof is all that is transmitted to the code receiver. In foundational PCC, on the other hand, everything else that VCGen does, and the proof that it does it correctly, is also embedded in the proof sent to the code receiver.

An essential difference between FPCC and the work described in this paper is the approach to *scalability*. Current implementations of VCGen-based PCC can handle programs of half a million lines of Java code; making this possible required certain engineering innovations (see e.g. [9]) which may be much more difficult to adapt to FPCC, which necessarily produces more complicated proofs. Clearly, scalability is vitally important to the success of a PCC system. We hope to retain the engineering work which allows the scalability of current implementations, while adding support for greater security and extensibility bit by bit. Taking the approach of FPCC, one starts with a maximally secure and flexible PCC system, and gradually scales to larger and larger examples. This may be a very slow and difficult process.

It is also worth pointing out a difference in our approach to formal type-safety proofs. Appel and Felty in [2] advocate a semantic approach: typing judgments are assigned a semantic truth-value relative to the state, such that typing rules are to be proven as lemmas, and the safety of a well-typed machine state follows immediately from the semantic definition of well-typedness. In contrast we have found that the syntactic approach (where we work directly with the inductive definitions of derivations of typing judgments) to be successful, and almost certainly conceptually simpler. In this our work bears some similarity to the work of Hamid et al. [5], who also aim to develop a full-fledged FPCC system, but advocate the syntactic approach. We note that this group also uses the Coq system, which has very strong handling of inductive types.

6   Conclusions and Future Directions

We have created the prototype of a general framework for stating a soundness theorem for the proof rules of PCC safety policies. Using the framework, we have produced a machine-checkable soundness proof for the typing axioms of a real safety policy for PCC. This soundness proof increases the security of PCC by removing from the trusted base one of the most specific, and thus least well-tested, parts of the system. This is done without giving up trust in more well-tested parts of the system; and there is no reduction of the ability of PCC to scale to large programs. The potentially general nature of the framework allows a more flexible PCC where new safety policies can be introduced by any code producer.

There are still certain issues to be resolved. An important one is the handling of trusted functions, which is still very specific to the Java safety policy. In order to generalize the framework to axiom systems where the trusted functions have different postconditions, we need to specify precisely how the trusted functions are to affect the pseudo-state, and what the corresponding clauses in the inductive definitions of the predicates must be. In order to generalize to different trusted functions altogether, we must specify how the machine behavior of the trusted functions is to be translated onto our abstract machine state. More generally, we need to make clear exactly what is involved in specifying a safety policy as a formal object.

Also, our framework so far is limited to proving the soundness of the proof rules, which is only a part of a typical safety policy. The rest of the policy is implemented as extensions to VCGen. In the case of the Java module, VCGen extensions handle discovering the trusted assumptions and requiring proofs of the consistency guarantees as needed, including handling of the initialization phase of the program where the virtual-method tables are allocated; and they handle novel (to VCGen) programming constructs such as dynamic dispatch, which the core VCGen is unable to deal with. An important step in future research will be to find an approach to proving the soundness of such extensions.

References

1. Andrew W. Appel. Foundational proof-carrying code. In *Proceedings of the 16th Annual IEEE Symposium on Logic in Computer Science*, pages 247–258, June 2001.
2. Andrew W. Appel and Amy P. Felty. A semantic model of types and machine instructions for proof-carrying code. In *POPL '00: The 27th ACM SIGPLAN-SIGACT Symposium on Principles of Programming Languages*, pages 243–253. ACM Press, January 2000.
3. Christopher Colby, Peter Lee, George C. Necula, Fred Blau, Mark Plesko, and Kenneth Cline. A certifying compiler for Java. *ACM SIGPLAN Notices*, 35(5):95–107, May 2000.
4. Coq Development Team. The Coq proof assistant reference manual, version 7.2. January 2002.
5. Nadeem A. Hamid, Zhong Shao, Valery Trifonov, Stefan Monnier, and Zhaozhong Ni. A syntactic approach to foundational proof-carrying code. Submitted for publication, January 2002.
6. Neophytos G. Michael and Andrew W. Appel. Machine instruction syntax and semantics in higher-order logic. In *Proceedings of the 17th International Conference on Automated Deduction*, pages 7–24. Springer-Verlag, June 2000.
7. George C. Necula. Proof-carrying code. In *The 24th Annual ACM Symposium on Principles of Programming Languages*, pages 106–119. ACM, January 1997.
8. George C. Necula. *Compiling with Proofs*. PhD thesis, Carnegie Mellon University, September 1998. Also available as CMU-CS-98-154.
9. George C. Necula. A scalable architecture for proof-carrying code. In *The 5th International Symposium of Functional and Logic Programming*, pages 21–39, March 2001.

Formal Verification of a Java Compiler in Isabelle[*]

Martin Strecker

Fakultät für Informatik, Technische Universität München
http://www.in.tum.de/~streckem

Abstract. This paper reports on the formal proof of correctness of a
compiler from a substantial subset of Java source language to Java bytecode in the proof environment Isabelle. This work is based on extensive
previous formalizations of Java, which comprise all relevant features of
object-orientation. We place particular emphasis on describing the effects
of design decisions in these formalizations on the compiler correctness
proof.

1 Introduction

The compiler correctness proof presented in this paper is part of a more comprehensive research effort aiming at formalizing and verifying key aspects of a
substantial subset of the Java programming language, in particular:

- the type system and operational semantics of Java, with a proof of type
  soundness [Ohe01a]
- an axiomatic semantics, with a proof of its equivalence to the operational
  semantics [Ohe01b]
- an abstract dataflow analyzer [Nip01], instantiated for Java bytecode, with
  a proof of correctness of Java bytecode verification [KN02].

All these formalizations and proofs have been carried out in the Isabelle system.
They will be briefly reviewed in Section 2, as far as relevant for our purpose.
  The present work links the existing Java source and bytecode formalizations,

- by defining an executable compiler from source to bytecode (Section 3), and
- by stating and proving a compiler correctness theorem with Isabelle (Section 4).

To date, there have been numerous machine-supported compiler correctness
proofs and several pen-and-paper formalizations of aspects of Java (cf. Section 5).
The current effort distinguishes itself from previous ones by being the first (to the
best of our knowledge) to formally establish such a result for a realistic object-
oriented language: our description of Java, even though incomplete in several
respects, comprises all essential features of object-orientation. In addition, the

---

[*] This research is funded by the EU project *VerifiCard*

A. Voronkov (Ed.): CADE-18, LNAI 2392, pp. 63–77, 2002.

source language model includes a notion of exceptions (which are, however, so far not taken into account in the correctness proof). To achieve a succinct presentation of the operational semantics, a few fundamental design decisions have been made. A recurring theme of this paper will be to analyse their consequences for compiler verification.

This paper can only give a survey of the overall effort – for details, consult the Isabelle sources at http://isabelle.in.tum.de/verificard/.

2 Language Formalizations

In this section, we give an overview of Isabelle and describe the existing formalizations of Java in Isabelle: the source language, μJava, and the Java virtual machine language, μJVM. This "micro" edition of Java (see [NOP00] for a gentle introduction) accommodates essential aspects of Java, like classes, subtyping, object creation, inheritance, dynamic binding and exceptions, but abstracts away from the wealth of arithmetic data types, interfaces, arrays, access modifiers, and multi-threading. It is a good approximation of the JavaCard dialect of Java, targeted at smart cards.

2.1 Isabelle Preliminaries

Isabelle is a generic framework for encoding different object logics. In this paper, we will only be concerned with the incarnation Isabelle/HOL [NPW02], which comprises a higher-order logic and facilities for defining datatypes as well as primitive and terminating general recursive functions.

Isabelle's syntax is reminiscent of ML, so we will only mention a few peculiarities: Consing an element x to a list xs is written as x#xs. Infix @ is the append operator, xs ! n selects the n-th element from list xs at position n.

We have the usual type constructors T1 $\times$ T2 for product and T1 $\Rightarrow$ T2 for function space. The long arrow $\Longrightarrow$ is Isabelle's meta-implication, in the following mostly used in conjunction with rules of the form $\llbracket$ P1; ...; Pn $\rrbracket$ $\Longrightarrow$ C to express that C follows from the premises P1 ... Pn. Apart from that, there is the implication $\longrightarrow$ of the HOL object logic, along with the standard connectives and quantifiers.

The polymorphic option type
datatype 'a option = None | Some 'a
is frequently used to simulate partiality in a logic of total functions: Here, None stands for an undefined value, Some x for a defined value x. Lifted to function types, we obtain the type of "partial" functions T1 $\rightsquigarrow$ T2, which just abbreviates T1 $\Rightarrow$ (T2 option).

The constructor Some has a left inverse, the function the :: 'a option $\Rightarrow$ 'a, defined by the sole equation the (Some x) = x. This function is total in the sense that also the None is a legal, but indefinite value.

2.2 μJava Source Language

We will now sketch the formalization of the μJava source language in Isabelle in the following stages:

- We will describe the *structure* of a μJava program, building on a formalization of its constituents, i.e. raw terms and types. Obviously, this is prerequisite to defining a translation from Java to Java bytecode (Section 3).
- Using a notion of *well-typedness*, it is possible to single out "legal" expressions, statements and (in extenso) programs. Only these will be considered for compiler correctness, see Section 4.1.
- The behaviour of μJava programs is defined by an *operational semantics* in the form of an evaluation relation. The semantics is essential for the statement of compiler correctness, and it determines the structure of the proof (Section 4.2), which is by induction on the evaluation relation.
- The correctness proof requires still another proviso, namely that during execution, program states *conform* to expected types. As it turns out, this precondition is purely technical and does not impose a genuine restriction. It is satisfied for well-typed programs anyway, due to the *type-safety* of μJava.

The Structure of Programs. The μJava language is embedded deeply in Isabelle, i.e. by an explicit representation of the Java term structure as Isabelle datatypes. We make the traditional distinction between expressions `expr` and statements `stmt`. The latter are standard, except maybe for `Expr`, which turns an arbitrary expression into a statement (this is a slight generalization of Java). For some constructs, more readable mixfix syntax is defined, enclosed in brackets and quotes.

```
datatype expr
   = NewC cname            | Cast cname expr
   | Lit val               | BinOp binop expr expr
   | LAcc vname            | LAss vname expr      ("_::=_")
   | FAcc cname expr vname | FAss cname expr vname
   | Call cname expr mname (ty list) (expr list)      ("{_}_._( {_}_)")

datatype stmt  = Skip      | Expr expr
   | Comp stmt stmt        ("_;; _" )
   | Cond expr stmt stmt   ("If (_) _ Else _")
   | Loop expr stmt        ("While (_) _" )
```

The μJava expressions form a representative subset of Java: `NewC` permits to create a new instance, given a class name `cname`; `Cast` performs a type cast; `Lit` embeds values `val` (see below) into expressions. μJava only knows a few binary operations `binop`: test for equality and integer addition. There is access to local variables with `LAcc`, given a variable name `vname`; assignment to local variables `LAss`; and similarly field access, field assignment and method call. The type annotations contained in braces { } are not part of the original Java syntax; they have been introduced to facilitate type checking. This concludes the description of μJava terms.

The type `val` of values is defined by

```
datatype val =  Unit  |  Null  |  Bool bool  |  Intg int  |  Addr loc
```

`Unit` is a (dummy) result value of void methods, `Null` a null reference. `Bool` and `Intg` are injections from the predefined Isabelle/HOL types `bool` and `int` into `val`, similarly `Addr` from an uninterpreted type `loc` of locations.

Let us briefly sketch the μJava type level, even though its deep structure is not modified by the compiler (which is reflected by some of the preservation lemmas of Section 4.2).

```
datatype prim_ty = Void | Boolean | Integer
datatype ref_ty  = NullT | ClassT cname
datatype ty      = PrimT prim_ty | RefT ref_ty
```

μJava types `ty` are either primitive types or reference types. `Void` is the result type of void methods; note that `Boolean` and `Integer` are not Isabelle types, but simply constructors of `prim_ty`. Reference types are the null pointer type `NullT` or class types.

On this basis, it is possible to define what is a field declaration `fdecl` and a method signature `sig` (method name and list of parameter types). A method declaration `mdecl` consists of a method signature, the method return type and the method body, whose type is left abstract. The method body type `'c` remains a type parameter of all the structures built on top of `mdecl`, in particular `class` (superclass name, list of fields and list of methods), class declaration `cdecl` (holding in addition the class name) and program `prog` (list of class declarations).

```
types   fdecl     = vname × ty
        sig       = mname × ty list
        'c mdecl = sig × ty × 'c
        'c class = cname × fdecl list × 'c mdecl list
        'c cdecl = cname × 'c class
        'c prog  = 'c cdecl list
```

By instantiating the method body type appropriately, we can use these structures both on the Java source and on the bytecode level. For the source level, we take `java_mb prog`, where `java_mb` consists of a list of parameter names, list of local variables (i.e. names and types), and a statement block, terminated with a single result expression (this again is a deviation from original Java).

```
types   java_mb = vname list × (vname × ty) list × stmt × expr
        java_prog = java_mb prog
```

Typing. Typing judgements come in essentially two flavours:
- $E \vdash e :: T$ means that expression e has type T in environment E. We write `wtpd_expr E e` for $\exists\ T.\ E \vdash e :: T$.

- $E \vdash c \surd$ means that statement c is well-typed in environment E.

The *environment* E used here is `java_mb env`, a pair consisting of a Java program `java_mb prog` and a local environment `lenv`.

A program G is well-formed (`wf_java_prog G`) if the bodies of all its methods are well-typed and in addition some structural properties are satisfied – mainly that all class names are distinct and the superclass relation is well-founded.

Operational Semantics. The operational semantics, in the style of a big-step (natural) semantics, describes how the evaluation of expressions and statements affects the program state, and, in the case of an expression, what is the result value. The semantics is defined as inductive relation, again in two variants:

- for expressions, $G \vdash s$ `-e>v->` s' means that for program G, evaluation of e in state s yields a value v and a new state s' (note that the evaluation of expressions may have side-effects).
- for statements, $G \vdash s$ `-c->` s' means that for program G, execution of c in state s yields a new state s'.

The *state* (of type `xstate`) is a triple, consisting of an optional exception component that indicates whether an exception is active, a heap `aheap` which maps locations `loc` to objects, and a local variable environment `locals` mapping variable names to values.

```
types   aheap  = loc ⤳ obj
        locals = vname ⤳ val
        state  = aheap × locals
        xstate = xcpt option × state
```

The semantics has been designed to be non-blocking even in the presence of certain errors such as type errors. For example, dynamic method binding is achieved via a method lookup function `method` that selects the method to be invoked, given the dynamic type `dynT` of expression e (whereas C is the static type) and the method signature (i.e. method name `mn` and parameter types `pTs`). Again, the method `m` thus obtained is indefinite if either `dynT` does not denote a valid class type or the method signature is not defined for `dynT`.

```
Call: ⟦ ...    m = the (method (G,dynT) (mn,pTs));    ... ⟧
      ⟹    G⊢Norm s0 -{C}e..mn({pTs}ps) ≻ v -> s'
```

The evaluation rules could be formulated differently so as to exclude indefinite values, at the expense of making the rules unwieldy, or they could block in the case of type errors, which would make a type correctness statement impossible (see [Ohe01a] for a discussion). Fortunately, the type safety results provided in the following show that this kind of values does not arise anyway. Unfortunately, the rules force us to carry along this type safety argument in the compiler correctness proof – see Section 4.2.

Conformance and Type-Safety. The type-safety statement requires as auxiliary concept the notion of *conformance*, which is defined in several steps:

- Conformance of a value v with type T (relative to program G and heap h), written $G,\ h \vdash v ::\preceq T$, means that the dynamic type of v under h is a subtype of T.
- Conformance of an object means that all of its fields conform to their declared types.
- Finally, a state s conforms to an environment E, written as $s ::\preceq E$, if all "reachable" objects of the heap of s conform and all local variables of E conform to their declared types.

The type safety theorem says that if evaluation of an expression e well-typed in environment E starts from a conforming state s, then the resulting state is again conforming; in addition, if no exception is raised, the result value v conforms to the static type T of e. An analogous statement holds for evaluation of statements.

2.3   Java Bytecode

For the Isabelle formalization of the Java Virtual Machine, μJVM, we have in principle to go through the same steps as for μJava, in particular definition of the language structure and operational semantics. There are however quite different mechanisms for dealing with typing issues; they are only skimmed in the following.

The μJava bytecode instructions manipulate data of type val, as introduced in Section 2.2. The instruction set is a simplification of the original Java bytecode in that the Load and Store instructions are polymorphic, i.e. operate on any type of value. In μJVM, there are so far only system exceptions; exceptions cannot be thrown explicitly and cannot be handled.[1]

```
datatype
  instr = Load nat          | Store nat
        | LitPush val       | New cname
        | Getfield vname cname  | Putfield vname cname
        | Checkcast cname    | Invoke cname mname (ty list)
        | Return             | Pop
        | Dup                | Dup_x1
        | Dup_x2             | Swap
        | IAdd               | Goto int
        | Ifcmpeq int
```

As mentioned in Section 2.2, much of the program structure is shared between source and bytecode level. Simply by exchanging the method body type, we can define the type of Java virtual machine programs:

```
types   bytecode = instr list
        jvm_prog = (nat × nat × bytecode) prog
```

Apart from the bytecode, the method body contains two numbers (maximum stack size and length of local variable array) which are required by the bytecode verifier but need not concern us here.

---

[1] This situation is currently being remedied.

The type *jvm_prog* reflects the structure of a Java class file rather directly up to minor differences, such as version numbers, redundant administrative information (e.g. methods count), and data related to interfaces, which are not handled in μJava and can thus be assumed to be void.

Ensuring type correctness of bytecode is the responsibility of the bytecode verifier. In analogy to the type safety result for the source level, it can be shown that if bytecode passes a correct bytecode verifier, it can be executed "safely" – see [KN02] for details.

The JVM operational semantics defines the effect of executing instructions on the *jvm_state*, which is a triple consisting of an optional component indicating the presence of an exception, a heap and a frame stack.

```
types    opstack    = val list
         locvars    = val list
         frame      = opstack ×  locvars × cname ×  sig × nat
         jvm_state  = xcpt option × aheap × frame list
```

Each frame holds an operand stack *opstack*, a list of local variables *locvars*, the class name and signature identifying the currently executing method, and the program counter. *xcpt*, *aheap* and *sig* are the same as on the source level. The only genuine data refinement is for the representation of local variables: In μJava, the method-local variables *locals* are a mapping from names to values. In μJVM, *locvars* is a list $this, p_1, \ldots, p_n, l_1, \ldots, l_m$ containing a reference *this* to the current class and the parameters $p_1, \ldots, p_n$ and local variable values $l_1, \ldots, l_m$ of the current method. This refinement is achieved by function *locvars_locals*, still needed further below.

The function *exec_instr* takes an instruction and the constituents of a state and computes the follow-up state. The *Load* instruction, for example, produces no exception (*None*), leaves the heap *hp* unmodified, and changes the topmost frame by pushing the contents of the local variable with index *idx* on the operand stack *stk* and incrementing the program counter *pc*.

```
exec_instr (Load idx) G hp stk vars C S pc frs =
    (None, hp, ((vars ! idx) # stk, vars, C, S, pc+1)#frs)
```

Function *exec* carries out a single step of computation: It looks up the current method, given μJVM program *G*, class name *C* and signature *S*, selects the instruction indicated by the program counter and executes it.

The relation *G ⊢ s -jvm-> t*, defined by means of the transitive closure of *exec*, expresses that state *t* can be reached from state *s* by a sequence of successful execution steps:

```
exec_all :: [jvm_prog,jvm_state,jvm_state] => bool  ("_ ⊢ _ -jvm-> _")
G ⊢ s -jvm-> t == (s,t) ∈ {(s,t). exec(G,s) = Some t}^*
```

3   Compiler Definition

Compilation is straightforwardly defined with the aid of a few directly executable functions. To begin with, `mkExpr :: java_mb => expr => instr list` and `mkStat :: java_mb => stmt => instr list`, defined in Figures 1 and 2, translate expressions resp. statements. The function `index` computes the index of variable name vn in method body jmb by looking up its position in a list of the form $this, p_1, \ldots, p_n, l_1, \ldots, l_m$.

```
mkExpr jmb (NewC c) = [New c]
mkExpr jmb (Cast c e) = mkExpr jmb e @ [Checkcast c]
mkExpr jmb (Lit val) = [LitPush val]
mkExpr jmb (BinOp bo e1 e2) = mkExpr jmb e1 @ mkExpr jmb e2 @
    (case bo of
        Eq => [Ifcmpeq 3,LitPush(Bool False),Goto 2,LitPush(Bool True)]
      | Add => [IAdd])
mkExpr jmb (LAcc vn) = [Load (index jmb vn)]
mkExpr jmb (vn::=e) = mkExpr jmb e @ [Dup , Store (index jmb vn)]
mkExpr jmb ( cne..fn ) = mkExpr jmb e @ [Getfield fn cn]
mkExpr jmb (FAss cn e1 fn e2 ) =
    mkExpr jmb e1 @ mkExpr jmb e2 @ [Dup_x1 , Putfield fn cn]
mkExpr jmb (Call cn e1 mn X ps) =
    mkExpr jmb e1 @ mkExprs jmb ps @ [Invoke cn mn X]
mkExprs jmb [] = []
mkExprs jmb (e#es) = mkExpr jmb e @ mkExprs jmb es
```

Fig. 1. Compilation of expressions

On this basis, compilation is extended to more complex structures, first method bodies, then classes and finally entire programs. `mkMethod` translates method bodies, essentially by appending code for the method body block blk and the result expression res and adding a `Return` instruction:

```
mkMethod :: java_mb => (nat * nat * bytecode)
mkMethod jmb == let (pn,lv,blk,res) = jmb
                in (0, 0,
                    (concat (map (mkInit jmb) lv)) @
                    (mkStat jmb blk) @ (mkExpr jmb res) @ [Return])
```

Prepended to this are instructions initializing the local variables lv to their default values – a complication which could be avoided if variables were known to be assigned to before being read. Such a check, as embodied in Java's "definite assignment" principle, is however not part of our current well-formedness condition of μJava programs. As mentioned in Section 2.3, the first two components of the result of `mkMethod` are only relevant for bytecode verification. Indeed, it can be shown that the compiler only produces bytecode which is type correct in the sense that it passes bytecode verification [Str02]. Since there is no space to discuss this issue here, we set these components to zero.

```
mkStmt jmb Skip = []
mkStmt jmb (Expr e) = (mkExpr jmb e) @ [Pop]
mkStmt jmb (c1;; c2) = (mkStmt jmb c1) @ (mkStmt jmb c2)
mkStmt jmb (If(e) c1 Else c2) =
    (let cnstf = LitPush (Bool False);
         cnd = mkExpr jmb e;
         thn = mkStmt jmb c1;
         els = mkStmt jmb c2;
         test = Ifcmpeq (int(length thn +2));
         thnex = Goto (int(length els +1))
    in [cnstf] @ cnd @ [test] @ thn @ [thnex] @ els)
mkStmt jmb (While(e) c) =
    (let cnstf = LitPush (Bool False);
         cnd = mkExpr jmb e;
         bdy = mkStmt jmb c;
         test = Ifcmpeq (int(length bdy +2));
         loop = Goto (-(int((length bdy) + (length cnd) +2)))
    in [cnstf] @ cnd @ [test] @ bdy @ [loop])
```

Fig. 2. Compilation of statements

Classes are translated by generating code for the method bodies and leaving the remaining structure untouched – recall that μJava and μJVM classes essentially differ in their method bodies.

```
mkClass :: java_mb cdecl  =>  (nat * nat * bytecode) cdecl
mkClass == λ(cn,cno,fdl,jmdl). (cn,cno,fdl,
            map (λ(s,t,mb). (s,t, mkMethod mb)) jmdl)


comp :: java_mb prog  =>  jvm_prog
comp jp == map mkClass jp
```

As mentioned in Section 2.3, the structure of *jvm_prog* is essentially the Java class file format. Even though the compiler only produces a symbolic class file and not an executable binary, this last step is relatively straightforward: It is possible to generate ML code from the Isabelle definition, using the code extraction facility described in [BN00], and then supply the print functions in ML.

4   Compiler Verification

4.1   Compiler Correctness Statement

In a rough sketch, the compiler correctness statement takes the form of the traditional "commuting diagram" argument: Suppose execution of a statement c transforms a μJava state s into a state s'. Then, for any μJVM state t corresponding to s, executing the bytecode resulting from a translation of c yields a state t' corresponding to s'.

This sketch has to be refined in that the notion of correspondence has to be made precise, both for expressions and for statements. Besides, compiler correctness depends on a few assumptions that will be spelled out here and further motivated in Section 4.2.

We first need a notion describing the effects of completely evaluating an expression or executing a statement on a μJVM state, in analogy to the evaluation and execution relations on the μJava level. We note the following:

- Apart from the exception indicator and the heap, only the topmost frame is affected, but not the remaining frame stack.
- When executing an instruction sequence `instrs`, the program counter advances by `length instrs`, provided `instrs` is part of the bytecode of a method body (which in particular implies that the start and end positions of the program counter are well-defined).

Of course, these observations do not hold for intermediate steps of a computation, e.g. when frames are pushed on the frame stack during a method call or when jumping back to the start of a while loop, but only after completion, when the frames have been popped off again or the whole while loop has finished.

This suggests a relation `progression`, defined as:

```
progression :: jvm_prog ⇒ cname ⇒ sig ⇒
               aheap ⇒ opstack ⇒ locvars ⇒
               bytecode ⇒
               aheap ⇒ opstack ⇒ locvars ⇒
               bool
               ("{_,_,_} ⊢ {_, _, _} >- _ → {_, _, _}" )
{G,C,S} ⊢ {hp0, os0, lvars0} >- instrs → {hp1, os1, lvars1} ==
∀ pre post frs.
(gis (gmb G C S) = pre @ instrs @ post) ⟶
G ⊢ (None,hp0,(os0,lvars0,C,S,length pre)#frs) -jvm->
  (None,hp1,(os1,lvars1,C,S,(length pre) + (length instrs))#frs)
```

Here, `{G, C, S} ⊢ {hp0, os0, lvars0} >- instrs → {hp1, os1, lvars1}` expresses that execution of instructions `instrs` transforms heap `hp0`, operand stack `os0` and local variables `lvars0` into `hp1`, `os1` and `lvars1`. Since exceptions are excluded from consideration here, the exception indicator of the states is invariantly `None`.

The instructions `instrs` are a subsequence of the instructions (selected by `gis`) of the method body (selected by `gmb`) of signature `S` in class `C` of program `G`. During execution, the program counter advances from the first position of `instrs` (at `length pre`) to the position right behind `instrs` (at `length pre + length instrs`). This indirect coding of the program counter movement not only makes the correctness statement more concise. It is also helpful in the proof, as it removes the need for engaging in complex "program counter arithmetic" – abstract properties like transitivity of `progression` are sufficient most of the time.

We are now prepared to clarify the notion of correspondence between μJava and μJVM states and present the correctness theorem for evaluation of expressions (the one for execution of statements is analogous).

Suppose that evaluation of expression ex in μJava state $(None, hp, loc)$ yields result val and state $(None, hp', loc')$, and some other conditions explained in a moment are met. We assume that ex is part of the method which can be identified by program G, class C and signature S. When running the bytecode $mkExpr$ $(gmb\ G\ C\ S)$ ex generated for ex in a μJVM state having the same heap hp, an (arbitrary) operand stack os and local variables as in loc, we obtain heap hp', the operand stack with val on top of it and local variables as in loc' (recall from Section 2.3 that the representation of local variables is refined by function $locvars\_locals$).

```
theorem compiler_correctness_eval:
 [ G ⊢ (None,hp,loc) -ex ≻val->(None,hp',loc');
 wf_java_prog G;
 class_sig_defined G C S;
 wtpd_expr (env_of_jmb G C S) ex;
 (hp,loc) ::≼ (env_of_jmb G C S) ] ⟹
 {(comp G), C, S} ⊢
   {hp, os, (locvars_locals G C S loc)}
     >- (mkExpr (gmb G C S) ex) →
   {hp', val#os, (locvars_locals G C S loc')}
```

The theorem is displayed diagramatically below – note the simplification regarding local variables on the bytecode level.

```
(None,hp,loc) -ex ──────────────────→ val -> (None,hp',loc')
      │                                          │
      │                                          │
      │                                          │
hp, os, loc  >- ──── mkExpr E ex ──────→ hp', val#os, loc'
```

Let us now take a look at the preconditions:

- The source program has to be well-formed as described in Section 2.2.
- The class signature has to be defined in the sense that C is a valid class in G and method lookup with S gives a defined result:
  ```
  class_sig_defined G C S ==
  is_class G C ∧ (∃ m. (method (G, C) S = Some m )
  ```
- Expression ex is well-typed in the environment of the method body. This environment $(env\_of\_jmb\ G\ C\ S)$ is essentially generated by the types of the local variables and the method parameters.
- Finally, the start state of the computation, (hp, loc), conforms (Section 2.2) to this environment.

These requirements are not very restrictive: the well-formedness and well-typing conditions are standard for compilers; the conformance condition is satisfied when a program is started with an empty heap and the local variables are initialized to their default values.

4.2   Compiler Correctness Proof

The correctness proof is by mutual induction on the evaluation relation $G \vdash$
$\_ \ -\_ \ \succ\_->\_$ resp. execution relation $\_ \vdash \_ \ -\_-> \_$. Apart from the rules that
pass on exceptions, which are dealt with trivially under our assumptions, we
essentially obtain a case distinction on the constructs of the source language.
These are handled uniformly and, except for pathological cases such as method
call, without difficulty:

- First, we establish preconditions so as to be able to use the induction hypotheses for subcomputations.
- After that, we apply the induction hypotheses, mostly exploiting transitivity
  of the relation *progression*, and then symbolically evaluate the bytecode with
  Isabelle's simplifier.

The reasoning for obtaining preconditions is as follows:

- *class_sig_defined* is obvious for most cases, when remaining within the
  same method body. An exception is the case "method call", where the preservation lemmas mentioned below are applied.
- Establishing *wtpd_expr* mostly requires showing that it holds for subexpressions (such as *wtpd_expr E e1*) when it is known to hold for a compound
  expression (such as *wtpd_expr E (BinOp op e1 e2)*), which is achieved by
  inversion of the typing rules. Again, method call is more intricate.
- Showing that conformance is still satisfied in the state reached after performing a number of subcomputations (e.g. after evaluating $G \vdash s0$ $-e1\succ$ $v1->$
  $s1$ and before evaluating $G \vdash s1$ $-e2\succ$ $v2->$ $s2$) requires repeated application of the type-soundness theorem.

Even though the proof is fairly straightforward, it has a few rough edges,
some of which can be directly traced back to object-oriented concepts such as
subclassing and dynamic method lookup: In the method *Call* rule of the operational semantics, we use a lookup function *method* which gives an indefinite
result under certain conditions (cf. Section 2.2), for example when being applied to a class that is not defined in the current program *G*. It is the purpose
of the preconditions of the correctness theorem, in particular the conformance
requirement, to exclude this situation.

The same *method* function is also used by the *Invoke* bytecode instruction in
the translated program *comp G*. To make sure that definedness of method lookup
in the source program carries over to the bytecode program, we have established
a series of *preservation lemmas* which incidentally formalize the claim that compilation leaves most of the structure of programs unmodified (cf. Section 3). The
preservation lemmas for the direct subclass relation *subcls1* and for method
lookup are:

```
lemma comp_subcls1: subcls1 G = subcls1 (comp G)
```

```
lemma comp_method : [ wf_prog wf_mb G; is_class G C] ⟹
```

```
(method (G, C) S) = Some (D, rT, mb) ⟶
(method (comp G, C) S) = Some (D, rT, mkMethod mb)
```

Method lookup for a program, a class C and signature S returns the defining class D, the return type rT and the source method body mb resp. the translated method body mkMethod mb.

In view of the above remarks, it may be surprising that the preconditions of the correctness theorem are not exclusively motivated by object-oriented features, but are rather a consequence of the particular style of semantics definition and resulting minor differences between μJava and μJVM semantics. They would – in a similar form – also be required for a much simpler language presented in the same fashion.

We illustrate this point with the translation of conditionals. Our limited μJVM instruction set forces us to translate the If statement to the Ifcmpeq operator, which compares the result of evaluating the condition with the constant Bool False. If evaluation of the condition did not leave behind a boolean value on top of the stack (which we know it does), Ifcmpeq would not be perturbed by the type-inconsistency, but would deterministically select the "else" branch. This is an example of an "offensive" JVM behaviour, close to an actual implementation, that does not bother to care for situations that cannot happen. In contrast, the behaviour of μJava is not determined in this case, so the source and bytecode level behave differently unless we assume that type inconsistencies cannot arise.

5 Conclusions

After a review of the existing Isabelle/HOL formalizations of Java, this paper has described the formalization and correctness proof of another key component, a compiler from source to bytecode. Because the compiler had to fit into an existing framework, the definitions of source and target language could not be "tuned" so as to suit the needs of compiler verification. Under these circumstances, the overall effort invested (4-5 months of work for a novice Isabelle user) can be considered moderate. This seems to indicate that

- proof assistant technology has progressed enough to allow for an analysis of realistic, complex languages.
- the existing formalizations are sufficiently mature to serve as a basis for further investigations.

On a technical level, this work has given insight into the interaction of language formalization and compiler correctness proofs:

- The big-step semantics leads to a concise, intuitive correctness theorem because only states at the end of a computation are compared. In contrast, a small-step (structural operational) semantics, such as the ASM formalization in [SSB01], requires juxtaposition of intermediate states, leading to a complex equivalence relation involving the contents of entire frame stacks.

- However, it is a (general) drawback of a big-step semantics that it only permits to talk about terminating computations and cannot express concurrency and related concepts.
- Object-orientation made the reasoning slightly more involved than it would have been for a plain imperative language, but had no decisive influence.
- A few places of the μJava operational semantics have a non-constructive flavour due to indefinite values resulting from functions like the. These make the evaluation rules more elegant, but buy us nothing in the compiler correctness proof – undefined situations have to be excluded a priori by preconditions of the theorem. Thus, we are confident that our proof could be easily recast in a constructive logic.
- Apart from that, the formalization uses few Isabelle specifics, as witnessed by the definitions and theorems presented in this paper. A transfer to other proof environments offering notions such as a higher-order logic, primitive recursion and inductive definitions should be possible without great effort.

There is a long history of mechanized compiler verification, conducted with different provers and for diverse language paradigms (imperative, functional) [MW72,Cur93,Bou95]. Gradually, the field is evolving away from a demonstration of feasibility to an analysis of complex artifacts: A "stack" of system components, ranging from a high-level language down to a microprocessor, has been examined in the ACL2 system [MBHY89]. Here, the emphasis is on a verified chain of refinements; the techniques employed in the individual phases [You89] are not substantially different from ours. Another direction, pursued in the Verifix project [DV01], is to refine the compiler program itself from an abstract "compiling specification" down to an executable version. Our work has still another focus: it aims at an in-depth investigation of aspects of the Java language.

Traditionally, languages have been studied semi-formally, with proofs in the form of pen-and-paper arguments. A very comprehensive account of this kind is given in [SSB01] for Java. This description covers far more language constructs and Java-specific concepts (multi-threading; class loading) than ours. The consequences of a purely technical difference, namely the use of the ASM formalism, akin to a small-step semantics, have already been discussed. Even though ASMs have previously been used in a fully formal verification [Sch99], it may be difficult to cope with the sheer amount of detail in Java.

Future work on our μJava compiler will add missing features, notably exceptions, however without trying to be complete in a literal sense. Also, it may be worth while to look at some compiler optimizations, for example mapping different source variables having different life times to a single bytecode variable. However, many optimizations that can sensibly be performed on the bytecode are already applicable on the source level.

Acknowledgements. The compiler presented in Section 3 has originally been written by Cornelia Pusch and Giampaolo Bella and only been slightly modified for the correctness proof. Johannes Pfeifroth has given a first version of the compiler correctness statement of Section 4.1. I am grateful to Axel Dold, Gerwin

Klein, Marko Luther and Norbert Schirmer for comments on a draft version of this paper.

References

[BN00]   Stefan Berghofer and Tobias Nipkow. Executing higher order logic. In *Proc. TYPES Working Group Annual Meeting 2000*, LNCS, 2000. Available from http://www4.in.tum.de/~berghofe/papers/TYPES2000.pdf.

[Bou95]   Samuel Boutin. Preuve de correction de la compilation de Mini-ML en code CAM dans le système d'aide à la démonstration COQ. Technical Report 2536, INRIA Rocquencourt, April 1995.

[Cur93]   Paul Curzon. A verified Vista implementation. Technical Report 311, University of Cambridge, Computer Laboratory, September 1993. Available from http://www.cl.cam.ac.uk/Research/HVG/vista/.

[DV01]   A. Dold and V. Vialard. A mechanically verified compiling specification for a Lisp compiler. In *Proc. FSTTCS 2001*, December 2001.

[KN02]   Gerwin Klein and Tobias Nipkow. Verified bytecode verifiers. *Theoretical Computer Science*, 2002. to appear.

[MBHY89]   J.S. Moore, W.R. Bevier, W. A. Hunt, and W. D. Young. System verification. *Special issue of J. of Automated Reasoning*, 5(4), 1989.

[MW72]   R. Milner and R. Weyhrauch. Proving compiler correctness in a mechanized logic. *Machine Intelligence*, 7:51–70, 1972.

[Nip01]   Tobias Nipkow. Verified bytecode verifiers. In M. Miculan F. Honsell, editor, *Foundations of Software Science and Computation Structures (FOSSACS 2001)*, volume 2030 of *Lecture Notes in Computer Science*. Springer Verlag, 2001.

[NOP00]   Tobias Nipkow, David von Oheimb, and Cornelia Pusch. μJava: Embedding a programming language in a theorem prover. In F.L. Bauer and R. Steinbrüggen, editors, *Foundations of Secure Computation. Proc. Int. Summer School Marktoberdorf 1999*, pages 117–144. IOS Press, 2000.

[NPW02]   Tobias Nipkow, Lawrence Paulson, and Markus Wenzel. *Isabelle/HOL. A Proof Assistant for Higher-Order Logic*. LNCS 2283. Springer, 2002.

[Ohe01a]   David von Oheimb. *Analyzing Java in Isabelle/HOL: Formalization, Type Safety and Hoare Logic*. PhD thesis, Technische Universität München, 2001. http://www4.in.tum.de/~oheimb/diss/.

[Ohe01b]   David von Oheimb. Hoare logic for Java in Isabelle/HOL. *Concurrency: Practice and Experience*, 13(13), 2001.

[Sch99]   G. Schellhorn. *Verifikation abstrakter Zustandsmaschinen*. PhD thesis, Universität Ulm, 1999.

[SSB01]   R. Stärk, J. Schmid, and E. Börger. *Java and the Java Virtual Machine – Definition, Verification, Validation*. Springer Verlag, 2001.

[Str02]   Martin Strecker. Compilation and bytecode verification in μJava. Forthcoming, preprint available from http://www4.in.tum.de/~streckem/Publications/compbcv02.html, 2002.

[You89]   William D. Young. A mechanically verified code generator. *J. of Automated Reasoning*, 5(4):493–518, 1989.

Embedding Lax Logic into Intuitionistic Logic*

Uwe Egly

Institut für Informationssysteme E184.3, TU Wien
Favoritenstraße 9–11, A–1040 Wien, Austria
uwe@kr.tuwien.ac.at

Abstract. Lax logic is obtained from intuitionistic logic by adding a single modality ○ which captures properties of necessity and possibility. This modality was considered by Curry in two papers from 1952 and 1957 and rediscovered recently in different contexts like verification of circuits and the computational λ-calculus. We show that lax logic can be faithfully embedded into the underlying intuitionistic logic and discuss (computational) properties of the embedding. Using the proposed polynomial-time computable embedding, PSPACE-completeness of the provability problem of propositional lax logic is shown.

1 Introduction

In the last decade, there has been an increasing interest in intuitionistic modal logics. One of them is lax logic (LL) which results from intuitionistic logic by adding the modality ○ (called *lax modality*) satisfying the following three additional axioms:

$$\circ\text{R}: M \to \circ M \qquad \circ\text{M}: \circ\circ M \to \circ M \qquad \circ\text{F}: (M \to N) \to (\circ M \to \circ N)$$

In contrast to other intuitionistic modal logics like intuitionistic S4, no new rule is necessary in a Frege-Hilbert-style formalization. The lax modality was first considered by Curry [2,3] and rediscovered recently by Mendler [13] in the context of verification of circuits and by Benton, Bierman, and de Paiva [1] as a result of a re-engineering process starting from the computational λ-calculus [14]. Applications for lax logic include reasoning about timing constraints for digital circuits. In order to automatize this reasoning process, an automated theorem prover for lax logic is required.

In this paper, we show that propositional (first-order) lax logic can be faithfully embedded into propositional (first-order) intuitionistic logic. This is to say that for each modal formula F, there exists an intuitionistic formula F^* such that F is provable in lax logic if and only if F^* is provable in intuitionistic logic. The translation of F into F^* is polynomial-time computable and preserves the length of cut-free proofs up to a polynomial in case of the translation from proofs of F to proofs of F^*. In case of the other direction, cut-free proofs of F^* are translated into proofs of F *with* cuts. Our embedding simplifies the usual embedding of lax logic into a bimodal (S4, S4) system [8,7] and the embedding of the fragment with implication and lax modality into intuitionistic S4 [15] considerably, because our embedding (together with well-known embeddings from intuitionistic logic into S4) result in an embedding of propositional (first-order) lax logic into classical propositional (first-order) mono-modal S4.

---

* The author would like to thank R. Dyckhoff, T. Eiter, D. Galmiche, D. Larchey-Wendling, and S. Woltran for discussions and the anonymous referees for questions and comments.

A. Voronkov (Ed.): CADE-18, LNAI 2392, pp. 78–93, 2002.
© Springer-Verlag Berlin Heidelberg 2002

Combining our faithful embedding with a "terminating" calculus for propositional intuitionistic logic like G4ip [4] yields a decision procedure (*without* loop-checks) even if proof search is performed from the end sequent towards the axioms. This is remarkable because no such decision procedure is known for propositional lax logic (see [11] for a discussion of the difficulties).

In contrast to other approaches, we show faithfulness of the embedding by purely proof-theoretical means. This has the desired consequence that additional properties like the preservation of proof length (up to a polynomial) and the recursive translation procedure itself result as a by-product. We use the proposed polynomial-time computable embedding in order to show that the provability problem of propositional lax logic is PSPACE-complete.

2   Preliminaries

Throughout this paper we use a first-order language consisting of *variables, function symbols, predicate symbols, logical connectives, falsum* ($\perp$), *quantifiers, the modality* $\circ$, *and punctuation symbols. Terms* and *formulae* are defined according to the usual formation rules. Negation is a defined concept, i.e., $\neg F$ is defined to be $F \to \perp$. We will identify 0-ary predicate symbols with *propositional atoms*, and 0-ary function symbols with (*object*) *constants*.

The *logical complexity* of a formula F, denoted by $lcomp(F)$, is the number of occurrences of connectives, quantifiers and modalities.

We use Gentzen systems (sequent systems) with and without the cut rule. The formal objects of our sequent systems are *intuitionistic sequents* $S \colon \Gamma \Longrightarrow \Sigma$, where Γ, Σ are finite multi-sets of formulae and Σ consists of at most one formula. (Γ is the *antecedent* of S, and Σ is the *succedent* of S.) Due to the use of multi-sets rather than sequences, no exchange rule is required.

The inference rules of the sequent system for first-order lax logic, called LL_1, are depicted in Fig. 1; it is a first-order extension of the sequent calculus for propositional lax logic from [6] with minor modifications. The axioms are of the form $\Gamma, \perp \Longrightarrow F$ or of the form $T \colon \Gamma, F \Longrightarrow F$. If F is atomic then T is called an *atomic* axiom. By LL_1+cut, we denote LL_1 extended by

$$\frac{\Gamma \Longrightarrow C \quad \Gamma, C \Longrightarrow \Delta}{\Gamma \Longrightarrow \Delta} \ cut$$

The formula C is called the *cut formula*. The cut rule is admissible in LL_1; this can be shown by an extension of Gentzen's *Hauptsatz* or cut elimination theorem.

The usual restrictions apply to the quantifier rules. The rules $\forall r$ and $\exists l$ must satisfy the *eigenvariable condition*, i.e., the *eigenvariable* y does not occur (free) in $\forall x A$, $\exists x A$, Γ, and Δ, respectively. Additionally, the term t in $\forall l$ and $\exists r$ is free for x in A.

We use the terms *principal formula* and *proof* in a sequent system in the usual way. By $\vdash_C S$, we mean provability of a sequent S in the sequent calculus C (with $C = i$ for intuitionistic logic, and with $C = l$ for lax logic). The length of a proof α, $l(\alpha)$, is defined to be the number of sequents occurring in α.

$$\frac{\Gamma, A, A \implies \Delta}{\Gamma, A \implies \Delta} \; cl \qquad \frac{\Gamma \implies \Delta}{\Gamma, A \implies \Delta} \; wl \qquad \frac{\Gamma \implies}{\Gamma \implies A} \; wr$$

$$\frac{\Gamma, A \implies \Delta}{\Gamma, A \wedge B \implies \Delta} \; \wedge l \qquad \frac{\Gamma, B \implies \Delta}{\Gamma, A \wedge B \implies \Delta} \; \wedge l \qquad \frac{\Gamma \implies A \quad \Gamma \implies B}{\Gamma \implies A \wedge B} \; \wedge r$$

$$\frac{\Gamma, A \implies \Delta \quad \Gamma, B \implies \Delta}{\Gamma, A \vee B \implies \Delta} \; \vee l \qquad \frac{\Gamma \implies A}{\Gamma \implies A \vee B} \; \vee r \qquad \frac{\Gamma \implies B}{\Gamma \implies A \vee B} \; \vee r$$

$$\frac{\Gamma \implies A \quad \Gamma, B \implies \Delta}{\Gamma, A \to B \implies \Delta} \; \to l \qquad \frac{\Gamma, A \implies B}{\Gamma \implies A \to B} \; \to r$$

$$\frac{\Gamma, A_t^x \implies \Delta}{\Gamma, \forall x A \implies \Delta} \; \forall l \qquad \frac{\Gamma \implies A_y^x}{\Gamma \implies \forall x A} \; \forall r \qquad \frac{\Gamma, A_y^x \implies \Delta}{\Gamma, \exists x A \implies \Delta} \; \exists l \qquad \frac{\Gamma \implies A_t^x}{\Gamma \implies \exists x A} \; \exists r$$

$$\frac{\Gamma, A \implies \circ B}{\Gamma, \circ A \implies \circ B} \; \circ l \qquad\qquad \frac{\Gamma \implies A}{\Gamma \implies \circ A} \; \circ r$$

Fig. 1. The inference rules of LL_1.

We later need formula occurrences, formula trees and replacements of a formula occurrence at position p in a tree. Formula trees are used in the usual way, i.e., trees whose nodes are labeled with atoms, falsum, connectives, quantifiers (together with the variable) or a modality. Moreover, we will associate with each node additional labels like the position of the node within the tree or a polarity. Sometimes, we will identify the node with its (main) label.

Let $\mathcal{T}_F^{p,q}$ denote the formula tree for a formula F at position p in polarity q. A *position* is a string over the alphabet $\{0, 1\}$. Polarities are denoted by $+$ (positive) and $-$ (negative). If q denotes a polarity, then $\bar{q}$ is $+$ when $q = -$, and $-$ otherwise. Formula trees (with position labels and polarity signs) are defined inductively as follows.

$$
\mathcal{T}_F^{p,q} =
\begin{cases}
A^{p,q} & \text{if } F \text{ is } A \text{ and } A \text{ is atomic or } \bot, \\[2ex]
\begin{array}{c} \circ^{p,q} \\ | \\ \mathcal{T}_G^{p1,q} \end{array} & \text{if } F \text{ is } \circ G, \\[3ex]
\begin{array}{c} \star^{p,q} \\ \diagup \quad \diagdown \\ \mathcal{T}_G^{p0,q} \quad \mathcal{T}_H^{p1,q} \end{array} & \text{if } F \text{ is } G \star H \text{ and } \star \in \{\wedge, \vee\}, \\[3ex]
\begin{array}{c} \to^{p,q} \\ \diagup \quad \diagdown \\ \mathcal{T}_G^{p0,\bar{q}} \quad \mathcal{T}_H^{p1,q} \end{array} & \text{if } F \text{ is } G \to H, \\[3ex]
\begin{array}{c} (Qx)^{p,q} \\ | \\ \mathcal{T}_G^{p1,q} \end{array} & \text{if } F \text{ is } QxG \text{ and } Q \in \{\forall, \exists\}.
\end{cases}
$$

Polarities and position labels are sometimes omitted in formula trees.

We use a prefix notation in order to denote formula trees: $N[S_1]$ and $N[S_1, S_2]$ mean that there is a node N with one successor tree S_1 and a node N with two successor trees S_1, S_2, respectively.

We use $p \preceq q$ if p is a prefix of q, i.e., there exists a (possibly empty) string r such that $pr = q$, where pr is the concatenation of p and r. Additionally, $p \prec q$ means $p \preceq q \wedge p \neq q$. Furthermore, $sl(p)$ denotes the *string length* of p, i.e., the number of occurrences of 0 and 1 in p.

An occurrence of a formula F at position p is sometimes denoted by F^p. L_p denotes a (globally new) predicate for a formula occurrence at position p. We say that an occurrence of a connective, a quantifier or a modality at position p *dominates* a subformula occurrence F^q, if $p \preceq q$.

The *principal connective*, the *principal quantifier* or the *principal modality* of a formula is the symbol associated with the root of the corresponding formula tree.

Definition 1. *Let F be a formula and let $\mathcal{T}_F^1$ be the corresponding formula tree with positions. Let*

$$(\mathcal{T}_K^r)_B^p = \begin{cases} \mathcal{T}_B^p & \text{if } r = p, \\ A^r & \text{if } \mathcal{T}_K^r = A^r,\ A \text{ is atomic or } \perp,\ \text{and } r \neq p, \\ (Qx)^r[(\mathcal{T}_L^{r1})_B^p] & \text{if } \mathcal{T}_K^r = (Qx)^r[\mathcal{T}_L^{r1}],\ Q \in \{\forall, \exists\},\ \text{and } r \neq p, \\ \circ^r[(\mathcal{T}_L^{r1})_B^p] & \text{if } \mathcal{T}_K^r = \circ^r[\mathcal{T}_L^{r1}]\ \text{and } r \neq p, \\ \star^r[(\mathcal{T}_L^{r0})_B^p, (\mathcal{T}_M^{r1})_B^p] & \text{if } \mathcal{T}_K^r = \star^r[\mathcal{T}_L^{r0}, \mathcal{T}_M^{r1}],\ \star \in \{\wedge, \vee, \rightarrow\},\ \text{and } r \neq p. \end{cases}$$

Then the replacement *of a formula occurrence at position p in F by B is $(\mathcal{T}_F^1)_B^p$.*

With a slight abuse of notation, we sometimes write F_B^p instead of $(\mathcal{T}_F^1)_B^p$.

We use $form(p, \mathcal{T})$ in order to denote the formula associated to the position p in $\mathcal{T}$; likewise for the polarity $pol(p, \mathcal{T})$.

Remark 1. In sequent systems, principal formulae are *reduced* when an inference rule is applied from the conclusion to the premise(s) in a backward search. Strictly speaking, *formula occurrences* occur in sequents, but position arguments are traditionally neglected.

3   An Embedding of Lax Logic into Intuitionistic Logic

Let $\mathcal{T}_0 = \mathcal{T}_F^1$ be the formula tree associated with F. Define the following sets:

$$\mathcal{P}_\circ^+(F) = \{p \mid form(p, \mathcal{T}_0) = \circ G,\ pol(p, \mathcal{T}_0) = +\} \tag{1}$$

$$\mathcal{P}_\circ^-(F) = \{p \mid form(p, \mathcal{T}_0) = \circ G,\ pol(p, \mathcal{T}_0) = -\} \tag{2}$$

$$\mathcal{S}_\circ^+(F) = \{form(p, \mathcal{T}_0) \mid p \in \mathcal{P}_\circ^+(F)\} \tag{3}$$

$$\mathcal{S}_\circ^-(F) = \{form(p, \mathcal{T}_0) \mid p \in \mathcal{P}_\circ^-(F)\} \tag{4}$$

Intuitively, $\mathcal{P}_\circ^q(F)$ is the set of all positions in polarity q in F labeled with $\circ$, and $\mathcal{S}_\circ^q(F)$ is the set of all subformulae corresponding to these positions.

With $fv(p)$, we denote the sequence of free variables of the formula $form(p, \mathcal{T}_0)$ in an arbitrary but fixed order; moreover, any two variables in $fv(p)$ are distinct. Let G be a subformula occurring at position p in F and let $fv(p) = x_1 \ldots x_n$. Then the *universal closure* of G, denoted by $\forall\, G$, is the formula $\forall x_1 \cdots \forall x_n G$.

Let $n^+(F) = |\mathcal{P}_o^+(F)|$, let $n^-(F) = |\mathcal{P}_o^-(F)|$, and let $n(F) = n^+(F) + n^-(F)$. Moreover, let

$$p_1, \ldots, p_{n(F)} \tag{5}$$

be an (ordered) sequence of all elements of $\mathcal{P}_o^+(F) \cup \mathcal{P}_o^-(F)$ such that

$$\forall i, j \text{ it holds that } sl(p_i) \geq sl(p_j) \text{ whenever } i < j.$$

Obviously, the positions are ordered in decreasing string length and therefore the formula occurrences associated with these positions are ordered in decreasing depth in which they occur in F.

Next, we construct a sequence of formula trees

$$\mathcal{T}_0, \mathcal{T}_1, \ldots, \mathcal{T}_{n(F)} \tag{6}$$

such that

(i) $\mathcal{T}_0$ is the formula tree of F;

(ii) $\mathcal{T}_i$ ($1 \leq i \leq n(F)$) is obtained from $\mathcal{T}_{i-1}$ by replacing the subtree at position p_i by a new formula N. If $pol(p_i, \mathcal{T}_{i-1}) = -$, then N is the new atom L_{p_i}. If $pol(p_i, \mathcal{T}_{i-1}) = +$, then N is $(form(p_i 1, \mathcal{T}_{i-1}) \to L_{p_i}) \to L_{p_i}$. In both cases, L_{p_i} has a globally new predicate symbol of arity r_i and arguments $fv(p_i) = x_1, \ldots, x_{r_i}$.

The formula which is replaced in (ii) is therefore $form(p_i, \mathcal{T}_{i-1})$ which is a formula with principal symbol $\circ$. Evidently, replacements of deeply occurring formulae are performed first and the free variables of any superformula of N in $\mathcal{T}_i$ coincides with the free variables of the corresponding superformula in each of $\mathcal{T}_0, \ldots, \mathcal{T}_{i-1}$.

In both subcases of (ii), L_{p_i} is called *corresponding* to $G = form(p_i 1, \mathcal{T}_{i-1})$, i.e., L_{p_i} corresponds to the unique occurrence of G at position $p_i 1$ in $\mathcal{T}_{i-1}$. It is immediately apparent that G does not contain $\circ$ and that G may contain new atoms L_{p_j} with $j < i$. $F_{n(F)}$ denotes $form(1, \mathcal{T}_{n(F)})$, i.e., it is the resulting formula after all replacements of occurrences of formulae of the form $\circ G$. Evidently, $F_{n(F)}$ does not contain $\circ$.

We construct the following set $\mathcal{D}(F)$ of (non-modal) formulae which will play an important role in the following. If $n^+(F) = 0$ or $n^-(F) = 0$, then simply set $\mathcal{D}(F)$ to the empty set. Otherwise

$$\mathcal{D}(F) = \{\, \forall\,((G \to L_q) \to (L_{p_i} \to L_q)) \mid$$
$$L_{p_i} \text{ corresponds to } G,\ p_i \in \mathcal{P}_o^-(F),\ q \in \mathcal{P}_o^+(F) \,\} \tag{7}$$

and $\forall\,((G \to L_q) \to (L_{p_i} \to L_q))$ is the intuitionistic formula for the provable modal formula $\forall\,((G \to \circ H) \to (\circ G \to \circ H))$. Obviously, $|\mathcal{D}(F)| = n^+(F) \cdot n^-(F)$.

Translation of Sequents. Recall that we annotate formula occurrences with their unique position in $\mathcal{T}_0$, i.e., G^p denotes the subformula occurrence G which occurs at position p in F. Let $[\![X]\!]_F$ denote the translation of X with respect to a formula F where X is a formula, a multi-set of formulae, or a sequent. The map $[\![\cdot]\!]_F$ is defined as follows.

1. If G^p is a formula of the form $\circ H^{p1}$ occurring negatively in F, then $[\![G]\!]_F = L_p$.
2. If G^p is a formula of the form $\circ H^{p1}$ occurring positively in F, then

$$[\![G]\!]_F = ([\![H]\!]_F \to L_p) \to L_p.$$

3. If G^p is a formula where $\circ$ is *not* the principal symbol (i.e., $p \notin \{p_1, \ldots, p_{n(F)}\}$), $[\![G]\!]_F$ is constructed by considering (a), (b), (c) until one case applies.
   (a) If $p \not\prec p_i$ (for all i with $1 \le i \le n(F)$), then $[\![G]\!]_F = form(p, \mathcal{T}_0)$.
   (b) If there exists no $i \in \{1, \ldots, n(F)\}$ with $p_i \prec p$, then $[\![G]\!]_F = form(p, \mathcal{T}_{n(F)})$.
   (c) Otherwise choose l from $\{1, \ldots, n(F)\}$ such that $p_l \prec p$ and $\forall k < l, p_k \not\prec p$. Then $[\![G]\!]_F = form(p, \mathcal{T}_{l-1})$.

Intuitively, we check in (a) whether modal formulae occur in G^p. If not, then $[\![G^p]\!] = G^p$ from the input formula. In (b), it is checked whether there exists an occurrence of $\circ$ position p_i which dominates p. If this is not the case, $[\![G^p]\!]$ is the formula at position p in the tree $\mathcal{T}_{n(F)}$. Otherwise, we select in (c) the unique "nearest" occurrence of $\circ$ dominating p and take as $[\![G^p]\!]$ the formula occurring at position p in the tree $\mathcal{T}_{l-1}$, which is the tree in which the formula at position p_l is changed resulting in $\mathcal{T}_l$.

The map is extended to multi-sets of formulae and sequents as follows. If Γ is the empty multi-set, then $[\![\Gamma]\!]_F = \Gamma$. If Γ is a non-empty multi-set of formulae of the form $G_1, \ldots, G_g$, then $[\![\Gamma]\!]_F = [\![G_1]\!]_F, \ldots, [\![G_g]\!]_F$. For a sequent $S: \Gamma \Longrightarrow C$ with $C \ne \circ D$, $[\![S]\!]_F$ is of the form $\mathcal{D}(F), [\![\Gamma]\!]_F \Longrightarrow [\![C]\!]_F$. For a sequent $S: \Gamma \Longrightarrow \circ C$ and $[\![\circ C]\!]_F = ([\![C]\!]_F \to L_p) \to L_p$, $[\![S]\!]_F$ is of the form $\mathcal{D}(F), [\![\Gamma]\!]_F, [\![C]\!]_F \to L_p \Longrightarrow L_p$. Observe that the free variables of S and $[\![S]\!]_F$ coincide. In the following, we usually omit the index F if it is clear from the context.

We will use the proof of the formula F:

$$(\circ G \vee \circ H) \to \circ(G \vee \circ H) \tag{8}$$

as the running example for the explanation of relevant properties of the embedding. The proof in the sequent calculus for lax logic is at the top of Fig. 2.

The modal formula (8) is translated into an intuitionistic formula. The formula tree $\mathcal{T}_0$ (with position labels and polarity signs) we are starting with is:

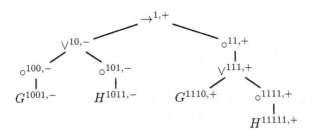

For this formula tree, we introduce the new atoms L_{11} and L_{1111} for the two positive occurrences of $\circ$, and the new atoms L_{100} and L_{101} for the two negative occurrences of $\circ$. Consider a sequence of positions

$$p_1, \; p_2, \; p_3, \; p_4 \; = \; 1111, \; 101, \; 100, \; 11 \qquad (9)$$

and observe that it satisfies (5). According to this sequence of positions, we get a sequence of formula trees as follows (we omit position labels and polarity signs and use I_{1111} to denote the formula tree for $(H \to L_{1111}) \to L_{1111}$ and I_{11} to denote the formula tree for $((G \vee I_{1111}) \to L_{11}) \to L_{11})$.

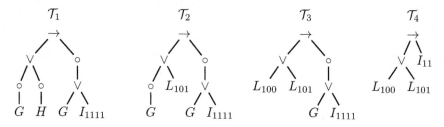

The following table relates the new atoms and their corresponding formulae.

atom	L_{1111}	L_{101}	L_{100}	L_{11}
formula	H	H	G	$G \vee ((H \to L_{1111}) \to L_{1111})$

Next, we define the translation of $S_e : \; \implies F$, i.e., $[\![S_e]\!] : \mathcal{D}(F) \implies [\![F]\!]_F$ where

$$[\![F]\!]_F = (L_{100} \vee L_{101}) \to (((G \vee ((H \to L_{1111}) \to L_{1111})) \to L_{11}) \to L_{11})$$
$$\mathcal{D}(F) = \{ (G \to L_{11}) \to (L_{100} \to L_{11}), (G \to L_{1111}) \to (L_{100} \to L_{1111}),$$
$$(H \to L_{11}) \to (L_{101} \to L_{11}), (H \to L_{1111}) \to (L_{101} \to L_{1111}) \}.$$

This concludes the discussion of the example for the moment; we will continue later.

The following structural property will be needed in the proof of Lemma 3 below.

Lemma 1. *Let $\mathcal{T}$ be the tree for a formula F. Let L be a subformula of F of the form $M \star N$, or QxM, where $\star \in \{ \wedge, \vee, \to \}$ and $Q \in \{ \forall, \exists \}$. Moreover, M, N do not contain $\circ$. Then $[\![M \star N]\!] = [\![M]\!] \star [\![N]\!]$, and $[\![QxM]\!] = Qx[\![M]\!]$.*

The proof of the lemma proceeds by induction on the logical complexity of L. Full details are presented in [5].

An important property of embeddings is *faithfulness*, i.e., the original formula is provable if and only if the translated formula is provable. In our context, faithfulness is rephrased as

$$\vdash_l F \qquad \text{if and only if} \qquad \vdash_i (\bigwedge_{D \in \mathcal{D}(F)} D) \to [\![F]\!].$$

Before we show a translation of proofs from lax logic into intuitionistic logic, we first translate the source proof into a specific normal form.

Definition 2. *Let α be a proof in the sequent calculus for lax logic. Then α is called simple if each axiom in α is atomic or of the form $\Gamma, \bot \implies \Delta$.*

The reason why we require *simple* proofs is easy. For non-atomic formulae G, an axiom of the form $\Gamma, G \implies G$ is *not* translated into an axiom in general because of the different new formulae introduced for modal subformula *occurrences*. For atomic axioms, the translation always results in atomic axioms.

In [5], we prove the following lemma.

Lemma 2. *Let α be a proof of a sequent $S :\implies F$ in the sequent calculus for lax logic. Then there is a simple proof α_a of S and $l(\alpha_a) \leq l(\alpha) \cdot (6 \cdot lcomp(F) + 4)$.*

The following lemma proves one part of the faithfulness of our embedding.

Lemma 3. *Let α be a proof of a sequent $T: \implies F$ in the sequent calculus for lax logic. If F is a propositional formula, then there exists a proof β of $[\![T]\!]_F$ in the sequent calculus for propositional intuitionistic logic and $l(\beta) \leq 7 \cdot l(\alpha) \cdot (6 \cdot lcomp(F) + 4)$. If F is a proper first-order formula, then there exists a proof β of $[\![T]\!]_F$ in the sequent calculus for intuitionistic logic and $l(\beta) < l(\alpha) \cdot (6 \cdot lcomp(F) + 4) \cdot (lcomp(F) + 7)$.*

Proof. By Lemma 2, it is sufficient to consider simple proofs. We first show that we can translate each initial subproof of α. The lemma follows then immediately. We proceed by induction on the length of the initial subproofs α_i of α with end sequent S.
Base: $l(\alpha_i) = 1$. Then α_i consists of a single axiom S.
CASE 1: $S: \Gamma, \bot \implies \Delta$. Then $[\![S]\!]$ is an axiom because $[\![\bot]\!] = \bot$.
CASE 2: $S: \Gamma, A \implies A$ for an atom A. Then $[\![S]\!]$ is an axiom because $[\![A]\!] = A$.

(IH) Let $l(\alpha_i) > 1$ and assume that for all simple (initial) proofs α_i of α with end sequent S and $l(\alpha_i) < n$, there exists a proof of $[\![S]\!]_F$ in the sequent calculus for intuitionistic logic.

Consider a proof α_i with $l(\alpha_i) = n$. We perform a case analysis depending on the last inference I in α_i. In all the cases below, the induction hypothesis provides a translated proof α'_1 for unary inferences and two translated proofs α'_1, α'_2 for binary inferences. We only show some main cases in the following; a proof with all details can be found in [5]. Due to space restrictions, we sometimes use Δ for $\mathcal{D}(F), [\![\Gamma]\!]$.

CASE 1: $I = \vee r$. We consider only one of the symmetric cases.

$$\frac{\begin{array}{c}\alpha_1\\ S: \Gamma \implies G\end{array}}{T: \Gamma \implies G \vee H} \vee r \, (G \neq \circ K) \qquad \frac{\begin{array}{c}\alpha'_1\\ [\![S]\!]: \mathcal{D}(F), [\![\Gamma]\!] \implies [\![G]\!]\end{array}}{[\![T]\!]: \mathcal{D}(F), [\![\Gamma]\!] \implies [\![G \vee H]\!]} \vee r$$

$$\frac{\begin{array}{c}\alpha_1\\ S: \Gamma \implies \circ G\end{array}}{T: \Gamma \implies \circ G \vee H} \vee r \qquad \frac{\dfrac{\begin{array}{c}\alpha'_1\\ [\![S]\!]: \mathcal{D}(F), [\![\Gamma]\!], [\![G]\!] \to L_p \implies L_p\end{array}}{\mathcal{D}(F), [\![\Gamma]\!] \implies ([\![G]\!] \to L_p) \to L_p} \to r}{[\![T]\!]: \mathcal{D}(F), [\![\Gamma]\!] \implies [\![\circ G \vee H]\!]} \vee r$$

CASE 2: $I = \vee l$.

$$\frac{\overset{\alpha_1}{S_1: \Gamma, G \Longrightarrow \Delta} \qquad \overset{\alpha_2}{S_2: \Gamma, H \Longrightarrow \Delta}}{T: \Gamma, G \vee H \Longrightarrow \Delta} \vee l \, (\Delta \neq \circ C)$$

is translated into

$$\frac{\overset{\alpha_1'}{[S_1]: \mathcal{D}(F), [\Gamma], [G] \Longrightarrow [\Delta]} \qquad \overset{\alpha_2'}{[S_2]: \mathcal{D}(F), [\Gamma], [H] \Longrightarrow [\Delta]}}{[T]: \mathcal{D}(F), [\Gamma], [G \vee H] \Longrightarrow [\Delta]} \vee l$$

$$\frac{\overset{\alpha_1}{S_1: \Gamma, G \Longrightarrow \circ C} \qquad \overset{\alpha_2}{S_2: \Gamma, H \Longrightarrow \circ C}}{T: \Gamma, G \vee H \Longrightarrow \circ C} \vee l$$

is translated into

$$\frac{\overset{\alpha_1'}{[S_1]: \Delta, [C] \to L_p, [G] \Longrightarrow L_p} \qquad \overset{\alpha_2'}{[S_2]: \Delta, [C] \to L_p, [H] \Longrightarrow L_p}}{[T]: \Delta, [C] \to L_p, [G \vee H] \Longrightarrow L_p} \vee l$$

CASE 3: $I = \circ r$.

$$\frac{\overset{\alpha_1}{S: \Gamma \Longrightarrow G}}{T: \Gamma \Longrightarrow \circ G} \circ r \qquad\qquad \frac{\overset{\alpha_1'}{[S]: \mathcal{D}(F), [\Gamma] \Longrightarrow [G]} \qquad \mathrm{ax}(L_p)}{\mathcal{D}(F), [\Gamma], [G] \to L_p \Longrightarrow L_p} \to l$$

CASE 4: $I = \circ l$.

$$\frac{\overset{\alpha_1}{S: \Gamma, G \Longrightarrow \circ H}}{T: \Gamma, \circ G \Longrightarrow \circ H} \circ l$$

is translated into

$$\frac{\dfrac{\overset{\alpha_1'}{[S]: \Delta, [H] \to L_q, [G] \Longrightarrow L_q}}{\dfrac{\Delta, [H] \to L_q, L_p, [G] \Longrightarrow L_q}{\Delta, [H] \to L_q, L_p \Longrightarrow [G] \to L_q} \to r} wl \qquad \dfrac{\mathrm{ax}(L_p) \qquad \mathrm{ax}(L_q)}{\Delta, [H] \to L_q, L_p, L_p \to L_q \Longrightarrow L_q} \to l}{\dfrac{\Delta, [H] \to L_q, L_p, ([G] \to L_q) \to (L_p \to L_q) \Longrightarrow L_q}{\vdots \; \forall l}} \to l$$
$$\frac{\Delta, [H] \to L_q, L_p, \forall(([G] \to L_q) \to (L_p \to L_q)) \Longrightarrow L_q}{[T]: \Delta, [H] \to L_q, L_p \Longrightarrow L_q} cl$$

By Lemma 2, any proof α can be transformed into a simple proof α_a with

$$l(\alpha_a) \leq l(\alpha) \cdot (6 \cdot lcomp(F) + 4).$$

For a propositional formula F, the manipulations introduce at most 6 additional sequents for each sequent in α_a. Therefore, the following relation holds.

$$l(\beta) \leq 7 \cdot l(\alpha_a) \leq 7 \cdot l(\alpha) \cdot (6 \cdot lcomp(F) + 4).$$

If F has variables, then the number of additional sequents depends on the number f of applications of $\forall l$ in case 4. Since $f < lcomp(F)$, the following relation holds.

$$l(\beta) < l(\alpha) \cdot (6 \cdot lcomp(F) + 4) \cdot (lcomp(F) + 7).$$

This concludes the proof of the lemma. □

We reconsider the formula F defined in (8) and continue our example with the translation of the proof of this formula. We start with a translation of each of the sequents S_1 to S_{10} from the proof in lax logic presented in Fig. 2 (top). The translated sequents are indicated by $[\![S_i]\!]$ in the second proof of this figure.

Reconsider the sequence of positions in (9) and let us consider S_8 and S_1 for a discussion of the translation.

$[\![S_1]\!]$: $\mathcal{D}(F), L_{100} \vee L_{101}, (G \vee ((H \rightarrow L_{1111}) \rightarrow L_{1111})) \rightarrow L_{11} \Longrightarrow L_{11}$

$[\![S_8]\!]$: $\mathcal{D}(F), H \Longrightarrow G \vee ((H \rightarrow L_{1111}) \rightarrow L_{1111})$

We start with S_8: $H \Longrightarrow G \vee \circ H$. The position argument of the antecedent formula H in the formula tree $\mathcal{T}_0$ for F is 1011. The succedent formula $G \vee \circ H$ occurs at position 111 in $\mathcal{T}_0$. Since this formula has a modal subformula (i.e., there exists a position $p_1 = 1111$ with $111 \prec 1111$) and there exists a position $p_4 = 11$ which dominates 111, case 3(c) applies. There, we take the position p_l of the lowmost occurrence of $\circ$ above 111 which is 11. Evidently, $11 \prec 111$ and $l = 4$. Hence, we take the formula at position 111 in $\mathcal{T}_3$.

For the antecedent formula of sequent S_1: $\circ G \vee \circ H \Longrightarrow \circ(G \vee \circ H)$, we have to consider case 3(b) because K: $\circ G \vee \circ H$ contains modal subformulae but it has no dominating occurrence of $\circ$. Since K occurs at position 10 in $\mathcal{T}_0$, we take the formula at position 10 in $\mathcal{T}_4$, which is $L_{100} \vee L_{101}$. For the succedent formula of S_1 which occurs at position 11 in $\mathcal{T}_0$, case 2 applies. The result is $([\![G \vee \circ H]\!] \rightarrow L_{11}) \rightarrow L_{11}$, where $[\![G \vee \circ H]\!]$ has been obtained above.

Finally, we translate the proof of S_e into a proof of $[\![S_e]\!]$ shown in Fig. 2. The sequents in the translated proof which are annotated by $[\![S_i]\!]$ form a kind of skeleton which is completed to a proof by adding the other sequents from the translations in the proof of Lemma 3.

Before we consider the second part for faithfulness of our embedding, we discuss a replacement theorem for first-order lax logic.

Definition 3. *Two formulae F and G are* provably equivalent *(denoted by $F \sim G$) iff $A \Longrightarrow B$ and $B \Longrightarrow A$ are both provable in* LL_1.

The relation $\sim$ is reflexive, symmetric and transitive.

Lemma 4. *Let F be a formula, $\mathcal{T}$ the corresponding formula tree and p a position in $\mathcal{T}$. Let A and B be two formulae satisfying $fv(A) = fv(B)$. Then $A \sim B$ imply $F_A^p \sim F_B^p$.*

Proof. The proof is by induction on the length, $sl(p)$, of p.
Base: $sl(p) = 1$. Then $F_X^p = X$ and the lemma holds trivially.

(IH) Let $sl(p) > 1$ and assume that for all positions q with $sl(q) < n$, $A \sim B$ implies $G_A^q \sim G_B^q$.

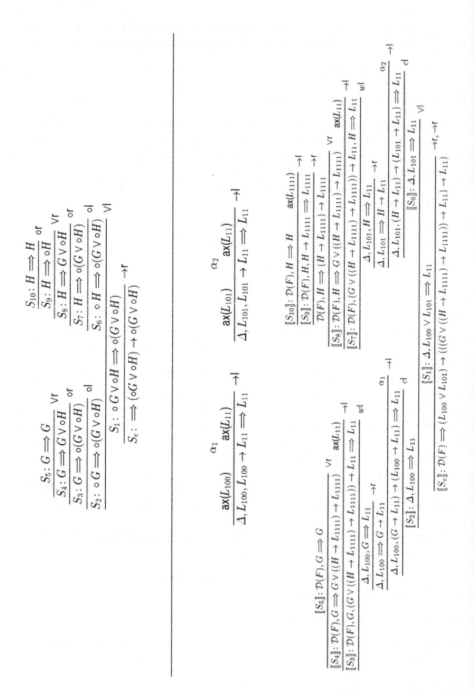

Fig. 2. The proofs for S_e and $[\![S_e]\!]$ (where Δ denotes $\mathcal{D}(F), (G \vee ((H \to L_{1111}) \to L_{1111})) \to L_{11}$ and cl is used to get duplications from $\mathcal{D}(F)$).

Consider $F_A^p \sim F_B^p$ where $sl(p) = n$. For the principal symbol of F, there are the following possibilities.

CASE 1: $F = H \wedge K$ and, without loss of generality, the replacement occurs in H. Obtain the position r of A respectively B in H by deleting the first bit from p and by changing the first bit in the resulting positions to 1. Obviously, $sl(r) = sl(p) - 1$. Then $A \sim B$ together with (IH) provide $H_A^r \sim H_B^r$. Applying $\wedge r$ (with axiom $K \implies K$), $\wedge l$ twice and cl yield the sequents $(H \wedge K)_A^p \implies (H \wedge K)_B^p$ and $(H \wedge K)_B^p \implies (H \wedge K)_A^p$.

CASE 2: $F = H \vee K$. Similar to case 1 with applications of $\vee r$ and $\vee l$.

CASE 3: $F = H \to K$. If the replacement occurs in H, then obtain the position r of A respectively B in H by deleting the first bit from p and by changing the first bit in the resulting positions to 1. Then $A \sim B$ together with (IH) provide $H_A^r \sim H_B^r$. One application of $\to l$ (with axiom $K \implies K$) and one application of $\to r$ yield the sequents $(H \to K)_B^p \implies (H \to K)_A^p$ and $(H \to K)_A^p \implies (H \to K)_B^p$ as desired.

If the replacement occurs in K, then obtain the position r of A respectively B in K by deleting the first bit from p. Then $A \sim B$ together with (IH) provide $K_A^r \sim K_B^r$. One application of $\to l$ (with axiom $H \implies H$) and one application of $\to r$ yield the sequents $(H \to K)_A^p \implies (H \to K)_B^p$ and $(H \to K)_B^p \implies (H \to K)_A^p$ as desired.

CASE 4: $F = \exists x H$. The position r of A respectively B in H is obtained by deleting the first bit from p. Then $A \sim B$ together with (IH) provide $H_A^r \sim H_B^r$. Observe that $fv(H_A^r) = fv(H_B^r)$ holds. One application of $\exists r$ and one application of $\exists l$ yield the sequents $(\exists x H)_A^p \implies (\exists x H)_B^p$ and $(\exists x H)_B^p \implies (\exists x H)_A^p$ as desired.

CASE 5: $F = \forall x H$. Similar to case 4.

CASE 6: $F = \circ H$. Similar to case 4. $\qquad\Box$

Recall that L_{p_i} and its corresponding formula C_{p_i} have exactly the same free variables. Let $\sigma_m = \{L_{p_m} \leftarrow \circ C_{p_m}\}$ denote the replacement of the atom L_{p_m} by $\circ C_{p_m}$. Then $\mathcal{T}_{n(F)} \sigma^{n(F)}$ denotes $(\cdots (\mathcal{T}_{n(F)} \sigma_{n(F)}) \cdots) \sigma_1$.

Lemma 5. *For all m ($0 \le m \le n(F)$), it holds that $\mathcal{T}_m \sigma^m \sim \mathcal{T}_0$.*

Proof. The proof proceeds by induction on $n(F)$.

Base: $n(F) = 0$. Then $\mathcal{T}_0 \sim \mathcal{T}_0$ holds trivially.

(IH) Let $n(F) > 0$ and assume that $\mathcal{T}_i \sigma^i \sim \mathcal{T}_0$ for all $i < m$.

Consider $\mathcal{T}_m \sigma^m$. By construction, $\mathcal{T}_m = (\mathcal{T}_{m-1})_{G_m}^{p_m}$.

CASE 1: $G_m = L_{p_m}$, i.e., $\mathcal{T}_m = (\mathcal{T}_{m-1})_{L_{p_m}}^{p_m}$ and p_m is the only position where L_{p_m} occurs in $\mathcal{T}_m$. The unique formula which is replaced by L_{p_m} is $\circ C_{p_m}$. Then

$$\mathcal{T}_m \sigma^m = (\mathcal{T}_{m-1})_{L_{p_m}}^{p_m} \{L_{p_m} \leftarrow \circ C_{p_m}\} \sigma^{m-1} = \mathcal{T}_{m-1} \sigma^{m-1}$$

and $\mathcal{T}_{m-1} \sigma^{m-1} \sim \mathcal{T}_0$ by (IH). Therefore, $\mathcal{T}_m \sigma^m \sim \mathcal{T}_0$ as desired.

CASE 2: $G_m = (C_{p_m} \to L_{p_m}) \to L_{p_m}$ and L_{p_m} occurs only twice in $\mathcal{T}_m$. Then

$$\mathcal{T}_m \sigma^m = (\mathcal{T}_{m-1})_{G_{p_m}}^{p_m} \{L_{p_m} \leftarrow \circ C_{p_m}\} \sigma^{m-1} = (\mathcal{T}_{m-1})_{(C_{p_m} \to \circ C_{p_m}) \to \circ C_{p_m}}^{p_m} \sigma^{m-1}.$$

Since $((C_{p_m} \to \circ C_{p_m}) \to \circ C_{p_m}) \sigma^{m-1} \sim \circ C_{p_m} \sigma^{m-1}$, it holds that

$$(\mathcal{T}_{m-1})_{(C_{p_m} \to \circ C_{p_m}) \to \circ C_{p_m}}^{p_m} \sigma^{m-1} \sim (\mathcal{T}_{m-1})_{\circ C_{p_m}}^{p_m} \sigma^{m-1}.$$

Then $\mathcal{T}_m \sigma^m \sim \mathcal{T}_0$ by $(\mathcal{T}_{m-1})_{\circ C_{p_m}}^{p_m} = \mathcal{T}_{m-1}$, (IH) and the transitivity of $\sim$. $\qquad\Box$

Lemma 6. *Let α be a proof of a sequent $[\![T]\!]_F$ in the sequent calculus for intuitionistic logic. Then there exists a proof of $T: \implies F$ in the sequent calculus for lax logic.*

Proof. Consider the end sequent S of α which can be of one of the two forms:

1. $\mathcal{D}(F) \implies [\![F]\!]_F$ if the principal symbol of F is not $\circ$;
2. $\mathcal{D}(F), [\![G]\!]_F \rightarrow L_p \implies L_p$ if F is of the form $\circ G$.

Take $\beta = \alpha$ for the first case, and add to α a final inference $\rightarrow r$ in order to construct β with end sequent $\mathcal{D}(F) \implies [\![F]\!]_F$ for the second case. Consider $\beta \sigma^{n(F)}$, i.e., replace all L_i by its modalized corresponding formula $\circ C_{p_i}$ in the order $p_{n(F)}, \ldots, p_1$. Observe that $\beta \sigma^{n(F)}$ is a correct proof of the end sequent $\mathcal{D}(F) \sigma^{n(F)} \implies [\![F]\!]_F \sigma^{n(F)}$ because only atoms are replaced by formulae and the free variables in L_{p_i} and C_{p_i} coincide. By Lemma 5, the sequent $[\![F]\!]_F \sigma^{n(F)} \implies F$ is provable in $LL_1 +$cut. Moreover, any element of $\mathcal{D}(F) \sigma^{n(F)}$ is provable in LL_1. Hence, $\beta \sigma^{n(F)}$ can be extended to a proof of $\implies F$ by additional applications of cut. Cut elimination yields the proof of $\implies F$ in LL_1. $\qquad\square$

Theorem 1. *The embedding $[\![\cdot]\!]_F$ from lax logic into intuitionistic logic is faithful.*

We continue our running example and perform the replacements of L_{11}, L_{100}, L_{101}, and L_{1111} (in that order) by their modalized corresponding formulae. We start with $[\![F]\!]_F = F_4$ and obtain F_3, F_2, F_1, F_0 as a result of the replacements. We get:

$$F_4 = (L_{100} \vee L_{101}) \rightarrow (((G \vee ((H \rightarrow L_{1111}) \rightarrow L_{1111})) \rightarrow L_{11}) \rightarrow L_{11})$$
$$F_3 = (L_{100} \vee L_{101}) \rightarrow ((C_{11} \rightarrow \circ C_{11}) \rightarrow \circ C_{11})$$
$$C_{11} = G \vee ((H \rightarrow L_{1111}) \rightarrow L_{1111})$$
$$F_2 = (\circ G \vee L_{101}) \rightarrow ((C_{11} \rightarrow \circ C_{11}) \rightarrow \circ C_{11})$$
$$F_1 = (\circ G \vee \circ H) \rightarrow ((C_{11} \rightarrow \circ C_{11}) \rightarrow \circ C_{11})$$
$$F_0 = (\circ G \vee \circ H) \rightarrow ((C'_{11} \rightarrow \circ C'_{11}) \rightarrow \circ C'_{11})$$
$$C'_{11} = G \vee ((H \rightarrow \circ H) \rightarrow \circ H)$$

Moreover, the sets $\mathcal{D}_i(F)$ (corresponding to F_i above) are as follows.

$$\mathcal{D}_4(F) = \{ (G \rightarrow L_{11}) \rightarrow (L_{100} \rightarrow L_{11}), (G \rightarrow L_{1111}) \rightarrow (L_{100} \rightarrow L_{1111}),$$
$$(H \rightarrow L_{11}) \rightarrow (L_{101} \rightarrow L_{11}), (H \rightarrow L_{1111}) \rightarrow (L_{101} \rightarrow L_{1111}) \}$$

$$\mathcal{D}_3(F) = \{ (G \rightarrow \circ C_{11}) \rightarrow (L_{100} \rightarrow \circ C_{11}), (G \rightarrow L_{1111}) \rightarrow (L_{100} \rightarrow L_{1111}),$$
$$(H \rightarrow \circ C_{11}) \rightarrow (L_{101} \rightarrow \circ C_{11}), (H \rightarrow L_{1111}) \rightarrow (L_{101} \rightarrow L_{1111}) \}$$
$$\mathcal{D}_2(F) = \{ (G \rightarrow \circ C_{11}) \rightarrow (\circ G \rightarrow \circ C_{11}), (G \rightarrow L_{1111}) \rightarrow (\circ G \rightarrow L_{1111}),$$
$$(H \rightarrow \circ C_{11}) \rightarrow (L_{101} \rightarrow \circ C_{11}), (H \rightarrow L_{1111}) \rightarrow (L_{101} \rightarrow L_{1111}) \}$$
$$\mathcal{D}_1(F) = \{ (G \rightarrow \circ C_{11}) \rightarrow (\circ G \rightarrow \circ C_{11}), (G \rightarrow L_{1111}) \rightarrow (\circ G \rightarrow L_{1111}),$$
$$(H \rightarrow \circ C_{11}) \rightarrow (\circ H \rightarrow \circ C_{11}), (H \rightarrow L_{1111}) \rightarrow (\circ H \rightarrow L_{1111}) \}$$
$$\mathcal{D}_0(F) = \{ (G \rightarrow \circ C_{11}) \rightarrow (\circ G \rightarrow \circ C_{11}), (G \rightarrow \circ H) \rightarrow (\circ G \rightarrow \circ H),$$
$$(H \rightarrow \circ C_{11}) \rightarrow (\circ H \rightarrow \circ C_{11}), (H \rightarrow \circ H) \rightarrow (\circ H \rightarrow \circ H) \}$$

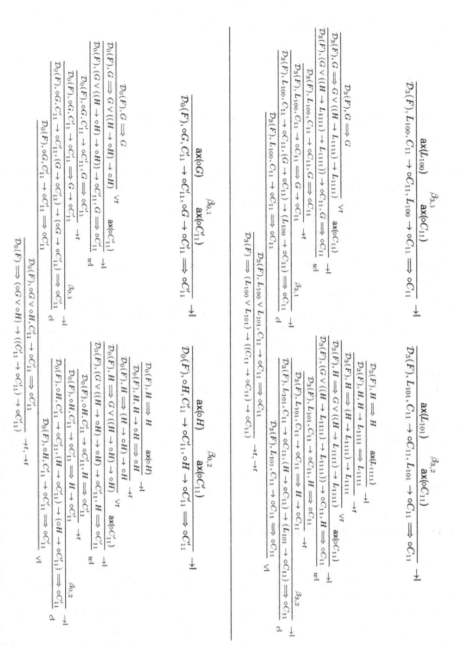

Fig. 3. The proof β_3 of $\mathcal{D}_3(F) \implies F_3$ and the proof β_0 of $\mathcal{D}_0(F) \implies F_0$.

We show in Fig. 3 top the proof β_3 of $\mathcal{D}_3(F) \implies F_3$. Additionally, the proof β_0 of $\mathcal{D}_0(F) \implies F_0$ is shown in Fig. 3 bottom. From the end sequent of β_0, all elements D

from $\mathcal{D}_0(F)$ can be eliminated by cut inferences because the sequent $\Longrightarrow D$ is provable in LL_1. The resulting sequent below the cut inferences is $\Longrightarrow F_0$. Since $F_0 \Longrightarrow F$ is provable in LL_1, one application of cut yields $\Longrightarrow F$. This concludes the discussion of the example.

4   The Complexity of the Provability Problem in PLL

This section has been added in order to answer the question raised by one of the anonymous referees about the complexity of (the provability problem of) propositional lax logic. In the following, we show that this problem is PSPACE-complete. The proof is remarkably simple and uses the proposed polynomial-time computable embedding from propositional lax logic into propositional intuitionistic logic.

For PSPACE-completeness of a decision problem, we have to show that this problem is PSPACE-hard (i.e., it resides in the class PSPACE or even in a higher complexity class), and that there exists an algorithm running in polynomial space which solves the decision problem.

Let us call PLL-PROV (PIL-PROV) the problem to decide the provability of a propositional lax (intuitionistic) formula. It is well known that PIL-PROV is PSPACE-complete (cf [16] for complexity results in propositional intuitionistic logic). Since any intuitionistic formula is also a lax formula (i.e., the "modal" language is an extension of the language of propositional intuitionistic logic by the new modality ∘), PLL-PROV is PSPACE-hard.

For the second part of completeness, let us take the (sound and complete) $(n \log n)$-space decision procedure for propositional intuitionistic logic in [12]. Before this procedure is invoked, the lax formula is translated into an intuitionistic formula by the proposed (faithful and polynomial-time computable) embedding. Therefore, the decision procedure returns yes if the original lax formula is provable (valid) and no otherwise.

Theorem 2. *The provability problem of propositional lax logic is PSPACE-complete.*

5   Conclusion and Future Work

We have shown that the lax modality can be interpreted by purely intuitionistic formulae. The proposed embedding of lax logic into intuitionistic logic has the advantage that "terminating" calculi can be used in order to search backwards for propositional proofs. Such calculi for propositional intuitionistic logic are available [4,12,9], but no satisfactory calculus is known so far for lax logic (see [10,11] for a discussion on questions related to proof search in lax logic). For first checks and experiments, we used the system STRIP [9] which combines terminating backward proof search and Kripke counter-model generation in a single system.

Future activities will include investigations on contraction-free calculi for propositional lax logic. Additionally, the translation of intuitionistic Kripke (counter-) models (found for instance with STRIP for propositional formulae) into constraint Kripke (counter-) models will be investigated.

References

1. P. N. Benton, G. M. Bierman, and V. C. V. de Paiva. Computational types from a logical perspective. *Journal of Functional Programming*, 8(2):177–193, 1998.
2. H. B. Curry. The elimination theorem when modality is present. *Journal of Symbolic Logic*, 17:249–265, 1952.
3. H. B. Curry. *A Theory of Formal Deducibility*, volume 6 of *Notre Dame Mathematical Lectures*. Notre Dame, Indiana, second edition, 1957.
4. R. Dyckhoff. Contraction-free sequent calculi for intuitionistic logic. *Journal of Symbolic Logic*, 57(3):795–807, 1992.
5. Uwe Egly. Embedding lax logic into intuitionistic logic. Technical report, Abteilung Wissensbasierte Systeme, TU Wien, 2002.
6. M. Fairtlough and M. Mendler. Propositional lax logic. *Information and Computation*, 137(1):1–33, 1997.
7. M. Fairtlough, M. Mendler, and M. Walton. First-order lax logic as a framework for constraint logic programming. Technical Report MIPS-9714, University of Passau, 1997.
8. M. Fairtlough and M. Walton. Quantified lax logic. Technical Report CS-97-11, University of Sheffield, Department of Computer Science, 1997.
9. D. Galmiche and D. Larchey-Wendling. Structural sharing and efficient proof-search in propositional intuitionistic logic. In *Asian Computing Science Conference, ASIAN'99*, volume 1742 of *Lecture Notes in Computer Science*, pages 101–112. Springer Verlag, 1999.
10. J. M. Howe. *Proof Search Issues in Some Non-Classical Logics*. PhD thesis, University of St Andrews, December 1998. Available as University of St Andrews Research Report CS/99/1.
11. J. M. Howe. Proof search in lax logic. *Mathematical Structures in Computer Science*, 11(4):573–588, August 2001.
12. J. Hudelmaier. An $O(n\log n)$-space decision procedure for intuitionistic propositional logic. *Journal of Logic and Computation*, 3(1):63–75, 1993.
13. M. Mendler. *A Modal Logic for Handling Behavioural Constraints in Formal Hardware Verification*. PhD thesis, Edinburgh University, Department of Computer Science, ECS-LFCS-93-255, 1993.
14. E. Moggi. Notion of computation and monads. *Information and Computation*, 93:55–92, 1991.
15. F. Pfenning and R. Davis. A judgemental reconstruction of modal logic. *Mathematical Structures in Computer Science*, 11(4):511–540, August 2001.
16. R. Statman. Intuitionistic propositional logic is polynomial-space complete. *Theoretical Computer Science*, 9:67–72, 1979.

Combining Proof-Search and Counter-Model Construction for Deciding Gödel-Dummett Logic

Dominique Larchey-Wendling

LORIA – Université Henri Poincaré
Campus Scientifique, BP 239
Vandœuvre-lès-Nancy, France

Abstract. We present an algorithm for deciding Gödel-Dummett logic. The originality of this algorithm comes from the combination of proof-search in sequent calculus, which reduces a sequent to a set of pseudo-atomic sequents, and counter-model construction of such pseudo-atomic sequents by a fixpoint computation. From an analysis of this construction, we deduce a new logical rule $[\supset_N]$ which provides shorter proofs than the rule $[\supset_R]$ of G4-LC. We also present a linear implementation of the counter-model generation algorithm for pseudo-atomic sequents.

1 Introduction

In [9], Gödel introduced the logic G_ω which was later axiomatized by Dummett in [4] and is known since as Gödel-Dummett logic LC. It is viewed as one of the most important intermediate logics, between intuitionistic logic IL and classical logic CL, with connections with the provability logic of Heyting's Arithmetics [14] and more recently fuzzy logic [10]. Starting from proof-search in intuitionistic logic IL, the development of efficient proof-search procedures for intermediate logics like Gödel-Dummett logic has been the subject of recent studies [1,6,2].

The first formulation of a cut-free Gentzen-type system for LC [13] does not terminate because of the duplication of formulae. The work of Dyckhoff [5] and Hudelmair [11] solved the termination problem for IL with a duplication-free sequent calculus now called G4-IL. This system was further refined by the author [8,12] in order to completely remove all the duplications, including those of sub-formulae. Dyckhoff [6] successfully applied the ideas of the duplication-free system G4-IL to the LC sequent calculus leading to a duplication-free sequent calculus called G4-LC. Moreover, he showed that there is a complete proof-search strategy which is deterministic, meaning that all the logical rules become invertible. In the same time, Avellone et al. [1] and Fiorino [7] investigated the ideas of the duplication-free system within the semantic tableaux approach and proposed corresponding tableaux calculi for various intermediate logics including LC. In [2], Avron claims that all these systems suffer from the serious drawback of using a rule, called $[\supset_R]$, with an arbitrary number of premises: this rule may introduce exponential blowup in the proof search process. Avron's solution to this problem is to use a hypersequent calculus for LC [2].

A. Voronkov (Ed.): CADE-18, LNAI 2392, pp. 94–110, 2002.

In this paper, we propose an original solution to the problem of rule $[\supset_R]$ which has an unbounded number of premises. It is based on the combination of a proof-search method in standard sequent calculus and a counter-model generation algorithm. We have a process in three steps: first the formula (resp. the sequent) to decide is converted into a *flat sequent*, the size of which is linearly bounded by the size of the initial problem. This step consists in an indexing of subformulae. Then, we apply a *proof-search process* to the flat sequent in which all the rules have one or two premises and are *strongly invertible*, i.e. they preserve counter-models top-down. It results in a set of *pseudo-atomic sequents* which is equivalent to the initial formula (resp. sequent). The last step consists of a *counter-model generation* algorithm to decide such pseudo-atomic sequents. The algorithm is based on a fixpoint computation, and either outputs a short proof or a (short) counter-model of the pseudo-atomic sequent. Then, from these steps, we have a new decision procedure for LC that leads to a solution of the problem of rule $[\supset_R]$. A surprising consequence of the fixpoint computation is the discovery of a *new logical rule* $[\supset_N]$ which efficiently replaces $[\supset_R]$. We briefly explain how this computation can be implemented in linear time.

Throughout this paper, we respect the following methodology: each time a transformation of a sequent $\mathcal{A}$ into a sequent $\mathcal{B}$ is given, we justify this transformation by giving the methods to convert a proof (resp. counter-model) of $\mathcal{B}$ into a proof (resp. counter-model) of $\mathcal{A}$. Thus, we fully describe a proof or counter-model generation algorithm.

2   Gödel-Dummett Logic LC

In this section, we present the propositional Gödel-Dummett logic LC, its algebraic semantics, and some admissible sequent calculus rules, including the contraction-free system G4-LC.

2.1   Formulae, Sequents, and Their Algebraic Semantic

The set of propositional *formulae*, denoted Form is defined inductively, starting from a set of propositional *variables* denoted by Var with an additional bottom constant $\perp$ denoting *absurdity* and using the connectives $\wedge$, $\vee$ and $\supset$. A *substitution* denoted by σ is any function that associates a formula to every propositional variable. We denote by A_σ the result of the application of σ to the variables in A. IL will denote the set of formulae that are provable in any intuitionistic propositional calculus (see [5]) and CL will denote the classically valid formulae. As usual an *intermediate propositional logic* [1] is a set of formulae $\mathcal{L}$ satisfying IL $\subseteq \mathcal{L} \subseteq$ CL and closed under the rule of modus ponens[1] and under arbitrary substitution.[2]

The Gödel-Dummett logic LC is an intermediate logic: in a Hilbert axiomatic system, it is the smallest intermediate logic satisfying the axiom formula

---

[1] If $A \in \mathcal{L}$ and $A \supset B \in \mathcal{L}$ then $B \in \mathcal{L}$.
[2] If $A \in \mathcal{L}$ and σ is any substitution then $A_\sigma \in \mathcal{L}$.

$$\frac{}{\Gamma, A \vdash A, \Delta} \; [\text{Ax}] \qquad \frac{\Gamma, A, B \vdash \Delta}{\Gamma, A \wedge B \vdash \Delta} \; [\wedge_L] \qquad \frac{\Gamma \vdash A, B, \Delta}{\Gamma \vdash A \vee B, \Delta} \; [\vee_R]$$

$$\frac{\Gamma, A, B \vdash \Delta}{\Gamma, A, A \supset B \vdash \Delta} \; [\supset^1_L] \qquad \frac{\Gamma, A \supset C, B \supset C \vdash \Delta}{\Gamma, (A \vee B) \supset C \vdash \Delta} \; [\supset^3_L] \qquad \frac{\Gamma, A \supset (B \supset C) \vdash \Delta}{\Gamma, (A \wedge B) \supset C \vdash \Delta} \; [\supset^2_L]$$

$$\frac{\Gamma, A \vdash \Delta \quad \Gamma, B \vdash G}{\Gamma, A \vee B \vdash \Delta} \; [\vee_L] \qquad \frac{\Gamma, B \supset C \vdash A \supset B, \Delta \quad \Gamma, C \vdash \Delta}{\Gamma, (A \supset B) \supset C \vdash \Delta} \; [\supset^4_L]$$

$$\frac{\Gamma \vdash A, \Delta \quad \Gamma \vdash B, \Delta}{\Gamma \vdash A \wedge B, \Delta} \; [\wedge_R] \qquad \frac{\dots \quad \Gamma, A_i \vdash B_i, \Delta^i \quad \dots}{\Gamma \vdash \Delta} \; [\supset_R]$$

Fig. 1. The cut-free terminating system G4-LC.

$(X \supset Y) \vee (Y \supset X)$. On the semantic side, intermediate logics are characterized by monotonic Kripke models and more particularly, LC is characterized by monotonic and *linear Kripke models* [4]. In this paper, we will rather use the algebraic semantic characterization of LC [2]. Let $\overline{\mathbb{N}} = \mathbb{N} \cup \{\infty\}$ be the set of natural numbers with its natural order $\leqslant$ augmented with a maximal element ∞. An interpretation $\llbracket \cdot \rrbracket : \mathsf{Var} \to \overline{\mathbb{N}}$ of propositional variables is inductively extended to formulae: $\perp$ interpreted by 0, the conjunction $\wedge$ is interpreted by the *minimum* function denoted $\wedge$, the disjunction $\vee$ by the *maximum* function $\vee$ and the implication $\supset$ by the operator $\to$ defined by $a \to b =$ if $a \leqslant b$ then ∞ else b. A formula is *valid* for the interpretation $\llbracket \cdot \rrbracket$ if the equality $\llbracket A \rrbracket = \infty$ holds and we write $\Vdash A$ when A is *universally valid*. This interpretation is complete for LC [9]. A *counter-model* of a formula A is an interpretation $\llbracket \cdot \rrbracket$ such that $\llbracket A \rrbracket < \infty$.

A *sequent* is a pair $\Gamma \vdash \Delta$ where Γ and Δ are multisets of formulae. Γ, Δ denotes the sum of the two multisets and if Γ is the empty multiset, we write $\vdash \Delta$. Substitutions may also be applied to multisets and sequents in the obvious way and we denote by $\Gamma_\sigma \vdash \Delta_\sigma$ the resulting sequent. Given a sequent $\Gamma \vdash \Delta$ and an interpretation $\llbracket \cdot \rrbracket$ of variables, we interpret $\Gamma \equiv A_1, \dots, A_n$ by $\llbracket \Gamma \rrbracket = \llbracket A_1 \rrbracket \wedge \cdots \wedge \llbracket A_n \rrbracket$ and $\Delta \equiv B_1, \dots, B_p$ by $\lceil \Delta \rceil = \llbracket B_1 \rrbracket \vee \cdots \vee \llbracket B_p \rrbracket$. This sequent is *valid*, with respect to the interpretation $\llbracket \cdot \rrbracket$, if $\llbracket \Gamma \rrbracket \leqslant \lceil \Delta \rceil$ and we write $\Gamma \Vdash \Delta$ when the sequent is universally valid. On the other hand, a *counter-model* to this sequent is an interpretation $\llbracket \cdot \rrbracket$ such that $\lceil \Delta \rceil < \llbracket \Gamma \rrbracket$, i.e, for any pair (i, j), the inequality $\llbracket B_j \rrbracket < \llbracket A_i \rrbracket$ holds. We denote by $\Gamma \nVdash \Delta$ when such a counter-model exists.

2.2 Sequent Calculi

In this section, we present sequent calculus rules to deal with proofs in LC. We only consider the $\perp$-free fragment of LC, i.e, atoms are propositional variables.[3] We present the terminating system G4-LC of Dyckhoff [6] in figure 1.[4] It is com-

---

[3] In section 6, we explain how to remove $\perp$ at the first step of the proof-search process.

[4] In G4-LC, the use of rule $[\supset^1_L]$ is restricted to the case A atomic, but this condition is not required for either soundness or completeness.

plete for LC and the structural rules of contraction [Contract], weakening [Weak], cut [Cut] and substitution [Subst$_\sigma$] are admissible.[5] All the rules of G4-LC are *strongly invertible*[6] [15] except rule [$\supset_R$]. Its restricted form called [$\supset'_R$] is invertible, making the system deterministic.

Let us analyze the use of the rule [$\supset_R$] and its restriction [$\supset'_R$] and its consequences in terms of complexity of proofs and proof-search. Δ is a multiset of for-

$$\frac{\cdots \quad \Gamma, A_i \vdash B_i, \Delta^i \quad \cdots}{\Gamma \vdash \Delta} \, [\supset_R]$$

mulae containing the sub-multiset $\Delta^\star$ of the implicational formulae $A_1 \supset B_1, \ldots, A_n \supset B_n$ of Δ. Δ may also contain some other kinds of formulae. The rule indicates that for each $i \in [1, n]$, there is premise $\Gamma, A_i \vdash B_i, \Delta^i$. Δ^i is the result of the removal of $A_i \supset B_i$ from $\Delta^\star$. So the rule instance has exactly n premises. The rule [$\supset'_R$] has the same form but its use is restricted to the case where no other rule of G4-LC is applicable.

Let us explore the logical implications of the rule [$\supset_R$]. Each premise of this rule corresponds to a particular choice of an $A_i \supset B_i$ formula. If we apply the same rule to each premise, we have to choose between the remaining $n-1$ implications, thus to each premise of the root sequent corresponds $n - 1$ premises, etc. We see that there is a proof-search branch for each particular choice sequence τ (i.e. permutation) of $[1, n]$. There are of course $n!$ such possible sequences. A proof search branch may stop (with an axiom for example) before all the sequence $\tau_1, \tau_2, \ldots$ has been explored but the proof size remains exponential: for example, consider the provable cycle sequent $\vdash X_1 \supset X_2, \ldots, X_n \supset X_1$. Within G4-LC, the proof of this sequent uses only the axiom rule [Ax] and the rule [$\supset_R$] and one can find at least $(n/2)!$ branches of length greater than $n/2$, so the size of this proof is bounded from below by an exponential.

3   Linear Reduction of Sequents into Flat Sequents

In this section, we describe how to convert a sequent into a *flat sequent* and in the next section, how to convert a flat sequent into a set of *pseudo-atomic sequents*. This first phase consists in indexing the initial sequent in order to have an equi-valid *flat sequent*. Propositions $\mathcal{P}$ and $\mathcal{Q}$ are *equi-valid* if they are both either valid or invalid. Propositions could be either formulae or sequents.

Definition 1 (Flat formula and sequent). *A formula is said to be flat if it is of one of the following forms: X or $X \supset Y$ or $Z \supset (X \otimes Y)$ or $(X \otimes Y) \supset Z$ where X, Y and Z are propositional variables and $\otimes \in \{\wedge, \vee, \supset\}$. A sequent $\Gamma \vdash \Delta$ is flat if all formulae of Γ are flat and Δ is only composed of formulae of the form X or $X \supset Y$ with X and Y variables.*

The process of flattening a formula D is quite standard, at least in classical logic. It consists in transforming D into an equi-valid flat sequent. The principle is to index the sub-formulae of D by new variables and to introduce the "axioms" that correspond to the subformula relation between those variables.

---

[5] [Subst$_\sigma$]: if σ is any substitution and $\Gamma \vdash \Delta$ is provable then $\Gamma_\sigma \vdash \Delta_\sigma$ is provable.

[6] A logical rule is invertible if the invalidity of any of its premise implies the invalidity of its conclusion and is strongly invertible if any counter-model of one of its premises is also a counter-model of the conclusion.

Let us fix a formula D for the rest of this section. We introduce a new variable X_C for every subformula C of D.[7] We do not distinguish between occurrences of subformulae. Moreover, if V is a variable occurring in D, we do not introduce a new variable X_V for it, i.e. we require the syntactic identity $X_V \equiv V$. We define two linear functions δ^+ and δ^- on the set of subformulae of D by the mutual induction with the following equations :

$$\delta^+(V) = \delta^-(V) = \emptyset \text{ when } V \text{ is a variable}$$

$$\delta^+(A \otimes B) = \delta^+(A), \delta^+(B), X_{A \otimes B} \supset (X_A \otimes X_B) \text{ when } \otimes \in \{\wedge, \vee\}$$
$$\delta^+(A \supset B) = \delta^-(A), \delta^+(B), X_{A \supset B} \supset (X_A \supset X_B)$$

$$\delta^-(A \otimes B) = \delta^-(A), \delta^-(B), (X_A \otimes X_B) \supset X_{A \otimes B} \text{ when } \otimes \in \{\wedge, \vee\}$$
$$\delta^-(A \supset B) = \delta^+(A), \delta^-(B), (X_A \supset X_B) \supset X_{A \supset B}$$

In this definition, $\delta^+(\cdot)$ and $\delta^-(\cdot)$ are multisets. The size of a formula is the number of occurrences of its subformulae, which is the number of nodes in its decomposition tree. Let C be a formula of size n. It is obvious to prove that the cardinals of $\delta^+(C)$ and $\delta^-(C)$ are smaller than n by mutual induction on C. Moreover, both of theses multisets are only composed of flat formulae, the size of which is 5, thus the size of either $\delta^+(C)$ or $\delta^-(C)$ is bounded by $5n$.

Proposition 1. *Any proof of the sequent $\delta^-(D) \vdash X_D$ can be transformed into a proof of the sequent $\vdash D$.*

Proof. Let σ be the substitution defined by $X_C \mapsto C$ for any subformula C of D. The result of applying the substitution σ to any formula of either $\delta^+(D)$ or $\delta^-(D)$ is a formula of the form $K \supset K$. Let us consider the following proof using one application of the rule [Subst$_\sigma$] and a repeated application of the cut rule [Cut]:

$$
\cfrac{
\cfrac{
\cfrac{\cdots}{\delta^-(D) \vdash X_D}
}{K_1 \supset K_1, \ldots, K_p \supset K_p \vdash D} \text{[Subst}_\sigma]
\qquad
\cfrac{
\cfrac{\overline{K_1 \vdash K_1} \text{[Ax]}}{\vdash K_1 \supset K_1} \text{[}\supset_R]
}{\cdots}
\text{[Cut]}
\qquad
\cfrac{\overline{K_p \vdash K_p} \text{[Ax]}}{\vdash K_p \supset K_p} \text{[}\supset_R]
}{\vdash D} \text{[Cut]}
$$

This last proof part describes the transformation of a proof of the flat sequent $\delta^-(D) \vdash X_D$ into a proof of the formula D.   □

Now we prove the converse result: a counter-model to the sequent $\delta^-(D) \vdash X_D$ is also a counter-model to the formula D. This justifies the equi-validity of the flattening of the formula D. For that, we introduce some useful derived rules to prove semantic properties of δ^+ and δ^-: these derived rules express the variance of the logical operators with respect to the validity preorder $\Vdash$.

---

[7] As D has a finite number of subformulae and Form is infinite, this is always possible.

Proposition 2. *The following rules (with $\otimes$ is either $\vee$ or $\wedge$) are admissible in* LC:

$$\frac{\Gamma, A \vdash B \qquad \Delta, A' \vdash B'}{\Gamma, \Delta, A \otimes A' \vdash B \otimes B'} \ [\otimes_M] \qquad \frac{\Gamma, B \vdash A \qquad \Delta, A' \vdash B'}{\Gamma, \Delta, A \supset A' \vdash B \supset B'} \ [\supset_M]$$

We do not give the proof of this standard result. From these rules, we derive a relation between C and $\delta^+(C)$ (resp. $\delta^-(C)$):

Lemma 1. *The sequents $\delta^+(C), X_C \vdash C$ and $\delta^-(C), C \vdash X_C$ are valid for any subformula C of D,*

Proof. By mutual induction on C. We only present the case of $C \equiv A \supset B$. Let us prove $\delta^+(A \supset B), X_{A \supset B} \Vdash A \supset B$. By induction hypothesis, we know that $\delta^-(A), A \Vdash X_A$ and $\delta^+(B), X_B \Vdash B$. Then by the proof

$$\frac{\dfrac{\delta^-(A), A \vdash X_A \qquad \delta^+(B), X_B \vdash B}{\delta^-(A), \delta^+(B), X_A \supset X_B \vdash A \supset B} \ [\supset_M]}{\dfrac{\delta^-(A), \delta^+(B), X_{A \supset B}, X_A \supset X_B \vdash A \supset B}{\delta^-(A), \delta^+(B), X_{A \supset B}, X_{A \supset B} \supset (X_A \supset X_B) \vdash A \supset B} \ [\supset_L^1]} \ [\text{Weak}]$$

and the soundness of the logical rules, we deduce the validity of the sequent $\delta^+(A \supset B), X_{A \supset B} \vdash A \supset B$. The other cases are similar. $\qquad \square$

Proposition 3. *Let $[\![\cdot]\!]$ be a counter-model of the sequent $\delta^-(D) \vdash X_D$. Then it is also a counter-model of D, i.e. $[\![D]\!] < \infty$.*

Proof. As $[\![\cdot]\!]$ is a counter-model, the relation $[\![X_D]\!] < \lfloor \delta^-(D) \rfloor$ holds. Moreover the relation $[\![D]\!] > [\![X_D]\!]$ would imply $[\![X_D]\!] < \lfloor \delta^-(D) \rfloor \wedge [\![D]\!]$ and $[\![\cdot]\!]$ would be a counter-model of the sequent $\delta^-(D), D \vdash X_D$ which is impossible by lemma 1. As a consequence, we have $[\![D]\!] \leqslant [\![X_D]\!] < \infty$. $\qquad \square$

Corollary 1. *Let D be any formula of size n, there exists a flat sequent which is equi-valid to D and of size smaller than $5n + 1$.*

Proof. We know by proposition 1 and 3 that D is equi-valid to $\delta^-(D) \vdash X_D$. This flat sequent is of size smaller than $5n + 1$. $\qquad \square$

We point out the fact that it is also possible to transform the sequent $A_1, \ldots, A_n \vdash B_1, \ldots, B_p$ into the flat sequent

$$\delta^+(A_1), \ldots, \delta^+(A_n), X_{A_1}, \ldots, X_{A_n}, \delta^-(B_1), \ldots, \delta^-(B_p) \vdash X_{B_1}, \ldots, X_{B_p}$$

4 From Flat to Pseudo-Atomic Sequents

In this section, we describe the second stage of our decision algorithm. It is a proof-search process that converts a flat sequent into a set of pseudo-atomic sequents such that the flat sequent is valid if and only if all the pseudo-atomic sequents are valid. Moreover, any counter-model of any of the pseudo-atomic sequents is also a counter-model to the flat sequent.

We present six strongly invertible rules to reduce any formula of the form $Z \supset (X \otimes Y)$ or $(X \otimes Y) \supset Z$ on the left-hand side of the $\vdash$ sign into variables X and/or implicational formulae $X \supset Y$ (all the X, Y and Z represent variables). But before, we introduce some logical equivalences holding in LC:[8]

Proposition 4. *The following equivalences hold in* LC*:*

1) $(A \wedge B) \supset C \dashv\vdash (A \supset C) \vee (B \supset C)$ 1') $A \supset (B \wedge C) \dashv\vdash (A \supset B) \wedge (A \supset C)$
2) $(A \vee B) \supset C \dashv\vdash (A \supset C) \wedge (B \supset C)$ 2') $A \supset (B \vee C) \dashv\vdash (A \supset B) \vee (A \supset C)$
3) $A \supset (B \supset C) \dashv\vdash (A \supset C) \vee (B \supset C)$

The reader can find proofs of similar equivalences in [2]. Now we introduce six rules that can decompose any flat formula on the left-hand side of $\vdash$ into implicational formula $(X \supset Y)$ or variables (X):

Proposition 5. *The following rules are sound and strongly invertible for* LC*:*

$$\frac{\Gamma, A \supset C \vdash \Delta \qquad \Gamma, B \supset C \vdash \Delta}{\Gamma, (A \wedge B) \supset C \vdash \Delta} \; [\supset_2] \qquad\qquad \frac{\Gamma, A \supset B, A \supset C \vdash \Delta}{\Gamma, A \supset (B \wedge C) \vdash \Delta} \; [\supset_2']$$

$$\frac{\Gamma, A \supset C, B \supset C \vdash \Delta}{\Gamma, (A \vee B) \supset C \vdash \Delta} \; [\supset_3] \qquad\qquad \frac{\Gamma, A \supset B \vdash \Delta \qquad \Gamma, A \supset C \vdash \Delta}{\Gamma, A \supset (B \vee C) \vdash \Delta} \; [\supset_3']$$

$$\frac{\Gamma, B \supset C \vdash A \supset B, \Delta \qquad \Gamma, C \vdash \Delta}{\Gamma, (A \supset B) \supset C \vdash \Delta} \; [\supset_4] \qquad\qquad \frac{\Gamma, A \supset C \vdash \Delta \qquad \Gamma, B \supset C \vdash \Delta}{\Gamma, A \supset (B \supset C) \vdash \Delta} \; [\supset_4']$$

Proof. The rule $[\supset_3]$ (resp. $[\supset_4]$) is included in G4-LC under the name $[\supset_L^3]$ (resp. $[\supset_L^4]$) so they are sound. For the other rules, we use the preceding equivalences. We prove soundness of rule $[\supset_3']$, using the cut rule [Cut] in conjunction with proposition 4, part 2'):

$$\frac{\dfrac{\Gamma, A \supset B \vdash \Delta \quad \Gamma, A \supset C \vdash \Delta}{\Gamma, (A \supset B) \vee (A \supset C) \vdash \Delta} \; [\vee_L] \qquad \dfrac{\cdots}{A \supset (B \vee C) \vdash (A \supset B) \vee (A \supset C)}}{\Gamma, A \supset (B \vee C) \vdash \Delta} \; [\text{Cut}]$$

Let us also prove the strong invertibility of rule $[\supset_2']$. Let $[\![\cdot]\!]$ be a counter-model of the premise, by proposition 4, part 1'), and soundness, we obtain the relation $[\![\Delta]\!] < [\![\Gamma]\!] \wedge [\![A \supset B]\!] \wedge [\![A \supset C]\!] = [\![\Gamma]\!] \wedge [\![(A \supset B) \wedge (A \supset C)]\!] \leqslant [\![\Gamma]\!] \wedge [\![A \supset (B \wedge C)]\!]$ and then, $[\![\cdot]\!]$ is a counter-model of the conclusion.   □

---

[8] The notation $A \dashv\vdash B$ means that both sequents $A \vdash B$ and $B \vdash A$ are valid in LC.

With the six preceding rules, we are able to decompose any flat sequent until all the formulae of the form $Z \supset (X \otimes Y)$ or $(X \otimes Y) \supset Z$ have been replaced by variables or atomic implications. What we obtain is called a pseudo-atomic sequent:

Definition 2 (Pseudo-atomic and atomic sequents). *An* atomic context *denoted by Γ_a is a multiset of the form $A_1, \ldots, A_l, B_1 \supset C_1, \ldots, B_m \supset C_m$ where all the A_i, B_i, C_i are (propositional) variables. An* atomic sequent *is a sequent of the form $\Gamma_a \vdash X_1, \ldots, X_n$ where Γ_a is an atomic context and all the X_i are variables. A* pseudo-atomic sequent *is a sequent of the form $\Gamma_a \vdash X_1 \supset Y_1, \ldots, X_n \supset Y_n, Z_1, \ldots, Z_q$ where all the X_i, Y_i and Z_i are variables.*

Proposition 6. *The bottom-up application of the rules of proposition 5 preserves flat sequents. If a flat sequent is irreducible by those rules then it is pseudo-atomic.*

Proof. The result of the conversion of a formula $Z \supset (X \otimes Y)$ or $(X \otimes Y) \supset Z$ is one or two formulae of the form $X \supset Y$ on the left-hand side of the $\vdash$ sign for all the rules except rule $[\supset_4]$. In this last case, we add $X \supset Y$ on the right-hand side (left premise) and the introduction of a variable X on the left-hand side (right premise). Then flat sequents are preserved.

Then it is clear that flat sequents without formulae of the form $Z \supset (X \otimes Y)$ or $(X \otimes Y) \supset Z$ in the left-hand side are in fact pseudo-atomic sequents.   □

5   Deciding Pseudo-Atomic Sequents

In this section we develop the last step of our decision algorithm for LC. We present a counter-model generation algorithm to decide pseudo-atomic sequents. Pseudo-atomic sequents are sequents to which only the rules $[\text{Ax}]$, $[\supset_L^1]$ or $[\supset_R]$ of the G4-LC calculus may be applied bottom-up. But as explained in section 6, the use of rule $[\supset_R]$ is not efficient in a decision algorithm. We propose a computationally efficient procedure which is based on counter-model generation.

Proposition 7. *The validity of the atomic sequent $\Gamma_a \vdash X_1, \ldots, X_n$ can be decided in linear time and is equivalent to the validity of one of the $\Gamma_a \vdash X_i$.*

Proof. We apply the rule $[\supset_L^1]$ in any order until this rule is no more applicable. As this rule is strongly invertible, the validity is preserved by this process. Each $B_i \supset C_i$ occurring in Γ_a may be reduced at most once and this algorithm is linear. If the obtained sequent is not an axiom, then it is necessarily of the form $A_1, \ldots, A_l, B_1 \supset C_1, \ldots, B_m \supset C_m \vdash X_1, \ldots, X_n$ where $\{A_1, \ldots, A_l\} \cap \{X_1, \ldots, X_n, B_1, \ldots, B_m\} = \emptyset$ and such a sequent has a classical counter-model: $[\![A_i]\!] = 1$ and $[\![X_i]\!] = [\![B_i]\!] = 0$ for any i. This interpretation is also a counter-model for all the $\Gamma_a \vdash X_i$ sequents.   □

The reader may have noticed that on atomic sequents, all intermediate logics collapse to classical logic and its boolean semantic. Of course, this is not the case for pseudo-atomic sequents.

5.1 Decision as a Fixpoint Computation

We present the general method to decide a fixed pseudo-atomic sequent with no variables on the right-hand side of the ⊢ sign, i.e. of the form

$$\Gamma_a \vdash X_1 \supset Y_1, \ldots, X_n \supset Y_n \qquad (n > 0)$$

Let $I \subseteq [1, n]$ be a subset of $[1, n]$. If I is the subset $\{i_1, \ldots, i_k\}$ then we denote by $\mathcal{X}_I$ the multiset of variables $\{X_{i_1}, \ldots, X_{i_k}\}$. We also denote by $\overline{I} = [1, n] - I$ the complement of I and by $\mathcal{S}_n$ the symmetric group i.e. the set of permutations of $[1, n]$. We define an increasing function φ on the complete (and finite) lattice of subsets of $[1, n]$, by:

$$\varphi \begin{cases} 2^{[1,n]} \to 2^{[1,n]} \\ I \mapsto \{i \mid \Gamma_a, \mathcal{X}_{\overline{I}} \not\vdash Y_i\} \end{cases}$$

We recall that the sequent $\Gamma_a, \mathcal{X}_{\overline{I}} \vdash Y_i$ is atomic and then $\varphi(I)$ can be computed in linear time using the method of proposition 7. Because of the two negations ($\overline{I}$ and $\not\vdash$), the function φ is monotonic. Then we can compute the least fixpoint[9] μ_φ of φ:

$$I_0 = \emptyset \subsetneq I_1 = \varphi(\emptyset) \subsetneq \cdots \subsetneq I_p = \varphi^p(\emptyset) = \mu_\varphi$$

This process takes a finite number of steps p which is less than the size of $[1, n]$: $0 \leqslant p \leqslant n$. The following theorem shows that the cardinal of the fixpoint μ_φ characterizes the validity of the pseudo-atomic sequent.

Theorem 1. *The three following propositions are equivalent:*

1. *The sequent $\Gamma_a \vdash X_1 \supset Y_1, \ldots, X_n \supset Y_n$ has a counter-model*
2. *$\exists \tau \in \mathcal{S}_n, \ \forall k \in [1, n] \quad \Gamma_a, X_{\tau_1}, \ldots, X_{\tau_k} \not\vdash Y_{\tau_k}$*
3. *$\mu_\varphi = [1, n]$*

In the following three subsections, we prove $1 \Rightarrow 2$, $2 \Rightarrow 3$ and finally $3 \Rightarrow 1$.

A necessary condition of invalidity.

Proposition 8 (1 ⇒ 2). *Let the interpretation $[\![\cdot]\!]$ be a counter-model of the pseudo-atomic sequent $\Gamma_a \vdash X_1 \supset Y_1, \ldots, X_n \supset Y_n$. Then there exists a permutation $\tau \in \mathcal{S}_n$ such that for any $k \in [1, n]$, $[\![\cdot]\!]$ is also a counter-model of $\Gamma_a, X_{\tau_1}, \ldots, X_{\tau_k} \vdash Y_{\tau_k}$.*

Proof. Let τ be any permutation such that $[\![X_{\tau_n}]\!] \leqslant \cdots \leqslant [\![X_{\tau_1}]\!]$, obtained by sorting all these values. As $[\![\cdot]\!]$ is a counter-model of $\Gamma_a \vdash X_1 \supset Y_1, \ldots, X_n \supset Y_n$, we obtain $[\![X_k \supset Y_k]\!] < [\![\Gamma_a]\!]$ for any $k \in [1, n]$. We fix a particular k and consider $\tau_k \in [1, n]$. We can then derive $[\![X_{\tau_k} \supset Y_{\tau_k}]\!] < \infty$ and thus $[\![X_{\tau_k}]\!] \to [\![Y_{\tau_k}]\!] < \infty$ holds. Then it is necessary that $[\![Y_{\tau_k}]\!] < [\![X_{\tau_k}]\!] = [\![X_{\tau_1}]\!] \wedge \cdots \wedge [\![X_{\tau_k}]\!]$ and thus $[\![Y_{\tau_k}]\!] = [\![X_{\tau_k} \supset Y_{\tau_k}]\!] < [\![\Gamma_a]\!]$. As a conclusion, $[\![Y_{\tau_k}]\!] < [\![\Gamma_a, X_{\tau_1}, \ldots, X_{\tau_k}]\!]$. We deduce that $[\![\cdot]\!]$ is a counter-model of $\Gamma_a, X_{\tau_1}, \ldots, X_{\tau_k} \vdash Y_{\tau_k}$. □

---

[9] Or equivalently, this is the greatest fixpoint of $I \mapsto \{i \mid \Gamma_a, \mathcal{X}_I \Vdash Y_i\}$.

Computing the fixpoint.

Proposition 9 (2 ⇒ 3). *If there exists a permutation $\tau \in \mathcal{S}_n$ satisfying the condition $\forall k \in [1, n]\ \Gamma_a, X_{\tau_1}, \ldots, X_{\tau_k} \not\Vdash Y_{\tau_k}$ then $\mu_\varphi = [1, n]$.*

Proof. We write μ for μ_φ. Let $k \in [1, n]$. We proceed by descending induction on $k \geqslant 1$. We prove the induction step:

$$\{\tau_{k+1}, \ldots, \tau_n\} \subseteq \mu \Rightarrow \tau_k \in \mu$$

The identity $\mathcal{X}_{\overline{\{\tau_{k+1}, \ldots, \tau_n\}}} = \{X_{\tau_1}, \ldots, X_{\tau_k}\}$ holds and $\Gamma_a, X_{\tau_1}, \ldots, X_{\tau_k} \not\Vdash Y_{\tau_k}$ also holds so $\tau_k \in \varphi(\{\tau_{k+1}, \ldots, \tau_n\})$ holds. With the induction hypothesis and the monotonicity of φ, we obtain $\tau_k \in \varphi(\{\tau_{k+1}, \ldots, \tau_n\}) \subseteq \varphi(\mu) = \mu$ which proves the induction step. Then it is trivial to prove $\tau_k \in \mu$ for all k: $\tau_n \in \mu$, then $\tau_{n-1} \in \mu$, ... and finally $\tau_1 \in \mu$. Thus we obtain $\mu = [1, n]$ □

From the fixpoint to the counter-model.

We now suppose that we have computed the fixpoint μ_φ and that it equals $[1, n]$. How to build a counter-model from this information? Let us consider the strictly increasing sequence $I_0 = \emptyset \subsetneq I_1 = \varphi(\emptyset) \subsetneq \cdots \subsetneq I_p = \varphi^p(\emptyset) = \mu_\varphi$. As μ_φ is not empty,[10] the inequation $p > 0$ holds. We show how to build a counter-model out of this strictly increasing sequence. We define a decreasing sequence $\mathcal{M}_0 \supseteq \mathcal{M}_1 \supseteq \cdots \supseteq \mathcal{M}_{p+1}$ of subsets of Var by

$$\mathcal{M}_0 = \mathsf{Var} \quad \text{and} \quad \mathcal{M}_{k+1} = \{Z \in \mathsf{Var} \mid \Gamma_a, \mathcal{X}_{\overline{I_k}} \Vdash Z\} \text{ for } k \in [0, p]$$

Then we define the following interpretation for any variable Z:

$$[\![Z]\!] = \max\{k \in [0, p+1] \mid Z \in \mathcal{M}_k\} \tag{1}$$

The next two propositions establish that $[\![\cdot]\!]$ is a counter-model of the sequent $\Gamma_a \vdash X_1 \supset Y_1, \ldots, X_n \supset Y_n$.

Proposition 10. *If the formula A is in Γ_a then $[\![A]\!] \geqslant p + 1$.*

Proof. Let A be an element of Γ_a, if A is a variable then $[\![A]\!]$ is given by equation (1). Since $A \in \Gamma_a$ holds, we deduce $\Gamma_a, \mathcal{X}_{\overline{I_p}} \Vdash A$ by the axiom rule [Ax], then $A \in \mathcal{M}_{p+1}$ and $[\![A]\!] = p + 1$.

Otherwise, A is of the form $P \supset Q$ where P and Q are variables. If $[\![P]\!] = 0$ then $[\![P \supset Q]\!] = \infty \geqslant p + 1$. Otherwise let $[\![P]\!] = k + 1$ with $k \in [0, p]$. Since P is a variable we obtain $P \in \mathcal{M}_{k+1}$, thus $\Gamma_a, \mathcal{X}_{\overline{I_k}} \Vdash P$ holds. Since $P \supset Q \in \Gamma_a$, $\Gamma_a, \mathcal{X}_{\overline{I_k}} \Vdash P \supset Q$ also holds. So, by application of the rule of modus ponens (which is admissible[11]) the validity of $\Gamma_a, \mathcal{X}_{\overline{I_k}} \Vdash Q$ holds. As Q is a variable, we deduce $Q \in \mathcal{M}_{k+1}$. $[\![Q]\!]$ is given by the equation (1) and we obtain $[\![Q]\!] \geqslant k + 1 = [\![P]\!]$. Finally $[\![P \supset Q]\!] = \infty$.   □

---

[10] We have supposed $n > 0$. The case $n = 0$ is treated separately in the proof of corollary 3, section 5.2.

[11] The modus ponens rule can be viewed as a combination of the cut rule [Cut] and the contraction rule [Contract] in G4-LC.

Proposition 11. *For any $i \in [1, n]$, the relation $[\![X_i \supset Y_i]\!] < p$ holds.*

Proof. Let us fix a particular $i \in [1, n]$. By the definition of the sequence $\emptyset = I_0 \subsetneq I_1 \subsetneq \cdots \subsetneq I_p = [1, n]$, there exists a unique $k \in [0, p-1]$ such that $i \in I_{k+1}$ and $i \notin I_k$. From $i \notin I_k$, we derive $i \in \overline{I_k}$, and then $\Gamma_a, \mathcal{X}_{\overline{I_k}} \Vdash X_i$. As X_i is a variable, $X_i \in \mathcal{M}_{k+1}$ holds thus $[\![X_i]\!] \geqslant k + 1$ holds by equation (1).

From $i \in I_{k+1} = \varphi(I_k)$, we deduce by definition of φ that $\Gamma_a, \mathcal{X}_{\overline{I_k}} \nVdash Y_i$ and $Y_i \notin \mathcal{M}_{k+1}$. Then, we have $[\![Y_i]\!] \leqslant k < [\![X_i]\!]$ and $[\![X_i \supset Y_i]\!] = [\![Y_i]\!] \leqslant k < p$ holds. $\square$

Corollary 2 (3 $\Rightarrow$ 1). *The semantic $[\![\cdot]\!]$ defined by equation (1) is a counter-model of the sequent $\Gamma_a \vdash X_1 \supset Y_1, \ldots, X_n \supset Y_n$.*

Proposition 12. *If Z is a variable such that $\Gamma_a \nVdash Z$ holds then $[\![Z]\!] \leqslant p$ holds.*

Proof. $I_p = [1, n]$, so $\overline{I_p} = \emptyset$ and finally $Z \notin \mathcal{M}_{p+1} = \{Z \mid \Gamma_a \Vdash Z\}$. $\square$

5.2   Deciding All Pseudo-Atomic Sequents

We have an algorithm to decide pseudo-atomic sequents with no variables on the right-hand side of the $\vdash$ sign. But it is straightforward to generalize it to any pseudo-atomic sequent.

Corollary 3. *Let $\Gamma_a \vdash X_1 \supset Y_1, \ldots, X_n \supset Y_n, Z_1, \ldots, Z_q$ be a pseudo-atomic sequent. It is provable in LC iff one of the sequents $\Gamma_a \vdash Z_i$ or the sequent $\Gamma_a \vdash X_1 \supset Y_1, \ldots, X_n \supset Y_n$ is provable.*

Proof. The (if) part is a simple application of a weakening rule on the right of the $\vdash$ sign of sequents. For the (only if) part, we distinguish between $n = 0$ and $n > 0$. In the former case, we use proposition 7. In the later case, suppose that neither the sequents $\Gamma_a \vdash Z_i$ nor the sequent $\Gamma_a \vdash X_1 \supset Y_1, \ldots, X_n \supset Y_n$ are provable (i.e. valid). We compute the fixpoint for this last sequent. Then by theorem 1, the fixpoint is $[1, n]$ and by proposition 12 and corollary 2, the semantics defined by equation (1) is also a counter-model of the sequent $\Gamma_a \vdash X_1 \supset Y_1, \ldots, X_n \supset Y_n, Z_1, \ldots, Z_q$. $\square$

5.3   A New Logical Rule Inspired by the Fixpoint Computation

From theorem 1, we know that $\mu_\varphi = [1, n]$ holds when the pseudo-atomic sequent $\Gamma_a \vdash X_1 \supset Y_1, \ldots, X_n \supset Y_n$ is not valid. When $\mu_\varphi \subsetneq [1, n]$, the sequent is provable and we aim to provide a proof of it. Unfortunately, with the rule $[\supset_R]$, we would not be able to provide a proof of reasonable size, as explained in section 6. Now, we propose a new rule in order to replace $[\supset_R]$. We show that the condition $\mu_\varphi \subsetneq [1, n]$ is the expression of a very natural logical rule.

Proposition 13. *If $\mu_\varphi \subsetneq [1, n]$ then there exists a non empty subset I of $[1, n]$ such that for any $i \in I$, the sequent $\Gamma_a, \mathcal{X}_I \vdash Y_i$ is valid.*

Proof. Let I be the complementary subset of μ_φ so I is not empty and $\overline{I} = \mu_\varphi$. Let $i \in I$ then $i \notin \overline{I} = \varphi(\overline{I})$ and thus $\Gamma_a, \mathcal{X}_I \Vdash Y_i$. $\qquad\square$

Then, with all the sequents $\Gamma_a, \mathcal{X}_I \vdash Y_i$ being valid, it would be nice to have a sound logical rule from which we could derive in only one step the conclusion $\Gamma_a \vdash X_1 \supset Y_1, \ldots, X_n \supset Y_n$. Now, we present a rule for decomposing implicational formulae on the right-hand side but, as opposed to the rule $[\supset_R]$, all the implications can be decomposed in only one step and for which there are no side conditions:[12]

Proposition 14. *Let $I = \{i_1, \ldots, i_k\}$ by a non empty subset of $[1, n]$, the following rule $[\supset_N]$ is sound for* LC:

$$\frac{\Gamma, A_{i_1}, \ldots, A_{i_k} \vdash B_{i_1} \quad \cdots \quad \Gamma, A_{i_1}, \ldots, A_{i_k} \vdash B_{i_k}}{\Gamma \vdash A_1 \supset B_1, \ldots, A_n \supset B_n, \Delta} \ [\supset_N]$$

Proof. We prove soundness by showing that any model $[\![\cdot]\!]$ of the premises is also a model of the conclusion. Let $[\![\cdot]\!]$ be a model of the premises. Then, for any $j \in [1, k]$, the inequality $\lfloor\Gamma\rfloor \wedge [\![A_{i_1}]\!] \wedge \cdots \wedge [\![A_{i_k}]\!] \leqslant [\![B_{i_j}]\!]$ holds. Let δ be the index such that $[\![A_{i_\delta}]\!]$ is minimal among the values $[\![A_{i_j}]\!]$. The property $[\![A_{i_\delta}]\!] = [\![A_{i_1}]\!] \wedge \cdots \wedge [\![A_{i_k}]\!]$ holds and also $\lfloor\Gamma\rfloor \wedge [\![A_{i_\delta}]\!] \leqslant [\![B_{i_\delta}]\!]$.

Now, we prove that we have $\lfloor\Gamma\rfloor \leqslant [\![A_{i_\delta} \supset B_{i_\delta}]\!]$. If $[\![A_{i_\delta}]\!] \leqslant [\![B_{i_\delta}]\!]$ then $[\![A_{i_\delta} \supset B_{i_\delta}]\!] = \infty$ and the property is trivially verified. On the other hand, suppose that $[\![A_{i_\delta}]\!] > [\![B_{i_\delta}]\!]$ holds. Then $[\![A_{i_\delta} \supset B_{i_\delta}]\!] = [\![B_{i_\delta}]\!]$ holds. The relation $\lfloor\Gamma\rfloor > [\![B_{i_\delta}]\!]$ is false because otherwise the relation $\lfloor\Gamma\rfloor \wedge [\![A_{i_\delta}]\!] > [\![B_{i_\delta}]\!]$ would hold. Therefore we obtain $\lfloor\Gamma\rfloor \leqslant [\![B_{i_\delta}]\!] = [\![A_{i_\delta} \supset B_{i_\delta}]\!]$.

The property $\lfloor\Gamma\rfloor \leqslant [\![A_1 \supset B_1]\!] \vee \cdots \vee [\![A_n \supset B_n]\!] \vee \lceil\Delta\rceil$ holds because $A_{i_\delta} \supset B_{i_\delta}$ is one of the $A_j \supset B_j$. $\qquad\square$

5.4   Remarks on Complexity

From the complexity point of view, this new rule $[\supset_N]$ has major advantages over the rule $[\supset_R]$: it allows to prove the sequent $\Gamma_a \vdash X_1 \supset Y_1, \ldots, X_n \supset Y_n$ in only one step using proposition 13:

$$\frac{\Gamma_a, \mathcal{X}_I \vdash Y_{i_1} \quad \cdots \quad \Gamma_a, \mathcal{X}_I \vdash Y_{i_k}}{\Gamma_a \vdash X_1 \supset Y_1, \ldots, X_n \supset Y_n} \ [\supset_N]$$

Compared to the $[\supset_R]$ rule, this $[\supset_N]$ rule avoids the exponential blowup which occurs because a proof-search algorithm based on $[\supset_R]$ needs to explore branches corresponding to all possible permutations of $[1, n]$ (see section 6). The case of pseudo-atomic sequents is a worst case example for the application of rule $[\supset_R]$. On the contrary, applicability of the $[\supset_N]$ rule can be decided using a fixpoint

---

[12] In rule $[\supset_N]$, Δ can be any multiset of formulae, i.e. it is not necessary that the $A_i \supset B_i$ enumerate all the implicational formulae on the right-hand side of $\vdash$.

computation and the fixpoint contains an instance of rule $[\supset_N]$. So in the case of pseudo-atomic sequent, the new rule $[\supset_N]$ is clearly much more efficient than $[\supset_R]$. Now what about replacing $[\supset_R]$ by $[\supset_N]$ in G4-LC ? This direct replacement does not lead to a complete cut-free calculus for LC. Indeed, the valid sequent $A \supset (B \vee C) \vdash (A \supset B) \vee (A \supset C)$ has no proof in such a system. So care has to be taken when designing a proof-search calculus based on $[\supset_N]$. We will investigate these logical properties in some future work. We have proposed a particular transformation of sequents into pseudo-atomic sequents. Other possible transformations will also be studied from a complexity point of view.

6   Removing the Constant $\perp$ from Formulae

In this section, we present a linear transformation of a formula into an equivalid sequent that does not contain $\perp$ as a subformula.[13] The idea is to replace $\perp$ by new variable α and to introduce hypothesis sufficient enough to be able to deduce "anything" from α. We denote by A_α the formula A where $\perp$ has been substituted by α, i.e. $A_\alpha = A_{\{\perp \mapsto \alpha\}}$. If $X_1, \ldots, X_n$ are the variables occurring in A, this idea is well described by the following rule

$$\frac{\vdash A}{\alpha \supset X_1, \ldots, \alpha \supset X_n \vdash A_\alpha} \quad [\alpha \text{ new variable}]$$

and we prove that it is sound and invertible in appendix A.

Theorem 2. *Let A be a formula, $\{X_1, \ldots, X_n\}$ its variables and α be another variable which is not one of the X_i's. Any proof (resp. counter-model) of the sequent $\alpha \supset X_1, \ldots, \alpha \supset X_n \vdash A_\alpha$ can be transformed into a proof (resp. counter-model) of $\vdash A$. The size of the former sequent is linear in the size of A.*

7   Computation of μ_φ

In this section, we describe an algorithm to compute the iterated sequence $I_0 = \emptyset \subsetneq I_1 = \varphi(\emptyset) \subsetneq \cdots \subsetneq I_p = \varphi^p(\emptyset) = \mu_\varphi$ in time linear to the size of the pseudo-atomic sequent. We do not give a full proof of the algorithm but rather explain the basic ideas. Suppose we want to compute the fixpoint for the sequent

$$A_1, \ldots, A_l, B_1 \supset C_1, \ldots, B_m \supset C_m \vdash X_1 \supset Y_1, \ldots, X_n \supset Y_n$$

We describe an algorithm that computes the fixpoint for this sequent. It can be seen as a *reference counting algorithm* [3]. In this scheme, an occurrence of an implication $B_i \supset C_i$ in the context represents a relative reference of the variable

---

[13] The proof search method we have described in the preceding sections can be easily extended to the $\perp$-case. But as it lengthens all the proofs, we have chosen to present a $\perp$-free decision procedure together with the removal of $\perp$ at the beginning of the process.

B_i to the variable C_i. An occurrence variable A_i or X_i in the context represents an absolute reference. For any variable X, the reference count of X equals the number of absolute references to X plus the number of relative references to X from any K which has a strictly positive reference count. The main point is that a variable is deducible from the context if and if only its reference count is strictly positive.

First, we represent this pseudo-atomic sequent by a graph $\mathcal{G}$: the *vertexes* are the variables occurring in the sequent and the *arrows* are $B_i \rightarrow C_i$ for all the implications $B_i \supset C_i$ on the left-hand side of the $\vdash$ sign. Let $\mathcal{S}$ be a multiset of vertexes (thus variables) and X a vertex. We represent the validity of the sequent $\mathcal{S}, B_1 \supset C_1, \ldots, B_m \supset C_m \vdash X$ by *accessibility* from $\mathcal{S}$ in the graph $\mathcal{G}$:

$$\mathcal{S}, B_1 \supset C_1, \ldots, B_m \supset C_m \Vdash X \quad \text{iff} \quad \exists Z \in \mathcal{S}, Z \rightarrow^* X \text{ in } \mathcal{G}$$

Thus, the computation of the fixpoint can be done on the contraction of the graph $\mathcal{G}$ where directed connected components are collapsed.[14] Then we suppose that the graph $\mathcal{G}$ is acyclic, i.e. there are no loops inside this graph.

We compute accessibility from $\mathcal{S}$ in $\mathcal{G}$ by a *reference counting function* $\mathcal{S}_Z$ defined inductively on the vertex Z:[15] this weight function counts the number of occurrences of the vertex Z in $\mathcal{S}$ plus the number of vertexes K below Z ($K \rightarrow Z \in \mathcal{G}$) such that $\mathcal{S}_K > 0$. There are three important facts: $\mathcal{S}_Z > 0$ holds iff Z is accessible from $\mathcal{S}$; the sum of all the weights $\sum_Z \mathcal{S}_Z$ is smaller than the number of arrows in $\mathcal{G}$ plus the cardinal of $\mathcal{S}$; $(\mathcal{S} \cup \{X\})_Z$ (resp. $(\mathcal{S} - \{X\})_Z$) can be computed incrementally from $\mathcal{S}_Z$ using a depth-first search algorithm and the total time to recompute $(\mathcal{S} \cup \{X\})_Z$ (resp. $(\mathcal{S} - \{X\})_Z$) is linearly bounded by the increase (resp. decrease) of the value $\sum_Z \mathcal{S}_Z$.

Let $\mathcal{A}$ be the multiset vertexes $\{A_1, \ldots, A_l\}$. For the computation of the fixpoint sequence, we first compute $(\mathcal{A}, \mathcal{X}_{\overline{I_0}})_Z = (\mathcal{A}, X_1, \ldots, X_n)_Z$ which takes a time linear in the size of $\mathcal{G}$ plus $l + n$, i.e. is linearly bounded by the size of the initial sequent. Then, I_1 is the set of indexes i such that $(\mathcal{A}, \mathcal{X}_{\overline{I_0}})_{Y_i} = 0$ holds. We remove those indexes from $\overline{I_0}$ obtaining $\overline{I_1}$ and recompute the corresponding weight function $(\mathcal{A}, \mathcal{X}_{\overline{I_1}})_Z$. Thus we can compute $\overline{I_2}$, etc. The total time for this computation is also linearly bounded by the size of the initial sequent because of the incremental computation of the sequence $(\mathcal{A}, \mathcal{X}_{\overline{I_0}})_Z, \ldots, (\mathcal{A}, \mathcal{X}_{\overline{I_p}})_Z$ of weight functions. In appendix B, we develop a complete execution of this algorithm.

What about the complexity of the three steps algorithm we have described ? Without entering the full details, it should appear that the final goal is to obtain an implementation with a complexity equivalent to that of a connection method for classical propositional logic. In this setting, atomic paths correspond to our pseudo-atomic sequents. To fulfill this design goal, we have to be able to compute the fixpoint on-the-fly, i.e. using a incremental reference count (garbage collection) algorithm so as to be able to decide pseudo-atomic sequent in constant time when we obtain an atomic path. For the moment, this step takes a linear

---

[14] Computing the connected components of a graph is a linear time process.
[15] That is why we need $\mathcal{G}$ acyclic.

time. But existing results in cyclic and incremental garbage collection techniques suggest the feasibility of such a design.

8 Conclusion

In this paper, we have proposed an algorithm, in three steps, that is able to compute either a proof or a counter-model of any formula of LC. The main contributions are: a counter-model generation algorithm for pseudo-atomic sequents than can be implemented in linear time and a new proof system where a new logical rule $[\supset_N]$ efficiently replaces $[\supset_R]$. The main perspectives of this work are the resource-conscious implementation of this algorithm and the study of the logical properties of the new rule. We would also like to investigate the extension of our methodology to some other intermediate logics.

References

1. Alessendro Avellone, Mauro Ferrari, and Pierangelo Miglioli. Duplication-Free Tableau Calculi and Related Cut-Free Sequent Calculi for the Interpolable Propositional Intermediate Logics. *Logic Journal of the IGPL*, 7(4):447–480, 1999.
2. Arnon Avron. A Tableau System for Gödel-Dummett Logic Based on a Hypersequent Calculus. In Roy Dyckhoff, editor, *Automated Reasoning with Analytic Tableaux and Related Methods*, volume 1847 of *Lecture Notes in Artificial Intelligence*, pages 98–111, St Andrews, Scotland, July 2000.
3. L. Peter Deutsch and Daniel G. Bobrow. A Efficient Incremental Automatic Garbage Collector. *Communications of the ACM*, 19(9):522–526, September 1976.
4. Michael Dummett. A Propositional Calculus with a Denumerable matrix. *Journal of Symbolic Logic*, 24:96–107, 1959.
5. Roy Dyckhoff. Contraction-free Sequent Calculi for Intuitionistic Logic. *Journal of Symbolic Logic*, 57(3):795–807, 1992.
6. Roy Dyckhoff. A Deterministic Terminating Sequent Calculus for Gödel-Dummett logic. *Logical Journal of the IGPL*, 7:319–326, 1999.
7. Fiorino. An $\mathcal{O}(n \log n)$-SPACE decision procedure for the propositional Dummett Logic. to appear in Journal of Automated Reasoning.
8. Didier Galmiche and Dominique Larchey-Wendling. Structural Sharing and Efficient Proof-Search in Propositional Intuitionistic Logic. In *Asian Computing Science Conference, ASIAN'99*, volume 1742 of *Lecture Notes in Computer Science*, pages 101–102, Phuket, Thaïland, December 1999.
9. Kurt Gödel. Zum intuitionistischen Aussagenkalkül. *Ergeb. Math. Koll*, 4:40, 1933.
10. P. Hajek. *Metamathematics of Fuzzy Logic*. Kluwer Academic Publishers, 1998.
11. Jörg Hudelmaier. An $\mathcal{O}(n \log n)$-space decision procedure for Intuitionistic Propositional Logic. *Journal of Logic and Computation*, 3(1):63–75, 1993.
12. Dominique Larchey, Daniel Méry, and Didier Galmiche. STRIP: Structural Sharing for efficient Proof-Search. In *International Joint Conference on Automated Reasoning, IJCAR 2001*, volume 2083 of *Lecture Notes in Artificial Intelligence*, pages 696–700, Siena, Italy, January 2001.
13. O. Sonobe. A Gentzen-type Formulation of Some Intermediate Propositional Logics. *Journal of Tsuda College*, 7:7–14, 1975.

14. A. Visser. On the Completeness Principle: A study of provability in Heyting's arithmetic. *Annals of Mathematical Logic*, 22:263–295, 1982.
15. Klaus Weich. Decisions Procedures for Intuitionistic Logic by Program Extraction. In *International Conference TABLEAUX'98*, volume 1397 of *Lecture Notes in Artificial Intelligence*, pages 292–306, Oisterwijk, The Netherlands, May 1998.

A   Proof of Theorem 2

Theorem 2. *Let A be a formula, $\{X_1, \ldots, X_n\}$ its variables and α be another variable which is not one of the X_i's. Any proof (resp. counter-model) of the sequent $\alpha \supset X_1, \ldots, \alpha \supset X_n \vdash A_\alpha$ can be transformed into a proof (resp. counter-model) of $\vdash A$. The size of the former sequent is linear in the size of A.*

Proof. We show how to transform a proof (resp. a counter-model) of $\alpha \supset X_1, \ldots, \alpha \supset X_n \vdash A_\alpha$ into a proof (resp. a counter-model) of $\vdash A$.

Suppose that we have a proof of $\alpha \supset X_1, \ldots, \alpha \supset X_n \vdash A_\alpha$. We remark that substituting $\bot$ for α in A_α produces A. Let σ be the substitution $\{\alpha \mapsto \bot\}$. We obtain the following proof of $\vdash A$:

$$
\cfrac{\cfrac{\cfrac{\cdots}{\alpha \supset X_1, \ldots, \alpha \supset X_n \vdash A_\alpha}}{\bot \supset X_1, \ldots, \bot \supset X_n \vdash A} \text{[Subst}_\sigma] \quad \cfrac{\cfrac{\cfrac{}{\bot \vdash X_1} \text{[}\bot_L]}{\vdash \bot \supset X_1} \text{[}\supset_R]}{\vdash \bot \supset X_1}}{\cfrac{\bot \supset X_2, \ldots, \bot \supset X_n \vdash A}{\cfrac{\cdots}{\vdash A}} \text{[Cut]} \quad \cdots \quad \cfrac{\cfrac{\cfrac{}{\bot \vdash X_n} \text{[}\bot_L]}{\vdash \bot \supset X_n} \text{[}\supset_R]}{} \text{[Cut]}}
$$

On the other hand, we suppose that $\llbracket \cdot \rrbracket$ is a counter-model of the sequent $\alpha \supset X_1, \ldots, \alpha \supset X_n \vdash A_\alpha$. Then for any i, the property $\llbracket \alpha \supset X_i \rrbracket > \llbracket A_\alpha \rrbracket$ holds. In the $n = 0$ case (i.e. A does not contain any variable) we get the property $\llbracket A_\alpha \rrbracket < \infty$, and this property also holds in the case $n > 0$.

We now prove that the identity $\llbracket \alpha \rrbracket \leqslant \llbracket X_i \rrbracket$ holds for any i. If $n = 0$, the property trivially holds. Otherwise, let i_0 an index such that the value of $\llbracket \alpha \supset X_i \rrbracket$ is minimal and let $\delta = \llbracket \alpha \supset X_{i_0} \rrbracket$ be this value. We prove by contradiction that $\llbracket \alpha \rrbracket \leqslant \delta$.

We suppose $\llbracket \alpha \rrbracket > \delta$. Then all the atoms of A_α are interpreted by values (the $\llbracket X_i \rrbracket$'s and $\llbracket \alpha \rrbracket$) which are greater than δ. Then by definition of $\llbracket \cdot \rrbracket$, $\llbracket A_\alpha \rrbracket$ is necessarily greater than δ. So $\llbracket \alpha \supset X_{i_0} \rrbracket > \llbracket A_\alpha \rrbracket \geqslant \delta$. But as $\llbracket \alpha \rrbracket > \llbracket X_{i_0} \rrbracket = \delta$, we obtain $\llbracket \alpha \supset X_{i_0} \rrbracket = \llbracket \alpha \rrbracket \to \llbracket X_{i_0} \rrbracket = \delta$ and a contradiction.

For any i, $\llbracket \alpha \rrbracket \leqslant \llbracket X_i \rrbracket$ holds. Thus we can define $\llbracket X \rrbracket' = \llbracket X \rrbracket - \llbracket \alpha \rrbracket$ for $X \in \{\alpha, X_1, \ldots, X_n\}$, the other values of the semantic function do not matter. In this new semantic, α is interpreted by 0 which is the same as $\bot$ and thus, $\llbracket A \rrbracket' = \llbracket A_\alpha \rrbracket'$. Moreover, by the definition of the semantic function $\llbracket \cdot \rrbracket$ on formulae, for any formula B, built with atoms in $\{\alpha, X_1, \ldots, X_n\}$, the identity $\llbracket B \rrbracket' = \llbracket B \rrbracket -$

$[\![\alpha]\!]$ holds.[16] In particular $[\![A_\alpha]\!]' = [\![A_\alpha]\!] - [\![\alpha]\!] < \infty$. Thus, since $[\![A]\!]' = [\![A_\alpha]\!]'$, the function $[\![\cdot]\!]'$ is a counter-model of A.

For the size of the sequent $\alpha \supset X_1, \ldots, \alpha \supset X_n \vdash A_\alpha$, it is linear in the size of A since the number of variables in A is lower than the size of A.   □

B   Example of Linear Computation of μ_φ

We develop an full example of computation of the fixpoint μ_φ on the graph of variables $\mathcal{G}$, see section 7. We choose the following sequent:

$$0 \supset 1, 1 \supset 2, 1 \supset 3, 2 \supset 4, 3 \supset 4$$
$$\vdash 2 \supset_1 1, 1 \supset_2 0, 4 \supset_3 2$$

In the graph on the right-hand side, the black arrows represent the real graph structure, the dashed (and numbered) arrows are only displayed to remind the reader of the implications on the right $(X_i \supset Y_i)$.

We display the weight function $\mathcal{S}_Z$ on $\mathcal{G}$ by marking the vertexes K such that K occurs in the multiset $\mathcal{S}$ and the arrows $K \to Z$ such that $\mathcal{S}_K > 0$. We also display the current value of $\mathcal{S}_Z$ beside the vertex Z

The first stage is to compute $(\mathcal{X}_{\{1,2,3\}})_Z = (2,1,4)_Z$. We start from $(\emptyset)_Z$ which is the zero weight function and compute successively $(2)_Z$ (two steps), $(2,1)_Z$ (three steps) and $(2,1,4)_Z$ (one step):

Thus, we obtain the value of I_1 which is $\{2\}$ because $1 \to_2 0$ is the only dashed arrow for which the end-vertex has weight 0. So, we have to compute $(\mathcal{X}_{\overline{I_1}}) = (\mathcal{X}_{\{1,3\}})_Z = (2,4)_Z$. We un-

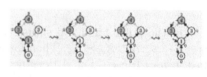

mark vertex 1 (corresponding to the dashed arrow $1 \to_2 0$) and recompute the weight function in 3 steps.

The computed value of I_2 is $\{1,2\}$ because $2 \to_1 1$ and $1 \to_2 0$ are the two arrows for which the end-vertex has weight 0. We unmark vertex 2 (corresponding to the dashed arrow $2 \to_1 1$) and recompute the weight function $(\mathcal{X}_{\overline{I_2}}) = (\mathcal{X}_{\{3\}})_Z = (4)_Z$ in 2 steps.

We obtain $I_3 = \{1,2,3\}$ and stop. The fixpoint is $[1,3]$. We can derive the counter-model: from the weights we obtain $\mathcal{X}_{\{1,2,3\}} \Vdash \{1,2,3,4\}$, $\mathcal{X}_{\{1,3\}} \Vdash \{2,4\}$, $\mathcal{X}_{\{3\}} \Vdash \{4\}$ and $\mathcal{X}_\emptyset \Vdash \emptyset$. Thus the counter-model is defined by $[\![0]\!] = 0$, $[\![1]\!] = [\![3]\!] = 1$, $[\![2]\!] = 2$ and $[\![4]\!] = 3$.

---

[16] This is trivial by induction on B, since the operation $x \mapsto x - [\![\alpha]\!]$ strictly preserves the order on the semantic values of atoms. Remark that the $-$ operator is defined in such a way that the identity $\infty - [\![\alpha]\!] = \infty$ holds.

Connection-Based Proof Search in Propositional BI Logic

Didier Galmiche and Daniel Méry

LORIA - Université Henri Poincaré
Campus Scientifique, BP 239
Vandœuvre-lès-Nancy, France

Abstract. We present a connection-based characterization of propositional **BI** (logic of bunched implications), a logic combining linear and intuitionistic connectives. This logic, with its sharing interpretation, has been recently used to reason about mutable data structures and needs proof search methods. Our connection-based characterization for **BI** is based on standard notions but involves, in a specific way, labels and constraints in order to capture the interactions between connectives during the proof-search. As **BI** is conservative w.r.t. intuitionistic logic and multiplicative intuitionistic linear logic, we deduce, by some restrictions, new connection-based characterizations and methods for both logics.

1 Introduction

The logic of bunched implications (**BI**) provides a logical analysis of the basic notion of resource, that is central in computer science, with well-defined proof-theoretic and semantic foundations [10,12]. Its propositional fragment freely combines multiplicative (or linear) $*$ and $-\!*$ connectives and additive (or intuitionistic) $\wedge$, $\rightarrow$ and $\vee$ connectives [11] and can be seen as a merging of intuitionistic logic (**IL**) and multiplicative intuitionistic linear logic (**MILL**). **BI** has a Kripke-style semantics (interpretation of formulae) [11] which combines the Kripke semantics of **IL** and Urquhart's semantics of **MILL**. The latter uses possible worlds, arranged as a commutative monoid and justified in terms of "pieces of information" [14]. The key property of the semantics is the *sharing interpretation*. The (elementary) semantics of the multiplicative conjunction, $m \models A * B$ iff there are n_1 and n_2 such that $n_1 \bullet n_2 \sqsubseteq m$, $n_1 \models A$ and $n_2 \models B$, is interpreted as follows: the resource m is sufficient to support $A * B$ just in case it can be divided into resources n_1 and n_2 such that n_1 is sufficient to support A and n_2 is sufficient to support B. Thus, A and B do not share resources. Similarly, the semantics of the multiplicative implication, $m \models A -\!* B$ iff for all n such that $n \models A$, $m \bullet n \models B$, is interpreted as follows: the resource m is sufficient to support $A -\!* B$ just in case for any resource n which is sufficient to support A the combination $m \bullet n$ is sufficient to support B. Thus, the function and its argument *do not share* resources. In contrast, if we consider the standard Kripke semantics

A. Voronkov (Ed.): CADE-18, LNAI 2392, pp. 111–128, 2002.

of the additives ∧ and → the resources are shared. Because of the interaction of intuitionistic and linear connectives and its sharing interpretation, **BI** is different from linear logic (LL) [11] and does not admit the usual number-of-uses reading. Proof-search methods dedicated to **IL** or multiplicative LL (**MLL**) introduced the notion of prefix in order to capture the order of rule applications from which a proof in the associated sequent calculus can be constructed [9,16]. Such an approach cannot be adapted to **BI** that needs more general notions, in order to capture the actual interactions between multiplicative and additive connectives. It appears that the introduction of labels and constraints is a natural way to do it. Recently, we have proposed a particular tableau method for propositional **BI** (without inconsistency) [6] with label and constraints attached to the expansion rules. This first proof search method for **BI** includes intrinsic and specific redundancies and their related problems. Our aim in this paper is to propose a connection (or matrix) characterization of provability in **BI** and a related connection-based proof method, knowing that connection methods drastically reduce the search space compared to calculi analyzing the outer structure of formulae such as sequent or tableau calculi [3,16].

In this setting, in addition to the standard notions, we introduce specific labels and constraints that in fact allow to capture the semantic consequence relation of **BI**. Such a constraint-based approach would provide powerful methods for substructural logics mixing different kinds of connectives, as in **BI** with intuitionistic and linear connectives. With connection methods based on labels and constraints, we propose an appropriate and natural way to capture the essence of the provability in **BI**, for which based-on prefixes methods, defined for instance in **IL** or **MLL** [9], cannot be easily extended. As **BI** is a new logical foundation for logic programming [1], interference in imperative programs [10] and reasoning about mutable data structures using pointers [7], our results could be fruitful in these settings. Moreover, as **BI** is conservative w.r.t. **IL** and **MILL**, the restriction and specialization of our results to both logics, provide new connection-based characterizations and proof methods for **IL** and **MILL**. The latter is strongly related to proof nets construction in **MILL** [2].

2 The Logic of Bunched Implications (BI)

The propositional language of **BI** consists of a multiplicative unit I, the multiplicative connectives $*$, $-\!\!*$, the additive units $\top$, $\bot$, the additive connectives $\wedge$, $\rightarrow$, $\vee$, a countable set $L = p, q, \ldots$ of propositional letters. $\mathcal{P}(L)$, the collection of **BI** propositions over L, is given by the following inductive definition:
$A ::= p \mid I \mid A * A \mid A -\!\!* A \mid \top \mid \bot \mid A \wedge A \mid A \rightarrow A \mid A \vee A$.
Judgements of **BI** are sequents of the form $\Gamma \vdash A$, where A is a proposition and Γ is what is called a "bunch", more precisely, a tree (rather than a list or a multiset) having propositions as leaves and whose internal nodes are labelled with ";" or ",". Therefore, we have two context-forming operations, namely, ";" and "," the key point being that ";" admits the structural rules of contraction and weakening while "," does not. More formally, bunches are given by the following grammar $\Gamma ::= A \mid \emptyset_m \mid \Gamma, \Gamma \mid \emptyset_a \mid \Gamma; \Gamma$.

– Identity and structures

$$\frac{}{A \vdash A} \, ax \qquad \frac{\Gamma \vdash A}{\Delta \vdash A} \, \Delta \equiv \Gamma \qquad \frac{\Gamma(\Delta) \vdash A}{\Gamma(\Delta; \Delta') \vdash A} \, w \qquad \frac{\Gamma(\Delta; \Delta) \vdash A}{\Gamma(\Delta) \vdash A} \, c$$

– Unities

$$\frac{}{\bot \vdash A} \, \bot_L \qquad \frac{\Gamma(\emptyset_m) \vdash A}{\Gamma(I) \vdash A} \, I_L \qquad \frac{}{\emptyset_m \vdash I} \, I_R \qquad \frac{\Gamma(\emptyset_a) \vdash A}{\Gamma(\top) \vdash A} \, \top_L \qquad \frac{}{\emptyset_a \vdash \top} \, \top_R$$

– Multiplicatives

$$\frac{\Gamma(A, B) \vdash C}{\Gamma(A * B) \vdash C} \, *_L \qquad \frac{\Gamma \vdash A \quad \Delta \vdash B}{\Gamma, \Delta \vdash A * B} \, *_R \qquad \frac{\Gamma \vdash A \quad \Delta(\Delta', B) \vdash C}{\Delta(\Delta', \Gamma, A \twoheadrightarrow B) \vdash C} \, \twoheadrightarrow_L \qquad \frac{\Gamma, A \vdash B}{\Gamma \vdash A \twoheadrightarrow B} \, \twoheadrightarrow_R$$

– Additives

$$\frac{\Gamma(A; B) \vdash C}{\Gamma(A \wedge B) \vdash C} \, \wedge_L \qquad \frac{\Gamma \vdash A \quad \Delta \vdash B}{\Gamma; \Delta \vdash A \wedge B} \, \wedge_R \qquad \frac{\Gamma \vdash A \quad \Delta(\Delta'; B) \vdash C}{\Delta(\Delta'; \Gamma; A \to B) \vdash C} \, \to_L$$

$$\frac{\Gamma; A \vdash B}{\Gamma \vdash A \to B} \, \to_R \qquad \frac{\Gamma(A) \vdash C \quad \Delta(B) \vdash C}{\Gamma(A \vee B); \Delta(A \vee B) \vdash C} \, \vee_L \qquad \frac{\Gamma \vdash A_{i\,(i=1,2)}}{\Gamma \vdash A_1 \vee A_2} \, \vee_{Ri}$$

Fig. 1. The **LBI** sequent calculus

We write $\Gamma(\Delta)$ to represent a bunch in which Δ is a subtree. Since bunches may be represented in various way, we consider them up to a structural equivalence ($\equiv$) defined as the least equivalence satisfying commutative monoid equations for $\emptyset_a$ and ";" and for $\emptyset_m$ and "," together with congruence: $\Delta \equiv \Delta'$ implies $\Gamma(\Delta) \equiv \Gamma(\Delta')$.

The **LBI** sequent calculus is given in figure 1. A proposition A is a theorem iff $\emptyset_m \vdash A$ is provable in **LBI**. Let us mention that an elementary Kripke semantics has been defined for **BI** but the completeness result only holds for **BI** without $\bot$. Some topological semantics have been proposed in order to have completeness for full propositional **BI** [11].

Proof-search in **BI** is difficult because of the interaction between additive and multiplicative connectives which, in the **LBI** calculus, results in sequents whose contexts are structured as bunches. Due to the properties of the context building operations, bunches admit various structural transformations which are delicate to handle, but on the other hand, often required during the proof-search process in order to achieve a proof. In order to alleviate each type of redundancies induced by proof-search in the **LBI** calculus, namely: notational redundancy, irrelevance and non-permutability [16], we propose a connection-based characterization of **BI** provability and a related proof-search method.

3   A Connection-Based Characterization of BI

The matrix (or connection) characterization of **BI** provability we propose is based on *labels* and *constraints* that are the appropriate concepts that allow to capture the consequence relation, and thus the interaction of connectives at a semantical level. Semantically speaking, the interaction between additive and multiplicative connectives can mainly be seen as a problem of sharing and distributing the resources and based-on prefixes methods, defined for instance in **IL** or **MLL** [9], cannot naturally deal with it.

3.1   Labels and Constraints

Given an alphabet C (for example $a, b, c, \cdots$), C^0, the set of *atomic labels over* C, is defined as the set C extended with the unit symbol 1. We then define C^*, the set of *labels over* C, as the smallest set containing C^0 and closed under composition ($x, y \in C^*$ implies $xy \in C^*$). Labels are defined up to associativity, commutativity and identity 1. Therefore, *aabcc*, *cbaca* and *cbcaa*1 are simply regarded as equivalent.

A *label constraint* is an expression $x \leq y$ where x and y are labels. A constraint of the form $x \leq x$ is called an *axiom* and we write $x = y$ to express that $x \leq y$ and $y \leq x$. We use the following inference rules to reason on constraints:

$$\frac{x \leq y}{xz \leq yz} \, func \qquad \qquad \frac{x \leq z \quad z \leq y}{x \leq y} \, trans$$

The *trans* rule formalizes the transitivity of $\leq$ while the *func* rule corresponds to the functoriality (also called compatibility) of label composition w.r.t. $\leq$. In this formal system, given a constraint k and a set of constraints H, we write $H \approx k$ if there is a deduction of k from H. The notation $H \approx K$, where K is a non-empty set of constraints, means that for any $k \in K$, $H \approx k$.

3.2   Labelled Indexed Formula Tree

Let us recall the standard notions of matrix characterizations of provability [9, 16]. In order to illustrate the concepts and results, we consider the **BI** formula $(p * ((q \to r) * s)) \mathbin{-\!*} ((p * (q \to r)) * s)$ as an example.

The *formula tree* for a formula A is its representation as a syntax tree the nodes of which are called *positions*. A position u exactly identifies a subformula of A, denoted $f(u)$. An *atomic position* is a position whose formula is atomic. The formula tree induces a partial ordering $\ll$ on positions, such that the root is the least element and if $u \ll v$ then u dominates v (u is in a path from the root to v) in the formula tree. In fact, we do not distinguish between a formula A and its formula tree. Thus, a position u in A is the position in its formula tree. A position u is assigned a polarity $pol(u)$, a principal type $ptyp(u)$ and a secondary type $styp(u)$. We identify in **BI** four principal types $\alpha, \beta, \pi\alpha, \pi\beta$ depending on the principal connective, the polarity and their related secondary types.

Specific concepts for BI. Depending on its principal type, we associate to a position u two notions, namely a label $slab(u)$ and possibly a (label) constraint $kon(u)$. Such a label is either a position or a position with a tilde superscript (in order to identify the formula that introduces the resource) and a label constraint is introduced in order to capture the composition and distribution of the formulae (seen as resources). For a position u, we define its *labelled signed formula* $lsf(u)$ as the triple $(slab(u), f(u), pol(u))$, denoted $slab(u) : f(u)^{pol(u)}$.

Figure 2 presents the inductive definition of such formulae, knowing that, given a **BI** formula A, we first consider the root position a_0 with polarity $pol(a_0) = 0$ and label $slab(a_0) = 1$, namely, the signed formula $1 : (A)^0$ (1 being the identity of the label composition). Let us note that u_1 and u_2 respectively stand for the first and second child of the position u. For example, if a position u has formula $A * B$, polarity 1 and label x, then u_1 has

$lsf(u)$	$ptyp(u)$	$kon(u)$	$lsf(u_1)$	$lsf(u_2)$
$x : (A \wedge B)^1$	α	$-$	$x : A^1$	$x : B^1$
$x : (A \vee B)^0$	α	$-$	$x : A^0$	$x : B^0$
$x : (A \rightarrow B)^0$	$\pi\alpha$	$x \leq u$	$u : A^1$	$u : B^0$
$x : (A \twoheadrightarrow B)^0$	$\pi\alpha$	$xu = \tilde{u}$	$u : A^1$	$\tilde{u} : B^0$
$x : (A * B)^1$	$\pi\alpha$	$u\tilde{u} \leq x$	$u : A^1$	$\tilde{u} : B^1$
$x : (A \wedge B)^0$	β	$-$	$x : A^0$	$x : B^0$
$x : (A \vee B)^1$	β	$-$	$x : A^1$	$x : B^1$
$x : (A \rightarrow B)^1$	$\pi\beta$	$x \leq u$	$u : A^0$	$u : B^1$
$x : (A \twoheadrightarrow B)^1$	$\pi\beta$	$xu = \tilde{u}$	$u : A^0$	$\tilde{u} : B^1$
$x : (A * B)^0$	$\pi\beta$	$u\tilde{u} \leq x$	$u : A^0$	$\tilde{u} : B^0$

Fig. 2. Signed formulae for **BI**

formula A, polarity 1 and label u while u_2 has formula B, polarity 1 and label $\tilde{u}$. Positions u_1 and u_2 inherit formulae and polarities from parent position u. The principal type of a position u is determined from its principal connective and polarity. Moreover, the labels are inherited by the positions u_1 and u_2, depending on the principal connective and label of u. The label constraint, associated to u, is computed from its principal connective and label.

Let us come back to our example. In fact the formula A is first represented as a syntax tree each node of which being identified with a position (tree on the right-hand side of figure 3). Moreover, we can associate an indexed formula tree (with labelled signed formulae as nodes), inductively built from $1 : (A)^0$ and the rules of Figure 2 (tree on the left-hand side of figure 3). In parallel, we have the generation of constraints for positions with principal type $\pi\alpha$ and $\pi\beta$ (see constraints $kon(u)$ in the array of figure 3).

Multiplicity. The **BI** logic deals with resource sharing and distribution. The LBI rules $*_R$, $\twoheadrightarrow_L$ and $\rightarrow_L$, related to $\pi\beta$ formulae, split the context and thus distribute the resources. Due to contraction and weakening, we may have to copy the resources (or formulae) before distribution and it could be necessary to have multiple instances of some formulae to achieve proofs. In our connection method for **BI** this necessity is captured by a notion of *multiplicity* μ attached to the $\pi\beta$ formulae. Similarly to [16], we now consider a formula A together with a multiplicity μ and we call this pair an *indexed formula* A^μ. The *indexed formula tree* for A^μ ($indt(A^\mu)$), which is a tree of indexed positions u^κ, κ being a sequence of positive integers, is defined as the following extension of the basic formula tree for A.

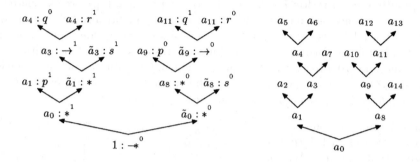

u	$pol(u)$	$f(u)$	$ptyp(u)$	$styp(u)$	$slab(u)$	$kon(u)$
a_0	0	$(p * ((q \to r) * s)) \twoheadrightarrow ((p * (q \to r)) * s)$	$\pi\alpha$	$-$	1	$1a_0 = \tilde{a}_0$
a_1	1	$p * ((q \to r) * s)$	$\pi\alpha$	$\pi\alpha_1$	a_0	$a_1\tilde{a}_1 \leq a_0$
a_2	1	p	$-$	$\pi\alpha_1$	a_1	$-$
a_3	1	$(q \to r) * s$	$\pi\alpha$	$\pi\alpha_2$	$\tilde{a}_1$	$a_3\tilde{a}_3 \leq a_1$
a_4	1	$q \to r$	$\pi\beta$	$\pi\alpha_1$	a_3	$a_3 \leq a_4$
a_5	0	q	$-$	$\pi\beta_1$	a_4	$-$
a_6	1	r	$-$	$\pi\beta_2$	a_4	$-$
a_7	1	s	$-$	$\pi\alpha_2$	$\tilde{a}_3$	$-$
a_8	0	$(p * (q \to r)) * s$	$\pi\beta$	$\pi\alpha_2$	$\tilde{a}_0$	$a_8\tilde{a}_8 \leq \tilde{a}_0$
a_9	0	$p * (q \to r)$	$\pi\beta$	$\pi\beta_1$	a_8	$a_9\tilde{a}_9 \leq a_8$
a_{10}	0	p	$-$	$\pi\beta_1$	a_9	$-$
a_{11}	0	$q \to r$	$\pi\alpha$	$\pi\beta_2$	$\tilde{a}_9$	$\tilde{a}_9 \leq a_{11}$
a_{12}	1	q	$-$	$\pi\beta_1$	a_{11}	$-$
a_{13}	0	r	$-$	$\pi\beta_2$	a_{11}	$-$
a_{14}	0	s	$-$	$\pi\beta_2$	$\tilde{a}_8$	$-$

Fig. 3. Indexed formula tree for $(p * ((q \to r) * s)) \twoheadrightarrow ((p * (q \to r)) * s)$

Definition 3.1. u^κ *is an* indexed position *of* $indt(A^\mu)$ *iff*
1) u is a position of the formula tree for A.
*2) let $u_1 \ll \cdots \ll u_n$ be all the $\pi\beta$-positions that dominate u in the formula
tree for A, then a) $\mu(u_i) \neq 0$, $1 \leq i \leq n$ and b) $\kappa = m_1 \cdots m_n$, $1 \leq m_i \leq n$,
$1 \leq i \leq n$.*

For example, having an indexed position u^{23} means that, in the basic formula
tree, u is dominated by a $\pi\beta$-position v_2 which is itself dominated by another
$\pi\beta$-position v_1. Moreover, in the indexed formula tree, u^{23} is the copy of u which
is in the subtree of the third copy of v_2 and of the second copy of v_1. The tree
ordering $\ll^\mu$ is given, for any two indexed positions u^κ and v^τ, by the following
definition: $u^\kappa \ll^\mu v^\tau$ iff $u \ll v$ and κ is an initial sequence of τ. Given an indexed
formula A^μ, we denote $\mathcal{O}cc(u^\kappa)$ the set of indexed positions $u^{\kappa\tau}$ occurring in
A^μ. All other notations straightforwardly extend to indexed formula trees and
indexed positions. Here, we only consider examples with a multiplicity of 1 and
we do not write indexes.

3.3 Paths and Connections

We adapt to **BI** the standard notions of path, connection and spanning set of connections defined for classical and intuitionistic logics [16].

Definition 3.2 (Path). *Let A^μ be an indexed formula, u^κ be an indexed position of indt(A^μ) and u_1, u_2 be the immediate successors of u in the basic formula tree of A, the set of* paths *through A^μ is inductively defined as the smallest set such that:*

1. *$\{a_0\}$ is a path, where a_0 is the root position;*
2. *if s is a path containing u^κ then*
a) *if $ptyp(u^\kappa) \in \{\alpha, \pi\alpha\}$ then, so is $(s \backslash u^\kappa) \cup \mathcal{O}cc(u_1^\kappa) \cup \mathcal{O}cc(u_2^\kappa)$,*
b) *if $ptyp(u^\kappa) \in \{\beta, \pi\beta\}$ then, so are $(s \backslash u^\kappa) \cup \mathcal{O}cc(u_1^\kappa)$ and $(s \backslash u^\kappa) \cup \mathcal{O}cc(u_2^\kappa)$.*

We say that a path s' obtained from a path s by decomposing a non-atomic position u^κ as explained in case 2 is obtained by *reduction* on u^κ. An *atomic path* is a path that cannot be reduced anymore and therefore only contains atomic positions.

Definition 3.3 (Connection). *A connection is a pair $\langle u, v \rangle$ of atomic positions such that $f(u) = f(v)$, $pol(u) = 1$ and $pol(v) = 0$[1].*
A set of connections spans *an indexed formula A^μ iff every atomic path through A^μ contains a connection from this set.*

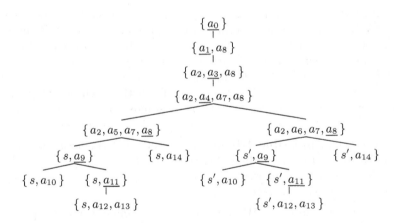

Fig. 4. Path reduction and connection sets

In our example, the reduction of the initial path $\{a_0\}$ results in six atomic paths as depicted in figure 4. At each step, we indicate the position which is reduced with an underscore. For conciseness, we write s and s' as shortcuts for a_2, a_5, a_7 and a_2, a_6, a_7. The set $\{\langle a_2, a_{10}\rangle, \langle a_{12}, a_5\rangle, \langle a_7, a_{14}\rangle, \langle a_6, a_{13}\rangle\}$ of connections spans the formula A^μ. Let us note that $\langle a_2, a_{10}\rangle$ and $\langle a_7, a_{14}\rangle$ both cover two paths at the same time.

---

[1] Note that the first position of the connection is the one with polarity 1.

3.4   Characterizing Validity in BI

Let A^μ be an indexed formula, Π_α (resp. Π_β) is the set of positions of A^μ with $\pi\alpha$ (resp. $\pi\beta$) as principal type. For $i = 1,2$, $\Pi_{\alpha i}$ (resp. Π_{β_i}) are the sets of positions of A^μ with $\pi\alpha_i$ (resp. $\pi\beta_i$) as secondary types. $\Sigma_\alpha = \{\, slab(u)/u \in (\Pi_{\alpha 1} \cup \Pi_{\alpha 2})\,\}$ and $\Sigma_\beta = \{\, slab(u)/u \in (\Pi_{\beta_1} \cup \Pi_{\beta_2})\,\}$ are respectively the sets of labels corresponding to positions of secondary types $\pi\alpha_i$ and $\pi\beta_i$.

In our example, $\Sigma_\alpha = \{\, a_0, \tilde{a}_0, a_1, \tilde{a}_1, a_3, \tilde{a}_3, a_{11}\,\}$ and $\Sigma_\beta = \{\, a_4, a_8, \tilde{a}_8, a_9, \tilde{a}_9\,\}$. Moreover, we split the set of constraints into two sets $\mathcal{K}_\alpha = \{\, kon(u)/u \in \Pi_\alpha\,\}$ and $\mathcal{K}_\beta = \{\, kon(u)/u \in \Pi_\beta\,\}$, by distinguishing constraints introduced by positions with $\pi\alpha$ and $\pi\beta$ as principal type.

Thus, we obtain $\mathcal{K}_\alpha = \{\, a_0 = \tilde{a}_0, a_1\tilde{a}_1 \le a_0, a_3\tilde{a}_3 \le \tilde{a}_1, \tilde{a}_9 \le a_{11}\,\}$ and $\mathcal{K}_\beta = \{\, a_8\tilde{a}_8 \le \tilde{a}_0, a_9\tilde{a}_9 \le a_8, a_3 \le a_4\,\}$.

The constraints of $\mathcal{K}_\alpha$ are called *assertions* and those of $\mathcal{K}_\beta$ are called *requirements*. We have already used a similar terminology in the labelled tableau calculus defined for **BI** without $\bot$ [6]. In our matrix-characterization, the resource distribution problem is handled via a so-called **BI**-*substitution* which provides a solution to the constraints derived from the set of connections $\mathcal{S}$ by considering the inequality $slab(u) \le slab(v)$ for each connection $\langle u, v\rangle$ in $\mathcal{S}$.

In our example, we have $\mathcal{S} = \{\, \langle a_2, a_{10}\rangle, \langle a_{12}, a_5\rangle, \langle a_7, a_{14}\rangle, \langle a_6, a_{13}\rangle\,\}$ and we generate the set of constraints $\mathcal{C}on = \{\, a_1 \le a_9, a_{11} \le a_4, \tilde{a}_3 \le \tilde{a}_8, a_4 \le a_{11}\,\}$.

A **BI**-*substitution* is a mapping $\sigma : \Sigma_\beta \to \Sigma_\alpha^\star$. Therefore, the elements of Σ_β play the role of variables that must be ground to labels built upon the elements of Σ_α which play the role of constants. It induces a relation $\sqsubseteq$ on $\Pi_\alpha \times \Pi_\beta$ in the following way: if $\sigma(u) = s$ then $pos(v) \sqsubseteq pos(u)$ for any v occurring in s, where pos is the function that returns the input u without tildes (i.e., $pos(\tilde{a}_3) = a_3$ and $pos(a_3) = a_3$). From this relation, we define the reduction ordering $\lhd := (\ll \cup \sqsubseteq)^+$, where $+$ stands for transitive closure and also the set $\mathcal{K}_\alpha^\lhd(u) = \{\, kon(v)/v \in \Pi_\alpha$ and $u \not\lhd v\,\}$ for a position u.

Definition 3.4 (admissible BI-substitutions). *Let A^μ be an indexed formula, a **BI**-substitution σ is admissible w.r.t. A^μ iff*
1. the induced reduction ordering $\lhd$ is irreflexive
2. $\forall\, u \in \Pi_\beta$, $\sigma(\mathcal{K}_\alpha^\lhd(u)) \mathrel{\vcenter{\hbox{$\approx$}}} \sigma(kon(u))$.

The condition 2. means that a **BI**-substitution σ is admissible if the requirements are derivable from the assertions by means of the constraint deduction system (see section 3.1), but with a precise order: the assertions involved in the proof of a requirement must correspond to $\pi\alpha$ positions that may be reduced, with the reduction ordering induced by σ, before the $\pi\beta$ position corresponding to this requirement.

Definition 3.5 (Complementarity). *Let A^μ be an indexed formula and σ be a **BI**-substitution, a connection $\langle u, v\rangle$ is said to be complementary under σ, or σ-complementary, iff $\sigma(\mathcal{K}_\alpha) \mathrel{\vcenter{\hbox{$\approx$}}} \sigma(slab(u)) \le \sigma(slab(v))$.*
A path is σ-complementary if it contains a σ-complementary connection. A set of paths is σ-complementary if all its paths are σ-complementary.

Theorem 3.1 (Connection-based characterization). *A formula A of* **BI** *is valid iff there is a multiplicity μ, an admissible* **BI**-*substitution σ and a set of σ-complementary connections that spans A^μ.*

Proof. see the next subsection.

Coming back to our example, from the set of connections that spans A^μ, we must find an admissible **BI**-substitution $\sigma : \Sigma_\beta \to \Sigma_\alpha{}^*$ which makes each connection σ-complementary, but how to compute such a substitution ?

The easiest way to satisfy the constraints of $\mathcal{C}on$ is to consider them as equalities, rather than inequalities, namely, $\sigma(a_9) = a_1, \sigma(a_4) = a_{11}, \sigma(\tilde{a}_8) = \tilde{a}_3, \sigma(a_4) = a_{11}, \sigma(a_8) = X, \sigma(\tilde{a}_9) = Y$. This substitution makes each connection of $\mathcal{C}on$ σ-complementary. and we have to find $X, Y \in \Sigma_\alpha{}^*$ such that σ is admissible in the sense of definition 3.4. Hence, we must verify that $\sigma(\mathcal{K}_\alpha) \mathrel{|\!\approx} \sigma(\mathcal{K}_\beta)$. It corresponds to show that

1. $a_0 = \tilde{a}_0, a_1\tilde{a}_1 \le a_0, a_3\tilde{a}_3 \le \tilde{a}_1, Y \le a_{11} \mathrel{|\!\approx} X\tilde{a}_3 \le \tilde{a}_0$
2. $a_0 = \tilde{a}_0, a_1\tilde{a}_1 \le a_0, a_3\tilde{a}_3 \le \tilde{a}_1, Y \le a_{11} \mathrel{|\!\approx} a_3 \le a_{11}$
3. $a_0 = \tilde{a}_0, a_1\tilde{a}_1 \le a_0, a_3\tilde{a}_3 \le \tilde{a}_1, Y \le a_{11} \mathrel{|\!\approx} a_1Y \le X$

A trivial solution for condition 2. is to consider $Y \equiv a_3$. Moreover, condition 3. is trivially verified with $X \equiv a_1a_3$ and condition 1. is also verified, because of

$$\cfrac{\cfrac{a_3\tilde{a}_3 \le \tilde{a}_1}{a_1a_3\tilde{a}_3 \le a_1\tilde{a}_1}\ func \qquad a_1\tilde{a}_1 \le a_0}{\cfrac{a_1a_3\tilde{a}_3 \le a_0 \qquad\qquad\qquad a_0 = \tilde{a}_0}{a_1a_3\tilde{a}_3 \le \tilde{a}_0}\ trans}\ trans$$

Let us remark that the proof of the constraint of a_8 ($a_1a_3\tilde{a}_3 \le \tilde{a}_0$) does not depend on the constraint of a_{11} ($a_3 \le a_{11}$) that is the only one that is $\lhd$-greater than a_8. Therefore, we deduce that $\sigma(a_8) = a_1a_3$ and $\sigma(\tilde{a}_9) = a_3$.

Finally, we have to show that the reduction ordering induced by σ is irreflexive. In fact, the relation $\sqsubset$ induced by σ is: $a_{11} \sqsubset a_4$, $a_1 \ll a_3 \sqsubset a_8 \ll a_9$. Combined with the relation $\ll$, which represents the tree ordering on the positions, we have the relation $\lhd$ depicted on figure 5, that is easily proved irreflexive (acyclic). The dotted arrows correspond to the parts of the relation coming from the substitution. Since the graph is acyclic, σ is admissible, and so, the formula is valid.

The present characterization can be extended to take the units into account. There is no problem with $\top$ and I since we can respectively translate all of their occurrences inside a formula A by the formulae $(\alpha \to \alpha)$ and $(\beta \mathbin{-\!\!*} \beta)$, where α and β are new propositional variables not occurring in A. The treatment of $\bot$ is more delicate [11] and needs the following additions to the notions of connection and complementarity: a $\bot$-*connection* is a pair $\langle u, v \rangle$ of atomic positions such that $pol(u) = 1$, $pol(v) = 0$ and $f(u) = \bot$. Let A^μ be an indexed formula and σ be a **BI**-substitution, a $\bot$-connection $\langle u, v \rangle$ is said to be *complementary* under σ iff $\sigma(\mathcal{K}_\alpha) \mathrel{|\!\approx} \sigma(slab(u))x \le \sigma(slab(v))$ for some label $x \in \Sigma_\alpha{}^*$. The next proof of our characterization is given for **BI** without units but with the previous extensions it can be easily adapted to **BI** with units.

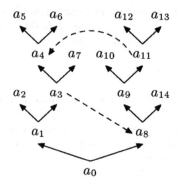

Fig. 5. Reduction ordering

3.5   Proof of the Matrix Characterization

Let us give the proof of the previous characterization of **BI** provability. It can be split in two parts, namely soundness and completeness. The proof of soundness follows the ideas given in [16] for modal logics, but we have to recall some points about **BI** validity. A *Kripke resource interpretation* $\mathcal{K} = \langle\,(M, \sqsubseteq, \bullet, e), \models, [\![-]\!]\,\rangle$ is a *Kripke resource monoid* $\langle\,(M, \sqsubseteq, \bullet, e)\,\rangle$, i.e., a preordered monoid in which $\bullet$ is order preserving (or functorial w.r.t. $\sqsubseteq$), together with a forcing relation $\models$ parametrized by an interpretation $[\![-]\!]$ of propositional variables. A formula A is *valid in* $\mathcal{K}$ iff $e \models A$. A formula A is *valid* if it is valid for all $\mathcal{K}$.

Let us introduce some appropriate definitions. A *reduction* is a finite sequence $(\mathcal{S}_i)_{0 \leq i \leq n} = \mathcal{S}_0, \cdots, \mathcal{S}_n$ where $\mathcal{S}_0$ is a set of paths and for any $i \geq 0$, $\mathcal{S}_{i+1}$ is obtained by reducing a position u_i in a path s_i of $\mathcal{S}_i$. We say that $\mathcal{S}_{i+1}$ is obtained by reduction of $\mathcal{S}_i$ on (s_i, u_i). Note that, given $\mathcal{S}_0$, $\mathcal{S}_{i+1}$ is completely determined by the sequence $(s_0, u_0), \cdots, (s_i, u_i)$. Moreover, for each $\mathcal{S}_i$, we define $\Pi_\alpha(\mathcal{S}_i)$ as the set of all the $\pi\alpha$-positions that were reduced before reaching $\mathcal{S}_i$ and $\Sigma_\alpha(\mathcal{S}_i)$ as the language of labels introduced by those reductions. More formally, $\Pi_\alpha(\mathcal{S}_i) = \{\,u_j/(j < i) \text{ and } ptyp(u_j) = \pi\alpha\,\}$ and $\Sigma_\alpha(\mathcal{S}_i) = \bigcup_{1 \leq j \leq i}\{\,slab(u)/u \in s, s \in \mathcal{S}_j\,\}$. $\mathcal{K}_\alpha(\mathcal{S}_i) = kon(\Pi_\alpha(\mathcal{S}_i))$ is the set of label-constraints introduced by the positions in $\Pi_\alpha(\mathcal{S}_i)$. Similarly for $\Pi_\beta(\mathcal{S}_i), \Sigma_\beta(\mathcal{S}_i)$ and $\mathcal{K}_\beta(\mathcal{S}_i)$ w.r.t. $\pi\beta$-positions. A reduction $(\mathcal{S}_i)_{0 \leq i \leq n}$ is *complete* if it cannot be further reduced, *i.e.*, if $\mathcal{S}_n$ only contains atomic paths.

Definition 3.6. *Let σ be a **BI**-substitution, a reduction $(\mathcal{S}_i)_{0 \leq i \leq n}$ is σ-proper if (i) for any $i \geq 0$, $\sigma(\mathcal{K}_\alpha(\mathcal{S}_i)) \not\approx \sigma(\mathcal{K}_\beta(\mathcal{S}_i))$ and (ii) for any $j > i \geq 0$, $u_j \not\triangleleft u_i$.*

Lemma 3.1. *A **BI**-substitution σ is admissible iff there exists a σ-proper reduction from $\{\,\{\,a_0\,\}\,\}$, where $\{\,a_0\,\}$ is the initial path containing the root position.*

Proof. The proof is direct since condition (ii) can only be satisfied if σ is irreflexive and condition (i) means that the assertions needed to deduce a requirement associated to a $\pi\beta$-position are the ones corresponding to previously reduced $\pi\alpha$-positions, *i.e.*, $\pi\alpha$-positions that are not $\lhd$-greater than this $\pi\beta$-position.

Definition 3.7. *Let σ be a **BI**-substitution and $(\mathcal{S}_i)_{0 \le i \le n}$ be a complete σ-proper reduction. An interpretation of $\mathcal{S}_i$ in a Kripke resource model $\mathcal{K}$ denoted $\langle (M, \sqsubseteq, \bullet, e), \models, \llbracket - \rrbracket \rangle$ is a mapping $\bar{\iota}: \Sigma_\alpha(\mathcal{S}_i) \to M$. The mapping ι obtained by homomorphic extension of $\bar{\iota}$ to $\Sigma_\alpha(\mathcal{S}_i)^\star$ is also called an interpretation. An interpretation ι realizes $\mathcal{S}_i$ under σ, or $\mathcal{S}_i$ is σ-realizable, if there is a path s in $\mathcal{S}_i$ such that:*

1. *for any $x \le y \in \mathcal{K}_\alpha(\mathcal{S}_i)$, $\iota\sigma(x) \sqsubseteq \iota\sigma(y)$.*
2. *for any $u \in s$ such that $lsf(u) = x : A^1$, $\iota\sigma(x) \models A$.*
3. *for any $u \in s$ such that $lsf(u) = x : A^0$, $\iota\sigma(x) \not\models A$.*

$\mathcal{S}_i$ is σ-realizable if it is σ-realizable for some interpretation.

Lemma 3.2. *If $\mathcal{S}_i$ is σ-realizable then $\mathcal{S}_{i+1}$ is σ-realizable.*

Proof. By case analysis on the position which is reduced.

Lemma 3.3. *If $(\mathcal{S}_i)_{0 \le i \le n}$ is a complete σ-proper reduction then, if $\mathcal{S}_n$ is σ-complementary it is not σ-realizable.*

Proof. Suppose $\mathcal{S}_n$ is σ-realizable for some interpretation ι. There is an atomic path $s \in \mathcal{S}_n$ which satisfies the conditions of definition 3.7. But, since $\mathcal{S}_n$ is σ-complementary, s contains a connection $\langle u, v \rangle$ such that, $f(u) = f(v)$, $pol(u) = 1$, $pol(v) = 0$ and $\sigma(\mathcal{K}_\alpha) \not\approx \sigma(slab(u)) \le \sigma(slab(v))$. $\mathcal{S}_n$ is σ-realizable and we have $\iota\sigma(slab(u)) \models f(u)$, $\iota\sigma(slab(v)) \not\models f(u)$.
Moreover, since the reduction is complete, $\mathcal{K}_\alpha = \mathcal{K}_\alpha(\mathcal{S}_n)$ and then $\iota\sigma(slab(u)) \sqsubseteq \iota\sigma(slab(v))$, which yields a contradiction because we should have $\iota\sigma(slab(v)) \models f(u)$ by Kripke monotonicity.

Theorem 3.2 (Soundness). *Let A be a **BI** formula, if there is a multiplicity μ, an admissible **BI**-substitution σ and a set of σ-complementary connections that spans A^μ then A is valid.*

Proof. Let us suppose that there is a multiplicity μ and an admissible **BI**-substitution σ which makes the set of atomic paths through A^μ σ-complementary. Let us assume that A does not hold in Kripke resource semantics. Then, there exists $\mathcal{K} = \langle (M, \sqsubseteq, \bullet, e), \models, \llbracket - \rrbracket \rangle$ such that $e \not\models A$ and the set $\mathcal{S}_0 = \{ \{ a_0 \} \}$ is therefore trivially σ-realizable. Since σ is admissible, lemma 3.1 ensures that there is a complete σ-proper reduction from $\mathcal{S}_0$. Because $\mathcal{S}_0$ is realizable, by lemma 3.2 the set of atomic paths is also realizable. Lemma 3.3 finally entails that this set cannot be σ-complementary, which is a contradiction.

Let us now consider the completeness. We say that a formula A is *connection-valid* if there is a multiplicity μ, an admissible **BI**-substitution σ and a set of σ-complementary connections that spans A^μ. A sequent $\Gamma \vdash A$ is *connection-valid* if the formula $\Phi_\Gamma \twoheadrightarrow A$ is connection-valid, where Φ_Γ is the formula obtained from Γ by replacing each $\emptyset_a$ by $\top$, each $\emptyset_m$ by I, each ";" by $\wedge$ and each "," by $*$. Now, we prove completeness by showing that connection-validity is closed under each rule of the **LBI** sequent calculus.

Lemma 3.4. *if $\Gamma \vdash A$ is **LBI**-provable then it is connection-valid.*

Proof. By induction on the derivation in **LBI** (see appendix A).

Theorem 3.3 (Completeness). *If a **BI** formula A is valid then there is a multiplicity μ, an admissible **BI**-substitution σ and a set of σ-complementary connections that spans A^μ.*

Proof. If A is valid then $\emptyset_m \vdash A$ is provable in **LBI**. Then, by lemma 3.4, we deduce that $I \twoheadrightarrow A$ is connection-valid and since $I \twoheadrightarrow A \dashv\vdash A$, there is a multiplicity μ, an admissible **BI**-substitution σ and a set of σ-complementary connections that spans A^μ.

3.6   The Related Connection Method

From this connection characterization of **BI** provability and as illustrated in the previous example, we can define a connection-based proof search method for **BI**. For that, we can follow the standard steps of connection methods proposed for intuitionistic logic or linear logic [9,16] but replace the procedures dedicated to the treatment of prefixes by procedures dealing with constraints. In the context of **BI** where intuitionistic and linear connectives cohabit, labels and constraints that capture the semantic consequence relation of the logic appears as a necessary generalization of prefixes that mainly capture the permutabilities of rules in a sequent calculus.

Let us focus now on the specific treatment of constraints in our method. A first step consists in computing the **BI**-substitutions (from a set of connections). As illustrated in the example, it mainly requires an unification algorithm on labels. First, we could use an existing T-string unification algorithm [9] or an AC-algorithm [4,13] on our labels. Further work will focus on this step in order to analyze if it is necessary to propose other unification algorithms, specially dedicated to our constraint-based method. The second step consists in proving the admissibility of such a substitution, *i.e.*, whether requirements hold w.r.t. assertions. For that, as illustrated in the example, we have to develop bottom-up proof search in the formal system including the inference rules *func* and *trans*, presented in section 3.1. What we can say about proof search in this calculus, in this step, is that it can be based on the following order of rule applications, namely, from the bottom we have all *trans* rules first and then a *func* rule with axioms or assertions as premises. Moreover, in the *trans* rules, the right-hand side premiss is always an assertion. Consequently, it reduces the possible instantiations of the left-hand side premiss $x \leq z$ from the known constraint $z \leq y$. From these results, that are not detailed here, we have significant improvements of the standard bottom-up proof search in the constraint calculus. This analysis of two specific steps of our method will lead to a first implementation that can be based on known and improved algorithms [9] but with specific modules dedicated to constraint generation and solving. Further work will be devoted to such an implementation with, in addition, a study of the effective use of multiplicity in this proof-search process. Here, we do not give an explicit bound but if we have enough copies of $\pi\beta$ formulae to have each atom involved in only one connection, we can show that it is sufficient to decide a **BI** formula with our method.

4   A New Connection-Based Characterization for IL

One important feature about **BI** is that it is conservative w.r.t. **IL** and **MILL** logics [11]. Thus, we propose a new characterization of **IL** provability which is directly derived from **BI** by restricting the formulae to the additive connectives. A main consequence is that $\pi\alpha$ and $\pi\beta$ positions respectively correspond to signed formulae of the form $(A \to B)^0$ and $(A \to B)^1$. Looking at figure 2, we can notice that such a restriction discards the need for atomic labels with a tilde and leads to constraints dealing only with *atomic* labels. Concerning the constraint deduction, this simplified constraints allow to forget about the *func* rule. Since the only rule is *trans*, checking whether a requirement is derivable from a set of assertions simply means checking whether this requirement belongs to the transitive closure of the assertions, which is a significant simplification. The necessary adaptations to substitutions, complementarity and validity are direct. All other definitions remain unchanged.

Let A^μ be an indexed formula, a **IL**-*substitution* is a mapping $\sigma : \Sigma_\beta \to \Sigma_\alpha$. The definitions of admissibility and complementarity are the same as for **BI** but involves the new (restricted) definition of **IL**-substitution. Thus, we obtain a new matrix characterization for **IL**.

Theorem 4.1 (Connection-based characterization). *A **IL** formula A is valid iff there is a multiplicity μ, an admissible **IL**-substitution σ and a set of σ-complementary connections that spans A^μ.*

The connection method for **BI** can directly be adapted to provide a new connection method for **IL**. Here, the label constraints involve either two Σ_α labels, two Σ_β labels or a Σ_α label and a Σ_β label. Therefore, the unification step is drastically simplified and the computation of **IL**-substitutions becomes quite immediate. Then, in the case of **IL**, the main step lies in the verification of the admissibility of the substitutions, which reduces to checking if the requirements belong to the transitive closure of the assertions.

Standard matrix characterizations of **IL** [9,16] consider prefixes that essentially describe the position of a subformula in the syntax tree. The order of rule applications in the search process is captured by an intuitionistic substitution which makes the prefixes of connected subformulae identical and a specialized string unification is required for this step. Deriving our method for **IL** from **BI** provides an alternative to this approach by considering constraints in place of prefixes.

Because of the simple form of the constraints in **IL**, we can refine and improve the specific steps dedicated to the constraints.

Further work will be devoted to a more accurate study of the constraints solving in **IL**. This new method emphasizes that, in a logic with a resource semantics like **BI** but also **IL**, labels can be used in order to capture, in a simple way, its consequence relation. It seems to be a more general approach than trying to capture the right order of rules applications in the sequent calculus, with prefixes for instance. This point will be more deeply analyzed but the interest of constraint-based proof calculi [15] for substructural logics is clearly confirmed.

5   A New Connection-Based Characterization for MILL

There exists connection-based characterizations and related connection methods for multiplicative (commutative) linear logic (**MLL**) [5,8] but not for its intuitionistic fragment, namely **MILL**. The matrix characterization proposed in [8] is based on particular prefixes and substitutions dedicated to **MLL**. In order to extend or adapt it to **MILL**, it would be necessary to add intuitionistic prefixes but it seems to be difficult and not natural. Since **BI** is conservative over **MILL** [11], we can define the first connection-based characterization for **MILL**, by restriction of the one for **BI** to the multiplicative connectives (see table 2). We only have to adapt all the definitions with such a restriction.

Theorem 5.1 (Connection-based characterization). *A* **MILL** *formula A is valid iff there is a multiplicity μ, an admissible* **MILL**-*substitution σ and a set of σ-complementary connections that spans A^μ.*

This result emphasizes the power of labels and constraints that are more natural and accurate than prefixes to capture the semantic consequence relation and consequently the order of rule applications in the related sequent calculus of **MILL**. From this characterization of provability, we can propose, like in **BI** a connection-based proof search method for **MILL**. As an example, we can consider the **BI** formula $(p * ((q \to r) * s)) \twoheadrightarrow ((p * (q \to r)) * s)$ in which we replace $\to$ by $\twoheadrightarrow$, namely $(p * ((q \twoheadrightarrow r) * s)) \twoheadrightarrow ((p * (q \twoheadrightarrow r)) * s)$. The development of the method on the example is the same as for **BI** with minor changes on the constraints to satisfy and thus we can show that this formula is provable.

We have previously defined a connection-based characterization of provability in **MLL** and studied the relationships between connection methods and proof nets construction in linear logic fragments [5]. We can show, like for **MLL**, that a connection-based method for **MILL** provides an algorithm for the construction of **MILL** proof nets [2]. Conversely, we have defined a connection method for **MLL** that is based on the automatic construction of proof nets (and of sequent proofs in parallel). This method starts with the formula (or decomposition) tree and builds, step by step and automatically, axiom-links (or connections) following particular strategies. We can define such an algorithm for **MILL** by taking into account labels and constraints attached to different positions in the formula tree. In this case, some steps of proof nets construction are only possible if some constraints are satisfied. It can be seen as another new connection method for **MILL**, that is based on proof nets construction.

6   Conclusion

In this paper, we define a connection-based characterization of propositional **BI** (logic of bunched implications) and a related proof-search method. In order to avoid redundancies of a labelled tableau method for propositional **BI** (without ⊥) [6], we design a connection method in which we introduce specific labels and constraints which naturally capture the semantic consequence relation of the logic. The fact to have such a simple connection method w.r.t. a sequent calculus with bunches emphasizes the power and the adequacy of methods based on labels and constraints, compared to more standard methods based on prefixes. As **BI** is conservative w.r.t. **IL** and **MILL** we also define, by restriction and refinements, new connection-based characterizations of provability for both logics. Including labels and constraints into connection-based methods appears as a necessary and general approach for some substructural logics as illustrated by **BI** and **MILL**. Further work will be devoted to the implementation of the method, mainly to the steps concerning constraints generation and solving. Moreover, we will study the problems about the management of the multiplicity in such methods.

References

1. P.A. Armelin and D. Pym. Bunched logic programming (extended abstract). In *First International Joint Conference on Automated Reasoning, IJCAR 2001, LNCS 2083*, pages 289–304, Siena, Italy, 2001.
2. V. Balat and D. Galmiche. *Labelled Deduction*, volume 17 of *Applied Logic Series*, chapter Labelled Proof Systems for Intuitionistic Provability. Kluwer Academic Publishers, 2000.
3. W. Bibel. On matrices with connections. *Journal of ACM*, 28(4):633–645, 1981.
4. K. Broda, M. Finger, and A. Russo. LDS-natural deduction for substructural logics (extended abstract). *Logic Journal of the IGPL*, 4(3):486–489, 1996.
5. D. Galmiche. Connection Methods in Linear Logic and Proof nets Construction. *Theoretical Computer Science*, 232(1-2):231–272, 2000.
6. D. Galmiche and D. Méry. Proof-search and countermodel generation in propositional BI logic - extended abstract -. In *4th Int. Symp. on Theoretical Aspects of Computer Software, TACS 2001, LNCS 2215*, pages 263–282, Sendai, Japan, 2001.
7. S. Ishtiaq and P. O'Hearn. BI as an assertion language for mutable data structures. In *28th ACM Symposium on Principles of Programming Languages, POPL 2001*, pages 14–26, London, UK, 2001.
8. C. Kreitz, H. Mantel, J. Otten, and S. Schmitt. Connection-based proof construction in linear logic. In *14th Int. Conference on Automated Deduction*, pages 207–221, Townsville, North Queensland, Australia, 1997.
9. C. Kreitz and J. Otten. Connection-based theorem proving in classical and non-classical logics. *Journal of Universal Computer Science*, 5(3):88–112, 1999.
10. P. O'Hearn. Resource interpretations, bunched implications and the $\alpha\lambda$-calculus. In *Typed Lambda Calculi and Applications, TLCA'99, LNCS 581*, pages 258–279, L'Aquila, Italy, 1999.
11. P.W. O'Hearn and D. Pym. The Logic of Bunched Implications. *Bulletin of Symbolic Logic*, 5(2):215–244, 1999.

126   D. Galmiche and D. Méry

12. D. Pym. On bunched predicate logic. In *14h Symposium on Logic in Computer Science*, pages 183–192, Trento, Italy, July 1999. IEEE Computer Society Press.
13. M. E. Stickel. A unification algorithm for associative-commutative functions. *Journal of ACM*, 28(3):423–434, 1981.
14. A. Urquhart. Semantics for relevant logic. *Journal of Symbolic Logic*, 37:159–169, 1972.
15. A. Voronkov. Proof-search in intuitionistic logic based on constraint satisfaction. In *Int. Workshop Tableaux'96, LNAI 1071*, pages 312–327, Terrasini, Italy, 1996.
16. L.A. Wallen. *Automated Proof search in Non-Classical Logics*. MIT Press, 1990.

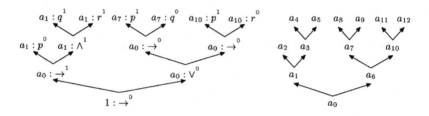

u	$pol(u)$	$f(u)$	$ptyp(u)$	$styp(u)$	$slab(u)$	$kon(u)$
a_0	0	$(p \to (q \wedge r)) \to ((p \to q) \vee (p \to r))$	$\pi\alpha$	–	1	$1 \leq a_0$
a_1	1	$p \to (q \wedge r)$	$\pi\beta$	$\pi\alpha_1$	a_0	$a_0 \leq a_1$
a_2	0	p	–	$\pi\beta_1$	a_1	–
a_3	1	$q \wedge r$	α	$\pi\beta_2$	a_1	–
a_4	1	q	–	α_1	a_1	–
a_5	1	r	–	α_1	a_1	–
a_6	0	$(p \to q) \vee (p \to r)$	α	$\pi\alpha_2$	a_0	–
a_7	0	$p \to q$	$\pi\alpha$	α_1	a_0	$a_0 \leq a_7$
a_8	1	p	–	$\pi\alpha_1$	a_7	–
a_9	0	q	–	$\pi\alpha_2$	a_7	–
a_{10}	0	$p \to r$	$\pi\alpha$	α_2	a_0	$a_0 \leq a_{10}$
a_{11}	1	p	–	$\pi\beta_1$	a_{10}	–
a_{12}	0	r	–	$\pi\beta_2$	a_{10}	–

Fig. 6. Indexed formula tree for $(p \to (q \wedge r)) \to ((p \to q) \vee (p \to r))$

A   Completeness of the BI Characterization

We say that a formula A is *connection-valid* if there is a multiplicity μ, an admissible **BI**-substitution σ and a set of σ-complementary connections that spans A^μ. To prove completeness we show that the connection-validity is closed under each rule of the **LBI** sequent calculus.

Lemma A.1. *if $\Gamma \vdash A$ is **LBI**-provable then it is connection-valid.*

Proof. The proof is by induction on the derivation in **LBI**.

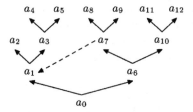

Fig. 7. Reduction ordering for $(p \to (q \wedge r)) \to ((p \to q) \vee (p \to r))$

- base case: an axiom $A \vdash A$, corresponding to $A \twoheadrightarrow A$, is connection-valid.
- induction step: let us consider the $\twoheadrightarrow_R$ case.

By induction hypothesis, we suppose that $\Gamma, A \vdash B$ is connection-valid and we show that $\Gamma \vdash A \twoheadrightarrow B$ is also connection-valid.

Since $\Gamma, A \vdash B$ is connection-valid, there exists a multiplicity μ and an admissible **BI**-substitution σ which makes σ-complementary every atomic path through $((\Phi_\Gamma * A) \twoheadrightarrow B)^\mu$. Therefore, we can construct a complete σ-proper reduction $\mathcal{R}_1$ from $\{\{a_0\}\}$, where $lsf(a_0) = 1 : ((\Phi_\Gamma * A) \twoheadrightarrow B)^0$, which results in σ-complementary atomic paths. From this reduction $\mathcal{R}_1$ we build a complete σ-proper reduction $\mathcal{R}_2$ for $\{\{a_0\}\}$, where $lsf(a_0) = 1 : (\Phi_\Gamma \twoheadrightarrow (A \twoheadrightarrow B))^0$. In the following figure, the first steps of $\mathcal{R}_1$ are shown on the left-hand side, while those of $\mathcal{R}_2$ are shown on the right-hand side. For clarity, we have represented paths as sets of labelled signed formulae rather than sets of positions.

$$\{1 : ((\Phi_\Gamma * A) \twoheadrightarrow B)^0\} \quad \Big| \quad \{1 : (\Phi_\Gamma \twoheadrightarrow (A \twoheadrightarrow B))^0\}$$
$$|\qquad\qquad\qquad\qquad\qquad |$$
$$\{a_0 : (\Phi_\Gamma * A)^1, \tilde{a}_0 : B^0\} \quad \Big| \quad \{a_0 : \Phi_\Gamma{}^1, \tilde{a}_0 : A \twoheadrightarrow B^0\}$$
$$|\qquad\qquad\qquad\qquad\qquad |$$
$$\{a_1 : \Phi_\Gamma{}^1, \tilde{a}_1 : A^1, \tilde{a}_0 : B^0\} \Big| \{a_1 : \Phi_\Gamma{}^1, a_i : A^1, \tilde{a}_i : B^0\}$$
$$\vdots \qquad\qquad\qquad\qquad\qquad \vdots$$

Both reductions result in a path containing the same signed formulae. The only problem is that they have distinct labels. However, if the relationships between the labels of $\mathcal{R}_2$ are the same or stronger than those between labels of $\mathcal{R}_1$, then, any constraint of $\mathcal{R}_2$, corresponding to a constraint of $\mathcal{R}_1$ which is derivable in $\mathcal{R}_1$, is derivable in $\mathcal{R}_2$. Consequently, if $\mathcal{R}_1$ can be properly continued to reach σ-complementary atomic paths, reusing the same continuation process for $\mathcal{R}_2$ results, upto the labels, in the same atomic paths. Moreover, these paths are also σ-complementary by the previous argument on the strength of the relationships. Now, the assertions generated by $\mathcal{R}_1$ after the first three steps are $\{a_0 = \tilde{a}_0, a_1\tilde{a}_1 \leq a_0\}$, while $\mathcal{R}_2$ generates $\{a_0 = \tilde{a}_0, \tilde{a}_0 a_i = \tilde{a}_i\}$. If we rewrite the labels more explicitly, those two sets respectively correspond to $\{slab(\Phi_\Gamma * A) = slab(B), slab(\Phi_\Gamma)slab(A) \leq slab(\Phi_\Gamma * A)\}$ and $\{slab(\Phi_\Gamma) = slab(A \twoheadrightarrow B), slab(A \twoheadrightarrow B)slab(A) =$

$slab(B)$ }. Simplifying synonyms introduced via the $\twoheadrightarrow$ connective, we can see that the relationship assumed in $\mathcal{R}_1$ is in fact $slab(\Phi_\Gamma)slab(A) \leq slab(B)$, while $\mathcal{R}_2$ assumes $slab(\Phi_\Gamma)slab(A) = slab(B)$, which is obviously stronger. The other cases are similar or immediate by the translation of bunches.

Theorem A.1 (Completeness). *If a formula A of* **BI** *is valid then there is a multiplicity μ, an admissible* **BI***-substitution σ and a set of σ-complementary connections that spans A^μ.*

Proof. If A is valid then $\emptyset_m \vdash A$ is provable in **LBI**. Then, by lemma A.1, we deduce that $I \twoheadrightarrow A$ is connection-valid and since $I \twoheadrightarrow A \dashv\vdash A$, there is a multiplicity μ, an admissible **BI**-substitution σ and a set of σ-complementary connections that spans A^μ.

B   An Example of the IL Characterization

Let us illustrate the new matrix characterization of **IL** provability with the following formula of **IL**: $A^\mu = (p \to (q \wedge r)) \to ((p \to q) \vee (p \to r))$.
The indexed formula tree is given in figure 6. Then we have the two sets of constraints $\mathcal{K}_\alpha = \{\, 1 \leq a_0, a_0 \leq a_7, a_0 \leq a_{10} \,\}$ and $\mathcal{K}_\beta = \{\, a_0 \leq a_1 \,\}$.
By application of the path reduction process to $\{\, a_0 \,\}$, we obtain two atomic paths, namely, $s_1 = \{\, a_2, a_8, a_9, a_{11}, a_{12} \,\}$ and $s_2 = \{\, a_4, a_5, a_8, a_9, a_{11}, a_{12} \,\}$. The path s_1 contains two connections $\langle\, a_8, a_2 \,\rangle$ and $\langle\, a_{11}, a_2 \,\rangle$ and s_2 contains $\langle\, a_4, a_9 \,\rangle$ and $\langle\, a_5, a_{12} \,\rangle$. Let us choose $\langle\, a_8, a_2 \,\rangle$ for s_1 and $\langle\, a_4, a_9 \,\rangle$ for s_2. From these connections, we can directly derive the following set of constraints $\mathcal{C}on = \{\, a_7 \leq a_1, a_1 \leq a_7 \,\}$ is directly derived.
Now, we must find an admissible **IL**-substitution. For that, we compute the two sets Σ_α and Σ_β which are respectively equal to $\{\, a_0, a_7, a_{10} \,\}$ and $\{\, a_1 \,\}$. By transitivity on constraints of $\mathcal{C}on$, we deduce that $\sigma(a_1) = a_7$. The next point is to show that $\sigma(\mathcal{K}_\alpha) \approx \sigma(\mathcal{K}_\beta)$. Since $a_0 \leq a_1$ is the only requirement and $\sigma(a_1) = a_7$, we only need to prove that $a_0 \leq a_7$ holds w.r.t. to the assertions, which is immediate because $a_0 \leq a_7$ is an assertion. The substitution $\sigma(a_1) = a_7$ induces the relation $a_7 \sqsubset a_1$, which, combined with the tree ordering of the positions, yields the relation $\lhd$ shown in figure 7. As the reader might check, the resulting graph is acyclic and the formula A^μ is therefore valid in **IL**.
This example illustrates how our connection method based on labels and constraints is an alternative to the standard methods based on prefixes as mentioned in section 4.

DDDLIB: A Library for Solving Quantified Difference Inequalities

Jesper B. Møller

Department of Innovation, IT University of Copenhagen
jm@it.edu

Abstract. DDDLIB is a library for manipulating formulae in a first-order logic over Boolean variables and inequalities of the form $x_1 - x_2 \leq d$, where x_1, x_2 are real variables and d is an integer constant. Formulae are represented in a semi-canonical data structure called difference decision diagrams (DDDs) which provide efficient algorithms for constructing formulae with the standard Boolean operators (conjunction, disjunction, negation, etc.), eliminating quantifiers, and deciding functional properties (satisfiability, validity and equivalence). The library is written in C and has interfaces for C++, Standard ML and Objective Caml.

1 Introduction

DDDLIB is a library for deciding functional properties of quantified difference inequalities which are formulae ϕ of the form

$$\phi ::= \mathbf{0} \mid \mathbf{1} \mid b \mid x_1 - x_2 \sim d \mid \neg\phi \mid \phi_1 \wedge \phi_2 \mid \phi_1 \vee \phi_2 \mid \phi_1 \Rightarrow \phi_2 \mid \exists b.\phi \mid \exists x.\phi \,,$$

where b is a Boolean variable, x is a real variable, d is an integer constant, and $\sim \in \{\leq, <, =, \neq, >, \geq\}$ is a relational operator. $\mathbf{0}$ and $\mathbf{1}$ denote false and true, respectively, and the symbols $\neg$ (negation), $\wedge$ (conjunction), $\vee$ (disjunction), $\Rightarrow$ (implication), and $\exists$ (existential quantification) have their usual meaning. We denote by $\phi[\boldsymbol{v}/\boldsymbol{v'}]$ the substitution of all occurrences of variable v'_i in ϕ by v_i, for $i = 1, \ldots, n$. The problem of determining whether a formula ϕ is a tautology, denoted $\models \phi$, is **PSPACE**-complete [11]. Formulae of this form occur in many areas of mathematics and computer science, some examples are logical formalisms for time, actions, events, and persistence [20,7,12,3], reasoning with temporal constraints [17], and planning and scheduling [2,10]. However, there are very few tools for performing quantifier elimination and validity checking for this logic efficiently. The primary focus has been on tools for either more expressive theories such as integers or reals with addition and order (e.g., Omega Library [21] and Redlog [8]), or less expressive theories such as quantified Boolean formulae (e.g., SATO [25] and BuDDy [16]).

This paper presents a library called DDDLIB for manipulating quantified difference inequalities. Formulae are represented in a graph data structure called DDDs [18], and the library implements a number of classical algorithms, such

A. Voronkov (Ed.): CADE-18, LNAI 2392, pp. 129–133, 2002.

as Bryant's Apply algorithm [6] for combining formulae with Boolean operators, Fourier–Motzkin's algorithm [9] for eliminating quantifiers, and Bellman–Ford's shortest-path algorithm [5] for determining satisfiability. A preliminary version of DDDLIB has been used to implement a verification tool for infinite-state systems [1], and a symbolic model checker for event-recording automata [23]. Larsen et al. [14] have described a data structure similar to DDDs called clock difference diagrams (CDDs); however, they do not define an algorithm for eliminating quantifiers in a CDD, and the algorithm for determining satisfiability of a CDD is different. CDDs have been implemented in the tool UPPAAL [4].

The paper is organized as follows: Section 2 gives an overview of the Standard ML (SML) interface, Section 3 is a short introduction to the implementation, and Section 4 presents a model checker for real-time systems written in SML.

2   Interface

This section gives an overview of the SML interface to DDDLIB. SML is a functional programming language with good support for modeling mathematical problems. The current version of DDDLIB uses Moscow ML [22] which is a lightweight implementation of SML. This implementation supports dynamic linkage with C functions, so each SML function simply delegates calls to the corresponding C function in DDDLIB. Variables in DDDLIB have type var:

```
type var
val RealVar : string -> var
val BoolVar : string -> var
```

Formulae have type ddd and are constructed as follows:

```
type ddd
datatype comp = EQ | NEQ | LEQ | GEQ | LE | GR
val False : ddd
val True : ddd
val BoolExpr : var -> ddd
val RealExpr : var * var * comp * int -> ddd
```

Boolean connectives and operators are defined as:

```
val Not : ddd -> ddd
val And : ddd * ddd -> ddd
val Or : ddd * ddd -> ddd
val Imp : ddd * ddd -> ddd
val Exists : var * ddd -> ddd
val Replace : ddd * var * var -> ddd
```

The following functions determine functional properties of a formula:

```
val Tautology : ddd -> bool
val Equivalent : ddd * ddd -> bool
```

3   Implementation

DDDLIB is based on DDDs [18] which are directed acyclic graphs with two terminal vertices, **0** and **1**, and a set of non-terminal vertices. Each non-terminal

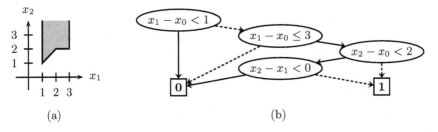

(a)   (b)

Fig. 1. The formula $\phi = (1 \leq x_1 - x_0 \leq 3) \wedge \big((x_2 - x_0 \geq 2) \vee (x_2 - x_1 \geq 0)\big)$ as (a) an (x_1, x_2)-plot for $x_0 = 0$, and (b) a difference decision diagram.

vertex $u = \alpha \rightarrow h, l$ denotes the formula $\phi^u = (\alpha \wedge \phi^h) \vee (\neg \alpha \wedge \phi^l)$. The test expression α is a difference constraint of the form $x_i - x_j < d$ or $x_i - x_j \leq d$. A Boolean variable b_i is represented as $x_i - x_i' \leq 0$, where x_i and x_i' are real variables used only in the encoding of b_i. Figure 1 shows an example of a DDD. As shown in [18], DDDs can be ordered and path reduced, yielding a semi-canonical form, which makes it possible to check for validity and satisfiability in constant time (as for BDDs). The DDD data structure is not canonical, however, so equivalence checking is performed as a validity check.

The operations for constructing DDDs are easily defined recursively on the DDD data structure. The function APPLY($\oplus, u_1, u_2$) combines two ordered DDDs rooted at u_1 and u_2 with a Boolean operator $\oplus$ (e.g., negation, conjunction, disjunction). APPLY is a generalization of the version used for BDDs [6] and has running time $O(|u_1||u_2|)$, where $|\cdot|$ denotes the number of vertices in a DDD.

The function EXISTS(v, u) is used to existentially quantify the variable v in a DDD rooted at u. The algorithm is an adoption of Fourier–Motzkin's quantifier-elimination algorithm [9], removing all vertices reachable from u containing v, while keeping all implicit constraints induced by v among the other variables, for example $\exists x_1.(x_0 - x_1 < 1 \wedge x_1 - x_2 \leq 0) \equiv x_0 - x_2 < 1$. EXISTS computes modified and additional constraints in polynomial time, but has an exponential worst-case running time since the resulting DDD must be ordered.

The function PATHREDUCE(u) removes all redundant vertices in a DDD rooted at u making it semi-canonical, which means that a formula ϕ^u is satisfiable if and only if PATHREDUCE(u) $\neq$ **0**. Similarly, ϕ^u is a tautology if and only if PATHREDUCE(u) = **1**. PATHREDUCE determines path feasibility using an incremental Bellman–Ford algorithm with dynamic programming, but has exponential worst-case running time.

4 Applications

This section shows how to implement a symbolic model checker for δ-programs using the SML interface. A δ-program [19] is a general notation for modeling real-time systems, and consists of a set of commands of the form $\delta v.\phi$, where v is a vector of variables, and ϕ is a formula over v and v'. A command $\delta(v_1, \ldots, v_n).\phi$ nondeterministically assigns to each variable v_i any value v_i', for $i = 1, \ldots, n$, such that ϕ is satisfied. It is straightforward to model timed systems as δ-programs. The key idea is to introduce a variable z interpreted as the common zero point of all clocks. A process in Fischer's protocol [13] can be modeled as follows:

$$\delta(a_i, b_i, x_i).\left(\neg b_i \wedge \neg a_i' \wedge b_i' \wedge x_i' - z = 0 \wedge \bigwedge_{j=1}^{N} \neg id_j\right)$$
$$\delta(a_i, b_i, x_i, id_i).\left(\neg a_i \wedge b_i \wedge a_i' \wedge \neg b_i' \wedge x_i - z \leq 10 \wedge x_i' - z = 0 \wedge id_i'\right)$$
$$\delta(a_i, b_i).\left(a_i \wedge \neg b_i \wedge a_i' \wedge b_i' \wedge x_i - z > 10 \wedge id_i \wedge \bigwedge_{j \neq i} \neg id_j\right)$$
$$\delta(a_i, b_i, id_i).\left(a_i \wedge b_i \wedge \neg a_i' \wedge \neg b_i' \wedge \neg id_i'\right)$$
$$\delta(z).\left(z' \leq z \wedge \left(\forall z''(z' \leq z'' \leq z) \Rightarrow \bigwedge_{i=1}^{N}(\neg a_i \wedge b_i \Rightarrow 0 \leq x_i - z'' \leq k)\right)\right),$$

where the last command is common for all processes and models the progression of time. The initial state is $\phi_0 = \bigwedge_{i=1}^{N}\left(\neg a_i \wedge \neg b_i \wedge \neg id_i \wedge x_i = z\right)$, and the property that only one process is in the critical section can be expressed as $I = \bigwedge_{i=1}^{N} \bigwedge_{j \neq i} \neg\left(a_i \wedge b_i \wedge a_j \wedge b_j\right)$.

We can model a δ-program in SML as an initial set of states phi0 of type ddd, and a list of commands cmds of type var list * var list * ddd (two lists of unprimed and primed variables, and a formula). Using the functions described in Section 2, Fischer's protocol can be modeled with less than 25 lines of SML code. As shown in [19], a formula I is invariant for a δ-program with initial state ϕ_0 if and only if $\not\models \mathbf{pre}^*(\neg I) \wedge \phi_0$, where

$$\mathbf{pre}^*(\neg I) = \mu X\left[\neg I \vee \bigvee_{\delta v.\phi} \exists v'.\left(\phi \wedge X[v'/v]\right)\right], \tag{1}$$

and where $\mu X[f(X)]$ is the least fixpoint of $f(X)$. We can use Eq. (1) directly to implement a symbolic model checker for δ-programs modeled in SML:

```
fun verify (cmds, phi0, I) =
    let val ReplaceL = ListPair.foldl (fn (v',v,d) => Replace(d,v',v))
        fun pre x = List.foldl (fn ((v,v'),d),r) =>
                Or(r, List.foldl Exists (And(d, ReplaceL r (v',v))) v')) x
        fun lfp f =
            let fun f' x =
                let val y = f x in if Equivalent(x,y) then y else f' y end
            in f' False end
        val prestar = lfp (fn x => Or(Not I, pre x cmds))
    in not (Tautology(And(phi0, prestar))) end
```

I have used verify to check that Fischer's protocol guarantees mutual exclusion. Within 1 hour it is possible to verify $N = 15$ processes on a 1 GHz Pentium III PC. This is comparable with other real-time verification tools (e.g., UPPAAL [15] and KRONOS [24]). The size of $\mathbf{pre}^*(\neg I)$ is 370,501 DDD vertices.

5   Conclusion

This paper has presented a library for manipulating quantified difference inequalities implemented using the data structure DDDs. I have demonstrated the applicability of the library in symbolic model checking of real-time systems by giving a 10-line SML function for verifying safety properties of δ-programs using backward reachability analysis. DDDLIB is available at www.it.edu/research/ddd.

References

1. P.A. Abdulla and A. Nylén. Better is better than well: On efficient verification of infinite-state systems. In *Proc. 15th LICS*, pages 132–140, 2000.
2. J.F. Allen, H. Kautz, R.N. Pelavin, and J. Tenenberg, editors. *Reasoning about Plans*. Morgan Kaufmann, San Mateo, California, 1991.
3. R. Alur, C. Courcoubetis, and D. Dill. Model-checking for real-time systems. In *Proc. 5th LICS*, pages 414–425, 1990.
4. G. Behrmann, K.G. Larsen, J. Pearson, C. Weise, and W. Yi. Efficient timed reachability analysis using clock difference diagrams. In *Proc. 11th Conference on Computer Aided Verification*, LNCS 1633, pages 341–353, 1999.
5. R. Bellman. On a routing problem. *Quarterly of Applied Math.*, 16(1):87–90, 1958.
6. R.E. Bryant. Graph-based algorithms for Boolean function manipulation. *IEEE Transactions on Computers*, C-35(8):677–691, 1986.
7. E.M. Clarke and E.A. Emerson. Design and synthesis of synchronization skeletons using branching time temporal logic. In *Proc. Workshop on Logics of Programs*, LNCS 131, pages 52–71. Springer-Verlag, 1981.
8. A. Dolzmann and T. Sturm. Redlog user manual. Technical Report MIP-9905, FMI, Universität Passau, D-94030 Passau, Germany, April 1999.
9. J.B.J. Fourier. Second extrait. In *Oeuvres*, pages 325–328. Gauthiers-Villars, 1890.
10. M.S. Fox. *Constraint-directed Search: A Case Study of Job-Shop Scheduling*. Morgan Kaufmann Publishers, 1987.
11. M. Koubarakis. Complexity results for first-order theories of temporal constraints. In *Principles of Knowledge Representation and Reasoning*, pages 379–390, 1994.
12. R.A. Kowalski and M.J. Sergot. A logic-based calculus of events. In *Proc. Foundations of Knowledge Base Management*, pages 23–55, 1985.
13. L. Lamport. A fast mutual exclusion algorithm. *ACM Trans. on Comp. Systems*, 5(1):1–11, 1987.
14. K.G. Larsen, J. Pearson, C. Weise, and W. Yi. Clock difference diagrams. *Nordic Journal of Computing*, 6(3):271–298, 1999.
15. K.G. Larsen, P. Pettersson, and W. Yi. Uppaal in a nutshell. *International Journal on Software Tools for Technology Transfer*, 1(1–2):134–152, 1997.
16. J. Lind-Nielsen. *BuDDy: Binary Decision Diagram package*. IT University of Copenhagen, Glentevej 67, DK-2400 Copenhagen NV, May 2001.
17. I. Meiri. Combining qualitative and quantitative constraints in temporal reasoning. *Artificial Intelligence*, 87(1–2):343–385, 1996.
18. J. Møller, J. Lichtenberg, H.R. Andersen, and H. Hulgaard. Difference decision diagrams. In *Proc. Computer Science Logic*, LNCS 1683, pages 111–125, 1999.
19. J.B. Møller. Simplifying fixpoint computations in verification of real-time systems. Technical Report TR-2002-15, IT University of Copenhagen, April 2002.
20. A. Pnueli. The temporal logic of programs. In *Proc. 18th IEEE Symposium on the Foundations of Computer Science*, pages 46–57, 1977.
21. W. Pugh. The Omega Test: A fast and practical integer programming algorithm for dependence analysis. *Comm. of the ACM*, 35(8):102–114, August 1992.
22. S. Romanenko, C. Russo, and P. Sestoft. *Moscow ML Owner's Manual*, June 2000.
23. M. Sorea. Tempo: A model-checker for event-recording automata. In *Proc. Workshop on Real-Time Tools*, August 2001. Also as SRI Technical Report CSL-01-04.
24. S. Yovine. Kronos: A verification tool for real-time systems. *International Journal on Software Tools for Technology Transfer*, 1(1–2):123–133, October 1997.
25. H. Zhang. SATO: An efficient propositional prover. In *Proc. Conference on Automated Deduction*, pages 272–275, 1997.

An LCF-Style Interface between HOL and First-Order Logic

Joe Hurd[*]

Computer Laboratory
University of Cambridge,
joe.hurd@cl.cam.ac.uk

1 Introduction

Performing interactive proof in the HOL theorem prover[1] [3] involves reducing goals to simpler subgoals. It turns out that many of these subgoals can be efficiently 'finished off' by an automatic first-order prover. To fill this niche, Harrison implemented a version of the MESON procedure [4] with the ability to translate proofs to higher-order logic. This was integrated as a HOL tactic in 1996, and has since become a standard workhorse of interactive proof. Today, building all the theories in the most recent distribution of HOL relies on MESON to prove 1726 subgoals.

Given this level of demand for automatic first-order proof by users performing interactive proof in HOL, it seems worthwhile to look for ways to narrow the gap between these two worlds. Consider the following high-level view of how a HOL goal g is proved using a first-order prover:

1. We first convert the negation of g to CNF; this results in a HOL theorem of the form

$$\vdash \neg g \iff \exists \boldsymbol{a}. \ (\forall \boldsymbol{v_1}. \ c_1) \wedge \cdots \wedge (\forall \boldsymbol{v_n}. \ c_n) \tag{1}$$

where each c_i is a HOL term having the form of a disjunction of literals, and may contain variables from the vectors $\boldsymbol{a}$ and $\boldsymbol{v_i}$.
2. Next, we create skolem constants for each variable in $\boldsymbol{a}$, and map each HOL term c_i to first-order logic. This produces the clause set

$$C = \{C_1, \ldots, C_n\}$$

3. The first-order prover runs on C, and finds a refutation ρ.
4. By proof translation, the refutation ρ is lifted to a HOL proof of the theorem

$$\{(\forall \boldsymbol{v_1}. \ c_1), \ldots, (\forall \boldsymbol{v_n}. \ c_n)\} \vdash \bot \tag{2}$$

5. Finally, some HOL primitive inferences use theorems (1) and (2) to derive

$$\vdash g \tag{3}$$

---

[*] Supported by EPSRC project GR/R27105/01
[1] HOL is available at http://www.cl.cam.ac.uk/Research/HVG/FTP/.

A. Voronkov (Ed.): CADE-18, LNAI 2392, pp. 134–138, 2002.
© Springer-Verlag Berlin Heidelberg 2002

Various logical incompatibilities manifest themselves in steps 2 and 4, when formulas and proofs must be mirrored in both logics. In this paper we present a generic interface between HOL and first-order logic, offering:

- an expressive representation of HOL terms in unsorted first-order logic, permitting many 'higher-order' goals to be proved by standard first-order deduction calculi;
- an automatic conversion from first-order refutations to HOL proofs, reducing the effort needed to integrate existing first-order provers with the HOL theorem prover;
- with a strong guarantee that soundness will not be violated.

2   Mapping HOL Terms to First-Order Logic

Seemingly the hardest problem with mapping HOL terms to first-order logic—dealing with λ-abstractions—can be smoothly dealt with as part of the conversion to CNF. Any λ-abstraction at or beneath the literal level is rewritten to combinatory form, using the set of combinators $\{S, K, I, C, \circ\}$.[2]

The mapping that we use makes explicit function application, so that the HOL term $m + n$ maps to the first-order term $@(@(+, m), n)$. Since in HOL there is no distinction between terms and formulas, we model this in first-order logic by defining a special relation called B (short for Boolean) that converts a first-order term to a first-order formula. For example, the HOL boolean term $m \leq n$ can be translated to the first-order formula $B(@(@(\leq, m), n))$. The only exception to this rule is equality: the HOL term $x = y$ can be mapped to the first-order logic formula $=(x, y)$.

The mapping described thus far includes no type information, but is still a useful way to map HOL terms to first-order logic. We also experimented with including types in the first-order representation of a HOL term. Using this idea, the HOL term $m + n$ would map to the first-order term

$$@(@(+ : \mathbb{N} \to \mathbb{N} \to \mathbb{N}, m : \mathbb{N}) : \mathbb{N} \to \mathbb{N}, n) : \mathbb{N}$$

where ':' is a binary function symbol (written infix for readability), and higher-order logic types are encoded as first-order terms.[3] As might be expected, this mapping produces much larger first-order clauses than omitting the types, and this results in first-order deduction steps taking longer to perform. However, we cannot conclude that including types is definitely harmful: the extra information may pay for itself by cutting down the search space.

---

[2] In principle we could use more combinators to guarantee a more compact translation, but HOL goals are normally small enough that this extra complication is not worth the effort.

[3] Encoding type variables as first-order logic variables allows polymorphic types to be dealt with in a straightforward manner.

Using this mapping, we can use a first-order prover to prove several 'higher-order' goals, such as the classic derivation of an identity function from combinator theory:

$$\vdash (\forall x, y.\ \mathsf{K}\ x\ y = x) \wedge (\forall f, g, x.\ \mathsf{S}\ f\ g\ x = (f\ x)\ (g\ x)) \Rightarrow \exists f.\ \forall x.\ f\ x = x$$

3 Translating First-Order Refutations to HOL

At first sight it may appear that the necessity of translating first-order refutations to higher-order logic proofs imposes a burden that hampers free experimentation with the first-order provers. However, by applying the technology of the LCF project [2], we can isolate the proof translation and make it invisible to the developer of first-order proof procedures. We have implemented this automatic proof translation for the mapping that preserves type information, and it has been successfully used in combination with ML versions of first-order calculi to prove many subgoals in the HOL theorem prover.

$$\frac{}{A_1 \vee \cdots \vee A_n}\text{AXIOM}\ [A_1, \ldots, A_n] \qquad\qquad \frac{}{L \vee \neg L}\text{ASSUME}\ L$$

$$\frac{A_1 \vee \cdots \vee A_n}{A_1[\sigma] \vee \cdots \vee A_n[\sigma]}\text{INST}\ \sigma \qquad\qquad \frac{A_1 \vee \cdots \vee A_n}{A_{i_1} \vee \cdots \vee A_{i_m}}\text{FACTOR}$$

$$\frac{A_1 \vee \cdots \vee L \vee \cdots \vee A_m \qquad B_1 \vee \cdots \vee \neg L \vee \cdots \vee B_n}{A_1 \vee \cdots \vee A_m \vee B_1 \vee \cdots \vee B_n}\text{RESOLVE}\ L$$

Fig. 1. The Primitive Rules of Inference of Clausal First-Order Logic.

This is achieved by defining a logical kernel of ML functions that execute a primitive set of deduction rules on first-order clauses. For our purposes, we use the five rules in Figure 1, which form a (refutation) complete proof system for clausal first-order logic.

The AXIOM rule is used to create a new axiom of the logical system; it takes as argument the list of literals in the axiom clause. The ASSUME rule takes a literal L and returns the theorem $L \vee \neg L$.[4] The INST rule takes a substitution σ and a theorem A, and applies the substitution to every literal in A.[5] The FACTOR rule takes a theorem and removes duplicate literals in the clause: note that no variable instantiation takes place here, two literals must be identical for one to be removed. Finally, the RESOLVE rule takes a literal L and two theorems A, B, and creates a theorem containing every literal except L from A and every literal except $\neg L$ from B. Again, no variable instantiation takes place here: only literals identical to L in A (or $\neg L$ in B) are removed.

---

[4] This rule is used to keep track of reductions in the model elimination procedure.

[5] In some presentations of logic, this uniform instantiation of variables in a theorem is called specialization.

```
signature Kernel =
sig
  type formula = Term.formula
  type subst   = Term.subst

  (* An ABSTRACT type for theorems *)
  eqtype thm

  (* Destruction of theorems is fine *)
  val dest_thm : thm -> formula list

  (* But creation is only allowed by these primitive rules *)
  val AXIOM   : formula list -> thm
  val ASSUME  : formula -> thm
  val INST    : subst -> thm -> thm
  val FACTOR  : thm -> thm
  val RESOLVE : formula -> thm -> thm -> thm
end
```

Fig. 2. The ML Signature of a Logical Kernel Implementing Clausal First-Order Logic.

The ML type system can be used to ensure that these primitive rules of inference represent the only way to create elements of an abstract thm type.[6] In Figure 2 we show the signature of an ML Kernel module that implements the logical kernel. We insist that the programmer of a first-order provers derive refutations by creating an empty clause of type thm. The only way to do this is to use the primitive rules of inference in the Kernel module: this is both easy and efficient for all the standard first-order proof procedures.

At this point it is simple to translate first-order refutations to HOL proofs. We add proof logs into the representation of theorems in the Kernel, so that each theorem remembers the primitive rule and theorems that were used to create it. When we complete a refutation, we therefore have a chain of proof steps starting at the empty clause and leading back to axioms. In addition, for each primitive rule of inference in Kernel, we create a higher-order logic version that works on HOL terms, substitutions and theorems.[7] The final ingredient needed to translate a proof is a HOL theorem corresponding to each of the first-order axioms. These theorems are the HOL clauses in the CNF representation of the original (negated) goal, which we mapped to first-order logic and axiomatized.

To summarize: by requiring the programmer of a first-order proof procedure to derive refutations using a logical kernel, lifting these refutations to HOL proofs can be done completely automatically.

---

[6] Indeed, the ability to define an abstract theorem type was the original reason that the ML type system was created.

[7] If we omit the types from our mapping of HOL terms to first-order logic, it is possible that the first-order refutation cannot be translated to a valid HOL proof. In this case we can either abort, or restart the whole procedure with types included.

4   Conclusions and Related Work

We tested the LCF-style kernel for clausal first-order logic by implementing ML versions of various first-order calculi, and found it to be more than just a convenient interface to a proof translator. Reducing the steps of proof procedures to primitive inferences clarified their behaviour, and also helped catch bugs early. Also, assuming the (52 line) ML Kernel module is correctly implemented and the programmer is careful about asserting axioms, loss of soundness arising from 'prover optimizations' can be completely avoided.

In addition to MESON in HOL, there have been many other examples of automatic first-order provers being used to prove problems in an interactive theorem prover, including: FAUST in HOL [5]; Paulson's blast in Isabelle [6]; and Bliksem in Coq [1].

In these link-ups, various mappings are used from theorem prover subgoals into problems of first-order logic, defining the class of subgoals that may be feasibly proved using the underlying first-order prover. The architecture presented in this paper for translating first-order refutations allows different first-order provers to be 'plugged-in' to the theorem prover, with small marginal effort. Moreover, if first-order provers emitted proofs in a standardized 'LCF-style' logical kernel for clausal first-order logic, then this would further simplify their integration into interactive theorem provers.

References

1. Marc Bezem, Dimitri Hendriks, and Hans de Nivelle. Automated proof construction in type theory using resolution. In David A. McAllester, editor, *Proceedings of the 17th International Conference on Automated Deduction (CADE-17)*, volume 1831 of *Lecture Notes in Computer Science*, pages 148–163, Pittsburgh, PA, USA, June 2000. Springer.
2. M. Gordon, R. Milner, and C. Wadsworth. *Edinburgh LCF*, volume 78 of *Lecture Notes in Computer Science*. Springer Verlag, 1979.
3. M. J. C. Gordon and T. F. Melham. *Introduction to HOL (A theorem-proving environment for higher order logic)*. Cambridge University Press, 1993.
4. John Harrison. Optimizing proof search in model elimination. In Michael A. McRobbie and John K. Slaney, editors, *13th International Conference on Automated Deduction (CADE-13)*, volume 1104 of *Lecture Notes in Artificial Intelligence*, pages 313–327, New Brunswick, NJ, USA, July 1996. Springer.
5. R. Kumar, T. Kropf, and K. Schneider. Integrating a first-order automatic prover in the HOL environment. In Myla Archer, Jeffrey J. Joyce, Karl N. Levitt, and Phillip J. Windley, editors, *Proceedings of the 1991 International Workshop on the HOL Theorem Proving System and its Applications (HOL '91), August 1991*, pages 170–176, Davis, CA, USA, 1992. IEEE Computer Society Press.
6. L. C. Paulson. A generic tableau prover and its integration with Isabelle. *Journal of Universal Computer Science*, 5(3), March 1999.

System Description: The MathWeb Software Bus for Distributed Mathematical Reasoning

Jürgen Zimmer[1] and Michael Kohlhase[2]

[1] FB Informatik, Universität des Saarlandes
jzimmer@mathweb.org
[2] School of Computer Science, Carnegie Mellon University,
kohlhase+@cs.cmu.edu

1 Introduction

Automated reasoning systems have reached a high degree of maturity in the last decade. Many reasoning tasks can be delegated to an automated theorem prover (ATP) by encoding them into its interface logic, simply calling the system and waiting for a proof, which will arrive in less than a second in most cases. Despite this seemingly ideal situation, ATPs are seldom actually used by people other than their own developers. The reasons for this seem to be that it is difficult for practitioners of other fields to find information about theorem prover software, to decide which system is best suited for the problem at hand, installing it, and coping with the often idiosyncratic concrete input syntax. Of course, not only potential outside users face these problems, so that, more often than not, existing reasoning procedures are re-implemented instead of re-used.

In a larger context, the same problems surface in many application domains, and have led to the emerging field of "web-services", where (parts of) applications are provided as so-called services on the Internet. The main problem is in providing a standardized infrastructure for identifying, discovering and calling these web services. Even though the field has got a lot of (industrial) attention because of potential applications in e-commerce, development and deployment are still in their early stages.

In [FK99], we have already reported on the MathWeb-SB service infrastructure specialized on deduction and symbolic computation services. The system MathWeb-SB[1] connects a wide-range of reasoning systems (*mathematical services*), such as ATPs, (semi-)automated proof assistants, Computer Algebra Systems (CASs), model generators (MGs), constraint solvers (CSs), human interaction units, and automated concept formation systems, by a common *mathematical software bus*. Reasoning systems integrated in the MathWeb-SB can therefore offer new services to the pool of services, and can in turn use all services offered by other systems.

---

[1] We used to call the MathWeb-SB simply MathWeb in earlier publications. The latter is now used for a whole set of projects cooperating to provide an infrastructure for web-based and semi-automated mathematics (see http://www.mathweb.org).

A. Voronkov (Ed.): CADE-18, LNAI 2392, pp. 139–143, 2002.

This system description summarizes the development in the last three years. We further extended the list of reasoning systems integrated in the MathWeb-SB, stabilized existing integrations and explored new application domains for the MathWeb-SB (see section 2). The main improvements are a more flexible architecture (section 3), and increased standards support in the communication protocols used in MathWeb-SB (section 4). As a consequence, it is much simpler now to use and integrate mathematical services into the MathWeb-SB infrastructure.

2   New Features and Reasoning Systems

The MathWeb-SB now offers an efficient version of the tptp2X utility [SSY94] that allows to transform first order problems in TPTP format (CNF of FOF) into the input format of most existing ATPs. With our tptp2X service (based on a servlet) we could reduce the transformation time from 3-4 seconds (of the tptp2X shell command) down to 100-200 ms (of the servlet) for a transformation of a medium size TPTP problem. This speedup is crucial since typical client applications produce thousands of first order conjectures and send them to the MathWeb-SB. All first order ATPs in the MathWeb-SB, such as *Bliksem*, E, OTTER, SPASS, and Vampire, now accept problems in TPTP format which they translate into their native format using the tptp2X service.

The HR program [Col00] performs automated theory formation in different domains. During concept formation, HR produces up to 3700 first order conjectures per minute. We integrated HR as a server and as a client into the Math-Web-SB. HR can now send its conjectures in TPTP format to single provers or to the concurrent ATP service. The latter allows to run several provers in parallel on one or several problems. An application using concurrent ATP, like HR, can specify whether it is interested in the first result returned by a prover or in all results to compare the success or the runtime of the ATPs.

Together with A. Adams, we integrated the specification and verification system PVS [ORS92] in the MathWeb-SB and defined a special provePVS service that uses the automated proof procedure of PVS. The provePVS service accepts conjectures in OPENMATH and PVS syntax. Using the provePVS service with the *transcendental library* of PVS [Got00], we proved conjectures about the continuity of real-valued functions in the ΩMEGA proof planner.

3   Architectural Improvements

Since [FK99], we have further modularized and stabilized the MathWeb-SB and have built a stable network of reasoning systems that is in everyday use at different Universities in Europe and the US (cf. Fig. 1, which we will use as a concrete example for our discussion).

While the first version of the MathWeb-SB was based on one central broker (a facilitator service that allows clients to discover services), it is now based on a dynamic net of brokers. Brokers maintain a database of local services offered by *meta-services* and can be given a set of URLs that refer to *remote brokers*, i.e. to other brokers available in the Internet. During startup, a broker tries to connect to his remote brokers and to inform them about his address in the Internet and about its local services. This registration mechanism significantly improved the stability and availability of the MathWeb-SB: even if one or more brokers become unavailable at the same time (e.g. due to machine- or network failure), there are still some others left that may offer the lost services.

Service requests by client applications, e.g. by the ΩMEGA proof assistant [SB02], are forwarded to all known remote brokers if the requested service is not available locally. This allows, e.g., an ΩMEGA client running at the University of Birmingham to use Computer Algebra Systems offered to a broker at the University of Saarbrücken.

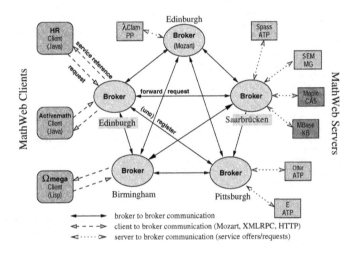

Fig. 1. The MathWeb Software Bus

4   Interfaces

At a conceptual level, MathWeb-SB now offers a uniform interface to all first order ATPs, abstracting away from system peculiarities. The main idea is that a generic **prove** service exports the state of the prover after processing a problem description given in a standard format (e.g., TPTP, DFG, or Otter). A call to the system is modeled as a request to the service to achieve a certain state (e.g. one, where a proof has been found). We have extended the specification of ATP states proposed in [AKR00] by states which describe errors, timeouts and situations where the search is exhausted for some reason. We extended all first order ATP services in the MathWeb-SB such that the **prove** service always returns one of the valid ATP states.

On a the protocol level, MathWeb-SB has been extended to include a native http interface and – building on that – an XML-RPC [XRP] interface. As a consequence MathWeb-SB services can, for instance, be accessed via HTML forms. We have chosen XML-RPC (an XML encoding of Remote Procedure Calls) to be the standard protocol for external access to MathWeb-SB since it is an independent standard that is easy to understand and has been implemented in many different programming languages (there are currently 56 independent implementations available). XML-RPC allows client applications outside the MathWeb-SB to request service objects and to use their service methods[2]. For instance, a client can simply request a service object for the ATP SPASS by sending the XML content in Fig. 2 via an http POST request to a MathWeb-SB XML-RPC server. An XML-RPC implementation in the client's implementation language

```
<methodCall><methodName>Broker.getService</methodName>
 <params><param><value><string>SPASS</string></value></param></params>
</methodCall>

<methodCall><methodName>prove</methodName>
 <params><param><struct>
  <member><name>i</name><value><string>
   include('Axioms/EQU001+0.ax').
   include('Axioms/GRP004+0.ax').
   input_formula(conjecture118,conjecture,(! [B,C,D] :
    ((equal(inverse(B),C) &amp; equal(multiply(C,B),D) ) &lt;=>
     (equal(multiply(B,C),D) &amp; equal(multiply(C,B),D) &amp; equal(inverse(C),B))))).
   </string></value></member>
  <member><name>syntax</name><value><string>tptp</string>
  <member><name>timeout</name><value><int>40</int></value></member>
 </struct></param></params>
</methodCall>
```

Fig. 2. Discovering SPASS and sending it a problem with XML-RPCs.

simplifies this process drastically since it abstracts from http protocol details and offers XML-RPCs using data structures of the host language. As a consequence, developing MathWeb clients is quite simple in such languages. Last but not least, both MS Internet Explorer and the open source WWW browser Mozilla now allows to perform XML-RPC calls within JavaScript. This opens new opportunities for building user interfaces based on web browsers.

5   Conclusion, Availability, and Future Work

We have presented new developments in the MathWeb-SB system, a framework for web-services specialized to deduction and symbolic computation services. The main new developments in the last three years have been a more flexible architecture and the support of standardized communication protocols.

---

[2] More information about service access via XML-RPC can be found at http://www.mathweb.org/mathweb/xmlrpc/howto.html.

The MathWeb-SB has been implemented in the concurrent constraint programming language MOZART [Moz] which is now available as Version 1.2.3 for many platforms (Unix, Linux, MacOS X, and Windows). An easy to install binary distribution of the compiled MathWeb-SB code and further information is available at http://www.mathweb.org/mathweb/. The system sources can be obtained via anonymous CVS under the GNU General Public License.

The MathWeb-SB is currently used in many automated reasoning groups around Europe and the US. Among other applications, it supports the use of external reasoning systems, such as CASs, ATPs, and MGs, in the ΩMEGA proof planner, as well as the use of MAPLE exercises in the web-based learning system *ActiveMath* [Mel00]. It offers an efficient access to state-of-the-art first order ATPs including an efficient transformation between different problem formats. This is crucial for applications that produce many first order conjectures, like, for instance, the HR system.

The next development steps in MathWeb-SB will be further support of standards (e.g. the emerging SOAP standard), and further agentification based on "service descriptions". These are machine-understandable specifications of the reasoning and computation capabilities of the web-services that can lead to service discovery and system-independent service requests. Our uniform interface to the first-order theorem provers in MathWeb-SB is a first step into this direction, but a lot of conceptual work remains to be done for more complex services, such as constraint solvers, decision procedures, or symbolic computation systems.

References

[AKR00]   A. Armando, M. Kohlhase, and S. Ranise. Communication protocols for mathematical services based on KQML and OMRS. In *Proc. of the Calculemus Symposium 2000)*, St. Andrews (Scotland), August 6–7, 2000.

[Col00]   S. Colton. *Automated Theory Formation in Pure Mathematics.* PhD thesis, University of Edinburgh, Edinburgh, Scotland, 2000.

[XRP]   XML Remote Procedure Call Specification. http://www.xmlrpc.com/.

[Moz]   The mozart programming system. http://www.mozart-oz.org.

[FK99]   A. Franke and M. Kohlhase. System description: MATHWEB, an agent-based communication layer for distributed automated theorem proving. In H. Ganzinger, ed., *Proc. CADE-16, LNAI* 1632, pp. 217–221. Springer 1999.

[Got00]   H. Gottliebsen. Transcendental Functions and Continuity Checking in PVS. In Proc. of TPHOLs'00, *LNCS* 1869, pp. 197–214, Springer 2000.

[Mel00]   E. Melis. The 'Interactive Textbook' project. In D. McAllester, ed., *Proc. of CADE WS "Deduction and Education;"*, *LNAI* 1831. Springer Verlag, 2000.

[ORS92]   S. Owre, J. M. Rushby, and N. Shankar. PVS: A Prototype Verification System. In D. Kapur, ed.*Proc. of CADE-11, LNCS* 607, pp. 748–752. Springer 1992.

[SB02]   J. Siekmann, C. Benzmüller et al. Proof development with ΩMEGA. In A. Voronkov, ed., *Proc. of CADE-18, LNAI* Springer 2002.

[SSY94]   G. Sutcliffe, C. Suttner, and T. Yemenis. The TPTP problem library. In A. Bundy, ed., *Proc. of CADE-12, LNAI* 814, pp. 252–266. Springer 1994.

Proof Development with ΩMEGA

Jörg Siekmann, Christoph Benzmüller, Vladimir Brezhnev,
Lassaad Cheikhrouhou, Armin Fiedler, Andreas Franke, Helmut Horacek,
Michael Kohlhase*, Andreas Meier, Erica Melis, Markus Moschner,
Immanuel Normann, Martin Pollet, Volker Sorge**, Carsten Ullrich,
Claus-Peter Wirth, and Jürgen Zimmer

omega@ags.uni-sb.de
FR 6.2 Informatik, Universität des Saarlandes, 66041 Saarbrücken, Germany

The ΩMEGA proof development system [2] is the core of several related and well integrated research projects of the ΩMEGA research group.

ΩMEGA is a mathematical assistant tool that supports proof development in mathematical domains at a user-friendly level of abstraction. It is a modular system with a central data structure and several complementary subsystems. ΩMEGA has many characteristics in common with systems like NuPRL [1], CoQ [23], HOL [13], and PVS [9]. However, it differs from these systems with respect to its focus on *proof planning* and in that respect it is similar to the systems at Edinburgh [6,20]. We present an overview of the architecture of the ΩMEGA system and sketch some of its novel features. Special features of ΩMEGA include (1) facilities to access a considerable number of different reasoning systems and to integrate their results into a single proof structure, (2) support for interactive proof development through some non-standard inspection facilities and guidance in the search for a proof, and (3) methods to develop proofs at a knowledge-based level.

1 System Overview

The ΩMEGA system (cf. Fig. 1) is a representative of the new paradigm of *proof planning* and combines interactive and automated proof construction in *mathematical domains*. ΩMEGA's inference mechanism is an interactive theorem prover based on a higher-order natural deduction (ND) variant of a sorted version of Church's simply typed λ-calculus [8]. The user can interactively construct proofs directly at the calculus level or at the more abstract level of *tactics* and *methods*. Proof construction can be supported by already proven assertions and lemmata and by calls to external systems to simplify or solve subproblems (see Sec. 2).

At the core of ΩMEGA is the *proof plan data structure* $\mathcal{PDS}$ [7] in which proofs and *proof plans* are represented at various levels of granularity and abstraction. The proof plans are classified with respect to a taxonomy of mathematical theories, which are currently being replaced by the mathematical data base

---

* now at Carnegie Mellon University, Pittsburgh, PA, USA
** now at University of Birmingham, Birmingham, UK

A. Voronkov (Ed.): CADE-18, LNAI 2392, pp. 144–149, 2002.

USER
INTERFACE

OMEGA CORE SYSTEM

EXTERNAL
REASONERS

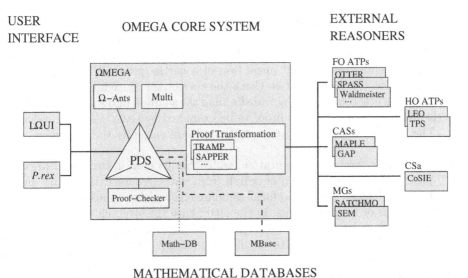

MATHEMATICAL DATABASES

Fig. 1. The architecture of the ΩMEGA proof assistant. Thin lines denote internal interfaces, thick lines denote communication via MATHWEB-SB. The thick dashed line indicates that MBASE is soon to be integrated via MATHWEB-SB. It will replace the current mathematical database (thin dotted line).

MBASE [12]. The user of ΩMEGA, or the proof planner MULTI [17], or the suggestion mechanism Ω-ANTS [3] modify the $\mathcal{PDS}$ during proof development. They can invoke external reasoning systems whose results are included in the $\mathcal{PDS}$ after appropriate transformation. After expansion of these high level proofs to the underlying ND calculus, the $\mathcal{PDS}$ can be checked by ΩMEGA's proof checker. User interaction is supported by the graphical user interface $\mathcal{LΩUI}$ [21] and the proof explainer $P.rex$ [10].

Fig. 1 illustrates the architecture of ΩMEGA: the previously monolithic system was split up and separated into several independent modules. These modules are connected via the mathematical software bus MATHWEB-SB [11]. An important benefit is that MATHWEB modules can be distributed over the Internet and are then accessible by other distant research groups as well.

2   External Systems

Proof problems require many different skills for their solution and it is therefore desirable to have access to several systems with complementary capabilities, to orchestrate their use, and to integrate their results. ΩMEGA interfaces heterogeneous external systems such as computer algebra systems (CASs), higher- and first-order automated theorem proving systems (ATPs), constraint solvers (CSs), and model generators (MGs). Their use is twofold: they may provide a solution to a subproblem, or they may give hints for the control of the proof search.

The output of an incorporated reasoning system is translated and inserted as a sub-proof into the $\mathcal{PDS}$, which maintains the proof plan. This is beneficial for interfacing systems that operate at different levels of abstraction, as well as for a human oriented display and inspection of a partial proof. When integrating partial results, it is important to check the correctness of each contribution. In ΩMEGA, this is accomplished by transforming the solution into a subproof, which is then refined to a logic-level proof to be examined by ΩMEGA's proof checker.

The integrated external systems in ΩMEGA are currently the following:

CASs provide symbolic computation, which can be used in two ways: to compute hints to guide the proof search (e.g., witnesses for existentially quantified variables); and to perform complex algebraic computation such as to normalize or simplify terms. In the latter case the symbolic computation is directly translated into proof steps in ΩMEGA. CASs are integrated via the transformation module SAPPER [22]. Currently, ΩMEGA uses the systems MAPLE and GAP.

ATPs are employed to solve subgoals. Currently, ΩMEGA uses the first-order ATPs BLIKSEM, EQP, OTTER, PROTEIN, SPASS, WALDMEISTER, and the higher-order systems TPS and $\mathcal{LEO}$. The first-order ATPs are connected via TRAMP [15], a proof transformation system that transforms resolution-style proofs into assertion level ND proofs to be integrated into ΩMEGA's $\mathcal{PDS}$. TPS already provides ND proofs, which can be further processed and checked with little transformational effort.

MGs guide the proof search. A model generator provides witnesses for existentially quantified variables or counter-models that show that some subgoal is not a theorem. Currently, ΩMEGA uses the MGs SATCHMO and SEM.

CSs construct mathematical objects with theory-specific properties, such as witnesses for existentially quantified variables. Moreover, a constraint solver can help to reduce the proof search by checking for inconsistencies of constraints. Currently, ΩMEGA employs $\mathcal{CoSIE}$ [19], a constraint solver for inequalities and equations over the field of real numbers.

3   Support for Proof Development

ΩMEGA supports the user while inspecting the state of a proof, and provides some guidance in the search.

ΩMEGA's graphical user interface $\mathcal{L\Omega UI}$ displays information on the current proof state in multiple (cross-linked) modalities: a graphical map of the proof tree, a linearized presentation of the proof nodes with their formulae and justifications, and a term browser. When inspecting portions of a proof by these facilities, the user can switch between alternative levels of abstraction, for example, by expanding a node in the graphical map of the proof tree, which causes appropriate changes in the other presentation modes. Moreover, a natural language explanation of the proof is provided by the system $P.\,rex$ [10], which is interactive and adaptive. The system explains a proof step at the most abstract level (which that user is assumed to know) and it reacts flexibly to questions and requests. While the explanation is in progress, the user can interrupt *P. rex* anytime, if the current explanation is not satisfactory. *P. rex* analyzes the user's interaction and enters into a clarification dialog when needed to identify the reason why the explanation was not satisfactory and re-plans a better explanation, for example, by switching to another level of abstraction.

Another feature of ΩMEGA is the guidance mechanism provided by the suggestion module Ω-ANTS [3]. This module finds a set of possible actions that may be helpful in finding a proof and orders them in a preference list. These actions are an application of particular calculus rules, tactics, or proof methods as well as external reasoners or facts from the knowledge base. Ω-ANTS is based on a hierarchical blackboard upon which data about the current proof state is collected. It is computed by concurrent computational threads, which communicate with the blackboard. This data is then processed by a multi-agent system, which compiles a list of possible actions. This provides not only a very flexible and robust mechanism but also the user does not have to wait until all possible next proof steps have been computed, but intermediate results are shown as they come up. The computation is anytime in the sense that the more time is spent on the computation the better and more complete is the result. A proof step can be executed interactively at any time either from the list of suggested actions or freely chosen by the user. Ω-ANTS can also be used in an automated mode. In this case the actions are ranked heuristically and the best rated action is automatically executed with a possibility to backtrack. These actions may perform proof steps at the natural deduction and tactic level as well as the automatic application of the various integrated external systems.

4   Proof Planning

ΩMEGA's main focus is on knowledge-based proof planning [5,18], where proofs are not conceived in terms of low level calculus rules but at a higher level of abstraction that highlights the main ideas and deemphasizes minor logical or mathematical manipulations on formulae. This viewpoint is realized in the system by proof tactics and abstract proof methods. In contrast to, for instance, the LCF philosophy, our tactics and methods are not necessarily always correct as they have heuristic elements incorporated that account for their strength, so that an informed use of these methods is unlikely to run into failures too often. Since an abstract proof plan may be incorrect for a specific case, its correctness has to be tested by refining it into a logical ND-proof in ΩMEGA's core calculus. This can then be verified by ΩMEGA's proof checker.

Tactics are annotated with partial specifications and then used as *methods* for the proof planner MULTI. Explicitly represented control knowledge helps to find high level proof plans. Traditional proof planning is enhanced in MULTI by using mathematical knowledge to prune the search. Methods are combined to form strategies, which then perform different proof techniques.

5   Case Studies

The novelties of the ΩMEGA system have been tested in several case studies. They particularly illustrate the useful interplay of the various components, such as proof planning supported by heterogeneous external reasoning systems.

A typical example for a class of problems that can not be solved by traditional automated theorem provers is the class of ϵ–δ–proofs [18]. This class was originally proposed by W. Beldsoe [4] and it comprises theorems such as LIM+ and LIM* where LIM+ states that the limit of the sum of two functions equals the sum of their limits and LIM* makes a similar statement for multiplication. The difficulty of this domain arises from the need for arithmetic computation and suitable instantiation of meta-variables (such as a δ depending on an ϵ). Crucial for the success of ΩMEGA's proof planning is the integration of suitable experts for these tasks: the arithmetic computations are done with the computer algebra system MAPLE, and an appropriate instantiation for δ is computed by the constraint solver $\mathcal{C}o\mathcal{SIE}$.

Another class of problems we tackled with proof planning is concerned with residue class problems [16]. In this domain we show theorems as e.g. the fact that the residue class structure $(\mathbb{Z}_5, \bar{+})$ is associative, has a unit element etc., where $\mathbb{Z}_5$ is the set of all congruence classes modulo 5 $\{\bar{0}_5, \bar{1}_5, \bar{2}_5, \bar{3}_5, \bar{4}_5\}$ and $\bar{+}$ is the addition on residue classes. Moreover, we prove for two given structures whether they are isomorphic or not. Although the problems in this domain are in the range of traditional automated theorem provers it is nevertheless an interesting domain for proof planning since multi strategy proof planning generates substantially different proofs based on different proof ideas. For instance, one strategy we realized in MULTI converts statements on residue classes into statements on numbers and then applies an exhaustive case analysis. Another strategy tries to reduce the original goal into sets of equations to which MAPLE is applied to check whether the equality actually holds. Moreover, the computer algebra systems MAPLE and GAP are employed to compute witnesses for particular elements, for instance, to compute $\bar{0}_5$, the unit element of $(\mathbb{Z}_5, \bar{+})$.

Another more recent case study is the proof of the *Irrationality of* $\sqrt{2}$. Here the user proposes interactively the main conceptual steps. Simple but painful logical subderivations are then passed to the ATPs and simple computations can be done by the CASs.

The ΩMEGA system is available at http://www.ags.uni-sb.de/~omega.

References

1. S. Allen, R. Constable, R. Eaton, C. Kreitz, and L. Lorigo. The Nuprl open logical environment. In *Proc. of CADE-17*, LNAI 1831. Springer, 2000.
2. C. Benzmüller et al. ΩMEGA: Towards a mathematical assistant. In *Proc. of CADE-14*, LNAI 1249. Springer, 1997.

3. C. Benzmüller and V. Sorge. Ω-ANTS – An open Approach at Combining Interactive and Automated Theorem Proving. In *Proc. of Calculemus-2000*. AK Peters, 2001.

4. W.W. Bledsoe. Challenge problems in elementary analysis. *Journal of Automated Reasoning*, 6:341–359, 1990.

5. A. Bundy. The Use of Explicit Plans to Guide Inductive Proofs. In *Proc. of CADE-9*, LNCS 310. Springer, 1988.

6. A. Bundy, F. van Harmelen, J. Hesketh, and A. Smaill. Experiments with proof plans for induction. *Journal of Automated Reasoning*, 7:303-324, 1991. Earlier version available from Edinburgh as DAI Research Paper No 413.

7. L. Cheikhrouhou and V. Sorge. *PDS* — A Three-Dimensional Data Structure for Proof Plans. In *Proc. of ACIDCA'2000*, 2000.

8. A. Church. A Formulation of the Simple Theory of Types. *The Journal of Symbolic Logic*, 5:56–68, 1940.

9. S. Owre et al. PVS: Combining specification, proof checking and model checking. In *Proc. of CAV-96*, LNCS 1102. Springer, 1996.

10. A. Fiedler. *P.rex*: An interactive proof explainer. In *Proc. of IJCAR 2001*, LNAI 2083. Springer, 2001.

11. M. Kohlhase and J. Zimmer. System description: The MathWeb Software Bus for Distributed Mathmatical Reasoning. In *Proc. of CADE-18*, LNAI. Springer, 2002.

12. A. Franke and M. Kohlhase. System description: MBASE, an open mathematical knowledge base. In *Proc. of CADE-17*, LNAI 1831. Springer, 2000.

13. M. Gordon and T. Melham. *Introduction to HOL – A theorem proving environment for higher order logic*. Cambridge University Press, 1993.

14. W. McCune. Otter 3.0 reference manual and guide. Technical Report ANL-94-6, Argonne National Laboratory, Argonne, Illinois 60439, USA, 1994.

15. A. Meier. TRAMP: Transformation of Machine-Found Proofs into Natural Deduction Proofs at the Assertion Level. In *Proc. of CADE-17*, LNAI 1831. Springer, 2000.

16. A. Meier, M. Pollet, and V. Sorge. Comparing Approaches to Explore the Domain of Residue Classes. *Journal of Symbolic Computations*, 2002. forthcoming.

17. E. Melis and A. Meier. Proof Planning with Multiple Strategies. In *Proc. of CL-2000*, LNAI 1861. Springer, 2000.

18. E. Melis and J. Siekmann. Knowledge-Based Proof Planning. *Artificial Intelligence*, 115(1):65–105, 1999.

19. E. Melis, J. Zimmer, and T. Müller. Integrating constraint solving into proof planning. In *Proc. of FroCoS 2000*, LNAI 1794. Springer, 2000.

20. J.D.C Richardson, A. Smaill, and I.M. Green. System description: Proof planning in higher-order logic with λ-CLAM. In *Proc. of CADE-15*, LNAI 1421, Springer, 1998.

21. J. Siekmann et al. *LOUI*: *L*ovely ΩMEGA *U*ser *I*nterface. *Formal Aspects of Computing*, 11:326–342, 1999.

22. V. Sorge. Non-Trivial Computations in Proof Planning. In *Proc. of FroCoS 2000*, LNAI 1794. Springer, 2000.

23. Coq Development Team. *The Coq Proof Assistant Reference Manual*. INRIA. see http://coq.inria.fr/doc/main.html.

LearnΩmatic: System Description

Mateja Jamnik[1,2], Manfred Kerber[2], and Martin Pollet[2,3]

[1] University of Cambridge Computer Laboratory
J.J. Thomson Avenue, Cambridge, CB3 0FD, England, UK
http://www.cl.cam.ac.uk/~mj201
[2] School of Computer Science, The University of Birmingham
Birmingham B15 2TT, England, UK
http://www.cs.bham.ac.uk/~mmk
[3] Fachbereich Informatik, Universität des Saarlandes, 66041 Saarbrücken, Germany
http://www.ags.uni-sb.de/~pollet

1 Introduction

We devised a framework within which a proof planning [1] system can learn frequently occurring patterns of reasoning automatically from a number of typical examples, and then use them in proving new theorems [2]. The availability of such patterns, captured as proof methods in a proof planning system, reduces search and proof length. We implemented this learning framework for the proof planner ΩMEGA [3], and present it in this paper – we call our system LEARNΩMATIC. The entire process of learning and using new proof methods in LEARNΩMATIC consists of the following steps:

1. The user chooses informative examples and gives them to ΩMEGA to be automatically proved. Traces of these proofs are stored.
2. Proof traces of typical examples are given to the learning mechanism which automatically learns so-called *method outlines.*
3. Method outlines are automatically enriched by adding to them additional information and performing search for information that cannot be reconstructed in order to get fully fleshed proof methods that ΩMEGA can use in proofs of new theorems.

2 Learning and Using Learnt Methods

The methods we aim to learn are complex and are beyond the complexity that can typically be tackled in the field of machine learning. Therefore, we simplify the problem and aim to learn *method outlines*, which are expressed in the following language L, where P is a set of known identifiers of primitive methods used in a method that is being learnt:

- for any $p \in P$, let $p \in L$,
- for any $l_1, l_2 \in L$, let $[l_1, l_2] \in L$,
- for any $l_1, l_2 \in L$, let $[l_1|l_2] \in L$,
- for any $l \in L$, let $l^* \in L$,
- for any $l \in L$ and $n \in \mathbb{N}$, let $l^n \in L$,
- for any *list* such that all $l_i \in list$ are also $l_i \in L$, let $T(list) \in L$.

A. Voronkov (Ed.): CADE-18, LNAI 2392, pp. 150–155, 2002.
© Springer-Verlag Berlin Heidelberg 2002

"[" and "]" are auxiliary symbols used to separate subexpressions, "," denotes a *sequence*, "|" denotes a *disjunction*, "*" denotes a *repetition* of a subexpression any number of times (including 0), n a fixed number of times, and T is a constructor for a branching point (*list* is a list of branches), i.e., for proofs which are not sequences but branch into a tree. For more information on the choice of this language, the reader is referred to [2].

Here is an example from group theory of a *simplify* method outline which applies the associativity left method, and then reduces the theorem by applying appropriate inverse and identity methods: [*assoc-l**, [*inv-r*| *inv-l*], *id-l*].

Learning Technique. Our learning technique considers some typically small number of positive examples which are represented in terms of sequences of identifiers for primitive methods (e.g., *assoc-l*, *inv-r*), and generalises them so that the learnt pattern is in language L (e.g., *simplify* given above). The pattern is of *smallest size* with respect to a defined heuristic measure of *size* [2], which essentially counts the number of primitives in an expression. The pattern is also *most specific* (or equivalently, least general) with respect to the definition of specificity *spec*. *spec* is measured in terms of the number of nestings for each part of the generalisation [2]. Again, this is a heuristic measure. We take both, the size (first) and the specificity (second), in account when selecting the appropriate generalisation. If the generalisations considered have the same rating according to the two measures, then we return all of them.

The algorithm is based on the generalisation of the simultaneous compression of well-chosen examples. Here is just an abstract description of the learning algorithm, but the detailed steps with examples of how they are applied can be found in [2]:

1. Split every example trace into sublists of all possible lengths.
2. If there is any branching in the examples, then recursively repeat this algorithm on every element of the list of branches.
3. For each sublist in each example find consecutive repetitions, i.e. patterns, and compress them using exponent representation.
4. Find compressed patterns that match in all examples.
5. If there are no matches in the previous step, then generalise the examples by joining them disjunctively.
6. For every match, generalise different exponents to a Kleene star, and the same exponents to a constant.
7. For every matching pattern in all examples, repeat the algorithm on both sides of the pattern.
8. Choose the generalisations with the smallest size and largest specificity.

For instance, the three sequences of method outlines [*assoc-l,assoc-l,inv-r,id-l*], [*assoc-l,inv-l,id-l*], and [*assoc-l,assoc-l,assoc-l,inv-r,id-l*] will be generalised to the *simplify* method [*assoc-l**, [*inv-r*| *inv-l*], *id-l*].

The learning algorithm is implemented in SML of NJ v.110. Its inputs are the sequences of methods extracted from proofs that were constructed in ΩMEGA. Its output are method outlines which are passed back to ΩMEGA. The algorithm was tested on several examples of proofs and it successfully produced the required method outlines. Properties of our learning algorithm are discussed in [2].

There are some disadvantages to our technique, mostly related to the run time of the algorithm relative to the length of the examples considered for learning. The algorithm can deal with relatively small examples, which we encounter in our application domain, in an optimal way. The complexity of the algorithm is exponential in the worst case. Hence, we use some heuristics for large and badly behaved examples [2].

Using learnt methods. From a learnt outline a learnt method can automatically be generated. The learnt method is applicable if some instantiation of the method outline, i.e., a sequence of methods, is applicable. Since methods are planning operators with pre- and postconditions, these conditions must be checked for the methods of the method outline. The complex structure of methods does not allow the precondition of a subsequent method of the learnt outline to be tested, without the instantiated postconditions of the previous methods. That is, the methods of an outline have to be applied to the current proof situation.

The applicability test performs a depth first search on the learnt outline. Besides the choice points from the operators of the outline language, i.e., disjunctions and number of repetitions for the Kleene operator, there can be more than one goal where a method of the learnt outline can be applied. Additionally, for methods containing parameters, an instantiation has to be chosen. The parameters of a method are instantiated by control rules that guide the proof search. Every control rule that gives an instantiation of parameters for the current method is evaluated and the resulting possibilities for parameters are added to the search space.

The application test is performed as the precondition of the learnt method. The application of a learnt method for which the test was successful will introduce the open nodes and hypotheses generated during the applicability test as postcondition of the learnt method to the current proof.

3   Examples and Evaluation

In order to evaluate our approach, we carried out an empirical study in different problem domains on a number of theorems. This test set includes the theorems from which new methods were learnt, but most of them are new and more complex. They are from the domains of residue classes (e.g, *commutativity* of the operation $\lambda x, y. x \bar{+} y$ on the residue class set of integers $\mathbb{Z}_2$), set theory (e.g., $\forall x, y, z. ((x \cup y) \cap z) = (x \cap z) \cup (y \cap z))$, and group theory (e.g., $group(G, \circ, e, i) \Rightarrow \forall a, b, c, d, f \in G. a \circ (((a^{-1} \circ b) \circ (c \circ d)) \circ f) = (b \circ (c \circ d)) \circ f)$. The learnt methods were added to the search space in a way that their applicability is checked first, before the existing standard methods are tried.

Table 1 compares the values of *matchings* and *proof length* for the three problem domains. It compares these measures when the planner searches for the proof with the standard set of available methods (column marked with S), and when in addition to these, there are also our newly learnt methods available to the planner (column marked with L). "—" means that the planner ran out of resources (four hours of CPU time) and could not find a proof plan. The counter *matchings* counts the successful and unsuccessful application tests of methods in the process of finding a complete successful proof plan. It also contains the method matchings performed by the search engine for learnt methods. *Matchings* provides an important measure, since on the one hand it indicates how directed was the performed search for a proof. On the other hand, checking the candidate methods that may be applied in the proof is by far the most expensive part of the proof search. Hence, *matchings* is a good measure to approximate the *time* needed by the two approaches (i.e., with and without learnt methods) while it is also independent of the concrete implementation inefficiencies.

We tested the system with (and without) the use of the following learnt methods: for residue classes we used two learnt methods, *tryanderror* and *choose*, for set theory we used one learnt method, and for group theory we learnt five new methods, but only used two, since these two are recursive applications of the others. As is evident from Table 1, the number of candidate methods that the planner has to check if they can be applied in the proof (i.e., *matchings*) is reduced in all domains where our newly learnt methods are available. In general, the more complicated the theorem, the better is the improvement made by the availability of the learnt methods. In the case of group theory, some complex theorems can be proved *only* within the resource limits when our learnt methods are available to the planner. Hence, the *coverage* of the system that uses learnt methods is increased. Furthermore, we noticed that for some very simple theorems of group theory, a larger number of *matchings* is required if the learnt methods are available in the search space. However, for more complex examples, this is no longer the case, and an improvement is noticed. The reason for this behaviour is that additional methods increase the search space, and the application test for learnt methods is expensive, especially when a learnt method is

Table 1. Evaluation results.

Domain	Theorems	Matchings S	Matchings L	Length S	Length L
Residue Class (using *tryanderror* method)	assoc-z3z-times	651	113	63	2
	assoc-z6z-times	4431	680	441	2
	average of all	1362.0	219.5	134.0	2.0
Residue Class (using *choose* method)	closed-z3z-plusplus	681	551	49	34
	closed-z6z-plusplus	3465	2048	235	115
	average of all	1438.8	918.3	101.0	57.3
Set theory	average of all	33.5	12.5	13.0	2.0
Group theory	average of all (simple)	94.2	79.0	15.5	8.3
Group theory	average of all (complex)	—	189.6	—	9.8

not applicable, but still all possible interpretations of the learnt method outline have to be checked by the search engine.

As expected, the *proof length* is much reduced by using learnt methods, since they encapsulate patterns in which several other methods are used in the proof.

On average, the *time* it took to prove theorems of residue classes and conjectures of set theory was up to 50% and 15% shorter, respectively, than without such methods. The search in group theory took approximately 100% longer than without the learnt methods. The time results reflect in principle the behaviour of the proof search measured by method *matchings*, but also contain the overhead due to the current implementation for the reuse of the learnt methods. For example, the current proof situation is copied for the applicability test of the learnt method, and the new open goals and hypotheses resulting from a successful application are copied back into the original proof.

The reason for the improvements described above is due to the fact that our learnt methods provide a structure according to which the existing methods can be applied, and hence they direct search. This structure also gives better explanation why certain methods are best applied in particular combinations. For example, the simplification method for group theory examples indicates how the methods for associativity, inverse and identity should be combined together, rather than be applied blindly in any possible combination.

4   Future Work and Availability

There are several limitations of our approach that could be improved in the future. Namely, the learning algorithm may overgeneralise, so we need to examine what are good heuristics for our generalisation and how suboptimal solutions can be improved. In order to reduce unnecessary steps, the preconditions of the learnt methods would ideally be stronger. Currently, we use an applicability test to search if the preconditions of the method outline are satisfied. In the future, preconditions should be learnt as well. Finally, in order to model the human learning capability in theorem proving more adequately it would be necessary to model how humans introduce new vocabulary for new (emerging) concepts.

A demonstration of LEARNΩMATIC implementation can be found on the following web page: `http://www.cs.bham.ac.uk/~mmk/demos/LearnOmatic/`. Further information, also with links to papers with more comprehensive references can be found on `http://www.cs.bham.ac.uk/~mmk/projects/MethodFormation/`.

Acknowledgements. We would like to thank Alan Bundy, Predrag Janičić, Achim Jung, and Stephen Muggleton for their helpful advice on our work, and Christoph Benzmüller, Andreas Meier, and Volker Sorge for their help with some of the implementation in ΩMEGA. This work was supported by EPSRC grant GR/M22031 and European Commission IHP Calculemus Project grant HPRN-CT-2000-00102.

References

1. Bundy, A.: The use of explicit plans to guide inductive proofs. In 9th Conference on Automated Deduction. LNCS 310, Springer (1988), 111–120.
2. Jamnik, M., Kerber, M., Pollet, M., Benzmüller, C.:   Automatic learning of proof methods in proof planning. Technical Report CSRP-02-05, School of Computer Science, The University of Birmingham, Birmingham, England, UK, (2002). ftp://ftp.cs.bham.ac.uk/pub/tech-reports/2002/CSRP-02-05.ps.gz
3. Benzmüller, C., et al.: ΩMEGA: Towards a mathematical assistant. In 14th Conference on Automated Deduction. LNAI 1249, Springer (1997), 252-255.

HyLoRes 1.0: Direct Resolution for Hybrid Logics

Carlos Areces and Juan Heguiabehere

Language and Inference Technology
Faculty of Science. University of Amsterdam
{carlos,juanh}@science.uva.nl

Hybrid languages are modal languages that allow direct reference to the elements of a model. Even the basic hybrid language ($\mathcal{H}(@)$), which only extends the basic modal language with the addition of nominals ($i, j, k, \dots$) and satisfiability operators ($@_i, @_j, @_k, \dots$), increases the expressive power: it can explicitly check whether the point of evaluation is a specific, named point in the model ($w \Vdash i$), and whether a named point satisfies a given formula ($w \Vdash @_i\varphi$). The extended expressivity allows one to define elegant decision algorithms, where nominals and @ play the role of labels, or prefixes, which are usually needed during the construction of proofs in the modal setup [5,3]. Note that they do so *inside* the object language. All these features we get with no increase in complexity: the complexity of the satisfiability problem for $\mathcal{H}(@)$ is the same as for the basic modal language, PSPACE [2]. When we move to very expressive hybrid languages containing binders, we obtain an impressive boost in expressivity, but usually we also move beyond the boundaries of decidability. Classical binders like $\forall$ and $\exists$ (together with @) make the logic as expressive as first-order logic (FOL) while adding the more "modal" binder $\downarrow$ gives a logic weaker than FOL [1]. We refer to the Hybrid Logic site at http://www.hylo.net for a broad on-line bibliography.

HyLoRes is a direct resolution prover for hybrid logics handling satisfiability of sentences in $\mathcal{H}(@,\downarrow)$; it implements the algorithm presented in [3]. The most interesting distinguishing feature of HyLoRes is that it is not based on tableau algorithms but on (direct) resolution. HyLoRes implements a version of the "given clause" algorithm, which has become the skeleton underlying most first-order provers. In contrast to translation based provers like MSPASS [8], HyLoRes performs resolution directly on the modal (or hybrid) input, with no translation into background logics. It is often said that hybrid logics combine interesting features from both modal and first-order logics. In the same spirit, HyLoRes fuses ideas from state-of-the-art first-order proving with the simple representation of the hybrid object language.

HyLoRes (and the Tcl/Tk interface xHyLoRes) is available for on-line use and downloading at http://www.illc.uva.nl/~carlos/HyLoRes.

1 Direct Resolution for Hybrid Logics

In [3] we presented a resolution calculus that uses the hybrid machinery to "push formulas out of modalities" and in this way, feed them into a simple and standard resolution rule. Nominals and @ introduce a limited form of equational reasoning:

A. Voronkov (Ed.): CADE-18, LNAI 2392, pp. 156–160, 2002.
© Springer-Verlag Berlin Heidelberg 2002

a formula like $@_{i}j$ is true in a model iff i and j are nominals for the *same* state. A paramodulation rule similar to the one used by Robinson and Wos [12] lets us handle nominals and $@$.

Very briefly, our resolution algorithm works as follows. First define the following rewriting procedure nf on hybrid formulas: $nf = \{\neg\neg\varphi \Rightarrow \varphi, \langle R\rangle\varphi \Rightarrow \neg([R]\neg\varphi), (\varphi_1 \vee \varphi_2) \Rightarrow \neg(\neg\varphi_1 \wedge \neg\varphi_2), \neg@_t\varphi \Rightarrow @_t(\neg\varphi)\}$. Further, for any formula φ in $\mathcal{H}(@, \downarrow)$, φ is satisfiable iff $@_t\varphi$ is satisfiable, for a nominal t not appearing in φ. We define the clause set $ClSet$ corresponding to φ to be $ClSet(\varphi) = \{\{@_t nf(\varphi)\}\}$, where t does not appear in φ. Next, let $ClSet^*(\varphi)$ (the saturated clause set corresponding to φ) be the smallest set containing $ClSet(\varphi)$ and closed under the following rules.

$$(\wedge) \frac{Cl \cup \{@_t(\varphi_1 \wedge \varphi_2)\}}{\begin{array}{c} Cl \cup \{@_t\varphi_1\} \\ Cl \cup \{@_t\varphi_2\} \end{array}} \qquad (\vee) \frac{Cl \cup \{@_t\neg(\varphi_1 \wedge \varphi_2)\}}{Cl \cup \{@_t nf(\neg\varphi_1), @_t nf(\neg\varphi_2)\}}$$

$$(\text{RES}) \frac{Cl_1 \cup \{@_t\varphi\} \quad Cl_2 \cup \{@_t\neg\varphi\}}{Cl_1 \cup Cl_2}$$

$$([R]) \frac{Cl_1 \cup \{@_t[R]\varphi\} \quad Cl_2 \cup \{@_t\neg[R]\neg s\}}{Cl_1 \cup Cl_2 \cup \{@_s\varphi\}} \qquad (\langle R\rangle) \frac{Cl \cup \{@_t\neg[R]\varphi\}}{\begin{array}{c} Cl \cup \{@_t\neg[R]\neg n\} \\ Cl \cup \{@_n nf(\neg\varphi)\} \end{array}}, \text{ for } n \text{ new.}$$

$$(@) \frac{Cl \cup \{@_t@_s\varphi\}}{Cl \cup \{@_s\varphi\}}$$

$$(\text{SYM}) \frac{Cl \cup \{@_t s\}}{Cl \cup \{@_s t\}} \qquad (\text{REF}) \frac{Cl \cup \{@_t\neg t\}}{Cl}$$

$$(\text{PARAM}) \frac{Cl_1 \cup \{@_t s\} \quad Cl_2 \cup \{\varphi(t)\}}{Cl_1 \cup Cl_2 \cup \{\varphi(t/s)\}}$$

The computation of $ClSet^*(\varphi)$ is in itself a sound and complete algorithm for checking satisfiability of $\mathcal{H}(@)$, in the sense that φ is unsatisfiable if and only if the empty clause $\{\}$ is a member of $ClSet^*(\varphi)$ (see [3]).

The hybrid binder $\downarrow$ binds variables to the point of evaluation, i.e., for a model $\mathcal{M}$, an assignment g and a state w, $\mathcal{M}, g, w \models \downarrow x.\varphi$ iff $\mathcal{M}, g^w_x, w \models \varphi$, where g^w_x is the assignment that coincides with g, but maps x to w. For example, a state w satisfies the formula $\downarrow x.\Diamond x$ if and only if w can reach itself through the accessibility relation.

Extending the system to account for hybrid sentences using $\downarrow$ is fairly straightforward. First, extend nf to handle $\downarrow$: $\neg\downarrow x.\varphi \Rightarrow \downarrow x.\neg\varphi$. Then consider the rule $(\downarrow)$ below

$$(\downarrow) \frac{Cl \cup \{@_t\downarrow x.\varphi\}}{Cl \cup \{@_t\varphi(x/t)\}}.$$

Notice that the rule transforms hybrid sentences into hybrid sentences. The full set of rules is a sound and complete calculus for checking satisfiability of sentences in $\mathcal{H}(@, \downarrow)$.

2   The "Given Clause" Algorithm for Hybrid Resolution

HyLoRes implements a version of the "given clause" algorithm (see, e.g., [13]).

---

input: init: set of clauses
var: new, clauses, inuse, inactive: set of clauses
var: given: clause

clauses := {}
new := init
simplify(&new, inuse ∪ inactive ∪ clauses)
if {} ∈ new **then return** "unsatisfiable"
clauses = computeComplexity(new)
while clauses != {} **do**
    given := select(clauses)
    clauses := clauses − {given}
    while subsumed(given, inuse) **do**
        if clauses = {}
            then return "satisfiable"
        else
            given := select(clauses)
            clauses := clauses − {given}
    simplify(&inuse, given)
    new := infer(inuse, given, &inactive)
    simplify(&new, inuse ∪ inactive ∪ clauses)
    if {} ∈ new **then return** "unsatisfiable"
    clauses = clauses ∪ computeComplexity(new)

simplify performs subsumption deletion (& marks the modified set). *compute-Complexity* determines length, modal depth, number of literals, etc. for each of the formulas; these values are used by *select*. *infer* applies the resolution rules to the given clause and each clause in inuse, if the ∧, ∨, ◇ or ↓-rules are applied, the given clause is added to inactive so that it's not generated again.

The implementation preserves the soundness and completeness of the calculus introduced in Section 1, and ensures termination for $\mathcal{H}(@)$.

HyLoRes is implemented in Haskell, and compiled with the Glasgow Haskell Compiler Version (GHC) 5.00, generating executable code which increases the usability of the prover.

The design of the algorithm is modular, both in the internal representation of the different kinds of data, and in the handling of new resolution rules (so that the prover can easily be made to handle new logical operators). We have used the Edison package (a library of efficient data types provided with GHC) to implement most of the data types representing sets. But while we represent clauses directly as `UnbalancedSet`, we have chosen different representations for each of the clause sets used by the algorithm: NEW and INUSE are simply lists of clauses (as they always have to be examined linearly one by one), CLAUSES and INACTIVE are UnbalancedSets of clauses.[1] In particular, CLAUSES is ordered by our selection criterion, which makes for an efficient selection of the given clause. The internal state of the given clause algorithm is represented as a combination of a state and an output monad. This allows the addition of further structure (hashing functions, etc.) to optimize search, with minimum recoding. With respect to the addition of further resolution rules, our main aim was not to disturb the modularity of the given clause algorithm. New rules can simply be added in the *infer* function without the need for any further modification of the code.

3   Testing and Comparison

The prototype is not yet meant to be competitive when compared with state of the art provers for modal and description logics like DLP, FaCT, MSPASS or RACER [11,7,8,6].

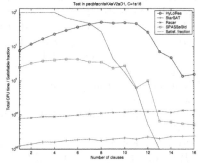

On the one hand, the system is still in a preliminary stage of development (only very simple optimizations for hybrid logics have been developed and implemented), and on the other hand the hybrid and description languages are related but different. $\mathcal{H}(@, \downarrow)$ is undecidable while the implemented description languages are mostly decidable. And even when comparing the fragment $\mathcal{H}(@)$ for which HyLoRes implements a decision algorithm, the expressive powers are incomparable ($\mathcal{H}(@)$ permits free Boolean combinations of @ and nominals but lacks the limited form of universal modality available in the T-Box of DL provers [1]). The plot shows some ongoing work on basic testing with the random QBF generator [10].

4   Future Work

There remain many things to try and improve in HyLoRes: 1) Develop both the theoretical and practical issues involved in performing direct *ordered* resolution for hybrid logics (ongoing). 2) Test and optimize the data types used (ongoing). 3) Make the prover aware of the characteristics of its input. At the moment, the prover always attempts to use the same set of rules and heuristics, disregarding syntactic properties of the input clause set (ongoing). 4) Extend the language with the universal modality A, which will let us perform inference in terms of full Boolean knowledge bases of the description logic $\mathcal{ALC}$, in HyLoRes (see [1]). 5)

---

[1] While `List` provides efficient sequential access to their elements, `UnbalancedSet` implements sets as unbalanced search trees to optimize search of single elements.

Implement some of the heuristics presented in [4]. 6) Display a concise refutation proof in case it finds one, or a model otherwise.

As we said in the introduction, HyLoRes fuses nicely some ideas from state-of-the-art first-order proving with the simplicity of hybrid languages; and it provides the basis for future developments on computational tools for hybrid logic. Already in its actual state, users find the tool useful for better understanding the formalisms.

Acknowledgement. C. Areces was supported by the NWO project # 612.069.006.

References

1. C. Areces. *Logic Engineering. The Case of Description and Hybrid Logics.* PhD thesis, ILLC, University of Amsterdam, The Netherlands, October 2000.
2. C. Areces, P. Blackburn, and M. Marx. Hybrid logic: Characterization, interpolation and complexity. *J. Symb. Logic*, 66(3):977–1010, 2001
3. C. Areces, H. de Nivelle, and M. de Rijke. Resolution in modal, description and hybrid logic. *J. Logic and Comp.*, 11(5):717–736, 2001.
4. Y. Auffray, P. Enjalbert, and J. Hebrard. Strategies for modal resolution: results and problems. *J. Autom. Reas.*, 6(1):1–38, 1990.
5. P. Blackburn. Internalizing labelled deduction. *J. Logic and Comp.*, 10(1):137–168, 2000.
6. V. Haarslev and R. Möller. RACE system description. In Lambrix et al. [9], pages 130–132.
7. I. Horrocks. FaCT and iFaCT. In Lambrix et al. [9], pages 133–135.
8. U. Hustadt, R. A. Schmidt, and C. Weidenbach. MSPASS: Subsumption testing with SPASS. In Lambrix et al. [9], pages 136–137.
9. P. Lambrix, A. Borgida, R. Möller M. Lenzerini, and P. Patel-Schneider, (eds.) *Proc. of the 1999 Int. Workshop on Description Logics (DL'99)*, 1999.
10. F Massacci. Design and results of the tableaux-99 non-classical (modal) systems comparison. In N. Murray, (ed.), *Proc. of TABLEAUX'99*, number 1617 of LNAI, pages 14–18. Springer, 1999.
11. P. Patel-Schneider. DLP system description. In E. Franconi, G. De Giacomo, R. MacGregor, W. Nutt, and C. Welty, (eds.), *Proc. of the 1998 Int. Workshop on Description Logics (DL'98)*, pages 87–89, 1998.
12. G. Robinson and L. Wos. Paramodulation and theorem-proving in first-order theories with equality. In *Mach. Int.* 4:135–150, 1969.
13. A. Voronkov. Algorithms, datastructures, and other issues in efficient automated deduction. In R. Goré, A. Leitsch, and T. Nipkow, (eds.), *Automated Reasoning. 1st. Int. Joint Conf., IJCAR 2001*, number 2083 of LNAI, pages 13–28, Italy, 2001.

Testing Satisfiability of CNF Formulas by Computing a Stable Set of Points

Eugene Goldberg

Cadence Berkeley Labs, 2001 Addison str., 3rd floor, Berkeley, California, 94704-1103,
phone: (510)-647-2825, fax: (510)-486-0205
egold@cadence.com

Abstract. We show that a conjunctive normal form (CNF) formula F is
unsatisfiable iff there is a set of points of the Boolean space that is stable
with respect to F. So testing the satisfiability of a CNF formula reduces
to looking for a stable set of points (SSP). We give some properties
of SSPs and describe a simple algorithm for constructing an SSP for
a CNF formula. Building an SSP can be viewed as a "natural" way
of search space traversal. This naturalness of search space examination
allows one to make use of the regularity of CNF formulas to be checked
for satisfiability. We illustrate this point by showing that if a CNF F
formula is symmetric with respect to a group of permutations, it is very
easy to make use of this symmetry when constructing an SSP. As an
example, we show that the unsatisfiability of pigeon-hole CNF formulas
can be proven by examining only a set of points whose size is quadratic
in the number of holes.

1   Introduction

A common belief is that there is no polynomial time algorithm for the satisfiability problem. Nevertheless, many classes of "real-life" CNF formulas have
structural properties that reduce (or may potentially reduce) the complexity of
checking these CNF formulas for satisfiability from exponential to polynomial.
However, the existing algorithms are not very good at taking into account structural properties of CNF formulas. One of the reasons is that currently there is
no "natural" way of traversing search space. For example, in the DPLL procedure [5], which is the basis of many algorithms used in practice, search is
organized as a binary tree. In reality, the search tree is used only to impose a
linear order on the points of the Boolean space to avoid visiting the same point
twice. However, this order may be in conflict with "natural" relationships between points of the Boolean space that are imposed by the CNF formula to be
checked for satisfiability (for example, if this formula has some symmetries).

In this paper, we introduce the notion of a stable set of points (SSP) that
we believe can serve as a basis for constructing algorithms that traverse the
search space in a "natural" way. We show that a CNF formula F is unsatisfiable
if and only if there is a set of points of the Boolean space that is stable with

A. Voronkov (Ed.): CADE-18, LNAI 2392, pp. 161–180, 2002.

respect to F. If F is satisfiable then any subset of points of the Boolean space is unstable, and an assignment satisfying F will be found in the process of SSP construction. We list some properties of SSPs and describe a simple algorithm for constructing an SSP. Interestingly, this algorithm is, in a sense, an extension of Papadimitriou's algorithm [11] (or a similar algorithm that is used in the well-known program called Walksat [13]).

A very important fact is that, generally speaking, a set of points that is stable with respect to a CNF formula F depends only on the clauses (i.e. disjunctions of literals) F consists of. So the process of constructing an SSP can be viewed as a "natural" way of traversing search space when checking F for satisfiability. In particular, if F has symmetries, they can be easily taken into account when constructing an SSP. To illustrate this point, we consider the class of CNF formulas that are symmetric with respect to a group of permutations. We show that in this case for proving the unsatisfiability of a CNF formula it is sufficient to construct a set of points that is stable modulo symmetry. In particular, as is shown in the paper, for pigeon-hole CNF formulas there is a stable modulo symmetry set of points whose size is linear in the number of holes. The unsatisfiability of pigeon-hole CNF formulas can be proven by examining only a set of points of quadratic size.

This notion of an SSP is the development of the idea of 1-neighborhood exploration introduced in [6]. There we described two proof systems based on the fact that for proving the unsatisfiability of a CNF formula F it suffices to examine the 1-neighborhood of all the clauses of F. (The 1-neighborhood of a clause C is the set of all points of the Boolean space that satisfy, i.e. set to 1, exactly one literal of C.) In this paper we show that it is not even necessary to examine the whole 1-neighborhood of clauses. It is sufficient to consider only a fraction of the 1-neighborhood that is an SSP. From the practical point of view the notion of an SSP (and, more generally, the notion of 1-neighborhood exploration) is important because it gives a new criterion for algorithm termination. Namely, once it is proven that the examined part of the Boolean space is an SSP (or contains an SSP) one can claim that the CNF under test is unsatisfiable.

The rest of the paper is organized as follows. In Section 2 we introduce the notion of an SSP. In Section 3 we describe some properties of SSPs. In Section 4 we describe a simple algorithm for constructing an SSP. In Section 5 we give some background on testing the satisfiability of symmetric CNF formulas. In Section 6 we show that our algorithm for constructing SSPs can be easily modified to take into account formula's symmetry. In Section 7 we apply the modified algorithm to a class of highly symmetric formulas called pigeon-hole CNF formulas. We conclude in Section 8 with a summary of results and directions for future research.

2   Stable Set of Points

In this section, we introduce the notion of an SSP. Let F be a CNF formula of n variables $x_1, \ldots, x_n$. Denote by B the set $\{0, 1\}$ of values taken by a Boolean variable. Denote by B^n the set of points of the Boolean space specified by variables $x_1,...,x_n$. A point of B^n is an assignment of values to all the n variables.

Definition 1. *A disjunction of literals (also called a clause) C is called satisfied by a value assignment (point) p if $C(p)=1$. Otherwise, clause C is called falsified by p.*

Definition 2. *Let F be a CNF formula. The satisfiability problem is to find a value assignment (point) satisfying all the clauses of F. This assignment is called a satisfying assignment.*

Definition 3. *Let p be a point of the Boolean space falsifying a clause C. The 1-neighborhood of point p with respect to clause C (written Nbhd(p,C)) is the set of points that are at Hamming distance 1 from p and that satisfy C.*

Remark 1. It is not hard to see that the number of points in $Nbhd(p,C)$ is equal to that of literals in C.

Example 1. Let $C = x_1 \lor \overline{x_3} \lor x_6$ be a clause specified in the Boolean space of 6 variables $x_1,\ldots,x_6$. Let $p = (x_1 = 0, x_2 = 1, x_3 = 1, x_4 = 0, x_5 = 1, x_6 = 0)$ be a point falsifying C. Then $Nbhd(p,C)$ consists of the following three points: $p_1 = (x_1\mathbf{=1}, x_2 = 1, x_3 = 1, x_4 = 0, x_5 = 1, x_6 = 0)$, $p_2 = (x_1 = 0, x_2 = 1, x_3\mathbf{=0}, x_4 = 0, x_5 = 1, x_6 = 0)$, $p_3 = (x_1 = 0, x_2 = 1, x_3 = 1, x_4 = 0, x_5 = 1, x_6\mathbf{=1})$. Points p_1, p_2, p_3 are obtained from p by flipping the value of variables x_1, x_3, x_6 respectively i.e. the variables whose literals are in C.

Denote by $Z(F)$ the set of points at which F takes value 0. If F is unsatisfiable, $Z(F) = B^n$.

Definition 4. *Let F be a CNF formula and P be a subset of $Z(F)$. Mapping g of P to F is called a transport function if, for any $p \in P$, clause $g(p) \in F$ is falsified by p. In other words, a transport function $g:P \to F$ is meant to assign each point $p \in P$ a clause that is falsified by p.*

Remark 2. We call mapping $P \to F$ a transport function because, as it is shown in Sect. 3, such a mapping allows one to introduce some kind of "movement" of points in the Boolean space.

Definition 5. *Let P be a nonempty subset of $Z(F)$, F be a CNF formula, and $g: P \to F$ be a transport function. Set P is called stable with respect to F and g if $\forall p \in P$, $Nbhd(p, g(p)) \subseteq P$.*

Remark 3. Henceforth, if we say that a set of points P is stable with respect to a CNF formula F without mentioning a transport function, we mean that there is a function $g:P \to F$ such that P is stable with respect to F and g.

Example 2. Consider an unsatisfiable CNF formula F consisting of the following 7 clauses: $C_1 = x_1 \vee x_2$, $C_2 = \overline{x_2} \vee x_3$, $C_3 = \overline{x_3} \vee x_4$, $C_4 = \overline{x_4} \vee x_1$, $C_5 = \overline{x_1} \vee x_5$, $C_6 = \overline{x_5} \vee x_6$, $C_7 = \overline{x_6} \vee \overline{x_1}$. Clauses of F are composed of literals of 6 variables: $x_1, \ldots, x_6$. The following 14 points form an SSP P: $p_1{=}000000$, $p_2{=}010000$, $p_3{=}011000$, $p_4{=}011100$, $p_5{=}111100$, $p_6{=}111110$, $p_7{=}111111$, $p_8{=}011111$, $p_9{=}011011$, $p_{10}{=}010011$, $p_{11}{=}000011$, $p_{12}{=}100011$, $p_{13}{=}100010$, $p_{14}{=}100000$. (Values of variables are specified in the order variables are numbered. For example, p_4 consists of assignments $x_1{=}0$, $x_2{=}1$, $x_3{=}1$, $x_4{=}1$, $x_5{=}0$, $x_6{=}0$.) Set P is stable with respect to the transport function g specified as: $g(p_1) = C_1$, $g(p_2) = C_2$, $g(p_3) = C_3$, $g(p_4) = C_4$, $g(p_5) = C_5$, $g(p_6) = C_6$, $g(p_7) = C_7$, $g(p_8) = C_4$, $g(p_9) = C_3$, $g(p_{10}) = C_2$, $g(p_{11}) = C_1$, $g(p_{12}) = C_7$, $g(p_{13}) = C_6$, $g(p_{14}) = C_5$. It is not hard to see that g indeed is a transport function i.e. for any point p_i of P it is true that $C(p_i){=}0$ where $C = g(p_i)$. Besides, for every point p_i of P, the condition $Nbhd(p, g(p)) \subseteq P$ of Definition 5 holds. Consider, for example, point $p_{10}{=}010011$. The value of $g(p_{10})$ is C_2, $C_2 = \overline{x_2} \vee x_3$ and the value of $Nbhd(p_{10}, C_2)$ is $\{p_{11}{=}000011, p_9{=}011011\}$, the latter being a subset of P.

Proposition 1. *If there is a set of points that is stable with respect to a CNF formula F, then F is unsatisfiable.*

Proofs of all the propositions are given in the appendix.

Proposition 2. *Let F be an unsatisfiable CNF formula of n variables. Then set $Z(F)$ is stable with respect to F and any transport function $Z(F) \to F$.*

Remark 4. From propositions 1 and 2 it follows that a CNF F is unsatisfiable if and only if there is a set of points stable with respect to F.

3   Some Properties of SSPs

In this section, we describe some properties of SSPs. Though Propositions 6-11 are not used in the rest of the paper, they are listed here because they might be useful for developing an algebra of SSPs.

Definition 6. *Let F be a CNF formula and $g: Z(F) \to F$ be a transport function. A sequence of k points $p_1, \ldots, p_k$, $k \geq 2$ is called a **path** from point p_1 to point p_k in set P with transport function g if points $p_1, \ldots, p_{k-1}$ are in P and $p_i \in Nbhd(p_{i-1}, g(p_{i-1}))$, $2 \leq i \leq k$. (Note that the last point of the path, i.e. p_k, does not have to be in P.) We will assume that no point repeats twice (or more) in a path.*

Example 3. Consider the CNF formula and transport function of Example 2. Let P be the set of points specified in Example 2. The sequence of points $p_1, p_{14}, p_{13}, p_{12}$ forms a path from p_1 to p_{12}. Indeed, it is not hard to check that $Nbhd(p_1, g(p_1)) = \{p_2, p_{14}\}$, $Nbhd(p_{14}, g(p_{14})) = \{p_{13}, p_1\}$, $Nbhd(p_{13}, g(p_{13})) = \{p_{14}, p_{12}\}$, $Nbhd(p_{12}, g(p_{12})) = \{p_{13}, p_{11}\}$. So each point p' of the path (except the starting point i.e. p_1) is contained in the set $Nbhd(p'', g(p''))$ where p'' is the preceding point.

Definition 7. *Let F be a CNF formula. Point p'' is called* **reachable** *from point p' by means of transport function $g : Z(F) \to F$ if there is a path from p' to p'' with transport function g. Denote by Reachable(p, g) the set consisting of point p and all the points that are reachable from p by means of transport function g.*

Proposition 3. *Let F be a satisfiable CNF formula, p be a point of $Z(F)$, and s be any closest to p (in Hamming distance) satisfying assignment. Let $g{:}Z(F) \to F$ be a transport function. Then in $Z(F)$ there is a path from p to s with transport function g i.e. solution s is reachable from p.*

Proposition 4. *Let P be a set of points that is stable with respect to CNF formula F and transport function $g : P \to F$. Then $\forall p \in P$, Reachable$(p, g) \subseteq P$.*

Proposition 5. *Let F be a CNF formula, $g : Z(F) \to F$ be a transport function, and p be a point from $Z(F)$. If $P = $ Reachable(p, g) does not contain a satisfying assignment, then P is stable with respect to F and g, and so F is unsatisfiable.*

Remark 5. From Proposition 5 it follows that a CNF F is satisfiable if and only if, given a point $p \in Z(F)$ and a transport function $g : Z(F) \to F$, set Reachable(p, g) contains a satisfying assignment.

Proposition 6. *Let F be a CNF formula, $P, P' \subseteq B^n$ be two sets of points, and $g : P \to F$, $g' : P' \to F$ be transport functions. Let P, P' be stable with respect to F and transport functions g and g' respectively. Then set $P'' = P \cup P'$ is also stable with respect to F and a transport function g''.*

Proposition 7. *Let F be an unsatisfiable CNF formula, $P = $ Reachable(p, g) be the set of points reachable from p by means of transport function $g : P \to F$. Denote by P^* a subset of P consisting of the points of P from which there is no path to p. (In particular, point p itself is not included in P^*). If P^* is not empty then it is stable with respect to CNF formula F and transport function g.*

Proposition 8. *Let F be an unsatisfiable CNF formula and $P = \{p_1, .., p_k\}$ be a subset of B^n that is stable with respect to F and transport function $g{:}P \to F$. Then $P = $ Reachable$(p_1, g) \cup \ldots \cup$ Reachable(p_k, g).*

Proposition 9. *Let F be an unsatisfiable CNF formula and $g : B^n \to F$ be a transport function. Let p' be reachable from p by means of transport function g. Then Reachable$(p', g) \subseteq$ Reachable(p, g).*

Proposition 10. *Let F be an unsatisfiable CNF formula and $g{:}B^n \to F$ be a transport function. Let p and p' be two points from B^n. Then, if set $P = $ Reachable$(p, g) \cap$ Reachable(p', g) is not empty, it is stable with respect to F and g.*

Proposition 11. *Let F be unsatisfiable and $g : B^n \to F$ be a transport function. Let P and P' be sets that are stable with respect to F and g. Then , if $P'' = P \cap P'$ is not empty, it is stable with respect to F and g.*

4   Testing Satisfiability of CNF Formulas by SSP Construction

In this section, we describe a simple algorithm for constructing an SSP that is based on Proposition 5. Let F be a CNF formula to be checked for satisfiability. The idea is to pick a point p of the Boolean space and construct set $Reachable(p, g)$. Since transport function $g : Z(F) \rightarrow F$ is not known beforehand, it is built on the fly. In the description of the algorithm given below, set $Reachable(p, g)$ is broken down into two parts: *Boundary* and *Body*. The *Boundary* consists of those points of the current set $Reachable(p, g)$ whose 1-neighborhood has not been explored yet. At each step of the algorithm a point p' of the *Boundary* is extracted and a clause C falsified by p' is assigned as the value of $g(p')$. Then the set $Nbhd(p', C)$ is generated and its points (minus those that are already in $Body \cup Boundary$) are added to the *Boundary*. This goes on until a stable set is constructed (F is unsatisfiable) or a satisfying assignment is found (F is satisfiable).

1. Generate a starting point p. $Boundary = \{p\}$. $Body = \emptyset$, $g = \emptyset$.
2. If the *Boundary* is empty, then the *Body* is an SSP and F is unsatisfiable. The algorithm terminates.
3. Pick a point $p' \in Boundary$. $Boundary = Boundary \setminus \{p'\}$.
4. Find a set M of clauses that are falsified by point p'. If $M = \emptyset$, then CNF formula F is satisfiable and p' is a satisfying assignment. The algorithm terminates.
5. Pick a clause C from M. Take C as the value of $g(p')$. Generate $Nbhd(p', C)$. $Boundary = Boundary \cup (Nbhd(p', C) \setminus Body)$. $Body = Body \cup \{p'\}$.
6. Go to step 2.

Interestingly, the described algorithm can be viewed as an extension of Papadimitriou's algorithm [11] (or a similar algorithm used in the program Walksat [13]) to the case of unsatisfiable CNF formulas. Papadimitriou's algorithm (and Walksat) can be applied only to satisfiable CNF formulas since it does not store visited points of the Boolean space. The remarkable fact is that the number of points that one has to explore to prove the unsatisfiability of a CNF formula can be very small. For instance, in Example 2 an SSP of a CNF formula of 6 variables consists only of 14 points while the Boolean space of 6 variables consists of 64 points. In general, it is not hard to show that for a subclass of the class of 2-CNF formulas (a clause of a 2-CNF formula contains at most 2 literals) there is always an SSP of linear size. This subclass consists of 2-CNF formulas analogous to the one described in Example 2. However, we have not proved (or disproved) this claim for the whole class of 2-CNF formulas yet.

A natural question to ask is: "What is the size of SSPs for "hard" CNF formulas?". One example of such formulas are random CNFs for which general resolution was proven to have exponential complexity [2]. Table 1 gives the results of computing SSPs for CNF formulas from the "hard" domain (the number of clauses is 4.25 times the number of variables [9]). For computing SSPs we used the algorithm described above enhanced by the following heuristic. When picking a clause to be assigned to the current point p' of the *Boundary* (Step 5), we give preference to the clause C (falsified by p') for which the maximum number of points of $Nbhd(p', C)$ are already in *Body* or *Boundary*. In other words, when choosing the clause C to be assigned to p', we try to minimize the number of new points we have to add to the *Boundary*.

We generated 10 random CNFs of each size (number of variables). The starting point was chosen randomly. Table 1 gives the average values of the SSP size and the share (percent) of the Boolean space taken by an SSP. It is not hard to see that the SSP size grows very quickly. So even for very small formulas it is very large. An interesting fact though is that the share of the Boolean space taken by the SSP constructed by the described algorithm steadily decreases as the number of variables grows.

Table 1. SSPs of "hard" random CNF formulas

number of variables	SSP size	#SSP/#All_Space (%)
10	430	41.97
11	827	40.39
12	1,491	36.41
13	2,714	33.13
14	4,931	30.10
15	8,639	26.36
16	16,200	24.72
17	30,381	23.18
18	56,836	21.68
19	103,428	19.73
20	195,220	18.62
21	392,510	18.72
22	736,329	17.55
23	1,370,890	16.34

Such a poor performance on random CNFs can be explained by the following two flaws of the described algorithm. First, an SSP is constructed point-by-point while computing an SSP in larger chunks of points (clustering "similar" points of the Boolean space) should be much more efficient. Second, the algorithm looks for a set of points that is stable with respect to the initial set of clauses. On the other hand, if an algorithm is allowed to resolve clauses of the initial CNF, it may find a much smaller set of points that is stable with respect to a set of resolvents. Nevertheless, there is a class of formulas for which even point-by-point SSP computation can be efficient. We mean the class of CNF formulas that are symmetric with respect to a group of variable permutations. Satisfiability testing of these formulas by SSP construction is considered in Sect. 6 and 7.

5   Testing Satisfiability of Symmetric CNF Formulas

In this section, we give some background on testing the satisfiability of symmetric CNF formulas. Methods for simplifying satisfiability check for symmetric formulas have received substantial attention in the past. In [8] it was shown that if the resolution system is enhanced by a "symmetry rule" then the complexity of proofs for some classes of formulas reduces from exponential to polynomial. This extra rule allows one to "shortcut" the deduction of implicates that are symmetric to ones deduced before. Pigeon-hole formulas was the first class of CNF formulas for which the resolution proof system was shown to have exponential complexity [7]. In [15] it was shown that in the resolution system with the symmetry rule, the satisfiability of pigeon-hole formulas can be refuted with a proof of length $(3n+1)n/2$ where n is the number of holes. Refutations of polynomial size can be also produced in other proof systems e.g. the cutting planes refutation system [3] and extended resolution [7]. Unfortunately, all these systems give only non-deterministic proofs and so the obtained results are not very helpful in designing deterministic algorithms.

Practical (and hence deterministic) algorithms for testing satisfiability of symmetric formulas were considered in [1,4,12,14]. In [1] a backtracking algorithm with some machinery for prunning symmetric branches was introduced. The problem of such an approach is that the ability to prune symmetric branches is obtained at the expense of losing the freedom of search tree examination. So if a new scheme of backtracking is found in the future a new algorithm would have to be designed to take into account symmetries of the CNF under test.

To solve the problem, in [4] it was suggested to add to the CNF formula F to be tested for satisfiability a set Q of "symmetry-breaking" clauses . The idea is to find such a set Q of clauses that only one point of each symmetry class satisfies all the clauses of Q. This way search in symmetric portions of the Boolean space is pruned earlier than without adding clauses of Q (if a clause of Q is falsified before any clause of F). The generation of symmetry-breaking clauses Q is done by a separate procedure performed before actual satisfiability testing. So this procedure (used as a preprocessor) can be run in combination with any SAT-solver to be developed in the future.

One of the flaws of the approach is that the problem of generating a full set of symmetry-breaking clauses is NP-hard [4]. Moreover, for some groups the number of all clauses that have to be generated to break all symmetris of the group is exponential [12]. This leads to the next problem. Since often one cannot break all the symmetries, it is reasonable to try to break only symmetries whose elimination would symplify satisfiability testing the most. However, since symmetry processing and satisfiability testing are performed separately, at the symmetry processing step we do not know which symmetries should be broken. This suggests that even though incorporating symmetry processing into the current backtracking algorithms is difficult, satisfiability testing and symmetry processing should be tightly linked. So, instead of separating symmetry processing and satisfiability testing steps it makes sense to try to find a search space traversal scheme that is more amenable to symmetry processing than backtracking. We believe that bulding an SSP could be such a scheme. The point is that an SSP of a CNF formula F is an inherent property of F. So if F has some symmetries, an SSP has these symmetries as well, which makes it easy to use them during satisfiability testing.

6   Testing Satisfiability of Symmetric CNF Formulas by SSP Construction

In this section we introduce the notion of a set of points that is stable modulo symmetry. This notion allows one to modify the algorithm of SSP construction given in Sect. 4 to take into account formula's symmetry. The modification itself is described in the end of the section. In the paper we consider only the case of permutations. However, a similar approach can be applied to a more general class of symmetries e.g. to the case when a CNF formula is symmetric under permutations combined with the negation of some variables.

Definition 8. *Let $X = \{x_1, \ldots, x_n\}$ be a set of Boolean variables. A **permutation** π defined on set X is a bijective mapping of X onto itself.*

Let $F = \{C_1, \ldots, C_k\}$ be a CNF formula. Let $p = (x_1, \ldots, x_n)$ be a point of B_n. Denote by $\pi(p)$ point $(\pi(x_1), \ldots, \pi(x_n))$. Denote by $\pi(C_i)$ the clause that is obtained from $C_i \in F$ by replacing variables $x_1, \ldots, x_n$ with variables $\pi(x_1), \ldots, \pi(x_n)$ respectively. Denote by $\pi(F)$ the CNF formula obtained from F by replacing each clause C_i with $\pi(C_i)$.

Definition 9. *CNF formula F is called **symmetric** with respect to permutation π if CNF formula $\pi(F)$ consists of the same clauses as F. In other words, F is symmetric with respect to π if each clause $\pi(C_i)$ of $\pi(F)$ is identical to a clause $C_k \in F$.*

Proposition 12. *Let p be a point of B_n and C be a clause falsified by p i.e. $C(p)=0$. Let π be a permutation of variables $\{x_1, \ldots, x_n\}$ and $C' = \pi(C)$ and $p' = \pi(p)$. Then $C'(p') = 0$.*

Remark 6. From Proposition 12 it follows that if F is symmetric with respect to a permutation π then $F(p) = F(\pi(p))$. In other words, F takes the same value at points p and $\pi(p)$.

The set of the permutations, with respect to which a CNF formula is symmetric, forms a group. Henceforth, we will denote this group by G. The fact that a permutation π is an element of G will be denoted by $\pi \in G$. Denote by 1 the identity element of G.

Definition 10. *Let B^n be the Boolean space specified by variables $X=\{x_1, \ldots, x_n\}$ and G be a group of permutations specified on X. Denote by **symm(p,p',G)** the following binary relation between points of B_n. A pair of points (p, p') is in $symm(p, p', G)$ if and only if there is $\pi \in G$ such that $p' = \pi(p)$.*

Remark 7. symm(p, p', G) is an equivalence relation and so breaks B^n into equivalence classes. In group theory the set of points that can be produced by applying to p the elements of group G (i.e. the set of points that are in the same equivalence class as p) is called the orbit of p.

Definition 11. *Points p and p' are called **symmetric points** if they are in the same equivalence class of symm(p,p',G).*

Definition 12. *Let F be a CNF formula and P be a subset of $Z(F)$. Set P is called **stable modulo symmetry** with respect to F and transport function g: $P \to F$ if for each $p \in P$, every point $p' \in Nbhd(p, g(p))$ is either in P or there is a point p'' of P that is symmetric to p'.*

Proposition 13. *Let B^n be the Boolean space specified by variables $X = \{x_1, \ldots, x_n\}$. Let p be a point of B^n, C be a clause falsified by p, and point $q \in Nbhd(p, C)$ be obtained from p by flipping the value of variable x_i. Let π be a permutation of variables from X, p' be equal to $\pi(p)$, C' be equal to $\pi(C)$, and $q' \in Nbhd(p', C')$ be obtained from p' by flipping the value of variable $\pi(x_i)$. Then $q' = \pi(q)$. In other words, for each point q of $Nbhd(p, C)$ there is a point q' of $Nbhd(p', C')$ that is symmetric to q.*

Proposition 14. *Let F be a CNF formula, P be a subset of $Z(F)$, and $g : P \to F$ be a transport function. If P is stable modulo symmetry with respect to F and g, then CNF formula F is unsatisfiable.*

Remark 8. The idea of the proof was suggested to the author by Howard Wong-Toi [16].

Proposition 15. *Let $P \subseteq B^n$ be a set of points that is stable with respect to a CNF formula F and transport function $g : P \to F$. Let P' be a subset of P such that for each point p of P that is not in P' there is a point $p' \in P'$ symmetric to p. Then P' is stable with respect to F and g modulo symmetry.*

Definition 13. *Let F be a CNF formula, G be its group of permutations, p be a point of $Z(F)$, and $g: P \to F$ be a transport function. A set $Reachable(p, g, G)$ is called the set of points **reachable from p modulo symmetry** if a) point p is in $Reachable(p, g, G)$ b) each point p' that is reachable from p by means of transport function g is either in $Reachable(p, g, G)$ or there exists point $p'' \in Reachable(p, g, G)$ that is symmetric to p'.*

Proposition 16. *Let F be a CNF formula, G be its group of permutations, p be a point of $Z(F)$, and $g : P \to F$ be a transport function. If set $P=Reachable(p, g, G)$ does not contain a satisfying assignment, then it is stable modulo symmetry with respect to F and g and so F is unsatisfiable.*

Remark 9. From Proposition 16 it follows that a CNF F is satisfiable if and only if, given a point $p \in Z(F)$, a transport function $g : Z(F) \to F$, and a group of permutations G, set *Reachable(p, g, G)* contains a satisfying assignment.

Let F be a CNF formula and G be its group of permutations. According to Proposition 16 when testing the satisfiability of F it is sufficient to construct set *Reachable(p, g, G)*. This set can be built by the algorithm of Sect. 4 in which step 5 is modified in the following way. Before adding a point p'' from *Nbhd(p', C)*\(*Body* $\cup$ *Boundary*) to the *Boundary* it is checked if there is a point p^* of *Boundary* $\cup$ *Body* that is symmetric to p''. If such a point exists, then p'' is not added to the *Boundary*.

7 Computing SSPs of Pigeon-Hole CNF Formulas

In this section, we apply the theory of Sect. 6 to a class of symmetric formulas called pigeon-hole formulas. Pigeon-hole CNF formulas, by means of propositional logic, describe the fact that if $n > m$, n objects (pigeons) cannot be placed in m holes so that no two objects occupy the same hole.

Definition 14. *Let Boolean variable $ph(i, k)$ specify if i-th pigeon is in k-th hole ($ph(i, k) = 1$ means that the pigeon is in the hole). **Pigeon-hole CNF formula** (written $PH(n, m)$) consists of the following two sets of clauses (denote them by $H_1(n, m)$ and $H_2(n, m)$). Set $H_1(n, m)$ consists of n clauses $ph(i, 1) \vee ph(i, 2) \vee \ldots \vee ph(i, m)$, $i = 1, \ldots, n$, i-th clause encoding the fact that i-th pigeon has to be in at least one hole. Set $H_2(n, m)$ consists of $m * n * (n - 1)/2$ clauses $\overline{ph(i, k)} \vee \overline{ph(j, k)}$, $i < j$, $1 \le i, j \le n$, $1 < k < m$, each clause encoding the fact that i-th and j-th pigeons , $i \ne j$, cannot be placed in the same k-th hole.*

Remark 10. Henceforth, we consider only the unsatisfiable CNF formulas $PH(n, m)$ i.e. those of them for which $n > m$.

CNF formula $PH(n, m)$ has $n * m$ variables. To "visualize" points of the Boolean space B^{n*m} we will assume that the variables of $PH(n,m)$ are represented by entries of a matrix M of n rows and m columns. Entry $M(i, j)$ of the matrix corresponds to variable $ph(i, j)$. Then each point of the Boolean space can be viewed as a matrix $n \times m$ whose entries take values 0 or 1. Denote by $M(p)$ the matrix representation of point p. Denote by $S(n,m)$ the following set of points of the Boolean space. $S(n,m)$ consists of two subsets of points denoted by $S_1(n, m)$ and $S_2(n, m)$. A point p is included in subset $S_1(n,m)$ if and only if each row and column of $M(p)$ contains at most one 1-entry. A point p is included in subset $S_2(n,m)$ if and only if matrix $M(p)$ has exactly one column containing two 1-entries and the rest of the columns have at most one 1-entry. Besides, $M(p)$ contains at most 1-entry per row.

It is not hard to see that for a point p from $S_1(n,m)$ there is a clause of $H_1(n,m)$ that p does not satisfy. The latter is true because, since $n > m$ and every column has at most one 1-entry, there is at least one row (say i-th row) of $M(p)$ consisting only of 0-entries. Then p does not satisfy clause $ph(i, 1) \vee$

$ph(i,2) \lor \ldots \lor ph(i,m)$ of $H_1(n,m)$. For each point p of $S_2(n,m)$ there is exactly one clause of $H_2(n,m)$ that p does not satisfy (and maybe some clauses of $H_1(n,m)$). Suppose for example, that in $M(p)$ entries $M(i,k)$ and $M(j,k)$ are equal to 1 (i.e. k-th column is the one containing two 1-entries). Then the only clause of $H_2(n,m)$ point p does not satisfy is $\overline{ph(i,k)} \lor \overline{ph(j,k)}$.

Definition 15. *Denote by g the following transport function mapping $S(n,m)$ to $PH(n,m)$. If $p \in S_1(n,m)$ then $g(p)$ is equal to a clause from $H_1(n,m)$ that p does not satisfy (no matter which). If $p \in S_2(n,m)$ then $g(p)$ is equal to the clause from $H_2(n,m)$ that p does not satisfy.*

Proposition 17. *Set of points $S(n,m) = S_1(n,m) \cup S_2(n,m)$ is stable with respect to the set of clauses $PH(n,m) = H_1(n,m) \cup H_2(n,m)$ and transport function g specified by Definition 15.*

Proposition 18. *Let p be the point all components of which are equal to 0. Let $g : B^{n*m} \to PH(n,m)$ be a transport function. Then set $Reachable(p,g)$ constructed by the algorithm described in Sect. 4 is a subset of $S(n,m)$ if the following heuristic is used when constructing an SSP. If a new point p to be added to the Boundary falsifies clauses from both $H_1(n,m)$ and $H_2(n,m)$, then a clause of $H_2(n,m)$ is selected as the value of $g(p)$.*

The group of permutations of CNF formula $PH(n,m)$ (denote it by $G(PH(n,m))$) is the direct product of groups $S(n)$ and $S(m)$ where $S(n)$ is the group of all the permutations of n pigeons and $S(m)$ is the group of all the permutations of m holes.

Definition 16. *Let p be a point of the Boolean space B^{n*m} of $n*m$ variables in which $PH(n,m)$ is specified. Vector $(c_1, \ldots, c_m)$ where c_j , $1 \leq j \leq m$ is the number of 1-entries in the j-th column of the matrix representation $M(p)$ of p, is called the **column signature** of p. We will say that column signature v' of p' and v'' of p'' are **identical modulo permutation** if vector v' can be transformed to v'' by a permutation.*

Proposition 19. *Let p' and p'' be points of B^{n*m} such that their column signatures are not identical modulo permutation. Then there is no permutation $\pi \in G(PH(n,m))$ such that $p'' = \pi(p')$ i.e. points p'' and p' are not symmetric.*

Proposition 20. *Let p and p' be points of $S(n,m)$ such that their column signatures are identical modulo permutation. Then there is a permutation $\pi^* \in G(PH(n,m))$ such that $p' = \pi^*(p)$ i.e. points p and p' are symmetric*

Proposition 21. *Set $S(n,m)$ contains $2*m+1$ equivalence classes of the relation $symm(p,p',G(PH(n,m)))$.*

Proposition 22. *There is a set of points that is stable with respect to $PH(n,m)$ and transport function g (specified by Definition 15) modulo symmetry, and that consists of $2*m+1$ points.*

Proposition 23. *Let $p \in S_1(n,m)$ be the point in which all variables are assigned 0. Let $Reachable(p, g, G(PH(n, m)))$ be the SSP built by the algorithm described in the end of Sect. 6 where the construction of the transport function is guided by the heuristic described in Proposition 18. Then set $Reachable(p, g, G(PH(n, m)))$ contains no more than $2 * m + 1$ points. The time taken by the algorithm for constructing such a set is $O(m^3 * f)$ where f is the complexity of checking if two points of $S(n, m)$ are symmetric. The number of points visited by the algorithm is $O(m^2)$.*

In Table 2 we compare the performance of SAT-solver Chaff [10] and the proposed algorithm of SSP computation on formulas $PH(n + 1, n)$ (i.e. $n + 1$ pigeons and n holes). Chaff is a general-purpose SAT-solver that is currently considered as the best solver based on the DPLL procedure [5]. We use Chaff not to compare with the proposed algorithm that is specially designed for symmetric formulas but to show that even small pigeon-hole formulas cannot be solved by the best general-purpose SAT-solver. Chaff takes about 1 hour to finish the formula of 12 holes. Besides, it is not hard to see that Chaff's runtime grows up at least 5 times as the size of the instance increases just by one hole. For each of the formulas of Table 2 a set of points that is stable modulo symmetry was computed using the algorithm described in the end of Sect. 6. This algorithm was implemented in a program written in C++. To check whether two points of the Boolean space were symmetric the algorithm just compared their column signatures. Points with identical (modulo permutation) column signatures were assumed to be symmetric. This means that the runtimes for computing SSPs given in Table 2 do not take into account the time needed for symmetry checks. By a symmetry check we mean checking if a point p to be added to the *Boundary* is symmetric to a point p' of the current set *Boundary* $\cup$ *Body*. A more general version of the algorithm, instead of comparing column signatures of p and points of *Boundary* $\cup$ *Body* , would have to check if there is a symmetry of $PH(n+1, n)$ that transforms p to a point of *Boundary* $\cup$ *Body* or vice versa. Nevertheless, Table 2 gives an idea of how easy formulas $PH(n, m)$ can be solved by contructing an SSP modulo symmetry.

8 Conclusions

We show that satisfiability testing of a CNF formula reduces to constructing a stable set of points (SSP). An SSP of a CNF formula can be viewed as an inherent characteristic of this formula. We give a simple procedure for constructing an SSP. We describe a few operations on SSPs that produce new SSPs. These operations can serve the basis of an SSP algebra to be developed in the future. As a practical application we show that the proposed procedure of SSP construction can be easily modified to take into account symmetry (with respect to variable permutation) of CNF formulas. In particular, we consider a class of symmetric CNF formulas called pigeon-hole formulas. We show that the proposed algorithm can prove their unsatisfiability in cubic (in the number of holes) time and there is a stable (modulo symmetry) set of points of linear size.

Table 2. Solving $PH(n+1, n)$ formulas

Number of holes	Number of variables	Chaff Time (sec.)	Computing SSPs modulo symmetry	
			Time (sec.)	Size of SSP modulo symmetry
8	72	2.2	0.05	17
9	90	10.6	0.07	19
10	110	51.0	0.09	21
11	132	447.9	0.13	23
12	156	3532.3	0.17	25
15	240	> 3600	0.38	31
20	420	> 3600	1.04	41
40	1640	> 3600	13.33	81

An interesting direction for future research is to relate SSPs of a CNF formula to the complexity of proving its unsatisfiability. On the practical side, it is important to develop methods that a) can use resolution to reduce the size of SSPs by producing "better" sets of clauses; b) are able to construct an SSP in "chunks" clustering points that are "similar";

References

1. C.A. Brown, L. Finkelstein, P.W. Purdom. *Backtrack searching in the presence of symmetry*. In "Applied algebra, algebraic algorithms and error correcting codes". Sixth international conference, P. 99-110. Springer-Verlag,1988.
2. V. Chvatal, E. Szmeredi. *Many hard examples for resolution*. J. of the ACM,vol. 35, No 4, pp.759-568.
3. W. Cook, C.R. Coullard, G. Turan.*On the complexity of cutting planes proofs*. Discrete Applied Mathematics, 18,1987,25-38.
4. J. Crawford, M. Ginsberg, E. Luks, A. Roy. *Symmetry breaking predicates for search problems*. Fifth International Conference on Principles of Knowledge Representation and Reasoning (KR'96).
5. M. Davis, G. Logemann, D. Loveland. *A Machine program for theorem proving*. Communications of the ACM. -1962. -V.5. -P.394-397.
6. E. Goldberg. *Proving unsatisfiability of CNFs locally*. Proceedings of LICS 2001 Workshop on Theory and Applications of Satisfiability Testing.
7. A.Haken. *The intractability of resolution*. Theor. Comput. Sci. 39 (1985),297-308.
8. B. Krishnamurthy. *Short proofs for tricky formulas*. Acta Informatica 22 (1985) 253-275.
9. D. Mitchell, B.Selman, and H.J. Levesque. *Hard and easy distributions of SAT problems*. Proceedings AAAI-92, San Jose,CA, 459-465.
10. M. Moskewicz, C. Madigan, Y. Zhao, L. Zhang, S. Malik. *Chaff: Engineering an Efficient SAT Solver*. Proceedings of DAC-2001.
11. C. Papadimitriou. *On selecting a satisfying truth assignment*. Proceedings of FOC-91.

12. A. Roy. *Symmetry breaking and fault tolerance in Boolean satisfiability*. PhD thesis. Downloadable from http://www.cs.uoregon.edu/~aroy/
13. B.Selman,H.Kautz,B.Cohen. *Noise strategies for improving local search*. Proceedings of AAAI-94.
14. I. Shlyakhter. *Generating effective symmetry breaking predicates for search problems*. Proceedings of LICS 2001 Workshop on Theory and Applications of Satisfiability Testing
15. A. Urquhart. *The symmetry rule in propositional logic*. Discrete Applied Mathematics 96-97(1999):177-193,1999.
16. H. Wong-Toi. *Private communication*.

9   Appendix

Proof (of Proposition 1). Assume the contrary. Let P be a set of points that is stable with respect to F and a transport function g, and p^* be a satisfying assignment i.e. $F(p^*) = 1$. It is not hard to see that $p^* \notin P$ because each point $p \in P$ is assigned a clause $C = g(p)$ such that $C(p){=}0$ and so $F(p){=}0$. Let p be a point of P that is the closest to p^* in Hamming distance. Denote by C the clause that is assigned to p by transport function g i.e. $C = g(p)$. Denote by Y the set of variables values of which are different in p and p^*.

Let us show that C can not have literals of variables of Y. Assume the contrary, i.e. that C contains a literal of $x \in Y$. Then, since P is stable with respect to F and g, it has to contain the point p' which is obtained from p by flipping the value of x. But then $p' \in P$ is closer to p^* than p. So we have a contradiction. Since $C(p){=}0$ and C does not contain literals of variables whose values are different in p and p^* we have to conclude that $C(p^*) = 0$. This means that p^* is not a solution and so we have a contradiction.   □

Proof (Proposition 2). Since F is unsatisfiable, then $Z(F) = B^n$. For each point $p \in B^n$, condition $Nbhd(p, g(p)) \subseteq B^n$ holds.   □

Proof (of Proposition 3). Denote by Y the set of variables whose values are different in p and s. Since $F(p){=}0$, then $p \in Z(F)$ and function g assigns a clause C to p where $C(p){=}0$. All literals of C are set to 0 by p. On the other hand, since s is a solution then at least one literal of C is set by s to 1. Then C has at least one literal of a variable from Y. Flipping the value of this variable of Y in p we obtain a point p' which is closer to point s by 1 (in Hamming distance). Point p' is reachable from p by means of transport function g. If $|Y| > 1$, then p' cannot be a satisfying assignment since, by our assumption, s is the closest to p satisfying assignment. Going on in this manner we reach satisfying assignment s in $|Y|$ steps.   □

Proof (of Proposition 4). Assume the contrary, i.e. that there is a point $p^* \in Reachable(p, g)$ that is not in P. Let H be a path from p to p^*. Denote by p'' the first point in the sequence of points specified by H that is not in P. (Points are numbered from p to p^*). Denote by p' the point preceding p'' in H. Point p' is in P and the latter is stable with respect to F and g. So $Nbhd(p', g(p')) \subseteq P$. Point p'' is in $Nbhd(p', g(p'))$ and so it has to be in P. We have a contradiction.   □

Proof (of Proposition 5). Assume the contrary, i.e. that $Reachable(p,g)$ is not stable. Then there exists a point p' of $Reachable(p,g)$ (and so reachable from p) such that a point p'' of $Nbhd(p',g(p'))$ is not in $Reachable(p,g)$. Since p'' is reachable from p' it is also reachable from p. We have a contradiction.   □

Proof (of Proposition 6). Denote by g'' the transport function $P'' \rightarrow F$ such that $g''(p) = g(p)$ if $p \in P$ and $g''(p) = g'(p)$ if $p \in P''\backslash P$. Let p be a point of P''. Consider the following two cases.

1) $p \in P$. Since P is stable with respect to g then $Nbhd(p, g(p)) \subseteq P$. Since $g''(p) = g(p)$ it is also true that $Nbhd(p, g''(p)) \subseteq P$ and so $Nbhd(p, g''(p)) \subseteq P''$.

2) $p \in P''\backslash P$. Since $P'' = P \cup P'$ then $P''\backslash P \subseteq P'$ and so $p \in P'$. Since P' is stable with respect to g' then $Nbhd(p, g'(p)) \subseteq P'$. Since $g''(p) = g'(p)$ it is also true that $Nbhd(p, g''(p)) \subseteq P'$ and so $Nbhd(p,g''(p)) \subseteq P''$.

Since for any point $p \in P''$ it is true that $Nbhd(p, g''(p)) \subseteq P''$, then P'' is stable with respect to F and transport function g''.   □

Proof (of Proposition 7). Assume the contrary, i.e. that set P^* is not stable. Then there is a point $p' \in P^*$ such that some point p'' from $Nbhd(p', g(p'))$ is not in P^*. Since P is stable then $p'' \in P$. Since $p'' \in P\backslash P^*$ point p is reachable from p'' (all points from which there is no path to p are in P^*). On the other hand, there is a path from p' to p''. This means that there is a path from p' to p going through p'', which contradicts the fact that $p' \in P^*$.   □

Proof (of Proposition 8). According to Proposition 4 for any point $p_i \in P$ set $Reachable(p_i, g)$ is a subset of P. So $Reachable(p_1, g) \cup \ldots \cup Reachable(p_k, g) \subseteq P$. On the other hand, set $Reachable(p_i, g)$ contains point p_i. So $Reachable(p_1, g) \cup \ldots \cup Reachable(p_k, g) \supseteq P$.   □

Proof (of Proposition 9). By definition, set $Reachable(p,g)$ includes all the points that are reachable from p. Since point p' is reachable from p, then any point that is reachable from p' is also reachable from p.   □

Proof (of Proposition 10). Let p'' be a point of P. Then $Reachable(p'', g) \subseteq Reachable(p, g)$ and $Reachable(p'', g) \subseteq Reachable(p', g)$ because any point reachable from p'' is also reachable from p and p'. Hence $Reachable(p'', g) \subseteq P$. Then P can be represented as $Reachable(p_1, g) \cup \ldots \cup Reachable(p_m, g)$ where $p_1, \ldots, p_m$ are the points from which P consists of. Hence P can be represented as the union of stable sets of points. According to Proposition 6 set P is stable as well.   □

Proof (of Proposition 11). Let $P = \{p_1, \ldots, p_k\}$ and $P' = \{p'_1, \ldots, p'_d\}$. From Proposition 8 it follows that $P = Reachable(p_1, g) \cup \ldots \cup Reachable(p_k, g)$ and $P' = Reachable(p'_1, g) \cup \ldots \cup Reachable(p'_d, g)$. Then set $P \cap P'$ can be represented as the union of $k * d$ sets $Reachable(p_i, g) \cap Reachable(p'_j, g)$, $i = 1, \ldots, k$, $j = 1, \ldots, d$. According to Proposition 10 set $Reachable(p_i, g) \cap Reachable(p'_j, g)$ is either empty or stable . Then set $P \cap P'$ is either empty (if every set $Reachable(p_i, g) \cap Reachable(p'_j, g)$ is empty) or it is the union of stable sets. In the latter case according to Proposition 6 set $P \cap P'$ is stable.   □

Proof (of Proposition 12). Let $\delta(x_i)$ be the literal of a variable x_i that is present in C. This literal is set to 0 by the value of x_i in p. Variable x_i is mapped to $\pi(x_i)$ in clause C' and point p'. Then the value of $\pi(x_i)$ at point p' is the same as that of x_i in p. So the value of literal $\delta(\pi(x_i))$ at point p' is the same as the value of $\delta(x_i)$ in p i.e. 0. Hence clause C' is falsified by p'.   □

Proof (of Proposition 13). The value of variable x_k, $k \neq i$ in q is the same as in p. Besides, the value of variable $\pi(x_k)$ in q' is the same as in p' (q' is obtained from p' by changing the value of variable $\pi(x_i)$ and since $k \neq i$ then $\pi(x_k) \neq \pi(x_i)$). Since $p' = \pi(p)$ then the value of x_k in q is the same as the value of variable $\pi(x_k)$ in q'. On the other hand, the value of variable x_i in q is obtained by negation of the value of x_i in p. The value of variable $\pi(x_i)$ in q' is obtained by negation of the value of $\pi(x_i)$ in p'. Hence the values of variable x_i in q and variable $\pi(x_i)$ in q' are the same. So $q' = \pi(q)$.   □

Proof (of Proposition 14). Denote by $K(p)$ the set of all points that are symmetric to point p i.e. that are in the same equivalence class of the relation *symm* as p. Denote by $K(P)$ the union of the sets $K(p)$, $p \in P$. Extend the domain of transport function g from P to $K(P)$ in the following way. Suppose p' is a point that is in $K(P)$ but not in P. Then there is a point $p \in P$ that is symmetric to p' and so $p' = \pi(p)$, $\pi \in G$. We assign $C' = \pi(C)$, $C = g(p)$ as the value of g at p'. If there is more than one point of P that is symmetric to p', we pick any of them.

Now we show that $K(P)$ is stable with respect to F and g: $K(P) \rightarrow F$. Let p' be a point of $K(P)$. Then there is a point p of P that is symmetric to p' and so $p' = \pi(p)$. Then from Proposition 13 it follows that for any point q of $Nbhd(p, g(p))$ there is a point $q' \in Nbhd(p', g(p'))$ such that $q' = \pi(q)$. On the other hand, since P is stable modulo symmetry, then for any point q of $Nbhd(p, g(p))$ there is a point $q'' \in P$ symmetric to q and so $q = \pi^*(q'')$, $\pi^* \in G$ (π^* may be equal to $1 \in G$ if q is in P). Then $q' = \pi(\pi^*(q''))$. Hence q' is symmetric to $q'' \in P$ and so $q' \in K(P)$. This means that $Nbhd(p', g(p')) \subseteq K(P)$ and so $K(P)$ is stable. Then according to Proposition 1 CNF formula F is unsatisfiable.   □

Proof (of Proposition 15). Let p' be a point of P'. Let q' be a point of $Nbhd(p', g(p'))$. Point p' is in P because $P' \subseteq P$. Since P is a stable set then $q' \in P$. From the definition of set P' it follows that if q' is not in P' then there is a point $r' \in P'$ that is symmetric to q'. So each point q' of $Nbhd(p', g(p'))$ is either in P' or there is a point of P' that is symmetric to q'.   □

Proof (of Proposition 16). Assume the contrary, i.e. that P is not stable modulo symmetry. Then there is a point $p' \in P$ (reachable from p modulo symmetry) such that a point p'' of $Nbhd(p', g(p'))$ is not in P and P does not contain a point symmetric to p''. On the other hand, p'' is reachable from p' and so it is reachable from p modulo symmetry. We have a contradiction.   □

Proof (of Proposition 17). Let p be a point from $S(n, m)$. Consider the following two alternatives.

1) $p \in S_1(n, m)$. Then the matrix representation $M(p)$ of p has at least one row (say i-th row) consisting only of 0-entries. Point p falsifies at least one clause C from $H_1(n,m)$. According to Definition 15 one of the clauses of $H_1(n, m)$ falsified by p is assigned to p by the transport function g. Assume that it is clause $C = \overline{ph(i, 1)} \vee \overline{ph(i, 2)} \vee ... \vee \overline{ph(i, m)})$. Let us show that $Nbhd(p, C) \subseteq S_1(n,m) \cup S_2(n,m)$. Denote by p' the point obtained from p by flipping the value of variable $ph(i, j)$, $1 \leq j \leq m$. By definition, no column of $M(p)$ contains more than one 1-entry. So we have two alternatives. a) If j-th column of $M(p)$ contains a 1-entry then the matrix representation $M(p')$ of p' contains exactly one column (namely, j-th column) that contains two 1-entries. Besides, all rows of $M(p')$ still contain at most one 1-entry. (We have added a 1-entry to the i-th row that did not contain any 1-entries in $M(p)$.) Then $p' \in S_2(n, m)$. b) If j-th column of $M(p)$ does not contain a 1-entry, then $M(p')$ does not contain columns having two 1-entries and so $p' \in S_1(n,m)$. In either case $Nbhd(p, C) \subseteq S_1(n, m) \cup S_2(n, m)$.

2) $p \in S_2(n,m)$. Then the matrix representation $M(p)$ of p has exactly one column (say j-th column) that has two 1-entries. Let us assume that j-th column $M(p)$ has 1-entries in i-th and k-th rows. Point p falsifies exactly one clause of $H_2(n,m)$, namely, clause $C = \overline{ph(i, j)} \vee \overline{ph(k, j)}$. According to Definition 15 this clause is assigned to p by the transport function g. Set $Nbhd(p, C)$ consists of two points obtained from p by flipping the value of $ph(i, j)$ or $ph(k, j)$. Let p' be either point of $Nbhd(p, C)$. Matrix $M(p')$ does not have a column of two 1-entries any more (because one 1-entry of j-th column has disappeared). Besides, $M(p')$ has at most one 1-entry per row. Then $p' \in S_1(n, m)$. Hence $Nbhd(p, C) \subseteq S_1(n, m)$ and so $Nbhd(p, C) \subseteq S_1(n, m) \cup S_2(n, m)$. $\qquad\square$

Proof (of Proposition 18). We prove the proposition by induction. Denote by *Boundary*(s) and *Body*(s) the sets *Boundary* and *Body* after performing s steps of the algorithm. Denote by g_s the transport function after performing s steps. Our induction hypothesis is that after performing s steps of the algorithm set *Boundary*$(s) \cup Body(s)$ is a subset of $S(n, m)$ and besides, g_s satisfies Definition 15 (at s points wherein the function g_s has been specified). First we need to check the that hypothesis holds for $s=1$. The starting point p is in $S_1(n, m)$. Besides, p falsifies only clauses from $H_1(n, m)$. So if we assign a clause C of $H_1(n, m)$ as the value of g_1 at point p, then function g_1 satisfies Definition 15.

Now we prove that from the fact the hypothesis holds after performing s steps of the algorithm, it follows that it also holds after $s + 1$ steps. Let p' be the point of *Boundary*(s) chosen at step $s + 1$. First let us show that transport function g_{s+1} satisfies Definition 15. If p' is in $S_1(n, m)$ then it falsifies only clauses from $H_1(n, m)$. So no matter which falsified clause is picked as the value of transport function g_{s+1} at point p', g_{s+1} satisfies Definition 15. If p' is in $S_2(n,m)$ then it falsifies exactly one clause of $H_2(n, m)$ and maybe some clauses of $H_1(n, m)$. Our heuristic makes us select the falsified clause of $H_2(n, m)$ as the value of g at point p'. So again transport function g_{s+1} satisfies Definition 15. Then we can apply arguments of Proposition 17 to show that from $p' \in S(n, m)$ it follows that $Nbhd(p', g_{s+1}(p'))$ is a subset of $S(n, m)$. Hence *Boundary*$(s + 1) \cup Body(s + 1)$ is a subset of $S(n, m)$. $\qquad\square$

Proof (of Proposition 19). Assume the contrary. Let points p and p' be symmetric but their signatures are not identical modulo permutation. Since p and p' are symmetric, then matrix $M(p')$ can be obtained by a permutation of rows and/or columns of $M(p)$. A permutation of rows cannot change the column signature of $M(p)$ while a permutation of columns can only permute components of the column signature of $M(p)$. So we have a contradiction.   □

Proof (of Proposition 20). Let us show that there are permutations $\pi,\pi' \in G(PH(n,m))$ such that $q = \pi(p)$ and $q = \pi'(p')$, i.e. that p and q and p' and q are in the same equivalence class. (This would mean that p and p' have to be in the same equivalence class as well and so p and p' are symmetric).

Since $p,p' \in S(n,m)$ then both p and p' have only columns containing no more than two 1-entries. Denote by $n_0(p),n_1(p),n_2(p)$ the numbers of columns of $M(p)$ containing zero, one and two 1-entries respectively ($n_2(p)$ can be equal only to 0 or 1). Since column signatures of p and p' are identical modulo permutation then $n_0(p) = n_0(p'),n_1(p) = n_1(p'),n_2(p) = n_2(p')$. Since we want to find q such that $q = \pi(p)$ and $q = \pi'(p')$ then $n_0(q),n_1(q),n_2(q)$ must be the same as for points p and p'. Let q be the point of $S(n,m)$ such that in $M(q)$ all the columns with one 1-entry go first, then they are followed by a column of two 1-entries (if such a column exists in $M(q)$) and the rest of the columns of $M(q)$ do not contain 1-entries. Besides, if j-th column of $M(q)$ contains only one 1-entry, then this 1-entry is located in the j-th row. If j-th column of $M(q)$ contains two 1-entries then they are located in j-th and $(j+1)$-th rows. It is not hard to see that each row of $M(q)$ contains at most one 1-entry and so $q \in S(n,m)$.

Point p can be transformed to q by a permutation $\pi = \pi_1\pi_2$ where π_1 and π_2 are defined as follows. π_1 is a permutation of columns of matrix $M(p)$ that makes $n_1(p)$ columns having only one 1-entry the first columns of $M(\pi_1(p))$. Besides, permutation π_1 makes the column of $M(p)$ that has two 1-entries (if such a column exists) the $(n_1(p)+1)$-th column of $M(\pi_1(p))$. π_2 is the permutation of rows of matrix $M(\pi_1(p))$ that places the 1-entry of j-th column, $1 \le j \le n_1(p)$ in the j-th row of $M(\pi_2(\pi_1(p)))$. Besides, permutation π_2 places the two 1-entries of the $(n_1(p)+1)$-th column of $M(\pi_1(p))$ (if such a column with two 1-entries exists) in $(n_1(p)+1)$-th and $(n_1(p)+2)$-th rows of $M(\pi_2(\pi_1(p)))$ respectively. Since all rows of $M(\pi_1(p))$ have at most one 1-entry, permutation π_2 always exists. It is not hard to see that $M(\pi_2(\pi_1(p)))$ is equal to $M(q)$ described above. The same procedure can be applied to point p'.   □

Proof (of Proposition 21). First of all, it is not hard to see that points from $S_1(n,m)$ and $S_2(n,m)$ have different column signatures (for a point p of $S_2(n,m)$ matrix $M(p)$ has a column with two 1-entries, while points of $S_1(n,m)$ do not have such columns in their matrix representation). This means that no equivalence class contains points from both $S_1(n,m)$ and $S_2(n,m)$. For a point p of $S_1(n,m)$ matrix $M(p)$ can have k columns with one 1-entry where k ranges from 0 to m. From Proposition 19 and Proposition 20 it follows that points with the same value of k in their signatures are in the same equivalence class while points with different values of k in their signatures are in different equivalence classes. So there are $m+1$ equivalence classes in $S_1(n,m)$.

For a point of $S_2(n, m)$ matrix $M(p)$ has exactly one column with two 1-entries. Besides, $M(p)$ can have k columns with one 1-entry where k ranges from 0 to $m - 1$. Points with the same value of k in their signatures are in the same equivalence class while points with different value of k in their signatures are in different equivalence classes. So there are m equivalence classes in $S_2(n, m)$. Hence the total number of equivalence classes in $S(n, m)$ is $2 * m + 1$.   □

Proof (of Proposition 22). According to Proposition 21 set $S(n,m)$ consists of $2*m+1$ equivalence classes. Let S' be a set consisting of $2*m+1$ points where each point is a representative of a different equivalence class. According to Proposition 15 set S' is stable with respect to F and g modulo symmetry.   □

Proof (of Proposition 23). The algorithm can have only two kinds of steps. At a step of the first kind at least one point of $Nbhd(p, g(p))$ (where p is the point of the *Boundary* picked at the current step) is added to the *Boundary*. At a step of the second kind no new points are added to the *Boundary* (because each point of p' of $Nbhd(p,g(p))$ is either in *Body* ∪ *Boundary* or the latter contains a point p'' that is symmetric to p'). The number of steps of the first kind is less or equal to $2*m+1$. Indeed, the total number of points contained in *Body* ∪ *Boundary* cannot exceed the number of equivalence classes (which is equal to $2*m+1$) because no new point is added to *Boundary* if it is symmetric to a point of *Body* ∪ *Boundary*. The number of steps of the second kind is also less or equal to $2*m+1$. The reason is that at each step of the second kind a point of the *Boundary* is moved to the *Body* and the total number of points that can appear in the *Boundary* is bounded by the number of equivalence classes in $S(n, m)$ i.e. by $2*m+1$. So the total number of steps in the algorithm is bounded by $2*(2*m+1)$. At each step of the first kind at most m neighborhood points can be generated. Each point is checked if it is symmetric to a point of *Body* ∪ *Boundary*. The complexity of this operation is bounded by $(2 * m + 1) * f$ where $2 * m + 1$ is the maximum number of points set *Body* ∪ *Boundary* can have and f is the complexity of checking whether two points of $S(n, m)$ are symmetric. So the time complexity of the algorithm is $O(m^3 * f)$. Since at most m points can be reached at each step, then the total number of points reached by the algorithm is bounded by $m * 2 * (2 * m + 1)$.   □

A Note on Symmetry Heuristics in SEM

Thierry Boy de la Tour

LEIBNIZ - IMAG
46, avenue Félix Viallet, 38031 Grenoble Cedex, FRANCE
Thierry.Boy-de-la-Tour@imag.fr

Abstract. We analyse two symmetry heuristics, i.e. heuristics that reduce the search space through properties of symmetry, in the finite model generator SEM. These are SEM's original LNH, and a recent extension XLNH. Our aim is to show how a simple group-theoretic framework brings much clarity in this matter, especially through group actions. Both heuristics can be seen as computationally efficient ways of applying a general symmetry pruning theorem. Moreover, simple combinatorics provide some insight into the relative performances of these heuristics. We finally expose a fundamental difficulty in making SEM symmetry efficient by symmetry pruning.

1   Introduction

It has become customary to consider mechanization of first-order logic not only under its provability problem, but also under its satisfiability problem, even though this is not semi-decidable. Many systems exist for the (decidable) bounded finite satisfiability problem, and there is no need to list them here. These systems rely on explicit representations of finite interpretations, which in some sense is naïve. The reason is that these interpretations are rather complex objects and do not have simple, straightforward, *canonical* representations. Hence the necessity to cope with many different, though *isomorphic* representations, which are indistinguishable from a logical point of view, and ought to be considered as redundant with respect to the satisfiability of a formula.

It has therefore been recognized that some amount of pruning could be obtained by granting some concern to this kind of redundancy. Indeed, the systems SEM (through LNH, see [9] and below) and FMC (see [6]) have been enriched with some mechanisms to handle some symmetries, and it has proved very successful. It is therefore a natural idea to try to extend these mechanisms so that they handle some more symmetries, as was done in [2] with XLNH.

However, the symmetries handled in [9] and [6] were relatively simple, and there was no need for a complex formalisation in order to present and justify them. The same cannot be said of [2], and as more and more complex symmetries may be put to use, the need for a clear and powerful framework is less and less avoidable. It is the aim of this paper to show that such a framework is to be found in group theory, especially through the notion of group actions.

A. Voronkov (Ed.): CADE-18, LNAI 2392, pp. 181–194, 2002.
© Springer-Verlag Berlin Heidelberg 2002

In Section 2 we develop the basic notions pertaining to SEM's search process. For sake of simplicity, we retain an abstract view of it, and assume very few properties, only as much as symmetry pruning requires. The following section develops the group theoretic notions we need; only subgroups of a given "group of reference" will be used, but these will act on different structures. By joining these formalisms in Section 4, it is easy to prove a general symmetry pruning theorem.

In this light we analyse LNH, which is fairly easy, in Section 5. More precisely, the pruning mechanism of LNH is a special case of the symmetry pruning theorem, and the cell ordering of LNH is an obvious way of keeping the amount of pruning high. In Section 6, we focus on the pruning part of XLNH, and show that it also stems from the general theorem, though in a much more subtle way than LNH. We next concentrate on the generating method in XLNH, first on a particularly manageable restriction in Section 7, and then on the general case in Section 8, where a generalized notion of search tree is introduced. We show how the generation of complex objects is somehow necessary and hardly compatible with SEM's search tree.

2   The Basic Search Tree

We are trying to build a model of a fixed formula, for a fixed signature Σ, in a fixed finite domain $\mathfrak{D}$. Σ is a sorted first-order signature, each symbol being defined with a typing rule. Σ_n is the set of symbols of arity n. $\mathfrak{D}$ is the disjoint union of the sorts' domains. We may use a distinguished boolean sort, whose domain contains the truth values. This allows to consider predicate symbols as function symbols whose range sort is the boolean sort. This formalisation makes things even simpler than by considering only non-sorted logic. Of course, we have restrictions on the typing rules: only first and second order types are admitted (constants and functions), and the boolean sort cannot occur as a domain sort.

A *cell* is an element of $\bigcup_{n \in \mathbb{N}} \Sigma_n \times \mathfrak{D}^n$, obeying the typing rules as given in the sorted signature Σ; the set of cells will be noted $\mathfrak{C}$. A cell $\langle f, v_1, \ldots, v_n \rangle$ will be noted $f[v_1, \ldots, v_n]$. A *partial interpretation* is a partial function from $\mathfrak{C}$ to $\mathfrak{D}$, obeying the typing rules. A *full interpretation* is a partial interpretation whose domain is $\mathfrak{C}$.

The set of partial interpretations will be noted $\mathfrak{I}$, its elements $\mathcal{I}, \mathcal{J}, \ldots$ Partial interpretations can be compared w.r.t. inclusion: we say that $\mathcal{J}$ *extends* $\mathcal{I}$, or is an *extension* of $\mathcal{I}$, iff $\mathcal{I} \subseteq \mathcal{J}$, meaning that the two functions are equal on the domain of $\mathcal{I}$. We note $\mathrm{Ext}(\mathcal{I})$ the set of full interpretations that are extensions of $\mathcal{I}$. For simplicity we note $+$ the disjoint union of partial interpretations, and $c \hookrightarrow v$ the partial interpretation of domain $\{c\}$ mapping $c \in \mathfrak{C}$ to $v \in \mathfrak{D}$.

For $n > 0$, $f \in \Sigma_n$ and $\mathcal{I} \in \mathfrak{I}$, we note $f_{\mathcal{I}}$ the partial function from $\mathfrak{D}^n$ to $\mathfrak{D}$, defined on the elements $\langle v_1, \ldots, v_n \rangle \in \mathfrak{D}^n$ such that the cell $f[v_1, \ldots, v_n]$ is in $\mathcal{I}$'s domain, by $f_{\mathcal{I}}(v_1, \ldots, v_n) = \mathcal{I}(f[v_1, \ldots, v_n])$.

Example 1. We consider a signature with one non boolean sort s, the boolean sort o, a constant symbol $c : s$ and a predicate symbol $P : s \to o$. We interpret

s as $\{0, 1, 2\}$ and o as $\{\top, \bot\}$; then $\mathfrak{D} = \{0, 1, 2, \top, \bot\}$. An example of partial interpretation is $\mathcal{I} = c \hookrightarrow 0 + P[0] \hookrightarrow \top + P[1] \hookrightarrow \bot$. Then $c_{\mathcal{I}} = 0$ and $P_{\mathcal{I}} = \{\langle 0, \top\rangle, \langle 1, \bot\rangle\}$.

It is clear that any Σ-formula gets a truth value through a full interpretation, but generally not through a partial interpretation. However, it is often the case that a partial interpretation is enough to compute the truth value of a formula; for example $\exists x\ P(x)$ only needs a one-cell partial interpretation to be satisfied. Hence we may assume a partial evaluation function Val (the formula being fixed) with the following basic property.

Definition 1. *Let* Val *be a partial function from $\mathfrak{I}$ to the set of truth values whose domain includes all full interpretations and, when defined on $\mathcal{I} \in \mathfrak{I}$, yields a value $v = \mathrm{Val}(\mathcal{I})$ such that $\mathrm{Val}(\mathrm{Ext}(\mathcal{I})) = \{v\}$.*

Notice that we do not require the domain of this evaluation function to include all extensions of its elements (as is the case in SEM), i.e. such that $\mathrm{Val}(\mathcal{I}) = v \Rightarrow \forall \mathcal{J} \supseteq \mathcal{I}, \mathrm{Val}(\mathcal{J}) = v$. This means that partial evaluations may be based on properties that are not stable by extension.

Neither do we require the converse of this basic property, that if the evaluation is invariant on $\mathrm{Ext}(\mathcal{I})$ (i.e. if $\mathrm{Val}(\mathrm{Ext}(\mathcal{I}))$ is a singleton) we should get this value as $\mathrm{Val}(\mathcal{I})$, resulting in a "complete" evaluation on partial interpretations. This would clearly be too strong a requirement for the evaluation to be efficiently computable: for example, any unsatisfiable formula would yield an evaluation function defined and false everywhere, and especially on the empty partial interpretation. Between this complete evaluation and SEM's, there may be some rewarding functions yielding better pruning. The following results would still apply.

The evaluation function is actually a fundamental part of SEM, and is rather complex: see [9], [8]. It works by turning the formula into constraints, and by simplifying these constraints each time an extension is proposed. Even if a truth value cannot be figured out, it simplifies the evaluations of further extensions, and therefore factorizes computational costs. It also yields restricted domains D_c for new cells c. Hence the program computing the evaluation function has other arguments than $\mathcal{I}$. However, we need only keep a very abstract view of this process in order to account for symmetry pruning in the search space.

We can now describe the basic search procedure. Starting from a partial interpretation $\mathcal{I}$, we backtrack if $\mathrm{Val}(\mathcal{I})$ yields a truth value (if true, the search for a model stops). Otherwise we consider a new cell c, and for each of its possible values $v \in D_c$ (this depends on $\mathcal{I}$) recursively search with $\mathcal{I} + c \hookrightarrow v$. The search space is therefore a tree[1], rooted at the empty partial interpretation; its maximal depth is the number of cells. It is of course important to select c with few possible values, the number of which is restricted in SEM by the propagation techniques used in the evaluation process.

---

[1] more precisely a planar tree: the descendants of a node are linearly ordered, according to chronology.

3   A Group Theoretic Framework

We now come to the notions we need in order to speak of *symmetries* (e.g. between elements of $\mathfrak{D}$) and *isomorphisms* (between partial interpretations). Isomorphisms are structure preserving bijective functions, a property preserved by function composition. Since $\mathfrak{D}$ is fixed, composition is untyped, and is therefore a (non commutative) group operation. It is in fact convenient to focus on this group structure (see for example [5]).

It is first interesting to question the fact that $\mathfrak{D}$ is fixed: why is it at all the case? We are searching for a model of a formula, having a fixed cardinality, but the domain of this model could be anything. The key point is that any interpretation whose domain has the same cardinality as $\mathfrak{D}$ is isomorphic to an interpretation on $\mathfrak{D}$, which is easy to prove. In other words: any isomorphism class of interpretations of a given cardinality meets the set of interpretations on a fixed domain of that cardinality. Restricting the search to a single domain, as is the case of all finite model builders, is at the root an application of pruning by isomorphisms.

Due to this restriction to $\mathfrak{D}$, the set of isomorphisms is a permutation group on $\mathfrak{D}$; it has a fundamental property to be expressed later[2]. It will be a subgroup[3] of the group of all permutations of $\mathfrak{D}$, known as the *symmetric* group on $\mathfrak{D}$, noted $\mathrm{Sym}(\mathfrak{D})$. Its identity is noted i; this is of course the identity function on $\mathfrak{D}$. For $\sigma \in \mathrm{Sym}(\mathfrak{D})$ and $v \in \mathfrak{D}$, the value of the function σ on v is noted v^σ. Consequently, for $\nu \in \mathrm{Sym}(\mathfrak{D})$, $(v^\sigma)^\nu$ is noted $v^{\sigma\nu}$, which explains why function composition is reversed, i.e. $\sigma\nu = \nu \circ \sigma$. It is standard to group theory to adopt the multiplicative notation for non commutative group operations.

An *action*[4] of a group G on a set O is a binary function from $O \times G$ to O, usually noted exponentially, such that $\forall o \in O, \forall \sigma, \nu \in G, o^i = o$ and $o^{\sigma\nu} = (o^\sigma)^\nu$. The exponential notation stresses the fact that function application is an action of a permutation group on the support set, here $\mathfrak{D}$. However, the notation may clearly be ambiguous if more than one action is being used, as will be the case in the sequel.

But no ambiguity will arise, due to the fact that only *natural* actions will be used, based on the structure of O. Suppose an action is defined on a set A, then the natural extension of the action of G to the power set 2^A is defined by: $\forall \sigma \in G, \forall S \subseteq A, S^\sigma = \{x^\sigma / x \in S\}$. The reader may check that this is indeed an action of G on 2^A. Consequently, if actions of G are defined on A and B, then the action on $A \times B$ is given by $\forall \langle x, y \rangle \in A \times B, \langle x, y \rangle^\sigma = \langle x^\sigma, y^\sigma \rangle$; and the action on partial functions f from A to B is given by $\forall x \in A, f^\sigma(x^\sigma) = f(x)^\sigma$ (i.e. $\langle x, y \rangle \in f \Leftrightarrow \langle x^\sigma, y^\sigma \rangle \in f^\sigma$). In general, the meaning of o^σ depends only on the type of o, so that for any set O we will refer to *the* action of G on O.

---

[2] We will actually consider this property as a *definition* of isomorphisms.

[3] A subset H of a group G is a subgroup iff $\forall a, b \in H, ab \in H$ and $a^{-1} \in H$. In finite groups, the latter is a consequence of the former.

[4] The literature also refers to this notion as a group *operation*, but there is a possible confusion with the operation *of* the group.

In case O is not build on $\mathfrak{D}$, we simply define this action as the *trivial* one, i.e. $\forall o \in O, \forall \sigma \in G, o^\sigma = o$.

In the example above, the set of partial functions from A to B is a subset of $2^{A \times B}$, and the action on partial functions is a restriction of the (natural) action on sets of tuples: this is only possible because the set of partial functions is stable through this natural action. Now we should note that, in order to define correctly an action on the set $\mathfrak{I}$ of partial interpretations on $\mathfrak{D}$, we have to do it on the set $\mathfrak{C}$ of cells, and we have the problem that for some permutation σ of $\mathfrak{D}$, and some cell $f[v_1, \ldots, v_n] \in \mathfrak{C}$, we may not have $f[v_1, \ldots, v_n]^\sigma = f[v_1^\sigma, \ldots, v_n^\sigma] \in \mathfrak{C}$, due to the typing rules. The solution is simply to restrict our attention to a group of σ that do preserve the set $\mathfrak{C}$ (the set of $\mathfrak{C}$- preserving permutations is indeed a group).

But we are not only interested in cells: our aim is basically to preserve the relation of satisfaction of the logic we consider. It is therefore natural to define the group $\mathfrak{G}$ by the following *fundamental property*.

Definition 2. $\mathfrak{G}$ *is the set of permutations σ of $\mathfrak{D}$ such that for any full interpretation $\mathcal{I}$ we have $\mathrm{Val}(\mathcal{I}^\sigma) = \mathrm{Val}(\mathcal{I})$. We call* isomorphisms *the elements of $\mathfrak{G}$, which is obviously a group.*

This implies that truth values are fixpoints of these permutations, and generally that sorts are preserved by the elements of $\mathfrak{G}$. Defining isomorphisms through the fundamental property avoids a convoluted definition of isomorphisms, which would involve sorts, function and predicate symbols, etc. Notice that the property is limited to full interpretations: we do not require the evaluation of partial interpretations to be invariant under isomorphisms.

We do not attempt here to describe explicitly the group $\mathfrak{G}$; it depends on the signature, the formula, the domain $\mathfrak{D}$. This could be complex, and the point in defining $\mathfrak{G}$ as above is chiefly to summon a formal apparatus that stands for clarity and expressive power. The few notions we need are now going to be introduced.

Definition 3. *For a set O on which an action of $\mathfrak{G}$ is defined, and $o \in O$, we note $\mathrm{Aut}(o) = \{\sigma \in \mathfrak{G}/o^\sigma = o\}$; this is obviously a subgroup of $\mathfrak{G}$, and is called the* automorphism group *of o. For any group G and set O on which G has an action, and for $o \in O$, the G-orbit o^G of o is the set $\{o^\sigma/\sigma \in G\}$. A G-orbit in O is the G-orbit of an element of O. A G-orbit is* trivial *if it is restricted to one element.*

The set of G-orbits in O is a partition of O. Particularly, the $\mathfrak{G}$-orbits in $\mathfrak{I}$ are the isomorphism classes we are interested in.

Example 2. Let us consider a small example. We consider a one-sort monadic function symbol f (i.e. the domain and range sorts are equal), to be interpreted in a five-elements domain, say $\{0, 1, 2, 3, 4\}$. Here $\mathfrak{G}$ is the set of permutations of $\{0, 1, 2, 3, 4\}$, that is the symmetric group S_5. Let $\mathcal{I} = f[0] \hookrightarrow 1 + f[1] \hookrightarrow 0$; this is a partial interpretation. We consider the permutation $(0\ 1)$ (swapping 0 and 1); we have $(f[0] \hookrightarrow 1)^{(0\ 1)} = f[1] \hookrightarrow 0$ and $(f[1] \hookrightarrow 0)^{(0\ 1)} = f[0] \hookrightarrow 1$, so obviously $\mathcal{I}^{(0\ 1)} = \mathcal{I}$, i.e. $(0\ 1) \in \mathrm{Aut}(\mathcal{I})$. It is easy to see that $\mathrm{Aut}(\mathcal{I})$ is generated[5] by $(0\ 1), (2\ 3\ 4)$ and $(3\ 4)$; it has 12 elements. The $\mathrm{Aut}(\mathcal{I})$-orbits in $\{0, 1, 2, 3, 4\}$ are $\{0, 1\}$ and $\{2, 3, 4\}$.

4   Symmetry Pruning

In this group theoretic framework it is very easy to prove a general theorem justifying some pruning in the search tree, by means of symmetries. We first prove a lemma to show that this tree behaves coherently under the action of $\mathfrak{G}$.

Lemma 1. *For all $\mathcal{I}, \mathcal{J} \in \mathfrak{I}, \sigma \in \mathfrak{G}, c \in \mathfrak{C}, v \in \mathfrak{D}$, we have*

1. $(c \hookrightarrow v)^\sigma = c^\sigma \hookrightarrow v^\sigma$,
2. *if C is the domain of $\mathcal{I}$, then $\mathcal{I}^\sigma$'s domain is C^σ,*
3. $(\mathcal{I} + \mathcal{J})^\sigma = \mathcal{I}^\sigma + \mathcal{J}^\sigma$,
4. $\mathrm{Ext}(\mathcal{I}^\sigma) = \mathrm{Ext}(\mathcal{I})^\sigma$.

Proof. 1. Trivial.
2. Let C' be the domain of $\mathcal{I}^\sigma$, for all $c \in \mathfrak{C}$, we have $\mathcal{I}^\sigma(c^\sigma) = \mathcal{I}(c)^\sigma$, and this is defined iff $\mathcal{I}(c)$ is defined. Hence $c^\sigma \in C'$ iff $c \in C$, i.e. $C' = C^\sigma$. A consequence is that $\mathcal{I} + \mathcal{J}$ is defined iff the domains of $\mathcal{I}$ and $\mathcal{J}$ are disjoint, hence exactly when $\mathcal{I}^\sigma + \mathcal{J}^\sigma$ is defined.
3. If $\mathcal{I}(c)$ is defined, then so is $\mathcal{I}^\sigma(c^\sigma) = \mathcal{I}(c)^\sigma$, and then $(\mathcal{I}^\sigma + \mathcal{J}^\sigma)(c^\sigma) = \mathcal{I}^\sigma(c^\sigma) = \mathcal{I}(c)^\sigma = (\mathcal{I} + \mathcal{J})(c)^\sigma = (\mathcal{I} + \mathcal{J})^\sigma(c^\sigma)$. The same holds if $\mathcal{J}(c)$ is defined, hence the result.
4. For $\mathcal{J} \in \mathrm{Ext}(\mathcal{I})$, we have $\mathcal{I} \subseteq \mathcal{J}$, hence $\mathcal{I}^\sigma \subseteq \mathcal{J}^\sigma$, and $\mathcal{J}^\sigma \in \mathrm{Ext}(\mathcal{I}^\sigma)$. This proves $\mathrm{Ext}(\mathcal{I})^\sigma \subseteq \mathrm{Ext}(\mathcal{I}^\sigma)$ for all $\mathcal{I}, \sigma$. Hence we may apply it to $\mathcal{I}^\sigma, \sigma^{-1}$, yielding $\mathrm{Ext}(\mathcal{I}^\sigma)^{\sigma^{-1}} \subseteq \mathrm{Ext}(\mathcal{I})$, to which we apply σ: $\mathrm{Ext}(\mathcal{I}^\sigma) \subseteq \mathrm{Ext}(\mathcal{I})^\sigma$.

We may now prove a general invariance property of truth values of extensions under symmetries.

Theorem 1.

$$\forall \sigma \in \mathrm{Aut}(\mathcal{I}) \cap \mathrm{Aut}(c), \mathrm{Val}(\mathrm{Ext}(\mathcal{I} + c \hookrightarrow v)) = \mathrm{Val}(\mathrm{Ext}(\mathcal{I} + c \hookrightarrow v^\sigma))$$

Proof. We have $\mathcal{I}^\sigma = \mathcal{I}$ and $c^\sigma = c$, therefore $(\mathcal{I} + c \hookrightarrow v)^\sigma = \mathcal{I} + (c \hookrightarrow v)^\sigma = \mathcal{I} + c \hookrightarrow v^\sigma$, and then $\mathrm{Ext}(\mathcal{I} + c \hookrightarrow v^\sigma) = \mathrm{Ext}(\mathcal{I} + c \hookrightarrow v)^\sigma$. The result follows by the fundamental property of $\mathfrak{G}$: $\forall \mathcal{J} \in \mathrm{Ext}(\mathcal{I} + c \hookrightarrow v), \mathrm{Val}(\mathcal{J}) = \mathrm{Val}(\mathcal{J}^\sigma)$ and $\mathcal{J}^\sigma \in \mathrm{Ext}(\mathcal{I} + c \hookrightarrow v^\sigma)$, and conversely $\forall \mathcal{J} \in \mathrm{Ext}(\mathcal{I} + c \hookrightarrow v^\sigma), \mathrm{Val}(\mathcal{J}) = \mathrm{Val}(\mathcal{J}^{\sigma^{-1}})$ and $\mathcal{J}^{\sigma^{-1}} \in \mathrm{Ext}(\mathcal{I} + c \hookrightarrow v)$.

---

[5] Meaning that $\mathrm{Aut}(\mathcal{I})$ is the smallest subgroup of $\mathfrak{G}$ containing these elements. Sets of generators provide a compact representation of groups. Here, we also use the standard cycles notation for permutations, e.g. $(0\ 4)(1\ 3)$ is the function $\{\langle 0, 4\rangle, \langle 4, 0\rangle, \langle 1, 3\rangle, \langle 3, 1\rangle, \langle 2, 2\rangle\}$.

This result yields the fundamental pruning technique w.r.t. symmetries in the basic search tree. It means that the possibility of extending $\mathcal{I} + c \hookrightarrow v$ to a model is independent of the particular v we choose in a $(\mathrm{Aut}(I) \cap \mathrm{Aut}(c))$-orbit in $\mathfrak{D}$. We will then obviously test only one value per orbit, i.e. we may restrict the search to one representative per orbit that contains a possible value.

But there still remains the task of computing these orbits. This obviously requires computing $\mathrm{Aut}(\mathcal{I})$ and $\mathrm{Aut}(c)$, and then their intersection: nice and efficient algorithms exist for computing with finite groups (see [5]). But we cannot generally guarantee that this can be done in polynomial time (see [3]), and there is no general relationship between $\mathrm{Aut}(\mathcal{I})$ and $\mathrm{Aut}(\mathcal{I} + c \hookrightarrow v)$: automorphisms are not preserved by extension.

5 LNH

However, it is not necessary to use Theorem 1 in its full generality. Any σ that provably belongs to $\mathrm{Aut}(\mathcal{I}) \cap \mathrm{Aut}(c)$ can be used for pruning, through the G-orbits, where G is the group generated by σ. These orbits are exactly the cycles of σ. More generally, any subgroup of $\mathrm{Aut}(\mathcal{I}) \cap \mathrm{Aut}(c)$ fits. LNH is based on the symmetries of elements which are *not* used in a partial interpretation.

Definition 4. *For* $c = f[v_1, \dots, v_n] \in \mathfrak{C}$ *let* $\mathrm{u}(c) = \{v_1, \dots, v_n\}$, *and for* $\mathcal{I} \in \mathfrak{I}$ *let* $\mathrm{u}(\mathcal{I}) = \mathrm{u}(A) \cup \mathcal{I}(A)$, *where* $A \subseteq \mathfrak{C}$ *is the domain of* $\mathcal{I}$; *these are the sets of domain elements used by* c *or* $\mathcal{I}$. *Let* D_c *be the set of possible values for* c *at the level of* $\mathcal{I}$ *in the search tree, and let* $S_{\mathcal{I},c} = \mathrm{Sym}(D_c \setminus (\mathrm{u}(\mathcal{I}) \cup \mathrm{u}(c)))$.

For any $\sigma \in \mathfrak{G}$ such that $\forall v \in \mathrm{u}(\mathcal{I}) \cup \mathrm{u}(c), v^\sigma = v$, we clearly have $\mathcal{I}^\sigma = \mathcal{I}$ and $c^\sigma = c$. We have just proved that $S_{\mathcal{I},c}$ is a subgroup of $\mathrm{Aut}(\mathcal{I}) \cap \mathrm{Aut}(c)$, and we may then apply symmetry pruning with $S_{\mathcal{I},c}$.

We are therefore interested in the $S_{\mathcal{I},c}$-orbits in D_c. For any $v \in D_c \cap (\mathrm{u}(\mathcal{I}) \cup \mathrm{u}(c))$ we have $v^{S_{\mathcal{I},c}} = \{v\}$, bringing no pruning. But for any $v \in D_c \setminus (\mathrm{u}(\mathcal{I}) \cup \mathrm{u}(c))$, we have $v^{S_{\mathcal{I},c}} = D_c \setminus (\mathrm{u}(\mathcal{I}) \cup \mathrm{u}(c))$, and according to Theorem 1 only one element of this set need be tested, say the smallest one ($D_c \subset \mathbb{N}$). This is exactly SEM's Least Number Heuristic, or LNH: see [9] (it also appeared in SEM's predecessor FALCON, see [7]).

It should be mentioned that Theorem 1 may have an influence on the search tree other than pruning, i.e. we may want to increase the chances of symmetry pruning when choosing the new cell c. The most promising cells in this respect may not be the most promising ones in other aspects (e.g. may not minimize the length of D_c). A wrong choice may make the symmetry-pruned tree bigger than an unpruned tree obtained with a different order of cells. This is an obvious remark, but it is important to bear in mind that we do not simply have a trade-off between some amount of pruning and the computational cost it requires. Adopting symmetry pruning is bound to change the cell ordering strategy.

This being said, Theorem 1 suggests a cell ordering strategy that would keep $\mathrm{Aut}(\mathcal{I}) \cap \mathrm{Aut}(c)$ as big as possible. In LNH, this translates into a strategy that would keep $\mathrm{u}(\mathcal{I}) \cup \mathrm{u}(c)$ as small as possible. This is indeed what happens in SEM, where the strategy is to keep $u(\mathcal{I}) \cup u(c)$ as consecutive integers from 0 to some mdn, and mdn as small as possible, so that D_c is pruned to $D_c \cap \{0, \ldots, mdn+1\}$. Experimentations in [9] support this strategy.

A search tree is *frugal* if it does not contain two isomorphic partial interpretations. Of course, a search tree may be frugal due to constraint propagation and backtracking (according to the formula), but it may also be the case that frugality is obtained independently from the formula, as in the following theorem.

Theorem 2. *If $\Sigma = \Sigma_0$, then SEM with LNH produces a frugal search tree.*

Proof. Due to LNH, at any node in the search tree we have built a partial interpretation $\mathcal{I}$ whose range is a set of integers $\{0, \ldots, i\}$ (see Figure 1).

Suppose there are two distinct isomorphic interpretations $\mathcal{J}, \mathcal{J}^\sigma$ at two distinct nodes in the tree, where $\sigma \in \mathfrak{G}$; let $\mathcal{I}$ be the interpretation at their greatest common ancestor. Since $\Sigma = \Sigma_0$, the action of $\mathfrak{G}$ on $\mathfrak{C}$ is trivial, so that the domains of $\mathcal{I}$ and $\mathcal{I}^\sigma$ are equal. Obviously we have $\mathcal{I} \subset \mathcal{J}$, so that $\mathcal{I}^\sigma \subset \mathcal{J}^\sigma$, and we also have $\mathcal{I} \subset \mathcal{J}^\sigma$. Hence $\mathcal{I}$ and $\mathcal{I}^\sigma$ are restrictions of $\mathcal{J}^\sigma$ on the same set of cells: $\mathcal{I} = \mathcal{I}^\sigma$.

Let i be the integer such that $\mathcal{I}$'s range is $\{0, \ldots, i\}$, then $\forall j \in \{0, \ldots, i\}, \exists c \in \mathfrak{C}$ such that $\mathcal{I}(c) = j$, and $j^\sigma = \mathcal{I}(c)^\sigma = \mathcal{I}^\sigma(c) = j$. Since $\mathcal{J} \neq \mathcal{J}^\sigma$, there is a constant a and a $v \in \mathfrak{D}$ such that $\mathcal{J}$ extends $\mathcal{I} + a \hookrightarrow v$, and therefore $\mathcal{J}^\sigma$ extends $\mathcal{I} + a \hookrightarrow v^\sigma$. Since we have $v, v^\sigma \in \{0, \ldots, i+1\}$ by LNH, we must have $v^\sigma = v$, which is impossible by definition of $\mathcal{I}$. This proves that two distinct partial interpretations in the tree cannot be isomorphic, i.e. that the tree is frugal.

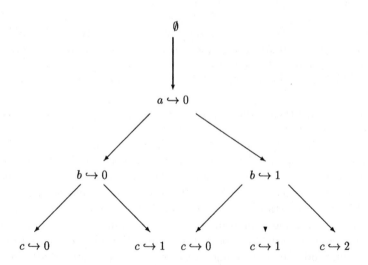

Fig. 1. SEM's search tree with 3 constants

This result does not generalize to more complex signatures. Considering Example 2 again, and starting from $\mathcal{I}$, SEM would select the cell $f[2]$ and consider the nodes $\mathcal{I} + f[2] \hookrightarrow v$ for all v in $\{0, 1, 2, 3\}$. In other words, LNH considers the symmetry $(3\ 4)$ but disregards the symmetry $(0\ 1)$ (we do have $f[2]^{(0\ 1)} = f[2]$), which according to Theorem 1 further prunes the search to $\{0, 2, 3\}$. The idea behind XLNH is precisely to recover this Lost Symmetry (and some others).

6 XLNH

XLNH focuses on monadic functions f with equal domain and range sorts, and more precisely on "bijective restrictions" (see [2]). We adopt here a different terminology: we call *cycle* of a partial function h from D to D any set $C = \{h^i(v)/0 \le i < l\}$ such that $h^l(v) = v$, and l its *length*. A cycle C is *pure* if $h^{-1}(C) = C$.

With each pure cycle C of $f_{\mathcal{I}}$ we associate the permutation $\gamma(C)$ on $\mathfrak{D}$ defined by $\forall v \in \mathfrak{D}, v^{\gamma(C)} = f_{\mathcal{I}}(v)$ if $v \in C$, and $v^{\gamma(C)} = v$ otherwise. Since $f_{\mathcal{I}}$ is cyclic on C, this is clearly a permutation. To any pair B, C of pure cycles of equal length l we associate a permutation $\tau(B, C)$ defined by first choosing arbitrarily $b \in B, c \in C$, and then, if $0 \le i < l$, let $(f_{\mathcal{I}})^i(b)^{\tau(B,C)} = (f_{\mathcal{I}})^i(c), (f_{\mathcal{I}})^i(c)^{\tau(B,C)} = (f_{\mathcal{I}})^i(b)$, and $\forall v \in \mathfrak{D} \setminus (B \cup C), v^{\tau(B,C)} = v$. Finally, we let $\mathrm{X}(f_{\mathcal{I}})$ be the subgroup of $\mathfrak{G}$ generated by these permutations[6] $\gamma(C)$ and $\tau(B, C)$; this group does not depend on the chosen $\tau(B, C)$.

Example 3. Let $h = f_{\mathcal{I}}$ be the permutation $(0\ 1)(2\ 3)$. h has two pure cycles $C = \{0, 1\}$ and $C' = \{2, 3\}$ of length 2. We have $\gamma(C) = (0\ 1)$ and $\gamma(C') = (2\ 3)$. We have either $\tau(C, C') = (0\ 2)(1\ 3)$ or $\tau(C, C') = (0\ 3)(1\ 2)$. In both cases, $\mathrm{X}(h)$ contains both versions of $\tau(C, C')$, and $\mathrm{X}(h) = \mathrm{Aut}(h)$. There is only one non-trivial $\mathrm{X}(h)$-orbit in $\mathfrak{D}$: this is $\{0, 1, 2, 3\}$.

More generally, any non trivial $\mathrm{X}(f_{\mathcal{I}})$-orbit in $\mathfrak{D}$ is the union of all pure cycles of $f_{\mathcal{I}}$ of a given length, and

Lemma 2. $\mathrm{X}(f_{\mathcal{I}})$ *is a subgroup of* $\mathrm{Aut}(f_{\mathcal{I}})$.

Proof. We prove that $f_{\mathcal{I}}$ is invariant under the generators of $\mathrm{X}(f_{\mathcal{I}})$, as defined above. Let C be a pure cycle of $f_{\mathcal{I}}$, then for all v, if $v \notin C$, then $f_{\mathcal{I}}(v) \notin C$, so they are both fixpoints of $\gamma(C)$. Therefore $f_{\mathcal{I}}^{\gamma(C)}(v) = f_{\mathcal{I}}^{\gamma(C)}(v^{\gamma(C)}) = f_{\mathcal{I}}(v)^{\gamma(C)} = f_{\mathcal{I}}(v)$. If $v \in C$, then $\exists u \in C$ such that $f_{\mathcal{I}}(u) = v$, so that $u^{\gamma(C)} = v$. Therefore $f_{\mathcal{I}}^{\gamma(C)}(v) = f_{\mathcal{I}}(u)^{\gamma(C)} = v^{\gamma(C)} = f_{\mathcal{I}}(v)$. We have proved that $f_{\mathcal{I}}^{\gamma(C)} = f_{\mathcal{I}}$.

Let B, C be two pure cycles of $f_{\mathcal{I}}$ of equal length, $b \in B, c \in C$ such that

$$\forall i, (f_{\mathcal{I}})^i(b)^{\tau(B,C)} = (f_{\mathcal{I}})^i(c) \text{ and } (f_{\mathcal{I}})^i(c)^{\tau(B,C)} = (f_{\mathcal{I}})^i(b).$$

As above, for all $v \notin B \cup C$, we have $f_{\mathcal{I}}(v) \notin B \cup C$, both are fixpoints of $\tau(B, C)$, so that $f_{\mathcal{I}}^{\tau(B,C)}(v) = f_{\mathcal{I}}(v)$. If $v \in B$, there is an i such that $v =$

---

[6] It is easy to see that they are indeed in $\mathfrak{G}$.

$(f_\mathcal{I})^i(b) = (f_\mathcal{I})^i(c)^{\tau(B,C)}$, and therefore

$$f_\mathcal{I}^{\tau(B,C)}(v) = f_\mathcal{I}^{\tau(B,C)}((f_\mathcal{I})^i(c)^{\tau(B,C)}) = (f_\mathcal{I})^{i+1}(c)^{\tau(B,C)} = (f_\mathcal{I})^{i+1}(b) = f_\mathcal{I}(v).$$

The same trivially holds for $v \in C$, and we have proved that $f_\mathcal{I}^{\tau(B,C)} = f_\mathcal{I}$.

Unfortunately, it is not generally true that $X(f_\mathcal{I})$ is a subgroup of $\mathrm{Aut}(\mathcal{I})$. In order to enforce this property, we will only consider the pure cycles of the restriction of $f_\mathcal{I}$ to elements of $\mathfrak{D}$ which are not used in $\mathcal{I}$ by other symbols than f. We need a few more notations to make this clear. For any partial function h on D, and any $C \subseteq D$, we note $h|C$ the restriction of h to C, and $h \setminus\!\setminus C = h|(D \setminus C)$. Let $\mathfrak{C}_f = \{f[v] \in \mathfrak{C}\}$, we note $\mathcal{I} \setminus\!\setminus f = \mathcal{I} \setminus\!\setminus \mathfrak{C}_f$.

Theorem 3. $X(f_\mathcal{I} \setminus\!\setminus \mathrm{u}(\mathcal{I} \setminus\!\setminus f))$ *is a subgroup of* $\mathrm{Aut}(\mathcal{I})$.

Proof. We must prove that $\mathcal{I}^\sigma = \mathcal{I}$ for the generators σ of $X(f_\mathcal{I} \setminus\!\setminus \mathrm{u}(\mathcal{I} \setminus\!\setminus f))$. We first note that this is a subgroup of $X(f_\mathcal{I})$, since every pure cycle of $f_\mathcal{I} \setminus\!\setminus \mathrm{u}(\mathcal{I} \setminus\!\setminus f)$ is a pure cycle of $f_\mathcal{I}$. By Lemma 2 we have $\sigma \in \mathrm{Aut}(f_\mathcal{I})$. Now $\forall c \in \mathfrak{C}_f$, we have $c = f[v]$, and

$$\mathcal{I}^\sigma(c) = \mathcal{I}^\sigma(f[v^{\sigma^{-1}}]^\sigma) = \mathcal{I}(f[v^{\sigma^{-1}}])^\sigma = f_\mathcal{I}(v^{\sigma^{-1}})^\sigma = f_\mathcal{I}(v) = \mathcal{I}(c).$$

We now prove the same for all $c \in \mathfrak{C} \setminus \mathfrak{C}_f$. If c is in the domain of $\mathcal{I}$, then $\mathrm{u}(c) \subseteq \mathrm{u}(\mathcal{I} \setminus\!\setminus f)$ and $\mathcal{I}(c) \in \mathrm{u}(\mathcal{I} \setminus\!\setminus f)$ as well. Therefore $\mathrm{u}(c) \cup \{\mathcal{I}(c)\}$ is disjoint from any pure cycle of $f_\mathcal{I} \setminus\!\setminus \mathrm{u}(\mathcal{I} \setminus\!\setminus f)$, so we have $c^\sigma = c$ and $\mathcal{I}(c)^\sigma = \mathcal{I}(c)$. This yields $\mathcal{I}^\sigma(c) = \mathcal{I}^\sigma(c^\sigma) = \mathcal{I}(c)^\sigma = \mathcal{I}(c)$, and also proves that c is in the domain of $\mathcal{I}^\sigma$.

Conversely, if c is in the domain of $\mathcal{I}^\sigma$, since $\mathcal{I}^\sigma(c) = \mathcal{I}(c^{\sigma^{-1}})^\sigma$, then $c^{\sigma^{-1}}$ is in the domain of $\mathcal{I}$, and from what precedes also in the domain of $\mathcal{I}^\sigma$. By induction this is true of all $c^{\sigma^{-n}}$, and in particular of c^σ (the degree d of σ verifies $\sigma^d = \mathrm{i}$, so that $\sigma^{-(d-1)} = \sigma$), but $\mathcal{I}^\sigma(c^\sigma) = \mathcal{I}(c)^\sigma$, and therefore c is in the domain of $\mathcal{I}$. We have proved that c is in the domain of $\mathcal{I}$ iff it is in the domain of $\mathcal{I}^\sigma$, and we can conclude that $\mathcal{I}^\sigma = \mathcal{I}$.

We also have $X(f_\mathcal{I} \setminus\!\setminus \mathrm{u}(c))$ is a subgroup of $\mathrm{Aut}(c)$, if $c \in \mathfrak{C} \setminus \mathfrak{C}_f$. This is rather trivial, since $\mathrm{u}(c)$ is disjoint from the pure cycles of $f_\mathcal{I} \setminus\!\setminus \mathrm{u}(c)$. We conclude that

Corollary 1. $X(f_\mathcal{I} \setminus\!\setminus (\mathrm{u}(c) \cup \mathrm{u}(\mathcal{I} \setminus\!\setminus f)))$ *is a subgroup of* $\mathrm{Aut}(\mathcal{I}) \cap \mathrm{Aut}(c)$.

Proof. $X(f_\mathcal{I} \setminus\!\setminus (A \cup B))$ is a subgroup of $X(f_\mathcal{I} \setminus\!\setminus A)$ since all pure cycles of $f_\mathcal{I} \setminus\!\setminus (A \cup B)$ are pure cycles of $f_\mathcal{I} \setminus\!\setminus A$. So $X(f_\mathcal{I} \setminus\!\setminus (A \cup B))$ is a subgroup of $X(f_\mathcal{I} \setminus\!\setminus A) \cap X(f_\mathcal{I} \setminus\!\setminus B)$, and we may then apply the previous results.

This result, together with Theorem 1, justifies the pruning of the search tree with respect to the $X(f_\mathcal{I} \setminus\!\setminus (\mathrm{u}(c) \cup \mathrm{u}(\mathcal{I} \setminus\!\setminus f)))$-orbits in $\mathfrak{D}$. This is basically what XLNH does; after producing a value for $f_\mathcal{I}$ (and we next see how this is done), it uses these orbits to prune the search tree, together with a cell ordering strategy that keeps $\mathrm{u}(\mathcal{I} \setminus\!\setminus f)$ as small as possible, consistently with LNH.

7   Counting the BIJ Restriction

SEM offers the option of restricting the search by asking that the monadic function symbol f should be only interpreted by bijective functions. On a domain of size n, this reduces the search space from n^n different functions to $n!$ permutations. In SEM, the restriction is implemented by adding constraints to the formula, so that, with the constraint propagation mechanism, only 1-1 partial functions are ever considered. But the interesting point is that, if the relevant cells are considered in priority, LNH is able to prune a considerable number of isomorphic permutations.

Indeed, suppose the first selected cell is in $\mathfrak{C}_f$; then it is $f[0]$ (here, $\mathfrak{D} = \{0, \ldots, n-1\}$), and according to LNH only two values need be considered: $f[0] \hookrightarrow 0$ and $f[0] \hookrightarrow 1$. Suppose at some level $\mathcal{I}$ is defined on $D_i = \{f[0], \ldots, f[i-1]\}$, and $\mathcal{I}(D_i) \subseteq \{0, \ldots, i\}$. Then we select the cell $f[i]$ and may consider all values in $\{0, \ldots, i+1\}$. However, the constraints coming from the BIJ restriction have propagated to reduce this set to $\{0, \ldots, i+1\} \setminus \mathcal{I}(D_i)$, i.e. to two values. Therefore the maximal search tree is binary on $\mathfrak{C}_f$, and the number of terminal nodes, hence of permutations considered in the search, is 2^{n-1}. This is of course much less than the $n!$ elements of $\mathrm{Sym}(\mathfrak{D})$, but still greater than the minimal number that can be achieved, which is of course the number of $\mathfrak{G}$-orbits in $\mathrm{Sym}(\mathfrak{D})$ (by considering the group operation as an action of $\mathfrak{G}$ on $\mathrm{Sym}(\mathfrak{D})$).

Let $\sigma \in \mathrm{Sym}(\mathfrak{D})$, we consider the cycles $C_1, \ldots, C_k$ of σ; they are mutually disjoint and $\bigcup_{i=1}^k C_i = \mathfrak{D}$. We next consider the length of these cycles, and sort them in a tuple $\langle l_1, \ldots, l_k \rangle$, noted $\mathrm{p}(\sigma)$; we have $l_1 \leq \ldots \leq l_k$ and $\sum_{i=1}^k l_i = n$. Thus each $\mathrm{p}(\sigma)$ is a *partition* of n.

Suppose $\mathrm{p}(\sigma) = \mathrm{p}(\sigma') = \langle l_1, \ldots, l_k \rangle$, let C_i (resp. C_i') be a cycle of length l_i in σ (resp. σ'). Then it is easy to prove that there is a $\rho \in \mathfrak{G}$ such that $\sigma\rho = \sigma'$; using the previous notations, we may take $\rho = \prod_{i=1}^k \tau(C_i, C_i')$. This proves that the function p is 1-1 from the set of $\mathfrak{G}$-orbits in $\mathrm{Sym}(\mathfrak{D})$ to the set of partitions of n. Moreover, this function is surjective, since to any partition $\langle l_1, \ldots, l_n \rangle$ of n it is easy to associate a σ such that $\mathrm{p}(\sigma) = \langle l_1, \ldots, l_n \rangle$; the first cycle of σ may be $(0 \ 1 \ \ldots \ l_1 - 1)$. This is exactly this way that the values of $f_{\mathcal{I}}$ are produced by XLNH on the BIJ restriction.

So we see that XLNH is frugal in this case (as mentioned in [2]), and that the number of terminal nodes of the maximal search tree is exactly the number of partitions of n. We do not have a simple formula expressing this number in function of n, which is known as one of the fundamental counting numbers. By writing it $S_n = \sum_{k=1}^n P_{n,k}$, where the *partition number* $P_{n,k}$ is the number of partitions of n of length k, we may easily compute those with the following recursion formulas (see e.g. [1] p. 95),

$$P_{n,1} = P_{n,n} = 1,$$
$$P_{n,k} = P_{n-k,1} + P_{n-k,2} + \cdots + P_{n-k,\max(k,n-k)}.$$

n	S_n	2^{n-1}	n!
10	42	512	3,628,800
20	627	524,288	2.43 10^{18}
30	5,604	536,870,912	2.65 10^{32}
40	37,338	5.5 10^{11}	8.16 10^{47}
50	204,226	5.63 10^{14}	3.04 10^{64}

Fig. 2. Sizes of maximal search trees with BIJ

Example 4. $P_{5,3} = P_{2,1} + P_{2,2} = 1 + 1 = 2$, and indeed we have two partitions of length 3: $5 = 1 + 1 + 3 = 1 + 2 + 2$.

So we may easily compare the sizes of the maximal search trees obtained with LNH and XLNH, and also with the tree that would be obtained without symmetry pruning; see Figure 2. This should confer a great advantage to XLNH compared to LNH[7].

8   The Extended Search Tree

It should be clear by now that XLNH does not work cell by cell when generating the values of $f_{\mathcal{I}}$. We may see why not by considering the search tree for the two cells $f[0]$ and $f[1]$, see Figure 3; notice that although this tree is minimal with respect to the symmetry pruning yielded by Theorem 1, we still get isomorphic partial interpretations. i.e $\mathcal{I}_1^{(0\ 1)} = \mathcal{I}_5$.

Since the search is depth-first, it is impossible to see a redundancy in $\mathcal{I}_5$, but for memorizing previous nodes... The flaw obviously comes from the fact that by providing values to cells one by one, the symmetries between cells (here $f[0]$ and $f[1]$) are broken.

So we have to extend our notion of a search tree in order to recover these symmetries: starting from a partial interpretation $\mathcal{I}$, we may consider any number of non empty partial interpretations $\mathcal{I}_1, \ldots, \mathcal{I}_m$ (with domains disjoint from $\mathcal{I}$'s), and recursively search $\mathcal{I} + \mathcal{I}_1, \ldots, \mathcal{I} + \mathcal{I}_m$. These extensions can obviously not be chosen at random, and we need to enforce a completeness property, that we make consistent with our group theoretic framework: $\forall \mathcal{J} \in \mathrm{Ext}(\mathcal{I}), \exists k, \exists \sigma \in \mathrm{Aut}(\mathcal{I})$ such that $\mathcal{J}^\sigma \in \mathrm{Ext}(\mathcal{I} + \mathcal{I}_k)$. Moreover, we say that this node is *frugal* if k is unique. Finding suitable extensions $\mathcal{I}_1, \ldots, \mathcal{I}_m$ at some level is called the *generating problem*.

This obviously generalizes the previous search tree, and allows the generation of many cell values at a single level of the search, as seen in the previous section.

---

[7] As the experimental results in [2] seem to confirm, but actually do not due to an unrepresentative sample: the bijective function considered is always a group inverse operation, which corresponds to partitions of the form $1 + \cdots + 1 + 2 + \cdots + 2$ with at least a 1 (for the group identity); that makes only $\frac{(n+1)}{2}$ among S_n partitions. A natural algorithm for generating the partitions would not evenly scatter these $\frac{(n+1)}{2}$ partitions among the S_n, and these results are therefore correlated with the order in which the partitions are generated.

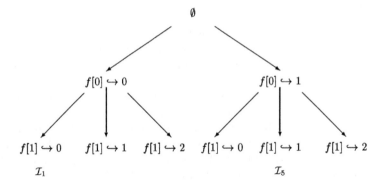

Fig. 3. Search tree for cells $f[0]$ and $f[1]$

The advantage is to keep a better view of the structure of the objects we need to generate. This structure is very different whether we consider constant symbols, monadic or polyadic function or predicate symbols, differences that are difficult to account for in the original search tree. The drawback is that it greatly increases the degree of the search tree, and consequently leaves fewer possibilities of pruning through partial evaluation.

We can for example evaluate the degree of the first node of the search tree obtained with XLNH[8]. The principle is, for each possible l as the total length of $f_{\mathcal{I}}$'s pure cycles, to generate all necessary values for the l first cells in $\mathfrak{C}_f$ as above (with the partitions of l), while the remaining $n - l$ cells will be provided values one by one, according to the given orbits (given by the partition). This late process may introduce pure cycles (in the $n - l$ remaining cells) that are not recognised, but the resulting subtree is symmetry pruned compared to what would be obtained by LNH.

The number of necessary values for each $l > 0$ is S_l. In particular, for $l = 1$ the only extension is $f[0] \hookrightarrow 0$. For $l = 0$, we only need the extension $f[0] \hookrightarrow 1$. The degree of the first node with XLNH is therefore $1 + \sum_{l=1}^{n} S_l$. It is clearly not frugal, since the two extensions for $l = 0$ and $l = 1$ are alone complete, according to LNH. Actually, starting from these two extensions the search trees obtained with XLNH are exactly the same as with LNH. This means that these two extensions must be tried after all others (with $l > 1$), if any improvement is expected from XLNH over LNH, and that none can be obtained if the input formula does not allow for pure cycles in $f_{\mathcal{I}}$.

This may be the place to mention that [4] presents an algorithm for generating a complete and frugal list of values for monadic functions, either from one sort to another sort, or to the same sort.

---

[8] we only consider here the case $\Sigma_0 = \emptyset$, for sake of simplicity, and of course with a monadic function symbol f, so that members of $\mathfrak{C}_f$ are selected first.

9   A Conclusion

Let us take a more abstract view of the extended search tree: at some point we have reached a partial interpretation $\mathcal{I}$, we select an object o and consider all possible values for it. In other words, we suppose we are able to solve (efficiently) the generating problem for o.

In SEM, the objects are as small as possible (cells are atoms in this respect), and LNH allows for a trivial approximation of the automorphism group. XLNH departs drastically from this paradigm, though only at the root of the search tree, by selecting as o a monadic one-sorted function, and then allows for more automorphisms than LNH. This is due to the necessity of getting insight into the *structure* of o, or more precisely its values.

So the dilemma is this: if we keep the objects o small, we only get a short-sighted view of the overall structure, and may produce many isomorphic interpretations without being able to notice; if we keep them big (a monadic function, a binary relation...), the nodes may have such huge degrees that all benefits of partial evaluations are lost, and no backtracking can yield a significant amount of pruning. Hence we need to consider small objects so that much is factorized in the search, but find some way to keep a clear view of the overall structures; we hope the reader is now convinced that this requires the use of groups and group actions.

References

1. Martin Aigner. *Combinatorial Theory*. Classics in Mathemathics. Springer-Verlag, 1997.
2. Gilles Audemard and Laurent Henocque. The extended least number heuristic. In Rajeev Goré, Alexander Leitsch, and Tobias Nipkow, editors, *First IJCAR*, LNAI 2083, pages 427–442, Siena, Italy, June 2001. Springer-Verlag.
3. Thierry Boy de la Tour. On the complexity of finite sorted algebras. In Ricardo Caferra and Gernot Salzer, editors, *Automated Deduction in Classical and Non-Classical Logics*, Lecture Notes in Artificial Intelligence 1761, pages 95–108. Springer Verlag, 2000.
4. Thierry Boy de la Tour. Some techniques of isomorph-free search. In *Artificial Intelligence and Symbolic Computation, International Conference AISC'2000*, pages 240–252. Springer Verlag, 2000. Lecture Notes in Artificial Intelligence 1930.
5. C. Hoffmann. *Group-theoretic algorithms and graph isomorphism*. Lecture Notes in Computer Science 136. Springer Verlag, 1981.
6. Nicolas Peltier. A new method for automated finite model building exploiting failures and symmetries. *Journal of Logic and Computation*, 8(4):511–543, 1998.
7. Jian Zhang. Constructing finite algebras with FALCON. *Journal of Automated Reasoning*, 17(1):1–22, August 1996.
8. Jian Zhang and Hantao Zhang. Constraint propagation in model generation. In Ugo Montanari and Francesca Rossi, editors, *Principles and practice of constraint programming - CP'95*, LNCS 976, Cassis, France, sep 1995. Springer-Verlag.
9. Jian Zhang and Hantao Zhang. SEM: a system for enumerating models. In Chris S. Mellish, editor, *Proceedings of the Fourteenth International Joint Conference on Artificial Intelligence*, pages 298–303. Morgan Kaufmann, aug 1995.

A SAT Based Approach for Solving Formulas over Boolean and Linear Mathematical Propositions*

Gilles Audemard[1,2], Piergiorgio Bertoli[1], Alessandro Cimatti[1],
Artur Kornilowicz[1,3], and Roberto Sebastiani[1,4]

[1] ITC-IRST, Povo, Trento, Italy
{audemard,bertoli,cimatti,kornilow}@itc.it
[2] LSIS, University of Provence, Marseille, France
[3] Institute of Computer Science, University of Białystok, Poland
[4] DIT, Università di Trento, Povo, Trento, Italy
roberto.sebastiani@dit.unitn.it

Abstract. The availability of decision procedures for combinations of boolean and linear mathematical propositions opens the ability to solve problems arising from real-world domains such as verification of timed systems and planning with resources. In this paper we present a general and efficient approach to the problem, based on two main ingredients. The first is a DPLL-based SAT procedure, for dealing efficiently with the propositional component of the problem. The second is a tight integration, within the DPLL architecture, of a set of mathematical deciders for theories of increasing expressive power. A preliminary experimental evaluation shows the potential of the approach.

1 Introduction

The definition of decision procedures for expressive logical theories, in particular theories combining constraints over boolean and real variables, is a very important and challenging problem. Its importance lies in the fact that problems arising from different real-world domains, ranging from formal verification of infinite state systems to planning with resources, can be easily encoded as decision problems for such theories. The challenge is to define automatic decision procedures, that are able to deal with a wide class of problems, but are also able to recognize easy problems and to deal with them efficiently.

In this paper, we tackle the decision problem for boolean combinations of linear mathematical propositions. We propose an approach based on the extension of efficient DPLL decision procedures for propositional satisfiability with a

---

* This work is sponsored by the CALCULEMUS! IHP-RTN EC project, contract code HPRN-CT-2000-00102, and has thus benefited of the financial contribution of the Commission through the IHP programme. We thank Andrew Goldberg, Stefano Pallottino and Romeo Rizzi for invaluable suggestions about the problems of solving linear (in)equalities.

A. Voronkov (Ed.): CADE-18, LNAI 2392, pp. 195–210, 2002.

set of mathematical deciders of increasing power. The approach is general and incremental. It allows for the structured integration of mathematical solvers of different expressive power within the DPLL decision procedure, with constraints learning and backjumping. The mathematical solvers have different expressive power, ranging from equalities, to binary linear inequalities, to full linear inequalities. More complex solvers come into play only when needed.

We implemented the approach in the MATH-SATsolver, based on the SIM package for propositional satisfiability. An experimental evaluation was carried out on tests arising from temporal reasoning [2] and formal verification of timed systems [3]. In the first class of problems, we compare our results with the results of the specialized system; although MATH-SAT is able to tackle a wider class of problems, it runs faster that the TSAT solver, that is specialized to a problem class. In the second class, we show the impact of a tighter degree of integration and the different optimization techniques on the ability of the solver. Although preliminary, the experimental evaluation is extremely promising.

The paper is structured as follows. In Section 2 we formalize the class of problems of interest. In Section 3.1 we discuss the general architecture of the solver, and the specific decision procedures that are currently integrated. In Section 4 we present an experimental evaluation, and in Section 5 we describe some related work and draw some conclusions.

2   MATH-SAT

By *math-terms* and *math-formulas* we denote respectively the linear mathematical expressions and formulas built on constants, variables and arithmetical operators over $\mathbb{R}$ and boolean connectives:

- a constant $c_i \in \mathbb{R}$ is a math-term;
- a variable v_i over $\mathbb{R}$ is a math-term;
- $c_i \cdot v_j$ is a math-term, $c_i \in \mathbb{R}$ and v_j being a constant and a variable over $\mathbb{R}$;
- if t_1 and t_2 are math-terms, then $-t_1$ and $(t_1 \otimes t_2)$ are math-terms, $\otimes \in \{+, -\}$.
- a boolean proposition A_i over $\mathbb{B} := \{\bot, \top\}$ is a math-formula;
- if t_1, t_2 are math-terms, then $(t_1 \bowtie t_2)$ is a math-formula, $\bowtie \in \{=, \neq, >, < , \geq, \leq\}$;
- if φ_1, φ_2 are math-formulas, then $\neg\varphi_1$ and $(\varphi_1 \wedge \varphi_2)$ are math-formulas.

The boolean connectives $\vee$, $\rightarrow$, $\leftrightarrow$ are defined from $\wedge$ and $\neg$ in the standard way. For instance, $A_1 \wedge ((v_1 + 5.0) \leq 2.0 \cdot v_3)$ is a math-formula.

An *atom* is any math-formula in one of the forms A_i or $(t_1 \bowtie t_2)$ above —respectively called *boolean atoms* and *mathematical atoms*. A *literal* is either an atom (a *positive* literal) or its negation (a *negative* literal). If l is a negative literal $\neg\psi$, then by "$\neg l$" we conventionally mean ψ rather than $\neg\neg\psi$. We denote by $Atoms(\phi)$ the set of mathematical atoms of a math-formula ϕ.

By *interpretation* is a map $\mathcal{I}$ which assigns real values and boolean values to math-terms and math-formulas respectively and preserves constants, arithmetical and boolean operators:

- $\mathcal{I}(A_i) \in \{\top, \bot\}$, for every $A_i \in \mathcal{A}$;
- $\mathcal{I}(c_i) = c_i$, for every constant $c_i \in \mathbb{R}$;
- $\mathcal{I}(v_i) \in \mathbb{R}$, for every variable v_i over $\mathbb{R}$;
- $\mathcal{I}(t_1 \otimes t_2) = \mathcal{I}(t_1) \otimes \mathcal{I}(t_2)$, for all math-terms t_1, t_2 and $\otimes \in \{+, -, \cdot\}$;
- $\mathcal{I}(t_1 \bowtie t_2) = \mathcal{I}(t_1) \bowtie \mathcal{I}(t_2)$, for all math-terms t_1, t_2 and $\bowtie \in \{=, \neq, >, <, \geq, \leq\}$;
- $\mathcal{I}(\neg \varphi_1) = \neg \mathcal{I}(\varphi_1)$, for every math-formula φ_1;
- $\mathcal{I}(\varphi_1 \wedge \varphi_2) = \mathcal{I}(\varphi_1) \wedge \mathcal{I}(\varphi_2)$, for all math-formulas φ_1, φ_2.

E.g., $\mathcal{I}((v_1 - v_2 \geq 4) \wedge (\neg A_1 \vee (v_1 = v_2)))$ is $(\mathcal{I}(v_1) - \mathcal{I}(v_2) \geq 4) \wedge (\neg \mathcal{I}(A_1) \vee (\mathcal{I}(v_1) = \mathcal{I}(v_2)))$. We say that $\mathcal{I}$ *satisfies* a math formula ϕ, written $\mathcal{I} \models \phi$, iff $\mathcal{I}(\phi)$ evaluates to true. E.g., $A_1 \rightarrow ((v_1 + 2v_2) \leq 4.5)$ is satisfied by an interpretation $\mathcal{I}$ s.t. $\mathcal{I}(A_1) = \top$, $\mathcal{I}(v_1) = 1.1$, and $\mathcal{I}(v_2) = 0.6$.

We call *MATH-SAT* the problem of checking the satisfiability of math-formulas. As standard boolean formulas are a strict subcase of math-formulas, it follows trivially that MATH-SAT is NP-hard.

A *truth assignment* for a math-formula ϕ is a truth value assignment μ to (a subset of) the atoms of ϕ. We represent truth assignments as set of literals

$$\mu = \{\alpha_1, \ldots, \alpha_N, \neg \beta_1, \ldots, \neg \beta_M, A_1, \ldots, A_R, \neg A_{R+1}, \ldots, \neg A_S\}, \quad (1)$$

$\alpha_1, \ldots, \alpha_N, \beta_1, \ldots, \beta_M$ being mathematical atoms and $A_1, \ldots, A_S$ being boolean atoms, with the intended meaning that positive and negative literals represent atoms assigned to true and to false respectively.

We say that μ *propositionally satisfies* ϕ, written $\mu \models_p \phi$, iff it makes ϕ evaluate to true. We say that an interpretation $\mathcal{I}$ satisfies an assignment μ iff $\mathcal{I}$ satisfies all the elements of μ. For instance, the assignment $\{(v_1 - v_2 \geq 4.0), \neg A_1\}$ propositionally satisfies $(v_1 - v_2 \geq 4.0) \wedge (\neg A_1 \vee (v_1 = v_2))$, and it is satified by $\mathcal{I}$ s.t. $\mathcal{I}(v_1) = 6.0$, $\mathcal{I}(v_2) = 1.0$, $\mathcal{I}(A_1) = \bot$. Intuitively, if we see a math-formula φ as a propositional formulas in its atoms, then $\models_p$ is the standard satisfiability in propositional logic.

Example 1. Consider the following math-formula φ:

$$\varphi = \{\neg \underline{(2v_2 - v_3 > 2)} \vee A_1\} \wedge$$
$$\{\underline{\neg A_2} \vee (2v_1 - 4v_5 > 3))\} \wedge$$
$$\{\underline{(3v_1 - 2v_2 \leq 3)} \vee A_2\} \wedge$$
$$\{\neg (2v_3 + v_4 \geq 5) \vee \underline{\neg (3v_1 - v_3 \leq 6)} \vee \neg A_1\} \wedge$$
$$\{A_1 \vee \underline{(3v_1 - 2v_2 \leq 3)}\} \wedge$$
$$\{\underline{(v_1 - v_5 \leq 1)} \vee (v_5 = 5 - 3v_4) \vee \neg A_1\} \wedge$$
$$\{A_1 \vee \underline{(v_3 = 3v_5 + 4)} \vee A_2\}.$$

The truth assignment given by the underlined literals above is:

$$\mu = \{\neg (2v_2 - v_3 > 2), \neg A_2, (3v_1 - 2v_2 \leq 3), (v_1 - v_5 \leq 1), \neg (3v_1 - v_3 \leq 6), (v_3 = 3v_5 + 4)\}.$$

μ is an assignment which propositionally satisfies φ, as it sets to true one literal of every disjunction in φ. Notice that μ is not satisfiable, as both the following sub-assignments of μ

$$\{(3v_1 - 2v_2 \le 3), \neg(2v_2 - v_3 > 2), \neg(3v_1 - v_3 \le 6)\} \qquad (2)$$

$$\{(v_1 - v_5 \le 1), (v_3 = 3v_5 + 4), \neg(3v_1 - v_3 \le 6)\} \qquad (3)$$

do not have any satisfying interpretation.   ◇

3   The Solver

3.1   General Idea

The key idea in our approach to solving the MATH-SAT problem consists in stratifying the problem over N layers $L_0, L_1, \ldots, L_{N-1}$ of increasing complexity, and searching for a solution "at a level as simple as possible". In our view, each level considers only an abstraction of the problem which interprets a subgrammar $G_0, G_1, \ldots, G_{N-1}$ of the original problem, G_{N-1} being the grammar G of the problem. Since L_n refines L_{n-1}, if the problem does not admit a solution at level L_n, then it does not at $L_0, \ldots, L_{n-1}$. If indeed a solution S exists at L_n, either n equals $N - 1$, in which case S solves the problem, or a refinement of S must be searched at L_{n+1}. In this way, much of the reasoning can be performed at a high level of abstraction. This results in an increased efficiency in the search of the solution, since low-level searches, which are often responsible for most of the complexity, are avoided whenever possible.

The simple and general idea above maps to an N-layered architecture of the solver. In general, a layer L_n is called by layer L_{n-1} to refine a (maybe partial) solution S of the problem. L_n must check for unsatisfiability of S and (a) return failure if no refinement can be found, or (b) invoke L_{n+1} upon a refinement S', unless n equals $N - 1$. An explanation for failure can be added in case (a), to help higher levels "not to try the same wrong solution twice". L_0 must behave slightly differently, by enumerating (abstract) solutions.

Our solver MATH-SAT realizes the ideas above over the *MATH-SAT* problem. MATH-SAT works on 5 refinement layers. L_0 takes into account only propositional connectives, and is realized by a DPLL propositional satisfiability procedure, modified to act as an enumerator for propositional assignments. To optimize the search, L_0 does not actually ignore mathematical atoms; rather, it abstracts them into boolean atoms, in order to reason upon them at an abstract level. As such, L_0 incorporates an association between newly introduced boolean atoms and originating mathematical atoms, which is used to communicate with L_1. L_1 considers also equalities, performing equality propagation, building equality-driven clusters of variables and detecting equality-driven unsatisfiabilities. L_2 handles also inequalities of the kind $(v_1 - v_2 \bowtie c)$, $\bowtie \in \{<, >, \le, \ge\}$, by a variant of the Bellman-Ford minimal path algorithm. L_3 considers also general inequalities —except negated equalities— using a standard simplex algorithm. Finally, L_4 considers also negated equalities.

The decomposition in MATH-SAT is significant both because it allows exploiting specialized efficient algorithms to deal with each layer, and because a number of significant problems can be expressed using one of the subgrammars

---

boolean MATH-SAT *(formula* φ, *interpretation* & $\mathcal{I}$)
  $\mu = \emptyset$;
  return MATH-DPLL$(\varphi, \mu, \mathcal{I})$;

boolean MATH-DPLL *(formula* φ, *assignment* & μ, *interpretation* & $\mathcal{I}$)
  if ($\varphi == \top$) {   /* base   */
      $\mathcal{I} = $ MATH-SOLVE(μ) ;
      return ($\mathcal{I} \neq Null$) ; }
  if ($\varphi == \bot$)   /* backtrack */
      return *False*;
  if {a literal l occurs in φ as a unit clause}   /* unit propagation */
      return MATH-DPLL$(assign(l, \varphi), \mu \cup \{l\}, \mathcal{I})$;
  $l = choose\text{-}literal(\varphi)$;   /* split   */
  return (MATH-DPLL$(assign(l, \varphi), \mu \cup \{l\}, \mathcal{I})$ **or**
      MATH-DPLL$(assign(\neg l, \varphi), \mu \cup \{\neg l\}, \mathcal{I})$);

Fig. 1. Pseudo-code of the basic version of the MATH-SAT procedure.

G_0, G_1, G_2. For instance, classical planning problems can be encoded in G_0, both the solving of disjunctive temporal constraints and the reachability of timed systems can be encoded in G_2. In those cases, the specialized search algorithms are used, so efficiency is not sacrificed to expressivity.

3.2 L_0: The Boolean Solver

To solve the satisfiability problem for our math-formulas, we have implemented a solver based on a variant of DPLL, along the guidelines described in [16]. The basic schema of such a procedure, called MATH-SAT, is reported in Figure 1. MATH-SAT is sound and complete [16].

MATH-SAT takes as input a math-formula φ and returns a truth value asserting whether φ is satisfiable or not, and in the former case an interpretation $\mathcal{I}$ satisfying φ. MATH-SAT is a wrapper for the main routine, MATH-DPLL. MATH-DPLL looks for a truth assignment μ propositionally satisfying φ which is satisfiable from the mathematical viewpoint. This is done recursively, according to the following steps:

- (base) If $\varphi = \top$, then μ propositionally satisfies φ. Thus, if μ is satisfiable, then φ is satisfiable. Therefore MATH-DPLL invokes MATH-SOLVE(μ), which returns an interpretation for μ if it is satisfiable, *Null* otherwise. MATH-DPLL returns *True* in the first case, *False* otherwise.
- (backtrack) If $\varphi = \bot$, then μ has lead to a propositional contradiction. Therefore MATH-DPLL returns *False*.
- (unit) If a literal l occurs in φ as a unit clause, then l must be assigned $\top$. Thus, MATH-DPLL is recursively invoked upon *assign(l, φ)* and the assignment obtained by adding l to μ. *assign(l, φ)* substitutes every occurrence of l in φ with $\top$ and propositionally simplifies the result.

– (split) If none of the above situations occurs, then *choose-literal(φ)* returns an unassigned literal l according to some heuristic criterion. Then MATH-DPLL is first invoked upon *assign(l, φ)* and $\mu \cup \{l\}$. If the result is *False*, then MATH-DPLL is invoked upon *assign(¬l, φ)* and $\mu \cup \{¬l\}$.

MATH-DPLL is a variant of DPLL, modified to work as an enumerator of truth assignments, whose satisfiability is recursively checked by MATH-SOLVE. The key difference wrt. standard DPLL is in the "base" step. Standard DPLL needs finding only one satisfying assignment μ, and thus simply returns *True*. MATH-DPLL instead also needs checking the satisfiability of μ, and thus it invokes MATH-SOLVE(μ). Then it returns *True* if a non-null interpretation satisfying μ is found, it returns *False* and backtracks otherwise.

The search space of the MATH-SAT problem for a math-formula φ is *infinite*. However, MATH-DPLL partitions such space into a *finite* number of regions, each induced by the mathematical constraints in one assignment μ propositionally satisfying φ. Each such region may contain an up-to-infinite set of satisfying interpretations. If so, MATH-SOLVE picks and returns one of them. Also, since MATH-SOLVE works in polynomial space, MATH-SAT works in polynomial space.

3.3 L_1-L_4: The Mathematical Solver

MATH-SOLVE takes as input an assignment μ, and returns either an interpretation $\mathcal{I}$ satisfying μ or *Null* if there is none. (For simplicity we assume to rewrite all the negated mathematical literals in μ into positive atoms, e.g., $¬(t_1 = t_2) \Longrightarrow (t_1 \neq t_2)$, $¬(t_1 > t_2) \Longrightarrow (t_1 \leq t_2)$, etc.)

L_1: **Eliminating equalities.** The first step eliminates from μ all equalities and simplifies μ accordingly. First, all atoms in the form $(v_i = v_j)$ are removed from μ and all variables occurring there are collected into equivalence classes $E_1, ..., E_i, ..., E_k$, and for each E_i a representant variable $v_i' \in E_i$ is designated. Then, for each E_i, all variables in E_i are substituted by their representant v_i' in the mathematical atoms of μ. All valid atoms (like, e.g., $(v_i - v_i \neq 2)$, $(v_i - v_i > -1)$) are removed, together with all duplicated atoms. If an inconsistent atom is found (like, e.g., $(v_i - v_i = 2)$, $(v_i - v_i \leq -1)$) then MATH-SOLVE terminates returning *Null*.

Second, each remaining atom in the form $(v_i = ...)$ in μ is removed, by applying equality propagation. Throughout this phase, all valid and duplicated atoms are removed, and, if an inconsistent atom is found, then MATH-SOLVE terminates returning *Null*.

L_2: **Minimal path plus negative cycle detection.** If only atoms in the form $(v_i - v_j \bowtie c)$ are left, $\bowtie \in \{>, <, \geq, \leq\}$, then the resulting problem is solved by invoking a minimum path algorithm with cycle detection, a variant of the Bellman-Ford algorithm described in [8], which either returns a satisfying interpretation for the variables v_i's or verifies there is none. In the former case

MATH-SOLVE decodes back the resulting interpretation and returns it, otherwise it returns *Null*. The algorithm is worst-case quadratic in time and linear in size.

L$_3$: Linear programming. Otherwise —unless some negated equality $(t_i \neq t_j)$ exist — a linear programming (LP) simplex algorithm is invoked, which, again, either returns a satisfying interpretation for the variables v_i's or verifies there is none. MATH-SOLVE behaves as in the previous case. This algorithm is worst-case exponential in time (but it is well-known that it exhibits polynomial behavior in non-pathological practical cases) and always requires polynomial memory.

L$_4$: Handling negated equalities. Neither minimal path nor LP procedures handle negated equality constraints like $(t_i \neq t_j)$. In many significant cases — including the ones of practical interest for us, see Section 4— it is always possible to avoid them.

However, in order to preserve expressiveness our design handles them. A trivial way to handle the problem is to split every negated equalities $(t_i \neq t_j)$ into the disjunction of the corresponding strict inequalities $(t_i > t_j) \vee (t_i < t_j)$, and handle the distinct problems separately. This is, of course, rather inefficient.

Instead, we first ignore negated equalities and run one of the algorithms on the remaining part. (i) if there is no solution, then the problem is unsatisfiable anyway, so that it is returned *Null*; (ii) if a solution $\mathcal{I}$ is found, then it is checked against the negated equalities: if it does not contradict them, then $\mathcal{I}$ is returned; (iii) if not, the negated equalities are split and the resulting problems are analyzed.

Notice that the latter event is extremely rare, for two reasons. First, MATH-SOLVE finds a solution at most once in the whole computation. All the other problems are unsatisfiable. Second, a constraint like $(t_i \neq t_j)$ covers only a null-measuring portion of the space of the variables in t_1 and t_2, while the space of the solutions of a solvable linear problem is typically a polyhedron containing infinitely many solutions. Thus $(t_i \neq t_j)$ makes a solvable problem unsolvable only if the solution space degenerates into a n-dimensional point.

3.4 Improvements & Optimizations

We describe some improvements and optimizations for MATH-SAT, some of which come from adapting to our domain improvements and optimizations of the DPLL-based procedures for modal logics [12,14,13] and for temporal reasoning and resource planning [2,19].

Preprocessing atoms. One potential source of inefficiency for the procedure of Figure 1 is the fact that semantically equivalent but syntactically different atoms are not recognized to be identical [resp. one the negation of the other] and thus they may be assigned different [resp. identical] truth values. This causes the undesired generation of a potentially very big amount of intrinsically unsatisfiable assignments (for instance, up to $2^{Atoms(\varphi)-2}$ assignments of the kind $\{(v_1 < v_2), (v_1 \geq v_2), ...\}$).

To avoid these problems, it is wise to preprocess atoms so that to map semantically equivalent atoms into syntactically identical ones:

- *exploit associativity* (e.g., $(v_1 + (v_2 + v_3))$ and $((v_1 + v_2) + v_3)) \implies (v_1 + v_2 + v_3))$;
- *sorting* (e.g., $(v_1 + v_2 \leq v_3 + 1)$, $(v_2 + v_1 - 1 \leq v_3) \implies (v_1 + v_2 - v_3 \leq 1))$;
- *exploiting negation* (e.g., $(v_1 < v_2)$, $(v_1 \geq v_2) \implies (v_1 < v_2)$, $\neg(v_1 < v_2))$.

Early Pruning (EP). If an assignment μ' is unsatisfiable, then all its supersets are unsatisfiable. If the unsatisfiability of an assignment μ' is detected during its recursive construction, then this prevents checking the satisfiability of all the up to $2^{|Atoms(\varphi)| - |\mu'|}$ truth assignments which extend μ'.

This suggests to introduce an intermediate satisfiability test on incomplete assignments just before the "split" step:

> **if** *Likely-Unsatisfiable(μ)*   /* early pruning */
>   **if** (MATH-SOLVE(μ) = *Null*)
>   **then return** *False;*

If the heuristic *Likely-Unsatisfiable* returns *True*, then MATH-SOLVE is invoked on the current assignment μ. If MATH-SOLVE(μ) returns *Null*, then all possible extensions of μ are unsatisfiable, and therefore MATH-DPLL returns *False* and backtracks, avoiding a possibly big amount of useless search.

In this case MATH-SOLVE needs not returning explicitly the interpretation $\mathcal{I}$, so that it can avoid decoding back the solution found by the solver. Moreover, negated equalities $(t_i \neq t_j)$, if any, can be ignored here, as they may only make a satisfiable problem unsatisfiable, not vice versa.

Example 2. Consider the formula φ of Example 1. Suppose that, in four recursive calls, MATH-DPLL builds, in order, the intermediate assignment:

$$\mu' = \{\neg(2v_2 - v_3 > 2), \neg A_2, (3v_1 - 2v_2 \leq 3), \neg(3v_1 - v_3 \leq 6)\}. \quad (4)$$

(rows 1, 2, 3 and 4 of φ), which contains the conflict set (2) and is thus unsatisfiable. If MATH-SOLVE is invoked on μ', it returns *Null*, and MATH-DPLL backtracks without exploring any extension of μ'. $\diamond$

Likely-Unsatisfiable avoids invoking MATH-SOLVE when it is very unlikely that, since last call, the new literals added to μ' can cause inconsistency. (For instance, when they are added only literals which either are purely-propositional or contain new variables.)

Enhanced early pruning (EEP). In early pruning, the call to MATH-SOLVE is not effective if μ is satisfiable. Anyway such a call can produce information which can be used to reduce search afterwords. In fact, the mathematical analysis of μ performed by MATH-SOLVE can allow to assign deterministically truth values to some mathematical atoms $\psi \notin \mu$, and this information can be returned by MATH-SOLVE as a new assignment η, which is unit-propagated away by MATH-DPLL.

For instance, assume that all the following mathematical atoms occur in the math-formula. If $(v_1 - v_2 \leq 4) \in \mu$ and $(v_1 - v_2 \leq 6) \notin \mu$, then MATH-SOLVE can derive deterministically that the latter is true, and thus return an assignment η containing $(v_1 - v_2 \leq 6)$. Similarly, if $(v_1 - v_2 > 2) \notin \mu$ and MATH-SOLVE(μ) finds that v_1 and v_2 belong to the same equivalence class, then it η contains $\neg(v_1 - v_2 > 2)$.

(Mathematical) Backjumping (BJ). An alternative optimization starts from the same observations as those of early pruning. Any branch containing a conflict set is unsatisfiable. Thus, suppose MATH-SOLVE is modified to return also a conflict set η causing the unsatisfiability of the input assignment μ. (As for L_2, a negative cycle represents a conflict set; as for L_3, a technique for returning a conflict sets in LP is hinted in [19].) If so, MATH-DPLL can jump back in its search to the deepest branching point in which a literal $l \in \eta$ is assigned a truth value, pruning the search space below.

Notice the difference w.r.t. early pruning. Both prune the search tree under a branch containing a conflict set. On one hand, backjumping invokes MATH-SOLVE only at the end of the branch, avoiding useless calls. On the other hand, early pruning prunes the search as soon as there is one conflict set in the assignment, whilst backjumping can prune a smaller search tree, as the conflict set returned by MATH-SAT is not necessarily the one which causes the highest backtracking.

Example 3. Consider the formula φ and the assignment μ of Example 1. Suppose that MATH-DPLL generates μ following the order of occurrence within φ, and that MATH-SOLVE(μ) returns the conflict set (2). Thus MATH-DPLL can backjump directly to the branching point $\neg(3v_1 - v_3 \leq 6)$ without branching first on $(v_3 = 3v_5 + 4)$ and $\neg(2v_2 - v_3 > 2)$, obtaining the same pruning effect as in example 2. If instead MATH-SOLVE(μ) returns the conflict set (3), forcing a branch on $(v_3 = 3v_5 + 4)$. $\diamond$

(Mathematical) Learning. When MATH-SOLVE returns a conflict set η, the clause $\neg\eta$ can be added in conjunction to φ. Since then, MATH-DPLL will never again generate any branch containing η.

Example 4. As in Example 3, suppose MATH-SOLVE(μ) returns the conflict set (2). Then the clause $\neg(3v_1 - 2v_2 \leq 3) \vee (2v_2 - v_3 > 2) \vee (3v_1 - v_3 \leq 6)$ is added in conjunction to φ. Thus, whenever a branch contains two elements of (2), then MATH-DPLL will assign the third to $\bot$ by unit propagation. $\diamond$

Learning is a technique which must be used with some care, as it may cause an explosion in size of φ. To avoid this, one has to introduce techniques for discarding learned clauses when necessary [4].

Notice the difference w.r.t. standard boolean backjumping and learning [4]. In the latter case, the conflict set propositionally falsifies the formula, while in our case it is inconsistent from the mathematical viewpoint.

Triggering. This technique is a generalization we propose of a technique adopted in [19]. It comes from the consideration (proved in [16]) that, if we

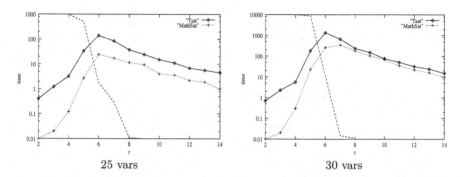

25 vars   30 vars

Fig. 2. Comparison between TSAT and MATH-SAT. $k = 2$, $n = 25, 30$, $L = 100$, $r := m/n$ in $[2, ..., 14]$. 100 sample formulas per point. Median CPU times (secs). Background: satisfiability rate.

have mathematical atoms occurring only positively [resp. negatively] in the input formulas, we can drop any negative [positive] occurrence of them from the assignment to be checked by MATH-SOLVE. This is particularly useful when we deal with equality atoms occurring only positively, as it avoids handling negated equalities.

4   Some Experimental Results

We've implemented MATH-SAT in C; MATH-DPLL is built on top of the SIM library [11]; MATH-SOLVE uses alternatively a home-made implementation of Bellman-Ford minimal path algorithm with negative cycle detection [8], and the Simplex LP library LP_SOLVE [5], as described in Section 3.3.

All experiments presented here were run under Linux RedHat 7.1 on a 4-processor PentiumIII 700MHz machine with more than 4GB RAM, with a time limit of 1 hour and a RAM limit of 1GB for each run. (All the math-formulas investigated here are available at www.science.unitn.it/~rseba/Mathsat.html, together with our implementation of MATH-SAT.)

4.1   Temporal Reasoning

As a first application example, we consider one of the most studied problems in the domain of temporal reasoning, that of solving the consistency of *disjunctive temporal problems* (DTP). Following [18], we encode the problem as a particular a MATH-SAT problem, where the math-formulas are in the restricted form:

$$\bigwedge_i \bigvee_j (v_{1_{ij}} - v_{2_{ij}} \leq c_{ij}), \tag{5}$$

$v_{k_{ij}}$ and c_{ij} being real variables and integer constants respectively. Notice that here (i) there are no boolean variables (ii) constraints are always in the form $(v_i - v_j \leq c)$ and (iii) they always occur positively.

[18] proposed as a benchmark a random generation model in which DTPs are generated in terms of four integer parameters k, m, n, L: a DTP is produced by randomly generating m distinct clauses of length k of the form (5); each atom is obtained by picking $v_{1_{ij}}$ and $v_{2_{ij}}$ with uniform probability $1/n$ and $c_{ij} \in [-L, L]$ with uniform probability $1/(2L + 1)$. Atoms containing the same variable like $(v_i - v_i \leq c)$ and clauses containing identical disjuncts are discharged.

[2] presented TSAT, a SAT based procedure ad hoc for DTPs like (5) based on Bohm SAT procedure [7] and the Simplex LP library LP_SOLVE [5]. In the empirical testing conducted on the same benchmarks as in [18], TSAT outperformed the procedure of [18]. TSAT is enhanced by a form of forward checking and of static learning, in which it learns binary constraints corresponding to pairs of mutually-inconsistent mathematical atoms.

We have run TSAT and MATH-SAT with enhanced early pruning and mathematical learning on the two hardest problems in [2]. The results are reported in Figure 2. As with TSAT, MATH-SAT curves have a peak around the value of r in which we have a 50% satisfiability rate. MATH-SAT is always faster than TSAT, up to one order of magnitude. Similarly to what happens with the optimizations of TSAT [2], when dropping either enhanced early pruning or mathematical learning in MATH-SAT the performances worsen significantly. Thus, although MATH-SAT is a general-purpose procedure, it turns out to be competitive —and even faster— than a current state-of-the-art specific procedure for this problem.

4.2   Model Checking Properties of Timed Systems

As a second application example, we consider the verification and debugging of properties for timed timed systems (e.g., real-time protocols). In short, a timed system is represented as a timed automaton [1], that is, an automaton augmented by real clock variables x, clock resetting statements in the form $(x := 0)$ and clock constraints in the form $(x \bowtie c)$, $\bowtie \in \{>, <, \geq, \leq\}$. The automaton can perform either instantaneous transitions, which are conditioned by clock constraint and can affect the value of boolean variables and resetting statements, or time elapse transition, which increment all clocks by the same value δ and keeps all values.

In [3] we have extended to timed systems the notion of bounded model checking (BMC) [6] and presented a way to encode such problem into a MATH-SAT problem. Given an automaton A, an LTL property f and an integer bound k, we consider the problem of finding an execution of A of up to length k verifying f, and we encode it into the satisfiability of a CNF math-formula $[[A, f]]_k$, s.t. any interpretation of $[[A, f]]_k$ corresponds to a desired execution path.

We introduce a new real variable z representing the current value of *zero*, and we rewrite every occurrence of a clock x with the difference $x - z$. Then, we replicate the propositional and real variables from 0 to k —e.g., x_i represents the variable x at step i— and "unroll" the transition relation from step 0 to step $k - 1$, so that we have

$$[[A, f]]_k := I_0 \wedge \bigwedge_{i=0}^{k-1} T_{i,i+1} \wedge [[f]]_k. \tag{6}$$

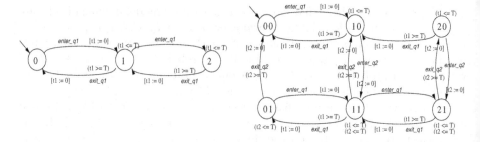

Fig. 3. Timed automata for the post-office problem, for N=1 (left) and N=2 (right).

I_0 is a math formula over the variables at step 0 representing the initial states; $T_{i,i+1}$ is a math formula over the variables at steps i and $i + 1$ representing the transition relation; $[[f]]_k$ is a math formula over all the variables from step 0 to step k representing the condition that the path must verify the LTL formula f. (See [6,3,9] for details.) The mathematical atoms in $[[A, f]]_k$ are all of the kind $(x = y)$, $(x_i - z_i = x_j - z_j)$ or $(x - y \bowtie c)$, $\bowtie \in \{\le, \ge, <, >\}$, such that:

1. every atom in the form $(x_i - z_i = x_j - z_j)$ occurs only positively in $[[A, f]]_k$,
2. for every atom $(x = y)$ in $[[A, f]]_k$, there is a corresponding atom $(x > y)$ in $[[A, f]]_k$ s.t. $\neg(x = y) \to (x > y)$ is a clause in $[[A, f]]_k$.

We have customized a version of MATH-SAT explicitly for this kind of problems. First, MATH-SOLVE(μ) ignores every negated equality in μ. In fact, by point 1., literals like $\neg(x_i - z_i = x_j - z_j)$ can be ignored because of triggering, and, by point 2., literals like $\neg(x = y)$ can be ignored because they are subsumed by $(x > y)$. Second, following [10,17], the encoder provides some semantic information on the boolean variable, so that the heuristic function *choose_literal()* of Figure 1 can split first on variables labeling transitions, and in order of their step index.

In [3] we presented some empirical tests on timed protocol verification, in which the approach of encoding such problems into math-formulas and running MATH-SAT over them turned out to be competitive wrt. using state-of-the-art verification systems. There the focus was on the encoding, and the goal was to show the effectiveness of our approach w.r.t. other verification approaches. Here instead we focus specifically on the effectiveness of MATH-SAT in solving math-formulas. As we are not aware of any existing decision procedure able to handle efficiently math-formulas of this kind, we restrict to showing how the various variants and optimizations affect the efficiency of MATH-SAT on this kind of formulas on an example.

Consider a post office with N desks, each desk serving a customer every T seconds. Every new customer chooses the desk with shorter queue and, when more than one queue has minimal length, the minimal queue with the minimum index. It is not possible to change a queue after entering it. We want to prove that, although all desks have the same serving time T and customers are "smart", one customer can get into the annoying situation of finding himself in queue

Table 1. MATH-SAT CPU times for the Post-office problem with various optimizations

$k\backslash N$	2	3	4	5	2	3	4	5	2	3	4	5	2	3	4	5
2	0.01	0.05	0.24	1.29	0.01	0.05	0.25	1.29	0.01	0.04	0.23	1.31	0.10	0.05	0.25	1.28
3	0.02	0.08	0.37	2.01	0.01	0.08	0.35	2.01	0.02	0.07	0.36	1.91	0.01	0.08	0.38	2.01
4	0.03	0.10	0.51	2.92	0.02	0.09	0.50	2.95	0.02	0.10	0.51	2.92	0.02	0.10	0.51	2.83
5	0.03	0.13	0.62	5.07	0.03	0.13	0.68	5.06	0.03	0.13	0.65	5.00	0.03	0.14	0.68	5.08
6	0.04	0.17	0.90	8.96	0.03	0.16	0.90	8.80	0.03	0.17	0.88	8.80	0.04	0.18	0.89	8.90
7	0.04	0.24	1.82	37	0.05	0.24	1.80	35	0.05	0.23	1.78	37	0.05	0.25	1.83	36
8	0.05	0.41	4.59	231	0.05	0.41	4.54	230	0.06	0.41	4.53	232	0.06	0.40	4.64	229
9		0.92	16	950		0.90	15	945		0.80	14	913		0.86	15	916
10		0.99	72	≥1h		0.98	73	≥1h		0.85	68	≥1h		0.83	70	≥1h
11			302	≥1h			299	≥1h			276	≥1h			288	≥1h
12			592	≥1h			592	≥1h			502	≥1h			529	≥1h
13				≥1h				≥1h				≥1h				≥1h
14				≥1h				≥1h				≥1h				≥1h
Σ	0.22	3.09	991	≥5h	0.20	3.04	990	≥5h	0.22	2.80	870	≥5h	0.22	2.89	911	≥5h
	Basic				Basic+BJ				Basic+EP				Basic+EEP			

Table 2. MATH-SAT CPU times for the Post-office problem with customized *choose_literal* and various optimizations

$k\backslash N$	2	3	4	5	2	3	4	5	2	3	4	5	2	3	4	5
2	0.01	0.05	0.25	1.28	0.01	0.05	0.24	1.29	0.01	0.05	0.24	1.30	0.01	0.05	0.24	1.30
3	0.01	0.08	0.38	1.98	0.02	0.07	0.37	1.98	0.01	0.07	0.36	2.05	0.01	0.07	0.37	1.97
4	0.02	0.10	0.49	2.65	0.02	0.10	0.49	2.65	0.02	0.10	0.50	2.73	0.02	0.10	0.49	2.68
5	0.02	0.13	0.63	3.48	0.03	0.13	0.64	3.45	0.03	0.13	0.62	3.51	0.03	0.13	0.61	3.48
6	0.03	0.16	0.74	4.27	0.03	0.16	0.75	4.22	0.03	0.16	0.76	4.33	0.03	0.15	0.78	4.26
7	0.04	0.19	0.88	5.21	0.05	0.19	0.91	5.13	0.04	0.19	0.87	5.19	0.04	0.19	0.90	5.02
8	0.04	0.24	1.09	6.46	0.03	0.23	1.10	6.43	0.05	0.22	1.07	6.40	0.05	0.23	1.07	6.10
9		0.36	1.48	8.98		0.36	1.44	9.08		0.28	1.28	8.15		0.28	1.29	7.54
10		0.29	2.78	16		0.29	2.81	16		0.28	1.83	11		0.28	1.80	9.97
11			8.43	42			8.45	42			2.89	19			2.94	15
12			5.10	159			5.03	155			2.07	47			1.80	33
13				685				742				115				80
14				208				207				38				23
Σ	0.17	1.60	22.2	1145	0.2	1.58	22.2	1199	0.19	1.48	12.5	265	0.19	1.48	12.3	194
	Basic				Basic+BJ				Basic+EP				Basic+EEP			

after one person, whilst all other queues are empty, and having to wait for a non-instantaneous period in this situation.

The corresponding timing automata for $N = 1$ and $N = 2$ are represented in Figure 3. Each location is labeled by N integers $l_1 l_2 ... l_N$, representing respectively the lengths of queues 1, 2, ... , N. For each queue i a clock variable t_i counts the serving time of the currently served customer. The property is encoded as

$$(20...0)_{k-1} \wedge (20...0)_k \wedge (\delta_{k-1} > 0)$$

for some step $k > 1$, that is, the system is in location 20...0 at both steps $k - 1$ and k and a non-null amount of time δ_{k-1} elapses between these two steps. We fix to 2 the maximum queue length of queue 1 and to 1 for the others; this will be enough to show that the problem has a solution, provided the queuing policy of customers. Although the problem is very simple, the size of the automata grow as $3 \cdot 2^N$.

We encoded this problem as described in [3], for increasing values of k and N, and we ran different versions of MATH-SAT on the resulting formulas. The resulting CPU times are reported in Tables 1 and 2. The last row Σ of each table represents the sum of the values in the corresponding column. Table 2 differs from Table 1 for the fact that in the latter we have used the customized version of *choose_literal()* described above.

All problems are unsatisfiable for $k < 2N + 4$ and satisfiable for $k \geq 2N + 4$, as the minimum path satisfying the property has length $2N + 4$. If we consider the case $N = 2$ of Figure 3, such a path is:

$$00 \xrightarrow{enter_{q1}} 10 \xrightarrow{enter_{q2}} 11 \xrightarrow{enter_{q1}} 21 \xrightarrow{\delta=T} 21 \xrightarrow{served_{q1}} 11 \xrightarrow{enter_{q1}} 21 \xrightarrow{served_{q2}} 20 \xrightarrow{\delta=T} 20$$

that is, customers C1,C2,C3 enter at time 0; after T seconds three new events occur sequentially within a null amount of time: C1 is served by desk 1, a new customer C4 enters queue 1 (as both queues are of length 1), and C2 is served by desk 2. After this, customers C3 and C4 are in queue 1 while nobody in queuing at desk 2, and C4 will have to wait another T seconds before starting being served.

The CPU times in Tables 1 and 2 suggest the following considerations.

First, MATH-SAT with the customized heuristic *choose_literal()* —which chooses transition variables first in order of their step index— dramatically out-performs the basic version, no matter the other optimizations. In fact, as in [10], initial states and transitions are the only sources of non-determinism: once their values are set, the truth values of all other atoms are either irrelevant or derive deterministically from them. This may drastically restrict the search space. Moreover, as in [17], selecting the transitions in forward [backward] step order allows to avoid selecting transition in intermediate steps whose firing conditions are not reachable from the initial states [resp. from whose consequences the goal states are not reachable].

Second, math backjumping is ineffective on these tests. This is due to the fact that, unlike with DTPs, with these math-formulas the conflict sets returned by MATH-SOLVE are very long and nearly always useless for both math backjumping and learning. In fact, when a (possibly small) conflict set is returned by Bellman-Ford, there is no obvious way to reconstruct back the corresponding minimum conflict set by undoing the variable substitutions over the equivalence classes.

Third, simple and enhanced early pruning improve CPU times slightly in Table 1 and very relevantly in Table 2. In particular, this synergy with the customized heuristics *choose_literal()* is due to the fact that the latter can often choose a "bad" transition whose mathematical prerequisites are not verified in the current state. Without early pruning, this causes the generation of a whole search tree of mathematically inconsistent assignments, whose inconsistency is verified one by one. With early pruning, MATH-DPLL invokes MATH-SOLVE and backtracks just after one sequence of unit propagations.

Fourth, whilst enhanced early pruning seems not faster that simple early pruning in the results of Table 1, a significant improvements appears in Table 2. This synergy with the customized heuristics *choose_literal()* is due to the fact that in many situations the value of a clock x is zero —($x = z$) in our encoding— because of either resetting or propagating a previous zero value. If so, performing an enhanced early pruning test before choosing the next transition allows to falsify all incompatible transition prerequisites on x —like, e.g., $(x - z \geq T)$— and thus to avoid choosing the corresponding "bad" transition.

A final consideration on the effectiveness of our layered architecture arises as soon as we do some profiling: a significant number of MATH-SOLVE calls —about 70% with basic MATH-SAT, 20-30% with EP, about 10% with EEP— are solved directly by propagating equalities (L_1), without calling Bellman-Ford (L_2).

5 Related Work and Conclusions

In this paper we have presented a new approach to the solution of decision problems for combinations of boolean propositions and linear equalities and inequalities over real variables. The approach is general, since it allows to integrate different levels of mathematical solving. This also allows for a significant degree of efficiency, since the more expensive solvers are called only when needed by the subproblem being analyzed. For instance, MATH-SAT is faster than TSAT on the specific class of problems for which the latter has been developed. The other closest related work is [19], where the LPSAT solver is presented, handling math-formulas in which all mathematical atoms occur only positively. The approach, however, is hardwired to the domain of planning, and there is no reference to the architectural issues. In [15], a data structure based on Binary Decision Diagrams (BDDs), combining boolean and mathematical constraints, is used to represent the state space of timed automata. The approach is sometimes very efficient, but it inherits the worst-case exponential memory requirements from BDDs.

In the future, we plan to extend the work presented in this paper along the following directions. First, we will tighten the integration of the different solvers within the SAT architecture. This will allow to incrementally construct the equivalence classes for equality reasoning, and reuse the previously constructed information. Then, we will explore the extensions of the approach to more complex (i.e., quadratic) mathematical constraints, and their applications to formal verification of programs.

References

1. R. Alur. Timed Automata. In *Proc. 11th International Computer Aided Verification Conference*, pages 8–22, 1999.
2. A. Armando, C. Castellini, and E. Giunchiglia. SAT-based procedures for temporal reasoning. In *Proc. European Conference on Planning, ECP-99*, 1999.
3. G. Audemard, A. Cimatti, A. Korniłowicz, and R. Sebastiani. Bounded Model Checking for Timed Systems. Technical Report 0201-05, ITC-IRST, Trento, Italy, January 2002. Submitted for publication.
4. R. J. Bayardo, Jr. and R. C. Schrag. Using CSP Look-Back Techniques to Solve Real-World SAT instances. In *Proc AAAI'97*, pages 203–208. AAAI Press, 1997.
5. Michel Berkelaar. The solver lp_solve for Linear Programming and Mixed-Integer Problems. Available at
http://elib.zib.de/pub/Packages/mathprog/linprog/lp-solve/.

6. A. Biere, A. Cimatti, E. Clarke, and Y. Zhu. Symbolic model checking without BDDs. In *Proc. CAV'99*, 1999.
7. M. Buro and H. Buning. Report on a SAT competition. Technical Report 110, University of Paderborn, Germany, November 1992.
8. Boris V. Cherkassky and Andrew V. Goldberg. Negative-cycle detection algorithms. *Mathematical Programming*, 85(2):277–311, 1999.
9. A. Cimatti, M. Pistore, M. Roveri, and R. Sebastiani. Improving the Encoding of LTL Model Checking into SAT. In *Proc. 3rd International Workshop on Verification, Model Checking, and Abstract Interpretation*, volume 2294 of *LNCS*. Springer, 2002.
10. E. Giunchiglia, A. Massarotto, and R. Sebastiani. Act, and the Rest Will Follow: Exploiting Determinism in Planning as Satisfiability. In *Proc. AAAI'98*, pages 948–953, 1998.
11. E. Giunchiglia, M. Narizzano, A. Tacchella, and M. Vardi. Towards an Efficient Library for SAT: a Manifesto. In *Proc. SAT 2001*, Electronics Notes in Discrete Mathematics. Elsevier Science., 2001.
12. F. Giunchiglia and R. Sebastiani. Building decision procedures for modal logics from propositional decision procedures – the case study of modal K. In *Proc. CADE13*, LNAI. Springer Verlag, August 1996.
13. F. Giunchiglia and R. Sebastiani. Building decision procedures for modal logics from propositional decision procedures – the case study of modal K(m). *Information and Computation*, 162(1/2), October/November 2000.
14. I. Horrocks and P. F. Patel-Schneider. FaCT and DLP. In *Proc. of Tableaux'98*, number 1397 in LNAI, pages 27–30. Springer-Verlag, 1998.
15. J. Moeller, J. Lichtenberg, H. Andersen, and H. Hulgaard. Fully Symbolic Model Checking of Timed Systems using Difference Decision Diagrams. In *Electronic Notes in Theoretical Computer Science*, volume 23. Elsevier Science, 2001.
16. R. Sebastiani. Integrating SAT Solvers with Math Reasoners: Foundations and Basic Algorithms. Technical Report 0111-22, ITC-IRST, November 2001.
17. Ofer Shtrichmann. Tuning SAT Checkers for Bounded Model Checking. In *Proc. CAV'2000*, volume 1855 of *LNCS*. Springer, 2000.
18. K. Stergiou and M. Koubarakis. Backtracking algorithms for disjunctions of temporal constraints. In *Proc. AAAI*, pages 248–253, 1998.
19. S. Wolfman and D. Weld. The LPSAT Engine & its Application to Resource Planning. In *Proc. IJCAI*, 1999.

Deductive Search for Errors in Free Data Type Specifications Using Model Generation

Wolfgang Ahrendt

Department of Computing Science,
Chalmers University of Technology, Göteborg, Sweden
ahrendt@cs.chalmers.se

Abstract. The presented approach aims at identifying false conjectures about free data types. Given a specification and a conjecture, the method performs a search for a model of an according *counter specification*. The model search is tailor-made for the semantical setting of free data types, where the fixed domain allows to describe models just in terms of *interpretations*. For sake of interpretation construction, a theory specific calculus is provided. The concrete rules are 'executed' by a procedure known as *model generation*. As most free data types have infinite domains, the ability of automatically solving the non-consequence problem is necessarily limited. That problem is addressed by limiting the *instantiation* of the axioms. This approximation leads to a restricted notion of model correctness, which is discussed. At the same time, it enables model completeness for free data types, unlike approaches based on limiting the domain size.

1 Introduction

The main approaches to abstract data type (ADT) specification have in common that, unlike in pure first order logic, only certain models are considered. In the *initial semantics* approach, the domain is identified with one particular quotient over the set of terms, where the size of the single equivalence classes is 'minimal'. In the *loose semantics* approach, the signature is split up into *constructors* and (other) *function symbols*. Here, the semantical domain is identified with any quotient over the set of *constructor terms*. The function symbols are interpreted as mappings over such domains. The term 'loose' refers the possibility of one specification having a 'polymorphic' meaning, i.e. owning different models, varying particularly in the *interpretation* of the (non-constructor) function symbols. In contrast to that, initial semantics is always 'monomorphic'. This paper is concerned with *free data type* specifications, which are an important special case of loose specifications. Free data types own the additional property that different constructor terms denote different elements. The domain is therefore fixed to be the set of constructor terms. The only thing which is left open is the interpretation of the function symbols. Given an ADT specification and a conjecture φ, we call it an error if φ is *not* a consequence of the axioms AX, regardless of whether the error intuitively lies in the axioms or the conjecture.

A. Voronkov (Ed.): CADE-18, LNAI 2392, pp. 211–225, 2002.

The issue of non-consequence translates to the existence of certain models. A formula φ is *not* a consequence of a set AX of axioms, if there exists a model of AX which violates φ. Our method performs the construction of such models, which in the case of free data types reduces to the *construction of interpretations*. The advantage of having fixed domains is opposed by the disadvantage of domain infinity, caused by recursive constructors. As interpretations over infinite domains are not even countable, an automated procedure can hardly solve the issue of non-consequence in a total way. Instead, the issue is approached by solving the non-consequence problem for an *approximation of the specification*. The method generates models for *finitely many, ground instantiated axioms*. To decide if the model found is extendible to the original axioms, i.e. if the model actually reveals an error, the user can vary the number of ground instances. In spite of these restrictions, the method is complete with respect to error detection. This means that the output will complain about a conjecture whenever the conjecture is faulty.

2   Free Data Types

In the described approach, the distinction between constructors and other function symbols is such important that we completely separate both. We simply call the non-constructor function symbols 'functions'. In the following, if $\mathcal{X}$ is a family of sets, $\overline{\mathcal{X}}$ denotes the union of all sets in $\mathcal{X}$.

Signature. An *ADT signature* Σ is a tuple $(S, \mathcal{C}, \mathcal{F}, \alpha)$, where S is a finite set of sort symbols, $\mathcal{C} = \{C_s | \ s \in S\}$ is a finite family of disjoint, S-indexed sets of constructor symbols, $\mathcal{F} = \{F_s | \ s \in S\}$ is a finite family of disjoint, S-indexed sets of functions $(\overline{\mathcal{C}} \cap \overline{\mathcal{F}} = \emptyset)$, and $\alpha : \overline{\mathcal{C}} \cup \overline{\mathcal{F}} \to S^*$ gives the argument sorts for every constructor or function symbol.

Example 1. We consider the following signature $\Sigma = (S, \mathcal{C}, \mathcal{F}, \alpha)$ for stacks of natural numbers (the constructors are written sans serif):

$$S = \{Nat, Stack\}$$
$$\mathcal{C} = \{\{\mathsf{zero}, \mathsf{succ}\}_{Nat}, \{\mathsf{nil}, \mathsf{push}\}_{Stack}\} \quad \mathcal{F} = \{\{pred, top\}_{Nat}, \{pop, del\}_{Stack}\}$$
$$\alpha(\mathsf{succ}) = Nat \quad \alpha(\mathsf{push}) = [Nat \ Stack] \quad \alpha(\mathsf{zero}) = \alpha(\mathsf{nil}) = \lambda \ \text{(no arguments)}$$
$$\alpha(pred) = Nat \quad \alpha(top) = \alpha(pop) = Stack \quad \alpha(del) = [Nat \ Stack]$$

A concrete syntax for Σ can look like:

sorts
$Nat ::= \mathsf{zero} \mid \mathsf{succ}(Nat);$
$Stack ::= \mathsf{nil} \mid \mathsf{push}(Nat; \ Stack);$

functions
$pred : \ Nat \to Nat;$
$top : \ Stack \to Nat;$
$pop : \ Stack \to Stack;$
$del : \ Nat \times Stack \to Stack;$

Terms. A signature induces terms in general, and constructor terms in particular. T_Σ is the set of all terms, T_s is the set of terms of sort s. V_s is the set of variables of sort s. CT_Σ is the set of all constructor terms, CT_s is the set of constructor terms of sort s, and $\mathcal{CT}_\Sigma = \{CT_s | \ s \in S\}$. We only consider signatures where $CT_s \neq \emptyset$ for all $s \in S$. For a term $t \in T_\Sigma$ with at least i arguments, $t{\downarrow}_i$ denotes the *i-th argument* of t, such that $l(t_1, \ldots, t_i, \ldots, t_n){\downarrow}_i = t_i$.

Semantics (of functions and terms). An $\mathcal{F}$-*interpretation* $\mathcal{I}$ assigns to each function symbol f, with $f \in F_s$ and $\alpha(f) = s_1 \ldots s_n$, a mapping $\mathcal{I}(f) : CT_{s_1} \times \ldots \times CT_{s_n} \to CT_s$. If $\mathcal{I}$ is an $\mathcal{F}$-interpretation, then the pair $(\mathcal{CT}_\Sigma, \mathcal{I})$ is a *freely generated* Σ-*algebra*. A *variable assignment* $\beta : V_\Sigma \to CT_\Sigma$ is a mapping, such that, for $x \in V_s$, $\beta(x) \in CT_s$. For every $\mathcal{F}$-interpretation $\mathcal{I}$ and variable assignment β, the *valuation* $val_{\mathcal{I},\beta} : T_\Sigma \to CT_\Sigma$ of terms is defined by:

$-\ val_{\mathcal{I},\beta}(x) = \beta(x)$, for $x \in V_\Sigma$.

$-\ val_{\mathcal{I},\beta}(f(t_1, \ldots, t_n)) = \mathcal{I}(f)(val_{\mathcal{I},\beta}(t_1), \ldots, val_{\mathcal{I},\beta}(t_n))$, for $f \in \overline{\mathcal{F}}$.

$-\ val_{\mathcal{I},\beta}(c(t_1, \ldots, t_n)) = c(val_{\mathcal{I},\beta}(t_1), \ldots, val_{\mathcal{I},\beta}(t_n))$, for $c \in \overline{\mathcal{C}}$.

We discuss some particular features of these definitions: (a) Only function, not the constructors are interpreted by $\mathcal{I}$. (b) For a given Σ, all freely generated Σ-algebras have the same domain, which is $\mathcal{CT}_\Sigma$, the sorted partitioning of the set of constructor terms. (Therefore, *val* is not indexed by the domain.) (c) The valuation of terms can be seen as a combination of standard valuations, see "$val_{\mathcal{I},\beta}(f(\cdot, \ldots)) = \mathcal{I}(f)(val_{\mathcal{I},\beta}(\cdot), \ldots)$", and Herbrand structure valuations, see "$val_{\mathcal{I},\beta}(c(\cdot, \ldots)) = c(val_{\mathcal{I},\beta}(\cdot), \ldots)$".

Equalities are the only atoms in our logic. For_Σ is the set of first order equality formulae, built from atoms by $\neg$, $\wedge$, $\vee$, $\to$, $\forall$ and $\exists$. Literals ($\in Lit_\Sigma$) are equalities and negated equalities. Clauses ($\in Cl_\Sigma$) are disjunctions of literals. The *contrary* of a formula φ, $Contr(\varphi)$, the free variables of which are $x_1, \ldots, x_n$, is defined by $Contr(\varphi) = \exists x_1 \ldots \exists x_n.\ \neg\varphi$. The valuation $val_{\mathcal{I},\beta}$ of terms and formulae is defined as usual. It is not indexed over some domain, as the domain is fixed. We just point out that in $\forall x.\varphi$ and $\exists x.\varphi$, the x is semantically quantified over CT_s, if $x \in V_s$. Given an $\mathcal{F}$-interpretation $\mathcal{I}$, a formula $\varphi \in For_\Sigma$ is *valid in* $\mathcal{I}$, abbreviated '$\mathcal{I} \models \varphi$', if for all variable assignments β it holds that $val_{\mathcal{I},\beta}(\varphi) = true$. A freely generated Σ-algebra $(\mathcal{CT}_\Sigma, \mathcal{I})$ is a *model* of $\varphi \in For_\Sigma$ resp. $\Phi \subseteq For_\Sigma$, if $\mathcal{I} \models \varphi$ resp. $\mathcal{I} \models \psi$ for all $\psi \in \Phi$. Given $\Phi \subseteq For_\Sigma$ and $\varphi \in For_\Sigma$, then φ *is a consequence of* Φ, abbreviated '$\Phi \models_\Sigma \varphi$', if every model of Φ is a model of φ. $\models_\Sigma \varphi$ abbreviates $\emptyset \models_\Sigma \varphi$.

Example 2. Let $\Sigma = (S, \mathcal{C}, \mathcal{F}, \alpha)$ be an ADT signature with
$S = \{Nat, Bool\}$ $\mathcal{C} = \{\{\text{zero}, \text{succ}\}_{Nat}, \{\text{tt}, \text{ff}\}_{Bool}\}$ $\mathcal{F} = \{\{\}_{Nat}, \{p\}_{Bool}\}$
$\alpha(\text{succ}) = \alpha(p) = Nat$ $\alpha(\text{zero}) = \alpha(\text{tt}) = \alpha(\text{ff}) = \lambda$ Then:

$-\ \models_\Sigma\ \text{succ}(\text{succ}(\text{succ}(\text{zero}))) \neq \text{succ}(\text{zero})$

$-\ \{p(\text{zero}) \doteq \text{tt},\ p(x) \doteq \text{tt} \to p(\text{succ}(x)) \doteq \text{tt}\} \models_\Sigma p(x) \doteq \text{tt}$

('$\doteq$' is the equality symbol of the object logic. '$\neq$' abbreviates negated equality.) An *ADT specification* is a pair $\langle \Sigma, AX \rangle$, where Σ is an ADT signature and $AX \subseteq For_\Sigma$. AX is the set of *axioms*. The notions of model and consequence are extended to specifications (while overloading '$\models$' a bit): $(\mathcal{CT}_\Sigma, \mathcal{I})$ is a *model* of $\langle \Sigma, AX \rangle$ if it is a model of AX. φ is a *consequence* of $\langle \Sigma, AX \rangle$, abbreviated '$\langle \Sigma, AX \rangle \models \varphi$', if $AX \models_\Sigma \varphi$.
'$\langle \Sigma, AX \rangle \not\models \varphi$' abbreviates that φ is *not* a consequence of $\langle \Sigma, AX \rangle$.

Example 3. The specification NatStack is given by $\langle \Sigma, AX \rangle$, where Σ is taken from *Example 1* and AX is given by

$$AX = \{ \ pred(\mathsf{succ}(n)) \doteq n \ , \ top(\mathsf{push}(n,st)) \doteq n \ , \ pop(\mathsf{push}(n,st)) \doteq st,$$
$$del(n, \mathsf{nil}) \doteq \mathsf{nil} \ , \ del(n, \mathsf{push}(n,st)) \doteq st \ ,$$
$$n \not\doteq n' \rightarrow del(n, \mathsf{push}(n',st)) \doteq \mathsf{push}(n', del(n,st)) \ \}$$

Given a specification SPEC and a formula φ, it may be that neither φ nor the opposite, $Contr(\varphi)$, is a consequence of a specification SPEC. For instance, neither (a) NatStack $\models pred(n) \not\doteq n$ nor (b) NatStack $\models \exists n. \ pred(n) \doteq n$ holds. This is due to the underspecification of *pred*. In one model of NatStack, $\mathcal{I}(pred)(\mathsf{zero})$ is zero, falsifying (a). In another model of NatStack, $\mathcal{I}(pred)(\mathsf{zero})$ is $\mathsf{succ}(\mathsf{zero})$, falsifying (b).

Proposition 1. *Let* $\Sigma = (S, \mathcal{C}, \mathcal{F}, \alpha)$ *be an ADT signature and* $\langle \Sigma, AX \rangle$ *an ADT specification. Then:*

$$\langle \Sigma, AX \rangle \not\models \varphi$$
$$\Longleftrightarrow$$
there exists an $\mathcal{F}$-interpretation with $\mathcal{I} \models AX \cup Contr(\varphi)$

In that context, we call $\langle \Sigma, AX \cup Contr(\varphi) \rangle$ a 'counter specification', and $\mathcal{I}$ the 'counter interpretation'. Our method mainly constructs such counter interpretations.

Given a specification $\langle \Sigma, AX \rangle$ and a conjecture φ, the method consists in three steps. The first is to construct *and normalise* the counter specification $\langle \Sigma, AX \cup Contr(\varphi) \rangle$. A specification is normalised if its axioms are clauses ($\in Cl_\Sigma$). Particularly, the existential quantifiers introduced by *Contr* are Skolemized away. The Skolemization handling has to respect our particular semantical setting, by adding the Skolem symbols to the *functions*, not to the constructors! The second and main step is the search for, and construction of, an according interpretation, see the following section. In the case of success, the last step consists in some post-processing, for sake of giving the user feedback in terms of the original specification and conjecture. We give examples for such output in section 7.

3   Explicit Reasoning about Interpretations

The core of the proposed method constructs $\mathcal{F}$-interpretations for normalised ADT specifications. We can think of an $\mathcal{F}$-interpretation $\mathcal{I}$ being a set of (in general infinite) tables, one for each function $f \in \overline{\mathcal{F}}$. The basic idea of our approach is to *perform reasoning about $\mathcal{F}$-interpretations using a representation that immediately describes individual lines of interpretation tables*. In particular, we represent lines of these tables as *atoms*, using the three argument predicate 'I'. I$(f, \langle ct_1, \ldots, ct_n \rangle, ct)$ represents the information that $\mathcal{I}(f)(ct_1, \ldots, ct_n)$ is ct. It is important to note that such atoms are *not* part of the object logic, used in formulae $\in For_\Sigma$, if only because the object signatures we consider do not contain predicate symbols. Instead, I-atoms are formulae *on the meta level*. These (and others) will be used for a kind of 'meta reasoning'. Beside 'I-atoms', we will use some others, calling them all 'meta atoms'. Each set of I-atoms represents a part of some $\mathcal{F}$-interpretation, if the set is *functional* in the last arguments, i.e. if there are no two I-atoms $I(g, \langle ct_1, \ldots, ct_n \rangle, ct_0)$ and $I(g, \langle ct_1, \ldots, ct_n \rangle, ct_0')$ with *different* constructor terms ct_0 and ct_0'. An arbitrary set of I-atoms, not necessarily being functional, describes an *interpretation candidate*. The search for proper interpretations consists mainly in the construction of interpretation candidates, by inferring new I-atoms using proof rules. Other proof rules reject candidates, e.g. as soon as they turn out not to be functional.

The inferred I-atoms do not have the pure form sketched above, in general. Some constructor terms may be unknown, initially, and must be searched for. They are represented by *place holders*, which are replaced later. Consider a function $f : Nat \to Nat$, and suppose we are searching for the value of $\mathcal{I}(f)(\text{zero})$. The following discussion is supported by the tree depicted here.

$$I(f,\ \langle \text{zero} \rangle,\ \text{val}(f(\text{zero})))$$

$$\text{search } Nat(\text{val}(f(\text{zero})))$$

$$\text{is}(\text{val}(f(\text{zero})),\ \text{zero}) \qquad\qquad \text{is}(\text{val}(f(\text{zero})),\ \text{succ}(\text{arg1}(\text{val}(f(\text{zero})))))$$

$$\boxed{I(f,\ \langle \text{zero} \rangle,\ \text{zero})} \qquad\qquad \text{search } Nat(\text{arg1}(\text{val}(f(\text{zero}))))$$

$$\text{is}(\text{arg1}(\text{val}(f(\text{zero}))),\ \text{zero}) \qquad :$$

$$\text{is}(\text{val}(f(\text{zero})),\ \text{succ}(\text{zero}))$$

$$\boxed{I(f,\ \langle \text{zero} \rangle,\ \text{succ}(\text{zero}))}$$

The search is initialised by creating the I-atom $I(f, \langle \text{zero} \rangle, \text{val}(f(\text{zero})))$. Its last argument, $\text{val}(f(\text{zero}))$, acts as a placeholder for the constructor term which we search for, and its syntax tells that it replaces the constructor term which equals '$\text{val}(f(\text{zero}))$'. As such, this atom does not contain much information. However, it is only meant to be a starting point. The search for a more informative last argument is initialised by adding another meta-atom, $\text{search\_}Nat(\text{val}(f(\text{zero})))$, to the model candidate. This atom causes a branching of the candidate, where each branch corresponds to one constructor of the sort Nat. On the first branch, we assume $val_{\mathcal{I}}(f(\text{zero}))$ to equal zero, by inferring $\text{is}(\text{val}(f(\text{zero})), \text{zero})$. On the second branch, we assume $val_{\mathcal{I}}(f(\text{zero}))$ to equal a constructor term starting with succ, by inferring an atom of the form $\text{is}(\text{val}(f(\text{zero})), \text{succ}(\ldots))$. The left out argument of $\text{succ}(\ldots)$ is explained now. On *this* branch $val_{\mathcal{I}}(f(\text{zero}))$ equals $\text{succ}(t)$ for some $t \in CT_{Nat}$. What we know about t is (a) that it is the *first argument* of $\text{succ}(t)$, i.e. $t = \text{succ}(t) \downarrow_1 = val_{\mathcal{I}}(f(\text{zero})) \downarrow_1$, and therefore represent t using the syntax $\text{arg1}(\text{val}(f(\text{zero})))$, such that we actually have $\text{is}(\text{val}(f(\text{zero})), \text{succ}(\text{arg1}(\text{val}(f(\text{zero})))))$. What we also know about t is (b) that t is a constructor term $\in CT_{Nat}$ which we have to search for further. Corresponding to the above discussion, we also add $\text{search\_}Nat(\text{arg1}(\text{val}(f(\text{zero}))))$ to the second branch. This search-atom causes another split, which is sketched in tree. Coming back to our first branch, it remains to propagate the information from is(val(f(zero)), zero) to the initial atom I(f, $\langle$zero$\rangle$, val(f(zero))), by inferring I(f, $\langle$zero$\rangle$, zero). A similar propagation happens twice on the first subbranch of the second branch, leading to the atom I(f, $\langle$zero$\rangle$, succ(zero)).

Looking at the leaves of the tree, we see that the different possible values of $\mathcal{I}(f)$(zero) are enumerated. If this was everything we wanted, we should not have chosen a deductive treatment. But at first, this mechanism will interfere with others explained below. And at second, the stepwise construction of constructor terms from the outer to the inner allows to *reject* a model candidate earlier, in some cases it enables rejection in finite time at all. In our example, the term succ(arg1(val(f(zero)))) represents all (i.e. infinitely many) terms starting with succ.

After this demonstration, we introduce the *rules* we used, denoting them in a tableaux style. x, y, z, fv and tv are rule variables.

$$\frac{\text{search\_}Nat(x)}{\text{is}(x, \text{zero}) \qquad \begin{array}{c} \text{is}(x, \text{succ}(\text{arg1}(x))) \\ \text{search\_}Nat(\text{arg1}(x)) \end{array}} \qquad \frac{\text{I}(fv,\ tv,\ x)}{\begin{array}{c}\text{is}(x,\ z)\\ \text{I}(fv,\ tv,\ z)\end{array}} \qquad \frac{\text{is}(x,\ \text{succ}(y))}{\begin{array}{c}\text{is}(y,\ z)\\ \text{is}(x,\ \text{succ}(z))\end{array}}$$

In the following, we turn over to use a linear notation for such rules, using the general pattern:

$$\underbrace{at_1,\dots,at_n}_{\text{premise}} \to \overbrace{\underbrace{at_{11},\dots,at_{1n_1}}_{\text{1.extension}} ; \ \dots \ ; \ \underbrace{at_{m_1},\dots,at_{mn_m}}_{\text{m.extension}}}^{\text{conclusion}} .$$

This simplifies the task of defining the transformation of specifications into rules. Moreover, this notation of rules is very close to the input notation of the tool we later use for rule execution.

4   Transforming the Signature

The linear notation of the above search_*Nat*-rule is:

search_$Nat(x)$ $\to$ is(x, zero) ; is(x, succ(arg1(x))), search_Nat(arg1(x)) .

We now define the general case.

Definition 1. *Let* $\Sigma = (S, \mathcal{C}, \mathcal{F}, \alpha)$ *be an ADT signature, with* $s \in S$ *and* $C_s = \{c_1, \dots, c_n\}$, *where* $|\alpha(c_i)| \leq |\alpha(c_j)|$ *for* $i \leq j$. *Then*

$$TransSort_\Sigma(s)$$
$$=$$
$$\text{search\_}s(x) \to TransConstr_\Sigma(x, c_1) ; \ \dots \ ; \ TransConstr_\Sigma(x, c_n) .$$

Note the semi-colon between the different extensions of the rule. The condition $|\alpha(c_i)| \leq |\alpha(c_j)|$ ensures that we order the extensions after the number of the constructor's arguments. The individual extensions are defined as follows.

Definition 2. *Let* Σ *be an ADT signature, with* $c \in C_\Sigma$.
– *if* $|\alpha(c)| = 0$, *then:* $TransConstr_\Sigma(x, c) = \{ \text{is}(x, c) \}$

– *if $\alpha(c) = s_1 \ldots s_n$, then:*

$$TransConstr_\Sigma(x, c)$$

$$=$$

{ is$(x, c(\text{arg}1(x), \ldots, \text{arg}n(x)))$, search_$s_1(\text{arg}1(x))$, $\ldots$, search_$s_n(\text{arg}n(x))$ }

In concrete rules resulting from the transformation, we skip the set braces. Here is the result of $TransSort_\Sigma(Stack)$:

$$\text{search\_}Stack(x) \ \rightarrow$$
$$\text{is}(x, \text{nil}) \ ;$$
$$\text{is}(x, \text{push}(\text{arg}1(x), \text{arg}2(x))) \ , \ \text{search\_}Nat(\text{arg}1(x)) \ , \ \text{search\_}Stack(\text{arg}2(x)) \ .$$

We now introduce the handling of (in)equality, discussing concrete rules, for *Nat* and *Stack* at first.

$$\text{same}(\text{succ}(x), \ \text{zero}) \ \rightarrow \ .$$
$$\text{same}(\text{push}(x_1, x_2), \ \text{push}(y_1, y_2)) \ \rightarrow \ \text{same}(x_1, y_1) \ , \ \text{same}(x_2, y_2) \ .$$
$$\text{different}(\text{zero}, \ \text{zero}) \ \rightarrow \ .$$
$$\text{different}(\text{push}(x_1, x_2), \ \text{push}(y_1, y_2)) \ \rightarrow \ \text{different}(x_1, y_1) \ ; \ \text{different}(x_2, y_2) \ .$$

The first and the third rule cause the proof procedure to *reject* a model candidate. Note that the last rule is a branching rule. We define the general case now:

Definition 3. *Let $\Sigma = (S, \mathcal{C}, \mathcal{F}, \alpha)$ be an ADT signature. The rules reflecting the 'freely generatedness', are contained in $FreeGen_\Sigma = TestSame_\Sigma \cup TestDiff_\Sigma$.*

– *$TestSame_\Sigma$ is the smallest set fulfilling:*
   - *for each two different constructors c_1, c_2 of the same sort ($\{c_1, c_2\} \subseteq C_s$), where $|\alpha(c_1)| = n$ and $|\alpha(c_2)| = m$,*
   $$\text{same}(c_1(x_1, \ldots, x_n), \ c_2(y_1, \ldots, y_m)) \ \rightarrow \ . \ \in TestSame_\Sigma$$
   - *for each constructor $c \in C_s$, where $|\alpha(c)| = n \neq 0$*
   $$\left. \begin{array}{l} \text{same}(c(x_1, \ldots, x_n), \ c(y_1, \ldots, y_n)) \\ \rightarrow \ \text{same}(x_1, \ y_1) \ , \ \ldots \ , \ \text{same}(x_n, \ y_n) \ . \end{array} \right\} \in TestSame_\Sigma$$
– *$TestDiff_\Sigma$ is the smallest set fulfilling:*
   - *for each constructor $c \in C_s$,*
     * *if $\alpha(c) = \lambda$, then*
     $$\text{different}(c, \ c) \ \rightarrow \ . \ \in TestDiff_\Sigma$$
     * *if $|\alpha(c)| = n \neq 0$, then:*
     $$\left. \begin{array}{l} \text{different}(c(x_1, \ldots, x_n), \ c(y_1, \ldots, y_n)) \\ \rightarrow \ \text{different}(x_1, \ y_1) \ ; \ \ldots \ ; \ \text{different}(x_n, \ y_n) \ . \end{array} \right\} \in TestDiff_\Sigma$$

The same- and different-atoms are introduced either by transformed axioms (see below), or by the following rule which 'checking' for *functionality*.

$$\text{I}(fv, tv, z) \ , \ \text{I}(fv, tv, z') \ \rightarrow \ \text{same}(z, z') \ .$$

In the end of section 3, we encountered the two rules:

$$\text{is}(x, \text{succ}(y)) \ , \ \text{is}(y, z) \ \rightarrow \ \text{is}(x, \text{succ}(z)) \ .$$
$$\text{I}(fv, tv, x) \ , \ \text{is}(x, z) \ \rightarrow \ \text{I}(fv, tv, z) \ .$$

The general case of such 'replacement' rules is described here only informally. The first rule must be provided for each constructor, and for each of a constructor's argument positions. The second rule is general enough. In addition, we need similar rules to replace each position in the tuples of I-atoms, as well as rules for replacing arguments of same() and different().

5   Transforming the Axioms

The rules discussed so far only consider the signature. But we actually are searching for a *model* of a specification, i.e. for a model of its *axioms*. In our approach, also (or particularly) the axioms are transformed to rules. We now explain this transformation, using very simple examples at the beginning. We start with ground equalities. Let $f_1(ct_1) \doteq f_2(ct_2)$ be an axiom, where f_1, f_2 are functions of some sort s, and ct_1, ct_2 are constructor terms. This equality can be represented by the rule:

$$\rightarrow \mathrm{I}(f_1, \langle ct_1 \rangle, \mathrm{val}(f_1(ct_1))) \ , \ \mathrm{search\_}s(\mathrm{val}(f_1(ct_1))) \ , \ \mathrm{I}(f_2, \langle ct_2 \rangle, \mathrm{val}(f_2(ct_2))) \ ,$$
$$\mathrm{search\_}s(\mathrm{val}(f_2(ct_2))) \ , \ \mathrm{same}(\mathrm{val}(f_1(ct_1)), \mathrm{val}(f_2(ct_2))) \ .$$

The rule intuitively says that we have to search for the two last arguments of the I-atoms, but with the constraint that they have to be the same. The empty premise means that the extension atoms can be added to *any* model candidate. In practice, the rule will be applied towards the beginning, before the initial model candidate branches. A transformation of $f_1(ct_1) \neq f_2(ct_2)$ results in almost the same rule, just that we have 'different' instead of 'same'.

The rule for $f_1(ct_1) \doteq f_2(ct_2)$ can be optimised, by loss of its symmetry. Instead of *twice* searching for something that should finally be the 'same' thing, it suffices to search for one of both:

$$\rightarrow \mathrm{I}(f_1, \langle ct_1 \rangle, \mathrm{val}(f_2(ct_2))) \ , \ \mathrm{I}(f_2, \langle ct_2 \rangle, \mathrm{val}(f_2(ct_2))) \ , \ \mathrm{search\_}s(\mathrm{val}(f_2(ct_2))) \ .$$

This is of course more efficient. Moreover, the examples are easier to understand when the resulting rules are as short as possible. On the other hand, the definition of the transformation is much simpler in a version that is not optimised and therefore more regular. In this paper, only define the unoptimised transformation formally. However, in the example transformations, we also show the optimised versions, which are more readable. A formal definition of the optimised transformation is given in [Ahr01, Sect. 3.2.3]. (Note that the rule for $f_1(ct_1) \neq f_2(ct_2)$ cannot be optimised similarly.)

The next example shows that, in general, we have to transform function terms in a recursive manner. The (again quite artificial) axiom $f_1(f_2(ct_1)) \doteq ct_2$ translates to the rule:

$$\rightarrow \mathrm{I}(f_2, \langle ct_1 \rangle, \mathrm{val}(f_2(ct_1))) \ , \ \mathrm{search\_}s(\mathrm{val}(f_2(ct_1))) \ , \ \mathrm{I}(f_1, \langle \mathrm{val}(f_2(ct_1)) \rangle, ct_2) \ .$$

Intuitively, this says that the last argument of $\mathrm{I}(f_2, \langle ct_1 \rangle, \mathrm{val}(f_2(ct_1)))$ is a not yet known constructor term, which has to be searched for. What *is* known about $\mathrm{val}(f_2(ct_1))$ is represented by the I-atom $\mathrm{I}(f_1, \langle \mathrm{val}(f_2(ct_1)) \rangle, ct_2)$.

So far, we discussed ground axioms, for simplicity. We now consider the axiom $f(x) \doteq ct$. The resulting rule is:

$$s(x) \ \rightarrow \ \mathrm{I}(f, \langle x \rangle, ct) \ .$$

'Binding' variables by *sort predicates* is a technique widely used. The operational meaning for the above rule is that, whenever we have $s(ct')$ on the current branch, for some ct', then we can infer $\mathrm{I}(f, \langle ct' \rangle, ct)$. In general, we can have functions on both side, as well as nested functions. The transformation then follows the same patterns as sketched above for the ground case, but finally 'binding ' all variables by providing sort atoms in the rule premise. We demonstrate this in another example: the commutativity axiom $f(x, y) \doteq f(y, x)$ becomes

$$s(x), \; s(y) \; \rightarrow$$
$$\mathsf{I}(f, \langle x, y \rangle, \mathsf{val}(f(y, x))) \; , \; \mathsf{I}(f, \langle y, x \rangle, \mathsf{val}(f(y, x))) \; , \; \mathsf{search\_}s(\mathsf{val}(f(y, x))) \; .$$

Note again that x and y are 'rule variables'. They do not appear on the branches, which are always ground. The application of this rule generates a *new* place holder $\mathsf{val}(f(ct, ct'))$ for every pair ct and ct' for which s-predicates are provided. The difference between our usage of val *terms*, and computing new place holder *symbols* in each rule application, is that we can possibly *reuse* the val terms, even when applying other rules. Therefore, the usage of val terms has similarities to the usage of ϵ-terms in free variable tableaux, described in [GA99]. In our context, the less place holders we produce, the less searches we start.

In the general case, axioms of normalised specifications are clauses, i.e. disjunctions of equalities and inequalities. The according rules can directly reflect the disjunction in the 'branching', by transforming each literal to a distinct extension of the rule.

Definition 4. *Be* $\Sigma = (S, \mathcal{C}, \mathcal{F}, \alpha)$ *an ADT signature and* $ax \in Kl_\Sigma$, *with* $ax = lit_1 \vee \ldots \vee lit_n$, $Var(ax) = \{x_1, \ldots, x_m\}$ *and* $sort(x_i) = s_i$. *Then:*

$$TransAxiom_\Sigma(ax) \; =$$
$$s_1(x_1) \; , \; \ldots \; , \; s_m(x_m) \; \rightarrow \; TransLit_\Sigma(lit_1) \; ; \; \ldots \; ; \; TransLit_\Sigma(lit_n) \; .$$

In the following definition of $TransLit_\Sigma$ and its subparts, we use '$Rep(t)$' to factor out a certain case distinction. The 'representation' of a term $t \in T_\Sigma$, $Rep(t)$, is defined to be t itself, if t contains only constructors and variables, or $\mathsf{val}(t)$, if t contains any functions. In particular, Rep is the identity for variables as well as for constructor terms.

Definition 5. *Let* $\Sigma = (S, \mathcal{C}, \mathcal{F}, \alpha)$ *be an ADT signature.*

- *Let* $t_1, t_2 \in T_s$ *for some* $s \in S$. *Then:*

$$TransLit_\Sigma(t_1 \doteq t_2) =$$
$$\{ \; \mathsf{same}(Rep(t_1), Rep(t_2)) \; , \; TransTerm_\Sigma(t_1) \; , \; TransTerm_\Sigma(t_2) \; \}$$

$$TransLit_\Sigma(t_1 \not\doteq t_2) =$$
$$\{ \; \mathsf{different}(Rep(t_1), Rep(t_2)) \; , \; TransTerm_\Sigma(t_1) \; , \; TransTerm_\Sigma(t_2) \; \}$$

- *Let* $t \in T_\Sigma$. *Then:*
  - *if* t *contains no functions, then:* $\quad TransTerm_\Sigma(t) \quad = \quad \emptyset$
  - *if* $t = a$ *with* $a \in F_s$, $\alpha(a) = \lambda$, *then:*

  $$TransTerm_\Sigma(t) = \{ \; \mathsf{I}(a, \langle \rangle, \mathsf{val}(a)), \; \mathsf{search\_}s(\mathsf{val}(a)) \; \}$$

  - *if* $t = f(t_1, \ldots, t_n)$ *with* $f \in F_s$, $\alpha(f) = s_1 \ldots s_n$, *then:*

  $$TransTerm_\Sigma(t) =$$
  $$\{ \; \mathsf{I}(f, \langle Rep(t_1), \ldots, Rep(t_n) \rangle, \mathsf{val}(t)) \; , \; \mathsf{search\_}s(\mathsf{val}(t)) \; \}$$
  $$\cup$$
  $$\bigcup_{i=1}^{n} TransTerm_\Sigma(t_i)$$

- *if* $t = c(t_1, \ldots, t_n)$ *with* $c \in C_s$, $\alpha(c) = s_1 \ldots s_n$, *and if* t *contains functions, then:*

$$TransTerm_\Sigma(t) =$$
$$\{ \text{ is}(\text{val}(t), c(Rep(t_1), \ldots, Rep(t_n))) \} \cup \bigcup_{i=1}^{n} TransTerm_\Sigma(t_i)$$

Note that $TransTerm_\Sigma(t)$ is empty exactly when $Rep(t)$ is t. This means that the recursion stops at terms that can be represented by themselves in the resulting rules. In contrast, function terms can only appear nested in val terms, i.e. place holders. Also note that we took the liberty to take over the variables as they are, even if in the rules they act as 'rule variables', to be matched/instantiated by rule application.

As an example, we show the result of transforming the (normalised) last axiom of NatStack (see Example 3).

$$TransAxiom_\Sigma(\ n \doteq m \ \lor \ del(n, \text{push}(m, st)) \doteq \text{push}(m, del(n, st))\ )$$
$$=$$
$$Nat(n),\ Nat(m),\ Stack(st)$$
$$\rightarrow$$
$$\text{same}(n, m)\ ;$$
$$\text{same}(\text{val}(del(n, \text{push}(m, st))),\ \text{val}(\text{push}(m, del(n, st)))),$$
$$\text{I}(del, \langle n, \text{push}(m, st)\rangle, \text{val}(del(n, \text{push}(m, st))))),$$
$$\text{search\_}Stack(\text{val}(del(n, \text{push}(m, st))))),$$
$$\text{is}(\text{val}(\text{push}(m, del(n, st))), \text{push}(m, \text{val}(del(n, st))))),$$
$$\text{I}(del, \langle n, st\rangle, \text{val}(del(n, st)))),$$
$$\text{search\_}Stack(\text{val}(del(n, st)))\ .$$

The optimised version results in a shorter rule:

$$Nat(n),\ Nat(m),\ Stack(st)$$
$$\rightarrow$$
$$\text{same}(n, m)\ ;$$
$$\text{I}(del, \langle n, \text{push}(m, st)\rangle, \text{val}(\text{push}(m, del(n, st))))),$$
$$\text{is}(\text{val}(\text{push}(m, del(n, st))), \text{push}(m, \text{val}(del(n, st))))),$$
$$\text{I}(del, \langle n, st\rangle, \text{val}(del(n, st)))),$$
$$\text{search\_}Stack(\text{val}(del(n, st)))\ .$$

We also show the transformation of another, simpler axiom:

$$TransAxiom_\Sigma(\ pop(\text{push}(n, st)) \doteq st\ )$$
$$=$$
$$nat(n), stack(st)$$
$$\rightarrow$$
$$\text{same}(\text{val}(pop(\text{push}(n, st))), st),$$
$$\text{I}(pop, \langle \text{push}(n, st)\rangle, \text{val}(pop(\text{push}(n, st))))),$$
$$\text{search\_}Stack(\text{val}(pop(\text{push}(n, st))))\ .$$

In this quite typical axiom pattern, the optimised transformation gains an enormous simplification:

$$nat(n) \; , \; stack(st) \; \rightarrow \; \mathrm{I}(pop, \langle \mathsf{push}(n, st) \rangle, st) \; .$$

6 Model Generation for Approximated Specifications

The rules transformed from the axioms can only be applied if the current model candidate contains appropriate sort atoms. Ideally, we would need to have $s(ct)$ for *every* constructor term ct of sort s, and that for each sort. This cannot be realized in finite time. But what we want is a method which *terminates in case there is a model*. This makes the real difference to the traditional (refutational) methods for *proving* conjectures. Our approach to the issue of model construction for free data type specifications does not solve the problem completely. An automated method hardly can. Instead we construct a model of an *approximation* of the specification.

Let us assume now that the constructors are recursive (which is mostly the case) and, therefore, determine an *infinite* domain. The set of (quantifier free) axioms is then equivalent to an *infinite set of ground axioms*, which results from instantiating the variables by all constructor terms. We now approximate the specification by considering a *finite subset* of these ground axioms, which results from instantiating the variables by a *finitely many constructor terms*. Particularly, we limit the number of instances by limiting their 'size', which is simply defined to be the number of constructors. '$\langle \Sigma, AX_{\leq n} \rangle$' denotes such an '$n$-restricted specification', where the axioms are instantiated by all constructor terms of maximal size n. The instantiation of axioms is reflected by applying the rules transformed from the axioms, where the arguments of the matched sort atoms are the instances. Therefore, to make the rules search for a model of '$\langle \Sigma, AX_{\leq n} \rangle$', we just initialise the first model candidate to be the set of sort atoms for all constructor terms up to size n. In the theorems below, we call this 'n-initialisation'. In practice, the n has to be rather small. But, depending on the signature, the *number* of terms is significantly bigger than their maximal size.

On this initial 'model candidate' (at first only containing sort atoms), the rules, transformed from a (counter) specification, are 'executed' by some procedure. We use a procedure known as *model generation* ([MB88], [FH91]), which can be seen positive, regular hyper tableaux. The regularity ensures termination in case every matching rule has *at least one extension* not adding anything new to the branch. If one branch cannot be extended further, model generation stops. In the theorems below, we call this 'termination by saturation' (in contrast to 'termination by rejection'). Our realization uses the tool 'MGTP' (model generation theorem prover, [FH91]) for executing the described rules. The input of a model generation procedure is a set of what they called 'clauses', which corresponds to what we called 'rules'. These 'clauses' have the general form depicted in the end of section 3. In addition, the rules must be 'range restricted', which means that each variable must also occur on the left side of '$\rightarrow$'. Our rules fulfil that restriction.

Taking the basic model generation procedure which is implemented in MGTP as an execution model for the transformed rules, we state the following

Theorem 1. *(n-restricted model correctness)*
Let $\langle \Sigma, AX \rangle$ be a normalised ADT spec., $n \in \mathbb{N}$ and $R = TransSpec(\langle \Sigma, AX \rangle)$.
If the n-initialised model generation procedure with input R terminates by saturation, then (a) $\langle \Sigma, AX_{\leq n} \rangle$ has a model, and (b) for every $\mathcal{F}$-interpretation $\mathcal{I}$ which corresponds to the I-atoms on the saturated branch, it holds that $\mathcal{I} \models \langle \Sigma, AX_{\leq n} \rangle$.

Theorem 2. *(model completeness)*
Let $\langle \Sigma, AX \rangle$ be a normalised ADT spec., $n \in \mathbb{N}$ and $R = TransSpec(\langle \Sigma, AX \rangle)$.
If $\langle \Sigma, AX \rangle$ has a model, then an n-initialised, fair model generation procedure with input R terminates by saturation, and for every $\mathcal{F}$-interpretation $\mathcal{I}$ which corresponds to the I-atoms on the saturated branch, it holds that $\mathcal{I} \models \langle \Sigma, AX_{\leq n} \rangle$.

The fairness in Theorem 2 is a requirement not implemented in MGTP. In practice, this is less important than in theory, as the search for constructor terms builds small terms first, and as small terms usually suffice to find a validating interpretation. However, the rules as such are complete, and this independent of n! Note that the theorem says "If $\langle \Sigma, AX \rangle$ has a model" instead of "If $\langle \Sigma, AX_{\leq n} \rangle$ has a model". We translate the completeness result to the non-consequence problem we are originally interested in. If it holds that '$\langle \Sigma, AX \rangle \not\models \varphi$, then model generation applied to the transformation of '$\langle \Sigma, AX \cup Contr(\varphi) \rangle$' terminates by saturation.

Both proofs for these theorems are nontrivial, particularly the completeness argument, which requires a termination argument, to be inferred from the model which is assumed to exist. The detailed proofs are given in [Ahr01].

7   Implementation and Examples

The method is implemented as a JAVA program, which, given a specification $\langle \Sigma, AX \rangle$ and a conjecture φ, (a) computes the transformation of the normalisation of $\langle \Sigma, AX \cup Contr(\varphi) \rangle$, (b) calls MGTP, and in case of saturation (c) analyses the saturated branch, producing an output both to the prompt and to a LATEX file, telling why φ might not be a consequence of $\langle \Sigma, AX \rangle$.

For instance, given NatStack and the conjecture $del(top(st), st) \doteq pop(st)$, the (abbreviated) LATEX output is:
the conjecture del(top(ST), ST) = pop(ST)
is violated by the following variable assignment: ST : nil
and by the following evaluation of conjecture subterms:
del(top(ST),ST) : nil
top(ST) : zero
pop(ST) : push(zero,nil)

The interpretation found by the system satisfies the axioms,
if instantiated by constructor terms with less than 4 constructors!
(*end of output*)
The warning reminds the user on what we called *n-restricted* correctness. Nevertheless, the system tells that the specification allows $pop(\mathsf{nil})$ being evaluated to $\mathsf{push}(\mathsf{zero}, \mathsf{nil})$, in which case $del(top(\mathsf{nil}), \mathsf{nil}) \doteq pop(\mathsf{nil})$ is false, and therefore the conjecture is false. This shows that either the conjecture or the specification has to be changed. Another example for a false conjecture on NatStack which the system complains about is $\mathsf{push}(top(st), pop(st)) \doteq st$.

Due to the *n-restricted* correctness, the system possibly can complain about a conjecture that actually *is* a consequence of the axioms. This happens for instance when we ask if $p(x) \doteq \mathsf{tt}$ is a consequence of (see Example 2, page 213):
$$\{p(\mathsf{zero}) \doteq \mathsf{tt}, \ p(x) \doteq \mathsf{tt} \rightarrow p(\mathsf{succ}(x)) \doteq \mathsf{tt}\}$$
The system complains about this conjecture, because it can always construct $\mathrm{I}(p, \langle \mathsf{succ}(ct) \rangle, \mathsf{ff})$ for a ct which is slightly bigger than the size restriction n.

The last example we mention here is based on a specification taken from [Thu98]. Even if [Thu98] also investigates errors in specifications, this error is neither discussed nor detected nor even intended there. We refer to that revealed error not to blame the author, but to demonstrate how easily such errors happen, even in a context where one is very aware of the possibility of errors. (In general, an more open exchange of errors that really happen would be of great benefit to the development of error revealing techniques.) The cited specification is intended to describe a 'merge sort' algorithm. The two main axioms are:
$sort(\mathsf{empty}) \doteq \mathsf{empty}$ and $sort(append(l, l')) \doteq merge(sort(l), sort(l'))$.

Our system, when being asked if the singleton list is stable under *sort*, i.e. $sort(\mathsf{cons}(n, \mathsf{empty})) \doteq \mathsf{cons}(n, \mathsf{empty})$, complains and suggests to evaluate $sort(\mathsf{cons}(n, \mathsf{empty}))$ to empty (!), as this is consistent with the specification, which does not specify at all how to sort a singleton. (To comprehend this, it suffices to know two more axioms: $merge(\mathsf{empty}, l') \doteq l'$ and $merge(l, \mathsf{empty}) \doteq l$.) As any other sorting reduces to sorting the singleton, the specification does not specify the sorting of *any* (but the empty) list.

8 Related Work and Conclusion

The works related to our task and approach can be divided in two (overlapping) fields: (1.) model construction and (2.) detecting faulty conjectures. In the first area, there are several methods searching for finite domain models. The methods described in [Sla94] and [ZZ96] search for models of a fixed size, whereas [BT98] dynamically extends the finite domain. As free data types usually have infinite domains, these finite domain methods cannot directly be applied to our setting. (A further discussion follows bellow.) Other methods in the first area are more syntax oriented, describing models by (extensions of) formulae ([FL96], [CP00]). These approaches construct models for *first order* formulae, usually not containing equalities. Our object logic, however, is completely equality based and, because of constructor generatedness, beyond first order. In the second area, a lot of work is done in the context of initial (or rewrite) semantics, where due to monomorphicity, the notions of proof and consistency are very close ([Bac88]). Also where monomorphicity is imposed by purely sysntactical means, the detection of faulty conjectures reduces to proving their opposite ([Pro92]). In that context, even the *correction* of faulty conjectures is examined ([Pro96], [MBI94]).

To the best knowledge of the author, the only work that is similarly dedicated to the detection of faulty conjectures in *loose* specifications (not even restricted to *free* data types), is [Thu98,RST01]. There, a 'counter example' is essentially a falsifying variable assignment, rather than a falsifying model. Unsurprisingly, that method, as well as ours, cannot totally solve the issue of non-consequence. During the construction of falsifying variable assignments, the method produces side condition, the consistence of which left to be judged by the user. Like in our approach, the user has to take the final decision. The assignment of values to axiom variables is included in our method (see the example outputs). Moreover, our method analyses possible valuation of function terms.

We conclude by stressing the main features of the presented approach and its implementation. We provide a fully automated method which is tailor-made for *detecting non-consequence* between a free data type specification and a conjecture. It searches for a counter model, basically by constructing an interpretation table and searching for its entries. The user receives feedback in form of variable assignments and subterm evaluations which falsify the conjecture. To enable termination, the property of a falsifying interpretation to actually *be* a model of the specification is approximated only. This is done by instantiating the axioms with terms of a limited size only. This size is a parameter of the method and its implementation. The price of the limited term size is a restricted model correctness: a model of a limited instantiation is not necessarily a model of the full specification. The user must attack this problem by (a) examining the proposed term evaluations and (b) varying the term size limit.

It is important not to confuse our limited instantiation of the axioms with a limited domain size. In our case, by increasing the limit we can only lose models, and by decreasing the limit, we can only gain models. This is the very reason why our model completeness result is *not* restricted by the chosen limit. Such a monotonous behaviour would not hold if we varied domain sizes. We could not gain model completeness by following a similar approach like [BT98] (see above). Model construction is the means rather that the purpose of our method. We finally want to detect faulty conjectures. From this pint of view, having model completeness is worth to pay a price for. The system indeed detects all non-consequences, even if it detects to many. At the same time, the restrictions are kept transparent to the user (see the example output above). In case the error is real, it is usually not difficulty to comprehend once one is pointed to. Providing unexpected valuations of function terms then helps to identify underspecified properties which are the source of errors.

Acknowledgements. I am grateful to Reiner Hähnle for his general support as well as for many, many, fruitful discussions, and for carefully checking the proofs in [Ahr01]. I am also grateful to Sonja Pieper for implementing the presented method.

References

[Ahr01]   Wolfgang Ahrendt. *Deduktive Fehlersuche in Abstrakten Datentypen*. 2001.
          Dissertation (preversion, in German), University of Karlsruhe, available un-
          der http://www.cs.chalmers.se/~ahrendt/cade02/diss.ps.gz.

[Bac88]   Leo Bachmair. Proof by consistency in equational theories. In *Proc. Third
          Annual Symposium on Logic in Computer Science, Edinburgh, Scotland*,
          pages 228–233. IEEE Press, 1988.

[BT98]   François Bry and Sunna Torge. A deduction method complete for refutation
          and finite satisfiability. In *Proc. 6th European Workshop on Logics in AI
          (JELIA)*, volume 1489 of *LNAI*, pages 122–136. Springer-Verlag, 1998.

[CP00]   Ricardo Caferra and Nicolas Peltier. Combining enumeration and deductive
          techniques in order to increase the class of constructible infinite models.
          Journal of Symbolic Computation, 29:177–211, 2000.

[FH91]   Hiroshi Fujita and Ryuzo Hasegawa. A model generation theorem prover
          in KL1 using a ramified-stack algorithm. In Koichi Furukawa, editor, *Pro-
          ceedings 8th International Conference on Logic Programming, Paris/France*,
          pages 535–548. MIT Press, 1991.

[FL96]   Christian Fermüller and Alexander Leitsch. Hyperresolution and automated
          model building. *Journal of Logic and Computation*, 6(2), 1996.

[GA99]   Martin Giese and Wolfgang Ahrendt. Hilbert's ε-terms in Automated Theo-
          rem Proving. In Neil V. Murray, editor, *Automated Reasoning with Analytic
          Tableaux and Related Methods, International Conference, Saratoga Springs,
          USA*, volume 1617 of *LNAI*, pages 171–185. Springer-Verlag, 1999.

[MB88]   Rainer Manthey and François Bry. SATCHMO: A theorem prover imple-
          mented in Prolog. In *Proceedings 9th Conference on Automated Deduction*,
          volume 310 of *LNCS*, pages 415–434. Springer-Verlag, 1988.

[MBI94]   Raul Monroy, Alan Bundy, and Andrew Ireland. Proof plans for the correc-
          tion of false conjectures. In Frank Pfenning, editor, *Proc. 5th International
          Conference on Logic Programming and Automated Reasoning, Kiev, Ukraine*,
          volume 822 of *LNAI*, pages 54–68. Springer-Verlag, 1994.

[Pro92]   Martin Protzen. Disproving conjectures. In D. Kapur, editor, *Proc. 11th
          CADE, Albany/NY, USA*, volume 607 of *LNAI*, pages 340–354. Springer-
          Verlag, 1992.

[Pro96]   Martin Protzen. Patching faulty conjectures. In Michael McRobbie and John
          Slaney, editors, *Proc. 13th CADE, New Brunswick/NJ, USA*, volume 1104
          of *LNCS*, pages 77–91. Springer-Verlag, 1996.

[RST01]   Wolfgang Reif, Gerhard Schellhorn, and Andreas Thums. Flaw detection in
          formal specifications. In Rajeev Goré, Alexander Leitsch, and Tobias Nipkow,
          editors, *Automated Reasoning, IJCAR 2001 Siena, Italy, June 18-23, 2001
          Proceedings*, volume 2083 of *LNAI*. Springer-Verlag, 2001.

[Sla94]   John Slaney. FINDER: finite domain enumerator. In Alan Bundy, edi-
          tor, *Proc. 12th CADE, Nancy/France*, volume 814 of *LNCS*, pages 798–801.
          Springer-Verlag, 1994.

[Thu98]   Andreas Thums. Fehlersuche in Formalen Spezifikationen. diploma thesis,
          Fakultät für Informatik, Universität Ulm, 1998.

[ZZ96]   Jian Zhang and Hantao Zhang. Generating models by SEM. In Michael
          McRobbie and John Slaney, editors, *Proc. 13th CADE, New Brunswick/NJ,
          USA*, volume 1104 of *LNCS*, pages 309–327. Springer-Verlag, 1996.

Reasoning by Symmetry and Function Ordering in Finite Model Generation

Gilles Audemard[1,2] and Belaid Benhamou[2]

[1] ITC-IRST, via Sommarive 16, 38050 Povo, Trento, Italy
[2] Laboratoire des Sciences de l'Information et des Systèmes de Marseille (LSIS)
39, Rue Joliot Curie - 13453 Marseille cedex 13 - France
{audemard, benhamou}@cmi.univ-mrs.fr

Abstract. Finite model search for first-order logic theories is complementary to theorem proving. Systems like Falcon, SEM and FMSET use the known LNH (Least Number Heuristic) heuristic to eliminate some trivial symmetries. Such symmetries are worthy, but their exploitation is limited to the first levels of the model search tree, since they disappear as soon as the first cells have been interpreted. The symmetry property is well-studied in propositional logic and CSPs, but only few trivial results on this are known on model generation in first-order logic.
We study in this paper both an ordering strategy that selects the next terms to be interpreted and a more general notion of symmetry for finite model search in first-order logic. We give an efficient detection method for such symmetry and show its combination with the trivial one used by LNH and LNHO heuristics. This increases the efficiency of finite model search generation. The method SEM with and without both the function ordering and symmetry detection is experimented on several interesting mathematical problems to show the advantage of reasoning by symmetry and the function ordering.

1 Introduction

A finite model of a first-order theory is an interpretation of the variables, the function symbols and the predicates over a finite domain of individuals that satisfies the axioms of the theory. A finite model generator is an automated tool which computes such interpretations. Model generation can be used to prove the consistency of a first-order theory (i.e., a model exists) or to find a counter model to disprove its validity. It can find a counter example of some expected conjecture and can help theorem provers to refute validity of formulas. In this sense, finite model generation is complementary to theorem proving.

Symmetry elimination is crucial in finite model generation. To get efficient model generators one has to detect and exploit symmetrical structures. Different approaches to symmetry elimination are used: For instance, the static approach used by James Crawford et al. in [5] for propositional logic theories consists of adding constraints expressing symmetry. The same technique is used by Masayuki Fujita et al. in [6] to search for finite models of quasigroup problems.

A. Voronkov (Ed.): CADE-18, LNAI 2392, pp. 226–240, 2002.
© Springer-Verlag Berlin Heidelberg 2002

One drawback of this approach is that only the structural symmetries appearing in the initial problem are considered.

The method FMC [7] eliminates some symmetries during the search to avoid isomorphic interpretations. Finite model generators like SEM [12] and FMSET[2] use the LNH (Least Number Heuristic) heuristic [12] to suppress some trivial symmetries existing between individuals of the domains. The previous methods use the CNF form of first-order logic where all the variables are universally quantified to express problems. As a consequence of this quantification, the individuals in the domains are all trivially symmetrical. That is, if during the search all the first individuals $\{0, \ldots, mdn\}$ of an ordered finite domain $D_n = \{0, \ldots, n-1\}$ (with $0 \leq mdn \leq n-1$) are used in the partial interpretation, then only the individuals of the part $\{mdn + 1, \ldots, n - 1\}$ remain symmetrical. All the individuals are symmetrical before starting the model search ($mdn = 0$). To keep a maximum number of symmetrical individuals, the LNH heuristic assigns in priority cells whose individuals have already been used.

Such trivial symmetries are very useful but they disappear as soon as the first cells are interpreted. The propagation process forces new individuals to be used, thus increases the $mdns$ and decreases the subset $\{mdn + 1, \ldots, n - 1\}$ of symmetrical individuals. This subset becomes empty when mdn reaches the value $n - 1$. On the other hand, the subset $\{0, \ldots, mdn\}$ of the used individuals increases and become quickly identical to the whole domain D_n.

A lot of other symmetries exist between individuals of the part $\{0, \ldots, mdn\}$ which can be exploited to increase the efficiency of model generation. In this article, we show how to detect and use such symmetries in combination with a function strategy that selects the terms to be interpreted and which preserves the trivial symmetries. This ordering gives a new heuristic that we call "LNHO" which improves the LNH one. We also show how to combine the detected symmetries with the trivial ones exploited by both LNH and LNHO heuristics to maximise the symmetry gain.

This article is organised as follows: In section 2, we give a short description of many-sorted first-order logic theories. In section 3, we study the principle of symmetry for finite model generation and prove that the trivial symmetry is a particular case of this study. We describe how to exploit such symmetry in section 4. Section 5 gives a short description of the method SEM. We describe in section 6 the function ordering strategy that we use in SEM to select the next terms to be interpreted. Section 7 presents an experimental evaluation of the known finite model generator SEM method with and without both advantages of symmetry and the function ordering on mathematical problems.

2   Background: Many-Sorted First-Order Logic Theories

2.1   Syntax

As a knowledge representation, we use the many-sorted first-order logic with equality in clausal normal form (CNF) where all the variables are universally quantified. Formally, a many-sorted theory is a triple $T = (S, F, C)$ where S is the set of sorts, F is the set of function symbols and C is the set of first order clause axioms. A function symbol $f \in F$ of arity k is specified by $f : s_1 \times \ldots \times s_k \mapsto s$ where $s_1, \ldots, s_k, s$ are in S. Constants are considered as 0-arity functions. Terms are built recursively with the function symbols and the variables. Predicates are considered as function symbols with the Boolean target sort. Problems are then expressed by the set C of first-order logic clause axioms. A clause is a disjunction of literals. A literal is an equation $t_1 = t_2$ or its negation $t_1 \neq t_2$ where t_1 and t_2 are terms or any predicate p. We denotes by C^t the expansion of the original theory axioms of C to the set of their ground instances (i.e. ground clauses).

2.2   Semantic

We consider only *finite* interpretations of a given theory T, i.e., the domain D_s of each sort $s \in S$ is finite. Without lost of generality, the corresponding domain to a sort $s \in S$ of cardinality n, is represented by the set $D_s = \{0, \ldots, n-1\}$ of natural numbers.

An interpretation of a function term $f : s_1 \times \ldots \times s_k \mapsto s$ is entirely specified by giving a value (in D_s) to each ground term $f(e_1, \ldots, e_n)$, called *cells*, where $(e_1, \ldots, e_n)$ is in $D_{s_1} \times \ldots \times D_{s_n}$. When it is not confusing, constants can be represented by some individuals of the domains. An interpreation is total if each cell is associated to a value, it is partial otherwise.

The set C^t of ground clauses is obtained by substituting each variable of the sort $s \in S$ in the terms by all the possible individuals in D_s. If I is a partial interpretation, then C_I^t denotes the remain set of ground clauses under the interpretation I (we say C^t simplified by I) , and T_I the resulting theory.

Example 1. Let be a theory T= $(\{s\}, \{h\}, C)$ where C contains the two following axioms.

- $\forall x, \quad h(x, x) = x$
- $\forall x, \forall y \quad h(h(x, y), x) = y$

Suppose $D_s = \{0, \ldots, 3\}$. This theory admits a lot of models, among which the one given by the function table of h (denoted I).

h	0 1 2 3
0	0 2 3 1
1	3 1 0 2
2	1 3 2 0
3	2 0 1 3

This is interpreted as: $h(0, 0) = 0$, $h(0, 1) = 2$, $\ldots$ etc.

The set of ground instances is $C^t = \{h(0, 0) = 0, h(1, 1) = 1, \ldots, h(h(0, 0), 0) = 0), h(h(1, 0), 1) = 0, h(h(0, 1), 0) = 1 \ldots\}$.

3   Permutations and Symmetries

First, we give some basic notions on permutations. We then define the symmetry principle for individuals of the domains.

Definition 1. *Given a finite set E, a permutation σ of E is a bijection mapping from E onto E. We note $Perm(E)$ the set of all permutations of E.*

The pair $(Perm(E), \circ)$ forms the permutation group of E. The composition of two permutations and the converse of a permutation are permutations. If σ is a permutation then σ^k denotes k compositions of σ. The order of a permutation σ is the smallest integer n such that $\sigma^n = Id_E$ (Id_E denotes the identity mapping). The permutation σ defined as $\sigma(a_1) = a_2$, $\sigma(a_2) = a_3 \ldots \sigma(a_n) = a_1$ forms a cycle on the elements $\{a_1, \ldots, a_n\}$ of E. We denote by $(a_1, \ldots, a_n)$ such a cycle, where n is its order. A permutation σ can be viewed as a composition of disjoint cycles.

Definition 2. *A permutation σ on individuals of the domains of the set of sorts S is a tuple $\sigma = (\sigma_1, \ldots, \sigma_n)$ where each $\sigma_i \in Perm(D_{s_i})$.*

Definition 3. *Let $f \in F$ be a function symbol specified by $f : s_{i_1} \times \ldots \times s_{i_k} \mapsto s_j$ and σ a permutation defined on the individuals of the domains of the corresponding sorts. If $f(e_{i_1}, \ldots, e_{i_k})$ is a cell then $\sigma(f(e_{i_1}, \ldots, e_{i_k})) = f(\sigma_{i_1}(e_{i_1}), \ldots \sigma_{i_k}(e_{i_k}))$.*

Therefore, the permutation σ of individuals can be easily generalised in the natural way to the set of ground clauses C^t of the theory T and to any partial interpretation I. This results from the individuals permutation in the ground terms forming C^t (resp. I). We now give the definition of symmetry.

Definition 4. *Let $T = (S, F, C)$ be a theory, I a partial interpretation, C_I^t the set of ground clauses corresponding to C which is simplified by I, and σ a permutation defined on the domains of the sorts of S. The permutation σ is a symmetry of T_I if the following two conditions hold:*

1. $\sigma(I) = I$, and
2. $\sigma(C_I^t) = C_I^t$

Definition 4 gives new conditions of symmetry in comparison to the propositional case [3]. To verify the symmetry conditions at a given node of the search tree, the permutation has to leave invariant both the partial set of ground clauses (C_I^t) and the partial interpretation I. Indeed, a partial interpretation is formed by a set of equations such as $f(e_1, \ldots, e_k) = e_j$, where $e_i \in D_{s_i}$, and which are generally sensitive to individual permutation. This is different from the propositional case where the partial interpretation is not concerned by the permutation.

Definition 5. *Let $T = (S, F, C)$ be a theory. Two individuals e_1 and e_2 of a sort domain D_s are symmetrical if there exists a symmetry σ of individuals of the domain D_s such that $\sigma(e_1) = e_2$.*

Definition 6. *Let $T = (S, F, C)$ be a theory. Two interpretations I and J are symmetrical if there exists a symmetry σ such that $\sigma(I) = J$.*

If I and J are symmetrical interpretations ($\sigma(I) = J$) of the theory T then I is a model of T if and only if J is a model of the theory T too.

3.1   Symmetry Detection

The symmetry detection algorithm consists in two steps: The first one partitions the individuals of the different sorts into primary classes with respect to the necessary conditions of Proposition 1. Two individuals will be candidates to symmetry if they are in the same primary class. The second step is a backtrack search which builds the symmetry.

Necessary Conditions. To be symmetrical, two individuals of a same domain have to satisfy some necessary conditions (Proposition 1).

Definition 7. *If I is a partial interpretation of the theory $T = (S, F, C)$, e an individual of a domain D_s and $f \in F$ a function symbol, then $\#_{I_{f_i}}(e)$ denotes the number of occurrences of e in I as the ith position argument of the function f and $\#_{I_{f_{val}}}(e)$ denotes the number of occurrences of e in I as a value of the function f.*

Example 2. In example 1, we have $\#_{I_{h_1}}(0) = 4$, $\#_{I_{h_2}}(0) = 4$, and $\#_{I_{h_{val}}}(0) = 4$. In this interpretation we have $\#_{I_{h_i}}(a) = 4$, $\forall i \in \{1,2\}$, $\forall a \in \{0,1,2,3\}$ and $\#_{I_{h_{val}}}(a) = 4$, $\forall a \in \{0,1,2,3\}$.

Proposition 1 (Necessary Conditions). *Let $T = (S, F, C)$ be a theory and a and b two individuals of a domain D_s. Let I be a partial interpretation of T. If the individuals a and b are symmetrical then the following condition hold:*

- $\forall f \in I \cap F, \quad \forall i \in \{1, \ldots, arity(f)\}, \quad \#_{I_{f_i}}(a) = \#_{I_{f_i}}(b)$
- $\forall f \in I \cap F, \quad \#_{I_{f_{val}}}(a) = \#_{I_{f_{val}}}(b).$

Proof. Let us prove the second condition. Let I be a partial interpretation of the theory T, σ a symmetry of T_I, and two individuals a and b of a domain D_s such that $\sigma(a) = b$. Suppose there exists a function f such that $\#_{I_{f_{val}}}(a) \neq \#_{I_{f_{val}}}(b)$. Thus we get $\sigma(I) \neq I$ since the number of occurrences of b as a value of f is different from the one of a. We can then deduce that σ is not a symmetry and we obtain a contradiction. The proof of the first condition can be done in a similar way. $\square$

Verification of the necessary conditions is an important step of the symmetry detection algorithm. They allow to reduce drastically the permutation search space, since they form domain partitions including the equivalence classes of individuals which are potential candidates for symmetry.

Symmetry Search (verification of the sufficient condition). In the second step, we compute the permutation (the symmetry) using the equivalence classes of the previous step. A symmetry in propositional calculus [3] is a variable permutation under which the set of clauses remains invariant. Such condition can be time consuming when the number of clauses grows. This condition is simplified in finite model generation. Indeed, if the set of clauses contains no individual constant, it is sufficient to look for permutations which leave invariant the partial model. The invariance of the partial set of clauses is guaranteed. This avoids checking its invariance. Formally:

Proposition 2. *Let $T = (S, F, C)$ be a theory, I a partial interpretation and σ a permutation on the domains of the sorts in S. If C contains no individual of any sort $s \in S$ and if $\sigma(I) = I$ then $\sigma(C_I^t) = C_I^t$.*

Proof. If C does not contain individuals then the permutation σ satisfies $\sigma(C^t) = C^t$. Thus, $\sigma(C_I^t) = \sigma(C^t)_{\sigma(I)} = C^t_{\sigma(I)} = C_I^t$.   □

Proposition 2 gives an important result for symmetry detection, which simplifies the sufficient condition of Definition 4. This increases drastically the efficiency of symmetry detection.

Remark 1. If some individuals appear in the set of clauses $C' \subset C$ of the theory T, then the permutation σ has to leave the subset $C' \subset C$ of clauses where the individuals occur invariant in addition to the invariance of the partial interpretation I (i.e. $\sigma(I) = I$ and $\sigma(C'^t) = C'^t$). The invariance of C'^t is checked in a preprocessing phase before starting the model search process.

We show now that the trivial symmetry (the one existing between the individuals not used so far) treated by the LNH heuristic is a particular case of our symmetry notion.

Proposition 3. *If $T = (S, F, C)$ is a theory, I a partial interpretation and σ a trivial symmetry, then $\sigma(I) = I$.*

Proof. The trivial symmetry σ is formed by the cycle $(mdn + 1, \ldots, n - 1)$ of the unused individuals. The permutation σ does not permute the individuals $\{0, \ldots, mdn\}$ which are the only ones used in I. I is independent of the permutation σ, thus $\sigma(I) = I$.   □

As the condition $\sigma(I) = I$ holds for each trivial symmetry σ then the symmetry exploited by the LNH heuristic is a particular case of our symmetry study (proposition 2). Such symmetries are very important, since they do not need detection. By the same way, we can show that the symmetry treated by the extension $XLNH$ [1] of LNH is also a particular case of our study. Algorithm 1 gives a short description of the symmetry detection method which is a backtrack procedure. Such algorithm has an exponential complexity in the worst case. But, in practice, when symmetry exists, it is computed with few backtracks and does not affect the run time of model generation. In theory the problem of symmetry detection is equivalent to the graph isomorphism detection [4] that still has an unknown complexity (between P and NP).

In Algorithm 1, the symbol $Cl(e, D_s)$ denotes the equivalence class of the individual $e \in D_s$ with respect to the necessary conditions (Proposition 1), and the function `Partition`(D_s) computes the equivalence classes of the individuals of D_s. The symbol $Mdn(D_s)$ denotes the Mdn number of D_s.

Algorithm 1 The symmetry search procedure

Function Sym(I : Interpretation; Var σ : permutation)
Return   : True if σ verify $\sigma(I) = I$
                False otherwise
        Function ConstructSym(Var σ : Permutation)
        Begin
            If $\sigma(I) = I$ **Then Return** True   %%σ is a symmetry
            Choose a sort s and $e \in D_s$ such that $e \leq Mdn(D_s)$ and
                                    $\sigma(e)$ is not interpreted
            For all $a \in Cl(e, D_s)$ **Do**
                $\sigma(e) = a$
                $Cl(e, D_s) = Cl(e, D_s) - a$
                If ConstructSym(σ)=True **Then Return** True
            Return False
        End
Begin
For all sort s **Do** Partition(D_s)   %%Necessary Condition
Return ConstructSym(σ)
End

---

4   Symmetry Exploitation

We now give some properties which allow to use the detected symmetries to improve finite model search efficiency.

Proposition 4. *Let I be a partial interpretation, a permutation σ such that $\sigma(I) = I$. If ce is a non interpreted cell, then both partial interpretations $I \cup \{ce = e\}$ and $I \cup \{\sigma(ce = e)\}$ are symmetrical.*

Proof. As I is invariant by the permutation σ then $\sigma(C_I^t) = C_I^t$ (proposition 2). The partial interpretation $I \cup \{ce = e\}$ and $\sigma(I \cup \{ce = e\})$ are symmetric (definition 6). Since $\sigma(I \cup \{ce = e\}) = I \cup \{\sigma(ce = e)\}$, then both extensions $I \cup \{ce = e\}$ and $I \cup \{\sigma(ce = e)\}$ are symmetrical.   □

Therefore, if we are looking for non symmetrical models then we keep only one of the previous extensions. As we are also interested in consistence of theories, we give in the following proposition the relationship between the previous extensions.

Proposition 5. *If the partial interpretation I of the theory $T = (S, F, C)$ is consistent[1], then [the extension $I \cup \{ce = e\}$ is consistent if and only if $I \cup \{\sigma(ce = e)\}$ is consistent]*

Proof. It is a consequence of the proposition 4 which guarantees that the two extensions are symmetrical, thus they are equivalence for consistency.   □

---

[1] I is not contradictory

Proposition 5 gives an important result that we exploit to reduce the search space of a finite model generation. That is, if the interpretation $ce = e$ is contradictory then the interpretation $\sigma(ce = e)$ is contradictory too. We avoid then exploring the branch corresponding to the assignment $\sigma(ce = e)$ (i.e. $\sigma(ce) = \sigma(e)$). That is what we call the symmetry cut.

Now, we prove that a symmetry of order k can make $k - 1$ cuts in a search tree. To be efficient, one has to detect symmetries with great orders.

Proposition 6. *Let $T = (S, F, C)$ be a theory, σ a permutation of individuals of the domains and I a partial interpretation. If $\sigma(I) = I$ then $\forall j \in \mathbb{N}$ $\sigma^j(I) = I$.*

Remark 2. If a partial interpretation I of the theory $T = (S, F, C)$ is invariant under σ ($\sigma(I) = I$) then $\forall j \in \mathbb{Z}$ $\sigma^j(C_I^t) = C_I^t$.

Now we can generalise the result of proposition 5 to any power of σ. Formally:

Proposition 7. *If a partial interpretation I of the theory $T = (S, F, C)$ is consistent then [the extension $I \cup \{ce = e\}$ is consistent if and only if $\forall j \in \mathbb{N}$, $I \cup \{\sigma^j(ce = e)\}$ is consistent]*

Proof. A trivial proof can be derived from propositions 5 and 6.   □

Proposition 7 gives a good exploitation of the symmetry σ. For each symmetry of order k, we cut $k - 1$ branches in the search tree. Indeed, when the assignment $ce=e$ is contradictory, all the assignments $\sigma^j(ce=e)$ for all $j \in \{1, \ldots, k-1\}$ are contradictory too. This leads to $k - 1$ symmetry cuts.

Many symmetries can be detected for a given theory. But, for efficiency reasons, we detect and exploit only one at each node of the search tree. This symmetry is combined with the trivial ones treated by both the LNH and LNHO heuristics to maximise the gain.

Combination of the detected symmetry (DSYM) with the trivial one.
Consider a theory with one sort whose individuals are in $D_n = \{0, \ldots, n-1\}$ and I the partial interpretation. If the individuals used (appear in some terms of I) at the current node of the search tree are all in the part $\{0, \ldots, mdn\}$, ($0 \le mdn \le n-1$), then all the extensions $I \cup \{t = mdn+1\}, \ldots, I \cup \{t = n-1\}$ are trivially symmetrical. These trivial symmetries are exploited with respect to both the LNH and the LNHO heuristics. We add to these the symmetries that we detect on the part $\{0, \ldots, mdn\}$ of used individuals. The trivial symmetry and the one we detect here are independent, since they are defined on two disjoint parts of the domain. Their combination is then straight forward and $n - mdn - 1 + k$ symmetry cuts can be made when they are associated.

5   SEM Description

As an initial preprocessing stage, SEM expands the original theory axioms to the set of their ground instances (i.e. ground clauses). SEM's efficiency relies on an efficient encoding of the terms and a direct access to the leaf terms. This allows fast upward propagation of cell assignments into embedded terms. The memory resources required by this transformation are far smaller than those needed by a propositional approach. In the latter case, the same kind of expansion is needed, but clause "flattening" (see [2] for instance) requires additional auxiliary variables at an obvious cost.

SEM naturally treats many-sorted theories as particular constraint satisfaction problems (CSP) where the variables are the cells, their associated domains are sorts and the constraints are specified by the resulting set of ground clauses.

Algorithm 2 SEM Search Algorithm

Function Search(A, B, C)
Return : True If C is satisfiable by A,
                otherwise False

Begin
If $B = \emptyset$ **Then Return** TRUE
Choose and delete (ce_i, D_i) from B %%with respect to LNH or LNHO heuristic
If $D_i = \emptyset$ **Then Return** FALSE
for All $e \in D_i$ **Do**
    $(A', B', C') = Propa(A \cup (ce_i, e), B, C)$
    If $C' \neq False$ **Then return** Search(A', B', C')
End

SEM's finite model search procedure is described in the algorithm 2. It uses the following parameters :

- A : a set of assignments $\{(ce, e)|e \in D_{sort(ce)}\}$
- B : a set of unassigned cells and their possible values $\{(ce, D)|D \subseteq D_{sort(ce)}\}$
- C : a set of clauses

Initially, A is empty and B contains all the cells $\{(ce, D_{sort(ce)})\}$. The backtrack procedure Search calls Propa and itself recursively. The procedure Propa propagates the assignments from A in C. This simplifies C and may force some cells in B to become assigned. It modifies (A, B, C) until a fixed point is reached or an inconsistency is detected, and returns the modified triple (A, B, C) upon success.

Before talking about the experiments we introduce the function ordering strategy that we use in SEM to select the terms to be interpreted first.

6   The Function Ordering Strategy

Interpretation of function symbols impacts on propagations, symmetry detection and then on computation times. We choose the next term to be interpreted in such a way as to maximise the amount of propagations and preserve the symmetry. The function ordering we propose is based on the *dependency graph* of the functions that we define below. Intuitively, if the formula $f(g(x), x) = x$ is one of the axioms of a given theory T then f depends on g and the function g will be before the function f in the ordering.

Definition 8. *Let $T = (S, F, C)$ be a theory. Let $G = (X, W)$ be the weighted and oriented dependency graph defined as follows:*

- *the set of vertices is the set F without constant symbols.*
- *the edge $(f_i \rightarrow f_j)$ belongs to W if there exists an axiom in C where f_i appears as a sub-term of f_j.*
- *the weight of the edge $(f_i \rightarrow f_j)$ equals the number of times there exists an axiom in C where f_i appears as a sub-term of f_j.*

Example 3. Consider the unit ring theory of table 1.
The axioms of the theory yields the following dependency graph:

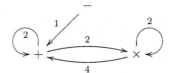

6.1   The Function Ordering

The function ordering that we perform in a preprocessing phase is defined with respect to the following strategy.

1. select first an n-ary function with no incoming arrow which has a minimal arity
2. secondly, select a function with the maximal sum of weights of arrows incoming from already selected functions
3. repeat recursively both step 1 and 2 on all the function symbols

For the example 3, the previous strategy, gives the following ordering: $-$, $+$ and $\times$. The choice of $-$ first is obvious, since it is a unary function without coming arrows. Secondly $+$ is chosen, because it depends on the already selected function $-$. Naturally the function $\times$ is the last in the ordering.

6.2   The Term Selection Heuristic (LNHO)

According to both the function ordering strategy and trivial symmetry preservation, we define the heuristic LNHO (LNH with function ordering) which chooses as a next cell to be interpreted the term $f(e_1, e_2, \dots, e_k)$ satisfying the following conditions:

1. The maximum of the individuals $\{e_1, e_2, \dots, e_k\}$ is the smallest.

2. The function f is the smallest in the function ordering
3. If more than one cell satisfies both condition 1 and 2, then choose the one with the smallest domain.

Constants (functions of arity 0) have to be considered. In LNHO, they are considered as 0-arity functions. They deserve a distinct treatment depending whether they appear in equations or disequations. On the former case constants are considered in prior (before other functions) to favour propagation. But on the second case, they are selected at last, since their interpretation breaks several symmetries.

7 Experimentations

We have experimented and compared both LNH and LNHO heuristics on the SEM finite model generator. We also compared the performances of SEM with and without the advantage of the detected symmetries (DSYM). First, we study the behaviour of the symmetry detection on different problems, which we describe in section 7.1. We also show the interest to combine this dynamic symmetry elimination with the LNHO heuristic which itself improves LNH heuristic. All CPU times are given in seconds and are obtained on a PC (K6II, 400Mhz, 128Mb) running under Linux 2.2.

The program source is available at
http://www.cmi.univ-mrs.fr/~audemard.

7.1 Problems

In a first time, our experiments are focused on mathematical problems. Some of them are described by Jian Zhang in [9,10], the other ones are picked up from the TPTP library [8]. The symbol AG denotes Abelian groups, NG denotes non Abelian groups, GRP100-1 (from the TPTP library) express one of the proposed conjectures to represent an Abelian group with one axiom. RU is for unit rings, RNB denotes a non Boolean ring ($a \times a \neq a$ for some constant a) which satisfies the additional axiom ($x^7 = x$), RNA contains the ring axioms where the associativity of the operator $\times$ is replaced by a counter example. RNG025-8 is picked up from the TPTP library. The axioms of both problems AG and RU are given in table 1 and most of the other problems are generated from the two previous ones by introducing or removing some axioms. In a second time, we deal with the linear-time temporal logic problems (LTL) expressed in first-order logic , see [11] for more details.

7.2 The Behaviour of the Symmetry Detection

Table 2 shows the behaviour of symmetry detection on three different problems when using SEM (with LNH) as a finite model generator. We can see for the Abelian groups that 82% of symmetry calls (i.e., the ratio between the result of the column "Find" to the result of the column "Calls" in table 2) succeed. This

Table 1. Problems AG and RU

	$x + 0 = x$
$x + 0 = x$	$x + y = y + x$
$0 + x = x$	$x + (-x) = 0$
$x + (-x) = 0$	$x + (y + z) = (x + y) + z$
$(-x) + x = 0$	$x \times 1 = x$
$x + (y + z) = (x + y) + z$	$x \times y = y \times x$
$x + y = y + x$	$(x \times y) + (x \times z) = x \times (y + z)$
	$(y \times x) + (z \times x) = (y + z) \times x$
	$x \times (y \times z) = (x \times y) \times z$
Abelian Group	Unit Ring

Table 2. Behaviour of the algorithm of symmetries detection

Pb	size	Time	Time for Sym	Nodes	Calls	Find	Suppressed
AG	24	117	55	124 753	12033	9803	118698
	25	132	59	130 644	13009	10737	133088
NAG	20	171	36	338 669	29388	25921	321123
	21	206	37	357 095	32480	27177	344578
RNA	8	5	0.4	51 491	7872	0	0
	9	10	0.8	81928	11 243	0	0
	10	62	5.3	252720	41 163	18 902	93184

eliminates a great number of isomorphic interpretations by symmetry cuts (see Column "Suppressed"). We can remark that symmetry detection is sometimes time consuming for the AG problems. This is because the necessary conditions of Proposition 1 does not reduce significantly the permutation search space.

Replacing the last axioms of the Abelian group (AG) (see table 1) by the clause $(1 + 2 \neq 2 + 1)$ yields the non Abelian group problem (NAG) and forces the individuals 1 and 2 to be permuted together (see remark 1). This strengthens the symmetry necessary conditions and the symmetry search space is substantially reduced. Symmetry detection is then more efficient for these problems.

For the non associative ring problems (RNA), the added clause $((2 \times 3) \times 4 \neq 2 \times (3 \times 4))$ forces the individuals $0 \ldots 4$ to be in the same class of symmetry. As in NAG, this clause reduce the symmetry search space and the detection time. We can see in table 2 that symmetries abound as the problem size grows.

Table 3 shows the behaviour of symmetry detection (DSYM) when using both LNH and LNHO heuristics. We remark that it is more profitable to use LNHO. When using LNHO heuristic, the constants of the axiom expressing non associativity in RNA problem are interpreted at the last. This helps to preserve symmetries.

Table 3. The impact of using LNHO heuristic on the symmetry detection

Problem	DSYM with LNH			DSYM with LNHO		
	Calls	Find	Suppressed	Calls	Find	Suppressed
RNA (8)	14 333	6 571	0	943	810	316
GRP100-1	129 521	0	0	29	9	15

7.3   The Advantage of the Detected Symmetries (DSYM) When Using Both LNH and LNHO Heuristics in SEM

In this section, we compare both LNH and LNHO heuristics and their combination with the detected symmetries (DSYM) on the problems described previously.

Table 4. Comparison – Group problems

Problem	size	LNH		LNHO		LNH + DSYM		LNHO + DSYM	
		Model	Time	Model	Time	Model	Time	Model	Time
AG	6	6	0.01	6	0.01	5	0.01	6	0.01
	32	2 295	962	2 295	1 086	551	1 298	1 037	1 429
	35	13	1 734	13	2 060	-	-	5	1 429
	37	-	-	1	3 425	-	-	1	3 018
	38	-	-	-	-	-	-	14	3 330
NAG	12	31	1.3	59	1	20	1.3	42	1.3
	24	1 130	2 671	3 786	587	493	1 777	1 654	473
	27	-	-	45	1 295	9	2 455	16	856
	30	-	-	301	3 191	-	-	135	1 853
GRP100-1	4	0	10.3	0	0.05	0	11.5	0	0.04
	5	0	2 008	0	0.05	-	-	0	0.56
	9	-	-	0	45	-	-	0	36
	10	-	-	-	-	-	-	0	2 284

Tables 4 and 5 show the results obtained when searching all the models (column model). The run time is limited to one hour. The mark (-) means that the program fails to answer the question in less than one hour time. We can see that SEM with the detected symmetry (DSYM) outperforms SEM without symmetry detection on the checked problems AG, NAG, GRP100-1, RU, RNA and RNB. With the advantage of the detected symmetry, we generate models of a great size that SEM cannot find in a reasonable time and several new isomorphic models that both LNH and LNHO heuristics do not consider, are detected. We remark that the function ordering improves the LNH heuristic (LNHO is generally better than LNH) on all the checked problems except for the RNB and RNG025-8 problems. Thus, the combination of LNHO with DSYM is better than the one of LNH with DSYM.

Table 6 shows the results obtained on the LTL problems. For an instance of size n we know that there exist exactly n non-isomorphic models. We can

Table 5. Comparison – Ring problems

Problem	size	LNH		LNHO		LNH + DSYM		LNHO + DSYM	
		Model	Time	Model	Time	Model	Time	Model	Time
RU	6	1	0.05	1	0.03	1	0.05	1	0.02
	16	1 745	165	1 745	70	355	49	1 119	55
	19	1	1323	1	113	1	225	1	91
	27	-	-	298	2 606	-	-	196	1 809
	28	-	-	29	3 338	-	-	29	2 314
RNG025-8	5	320	6	20	930	320	7	20	1 026
	6	960	48	144	3 332	960	49	-	-
RNA	6	0	0.86	0	0.02	0	0.9	0	0.02
	8	2 496	10	280	0.74	2 496	11	224	0.74
	10	0	90	0	1	0	105	0	0.9
	15	0	1 047	0	20	0	1 061	0	18
RNB	16	90	8.3	800	132	30	3.5	331	60
	18	0	10	0	170	0	4	0	80
	30	0	79	-	-	0	30	-	-
	32	3 550	2 517	-	-	464	417	-	-
	34	-	-	-	-	0	465	-	-

see that the LNHO heuristic eliminates more isomorphic models than the LNH one and the advantage of the detected symmetry (DSYM) on these problems is substantial. The combination of DSYM with both LNHO and LNH increases individually their performances and DSYM with LNHO seems to be the best.

Table 6. Comparison – LTL problems

size	LNH		LNHO		LNH + DSYM		LNHO + DSYM	
	Model	Time	Model	Time	Model	Time	Model	Time
4	23	0.01	19	0.01	12	0.01	11	0.01
5	71	0.01	47	0.01	24	0.01	19	0.01
6	243	0.11	117	0.05	55	0.11	42	0.03
7	988	1.3	289	0.34	117	1	92	0.15
8	4 950	23	724	5	299	11	205	2.5
9	30 556	629	1 836	98	719	150	479	61
10	-	-	-	-	-	-	1 161	1955

8   Conclusion

We have shown some new results on symmetry for finite model generation in many-sorted first-order logic theories. The trivial symmetry is shown to be a particular case of our symmetry notion and a symmetry detection algorithm is given. A function ordering resulting in a new heuristic LNHO which improves the LNH heuristic is studied. The trivial symmetry treated by both LNH and LNHO heuristics is combined with the detected symmetry (DSYM) to maximise the gain. The method SEM augmented with the property of the detected symmetry is experimented on several problems. The experimental results obtained with our first implementation are satisfactory and confirmed the advantage of using the detected symmetry. Many improvements of the implementation are possible. One can refine the necessary symmetry conditions to increase the efficiency of symmetry detection. Another point of interest is to exploit some other trivial symmetries (like the ones of XLNH) which do not need detection and combine them with the detected ones. Our experiments are still in progress. We also aim to apply our results for finite model generation of modal logics and planing problems.

Acknowledgements. Many thanks to the referees for their comments which helped us to provide the final version of this paper.

References

1. G. Audemard and L. Henocque. The extended least number heuristic. *Proceedings of the first International Joint Conference in Automated Reasoning (IJCAR)*, Springer Verlag, 2001.
2. B. Benhamou and L. Henocque. A hybrid method for finite model search in equational theories. *Fundamenta Informaticae*, 39(1-2):21–38, 1999.
3. B. Benhamou and L. Sais. Tractability through symmetries in propositional calculus. *Journal of Automated Reasoning*, 12(1):89–102, 1994.
4. J. Crawford. A theorical analisys of reasoning by symmetry in first-order logic. In *Proceedings of Workshop on Tractable Reasonning, AAI92*, pages 17–22, 1992.
5. J. Crawford, M. L. Ginsberg, E. Luck, and A. Roy. Symmetry-breaking predicates for search problems. In *proceedings of KR'96*, pages 148–159. 1996.
6. M. Fujita, J. Slaney, and F. Bennett. Automatic generation of some results in finite algebra. In *Proceedings of International Joint Conference on Artificial Intelligence*, pages 52–57. Morgan Kaufmann, 1993.
7. N. Peltier. A new method for automated finite model building exploiting failures and symmetries. *Journal of Logic and Computation*, 8(4):511–543, 1998.
8. C. Suttner and G. Sutcliffe. The TPTP Problem Library. Technical Report, J. Cook University, 1997. http://www.cs.jcu.edu.au/ftp/pub/techreports/97-8.ps.gz
9. J. Zhang. Problems on the Generation of Finite Models. In *proceedings of the 12th International Conference on Automated Deduction*, LNAI 814, pages 753–757, Nancy, France, 1994. Springer-Verlag.
10. J. Zhang. Constructing finite algebras with FALCON. *Journal of Automated Reasoning*, 17(1):1–22, August 1996.
11. J. Zhang. Test Problems and Perl Script for Finite Model Searching. Association of Automated Reasoning , Newsletter 47, 2000.
    http://www-unix.mcs.anl.gov/AAR/issueapril00/issueapril00.html
12. J. Zhang and Hantao Zhang. SEM: a system for enumerating models. In *Proceedings of the Fourteenth International Joint Conference on Artificial Intelligence*, pages 298–303, 1995.

Algorithmic Aspects of Herbrand Models Represented by Ground Atoms with Ground Equations

Bernhard Gramlich and Reinhard Pichler

Technische Universität Wien, Inst. f. Computersprachen, AG Theoretische Informatik
und Logik, Favoritenstrasse 9 – E185/2, A-1040 Wien, Austria,
{gramlich|reini}@logic.at

Abstract. *Automated model building* has evolved as an important sub-discipline of *automated deduction* over the past decade. One crucial issue in automated model building is the selection of an appropriate (finite) representation of (in general infinite) models. Quite a few such formalisms have been proposed in the literature. In this paper, we concentrate on the representation of Herbrand models by ground atoms with ground equations (GAE-models), introduced in [9]. For the actual work with any model representation, efficient algorithms for two decision problems are required, namely: The *clause evaluation problem* (i.e.: Given a clause C and a representation $\mathcal{M}$ of a model, does C evaluate to "true" in this model?) and the *model equivalence problem* (i.e.: Given two representations $\mathcal{M}_1$ and $\mathcal{M}_2$, do they represent the same model?). Previously published algorithms for these two problems in case of GAE-models require exponential time. We prove that the clause evaluation problem is indeed intractable (that is, coNP-complete), whereas the model equivalence problem can be solved in polynomial time. Moreover, we show how our new algorithm for the model equivalence problem can be used to transform an arbitrary GAE-model into an equivalent one with better computational properties.

1 Introduction

One of the principal goals of automated deduction is the construction of algorithms to detect the validity of a first-order formula (or, equivalently, the unsatisfiability of a corresponding clause set). The use of *models* in this activity can be essentially twofold: First, by constructing a counter-model (rather than just answering "NO"), the user not only learns *that* a given formula is not a theorem but also gets some insight as to *why* it is not a theorem. Second, models can be used to speed up the deduction process itself, e.g. by taking a model of parts of a given clause set as an input to a theorem prover based on semantic resolution or semantic clash resolution. The former use of models was the main motivation for early attempts towards automated model building (cf. [22]). The latter one was studied e.g. in [3]. Many research activities in this area over the past years

A. Voronkov (Ed.): CADE-18, LNAI 2392, pp. 241–259, 2002.
© Springer-Verlag Berlin Heidelberg 2002

demonstrate the increasing interest in this subfield of automated deduction (cf. e.g. [4], [21], [19,13], [5], [23], [3], [8,9], [14,15], [2]).

A crucial issue in automated model building is the selection of an appropriate representation of models. Quite a few such formalisms have been proposed in the literature, e.g.: linear atomic representations, general atomic representations, literals with equational constraints, finite tree automata, regular term grammars, term schematizations via R-terms or I-terms, ground atoms with ground equations. A comprehensive overview of these formalisms and a comparison of their expressive power is given in [14,15] (cf. also [6]). In this work, we concentrate on the representation of models[1] by ground atoms with ground equations (GAE-models, for short) introduced in [9]. A GAE-model $\mathcal{M}$ over some finite signature Σ, consisting of a set $\mathcal{F}$ of constant and function symbols and a (disjoint) set $\mathcal{P}$ of uninterpreted predicate symbols ($\Sigma = \mathcal{F} \uplus \mathcal{P}$), is given through a finite set $\mathcal{A} = \{A_1, \ldots, A_m\}$ of ground atoms and a finite set $\mathcal{E} = \{s_1 = t_1, \ldots, s_n = t_n\}$ of ground equations over $\mathcal{F}$. A ground atom B over Σ evaluates to "true" in the model $\mathcal{M}$ iff B is equal to some atom $A_i \in \mathcal{A}$ in the equational theory defined by $\mathcal{E}$.[2]

Example 1. Let $\mathcal{C} = \{P(x) \vee P(f(x)), \neg P(x) \vee \neg P(f(x))\}$ be a clause set over the signature $\Sigma = \{P, f, a\}$. Then $\mathcal{M} = (\mathcal{A}, \mathcal{E})$ with $\mathcal{A} = \{P(a)\}$ and $\mathcal{E} = \{a = f(f(a))\}$ is a model of the clause set $\mathcal{C}$. Note that the set of ground atoms that are "true" in $\mathcal{M}$ is $\{P(a), P(f^2(a)), P(f^4(a)), \ldots\}$. Another model of $\mathcal{C}$ would be $\mathcal{M}' = (\mathcal{A}', \mathcal{E}')$ with $\mathcal{A}' = \{P(f(a))\}$ and $\mathcal{E}' = \{a = f(f(a))\} = \mathcal{E}$. In this case, the set of ground atoms that evaluate to "true" in $\mathcal{M}'$ is $\{P(f(a)), P(f^3(a)), P(f^5(a)), \ldots\}$.

For the actual work with any model representation formalism, efficient algorithms for the following decision problems are crucial:

- *Clause Evaluation*: Given a clause C and a model representation $\mathcal{M}$, does C evaluate to "true" in the model represented by $\mathcal{M}$.
- *Model Equivalence*: Given two model representations $\mathcal{M}_1$ and $\mathcal{M}_2$, do they represent the same model, i.e.: Does every clause (over the given signature) have the same truth value in both models.

The importance of the first decision problem is obvious. Without an efficient clause evaluation procedure, semantic resolution or semantic clash resolution based on such models would not be feasible. The importance of the latter decision problem comes from the following observation: In general, the cost of clause

---

[1] For simplicity, but slightly abusing common terminology, throughout the paper we will speak of *models* rather than of *interpretations* sometimes tacitly assuming there is some (implicitly given) clause set for which the considered interpretation is indeed a model.

[2] Note that in contrast to [9] our notion of GAE-model uses (ground) equality only as a representation formalism but doesn't allow (ground) equations as (ground) atoms. The results, however, can be partially extended to cover this case, too (cf. Section 6).

evaluation heavily depends on the *representation* of the model rather than just on the model itself. We shall see that also in case of GAE-models, it is important to look for transformations of a given model representation into an equivalent one with "better" computational properties. But then we have to make sure, of course, that the model representation resulting from such a transformation is equivalent to the original one.

In [9], a clause evaluation procedure for GAE-models was presented. The computational complexity of this procedure was not explicitly analyzed, but it is clearly exponential. In [14], it is shown that GAE-models have the same expressive power as finite tree automata and regular tree grammars. In particular, a transformation of GAE-models into equivalent finite tree automata and vice versa is given there. Hence, one way to decide the equivalence of two GAE-models $\mathcal{M}_1$ and $\mathcal{M}_2$ is to construct equivalent finite tree automata A_1 and A_2, respectively, and to check whether they generate the same languages L_1 and L_2. Yet, the naive approach of proceeding like that yields an exponential time algorithm ([14,15,18]), cf. the detailed discussion at the end of Section 4.

In this paper, we give a new algorithm for the model equivalence problem, which works in polynomial time. As to clause evaluation, we cannot expect to do equally well by the coNP-completeness, that we are going to prove here. However, we shall provide a transformation of an arbitrary GAE-model into an equivalent one with better computational properties. In many cases, this should lead to a significant speed-up of clause evaluation, even though the exponential worst-case complexity can clearly not be avoided.

The remainder of this work is organized as follows: In Section 2 we recall some basic notions and results on ground term rewrite systems and on GAE-models. In Sections 3 and 4, we analyze the complexity of the clause evaluation problem and we provide a new algorithm for the model equivalence problem of GAE-models as well as a detailed complexity analysis and comparison with tree automata based approaches. In Section 5 we suggest a transformation of GAE-models into computationally better ones via the model equivalence algorithm of Section 4. Finally, in Section 6, we briefly discuss the obtained results and related topics. Due to lack of space, some proofs have been omitted.[3]

2   Preliminaries

2.1   Ground Term Rewrite Systems

We assume familiarity with the basic terminology and theory in (ground) term rewriting, cf. e.g. [1], [7]. For the sake of readability we just recall a few notions needed. A term rewrite system (TRS) $\mathcal{R}$ is *convergent* iff it is *confluent* and *terminating*. $\mathcal{R}$ is *canonical* iff it is convergent and *(inter)reduced*[4] . The *normal form* of a term t w.r.t. some (convergent) TRS $\mathcal{R}$ is denoted by $NF_{\mathcal{R}}(t)$. The *size*

---

[3] Complete proofs are given in the full version [12] of this paper.

[4] This means that all right-hand sides of rules in $\mathcal{R}$ are irreducible and the left-hand side of every rule $l \to r$ in $\mathcal{R}$ is irreducible w.r.t. $\mathcal{R} \setminus \{l \to r\}$.

$|t|$ and *depth* $\tau(t)$ of t are defined as usual. A ground term rewrite system (GTRS) is a TRS without variables in its rules. It is well-known, that any finite system of *ground* term equations (GTES) can be turned into a (logically) equivalent canonical finite GTRS. This can even be achieved quite efficiently, namely in polynomial time (w.r.t. the size of the original system). The earlier *completion* algorithms for that purpose are in essence *congruence closure* based methods (cf. e.g. [10]) where the original signature is extended by fresh constants in order to name certain congruence classes. Yet, direct polynomial completion without extending signatures is also possible via a more sophisticated approach as demonstrated in [17] (cf. also [20]).

Next we summarize those basic results that will frequently be used in subsequent sections (cf. [17], [20]):

(a) Any finite GTES $\mathcal{E}$ can be completed into a canonical GTRS $\mathcal{R}$ (over the same signature) in polynomial (more precisely: quadratic) time (w.r.t. the size of $\mathcal{E}$). Moreover, the size of the completed system is bounded by the size of the original one: $|\mathcal{R}| \leq |\mathcal{E}|$.

(b) If, by a canonical GTRS $\mathcal{R}$, a term t reduces at the root to t', then t' is in normal form.[5]

(c) Given a term t and a canonical GTRS $\mathcal{R}$, computing $NF_{\mathcal{R}}(t)$ can be done in at most $|t|$ steps.[6]

(d) Let $\mathcal{M} = (\mathcal{A}, \mathcal{E})$ be a GAE-model over some Herbrand universe $H = \mathcal{T}(\mathcal{F})$ with signature Σ ($\mathcal{F} \subseteq \Sigma$), s.t. $\mathcal{A}$ is a finite set of ground atoms over Σ, $\mathcal{E}$ is a finite set of ground equations over $\mathcal{F}$, and $\mathcal{U}$ is the set of all terms and subterms occurring in $\mathcal{A} \cup \mathcal{E}$. Then it is possible to compute the triple $(\mathcal{R}, \widehat{\mathcal{A}}, \widehat{\mathcal{U}})$ in quadratic time, where $\mathcal{R}$ is a canonical GTRS equivalent to $\mathcal{E}$, $\widehat{\mathcal{A}}$ is the set of normal forms w.r.t. $\mathcal{R}$ of the atoms in $\mathcal{A}$ and $\widehat{\mathcal{U}}$ is the set of normal forms w.r.t. $\mathcal{R}$ of $\mathcal{U}$.[7]

(e) If $t \in H$ normalizes into $\widehat{\mathcal{U}}$, then every subterm of t also has its normal form in $\widehat{\mathcal{U}}$. Hence, in particular, $\widehat{\mathcal{U}}$ is closed w.r.t. subterms, i.e.: If $t \in \widehat{\mathcal{U}}$, then every subterm of t is in $\widehat{\mathcal{U}}$.[8]

2.2   GAE-Models

The representation of models by ground atoms with ground equations (GAE-models, for short) was introduced in [9] in order to provide a model construction algorithm for a certain syntactical class of clauses, the so-called class $\mathrm{PVD}_g^{=}$. Actually, GAE-models are a powerful mechanism which allow us to represent

---

[5] Obvious, since $\mathcal{R}$ is interreduced.

[6] Note that contracting a subterm in t makes the corresponding subterm in the resulting term irreducible. Hence, the statement follows by (b).

[7] This is a consequence of (a)-(c), where, in order to guarantee the complexity bound we need to employ a ground total reduction ordering for completion that is size decreasing.

[8] Property (e) follows from the subterm closedness of $\mathcal{U}$ and the fact that $\mathcal{R}$ is canonical. The details are worked out in the full version [12] of the paper.

models of clause sets where other formalisms would fail, e.g.: The clause set $C = \{P(x) \vee P(f(x)), \neg P(x) \vee \neg P(f(x))\}$ in Example 1 has a simple GAE-model, whereas it is impossible to represent a model of C via atomic representations or even via the much more powerful formalism of literals with equational constraints (cf. [16]).

In this section, we briefly recall the clause evaluation algorithm from [9] for GAE-models. It has already been mentioned in Section 2.1, that the evaluation of ground atoms is done via a canonical GTRS, i.e.: Let a GAE-model $\mathcal{M}$ be given through a set of ground atoms $\mathcal{A}$ and a set of ground equations $\mathcal{E}$. Moreover, let $\mathcal{R}$ be a canonical GTRS equivalent to $\mathcal{E}$ and let $\widehat{\mathcal{A}}$ denote the set of normal forms of $\mathcal{A}$ w.r.t. $\mathcal{R}$. Then a ground atom B evaluates to "true" in $\mathcal{M}$, iff $NF_{\mathcal{R}}(B) \in \widehat{\mathcal{A}}$. The evaluation of ground clauses $B_1 \vee \ldots \vee B_k \vee \neg B_{k+1} \vee \ldots \vee \neg B_l$ is then also obvious.

Now let $\mathcal{U}$ denote the set of all terms and subterms occurring in $\mathcal{A}$ and $\mathcal{E}$. Moreover, let $\widehat{\mathcal{U}}$ denote the set of normal forms w.r.t. $\mathcal{R}$ of the terms in $\mathcal{U}$. The key to the evaluation of a non-ground clause C are the following lessons learned from the evaluation of a ground atom B:

1. Any subterm u occurring in B may be replaced by its normal form $NF_{\mathcal{R}}(u)$ without affecting the truth value of B. Hence, suppose that all terms of H can be normalized into $\widehat{\mathcal{U}}$. Then it is not necessary to check all possible ground instances $C\vartheta$ of C, that are obtained by substituting all possible terms in H for the variables in C. Instead, it suffices to check the truth value of those ground instances $C\vartheta$ of C, where the range of ϑ is restricted to the *finite* set $\widehat{\mathcal{U}}$.

2. Suppose that some subterm u occurring in B does not normalize into $\widehat{\mathcal{U}}$. In this case, the normal form $NF_{\mathcal{R}}(B)$ will definitely lie outside $\widehat{\mathcal{A}}$. In other words, normalization of any subterm in B into the set $\widehat{\mathcal{U}}$ is a necessary condition for B to have the truth value "true". So let t be an arbitrary term in H with $NF_{\mathcal{R}}(t) \notin \widehat{\mathcal{U}}$. Then we may in fact substitute t for any subterm u in B with $NF_{\mathcal{R}}(u) \notin \widehat{\mathcal{U}}$ without changing the truth value of B (which is "false"). But then, it is again not necessary to check all possible ground instances $C\vartheta$ of C, that are obtained by substituting all possible terms in H for the variables in C. Instead, it suffices to consider those ground instances $C\vartheta$ of C, where the range of ϑ is restricted to the *finite* set $\widehat{\mathcal{U}} \cup \{t\}$.

Thus, the clause evaluation procedure in [9] for an arbitrary clause C in a GAE-model $\mathcal{M}$ consists of two steps: First, we have to check, whether the whole Herbrand universe H normalizes into $\widehat{\mathcal{U}}$ or not. This is done by the simple procedure CHECK_TOTAL_COVER displayed in Figure 1. Depending on the outcome of this procedure, we have to distinguish two cases:

- *Case 1*: If $\forall t \in H$, $NF_{\mathcal{R}}(t) \in \widehat{\mathcal{U}}$ holds, then the truth value of C can be determined via the following equivalence: C evaluates to "true" in $\mathcal{M}$, iff every ground instance $C\vartheta$ does, where ϑ is an arbitrary ground substitution with range $rg(\vartheta) \subseteq \widehat{\mathcal{U}}$.

CHECK IF $\widehat{\mathcal{U}}$ CONTAINS ALL POSSIBLE NORMAL FORMS
input: Σ, $\mathcal{R}$, $\widehat{\mathcal{U}}$
output: "true", if the whole universe of ground terms (over Σ) normalizes into $\widehat{\mathcal{U}}$;
   "t" with $t \in \mathcal{T}(\mathcal{F})$, $NF_{\mathcal{R}}(t) \notin \widehat{\mathcal{U}}$, otherwise.

begin

   for all $f \in \Sigma$ with arity $k \geq 0$ **do**
      if $\exists f(t_1, \ldots, t_k)$, s.t. $(\forall i \in \{1, \ldots, k\}, t_i \in \widehat{\mathcal{U}})$ **and** $NF_{\mathcal{R}}(f(t_1, \ldots, t_k)) \notin \widehat{\mathcal{U}}$
         then return $f(t_1, \ldots, t_k)$;
   return "true";

end.

Fig. 1. Procedure CHECK_TOTAL_COVER

– *Case 2*: If $\exists t \in H$, s.t. $NF_{\mathcal{R}}(t) \notin \widehat{\mathcal{U}}$ holds, then the truth value of C can be determined via another equivalence, namely: C evaluates to "true" in $\mathcal{M}$, iff every ground instance $C\vartheta$ does, where ϑ is an arbitrary ground substitution with range $rg(\vartheta) \subseteq \widehat{\mathcal{U}} \cup \{t\}$.

Based on these considerations, the correctness of procedure CHECK_TOTAL_COVER is not difficult to verify.

3   Clause Evaluation in GAE-Models

In the previous section, we recalled the clause evaluation procedure from [9]. It is clear "at a glance", that this procedure requires exponential time since, in general, we will have to test exponentially many ground instances of the form $C\vartheta$ of a given clause C. However, no precise complexity analysis of this procedure or of the clause evaluation problem itself is given in [9]. In this section, we shall show that clause evaluation in GAE-models is coNP-complete. Formally, we investigate the following decision problem:

GAE-CLAUSE-EVALUATION
Instance: A tuple $(\Sigma, \mathcal{M}, C)$, where $\mathcal{M}$ is a GAE-model over the universe H with signature Σ and C is a clause over Σ.
Question: Does C evaluate to "true" in $\mathcal{M}$.

Note that for the GAE-CLAUSE-EVALUATION above as well as for the decision problems to be defined in Section 4, we are considering the signature Σ as part of the input. This decision was mainly motivated by the fact that, when we have in mind the model construction process for some clause set $\mathcal{C}$, then the signature is usually not explicitly given either. Instead, it is implicit in the input $\mathcal{C}$. However, it can be easily verified that all the results derived in Sections 3 to 5 hold for any non-trivial signature, also if Σ is not part of the input.

In the following theorem, we show the coNP-completeness of the decision problem GAE-CLAUSE-EVALUATION. As to coNP-membership, it turns out that no new ideas are required. All that is needed is a careful analysis of the algorithm of [9]. The proof of the coNP-hardness works by a straightforward reduction from the 3-SAT problem.

Theorem 1. *The* GAE-CLAUSE-EVALUATION *problem is coNP-complete.*

Proof. As to coNP-membership, we have to show that checking whether a clause C evaluates to "false" in a model $\mathcal{M}$ can be done in non-deterministic polynomial time. To this end, we have a closer look at the algorithm of [9] recalled in Section 2.2: As was already mentioned in Section 2.1, we can compute a canonical GTRS $\mathcal{R}$ as well as the sets $\widehat{\mathcal{A}}$ and $\widehat{\mathcal{U}}$ of atoms and terms, respectively, in normal form w.r.t. $\mathcal{R}$, in polynomial time. Moreover, we claim that also the procedure CHECK_TOTAL_COVER works in polynomial time. This can be seen as follows: For every $f \in \Sigma$ and every term of the form $f(t_1, \ldots, t_k)$ with $t_i \in \widehat{\mathcal{U}}$, we have to check, whether $NF_{\mathcal{R}}(f(t_1, \ldots, t_k)) \in \widehat{\mathcal{U}}$ or not. Note that, in principle, there are exponentially many terms of the form $f(t_1, \ldots, t_k)$, since we are considering the signature Σ as part of the input. However, we only have to search through these terms $f(t_1, \ldots, t_k)$ until we finally find one whose normal form w.r.t. $\mathcal{R}$ is outside $\widehat{\mathcal{U}}$. Moreover, all of the arguments t_i thus considered are in normal form w.r.t. $\mathcal{R}$. Hence, for $NF_{\mathcal{R}}(f(t_1, \ldots, t_k))$ to be in $\widehat{\mathcal{U}}$, either $f(t_1, \ldots, t_k) \in \widehat{\mathcal{U}}$ holds or there exists a rule of the form $f(t_1, \ldots, t_k) \to t$ in $\mathcal{R}$, s.t. $t \in \widehat{\mathcal{U}}$. But then, the number of such terms $f(t_1, \ldots, t_k)$ that can be normalized into $\widehat{\mathcal{U}}$ is bounded by $|\widehat{\mathcal{U}}| + |\mathcal{R}|$. In other words, the procedure CHECK_TOTAL_COVER has to check at most $|\widehat{\mathcal{U}}| + |\mathcal{R}| + 1$ terms, provided that it halts when the first term with normal form outside $\widehat{\mathcal{U}}$ is detected. Therefore, it only remains to show that for both possible outcomes of the procedure CHECK_TOTAL_COVER, the evaluation of C to "false" can be checked in non-deterministically polynomial time. But this is easy to prove, namely: Suppose that all ground terms of H normalize into $\widehat{\mathcal{U}}$. Then we just have to guess a ground substitution ϑ with $rg(\vartheta) \subseteq \widehat{\mathcal{U}}$ and check in polynomial time that the resulting *ground* clause $C\vartheta$ evaluates to "false" in $\mathcal{M}$. On the other hand, if there exists some $t \in H$ with $NF_{\mathcal{R}}(t) \notin \widehat{\mathcal{U}}$, then we have to guess a ground substitution ϑ with $rg(\vartheta) \subseteq \widehat{\mathcal{U}} \cup \{t\}$ and again check in polynomial time that the resulting *ground* clause $C\vartheta$ evaluates to "false" in $\mathcal{M}$.

In order to prove the coNP-hardness, we reduce the well-known NP-complete problem 3-SAT to the complementary problem of GAE-CLAUSE-EVALUATION: Let $F = (l_{11} \vee l_{12} \vee l_{13}) \wedge \ldots \wedge (l_{n1} \vee l_{n2} \vee l_{n3})$ be a Boolean formula with propositional variables in $X = \{x_1, \ldots, x_m\}$, s.t. the literals $l_{\alpha\beta}$ in F are either non-negated propositional variables x_i or negated propositional variables $\bar{x}_i$ for some $x_i \in X$. Then we construct the instance $(\Sigma, \mathcal{M}, C)$ of the GAE-CLAUSE-EVALUATION problem, where $\Sigma = \{P, Q, a, b\}$, $C = P(l_{11}, l_{12}, l_{13}) \vee \ldots \vee P(l_{n1}, l_{n2}, l_{n3}) \vee Q(x_1, \bar{x}_1) \vee \ldots \vee Q(x_m, \bar{x}_m)$, and the GAE-model is given through the atom set $\mathcal{A} = \{P(a, a, a), Q(b, b)\}$ and the empty set $\mathcal{E} = \emptyset$ of equations. Of course, this transformation can be done in polynomial time. Hence, it only remains to show the following equivalence: F is satisfiable $\Leftrightarrow$ C evaluates to "false" in $\mathcal{M}$.

Note that in the above problem definitions, we write x_i and $\bar{x}_i$ both to denote propositional literals in F and first-order variables in C. This dual use of the notation was chosen in order to stress the main idea of the equivalence proof below, namely: The propositional literals x_i and $\bar{x}_i$ will have the truth value "true", iff the first-order variables x_i and $\bar{x}_i$ are instantiated to b. Likewise, the constant term a will be used to encode the truth value "false".

With these preparations it is not difficult to show the above transformation equivalence (cf. [12]).   □

4   Model Equivalence

In this section, we investigate the problem of deciding whether two GAE-models $\mathcal{M}_1$ and $\mathcal{M}_2$ over some signature Σ with universe $H = \mathcal{T}(\mathcal{F})$, $\mathcal{F} \subseteq \Sigma$, are equivalent, i.e., whether all H-ground atoms have the same truth value in these two GAE-models. In this case, we write $\mathcal{M}_1 \equiv \mathcal{M}_2$. Actually, it suffices to provide a decision procedure for testing the inclusion of a GAE-model by another one, i.e.: Is every H-ground atom that is "true" in $\mathcal{M}_1$ also "true" in $\mathcal{M}_2$? By abuse of notation, we denote this by $\mathcal{M}_1 \subseteq \mathcal{M}_2$. Of course, $\mathcal{M}_1 \equiv \mathcal{M}_2$ holds iff both $\mathcal{M}_1 \subseteq \mathcal{M}_2$ and $\mathcal{M}_2 \subseteq \mathcal{M}_1$ hold. We thus study the following problems:

GAE-MODEL-EQUIVALENCE
Instance: A tuple $(\Sigma, \mathcal{M}_1, \mathcal{M}_2)$, where $\mathcal{M}_1$ and $\mathcal{M}_2$ are GAE-models over the universe H with signature Σ.
Question: Does $\mathcal{M}_1 \equiv \mathcal{M}_2$ hold?

GAE-MODEL-INCLUSION
Instance: A tuple $(\Sigma, \mathcal{M}_1, \mathcal{M}_2)$, where $\mathcal{M}_1$ and $\mathcal{M}_2$ are GAE-models over the universe H with signature Σ.
Question: Does $\mathcal{M}_1 \subseteq \mathcal{M}_2$ hold?

Recall from Section 2.1, that the GAE-model $\mathcal{M}_1 = (\mathcal{A}, \mathcal{E}_1)$ can efficiently (i.e., in quadratic time) be brought into the form $(\mathcal{P}, \widehat{\mathcal{A}}, \widehat{\mathcal{S}})$, where $\mathcal{P}$ is a canonical GTRS equivalent to $\mathcal{E}_1$, $\widehat{\mathcal{A}}$ is the set of ground atoms $\mathcal{A}$ in normal form, and $\widehat{\mathcal{S}}$ is the set of ground normal forms of all subterms in $\mathcal{A} \cup \mathcal{E}_1$. Likewise, $\mathcal{M}_2 = (\mathcal{B}, \mathcal{E}_2)$ can be transformed into $(\mathcal{R}, \widehat{\mathcal{B}}, \widehat{\mathcal{U}})$. Our GAE-MODEL-INCLUSION algorithm will be based on the construction of the following sets COMP$_1$ and COMP$_2$:

Definition 1. (compatible terms) *The sets* COMP$_1 \subseteq (\widehat{\mathcal{S}} \times \widehat{\mathcal{U}})$ *and* COMP$_2 \subseteq (\widehat{\mathcal{S}} \times \{\perp\})$ *are defined as follows:*

- $(s, t) \in$ COMP$_1$, *iff* $\exists r \in H$, *s.t.* $NF_{\mathcal{P}}(r) = s$ *and* $NF_{\mathcal{R}}(r) = t$.
- $(s, \perp) \in$ COMP$_2$, *iff* $\exists r \in H$, *s.t.* $NF_{\mathcal{P}}(r) = s$ *and* $NF_{\mathcal{R}}(r) \notin \widehat{\mathcal{U}}$.

In other words, we call a term $s \in \widehat{\mathcal{S}}$ "compatible" with a term $t \in \widehat{\mathcal{U}}$, iff s and t can be obtained as the normal forms w.r.t. $\mathcal{P}$ and $\mathcal{R}$, respectively, of some "common predecessor" $r \in H$. Likewise, a term $s \in \widehat{\mathcal{S}}$ is called "compatible" with the auxiliary symbol $\perp$, iff s is the normal form w.r.t. $\mathcal{P}$ of some term r, whereas the normal form of r w.r.t. $\mathcal{R}$ is outside $\widehat{\mathcal{U}}$. In Figure 2, we provide an algorithm for computing these sets COMP_1 and COMP_2.

The idea of the computation of COMP_1 in Step 1 in Figure 2 is as follows: If some term r is contained both in $\widehat{\mathcal{S}}$ and $\widehat{\mathcal{U}}$, then (r, r) is in COMP_1. Now suppose that f is a k-ary function symbol with $k \geq 0$ and (s_1, t_1), ..., (s_k, t_k) are pairs of compatible terms in COMP_1. Then also $f(s_1, \ldots, s_k)$ and $f(t_1, \ldots, t_k)$ are compatible. Finally, suppose that (s_i, t_i), $1 \leq i \leq k$, have already been found to be compatible and let $s = f(s_1, \ldots, s_k)$, $t = f(t_1, \ldots, t_k)$. Moreover, suppose that $\mathcal{P}$ contains a rule $s \to s'$. Then also $(s', t) \in \text{COMP}_1$ holds. Likewise, if there exists a rule $t \to t'$ in $\mathcal{R}$ then $(s, t') \in \text{COMP}_1$ holds.

Lemma 1. *(computation of* COMP_1*) Let* $\mathcal{M}_1$ *and* $\mathcal{M}_2$ *be two GAE-models over some H with signature Σ. Moreover, let $(\mathcal{P}, \widehat{\mathcal{A}}, \widehat{\mathcal{S}})$ and $(\mathcal{R}, \widehat{\mathcal{B}}, \widehat{\mathcal{U}})$ be the normal form representations of $\mathcal{M}_1$ and $\mathcal{M}_2$, respectively, according to Property (d) in Section 2.1. Then STEP 1 of the procedure* COMPUTE_COMP *in Figure 2 computes the set* $\text{COMP}_1 \subseteq \widehat{\mathcal{S}} \times \widehat{\mathcal{U}}$ *of Definition 1 in time $O(|\widehat{\mathcal{S}}| * |\widehat{\mathcal{U}}| * (|\widehat{\mathcal{S}}| + |\mathcal{P}|) * (|\widehat{\mathcal{U}}| + |\mathcal{R}|) * K)$, where K denotes the maximum arity of (function) symbols in Σ.*

Proof. A complete proof of the correctness and of the upper bound on the complexity of STEP 1 of procedure COMPUTE_COMP is given in the full paper [12]. We only sketch the complexity proof here. By construction, $\text{COMP}_1 \subseteq \widehat{\mathcal{S}} \times \widehat{\mathcal{U}}$. Hence, the fixed point is reached after at most $|\widehat{\mathcal{S}} \times \widehat{\mathcal{U}}|$ iterations of the repeat-loop. The (nested) loops "for all $s = f(s_1, \ldots, s_k) \in \widehat{\mathcal{S}}$" and "for all $(f(s_1, \ldots, s_k) \to s) \in \mathcal{P}$" on the one hand, and "for all $t = f(t_1, \ldots, t_k) \in \widehat{\mathcal{U}}$" and "for all $(f(t_1, \ldots, t_k) \to t) \in \mathcal{R}$" on the other hand, come down to touching $(|\widehat{\mathcal{S}}| + |\mathcal{P}|) * (|\widehat{\mathcal{U}}| + |\mathcal{R}|)$ pairs of terms of the form $(f(s_1, \ldots, s_k), f(t_1, \ldots, t_k))$. For each such pair, we have to carry out at most K checks as to whether $(s_i, t_i) \in \text{COMP}_1$ holds. Each such check can be done in constant time, provided that COMP_1 is represented appropriately (e.g., as a matrix $M \in \{0, 1\}^{|\widehat{\mathcal{S}}| \times |\widehat{\mathcal{U}}|}$, s.t. $M_{\alpha\beta} = 1$, iff $(s_\alpha, t_\beta) \in \text{COMP}_1$). The desired upper bound follows easily. □

The computation of COMP_2 in Step 2 of the algorithm in Figure 2 is based on the following idea: Let $s \in \widehat{\mathcal{S}}$ be of the form $s = f(s_1, \ldots, s_k)$. Then there can be basically two reasons why the pair $(s, \perp)$ is in COMP_2: Suppose that for some i we have already shown $(s_i, \perp) \in \text{COMP}_2$. Then, by the subterm closedness of $\widehat{\mathcal{U}}$ (cf. Property (e) in Section 2.1), also $(s, \perp) \in \text{COMP}_2$ holds. On the other hand, suppose that there exist k pairs (s_1, t_1), ..., $(s_k, t_k) \in \text{COMP}_1$, s.t. $NF_{\mathcal{R}}(f(t_1, \ldots, t_k)) \notin \widehat{\mathcal{U}}$. By the definition of COMP_1 we know that for every $i \in \{1, \ldots, k\}$ the terms s_i and t_i have a common predecessor r_i w.r.t. $\mathcal{P}$ and $\mathcal{R}$, respectively. Hence, also s and $f(t_1, \ldots, t_k)$ have a common predecessor $f(r_1, \ldots, r_k)$ and thus $(s, \perp) \in \text{COMP}_2$. Of course, if some term s is compatible with $\perp$ and $\mathcal{P}$ contains a rule $s \to s'$, then also s' is compatible with $\perp$.

Lemma 2. *(computation of* COMP_2*) Let* $\mathcal{M}_1$ *and* $\mathcal{M}_2$ *be two GAE-models over H with signature Σ and let $(\mathcal{P}, \widehat{\mathcal{A}}, \widehat{\mathcal{S}})$ and $(\mathcal{R}, \widehat{\mathcal{B}}, \widehat{\mathcal{U}})$ be as above. Then STEP 2 of*

COMPUTATION OF COMP$_1$ **AND** COMP$_2$
input: Σ, $\mathcal{P}$, $\widehat{\mathcal{S}}$, $\mathcal{R}$, $\widehat{\mathcal{U}}$
result: COMP$_1$ and COMP$_2$

STEP 1: /* computation of COMP$_1$ */

    COMP$_1$:= $\emptyset$;

    repeat

        for all $s = f(s_1, \ldots, s_k) \in \widehat{\mathcal{S}}$ **do**
            for all $t = f(t_1, \ldots, t_k) \in \widehat{\mathcal{U}}$ **do**
                if $\forall i \in \{1, \ldots, k\}$, $(s_i, t_i) \in$ COMP$_1$ **then** COMP$_1$:= COMP$_1 \cup \{(s,t)\}$;
            for all $(f(t_1, \ldots, t_k) \to t) \in \mathcal{R}$ **do**
                if $\forall i \in \{1, \ldots, k\}$, $(s_i, t_i) \in$ COMP$_1$ **then** COMP$_1$:= COMP$_1 \cup \{(s,t)\}$;
        od;

        for all $(f(s_1, \ldots, s_k) \to s) \in \mathcal{P}$ **do**
            for all $t = f(t_1, \ldots, t_k) \in \widehat{\mathcal{U}}$ **do**
                if $\forall i \in \{1, \ldots, k\}$, $(s_i, t_i) \in$ COMP$_1$ **then** COMP$_1$:= COMP$_1 \cup \{(s,t)\}$;
            for all $(f(t_1, \ldots, t_k) \to t) \in \mathcal{R}$ **do**
                if $\forall i \in \{1, \ldots, k\}$, $(s_i, t_i) \in$ COMP$_1$ **then** COMP$_1$:= COMP$_1 \cup \{(s,t)\}$;
        od;

    until a fixed point is reached;

STEP 2: /* computation of COMP$_2$ */

    COMP$_2$:= $\emptyset$;

    for all $s = f(s_1, \ldots, s_k) \in \widehat{\mathcal{S}}$ **do**
        if $\exists f(t_1, \ldots, t_k)$, s.t. $(\forall i \in \{1, \ldots, k\}$, $(s_i, t_i) \in$ COMP$_1)$
            and $NF_{\mathcal{R}}(f(t_1, \ldots, t_k)) \notin \widehat{\mathcal{U}}$ **then** COMP$_2$:= COMP$_2 \cup \{(s, \perp)\}$;

    for all $(f(s_1, \ldots, s_k) \to s) \in \mathcal{P}$ **do**
        if $\exists f(t_1, \ldots, t_k)$, s.t. $(\forall i \in \{1, \ldots, k\}$, $(s_i, t_i) \in$ COMP$_1)$
            and $NF_{\mathcal{R}}(f(t_1, \ldots, t_k)) \notin \widehat{\mathcal{U}}$ **then** COMP$_2$:= COMP$_2 \cup \{(s, \perp)\}$;

    repeat

        for all $s = f(s_1, \ldots, s_k) \in \widehat{\mathcal{S}}$ **do**
            if $\exists i \in \{1, \ldots, k\}$, $(s_i, \perp) \in$ COMP$_2$ **then** COMP$_2$:= COMP$_2 \cup \{(s, \perp)\}$;

        for all $(f(s_1, \ldots, s_k) \to s) \in \mathcal{P}$ **do**
            if $\exists i \in \{1, \ldots, k\}$, $(s_i, \perp) \in$ COMP$_2$ **then** COMP$_2$:= COMP$_2 \cup \{(s, \perp)\}$;

    until a fixed point is reached;

Fig. 2. Procedure COMPUTE_COMP

the procedure COMPUTE_COMP *in Figure 2 computes the set* COMP$_2 \subseteq \widehat{\mathcal{S}} \times \{\perp\}$
of Definition 1 in time $O((|\widehat{\mathcal{S}}| + |\mathcal{P}|) * (|\widehat{\mathcal{U}}| + |\mathcal{R}|) * K)$, *where* K *denotes the*
maximum arity of (function) symbols in Σ.

Proof. Again, we only sketch the complexity proof here. For details and for
a correctness proof, see [12]. As to the for-loops in front of the repeat-loop,

note that the number of iterations of the for-loops is bounded by $|\widehat{\mathcal{S}}|$ and $|\mathcal{P}|$, respectively. We only have to be a bit careful with the checks inside these for-loops: In principle, there are exponentially many terms of the form $f(t_1, \ldots, t_k)$ with $(s_i, t_i) \in \text{COMP}_1$, since we are considering the signature Σ as part of the input. However, we only have to search through these terms $f(t_1, \ldots, t_k)$ until we finally find one whose normal form w.r.t. $\mathcal{R}$ is outside $\widehat{\mathcal{U}}$. In other words, the number of terms $f(t_1, \ldots, t_k)$ thus tested is bounded by 1 plus the number of such terms that can be normalized into $\widehat{\mathcal{U}}$. Recall that by definition of COMP_1, all arguments t_i are in normal form w.r.t. $\mathcal{R}$. Hence, for $NF_{\mathcal{R}}(f(t_1, \ldots, t_k))$ to be in $\widehat{\mathcal{U}}$, either $f(t_1, \ldots, t_k) \in \widehat{\mathcal{U}}$ holds or there exists a rule $f(t_1, \ldots, t_k) \to t$ in $\mathcal{R}$. Thus, the cost of searching for a term $f(t_1, \ldots, t_k)$ with $(s_i, t_i) \in \text{COMP}_1$ and $NF_{\mathcal{R}}(f(t_1, \ldots, t_k)) \notin \widehat{\mathcal{U}}$ is bounded by $O((|\widehat{\mathcal{U}}| + |\mathcal{R}|) * K)$ for each iteration of each of the two for-loops.

Now consider the repeat-loop. By construction, $\text{COMP}_2 \subseteq \widehat{\mathcal{S}} \times \{\perp\}$. Hence, the fixed point is reached after at most $|\widehat{\mathcal{S}}|$ iterations. In the first for-loop, we have to run through the terms $s \in \widehat{\mathcal{S}}$ and check whether one of the arguments of s already occurs in COMP_2. There are at most $|\widehat{\mathcal{S}}| * K$ such checks required. Likewise, in the second for-loop, we have to run through the terms s occurring as left-hand sides of rules in $\mathcal{P}$. Hence, in this case, we end up with an upper bound of $|\mathcal{P}| * K$ on the number of checks. But then the asymptotic complexity of STEP 2 is fully determined by the complexity $O((|\widehat{\mathcal{S}}| + |\mathcal{P}|) * (|\widehat{\mathcal{U}}| + |\mathcal{R}|) * K)$ of the for-loops in front of the repeat-loop. $\qquad\square$

We are now ready to solve the GAE-MODEL-INCLUSION problem. The idea of our decision procedure is to search for an atom $P(r_1, \ldots, r_k)$, whose truth value is "true" in $\mathcal{M}_1$ and "false" in $\mathcal{M}_2$. This can be done via the sets of compatible terms in $\text{COMP}_1 \cup \text{COMP}_2$ as follows: Suppose that $P(s_1, \ldots, s_k)$ is in $\widehat{\mathcal{A}}$ but some argument s_i is compatible with $\perp$. Then $P(s_1, \ldots, s_k)$ has a predecessor $P(r_1, \ldots, r_k)$, whose truth value is "true" in $\mathcal{M}_1$ and "false" in $\mathcal{M}_2$. Likewise, suppose that $P(s_1, \ldots, s_k)$ is compatible with an atom $P(t_1, \ldots, t_k)$ (i.e.: all pairs (s_i, t_i) are in COMP_1), s.t. $P(s_1, \ldots, s_k)$ evaluates to "true" in $\mathcal{M}_1$, whereas $P(t_1, \ldots, t_k)$ evaluates to "false" in $\mathcal{M}_2$. Then, by the definition of COMP_1, the atoms $P(s_1, \ldots, s_k)$ and $P(t_1, \ldots, t_k)$ have a common predecessor that is a witness for $\mathcal{M}_1 \not\subseteq \mathcal{M}_2$. Similarly to Lemma 2, it can be shown that such a procedure works in polynomial time. More precisely, we get the following.

Lemma 3. *(GAE-MODEL-INCLUSION) Let $\mathcal{M}_1$ and $\mathcal{M}_2$ be two GAE-models over H with signature Σ and let $(\mathcal{P}, \widehat{\mathcal{A}}, \widehat{\mathcal{S}})$ and $(\mathcal{R}, \widehat{\mathcal{B}}, \widehat{\mathcal{U}})$ as above. Moreover, suppose that the sets COMP_1 and COMP_2 of Definition 1 have already been computed. Then the GAE-MODEL-INCLUSION problem can be decided in time $O(|\widehat{\mathcal{A}}| * |\widehat{\mathcal{B}}| * K)$, where K is the maximum arity of (predicate) symbols in Σ.*

Proof. By the above considerations, the GAE-MODEL-INCLUSION problem can be solved with the following piece of program code:

> **for all** $P(s_1, \ldots, s_k) \in \widehat{\mathcal{A}}$ **do**
>   **if** $\exists i \in \{1, \ldots, k\}$, s.t. $(s_i, \bot) \in \text{COMP}_2$
>   **then return** "false";
>   **if** $\exists P(t_1, \ldots, t_k)$, s.t. $(\forall i \in \{1, \ldots, k\}, (s_i, t_i) \in \text{COMP}_1)$
>   and $P(t_1, \ldots, t_k) \notin \widehat{\mathcal{B}}$ **then return** "false";
> **od**;
> **return** "true";

For the correctness of this procedure, see [12]. As to the complexity, note that the for-loop is iterated at most $|\widehat{\mathcal{A}}|$ times. Moreover, in the first if-statement, we have to check for at most K arguments s_i whether $(s_i, \bot) \in \text{COMP}_2$ holds. Now let us consider the second if-statement. Similarly to Lemma 2, we have to be a bit careful since, in principle, there are exponentially many atoms of the form $P(t_1, \ldots, t_k)$ to be checked. However, we stop this search as soon as we find an atom $P(t_1, \ldots, t_k)$ whose normal form w.r.t. $\mathcal{R}$ is outside $\widehat{\mathcal{B}}$. Hence, analogously to Lemma 2, we get an upper bound $O(|\widehat{\mathcal{B}}| * K)$ on the time required for processing each atom $P(s_1, \ldots, s_k) \in \widehat{\mathcal{A}}$. In total, we thus get the desired upper bound $O(|\widehat{\mathcal{A}}| * |\widehat{\mathcal{B}}| * K)$. □

The main result of this section is now easily established. Recall that by Property (d) in Section 2.1, the computation of $(\mathcal{P}, \widehat{\mathcal{A}}, \widehat{\mathcal{S}})$ from $\mathcal{M}_1$ and of $(\mathcal{R}, \widehat{\mathcal{B}}, \widehat{\mathcal{U}})$ from $\mathcal{M}_2$ can be done in polynomial time, more precisely in quadratic time. Hence, together with the Lemmas 1 through 3, we immediately get

Theorem 2. *The* GAE-MODEL-EQUIVALENCE *problem can be decided in polynomial time, i.e.: Let* $\mathcal{M}_1 = (\mathcal{A}_1, \mathcal{E}_1)$ *and* $\mathcal{M}_2 = (\mathcal{A}_2, \mathcal{E}_2)$ *be two arbitrary GAE-models over some* H *with signature* Σ. *Then it can be decided in polynomial time w.r.t. the input* $(\Sigma, (\mathcal{A}_1, \mathcal{E}_1), (\mathcal{A}_2, \mathcal{E}_2))$ *whether* $\mathcal{M}_1 \equiv \mathcal{M}_2$ *holds.*

Remark (Comparison with other methods): An alternative way of solving the equivalence problem of GAE-models would be to transform the GAE-models into finite tree automata (FTA, for short) and to apply an equivalence test to the resulting FTA. In [14,15], such a transformation from the normal form representation $(\mathcal{P}, \widehat{\mathcal{A}}, \widehat{\mathcal{S}})$ of a GAE-model $\mathcal{M}_1$ into an equivalent deterministic FTA $A_1 = (\Sigma, Q, Q_f, \delta)$ (i.e.: A_1 recognizes exactly those ground atoms over Σ which are "true" in $\mathcal{M}_1$) is presented. The number $|Q|$ of states of A_1 basically corresponds to the number $|\widehat{\mathcal{S}}|$ of normalized subterms in the GAE-model. Moreover, the number of state transitions in δ basically corresponds to $|\mathcal{P}| + |\widehat{\mathcal{A}}|$.

Now suppose that we have transformed both GAE-models $\mathcal{M}_1$ and $\mathcal{M}_2$ into equivalent FTA A_1 and A_2. Let N denote the total number of states of these automata and let M denote their total size. With the construction of [14,15], N depends linearly on $|\widehat{\mathcal{S}}| + |\widehat{\mathcal{U}}|$ and M depends linearly on the total size of $(\mathcal{P}, \widehat{\mathcal{A}}, \widehat{\mathcal{S}})$ and $(\mathcal{R}, \widehat{\mathcal{B}}, \widehat{\mathcal{U}})$. In order to test the equivalence of these two FTA, we could follow the way suggested in [6], i.e., first transform the FTA into equivalent *complete* FTA A_1' and A_2'. Then the equivalence of A_1' and A_2' can be checked in quadratic time. However, recall that we are considering the signature as part of a problem instance here. Hence, the straightforward process of completing an FTA may add exponentially many new transition rules in the worst-case.

Alternatively, we may test the equivalence of A_1 and A_2 via the method presented in [18]. A careful analysis of [18] reveals that in our setting this method works in time $O(N^{K+2} * M)$, where K denotes the maximum arity of the symbols in Σ. Moreover, it is shown in [18] how the maximum arity K can be reduced to 2. Note however, that this reduction of the arity leads to a multiplication of the number of states, i.e., we get automata A_1' and A_2' whose total number of states is basically $N * K$. Hence, we end up with an upper bound $O((N * K)^4 * M)$ on the time complexity.

The main source of complexity of our model equivalence test is the computation of the sets COMP_1 and COMP_2. By Lemma 1, this can be done in time $O(|\widehat{\mathcal{S}}| * |\widehat{\mathcal{U}}| * (|\widehat{\mathcal{S}}| + |\mathcal{P}|) * (|\widehat{\mathcal{U}}| + |\mathcal{R}|) * K)$. In terms of the FTA, this corresponds to $O(N^2 * M^2 * K)$. The computations according to the Lemmas 2 and 3 can also be done within this bound. Actually, if the original GAE-model contains a huge number of equations on comparatively few and small terms, then the algorithm of [18] may possibly be more efficient than ours. Otherwise (i.e., in particular, when the number of subterms occurring in the GAE-model is of the same order of magnitude as the number of equations) our algorithm should actually outperform the one hidden in [18]. Moreover, the dependence on the signature is clearly smaller in our algorithm.

5   Construction of an Almost Minimal Finite Model

In [9], an algorithm is provided that constructs a GAE-model $\mathcal{M}$ for any satisfiable clause set from the so-called class $\text{PVD}_g^{=}$. Of course, if the signature Σ contains at least one proper function symbol, then in general the model $\mathcal{M}$ has an infinite domain, namely the Herbrand universe over Σ. However, it is shown in [9], how one can derive from $\mathcal{M}$ an equivalent finite model $\mathcal{M}_{\mathcal{F}}$. This extraction of a finite model is based on the following idea: First of all, the model $\mathcal{M}$ given through a set of ground atoms $\mathcal{A}$ and ground equations $\mathcal{E}$ is transformed into the form $(\mathcal{R}, \widehat{\mathcal{A}}, \widehat{\mathcal{U}})$, where $\mathcal{R}$ is a canonical GTRS equivalent to $\mathcal{E}$, $\widehat{\mathcal{A}}$ contains the normal forms of the atoms in $\mathcal{A}$, and $\widehat{\mathcal{U}} = \{t_1, \ldots, t_N\}$ contains the normal forms of all terms and subterms occurring in $\mathcal{A}$ and $\mathcal{E}$. Then, analogously to the clause evaluation procedure recalled in Section 2.2, we first have to check, whether the whole universe H over the signature Σ normalizes into $\widehat{\mathcal{U}}$ or not. This can be done with the procedure CHECK_TOTAL_COVER in Figure 1. Then we have to distinguish two cases:

- Case 1: If $\forall t \in H, NF_{\mathcal{R}}(t) \in \widehat{\mathcal{U}}$, then $\mathcal{M}_{\mathcal{F}}$ has the domain $D = \{a_1, \ldots, a_N\}$ (i.e., D has the same cardinality as $\widehat{\mathcal{U}}$), s.t. every ground term $s \in H$ with normal form $NF_{\mathcal{R}}(s) = t_i$ is interpreted by a_i. Moreover, each predicate symbol $P \in \Sigma$ with arity $k \geq 1$ is interpreted in $\mathcal{M}_{\mathcal{F}}$ by the relation $\mathcal{M}_{\mathcal{F}}(P) \subseteq D^k$ with $\mathcal{M}_{\mathcal{F}}(P) = \{(a_{i_1}, \ldots, a_{i_k}) \mid P(t_{i_1}, \ldots, t_{i_k}) \in \widehat{\mathcal{A}}\}$.

- Case 2: If $\exists t \in H$ with $NF_{\mathcal{R}}(t) \notin \widehat{\mathcal{U}}$, then $\mathcal{M}_{\mathcal{F}}$ has the domain $D = \{a_1, \ldots, a_N\} \cup \{d\}$ for some new element d (i.e., $|D| = |\widehat{\mathcal{U}}| + 1$), s.t. every ground term $s \in H$ with normal form $NF_{\mathcal{R}}(s) = t_i \in \widehat{\mathcal{U}}$ is interpreted by a_i and every ground term $s \in H$ with normal form $NF_{\mathcal{R}}(s) \notin \widehat{\mathcal{U}}$ is interpreted by d. Analogously to Case 1 above, each predicate symbol $P \in \Sigma$ with arity $k \geq 1$ is interpreted by the relation $\mathcal{M}_{\mathcal{F}}(P) = \{(a_{i_1}, \ldots, a_{i_k}) \mid P(t_{i_1}, \ldots, t_{i_k}) \in \widehat{\mathcal{A}}\}$.

Recall from Section 3, that the computational cost of evaluating clauses over a GAE-model $\mathcal{M}$ heavily depends on the size of $\widehat{\mathcal{U}}$. In particular, if C is a clause with k variables, then we have to check $k^{|\widehat{\mathcal{U}}|}$ ground instances of C (in Case 1 above) or $k^{(|\widehat{\mathcal{U}}|+1)}$ instances (in Case 2 above), respectively, in order to show that C indeed evaluates to "true" in $\mathcal{M}$. Likewise, if we do the clause evaluation in the corresponding finite model, then the computational cost is mainly determined by the size of the finite domain D. Consequently, before we actually start evaluating clauses in a GAE-model $\mathcal{M}$ (e.g., when $\mathcal{M}$ is used by theorem prover based on semantic resolution), it would be desirable to first transform $\mathcal{M}$ into an equivalent GAE-model $\mathcal{M}'$ with a smaller set $\widehat{\mathcal{U}}'$. Likewise, if the clause evaluation is done in the finite model $\mathcal{M}_{\mathcal{F}}$ obtained from $\mathcal{M}$ via the algorithm of [9], then we should first search for an equivalent finite model $\mathcal{M}'_{\mathcal{F}}$ with a smaller domain.

Actually, searching for a finite model whose domain is minimal by checking all possible domains D with $|D| = 1, 2, 3, \ldots$ and all possible interpretations of the signature Σ is out of the question. It was already pointed out in [9] that constructing a GAE-model first and extracting a finite model afterwards is the only reasonable way. However, it was also mentioned in [9] that this method has the disadvantage that the size of the domain of the resulting finite model is possibly far bigger than actually necessary. In this section, we show how this drawback can be remedied to a certain extent. Of course, it is infeasible to start from scratch and compute a completely different model. However, what we can do is to take a GAE-model $\mathcal{M}$ resulting from the model construction procedure in [9] and transform it into an equivalent model $\mathcal{M}'$ with a possibly much smaller set $\widehat{\mathcal{U}}'$ of terms in normal form. Consequently, also the finite model $\mathcal{M}'_{\mathcal{F}}$ obtained from $\mathcal{M}'$ by the above recalled method of [9] possibly has a much smaller domain than the finite model $\mathcal{M}_{\mathcal{F}}$ extracted from $\mathcal{M}$. In Figure 3 we provide an algorithm that takes a GAE-model $\mathcal{M}$ as an input and transforms it into an equivalent model $\mathcal{M}'$ that is "almost minimal" in the following sense.

Definition 2. (almost minimal GAE-model) *Let $\mathcal{M}$ be a GAE-model and let $\mathcal{M}_{\mathcal{F}}$ with domain D be the corresponding finite model that is obtained via the algorithm of [9]. Furthermore, let $\mathcal{M}_{\min}$ be an equivalent finite model with minimal domain $D_{\min}$. Then we call $\mathcal{M}$ a minimal GAE-model, if $|D| = |D_{\min}|$ holds. Moreover, $\mathcal{M}$ is called an almost minimal GAE-model if $|D| \leq |D_{\min}| + 1$ holds.*

COMPUTATION OF AN ALMOST MINIMAL GAE-MODEL

input: Σ, $\mathcal{M} = (\mathcal{A}, \mathcal{E})$

output: $\mathcal{M}' = (\mathcal{A}', \mathcal{E}')$, s.t. $\mathcal{M}'$ is almost minimal and equivalent to $\mathcal{M}$

begin

   compute $(\mathcal{R}, \widehat{\mathcal{A}}, \widehat{\mathcal{U}})$ according to $(\mathcal{A}, \mathcal{E})$;   /* cf. Property (d) in Section 2.1 */

   repeat

      if $\exists$ distinct terms s, t in $\widehat{\mathcal{U}}$, s.t.

        $\mathcal{M} = (\mathcal{A}, \mathcal{E})$ and $\mathcal{M}' = (\mathcal{A}, \mathcal{E} \cup \{s = t\})$ are equivalent **then**

      begin

        $\mathcal{E} := \mathcal{E} \cup \{s = t\}$;

        compute $(\mathcal{R}, \widehat{\mathcal{A}}, \widehat{\mathcal{U}})$ according to $(\mathcal{A}, \mathcal{E})$;

      end;

   until no such pair (s, t) is found;

   return $(\mathcal{A}, \mathcal{E})$;

end.

Fig. 3. Procedure FIND_ALMOST_MINIMAL_MODEL

The procedure FIND_ALMOST_MINIMAL_MODEL in Figure 3 is based on the following idea: Let $\mathcal{M}$ be given in the form $(\mathcal{R}, \widehat{\mathcal{A}}, \widehat{\mathcal{U}})$. Now suppose that all terms in $\widehat{\mathcal{U}}$ are interpreted in $\mathcal{M}_{\min}$ by pairwise distinct elements of $D_{\min}$. In this case, we have $|\widehat{\mathcal{U}}| \leq |D_{\min}|$ and, therefore, $|D| \leq |D_{\min}| + 1$. Hence, $\mathcal{M}$ is already almost minimal. On the other hand, suppose that there are two distinct terms s and t in $\widehat{\mathcal{U}}$, that are interpreted by the same domain element $a_i \in D_{\min}$. In this case, it is easy to show that adding the equation $s = t$ to the GAE-model yields an equivalent model. Hence, in order to transform $\mathcal{M}$ into an almost minimal GAE-model we just have to take all pairs (s, t) from $\widehat{\mathcal{U}}$ and check whether the equation $s = t$ can be added to the GAE-model without changing the truth value of any ground atom (of $\mathcal{M}$) over this signature.[9]

Theorem 3. *(termination and correctness of* FIND_ALMOST_MINIMAL_MODEL*)*
Let $\mathcal{M} = (\mathcal{A}, \mathcal{E})$ *be a GAE-model over the signature* Σ*. Then the procedure* FIND_ALMOST_MINIMAL_MODEL *with input* $(\Sigma, \mathcal{M})$ *terminates and returns an almost minimal GAE-model* $\mathcal{M}'$ *that is equivalent to* $\mathcal{M}$*.*

Proof: As to <u>termination</u>, recall from Property (e) in Section 2.1, that $\widehat{\mathcal{U}}$ is closed w.r.t. subterms. By construction, the terms in $\widehat{\mathcal{U}}$ correspond to equivalence classes of all subterms occurring in $\mathcal{A}$ and $\mathcal{E}$ w.r.t. the equations in $\mathcal{E}$. Of course, we get exactly the same set of equivalence classes w.r.t. the equations in $\mathcal{E}$, if we consider the subterms of $\mathcal{A}$ and $\mathcal{E}$ plus the subterms of $s, t \in \widehat{\mathcal{U}}$. Moreover,

---

[9] Note that, in practice and from an efficiency point of view, an incremental completion in procedure FIND_ALMOST_MINIMAL_MODEL is of course preferable. That is, instead of completing $\mathcal{E} \cup \{s = t\}$ it is generally better to use the already computed canonical GTRS $\mathcal{R}$ for $\mathcal{E}$ and complete $\mathcal{R} \cup \{s = t\}$ (using the same completion parameters, in particular, the same reduction ordering).

adding an equation $s = t$ to $\mathcal{E}$ with $s, t \in \widehat{\mathcal{U}}$, $s \neq t$, has the following effect: On the one hand, the two distinct equivalence classes corresponding to s and t collapse into a single one and, on the other hand, no new equivalence class can arise by adding an equation to $\mathcal{E}$. Hence, the number of equivalence classes w.r.t. $\mathcal{E} \cup \{s = t\}$ of the subterms in $\mathcal{A}$ and $\mathcal{E} \cup \{s = t\}$ is strictly smaller than the number of equivalence classes w.r.t. $\mathcal{E}$ of the subterms in $\mathcal{A}$ and $\mathcal{E}$. But then, the number of iterations of the repeat-loop is clearly restricted by $|\widehat{\mathcal{U}}|$ of the input GAE-model $\mathcal{M}$.

As to <u>correctness</u> of the procedure FIND_ALMOST_MINIMAL_MODEL, we have to show that the resulting GAE-model $\mathcal{M}'$ is almost minimal and equivalent to $\mathcal{M}$. Actually, the equivalence is trivial since, in each iteration of the repeat-loop, we only add an equation $s = t$ to $\mathcal{E}$ after checking that the GAE-models $(\mathcal{A}, \mathcal{E})$ and $(\mathcal{A}, \mathcal{E} \cup \{s = t\})$ are indeed equivalent. It only remains to show that the final model $\mathcal{M}'$ is almost minimal. To this end, it suffices to show that $|\widehat{\mathcal{U}}'| \leq |D_{\min}|$ holds. In other words, any two distinct terms in $\widehat{\mathcal{U}}'$ are interpreted by distinct domain elements in $D_{\min}$. Suppose on the contrary, that $\widehat{\mathcal{U}}'$ contains two distinct terms s, t, which are interpreted by the same domain element in $D_{\min}$. Now let $r[s]$ be an arbitrary ground term with subterm s and let $r[t]$ be the term obtained from $r[s]$ by replacing the subterm s with t. Then the interpretation $\mathcal{M}_{\min}$ maps the terms $r[s]$ and $r[t]$ to identical domain elements in $D_{\min}$. Likewise, if $A[s]$ is a ground atom with subterm s and if $A[t]$ is obtained from $A[s]$ by replacing the subterm s with t, then the interpretation $\mathcal{M}_{\min}$ clearly assigns the same truth value to $A[s]$ and $A[t]$. In other words, ground atoms that are equivalent w.r.t. the equation $s = t$ are assigned the same truth value by the interpretation $\mathcal{M}_{\mathcal{F}}$. Hence, they are also assigned the same truth value by $\mathcal{M}'$. Thus we may in fact add the equation $s = t$ to $\mathcal{E}'$ without changing the model $\mathcal{M}'$. But this contradicts the assumption, that $\mathcal{M}'$ is the final result of procedure FIND_ALMOST_MINIMAL_MODEL. $\square$

The algorithm FIND_ALMOST_MINIMAL_MODEL is put to work in the following example:

Example 2. Let $\mathcal{M} = (\mathcal{A}, \mathcal{E})$ be a GAE-model over the signature $\Sigma = \{a, b, f\}$ with $\mathcal{A} = \{P(f^2(a)), P(a)\}$ and $\mathcal{E} = \{f^2(a) = f^4(a), f^2(b) = a\}$. Clearly, $\mathcal{U} = \{a, f(a), f^2(a), f^3(a), f^4(a), b, f(b), f^2(b), f^3(b), f^4(b)\}$. Moreover, completing $\mathcal{E}$ into a canonical GTRS $\mathcal{R}$ and normalizing $\mathcal{T}$ yields $\mathcal{R} = \{f^4(a) \rightarrow f^2(a), f^2(b) \rightarrow a\}$,[10] $\widehat{\mathcal{U}} = \{a, f(a), f^2(a), f^3(a), b, f(b)\}$. In the repeat-loop of procedure FIND_ALMOST_MINIMAL_MODEL, we search for a pair $s = t$ of terms in $\widehat{\mathcal{U}}$, s.t. $(\mathcal{A}, \mathcal{E})$ and $(\mathcal{A}, \mathcal{E} \cup \{s = t\})$ are equivalent: We first check the equation $a = f(a)$. Actually, it can be easily checked "by hand" that $(\mathcal{A}, \mathcal{E})$ and $(\mathcal{A}, \mathcal{E} \cup \{s = t\})$ are not equivalent. This is due to the fact that $P(a)$ and $P(f(a))$ clearly have the same truth values in $(\mathcal{A}, \mathcal{E} \cup \{s = t\})$, but different ones in $\mathcal{M}$. Now we check the equation $a = f^2(a)$. In fact, this equation may be added to $\mathcal{E}$. Hence, we have to update the variables $\mathcal{E}$, $\mathcal{R}$, and $\widehat{\mathcal{U}}$ in the procedure

---

[10] For the construction of $\mathcal{R}$, we assume here that $b > a$ holds, w.r.t. to the underlying reduction ordering used.

FIND_ALMOST_MINIMAL_MODEL as follows:

$$\mathcal{E} = \{f^2(a) = f^4(a), f^2(b) = a, f^2(a) = a\},$$
$$\mathcal{R} = \{f^2(a) \to a, f^2(b) \to a\},$$
$$\widehat{\mathcal{U}} = \{a, f(a), b, f(b)\}.$$

In the next iteration of the repeat-loop, we check whether the equation $a = b$ may be added to the new set $\mathcal{E}$. The answer is again yes. Hence, the new values of the variables $\mathcal{E}$, $\mathcal{R}$, and $\widehat{\mathcal{U}}$ are:

$$\mathcal{E} = \{f^2(a) = f^4(a), f^2(b) = a, f^2(a) = a, b = a\},$$
$$\mathcal{R} = \{f^2(a) \to a, b \to a\},$$
$$\widehat{\mathcal{U}} = \{a, f(a)\}.$$

We have already mentioned above, that the equation $a = f(a)$ must not be added. Hence, the repeat-loop terminates and returns the final result $\mathcal{M}' = (\mathcal{A}', \mathcal{E}')$ with $\mathcal{A}' = \mathcal{A}$ and $\mathcal{E}' = \{f^2(a) = f^4(a), f^2(b) = a, f^2(a) = a, b = a\}$.

6 Discussion

The aim of this paper was to improve upon previous algorithms for the clause evaluation problem and the model equivalence problem of GAE-models. As to model equivalence, we have presented a polynomial time algorithm whereas all previously published methods require exponential time. Yet, as we have pointed out in Section 4, a careful analysis of previous work and results on tree automata and of their relation to GAE-models (cf. [18], [6], [14,15]) has revealed that an appropriate combination of such known results also yields indeed a polynomial time algorithm for the model equivalence problem of GAE-models. A comparison of this "hidden" generic approach with our special purpose algorithm seems to indicate that ours should usually outperform the former one.

As to clause evaluation we have established a clear limit for possible improvements by proving the coNP-completeness. Nevertheless, the computation of an "almost minimal" GAE-model presented in Section 5 may lead to a considerable speed-up in many cases. It has already been mentioned that our notion of GAE-models slightly differs from the definition in [9] in that we consider (ground) equality only as a representation formalism but we do not consider (ground) equations as (ground) atoms. Actually, if we consider the notion of GAE-models from [9] then all of the results in Sections 3 and 4 should easily carry over to this case. The transformation of GAE-models in Section 5 does not become wrong but it gets useless. Namely, if we consider ground equations as atoms that may occur in the clauses, then we will never be allowed to add any equations (as in Fig. 3) to the set $\mathcal{E}$ without changing the model.[11]

Let us finally compare our results with algorithms and complexity results for a few other model representation formalisms. The complexity behaviour of linear or general atomic representations (i.e., LARs and ARs, for short) of Herbrand

---

[11] In this setting, identification of distinct ground term congruence classes clearly destroys (at least the equational part of) the original model.

models is different from GAE-models. In [8], ARs are defined as finite sets of atoms $\mathcal{A} = \{A_1, \ldots, A_n\}$ with the intended meaning that the ground atoms that evaluate to "true" in such a model are precisely the ground instances of the atoms in $\mathcal{A}$. In an LAR, each atom $A_i \in \mathcal{A}$ has to be linear (i.e.: A_i contains no multiple occurrences of variables). It can be shown that LARs have strictly less expressive power than GAE-models while ARs are incomparable with GAE-models (cf. [15]). In contrast to GAE-models, both the clause evaluation problem *and* the model equivalence problem have been shown to be coNP-complete for LARs and ARs (cf. [11]).

Apart from the model representation formalisms mentioned above, there are many more in the literature. In [15] (and partly also in [14]) a comparison of quite a few such formalisms is given from the point of view of their expressive power. However, rather little attention has been paid so far to algorithmic and complexity-theoretic aspects of most of these formalisms, although the construction of efficient algorithms is decisive for their practical value. Hence, a lot of work remains to be done this area.

Acknowledgement. We would like to thank the anonymous referees for a couple of useful hints and constructive criticisms.

References

1. F. Baader and T. Nipkow. *Term rewriting and All That.* Cambridge University Press, 1998.
2. P. Baumgartner, C. Fermüller, N. Peltier, and H. Zhang. Workshop: Model Computation – Principles, Algorithms, Applications. In D. McAllester, ed., *Proc. 17th Int. Conf. on Automated Deduction (CADE'00)*, LNAI 1831, p. 513, Pittsburgh, PA, USA, June 2000. Springer-Verlag.
3. R. Caferra and N. Peltier. Extending semantic resolution via automated model building: Applications. In *Proc. 14th Int. Conf. on Artificial Intelligence (IJCAI'95)*, pp. 328–334, Montréal, Québec, Canada, Aug. 1995. Morgan Kaufmann.
4. R. Caferra and N. Zabel. A method for simultanous search for refutations and models by equational constraint solving. *Journal of Symbolic Computation*, 13:613–642, 1992.
5. H. Chu and D. Plaisted. CLIN-S - a semantically guided first-order theorem prover. *Journal of Automated Reasoning*, 18(2):183–188, 1997.
6. H. Comon, M. Dauchet, R. Gilleron, F. Jacquemard, D. Lugiez, S. Tison, and M. Tommasi. Tree automata techniques and applications. Preliminary version from October, 14 1999, available at: http://www.grappa.univ-lille3.fr/tata.
7. N. Dershowitz and D. Plaisted. Rewriting. In J. Robinson and A. Voronkov, eds., *Handbook of Automated Reasoning*, volume 1, chapter 9, pp. 535–610. Elsevier and MIT Press, 2001.
8. C. G. Fermüller and A. Leitsch. Hyperresolution and automated model building. *Journal of Logic and Computation*, 6(2):173–230, 1996.
9. C. G. Fermüller and A. Leitsch. Decision procedures and model building in equational clause logic. *Logic Journal of the IGPL*, 6(1):17–41, 1998.

10. Z. Fülöp and S. Vágvölgyi. Ground term rewriting rules for the word problem of ground term equations. *Bulletin of the European Association for Theoretical Computer Science*, 45:186–201, Oct. 1991.
11. G. Gottlob and R. Pichler. Hypergraphs in model checking: Acyclicity and hypertree-width versus clique-width. In F. Orejas, P. Spirakis, and J. Leeuwen, eds., *Proc. 28th International Colloquium on Automata, Languages and Programming (ICALP'01)*, LNCS 2076, pp. 708–719, Crete, Greece, July 201. Springer-Verlag.
12. B. Gramlich and R. Pichler. Algorithmic aspects of Herbrand models represented by ground atoms with ground equations. Technical report, Institut für Computersprachen, TU Wien, May 2002. Full version of this paper.
13. K. Hodgson and J. Slaney. System description: Scott-5. In R. Goré, A. Leitsch, and T. Nipkow, eds., *Proc. 1st Int. Joint Conf. on Automated Reasoning (IJCAR'01)*, LNAI 2083, pp. 443–447, Siena, Italy, June 2001. Springer-Verlag.
14. R. Matzinger. Comparing computational representations of Herbrand models. In G. Gottlob, A. Leitsch, and D. Mundici, eds., *Proc. 5th Kurt Gödel Colloquium – Computational Logic and Proof Theory (KGC'97)*, LNCS 1289, pp. 203–218, Vienna, Austria, Aug. 1997. Springer-Verlag.
15. R. Matzinger. *Computational Representations of Models in First-Order Logic*. PhD thesis, Vienna University of Technology, 2000.
16. N. Peltier. Tree automata and automated model building. *Fundamenta Informaticae*, 30(1):59–81, 1997.
17. D. Plaisted and A. Sattler-Klein. Proof lengths for equational completion. *Information and Computation*, 125(2):154–170, 1996.
18. H. Seidl. Deciding equivalence of finite tree automata. *SIAM Journal on Computing,*, 19(3):424–437, June 1990.
19. J. Slaney. FINDER: Finite domain enumerator – system description. In A. Bundy, ed., *Proc. 12th Int. Conf. on Automated Deduction (CADE'94)*, LNAI 814, pp. 798–801, Nancy, France, June 26 – July 1 1994. Springer-Verlag.
20. W. Snyder. A fast algorithm for generating reduced ground rewriting systems from a set of ground equations. *Journal of Symbolic Computation*, 15:415–450, 1993.
21. T. Tammet. *Resolution Methods for Decision Problems and Finite Model Building*. PhD thesis, Chalmers University of Technology, Göteborg, Sweden, 1992.
22. S. Winker. Generation and verification of finite models and counterexamples using an automated theorem prover answering two open questions. *Journal of the ACM*, 29(2):273–284, 1982.
23. J. Zhang and H. Zhang. System description: Generating models by SEM. In M. McRobbie and J. Slaney, eds., *Proc. 13th Int. Conf. on Automated Deduction (CADE'96)*, LNAI 1104, pp. 308–312, New Brunswick, NJ, USA, July 30 – August 3 1996. Springer-Verlag.

A New Clausal Class Decidable by Hyperresolution*

Lilia Georgieva[1,2], Ullrich Hustadt[3], and Renate A. Schmidt[1,2]

[1] Department of Computer Science, University of Manchester, UK
{georgiel,schmidt}@cs.man.ac.uk
[2] Max-Planck-Institut für Informatik, Saarbrücken, Germany
{georgie,schmidt}@mpi-sb.mpg.de
[3] Department of Computer Science, University of Liverpool, UK
U.Hustadt@csc.liv.ac.uk

Abstract. In this paper we define a new clausal class, called $\mathcal{BU}$, which can be decided by hyperresolution with splitting. We also consider the model generation problem for $\mathcal{BU}$ and show that hyperresolution plus splitting can also be used as a Herbrand model generation procedure for $\mathcal{BU}$ and, furthermore, that the addition of a local minimality test allows us to generate only minimal Herbrand models for clause sets in $\mathcal{BU}$. In addition, we investigate the relationship of $\mathcal{BU}$ to other solvable classes.

1 Introduction

In recent work [13,14] we have considered the fragment GF1$^-$ of first-order logic which was introduced by Lutz, Sattler, and Tobies [21]. GF1$^-$ is a restriction of the guarded fragment which incorporates a variety of modal and description logics via standard or non-standard translations, and can be seen as a generalisation of these logics. In contrast to the guarded fragment [1], GF1$^-$ allows for the development of a space-efficient decision procedure. Under the assumption that either (i) there is a bound on the arity of predicate symbols in GF1$^-$ formulae, or (ii) that each subformula of a GF1$^-$ formula has a bounded number of free variables, the satisfiability problem of GF1$^-$ is PSPACE-complete [21], while under identical assumptions the satisfiability problem of the guarded fragment is EXPTIME-complete [15]. Thus, GF1$^-$ has the same complexity as the modal and description logics it generalises.

In [13] we have shown that hyperresolution plus splitting provides a decision procedure for GF1$^-$. One of the interesting features of GF1$^-$ is that it is one of the few solvable classes where, during the deduction by the resolution decision procedure, derived clauses can contain terms of greater depth than the clauses in the initial set of clauses. In [14] we have shown that a modification of the main procedure of a standard saturation based theorem prover with splitting can provide a polynomial space decision procedure for GF1$^-$. We also describe several solutions to the problem of generating minimal Herbrand models for GF1$^-$.

---

* We thank the referees for helpful comments and suggestions. The work is supported by research grants GR/M36700 and GR/R92035 from the EPSRC, UK.

A. Voronkov (Ed.): CADE-18, LNAI 2392, pp. 260–274, 2002.
© Springer-Verlag Berlin Heidelberg 2002

In [13,14] we have used structural transformation (or definitional form transformation, cf. e.g. [3,18]), to transform GF1⁻ formulae into clausal form. While it is straightforward to give a schematic characterisation of the resulting sets of clauses, it is much more difficult to state the conditions which an arbitrary set of clauses needs to satisfy so that it shares most or all the properties of the clauses sets we obtain from the definitional form transformation of GF1⁻ formulae.

In this paper we define a new clausal class $\mathcal{BU}$ which generalises the set of all clause sets we can obtain from GF1⁻ via the definitional form transformation. $\mathcal{BU}$ is defined such that hyperresolution plus splitting is still a decision procedure. Since hyperresolution is implemented in many state-of-the-art theorem provers, e.g. Otter, SPASS, and Vampire, this gives a practical decision procedure for the class. We also show that if an input clause set from $\mathcal{BU}$ is not refuted, an adequate representation of a model and of a minimal model of the clausal class can be extracted from the information produced by the prover.

A main motivation for studying classes like GF1⁻ and $\mathcal{BU}$ is that a variety of expressive modal and description logics can be embedded into them. Expressive modal and description logics have found applications in such varied areas as, for example, verification, program analysis, knowledge representation, deductive data bases and the semantic web. However, there are a number of alternative solvable classes for which the same is true. We will discuss the relationship of $\mathcal{BU}$ to some of these alternative classes.

The paper is organised as follows. Section 2 defines the notation used, some basic concepts and a hyperresolution calculus with splitting. The clausal class $\mathcal{BU}$ is defined in Section 3, and the relationship of $\mathcal{BU}$ to other solvable classes is discussed in Section 4. The applicability of the hyperresolution calculus as a decision procedure for the class, model building by hyperresolution and in particular, minimal model building are investigated in Sections 5 and 6. The final section is the Conclusion.

2   Fundamentals and Hyperresolution

Notation. The notational convention is as follows. We use the symbols x, y, z for first-order variables, s, t, u for terms, a, b for constants, f, g, h for functions, P, Q for predicate symbols, A for atoms, L for literals, C for clauses, φ, ϕ, ψ, for formulae, and N for sets of clauses.

An over-line indicates a sequence. An *i-sequence* is a sequence with i elements. If $\bar{s}$ and $\bar{t}$ are two sequences of terms and X is a set of terms, then the notation $\bar{s} \subseteq \bar{t}$ ($\bar{s} \subseteq X$) means that every term in $\bar{s}$ also occurs in $\bar{t}$ (X). By definition, $\bar{s} = \bar{t}$ ($\bar{s} = X$) iff $\bar{s} \subseteq \bar{t}$ and $\bar{t} \subseteq \bar{s}$ ($\bar{s} \subseteq X$ and every term in X occurs in $\bar{s}$). The union of the terms in $\bar{s}$ and $\bar{t}$ is denoted by $\bar{s} \cup \bar{t}$. Given a sequence $\bar{s}$ of terms, $\overline{f_{\bar{s}}(\bar{u}_i)}$ denotes a sequence of terms of the form $f_1(\bar{u}_1), \ldots, f_k(\bar{u}_k)$, where $\bar{u}_i \subseteq \bar{s}$ for every $1 \leq i \leq k$.

Terms, literals, clauses and orderings. The term depth $dp(t)$ of a term t, is inductively defined as follows. (i) If t is a variable or a constant, then $dp(t) = 1$.

(ii) If $t = f(t_1, \ldots, t_n)$, then $dp(t) = 1 + max\{ dp(t_i) \mid 1 \leq i \leq n \}$. The term depth of a literal is defined by the maximal term depth of its arguments, and the term depth of a clause is defined by the maximal term-depth of all literals in it.

A *literal* is an atomic formula A (a *positive* literal) or the negation $\neg A$ of an atomic formula A (a *negative* literal). We regard a *clause* as a multiset of literals and consider two clauses C and D to be identical if C can be obtained from D by variable renaming. A *multiset* over a set $\mathcal{L}$ is a mapping C from $\mathcal{L}$ to the natural numbers. We write $L \in C$ if $C(L) > 0$ for a literal L. We use $\perp$ to denote the empty clause. A *positive* (*negative*) clause contains only positive (negative) literals. The *positive* (*negative*) *part* of a clause is the subclause of all positive (negative) literals. A *split component* of a clause $C \vee D$ is a subclause C such that C and D do not have any variables in common, i.e. are *variable disjoint*. A *maximally split* (or variable indecomposable) clause cannot be partitioned (or split) into subclauses which do not share variables.

A clause C is said to be *range restricted* iff the set of variables in the positive part of C is a subset of the set of variables of the negative part of C. A clause set is range restricted iff it contains only range restricted clauses. This means that a positive clause is range restricted only if it is a ground clause.

A strict partial ordering $\succ$ on a set $\mathcal{L}$ (i.e. an irreflexive and transitive relation) can be extended to an ordering $\succ^{mul}$ on (finite) multisets over $\mathcal{L}$ as follows: $C \succ^{mul} D$ if (i) $C \neq D$ and (ii) whenever $D(x) > C(x)$ then $C(y) > D(y)$, for some $y \succ x$. $\succ^{mul}$ is called the *multiset extension of* $\succ$.

Given an ordering $\succ$ on literals we define a maximal literal in a clause in the standard way: A literal L in a clause C is *maximal* in C, if there is no literal L' in C, for which $L' \succ L$. A literal L is *strictly maximal* in C if it is the only maximal literal in C.

A term, an atom, a literal or a clause is called *functional* if it contains a constant or a function symbol, and *non-functional*, otherwise.

A hyperresolution calculus with splitting. We denote the calculus by $\mathsf{R}^{\mathsf{hyp}}$. Inferences are computed with the following expansion rules:

Deduce: $\dfrac{N}{N \cup \{C\}}$

where C is a resolvent or a factor.

Splitting: $\dfrac{N \cup \{C_1 \vee C_2\}}{N \cup \{C_1\} \mid N \cup \{C_2\}}$

where C_1 and C_2 are variable disjoint.

The resolution and factoring inference rules are:

Hyperresolution: $\dfrac{C_1 \vee A_1 \quad \ldots \quad C_n \vee A_n \quad \neg A_{n+1} \vee \ldots \vee \neg A_{2n} \vee D}{(C_1 \vee \ldots \vee C_n \vee D)\sigma}$

where (i) σ is the most general unifier such that $A_i\sigma = A_{n+i}\sigma$ for every i, $1 \leq i \leq n$, and (ii) $C_i \vee A_i$ and D are positive clauses, for every i, $1 \leq i \leq n$. The rightmost premise in the rule is referred to as the *negative* premise and all other premises are referred to as *positive* premises.

Factoring: $\dfrac{C \vee A_1 \vee A_2}{(C \vee A_1)\sigma}$

where σ is the most general unifier of A_1 and A_2.

A *derivation* in $\mathsf{R}^{\mathsf{hyp}}$ from a set of clauses N is a finitely branching, ordered tree T with root N and nodes which are sets of clauses. The tree is constructed by applications of the expansion rules to the leaves. We assume that no hyper-resolution or factoring inference is computed twice on the same branch of the derivation. Any path $N(= N_0), N_1, \ldots$ in a derivation T is called a *closed branch* in T iff the clause set $\bigcup_{j \geq 0} N_j$ contains the empty clause, otherwise it is called an *open branch*. We call a branch B in a derivation tree *complete* (with respect to $\mathsf{R}^{\mathsf{hyp}}$) iff no new successor nodes can be added to the endpoint of B by $\mathsf{R}^{\mathsf{hyp}}$, otherwise it is called an *incomplete branch*. A derivation T is a *refutation* iff every path $N(= N_0), N_1, \ldots$ in it is a closed branch, otherwise it is called an *open derivation*.

In general, the calculus $\mathsf{R}^{\mathsf{hyp}}$ can be enhanced with standard simplification rules such as tautology deletion and subsumption deletion, in fact, it can be enhanced by any simplification rules which are compatible with a general notion of redundancy [4,5]. A set N of clauses is *saturated up to redundancy* with respect to a particular refinement of resolution if the conclusion of every inference from non-redundant premises in N is either contained in N, or else is redundant in N. A derivation T from N is called *fair* if for any path $N(= N_0), N_1, \ldots$ in T, with limit $N_\infty = \bigcup_{j \geq 0} \bigcap_{k \geq j} N_k$, it is the case that each clause C which can be deduced from non-redundant premises in N_∞ is contained in some N_j. Intuitively, fairness means that no non-redundant inferences are delayed indefinitely. For a finite complete branch $N(= N_0), N_1, \ldots N_n$, the limit N_∞ is equal to N_n.

Theorem 1 ([5]). *Let T be a fair $\mathsf{R}^{\mathsf{hyp}}$ derivation from a set N of clauses. Then: (i) If $N(= N_0), N_1, \ldots$ is a path with limit N_∞, then N_∞ is saturated (up to redundancy). (ii) N is satisfiable if and only if there exists a path in T with limit N_∞ such that N_∞ is satisfiable. (iii) N is unsatisfiable if and only if for every path $N(= N_0), N_1, \ldots$ the clause set $\bigcup_{j \geq 0} N_j$ contains the empty clause.*

3   The Clausal Class $\mathcal{BU}$

The language of $\mathcal{BU}$ is that of first-order clausal logic. Additionally, each predicate symbol P is uniquely associated with a pair (i, j) of non-negative integers, such that if the arity of P is n then $i + j = n$. The pair is called the *grouping* of the predicate symbol. Sometimes the grouping (i, j) of a predicate symbol P will be made explicit by writing $P^{(i,j)}$. The notion of grouping is extended to literals in the following way. A literal L is said to satisfy the *grouping condition with respect to the sequences $\overline{x}$ and $\overline{s}$*, if $L = (\neg)P^{(i,j)}(\overline{x}, \overline{s})$ or $L = (\neg)P^{(j,i)}(\overline{s}, \overline{x})$, where $\overline{x}$ is an i-sequence of variables, and $\overline{s}$ is either a j-sequence of variables disjoint from $\overline{x}$ or a j-sequence of terms of the form $f(\overline{z})$ where $\overline{z} \subseteq \overline{x}$, and $\overline{x}$ is non-empty. Repetitions of variables and terms in any of the sequences are allowed.

Furthermore, an acyclic relation $\succ_d$, called an *acyclic dependency relation*, is defined over the predicate symbols. Let $\succ_d^+$ be the transitive closure of $\succ_d$. Then $\succ_d^+$ is an ordering on predicate symbols. This ordering extends to atoms, literals and clauses by the following definitions. Given two literals $L_1 = (\neg)P_1(\overline{s})$ and $L_2 = (\neg)P_2(\overline{t})$, $L_1 \succ_D L_2$ iff $P_1 \succ_d^+ P_2$. The multiset extension of the ordering $\succ_D$, also denoted by $\succ_D$, defines an ordering on ground clauses. The acyclicity of $\succ_d$ implies that $\succ_D$ is also acyclic.

Given a finite signature Σ such that (i) any predicate symbol has a unique grouping, and (ii) there is an acyclic dependency relationship $\succ_d$ on the predicate symbols in Σ, we define the *class* $\mathcal{BU}$ of clausal sets over Σ as follows.

A clausal set N belongs to $\mathcal{BU}$ if any clause C in N satisfies one of the three conditions below as well as the following. If C is a non-ground and non-positive clause then C is required to contain a strictly $\succ_D$-maximal literal, which is negative and non-functional. This literal is called the *main literal* of the clause. The predicate symbol P of the main literal must either have the grouping $(0, i)$ or $(i, 0)$, where i is the arity of P.

Condition 1: C is a non-positive, non-ground and non-functional clause and the following is true.
  (a) The union of the variables of the negative part can be partitioned into two disjoint subsets X and Y, at least one of which is non-empty.
  (b) For every literal L in C, either the variables of L are (i) subsets of X, or (ii) subsets of Y, or (iii) there are non-empty sequences $\overline{x}$, $\overline{y}$, such that $\overline{x} \subseteq X$, $\overline{y} \subseteq Y$ and L satisfies the grouping condition with respect to $\overline{x}$ and $\overline{y}$.
  (c) Either the main literal contains all the variables of the clause, or it contains all the variables from one of the sets X and Y, and there is a negative literal L whose arguments satisfy (b.iii) and which contains all the variables from Y if the main literal contains all the variables from X, or all the variables from X if the main literal contains all the variables from Y.

Condition 2: C is a non-positive and non-ground functional clause and the following is true.
  (a) The main literal of C contains all the variables of C.
  (b) Every other literal L in C satisfies the grouping condition with respect to two disjoint sequences of variables $\overline{x}$ and $\overline{y}$, or with respect to two sequences $\overline{x}$ and $\overline{f_{\overline{x}}(\overline{u}_i)}$, where $\overline{x}$ is a sequence of variables and $\overline{f_{\overline{x}}(\overline{u}_i)}$ is a sequence of terms $f_i(\overline{u}_i)$ such that $\overline{u}_i \subseteq \overline{x}$.

Condition 3: C is a positive ground unit clause, its arguments are constants and its predicate symbol has grouping $(0, i)$ or $(i, 0)$.

Consider the following clauses.

1. $\neg P(x, y) \vee \neg Q(x) \vee \neg R(x, x, y, z)$
2. $\neg P(x, y, z) \vee \neg Q(y, x) \vee R(x, x, y, z)$
3. $\neg P(x, y) \vee \neg Q(y, z) \vee \neg R(x, x, y, z)$
4. $\neg P(x, y) \vee \neg Q(y, z) \vee \neg R(x, y, z, x)$
5. $\neg P(x, y) \vee Q(x, x, y, f(x, y))$
6. $\neg P(x, y) \vee Q(x, x, y, g(y))$
7. $\neg P(x, y) \vee Q(x, x, g(y), y)$
8. $\neg P(x) \vee P(f(x))$

It follows from the definition of $\mathcal{BU}$ that all non-positive clauses must contain a *covering* negative literal which contains all the variables of the clause. This negative literal can be the main literal, or it is a literal satisfying Condition 1.(b.iii).

In the latter case the clause must contain another negative literal which is the main literal. In Clause 1 the literal $\neg R(x, x, y, z)$ is the covering negative literal. If R has the grouping $(4,0)$ or $(0,4)$ and R is maximal then it is the main literal. Another possibility is that R has the grouping $(3,1)$ and $\neg P(x, y)$ is the main literal (hence $P \succ_D R, Q$). $\neg Q(x)$ cannot be the main literal. In Clause 2 there is one covering negative literal, namely $\neg P(x, y, z)$, which must also be the main literal. Hence P is maximal and has grouping $(3,0)$ or $(0,3)$. The grouping of Q and R are immaterial; and the signs of the Q and R literals are also immaterial. But observe that in Clause 3, if $\neg P(x, y)$ is the main literal then the grouping condition must hold for the Q and R literals, i.e. the grouping of Q and R must be $(1,1)$ and $(3,1)$, respectively. In Clause 4, if $\neg P(x, y)$ is the main literal then the sequence (x, y, z, x) cannot be divided into disjoint non-empty subsequences, because the variable x would appear in both of the subsequences. Clauses 5 and 6 are examples of clauses which satisfy Condition 2, provided P has grouping $(2,0)$ or $(0,2)$, Q has grouping $(3,1)$, and $P \succ_D Q$. Clause 7 on the other hand violates Condition 2 because the Q literal does not satisfy the grouping condition. Clause 8 violates Condition 2, because it does not contain a strictly maximal negative literal, with respect to any acyclic dependency relation. In general, this excludes clauses where the predicate symbol of the main literal occurs both positively and negatively. Thus the transitivity clause and the symmetry clause do not belong to any clausal set in $\mathcal{BU}$. Also the reflexivity clause and the seriality clause are excluded from $\mathcal{BU}$ clause sets, because every non-ground clause must contain a negative main literal. Thus, other than irreflexivity $\neg R(x, x)$, none of the standard properties of relations except forms of relational inclusion (e.g. $\neg R(x, y) \vee S(y, x)$) can be formulated in $\mathcal{BU}$. We comment on this 'apparent' limitation in the next section.

4   Relationships to Other Solvable Classes

One of the main motivations for studying $\mathcal{BU}$ is that a variety of modal and description logics can be embedded into it. Simple examples are the basic multimodal logic $\mathsf{K}_{(m)}$ and the corresponding description logic $\mathcal{ALC}$ [24]. For example, if we translate formulae of $\mathsf{K}_{(m)}$ into first-order logic and transform the resulting formulae into clausal form using structural transformation, then the clauses we obtain take one of the following forms [10,17,18].

$$
\begin{array}{lll}
Q_1(a) & \neg Q_1(x) \vee Q_2(x) & \neg Q_1(x) \vee Q_2(x) \vee Q_3(x) \\
\neg Q_1(x) \vee \neg R(x, y) \vee Q_2(y) & \neg Q_1(x) \vee R(x, f(x)) & \neg Q_1(x) \vee Q_2(f(x))
\end{array}
$$

Furthermore, we can always define an acyclic dependency relation on the predicate symbols in these clauses and associate groupings $(0,1)$ and $(1,1)$ with every unary and binary predicate symbol, respectively, such that the clause set satisfies the conditions for clause sets in $\mathcal{BU}$. Much more expressive logics like the multi-modal logic $K_{(m)}(\cap, \cup, \smile)$ which is defined over families of relations closed under intersection, union, and converse, and the corresponding extension of $\mathcal{ALC}$ can also be embedded into $\mathcal{BU}$.

We have already mentioned in the previous section that clauses expressing most of the standard properties of binary relations like reflexivity, seriality, symmetry, and transitivity cannot occur in $\mathcal{BU}$ clause sets. Consequently, the standard translation of formulae in modal logics extending $\mathsf{K}_{(m)}$ by one or more of the axiom schemata T (reflexivity), D (seriality), B (symmetry) and 4 (transitivity) do not result in $\mathcal{BU}$ clause sets. However, for the extensions of $\mathsf{K}_{(m)}$ by any combination of the axiom schemata T, D, and B, a non-standard translation proposed by De Nivelle [9] exists which together with structural transformation allows us to translate formulae of these modal logics into $\mathcal{BU}$ in a satisfiability equivalence preserving way. Although this non-standard translation also provides an alternative approach for the modal logic $\mathsf{K4}_{(m)}$, the resulting clause sets are still not in $\mathcal{BU}$, since it is in general impossible to define the required acyclic dependency relationship. This negative result is not surprising, since tableau decision procedures for $\mathsf{K4}_{(m)}$ require an auxiliary loop checking mechanism besides the tableau expansion rules to ensure termination.

Another example of a reasoning problem in description logics that can be solved by embedding into the class $\mathcal{BU}$ is the satisfiability problem of $\mathcal{ALC}$ concepts with respect to acyclic TBoxes. This problem has recently been shown to be PSPACE-complete [20]. Here the acyclicity of a TBox $\mathcal{T}$ allows us to define an acyclic dependency relation on predicate symbols occurring in the translation of $\mathcal{T}$ such that the conditions for $\mathcal{BU}$ clause sets are satisfied. Note that the standard translation of $\mathcal{T}$, which contains closed first-order formulae, is not in GF1⁻.

There are a number of other fragments of first-order logic and clausal classes which would cover the same modal and description logics, including the guarded fragment [1], the dual of Maslov's class K [16], and fluted logic [23]. The clausal classes corresponding to the guarded fragment [12] and the dual of Maslov's class K contain only clause sets where every non-constant functional term t contains all the variables of the clause C it occurs in. Clause 6 on page 264 illustrates that this is not the case for $\mathcal{BU}$ clause sets. Fluted logic requires a certain ordering on variable occurrences which means that a clause like $\neg R(x, y) \vee Q(y, x)$ is not fluted, but could occur in a $\mathcal{BU}$ clause set. On the other hand, we can also give examples for each of these three classes showing that $\mathcal{BU}$ subsumes neither of them. Thus, all four classes are distinct from each other. However, $\mathcal{BU}$ is the only class among them for which a hyperresolution decision procedure is known.

Other syntactically defined clausal classes which are also decidable by hyperresolution include the classes $\mathcal{PVD}$ and $\mathcal{KPOD}$ [11,19]. For $\mathcal{PVD}$ the syntactic restrictions on the class imply that during a derivation by hyperresolution the depth of a derived clause does not exceed the depth of its parent clauses. An example of a clause set which is in $\mathcal{BU}$ but not in $\mathcal{PVD}$ is $\{\neg Q(x) \vee \neg R(x, y), \neg P(x) \vee R(x, f(x))\}$, while $\{\neg R(x, y) \vee R(y, x)\}$ is an example of a $\mathcal{PVD}$ clause set which is not in $\mathcal{BU}$. For $\mathcal{KPOD}$, like $\mathcal{BU}$, the term depth of derived clauses can increase during the derivation. Essential for $\mathcal{KPOD}$ is the restriction of clauses to Krom form ($|C| \leq 2$), while $\mathcal{BU}$ has no restriction on the number of literals in a clause. On the other hand, $\mathcal{KPOD}$ does not require an acyclic dependency relation on predicate symbols or any grouping restriction. Therefore, $\mathcal{BU}$, $\mathcal{PVD}$, and $\mathcal{KPOD}$ are all distinct from each other.

5   Deciding $\mathcal{BU}$

To decide $\mathcal{BU}$ we use the calculus $\mathsf{R}^{\mathsf{hyp}}$, described in Section 2, which consists of hyperresolution, factoring, and splitting (though factoring is optional). We assume in the following that a hyperresolution inference cannot use a clause C as a positive premise if the splitting rule or, if present, the factoring rule can be applied to C. As usual we make a minimal assumption that no inference rule is applied twice to the same premises during the derivation.

For the classes of clause sets we consider in the present paper the positive premises are always ground, in particular, because we use splitting, the positive premises are always ground *unit* clauses, and the conclusions are always positive ground clauses. Crucial for termination is that the unit clauses are always either *uni-node* or *bi-node*. These notions are adapted and extended from similar notions in [21] and [13,14].

A sequence $\bar{t} = (t_1, \ldots, t_n)$ (or multiset $\{t_1, \ldots, t_n\}$) of ground terms is called a *uni-node* iff all terms in the sequence (or multiset) have the same depth, that is, $dp(t_i) = dp(t_j)$ for every $1 \leq i, j \leq n$. If $\bar{t}$ and $\bar{s}$ are uni-nodes and $\bar{t} \subseteq \bar{s}$, we say $\bar{t}$ is a *uni-node defined over* $\bar{s}$. A sequence $\bar{t} = (t_1, \ldots, t_m)$ (or multiset) is called a *direct successor* of a sequence $\bar{s} = (s_1, \ldots, s_n)$ (or multiset) iff for each t_i, $1 \leq i \leq m$, there is a function symbol f such that t_i is of the form $f(\bar{u})$, where $\bar{u} \subseteq \bar{s}$, and $\bar{u}$ is non-empty. A sequence (or multiset) of ground terms is called a *bi-node* (*over* $\{X_1, X_2\}$) iff it can be presented as a union $X_1 \cup X_2$ of two non-empty disjoint uni-nodes X_1 and X_2 such that X_2 is a direct successor of X_1.

A ground literal (unit clause) is a *uni-node* iff the set of its arguments is a uni-node. The empty clause $\bot$ is a special type of uni-node literal (with no direct successors). A ground literal L (unit clause) is a *bi-node* iff the set of its arguments is a bi-node over $\{\bar{s}, \bar{t}\}$ and has the form $L = (\neg)P^{(i,j)}(\bar{s}, \bar{t})$, where $\bar{s}$ is an i-sequence and $\bar{t}$ is a j-sequence of terms. If the latter is true we say L satisfies the *grouping condition with respect to $\bar{s}$ and $\bar{t}$* (this extends the definition in Section 3 to ground literals). Subsequently, when we write $(\neg)P^{(i,j)}(\bar{s}, \bar{t})$ we mean that this literal satisfies the grouping condition with respect to $\bar{s}$ and $\bar{t}$.

The following table gives examples of uni-nodes and bi-nodes.

Uni-nodes: $\{a, a, b\}$, $\{g(a, b)\}$, $\{g(a, b), f(b, b)\}$

Bi-nodes: $\{a, b, f(b)\}$, $\{a, b, g(a, b), h(a, b, b)\}$, $\{a, b, f(b), h(b, a, b)\}$

The notions of uni-node and direct successor are more general than the notions defined in [13,14,21]. For example, $\{a, b, f(b)\}$ is not a bi-node (nor a uni-node) under the previous definitions. The set $\{a, f(a, b)\}$ is not a bi-node (or a uni-node) under either definitions.

In the rest of the section, assume N is a given (finite) clausal set in $\mathcal{BU}$. The aim is to show that any derivation from N by $\mathsf{R}^{\mathsf{hyp}}$ terminates. The following properties are characteristic about hyperresolution inferences for the class $\mathcal{BU}$:

1. All conclusions are ground.
2. Each of the split components of the derived clauses are ground unit clauses which are either uni-nodes or bi-nodes.
3. Each of the ground unit clauses used as a positive parent produces a bounded number of different conclusions.

These properties are key to the termination proof given below. The first property is easy to see, since any $\mathcal{BU}$ clause set is range restricted and if all positive premises of hyperresolution inference steps are ground, and all non-ground clauses are range restricted, the conclusion of any inference step by $\mathsf{R}^{\mathsf{hyp}}$ is either the empty clause, or a positive ground unit clause, or a positive ground clause which can be split into positive ground unit clauses. The second property is established in Lemma 2.2. (This property is the reason for choosing the name $\mathcal{BU}$ for the considered clausal class.) The third property is a consequence of Lemma 1.

As factoring is applied only to positive clauses, and positive clauses in any $\mathsf{R}^{\mathsf{hyp}}$ derivation for $\mathcal{BU}$ clauses are always ground, factoring has the effect of eliminating duplicate literals in ground clauses. For this reason no special consideration is given to factoring inference steps in subsequent proofs.

Given a finite signature the following can be proved using the same argument as in the corresponding lemma for $\mathsf{GF1}^-$ in [13].

Lemma 1. *1. The cardinality of any uni-node set is finitely bounded.*
2. Every uni-node has a bounded number of direct successors which are uni-nodes.
3. For any given uni-node $\bar{s}$, the number of the uni-nodes and bi-nodes that have terms in $\bar{s}$ as elements is finitely bounded.

Lemma 2. *In any $\mathsf{R}^{\mathsf{hyp}}$ derivation from a clause set in $\mathcal{BU}$:*

1. *At least one of the positive premises of any hyperresolution inference step is a uni-node.*
2. *Maximally split conclusions are either uni-nodes or bi-nodes.*
3. *If $P(\bar{s},\bar{t})$ is a bi-node over $\{\bar{s},\bar{t}\}$ and occurs in the derivation and $\bar{t}$ is a direct successor of $\bar{s}$, then all terms in $\bar{s}$ have the same depth d and all terms in $\bar{t}$ have the same depth $d+1$.*

Proof. The proof is by induction. In the first step of any $\mathsf{R}^{\mathsf{hyp}}$ derivation the only possible positive premises are uni-nodes. Since all their arguments are constants, they have the same depth. The induction hypothesis is that the above properties are true for the premises and conclusions of the first n inference steps in any derivation.

Now consider the different inference possibilities in step $n+1$. First, a general observation. The grouping restriction on the main literal of any non-positive $\mathcal{BU}$

clause implies that the premise associated with the main literal, generally, we call it the *main premise*, must be a unit clause whose literal has grouping $(0, i)$ or $(i, 0)$. This means the main premise is a uni-node. This proves property 1.

Consider an inference step by hyperresolution involving a non-positive clause C satisfying Condition 1, as negative premise. Assume the main premise is a uni-node of the form $Q(\overline{s})$. If the main literal contains all the variables of the clause then each variable in C is unified with a term from $\overline{s}$. It follows immediately that all other premises and all maximally split conclusions are uni-nodes and the depths of all arguments are the same, since by the induction hypothesis the depth of all arguments in $Q(\overline{s})$ are the same.

Let X and Y be as in Condition 1.(a). Assume the main literal does not contain all the variables of C, instead it contains all the variables from $X (\neq \emptyset)$. Then C has a negative literal that satisfies 1.(b.iii) of the definition of $\mathcal{BU}$ and contains all the variables of Y. Suppose this literal has the form $\neg P^{(i,j)}(\overline{x}, \overline{y})$, where $\overline{x} \subseteq X$ and $\overline{y} = Y$, and the corresponding premise has the form $P(\overline{u}, \overline{t})$. The grouping restriction ensures that the sequences of variables $\overline{x}$ and $\overline{y}$ have the same length as the sequences of terms $\overline{u}$ and $\overline{t}$, respectively. Then $\overline{u} \subseteq \overline{s}$. If $P(\overline{u}, \overline{t})$ is a uni-node then, as above, it is easy to see that all other premises and all maximally split conclusions are uni-nodes and the depths of all arguments are the same. If not, then $P(\overline{u}, \overline{t})$ is a bi-node over $\{\overline{u}, \overline{t}\}$ (by the induction hypothesis and because the grouping associated with a predicate symbol is unique). Hence, $\overline{u}$ and $\overline{t}$ are distinct uni-nodes and $\overline{u}$ (and $\overline{s}$) is a direct successor of $\overline{t}$, or vice versa. As X and $\overline{y}$ together cover all the variables of C, all other premises and all maximally split conclusions are either uni-nodes defined over $\overline{s}$ or $\overline{t}$ (more precisely, uni-nodes of the form $P(\overline{w})$ where $\overline{w} \subseteq \overline{s}$ or $\overline{w} \subseteq \overline{t}$), or they are bi-nodes over $\{\overline{w}, \overline{v}\}$, where $\overline{w} \subseteq \overline{s}$ and $\overline{v} \subseteq \overline{t}$. This proves property 2. As $\overline{s}$ is a direct successor of $\overline{t}$, or vice versa, the difference in depth between terms in $\overline{u}$ (or $\overline{s}$) and terms in $\overline{t}$ is one. Property 3 is evident.

The proof for inferences with a negative premise satisfying Condition 2 is by a similar case analysis.   □

The analysis in the proof of the previous lemma allows us to conclude:

Lemma 3. *In any* $\mathsf{R}^{\mathsf{hyp}}$ *derivation, if C and D are uni-nodes, such that D is a direct successor of C, then D is derived from C and a bi-node.*

The importance of the acyclic dependency relationship on the predicate symbols for decidability will become apparent in the proof of Lemma 4. By the definition of $\mathcal{BU}$ the negative premise of a hyperresolution inference step always contains a main literal, which is strictly maximal with respect to the ordering $\succ_D$. Hence a non-empty conclusion is always smaller than the main premise resolved with the main literal. However, for termination this property is not sufficient. Instead, we need the following result.

Lemma 4. *There is a bound on the term depth of any clause in a* $\mathsf{R}^{\mathsf{hyp}}$ *derivation from N belonging to $\mathcal{BU}$.*

Proof. Define a complexity measure μ on non-empty, ground unit clauses by:

$$\mu(C) = \begin{cases} Q & \text{if } C = Q(\overline{s}) \text{ and } Q \text{ has grouping } (0,i) \text{ or } (i,0), \\ P & \text{otherwise, where } P \text{ is the predicate symbol of the main} \\ & \text{premise with which } C \text{ was derived.} \end{cases}$$

Thus the complexity measure of any non-empty, ground unit clause is determined by a predicate symbol with grouping $(0,i)$ or $(i,0)$. By definition these complexity measures are related by $\succ_d$. This is an acyclic relationship, which can always be linearised. Suppose therefore that $\succ_c$ is an arbitrary total ordering on the $(0,i)$ or $(i,0)$ type predicate symbols in N and $\succ_d \subseteq \succ_c$. The proof is by induction with respect to the enumeration of the type $(0,i)$ or $(i,0)$ predicate symbols in N as determined by $\succ_c$. Technically, let the enumeration be $Q_1 \succ_c Q_2 \succ_c \cdots \succ_c Q_n$ where n is the number of type $(0,i)$ or $(i,0)$ predicate symbols in N. Let $\overline{\mu}$ be a function from ground unit clauses to $\{1, \ldots, n\}$ such that $\overline{\mu}(C) = i$, provided $\mu(C) = Q_i$. In a sense $\overline{\mu}$ preserves μ, but reverses the ordering. We prove the following property is true for every non-empty, ground unit clause C derived from N.

$$dp(C) \leq \begin{cases} \overline{\mu}(C) & \text{if } C = Q(\overline{s}) \text{ and } Q \text{ has grouping } (0,i) \text{ or } (i,0), \\ \overline{\mu}(C) + 1 & \text{otherwise.} \end{cases} \tag{†}$$

Initially the only ground unit clauses in N are those which have depth 1. For any of these clauses C, $dp(C) \leq \overline{\mu}(C)$. Suppose the induction hypothesis is: Let D be an arbitrary ground unit clause in the derivation and suppose (†) is true for all ground unit clauses C in the derivation with larger measure, i.e. $\mu(C) \succ_D \mu(D)$.

Assume D is a maximally split conclusion of an inference with the main premise $Q(\overline{s})$ and negative premise C. Then $Q(\overline{s}) \succ_D D$ and the inductive hypothesis applies to $Q(\overline{s})$. (a) D can either have a predicate symbol with grouping $(0,i)$ or $(i,0)$. Then $\overline{\mu}(Q(\overline{s})) < \overline{\mu}(D)$ as Q is larger than any other predicate symbol in C. (b) Otherwise, by the definition of μ, $\mu(Q(\overline{s})) = Q = \mu(D)$ as Q is the predicate symbol of the main premise with which D is derived, and consequently, $\overline{\mu}(Q(\overline{s})) = \overline{\mu}(D)$. So, in either case, i.e. for any D, we have the property:

$$\overline{\mu}(Q(\overline{s})) \leq \overline{\mu}(D). \tag{‡}$$

Now suppose C is a clause which satisfies Condition 1. If the main literal contains all the variables of C, then D is a uni-node, $P'(\overline{w})$, say, where $\overline{w} \subseteq \overline{s}$ (by the same argument as in the proof of Lemma 2). Thus, $dp(D) = dp(Q(\overline{s}))$ since $dp(\overline{w}) = dp(\overline{s})$, $dp(Q(\overline{s})) \leq \overline{\mu}(Q(\overline{s}))$ by the inductive hypothesis, and $\overline{\mu}(Q(\overline{s})) \leq \overline{\mu}(D)$ by (‡). Consequently, $dp(D) \leq \overline{\mu}(D)$. Hence, (†) holds for D in this case.

If the main literal in C does not contain all the variables, w.l.o.g. assume the main literal contains all the variables from $X(\neq \emptyset)$ and there is a negative literal in C which satisfies 1.(b.iii) and contains all the variables of Y, where X and Y are defined as in 1.(a) of the definition of $\mathcal{BU}$. Suppose this literal has the form $\neg P^{(i,j)}(\overline{x}, \overline{y})$ where $\overline{x} \subseteq X$ and $\overline{y} = Y$, and the corresponding premise is $P^{(i,j)}(\overline{u}, \overline{t})$. Hence, $\overline{u} \subseteq \overline{s}$.

If $P(\overline{u}, \overline{t})$ is a uni-node then $dp(\overline{u}) = dp(\overline{s}) = dp(\overline{t})$. D is an instance of a positive literal L in C and by Condition 1.(b) all variables of D are in $X \cup Y$. So, all the arguments of D are among the arguments of $Q(\overline{s})$ and $P(\overline{u}, \overline{t})$. Therefore, $dp(D) = dp(P(\overline{u}, \overline{t})) = dp(Q(\overline{s})) \leq \overline{\mu}(Q(\overline{s})) \leq \overline{\mu}(D)$ (as above, by the inductive hypothesis and ($\ddagger$)). Hence, ($\dagger$) holds in this case.

If $P^{(i,j)}(\overline{u}, \overline{t})$ is a bi-node, and $\overline{u}$ is a direct successor of $\overline{t}$, then $dp(\overline{u}) = dp(\overline{t}) + 1$. By Condition 1.(b), if D is a uni-node, then all arguments of D are either all among $\overline{s}$ or all among $\overline{t}$. In the first case because $dp(\overline{u}) = dp(\overline{s})$, $dp(D) = dp(Q(\overline{s})) \leq \overline{\mu}(Q(\overline{s})) \leq \overline{\mu}(D)$ (again, by the inductive hypothesis and ($\ddagger$)). Similarly, when D is a uni-node over $\overline{t}$, $dp(D) = dp(Q(\overline{s})) - 1$, because $dp(\overline{s}) = dp(\overline{u}) = dp(\overline{t}) + 1$. Then $dp(D) \leq \overline{\mu}(Q(\overline{s})) - 1 \leq \overline{\mu}(D) - 1$. This implies that $dp(D) \leq \overline{\mu}(D)$. Otherwise, D is a bi-node over $\{\overline{w}, \overline{v}\}$ where $\overline{w} \subseteq \overline{s}$ and $\overline{v} \subseteq \overline{t}$ (by the same argument as in the proof of Lemma 2). Then $dp(D) = dp(Q(\overline{s})) \leq \overline{\mu}((Q(\overline{s})) \leq \overline{\mu}(D)$. This proves ($\dagger$).

If, on the other hand, $\overline{t}$ is a direct successor of $\overline{u}$, then $dp(\overline{t}) = dp(\overline{u}) + 1 = dp(\overline{s}) + 1$. Similarly as above, D is either a uni-node over $\overline{s}$, a uni-node over $\overline{t}$, or a bi-node over $\{\overline{w}, \overline{v}\}$ where $\overline{w} \subseteq \overline{s}$ and $\overline{v} \subseteq \overline{t}$. Then $dp(D) = dp(Q(\overline{s})) \leq \overline{\mu}(Q(\overline{s})) \leq \overline{\mu}(D)$ in the first case. In the second and third case, $dp(D) = dp(Q(\overline{s})) + 1 \leq \overline{\mu}(Q(\overline{s})) + 1 \leq \overline{\mu}(D) + 1$. This proves ($\dagger$).

A similar case analysis is needed to prove the claim for conclusions of inferences with a negative premise satisfying Condition 2.   □

Theorem 2 (Termination, soundness, completeness). *Let N be a finite set of $\mathcal{BU}$ clauses. Then:*

1. *Any $\mathsf{R}^{\mathsf{hyp}}$ derivation from N terminates.*
2. *If T is a fair derivation from N then: (i) If $N(= N_0), N_1, \ldots$ is a path with limit N_∞, N_∞ is saturated up to redundancy. (ii) N is satisfiable if and only if there exists a path in T with limit N_∞ such that N_∞ is satisfiable. (iii) N is unsatisfiable if and only if for every path $N(= N_0), N_1, \ldots$ the clause set $\bigcup_j N_j$ contains the empty clause.*

This theorem subsumes corresponding results for GF1$^-$ [13] and the first-order fragment encoding the extended modal logic $K_{(m)}(\cap, \cup, \smile)$ [10,18].

The calculus $\mathsf{R}^{\mathsf{hyp}}$ (with optional factoring) is the simplest calculus with which the class $\mathcal{BU}$ can be decided. In practice, one wants to improve the efficiency. For this purpose, the result permits the use of any refinements and simplification rules based on the resolution framework of [4]. The result also permits the use of stronger versions of the splitting rule which ensure the branches in a derivation tree are disjoint. Such splitting rules cause branches to close earlier.

6   Minimal Herbrand Model Generation

It is well-known that hyperresolution, like tableaux methods, can be used to construct models for satisfiable formulae [11] and minimal Herbrand models for satisfiable formulae and clausal classes [2,6].

A *Herbrand interpretation* is a set of ground atoms. By definition a ground atom A is *true* in an interpretation H if $A \in H$ and it is *false* in H if $A \notin H$, $\top$ is true in all interpretations and $\bot$ is false in all interpretations. A literal $\neg A$ is true in H iff A is false in H. A conjunction of two ground atoms A and B is true in an interpretation H iff both A and B are true in H and respectively, a disjunction of ground atoms is true in H iff at least one of A or B is true in the interpretation. A clause C is true in H iff for all ground substitutions σ there is a literal L in $C\sigma$ which is true in H. A set N of clauses is true in H iff all clauses in N are true in H. If a set N of clauses is true in an interpretation H then H is referred to as a *Herbrand model* of N. H is a *minimal Herbrand model* for a set N of clauses iff H is a Herbrand model of N and for no Herbrand model H' of N, $H' \subset H$ holds.

For $\mathcal{BU}$ (more generally, range restricted clauses), the procedure $\mathsf{R^{hyp}}$ implicitly generates Herbrand models. If $\mathsf{R^{hyp}}$ terminates on a clause set N in $\mathcal{BU}$ without having produced the empty clause then a model can be extracted from any open branch in the derivation. The model is given by the set of ground unit clauses in the limit of the branch, i.e. the clause set at the leaf of the branch.

Bry and Yahya [8] have proved the following even stronger result: For every minimal model H of a satisfiable, range restricted clause set N, there exists a branch in the $\mathsf{R^{hyp}}$ derivation tree for N, such that the set of ground unit clauses in the limit of the branch coincides with the ground atoms in H. Since by definition every clause set in $\mathcal{BU}$ is range restricted, this result also applies to $\mathcal{BU}$ clause sets.

Consequently, if we want to turn $\mathsf{R^{hyp}}$ into a procedure which generates only minimal models for satisfiable clause sets in $\mathcal{BU}$, it is sufficient to modify the calculus in a way that eliminates all those branches of a derivation that would generate non-minimal models. In [14] we have discussed various ways of how this can be achieved, including (i) an approach which extends $\mathsf{R^{hyp}}$ by a *model constraint propagation rule*, (ii) a modification of the extension of $\mathsf{R^{hyp}}$ by the model constraint propagation rule which replaces the splitting rule by a *complement splitting rule* and investigates the derivation tree in a particular order [8], and finally, (iii) a variant of Niemelä's groundedness test [22] which tests the minimality of a model locally for each branch by invoking another theorem proving derivation. We have compared the worst case space requirements of these approaches for clause sets associated with GF1$^-$ formulae and concluded that Niemelä's groundedness test has the best worst case space requirement among the three approaches [14]. This observation carries over to $\mathcal{BU}$.

The groundedness test is based on the following observation. Given a (finite) set H of ground atoms (or positive unit clauses) define: $\neg H = \{\neg A \mid A \in H\}$ and $\overline{H} = \bigvee_{A \in H} \neg A$. Let N be a set of clauses and U the set of all atoms over the Herbrand universe of N. Let H be a finite Herbrand model of N. Then H is a minimal Herbrand model of N iff $MMT(N, H) = N \cup \neg(U - H) \cup \{\overline{H}\}$ is unsatisfiable. This model minimality test is called *groundedness test*. Thus, we can use $\mathsf{R^{hyp}}$ to enumerate all models of a $\mathcal{BU}$ clause set N and also use $\mathsf{R^{hyp}}$

to test each model H for minimality by testing $MMT(N,H)$ for unsatisfiability. This approach has also been applied in [2,7], for ground clause logic.

A problem in applying the groundedness test to $\mathcal{BU}$ is that the set U of all atoms over the Herbrand universe of a $\mathcal{BU}$ clause set N is usually infinite. Consequently, $\neg(U - H)$ and $MMT(N,H)$ are usually infinite sets of clauses. However, in the case of an $\mathsf{R^{hyp}}$ derivation from $MMT(N,H)$, we observe the clauses in $\neg(U - H)$ have only the effect of deriving a contradiction for any clause set N' derivable from N which contains a positive unit clause not in H. Since H itself is finite, this effect is straightforward to implement. A detailed presentation of the approach and an algorithmic description is given in [14].

Theorem 3. *Let N be a clausal set in $\mathcal{BU}$. Let N_∞ be the limit of any branch B in an $\mathsf{R^{hyp}}$ derivation tree with root N and let H be the set of all positive ground unit clauses in N_∞. Then, the satisfiability of $MMT(N,H)$ can be tested in finite time and H is a minimal model of N iff $MMT(N,H)$ is unsatisfiable.*

7   Conclusion

The definition of the class $\mathcal{BU}$ attempts to capture characteristic properties for ensuring decidability by hyperresolution (or if the reader prefers hypertableaux or ground tableaux calculi, which are closely related, see [13,14]), while permitting term depth growth during the inference process. $\mathcal{BU}$ covers many familiar description logics and the corresponding extended propositional modal logics, for example the description logic $\mathcal{ALC}$ with inverse roles, conjunctions and disjunctions of roles and the corresponding modal logics below $K_{(m)}(\cap, \cup, \smile)$. Although recent results (see e.g. [10,11,12,16,17,18,23]) show that ordered resolution is the more powerful method when decidability is an issue, an advantage of hyperresolution is that it can be used for Herbrand model generation without the need for extra machinery, except when we want to generate minimal Herbrand models for which a modest extension is needed (cf. Section 6).

An open question is the complexity of the decision problem of $\mathcal{BU}$. One of the advantages of $\mathsf{GF1^-}$ compared to other solvable classes such as the guarded fragment or fluted logic is the low complexity of its decision problem, which is PSPACE-complete. Intuitively, due to the more restricted form of bi-nodes in $\mathsf{GF1^-}$ it is possible to investigate bi-nodes independently of each other. For details see [14]. In contrast, the very general definition of bi-nodes given in this paper makes it difficult to establish whether the same approach is possible for $\mathcal{BU}$.

References

1. H. Andréka, J. van Benthem, and I. Németi. Back and forth between modal logic and classical logic. *Bull. IGPL*, 3(5):685–720, 1995.
2. C. Aravindan and P. Baumgartner. Theorem proving techniques for view deletion in databases. *J. Symbolic Computat.*, 29(2):119–147, 2000.

3. M. Baaz, U. Egly, and A. Leitsch. Normal form transformations. In *Handbook of Automated Reasoning*, pp. 273–333. Elsevier, 2001.
4. L. Bachmair and H. Ganzinger. Resolution theorem proving. In *Handbook of Automated Reasoning*, pp. 19–99. Elsevier, 2001.
5. L. Bachmair, H. Ganzinger, and U. Waldmann. Superposition with simplification as a decision procedure for the monadic class with equality. In *Proc. KGC'93*, vol. 713 of *LNCS*, pp. 83–96. Springer, 1993.
6. P. Baumgartner, P. Fröhlich, U. Furbach, and W. Nejdl. Semantically guided theorem proving for diagnosis applications. In *Proc. IJCAI'97*, pp. 460–465. Morgan Kaufmann, 1997.
7. P. Baumgartner, J. Horton, and B. Spencer. Merge path improvements for minimal model hyper tableaux. In *Proc. TABLEAUX'99*, vol. 1617 of *LNAI*. Springer, 1999.
8. F. Bry and A. Yahya. Positive unit hyperresolution tableaux for minimal model generation. *J. Automated Reasoning*, 25(1):35–82, 2000.
9. H. de Nivelle. Translation of S4 into GF and 2VAR. Manuscript, 1999.
10. H. de Nivelle, R. A. Schmidt, and U. Hustadt. Resolution-based methods for modal logics. *Logic J. IGPL*, 8(3):265–292, 2000.
11. C. G. Fermüller, A. Leitsch, U. Hustadt, and T. Tammet. Resolution decision procedures. In *Handbook of Automated Reasoning*, pp. 1791–1849. Elsevier, 2001.
12. H. Ganzinger and H. de Nivelle. A superposition decision procedure for the guarded fragment with equality. In *Proc. LICS'99*, pp. 295–303. IEEE Computer Society Press, 1999.
13. L. Georgieva, U. Hustadt, and R. A. Schmidt. Hyperresolution for guarded formulae. To appear in *J. Symbolic Computat.*
14. L. Georgieva, U. Hustadt, and R. A. Schmidt. Computational space efficiency and minimal model generation for guarded formulae. In *Proc. LPAR 2001*, vol. 2250 of *LNAI*, pp. 85–99. Springer, 2001.
15. E. Grädel. On the restraining power of guards. *J. Symbolic Logic*, 64:1719–1742, 1999.
16. U. Hustadt and R. A. Schmidt. Maslov's class K revisited. In *Proc. CADE-16*, vol. 1632 of *LNAI*, pp. 172–186. Springer, 1999.
17. U. Hustadt and R. A. Schmidt. Issues of decidability for description logics in the framework of resolution. In *Automated Deduction in Classical and Non-Classical Logics*, vol. 1761 of *LNAI*, pp. 191–205. Springer, 2000.
18. U. Hustadt and R. A. Schmidt. Using resolution for testing modal satisfiability and building models. In *SAT 2000: Highlights of Satisfiability Research in the Year 2000*, pp. 459–483. IOS Press, Amsterdam, 2000.
19. A. Leitsch. Deciding clause classes by semantic clash resolution. *Fundamenta Informaticae*, 18:163–182, 1993.
20. C. Lutz. Complexity of terminological reasoning revisited. In *Proc. LPAR'99*, vol. 1705 of *LNAI*, pp. 181–200. Springer, 1999.
21. C. Lutz, U. Sattler, and S. Tobies. A suggestion of an *n*-ary description logic. In *Proc. DL'99*, pp. 81–85. Linköping University, 1999.
22. I. Niemelä. A tableau calculus for minimal model reasoning. In *Proc. TABLEAUX'96*, vol. 1071 of *LNAI*, pp. 278–294. Springer, 1996.
23. R. A. Schmidt and U. Hustadt. A resolution decision procedure for fluted logic. In *Proc. CADE-17*, vol. 1831 of *LNAI*, pp. 433–448. Springer, 2000.
24. M. Schmidt-Schauß and G. Smolka. Attributive concept descriptions with complements. *J. Artificial Intelligence*, 48:1–26, 1991.

SPASS Version 2.0

Christoph Weidenbach, Uwe Brahm, Thomas Hillenbrand, Enno Keen,
Christian Theobald, and Dalibor Topić

Max-Planck-Institut für Informatik,
Stuhlsatzenhausweg 85, 66123 Saarbrücken, Germany,
spass@mpi-sb.mpg.de

Abstract. SPASS is an automated theorem prover for full first-order logic with equality. This system description provides an overview of recent developments in SPASS 2.0, including among others an implementation of contextual rewriting, refinements of the clause normal form transformation, and enhancements of the inference engine.

1 Introduction

SPASS is an automated theorem prover for full sorted first-order logic with equality that extends superposition by sorts and a splitting rule for explicit case analysis (Weidenbach, Afshordel, Brahm, Cohrs, Engel, Keen, Theobalt & Topic 1999). The prover runs on almost any recent computer platform (see Section 2.5).

SPASS is meant to be useful for two groups of users: people using it as a theorem-proving tool and people using it as a development platform for theorem-proving tools. Many of our recent efforts went into improving value and ease of use for both groups.

2 New Features

Compared to SPASS version(s) 1.0.x described earlier by Weidenbach et al. (1999), we added the functionality described in the following subsections. Most of the underlying theory is explained by Nonnengart & Weidenbach (2001) and Weidenbach (2001). The notation and notions of these handbook chapters are used throughout this article.

2.1 Reduction Rules

Although contextual rewriting is a rather old concept (Bachmair & Ganzinger 1994), refining and instantiating and actually implementing this reduction rule such that it performs well in relevant application areas is a difficult task.

    The reduction rule contextual rewriting[1]

---

[1] This is a simplified version, hiding our integrated sort concept, and only the left variant of the rule.

A. Voronkov (Ed.): CADE-18, LNAI 2392, pp. 275–279, 2002.

$$\mathcal{R}\frac{\Gamma_1 \to \Delta_1, s \approx t \quad \Gamma_2, E[s']_p \to \Delta_2}{\begin{array}{c} \Gamma_1 \to \Delta_1, s \approx t \\ \Gamma_2, E[p/t\sigma] \to \Delta_2 \end{array}}$$

allows a reduction of the term $s' = s\sigma$ provided among other restrictions that the literals in $\Gamma_1 \to \Delta_1$ can be shown to be logically implied by $\Gamma_2 \to \Delta_2$ and all other smaller clauses: $N_C \models \Gamma_2 \to E$ for all atoms $E \in \Gamma_1\sigma$ ($N_C \models E \to \Delta_2$ for all atoms $E \in \Delta_1\sigma$) where N_C denotes all available clauses smaller than $C = \Gamma_1 \to \Delta_1, s \approx t$.

This semantic test could easily be approximated recursively, e.g. by considering only syntactically smaller clauses with respect to variable renaming and by replacing the models relation $\models$ by recursive application of contextual rewriting and congruence closure. But this approach, although effective, is not without problems. In relevant cases too much time is spent to test the applicability of the rule or the prover even gets stuck in searching for contextual rewriting applications. Therefore, we decided to start with stronger restrictions that still give many benefits in practice, but can be much more efficiently computed. Our restrictions to the rule are: (i) $s\sigma = s'$, (ii) $s \succ t$, (iii) for any term t' in $\Gamma_1 \to \Delta_1, s \approx t$ we require $s \succ t'$, (iv) $\models \mathit{fred}(\Gamma_2 \to E)$ for all atoms $E \in \Gamma_1\sigma$, (v) $\models \mathit{fred}(E \to \Delta_2)$ for all atoms $E \in \Delta_1\sigma$.

The conditions (ii) and (iii) guarantee the necessary ordering restrictions, while the conditions (iv) and (v) force the context of $s \approx t$ to be valid. The function fred, for $\mathit{forward\ reduction}$, (recursively) applies the reduction rules of SPASS to the constructed subclauses before they are checked as tautologies. This is a weaker but much more efficient variant of the above-mentioned syntactic test. The tautology check itself is highly efficiently integrated into SPASS 2.0 by the implementation of a variant of the well-known congruence closure algorithm (Downey, Sethi & Tarjan 1980, Brinker 2000) on top of the SPASS datastructures. The performance of fred, i.e., which reduction rules are actually selected by the user for a SPASS run, determines the strength as well as the cost for testing and applying contextual rewriting.

One nice result of this enhancement is that SPASS is now able to finitely saturate Balbiani's (Balbiani 1995) formulation of a certain fragment of the Euclidean geometry (Brinker 2000). Currently we are investigating examples from formal system analysis, e.g. using SPASS as the reasoning backend in static analysis of list-processing C programs (Topić 2002), to get an appropriate mix of reduction rules for the fred function in this application domain.

As an additional reduction mechanism we integrated the so-called $\mathit{terminator}$ suggested by Antoniou & Ohlbach (1983) into SPASS 2.0. The idea is to exhaustively search for a unit refutation with a bounded use of non-unit clauses.

2.2 Clause Normal Form Translation

In addition to the theory now described in full detail by Nonnengart & Weidenbach (2001) and presented in our previous system description (Weidenbach et al. 1999), we improved the renaming selection. Recall that we rename a formula if the introduction of a new atom for the formula plus the definition equivalence reduces the number of eventually generated clauses. Once a formula ϕ is detected as such a renaming candidate, we now first search for a more general formula ψ that occurs in the overall formula. We generalize terms in ϕ by free variables that have to be properly universally bound in ψ. If we find such a formula, we use it instead of ϕ as the renaming formula and rename ϕ and potential further hits as instances of ψ.

We revisited our notion of an atom definition extended by a guard as in
$$\forall x_1, \ldots, x_m \, (\phi \supset (P(t_1, \ldots, t_n) \equiv \psi)).$$
The theory is now described in full detail in a paper by Afshordel, Hillenbrand & Weidenbach (2001) and implemented exactly that way in SPASS 2.0. For the proof of the guard formulae we use SPASS as a proper sub proof procedure, now possible in SPASS 2.0, as indicated in Section 2.4.

2.3 Inference Engine

Theorem provers tend to be sensitive to the addition of even single new clauses or just a reordering of the clauses in the input problem. We want the behavior of SPASS to be more robust against such changes. To this end we implemented an initial clause ordering that is not simply based on the weight of the clauses, but their syntactic characteristics. Part of it is an abstraction of a clause as nested multiset of its literal and term structure, where all symbols are eventually abstracted by their arity. These nested multisets are then used, in addition to the weight, to get the initial ordering of the clause set. The technique is a generalization of what is implemented in WALDMEISTER (Hillenbrand, Jaeger & Löchner 1999) for equations.

The automatic selection of the precedence for the term ordering is no longer simply based on function symbol arity in SPASS 2.0. The overall idea here is to orient as many equations (get unique maximal literals in clauses) as possible. To this end a graph is built based on the left- and right-hand side terms of positive equations. Whenever there is an equation $f(t_1, \ldots, t_n) \approx g(s_1, \ldots, s_m)$ a link between f and g is established annotated with the equation. Then it is tried to turn the resulting graph into a directed acyclic graph with an appropriate precedence, where a link can be oriented if all annotated equations can be appropriately oriented with respect to the selected precedence. The strategy for the precedence search is a hill-climbing approach.

SPASS performs explicit splitting of clauses whenever a clause can be separated into two variable disjoint parts that both contain at least one positive literal. The selection of such a clause in SPASS 1.0.x was determined by the selection of the next *given* clause for inference selection (Weidenbach 2001). The main motivation for splitting a clause is to use the separated parts for exhaustive reduction, e.g. subsumption. SPASS 2.0 now selects the clause for splitting by this criterion. The clause with the highest reduction potential for subsumption and unit reductions after splitting is selected for splitting.

With SPASS 2.0 we do not only provide an inference/reduction procedure with complete interreduction, but also a variant where the set of *usable* clauses is not interreduced (Weidenbach 2001). Although we do not support memory compression techniques for this case, the time for interreduction of the *usable* clauses is saved in this mode.

2.4   Code Development

One of our long-term goals is to provide as much as possible of the functionality of SPASS in form of a documented C library. Towards this end, we improved modularization, debugging support and code documentation. And as is always the case for such a complex piece of software, we fixed several bugs in the code, thanks to reports from our users.

In SPASS 2.0 we now introduced a PROOFSEARCH datatype that holds all information about a particular proof attempt. This includes the input problem, options, ordering settings, clause data bases, etc. For example, any clause belongs to exactly one PROOFSEARCH object (via labelling). The search engine is parameterized by the PROOFSEARCH object. This was made possible by further modularizations of the underlying source code resulting in the elimination of almost all global variables. So we can now run several proof attempts completely independently at the same time within SPASS. The test of the guard formula, see Section 2.2, or our soft typing approach (Ganzinger, Meyer & Weidenbach 1997) are examples of such a usage.

SPASS 2.0 has a complete documentation of its search engine, inference rules and options with pointers into the source code.

2.5   Web Interface and Distribution

The Web interface available from the SPASS homepage:
                                    http://spass.mpi-sb.mpg.de/
is now also updated to version 2.0 and has links to the new documentation.

The SPASS distribution contains binaries for SUN Sparc Solaris, PC Linux and PC Windows 95/Windows 98/Windows NT/Windows 2000 and Windows XP. For the Windows versions we moved our GUI to Qt Version 3.0[2] and this GUI is also available as a SUN Sparc Solaris binary. Under a Unix environment, the source code (excluding the GUI) should compile without any problems if recent versions of the standard GNU[3] tools bison, flex, make and gcc are available. The distribution is available from the above-mentioned SPASS homepage where also links to the Web interface, documentation and problem libraries exist.

The distribution of SPASS contains texinfo-based documentation in different formats: man pages, info pages and HTML pages. Furthermore, full documentation of the search engine, inference rules and underlying theory with pointers into the source code is available in PDF format.

---

[2] See http://www.trolltech.com/
[3] See http://www.gnu.org/

3   Future Directions

Further development of SPASS will concentrate on enhancements towards improved performance on problems from concrete application domains, like static program analysis.

References

Afshordel, B., Hillenbrand, T. & Weidenbach, C. (2001), First-order atom definitions extended, *in* R. Nieuwenhuis & A. Voronkov, eds, 'Logic for Programming, Artificial Intelligence, and Reasoning, LPAR 2001', Vol. 2250 of *LNAI*, Springer, pp. 309–319.

Antoniou, G. & Ohlbach, H. J. (1983), Terminator, *in* A. Bundy, ed., 'Proceedings of 8th International Joint Conference on Artificial Intelligence, IJCAI-83', pp. 916–919.

Bachmair, L. & Ganzinger, H. (1994), 'Rewrite-based equational theorem proving with selection and simplification', *Journal of Logic and Computation*.

Balbiani, P. (1995), Equation solving in geometrical theories, *in* N. Dershowitz & N. Lindenstrauss, eds, 'Proceedings of the 4th international workshop on conditional and typed rewriting systems', Vol. 968 of *LNCS*, Springer.

Brinker, C. (2000), Geometrisches Schliessen mit SPASS, Diplomarbeit, Universität des Saarlandes and Max-Planck-Institut für Informatik, Saarbrücken, Germany.

Downey, P. J., Sethi, R. & Tarjan, R. E. (1980), 'Variations on the common subexpression problem', *Journal of the ACM* **27**(4), 758–771.

Ganzinger, H., Meyer, C. & Weidenbach, C. (1997), Soft typing for ordered resolution, *in* 'Proceedings of the 14th International Conference on Automated Deduction, CADE-14', Vol. 1249 of *LNAI*, Springer, Townsville, Australia, pp. 321–335.

Hillenbrand, T., Jaeger, A. & Löchner, B. (1999), WALDMEISTER – improvements in performance and ease of use, *in* H. Ganzinger, ed., '16th International Conference on Automated Deduction, CADE-16', LNAI, Springer, pp. 232–236.

Nonnengart, A. & Weidenbach, C. (2001), Computing small clause normal forms, *in* A. Robinson & A. Voronkov, eds, 'Handbook of Automated Reasoning', Vol. 1, Elsevier, chapter 6, pp. 335–367.

Topić, D. (2002), Static analysis of list-processing C programs, Diplomarbeit, Universität des Saarlandes and Max-Planck-Institut für Informatik, Saarbrücken, Germany.

Weidenbach, C. (2001), Combining superposition, sorts and splitting, *in* A. Robinson & A. Voronkov, eds, 'Handbook of Automated Reasoning', Vol. 2, Elsevier, chapter 27, pp. 1965–2012.

Weidenbach, C., Afshordel, B., Brahm, U., Cohrs, C., Engel, T., Keen, E., Theobalt, C. & Topic, D. (1999), System description: SPASS version 1.0.0, *in* H. Ganzinger, ed., '16th International Conference on Automated Deduction, CADE-16', Vol. 1632 of *LNAI*, Springer, pp. 314–318.

System Description: GrAnDe 1.0

Stephan Schulz[1] and Geoff Sutcliffe[2]

[1] Institut für Informatik, Technische Universität München
schulz@informatik.tu-muenchen.de
[2] Department of Computer Science, University of Miami
geoff@cs.miami.edu

1 Introduction

The validity problem for full first-order logic is only semi-decidable. However, there are many interesting problems that, when expressed in clause normal form, have a finite Herbrand universe. They fall into a decidable subclass of first-order logic. Traditionally, such problems have been tackled using conventional first-order techniques. Some implementations, e.g. DCTP [SL01], are decision procedures for this class of problems. An alternative approach, justified by Herbrand's theorem, is to generate the ground instances of such a problem and use a propositional decision system to determine the satisfiability of the resulting propositional problem. The applicability of the grounding approach has led to these problems being called "effectively propositional" (EPR) problems. The TPTP problem library [SS98] v2.4.1 contains 574 EPR problems. Many of these are group theory problems (101 problems) and CNF translations of formulae in propositional multi-modal logic (206 problems).

There have been claims that first-order techniques are at least as good as the grounding approach on EPR problems. In order to test these claims we implemented the grounding approach in the system PizEAndSATO, and entered it (as a demonstration system) into the EPR division of CASC-JC [SSP02,Sut01]. Despite its prototypical nature, PizEAndSATO 0.2 achieved second place. The winner, E-SETHEO csp01, is a compositional system that used both a grounding approach and several different first-order procedures sequentially.

This paper describes the latest incarnation of our system, GrAnDe 1.0 (short for *Ground And Decide*). GrAnDe has two principal components: the grounding procedure eground [Sch02] and the propositional prover ZChaff [MMZ+01]. ZChaff was chosen from a field of powerful and mature propositional systems [HS01].[1] The absence of an adequately powerful and accessible grounding tool, on the other hand, necessitated the development of eground from scratch.

This paper provides details of our contributions: The construction of eground, the combination of the systems, and an evaluation. For details about ZChaff, see [MMZ+01]. GrAnDe is available on the web at

http://www.cs.miami.edu/~tptp/ATPSystems/GrAnDe/

---

[1] ZChaff replaced SATO [ZS00] due to ZChaff's ability to deal with larger proposition numbers.

A. Voronkov (Ed.): CADE-18, LNAI 2392, pp. 280–284, 2002.
© Springer-Verlag Berlin Heidelberg 2002

2   The Grounding Procedure `eground`

An EPR problem is certainly (un)satisfiable if the set of *all* ground instances of its clauses is (un)satisfiable. However, with n constant symbols, a single clause with m variables has n^m ground instances. Thus, the set of all ground instances is often too large to compute with reasonable (or even reasonably unreasonable) resources. An aim in developing `eground` was to find smaller sets of ground instances that are still equiconsistent with the original set of clauses. In order to achieve this, three techniques were combined: clause splitting, structural constraints on variable instantiation, and propositional simplification.

Basic *clause splitting* takes a clause $C \vee D$, in which C and D do not share any variables, and replaces it by two clauses $C \vee p$ and $D \vee \neg p$, where p is a new propositional symbol. This does not change the satisfiability of the clause set – any model of the original clause set can be extended to a model of the modified clause set, and any model of the modified clause set satisfies the original one [Sch02]. The latest version of `eground` also splits a clause if C and D have common variables, but each part has some variables not occurring in the other. In this case, the variables occurring in both C and D are the arguments of p. If a clause has more than two parts that can be separated then *hyper-splitting* [RV01] is used, i.e., a clause with k parts is replaced in one step by k split clauses and a single link clause.

Clause splitting is performed in `eground` before starting to instantiate the clauses. Although splitting increases the number of clauses, it typically significantly reduces the number of ground instances. If C contains m_C variables, and D contains m_D variables, $C \vee D$ has $n^{m_C} n^{m_D}$ ground instances, where n is the number of constants. The two split clauses have only $n^{m_C} + n^{m_D}$ ground instances.

Structural constraints are used to prohibit variable instantiations that would lead to the generation of pure literals in the resulting ground clauses, and thus approximate the hyper-linking condition [LP92]. An overview of structural constraints is given here; for a full formal definition see [Sch02]. A *local structural constraint* is induced for each triple polarity/predicate symbol/position. Consider a symbol P with arity k. The local structural constraint with positive polarity at position $p \in \{1 \ldots k\}$ is induced by all negative literals with symbol P. If there exists such a negative literal L such that $L|_p$ is a variable, the position is unconstrained. Otherwise, the constraint has the form $P|_p = c_1 \vee \ldots \vee P|_p = c_i$, where the c_i are exactly the constants that appear at position p in the negative literals with predicate symbol P. Any instance of a positive literal with symbol P that does not fulfill the structural constraint will be pure, and hence ground clauses containing such instances are not needed. Constraints with negative polarity are induced by all positive literals in the same way. The local structural constraints for each variable in a clause are conjoined and simplified into a minimal conjunctive normal form. The acceptable instantiations for each variable can then be read directly off the constraints, so that the generation of the ground instances is done very efficiently. If there are no possible instantiations for some variable in a clause, then no instances of the clause are generated.

Splitting and structural constraints are somewhat complementary. Clause splitting works one clause at a time, while structural constraints are induced by the whole clause set. If variables occur in only a small number of literals, the chance that the clause can be split increases. If a variable occurs in many positions, the likelihood that it is constrained increases.

The third technique used to reduce the size of the ground clause set is *propositional simplification*. Tautology deletion and forward unit subsumption are used to delete redundant ground clauses, and forward unit resolution is used to reduce the size of the generated ground clauses. The forward unit simplifications use existing propositional units to subsume and simplify newly generated ground clauses. Due to the internal data structures used, these simplifications are done at negligible cost.

Despite the optimizations, there are still problems where **eground** runs out of time or, more often, out of memory.[2] However, this does not necessarily mean that the effort has been in vain. While the satisfiability of the original clause set can be shown only by satisfying *all* non-redundant ground instances, unsatisfiability may be shown using only a subset of the instances. In order to allow GrAnDe to take advantage of this possibility, **eground** can be configured to output a set of ground clauses when it runs out of time or memory. In this situation the normal generation procedure is stopped, and a single ground instance of each input clause is added to the already generated clause set. The resultant clause set is *incomplete* (with respect to the test for unsatisfiability).

The ground clauses generated are converted to propositional clauses and output in DIMACS format [DIM], followed by a message indicating whether the clause set is complete or incomplete.

3   Combining the Systems

A **Perl** script called **And** is used to combine **eground** and ZChaff. The script invokes **eground** on the EPR problem, allowing it maximally 66% of the CPU time limit. The propositional clauses written by **eground** are captured into a temporary file, which is used as the input for ZChaff. ZChaff is allowed whatever CPU time has not been used by **eground** (more than 34% of the CPU time limit in the cases where **eground** terminates early, either because it runs out of memory or because it has generated a complete ground clause set). The completeness marker line written by **eground** is used by **And** for interpreting the output of ZChaff. If **eground** has generated an incomplete clause set and ZChaff reports that it is satisfiable, then no result is reported by GrAnDe. If **eground** has generated an incomplete clause set and ZChaff reports that it is unsatisfiable, or if **eground** has generated a complete clause set, then ZChaff's result is reported by GrAnDe as the overall result.

---

[2] Because **eground** generates output in DIMACS format, it can only print the result once the number of clauses and the largest proposition number are known.

4   Experimental Results

GrAnDe 1.0 has been tested on the 574 CNF EPR problems in TPTP v2.4.1. Of
these, 413 are unsatisfiable and 161 are satisfiable. Three systems that use first-
order techniques were also tested: DCTP 1.0 [SL01], SPASS 1.03 [Wei99], and
Vampire 2.0 [RV99]. DCTP is a decision procedure for EPR problems; SPASS is
complete for unsatisfiable problems and known to be very strong on satisfiable
problems in general; Vampire 2.0 was the winner of the MIX division of CASC-
JC. Unfortunately, we were unable to get a working hyper-linking prover, as
e.g., OSHL [PZ00], for comparison. PizEAndSATO 0.2 was also tested, to gauge
progress in our development. The testing was done on a SUN Ultra-80, with a
450MHz CPU and 400 MB of RAM. A 300 second overall CPU time limit was
imposed for each problem. The results are summarized in Table 1.

Table 1. Results

System	Total	Unsatisfiable	Satisfiable
	574	413	161
DCTP 1.0	489	352	137
SPASS 1.03	498	397	101
Vampire 2.0	498	403	95
PizEAndSATO 0.2	543	407	136
GrAnDe 1.0	546	408	138

Of the 574 problems, eground was able to create a complete ground clause
set for 546 problems. Of these, ZChaff reported 138 as satisfiable, 407 as unsatisfiable, and timed out on one problem. Of the 28 problems for which eground
was unable to create a complete clause set, ZChaff reported 8 as satisfiable (i.e.
no result for GrAnDe), one as unsatisfiable (i.e. the problem was solved despite
eground being unable to generate a complete clause set), and timed out on 19
problems.

509 of the problems solved by GrAnDe were solved in less than one second
of CPU time, and only 16 problems required more than 10 seconds. Of these 16
"hard" problems, only one required more than 60 seconds. This is the problem
for which eground generated an incomplete clause set that ZChaff still found to
be unsatisfiable. For the other 15 "hard" problems, eground always took most
of the CPU time, but never more than 40 seconds. There thus seem to be three
major scenarios (with the 300 second CPU time limit): either i) the problem
is easy for GrAnDe, or ii) eground completes reasonably quickly (within 40
seconds) and ZChaff can decide the clause set, or iii) eground hits a resource
limit and ZChaff is unable to decide the resulting incomplete, typically very
large, clause set in the remaining time.

5   Possible Improvements

Despite the fact that eground is the most powerful grounding procedure we
are aware of, at the moment it still is the weakest link in GrAnDe. There are

a number of possible improvements to the program. Two important ideas are the use of more simplification in **eground**, e.g., the use of simple indexing for non-unit subsumption (and possibly subsumption resolution), and the use of more restrictive local unification constraints instead of the simple structural constraints. Additionally, it might be possible to generate better (smaller and more diverse) incomplete clause sets if complete grounding is not possible.

References

[DIM]   DIMACS. Satisfiability Suggested Format. ftp://dimacs.rutgers.edu/ pub/challenge/satisfiability/doc/satformat.tex.

[HS01]   H. Hoos and T. Stützle. SATLIB: An Online Resource for Research on SAT. In I. Gent, H. van Maaren, and T. Walsh, editors, *Proc. of the 3rd Workshop on the Satisfiability Problem*, 2001. http://www.satlib.org/.

[LP92]   S-J. Lee and D.A. Plaisted. Eliminating Duplication with the Hyper-Linking Strategy. *Journal of Automated Reasoning*, 9(1):25–42, 1992.

[MMZ⁺01] M. Moskewicz, C. Madigan, Y. Zhao, L. Zhang, and S. Malik. Chaff: Engineering an Efficient SAT Solver. In D. Blaauw and L. Lavagno, editors, *Proc. of the 39th Design Automation Conference*, pages 530–535, 2001.

[PZ00]   D.A. Plaisted and Y. Zhu. Ordered Semantic Hyper-linking. *Journal of Automated Reasoning*, 25(3):167–217, 2000.

[RV99]   A. Riazanov and A. Voronkov. Vampire. In H. Ganzinger, editor, *Proc. of the 16th International Conference on Automated Deduction*, number 1632 in Lecture Notes in Artificial Intelligence, pages 292–296. Springer, 1999.

[RV01]   A. Riazanov and A. Voronkov. Splitting without Backtracking. In B. Nebel, editor, *Proc. of the 17th International Joint Conference on Artificial Intelligence* , pages 611–617. Morgan Kaufmann, 2001.

[Sch02]   S. Schulz. A Comparison of Different Techniques for Grounding Near-Propositional CNF Formulae. In S. Haller and G. Simmons, editors, *Proc. of the 15th Florida Artificial Intelligence Research Symposium*. AAAI Press, 2002. To appear.

[SL01]   G. Stenz and R. Letz. DCTP - A Disconnection Calculus Theorem Prover. In R. Gore, A. Leitsch, and T. Nipkow, editors, *Proc. of the International Joint Conference on Automated Reasoning*, number 2083 in Lecture Notes in Artificial Intelligence, pages 381–385. Springer, 2001.

[SS98]   G. Sutcliffe and C.B. Suttner. The TPTP Problem Library: CNF Release v1.2.1. *Journal of Automated Reasoning*, 21(2):177–203, 1998.

[SSP02]   G. Sutcliffe, C. Suttner, and J. Pelletier. The IJCAR ATP System Competition. *Journal of Automated Reasoning*, To appear, 2002.

[Sut01]   G. Sutcliffe. CASC-JC. http://www.cs.miami.edu/ tptp/CASC/JC/, 2001.

[Wei99]   C. Weidenbach, et al. SPASS Version 1.0.0. In H. Ganzinger, editor, *Proc. of the 16th International Conference on Automated Deduction*, number 1632 in Lecture Notes in Artificial Intelligence, pages 378–382. Springer, 1999.

[ZS00]   H. Zhang and M. Stickel. Implementing the Davis-Putnam Method. *Journal of Automated Reasoning*, 24(1/2):277–296, 2000.

The HR Program for Theorem Generation

Simon Colton*

Division of Informatics, University of Edinburgh, UK. simonco@dai.ed.ac.uk

1 Introduction

Automated theory formation involves the production of objects of interest, concepts about those objects, conjectures relating the concepts and proofs of the conjectures. In group theory, for example, the objects of interest are the groups themselves, the concepts include element types, subgroup types, etc., the conjectures include implication and if-and-only-if conjectures and these become theorems if they are proved, non-theorems if disproved. Similar to Zhang's MCS program [11], the HR system [1] – named after mathematicians Hardy and Ramanujan – performs theory formation in mathematical domains. It works by (i) using the MACE model generator [9] to generate objects of interest from axiom sets (ii) performing the concept formation and conjecture making itself and (iii) using the Otter theorem prover [8] to prove conjectures. In domains where Otter and MACE are effective, HR can produce large numbers of theorems for testing automated theorem provers (ATPs), or smaller numbers of prime implicates, which represent some of the fundamental facts in a domain. We explain how HR operates in §2 and give details of a representative session in §3. As discussed in §4, the applications of HR to automated reasoning include the generation of constraints for constraint satisfaction problems, the generation of lemmas for automated theorem proving, and the production of benchmark theorems for the TPTP library of test problems for ATP systems [10]. HR is a Java program available for download here: www.dai.ed.ac.uk/~simonco/research/hr.

2 Automated Theorem Generation

Initialising from Axioms

HR can be given background information in a number of different formats. In particular, it can form a theory from the bare minimum of a domain: the axiom set, which must be supplied in MACE input syntax. HR calls MACE in order to produce a single model satisfying the axioms, which becomes the first object of interest in the theory. Using the -N8 -m1 flags, HR asks MACE to look for a model of size 1, 2, 3, etc. until it finds a single one (stopping after size 8). MACE presents the model in terms of the concepts embedded in the axioms, e.g., in ring theory, MACE produces a single ring of size 1, described by four concepts: the addition and multiplication operations, the additive inverse of elements, and the additive identity. To initialise the theory, HR takes the concepts from MACE's output as the initial concepts in the domain and uses the model from MACE's output to calculate the first examples for these concepts. All future concepts and conjectures are built from the initial concepts.

* This work is supported by EPSRC Grant GR/M98012.

A. Voronkov (Ed.): CADE-18, LNAI 2392, pp. 285–289, 2002.

Inventing Concepts

HR invents concepts by passing old concepts through one of 10 production rules (PRs). This mechanism is described in detail in [2] and we give only a brief overview of 4 PRs here. The `match` PR equates variables in definitions, e.g., it could start with the multiplication operation $(a * b = c)$ in group theory and equate $a = b = c$ to invent the concept of idempotent elements $(a * a = a)$. The `compose` PR uses conjugation to compose two old concepts into a new one which describes objects satisfying both definitions. For example, it starts with the concept of self inverse elements in group theory $(a^{-1} = a)$ and composes it with the squaring operation $(a * a = b)$, to produce either the square of self inverse elements $(a * a = b \wedge a^{-1} = a)$, or elements which square to give a self inverse element $(a * a = b \wedge b^{-1} = b)$. The `negate` PR negates certain clauses in a definition, e.g., it produces the concept of non-self-inverse elements $(a^{-1} \neq a)$. Finally, the `exists` production rule introduces existential quantification into a definition. For example, this PR invents the concept of elements appearing on the diagonal of a group's multiplication table $(\exists \, b \text{ s.t. } b * b = a)$. Other production rules count set sizes and introduce constants, but produce concepts which are not easily expressible for first order provers, so we omit details here. Also, in future, we intend to enable HR to extract concepts from proofs.

Theory formation is driven by a heuristic search: more interesting concepts are used to build new concepts before less interesting ones. The heuristic measures include both properties of concepts, such as the complexity of the definition, and properties of the conjectures about the concepts, with details given in [3]. In previous versions of HR, in order to avoid repetitions, we specified forbidden paths, namely routes which HR was not allowed to take, so that certain concepts could only be produced in one way. However, we found that this interfered with the heuristic search – often hindering the development of the most interesting concepts. Hence, we removed the forbidden paths, and enabled HR to efficiently prune concepts at the definition stage. That is, if it invents a concept with the same definition as a previous one, the new concept is discarded. Also, if HR invents a concept with a negation conflict, such as $(a * a = a \wedge -(a * a = a))$ or a function conflict, such as $(a * a = b \wedge a * a = c \wedge b \neq c)$, the concept is also discarded, because such concepts trivially have no examples.

Empirical Conjecture Making

If a new concept passes the pruning stage, HR calculates the examples for it, and one of 3 situations will occur. In the first case, the example set is empty and HR makes a *non-existence* conjecture stating that the concept's definition is inconsistent with the axioms. For example, when HR invents the concept of non-identity idempotent elements, it cannot find any, so makes the conjecture: $\nexists \, a \text{ s.t. } (-(a = id) \wedge a * a = a)$. Proved non-existence theorems are used later to prune concepts at the definition stage, i.e., they are used to show that a concept will have no examples before the examples are calculated.

In the second case, the example set is exactly the same as that for a concept already in the theory, and HR makes the *equivalence* conjecture that the new and old concepts have logically equivalent definitions. For example in group theory, HR invents the concept of idempotent elements, notices that for all the groups it has, the idempotent elements are the identity elements, and makes the conjecture: $a * a = a \leftrightarrow a = identity$.

In the third case, the example set is non-empty and different to those of all previous concepts, and HR adds the concept to the theory. It then endeavours to find some conjectures about the new concept. To do this, HR looks for subsumption conjectures by finding old concepts where the examples are a subset of the examples for the new concept. For each it finds, it makes the implication conjecture that the definition of the old concept implies the definition of the new concept. Accordingly, HR makes an appropriate implication conjecture if an old concept has examples which are a superset of the examples for the new concept.

Extracting Prime Implicates

Given an implication conjecture of the form $A \wedge B \wedge C \rightarrow D \wedge E \wedge F$, HR extracts the implicates $A \wedge B \wedge C \rightarrow D$, $A \wedge B \wedge C \rightarrow E$ and so on. The left-hand and right-hand implication conjectures which make up an equivalence conjecture are dealt with similarly. Given a non-existence conjecture of the form $\not\exists (A \wedge B \wedge C)$, HR extracts implicates of the form $A \wedge B \rightarrow \neg C$ and so on. HR discards any implicate if it has already proved a stronger conjecture, i.e., with the same goal but a subset of the premises. From each implicate which survives, HR employs Otter to try to prove it, with a time limit set by the user (usually 10 seconds). If the implicate is true, HR then tries to extract prime implicates, which are implicate theorems such that no subset of the premises implies the goal. While there are more sophisticated methods for finding prime implicates [7], HR employs a naive search for prime implicates: using Otter to try to prove that ever larger subsets of the premises imply the goal, stopping when such a subset is found or the subset becomes the entire set of premises.

Introducing Counterexamples

HR employs MACE to find a counterexample to any implicate extracted from the empirical conjectures that Otter fails to prove. Each counterexample is added to the theory and examples for all the concepts are re-calculated so that similar non-theorems are avoided later. Prime implicates which are extracted from the implicates are assumed to be false if Otter does not prove them, and MACE is not used to find a counterexample. This is because the extracted prime implicates are not supported by empirical evidence, and in practice we have found that, as they are simply stated, if Otter cannot prove them quickly, then they are false in the vast majority of cases (we have yet to see an exception to this rule).

3 A Representative Session

We ran HR with the RNG-004 ring theory axioms from the TPTP library [10] for 1000 theory formation steps, which took 6481 seconds on a Pentium 1Ghz processor. We used the compose, match, exists and negate PRs in a breadth first search, as we were interested in finding prime implicates, rather than interesting concepts. 340 steps resulted in concepts which were discarded due to their definitions, 255 resulted in new concepts, 401 resulted in equivalence conjectures and 4 resulted in non-existence conjectures. This highlights that there is a fair amount of redundancy in the theory formation, as 340 steps resulted in discarded concepts. Fortunately, such steps are carried out very quickly. The high number of equivalence conjectures is indicative of algebras constrained with many axioms, as many concepts can be proved equivalent. The low number of non-existence conjectures is because rings have an additive identity: it is rare for a concept to not be satisfied by the identity element or some derivative of it.

From the non-existence and equivalence conjectures, HR extracted 275 proved prime implicates, of which 39 had a proof length of 10 or more (indicating the complexity of the theorem). Hence the prime implicates were mostly easy for Otter to prove, but a few managed to tax it. This theorem had a proof length of 40, which was the longest: $\forall\ b, c\ (b*c = c \wedge c*b = b \wedge c+c = b \rightarrow b+b = c)$, and we found that, like this one, the most difficult to prove conjectures involved both the addition and multiplication operations. MACE introduced counterexamples to 30 non-theorems, with 2 models of size 2 and of size 3, 25 models of size 4 and 1 model of size 7, given below along with the conjecture which it disproved.

$$\forall\ b, c \in G$$
$$(b*b = c \wedge b+b =$$
$$c \wedge c*c = b\ \rightarrow$$
$$b^{-1} = c)$$

*	0	1	2	3	4	5	6
0	0	0	0	0	0	0	0
1	0	2	5	4	6	1	3
2	0	5	1	6	3	2	4
3	0	4	6	5	1	3	2
4	0	6	3	1	2	4	5
5	0	1	2	3	4	5	6
6	0	3	4	2	5	6	1

+	0	1	2	3	4	5	6
0	0	1	2	3	4	5	6
1	1	2	3	5	0	6	4
2	2	3	5	6	1	4	0
3	3	5	6	4	2	0	1
4	4	0	1	2	6	3	5
5	5	6	4	0	3	1	2
6	6	4	0	1	5	2	3

id = 0

inv 0 1 2 3 4 5 6
    0 4 6 5 1 3 2

4   Applications

Automated theory formation has much potential for automated reasoning. Firstly, we have used HR to improve efficiency in solving constraint satisfaction problems (CSPs) [4]. HR extracts concepts and axioms from the basic CSP specification and forms a theory. Then, using various measures of interestingness in HR, we identify concepts and theorems to use as additional constraints for the CSP. When interpreted as constraints, the theorems can be added as implied constraints with no loss of generality. In contrast, the concepts suggest induced constraints, which act as case splits for the problem. Adding both implied and induced constraints can have a dramatic effect on the time taken to solve a CSP. For example, for QG3-quasigroups (where every element appears in each row and column, and additionally: $\forall\ a, b, (a*b)*(b*a) = a$), HR identified (i) an all-different constraint on the diagonal of the multiplication table (ii) a symmetry constraint on the diagonal: $a*a = b \rightarrow b*b = a$ and (iii) that QG3-quasigroups are anti-Abelian, i.e., $a*b = b*a \rightarrow a = b$. These additional constraints greatly improved efficiency, producing a 10-times speedup for some solution sizes.

We have also used HR to generate benchmark problems for the TPTP library of theorems for ATP systems, the de facto standard for assessing ATP systems [10]. Our challenge was to use HR to find theorems that some state of the art provers were able to prove, but others were not. Working in group theory, our first attempt involved a brute force search for theorems. We gave HR the non-isomorphic groups up to order 8 and turned off the theorem proving and counterexample finding abilities. As discussed in [5], HR produced 46,000 distinct equivalence conjectures in a ten minute session. These were passed to Geoff

Sutcliffe (who maintains the TPTP library), who tested them on the Spass, E, Vampire, Gandalf and Otter provers. Spass was able to prove all of them, but 40 were rated 0.8 and 144 were rated 0.6 (provable by only 1 out of 5 and 2 out of 5 provers respectively), and these 184 were accepted into the TPTP library. The next challenge was to find theorems which E could prove, but not Spass. Working again in group theory, we added HR to the MathWeb Software Bus [6], which gave HR direct access to E and Spass (taking Sutcliffe out of the loop). We allowed both provers 120 seconds to prove theorems and ran HR until it had produced 12,000 equivalence conjectures. This managed to produce just four theorems which E proved, but Spass could not prove in 120 seconds, including:

$$\forall \ b,c,d \ (b{*}c = d{\wedge}b^{-1} = c{\wedge}b{*}d = c{\wedge}\exists \ e,f \ (e^{-1} = f{\wedge}e{*}b = f){\wedge}\exists \ g \ (g \neq id){\wedge}d^{-1} = d$$
$$\Leftrightarrow b^{-1} = c{\wedge}c{*}b = d{\wedge}b{*}d = c{\wedge}\exists \ e,g \ (e^{-1} = f \wedge e{*}b = f) \wedge \exists \ g \ (g \neq id) \wedge d{*}b = c).$$

Our third application is to automated theorem proving itself. Given the axioms for a theorem, we use HR to form a theory containing many prime implicates, such as the theory described above. Using their proof lengths, we select certain prime implicates to be added to the original problem as lemmas. We aim to show that the time using HR can be compensated for by the decrease in time taken to prove the theorem (or, indeed, sets of theorems) when the lemmas are added. We have positive results with the group theory TPTP theorems supplied by HR itself, but an initial application to TPTP ring theorems (not supplied by HR) has been less successful. Working with ATP designers, we hope to make HR generate and choose lemmas more intelligently to improve the results.

References

1. S.Colton. *Automated Theory Formation in Pure Mathematics*. PhD thesis, Department of Artificial Intelligence, University of Edinburgh, 2000.
2. S.Colton, A.Bundy, and T.Walsh. Automatic identification of mathematical concepts. In *Machine Learning: Proceedings of the 17th International Conference*, 2000.
3. S.Colton, A.Bundy, and T.Walsh. On the notion of interestingness in automated mathematical discovery. *IJHCS*, 53(3):351–375, 2000.
4. S. Colton and I Miguel. Constraint generation via automated theory formation. In *Proceedings of CP-01*, 2001.
5. S.Colton and G.Sutcliffe. Automatic Generation of Benchmark Problems for ATP Systems. In *Proceedings of the 7th Symposium on AI and Mathematics*, 2002.
6. Andreas Franke and Michael Kohlhase. Mathweb, an agent-based communication layer for distributed automated theorem proving. In *CADE 16*, 1999.
7. P.Jackson. Computing prime implicates incrementally. In *CADE 11*, 1992.
8. W.McCune. The OTTER user's guide. Technical Report ANL/90/9, Argonne National Laboratories, 1990.
9. W.McCune. A Davis-Putnam program and its application to finite first-order model search. Technical Report ANL/MCS-TM-194, Argonne National Laboratories, 1994.
10. G.Sutcliffe and C.Suttner. The TPTP Problem Library: CNF Release v1.2.1. *Journal of Automated Reasoning*, 21(2):177–203, 1998. www.cs.miami.edu/~tptp/.
11. J.Zhang. MCS: Model-based conjecture searching. In *CADE-16*, 1999.

AutoBayes/CC — Combining Program Synthesis with Automatic Code Certification — System Description —

Michael Whalen[1], Johann Schumann[2], and Bernd Fischer[2]

[1] Department of Computer Science and Engineering
Univ. of Minnesota, Minneapolis, MN 55455 whalen@cs.umn.edu
[2] RIACS / NASA Ames, Moffett Field, CA 94035
{schumann|fisch}@email.arc.nasa.gov

1 Introduction

Code certification is a lightweight approach to formally demonstrate software quality. It concentrates on aspects of software quality that can be defined and formalized via properties, e.g., operator safety or memory safety. Its basic idea is to require code producers to provide formal *proofs* that their code satisfies these quality properties. The proofs serve as *certificates* which can be checked independently, by the code consumer or by certification authorities, e.g., the FAA. It is the idea underlying such approaches as proof-carrying code [6].

Code certification can be viewed as a more practical version of traditional Hoare-style program verification. The properties to be verified are fairly simple and regular so that it is often possible to use an automated theorem prover to automatically discharge *all* emerging proof obligations. Usually, however, the programmer must still splice auxiliary annotations (e.g., loop invariants) into the program to facilitate the proofs. For complex properties or larger programs this quickly becomes the limiting factor for the applicability of current certification approaches.

Our work combines code certification with automatic program synthesis [4] which makes it possible to automatically generate both the code and all necessary annotations for fully automatic certification. By *generating* detailed annotations, one of the biggest obstacles for code certification is removed and it becomes possible to automatically check that synthesized programs obey the desired safety properties.

Program synthesis systems are built on the notion of "correctness-by-construction", i.e., generated programs always implement the specifications correctly. Hence, verifying these programs may seem redundant. However, a synthesis system ensures only that code fragments are assembled correctly while the fragments themselves are included in the domain theory and thus not directly verified by the synthesis proof. Our approach can verify properties about the instantiated code fragments, and so provides additional guarantees about the generated code.

A. Voronkov (Ed.): CADE-18, LNAI 2392, pp. 290–294, 2002.
© Springer-Verlag Berlin Heidelberg 2002

2   The AutoBayes/CC System

AUTOBAYES/CC (Fig. 1) is a code certification extension to the AUTOBAYES synthesis system, which is used in the statistical data analysis domain[2]. Its input specification is a statistical model, i.e., it describes how the statistical variables are distributed and depend on each other and which parameters have to be estimated for the given task. AUTOBAYES synthesizes code by exhaustive, layered application of *schemas*. A schema consists of a code fragment with open slots and a set of applicability conditions. The synthesis system fills the slots with code fragments by recursively calling schemas. The conditions constrain how the slots can be filled; they must be proven to hold for the specification model before the schema can be applied. Some of the schemas contain calls to symbolic equation solvers, others contain entire skeletons of statistical or numerical algorithms. By recursively invoking schemas and composing the resulting code fragments, AUTOBAYES is able to automatically synthesize programs of considerable size and internal complexity (currently up to 1,400 lines of commented C++ code).

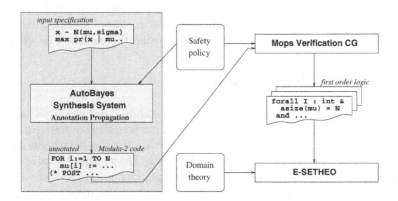

Fig. 1. The AUTOBAYES/CC system architecture

At the core of the CC-extension lie "certification augmentations" to the AUTOBAYES-schemas; these augmentations are schematic Hoare-style code annotations that describe how the schema-generated code locally affects properties of interest to our safety policy (currently memory and operator safety). For example, a loop is annotated with a schematic invariant and schematic pre- and postconditions describing how its body changes the variables of the program. During synthesis, the annotations are instantiated in parallel with the original schemas. The domain knowledge encoded in each schema is detailed enough to provide all information required for the instantiation. These annotations are also used to partition the safety proofs into small, automatically provable segments.

Unfortunately, these schema-local annotations are in general insufficient to prove the postconditions at the end of recursively composed fragments—an "inner" loop-invariant may not be aware of proof obligations that are relevant to an "outer" loop-invariant. AUTOBAYES overcomes this problem by *propagating* any unchanged information through the annotations. Since program synthesis restricts aliasing to few, known places, testing which statements influence which annotations can be accomplished easily without full static analysis of the synthesized program.

As a next step, the synthesized annotated code is processed by a verification condition generator (VCG). Here we use the VCG of the *Modula Proving System* MOPS [3], a Hoare-calculus based verification system for a large subset of the programming language Modula-2,[1] including pointers, arrays, and other data structures. MOPS uses a subset of VDM-SL as its specification language; this is interpreted here only as syntactic sugar for classical first-order logic.

The proof obligations generated by MOPS are then fed (after automatic syntactic transformation and addition of domain axioms) into the automated theorem prover E-SETHEO, version csp01 [1]. E-SETHEO is a compositional theorem prover for formulas in first-order logic, combining the systems E [8] and SETHEO [5]. The individual subsystems are based on the superposition, model elimination, and semantic tree calculi. Depending on syntactic characteristics of the input formula, an optimal schedule for each of the different strategies is selected. Because all of the subsystems work on formulas in clausal normal form (CNF), the first-order formula is converted into CNF using the module Flotter [10].

3   A Certification Example

We illustrate the operation of our system on a standard data analysis task: classify normally (Gaussian) distributed data from a mixture of sources (e.g., photon energy levels in a spectrum). A straightforward 19-line specification is sufficient to describe the problem in domain-specific terms. The synthesized program uses an iterative EM (expectation maximization) algorithm and consists of roughly 380 lines of code, 90 of which are auto-generated comments to explain the code. For details see http://ase.arc.nasa.gov/schumann/AutoBayesCC and [2]. The code is annotated to prove division-by-zero and array-bounds safety. With all annotations (including the propagated annotations), the code grows to 2,116 lines—a clear indication that manual annotation is out of question. For an excerpt of the code see Figure 2.

The MOPS verification condition generator takes this annotated code file and produces 69 proof tasks in first-order logic. Initially, E-SETHEO could solve 65 of the 69 tasks automatically. The remaining four proof tasks were of the general form $Ax \wedge A \wedge B \rightarrow A' \wedge C$ where Ax, A, A', B, C are variable-disjoint first-order formulas. This form is a consequence of the task generation process: Ax represents the domain axioms, A and A' are propagated annotations, and $B \rightarrow C$ is the "proper" proof obligation itself. In order to reduce the formula size, a preprocessing script was used to split each of these proof tasks into two separate tasks, namely $Ax \wedge A \wedge B \rightarrow A'$ and $Ax \wedge A \wedge B \rightarrow C$; these were then processed

---

[1] We extended AUTOBAYES to generate the Modula-2 code. Usually, AUTOBAYES synthesizes C/C++ programs for Matlab and Octave (http://www.octave.org).

separately and proven automatically by E-SETHEO. After conversion into CNF the formulas had on average 131 clauses (between 112 and 166); roughly half of the clauses were non-Horn. The terms had a syntactically rich structure with an average number of 51 function symbols and 39 constant symbols. Equality and relational operators were the only predicate symbols in the original formula; additional predicate symbols were introduced by Flotter during the conversion into CNF. Despite the size of the formula and their syntactic richness, most of the proofs were relatively short and were basically found by only two of E-SETHEO's strategies, namely using the E-prover, and an iterative combination of the E-prover and scheme-SETHEO.

```
 1 (*{ assert i=N and j=M and
 2 (forall a,b : int & ((0<=a and a<N) and
 3    (0<=b and b<M)) => q[a,b]=0.0) }*)
 4 (*{ loopinv  0<=k and k<=N-1 and
 5 (forall a,b: int &  ((0<=a and a<N) and
 6    (0<=b and b<M) => 0<=q[a,b] and
 7      q[a,b]<=1.0) }*)
 8 FOR k := 0 to N - 1 DO
 9    q[k,c[k]] := 1.0;
10 END
11 (*{ post (forall a,b : int &
12 ((0<=a and a<N) and (0<=b and b<M))
13    => 0 <= q[a,b] and q[a,b] <=  1.0) }*)
```

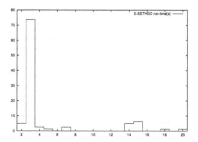

Fig. 2. *Left*, excerpt of annotated code produced by AUTOBAYES/CC. Annotations are enclosed in (*{ ... }*). *Right*, distribution of E-SETHEO proof times (% solved over runtime in seconds).

Fig. 2 shows the runtime distribution for the proof tasks.[2] Most tasks were solved in about two to three seconds, but some tasks took up to 20 seconds. The smaller second peak visible around 15 seconds is due to a non-optimal schedule. We expect that a re-training of E-SETHEO's internal scheduler could help to avoid such long runtimes (cf. [9]). The overall proof time of 323 seconds indicates that our approach is feasible.

In order to compare our approach to certification techniques based on static analysis, we analyzed the equivalent C-version of our example program with the commercial tool PolySpace [7]. PolySpace was capable of declaring most of the code safe with respect to memory/operator safety. However, it could not clear several crucial parts of the code, most notably the nested indexing (q[k,c[k]], see line 9 in Fig. 2) and the initialization of some variables in the main loop. In these cases, certification requires annotation propagation as it is done in our work; Polyspace does not require or support annotations. On the other hand, PolySpace detected a possible integer overflow error of a loop counter in the synthesized code, something that our safety policy does not (yet) check. The runtime of PolySpace for this example (about one hour of wall-clock time on the

---

[2] All runtimes have been obtained with a total CPU-time limit of 120 seconds on a 1000 MHz SunBlade workstation. Due to the internal scheduling of E-SETHEO, substantially different runtimes can result if this limit is changed.

same 1000MHz SunBlade) demonstrates that our approach can be competitive to commercial tools.

4 Conclusions

In this paper, we have described AUTOBAYES/CC, a novel combination of automated program synthesis and automated program verification. Our idea is to use the knowledge of the domain which is formalized in the program synthesis system to generate the program together with the necessary detailed formal annotations required for a fully automatic safety proof. The underlying approach is general and we expect it to be applicable to other code-generation systems as well. The major benefit of this combination of program synthesis and program verification is obviously the additional verification of important quality aspects of the synthesized code which comes at no cost for the user.

AUTOBAYES/CC is still work in progress; currently, the certification extension covers only those parts of the domain theory required to generate EM-variants. However, we see no fundamental obstacles in extending the approach to the entire (still growing) domain theory. Also, the safety policy is still hard-coded in the way the annotations are generated within the synthesis schemas. We will work on ways to explicitly represent safety policies (e.g., using higher-order formulations) and use this to tailor the annotation generation in AUTOBAYES/CC. We also plan to implement a preprocessing and simplification component which can substantially reduce size and complexity of the proof tasks.

References

[1]   CASC-JC Theorem Proving Competition. www.cs.miams.edu/~tptp/CASC/JC, 2001.

[2]   B. Fischer and J. Schumann. AutoBayes: A System for Generating Data Analysis Programs from Statistical Models. *JFP*, to appear 2002. Preprint available at http://ase.arc.nasa.gov/people/fischer/papers.html.

[3]   T. Kaiser, B. Fischer, and W. Struckmann. "MOPS: Verifying Modula-2 programs specified in VDM-SL". *Proc. 4th Workshop Tools for System Design and Verification*, pp. 163–167, 2000.

[4]   C. Kreitz. "Program Synthesis". In W. Bibel and P. H. Schmitt, (eds.), *Automated Deduction – A Basis for Applications*, Vol III, pp. 105–134. 1998.

[5]   M. Moser, O. Ibens, R. Letz, J. Steinbach, C. Goller, J. Schumann, and K. Mayr. "The Model Elimination Provers SETHEO and E-SETHEO". *JAR*, **18**:237–246, 1997.

[6]   G. C. Necula. "Proof-Carrying Code". *Proc. 24th POPL*, pp. 106–119. 1997.

[7]   PolySpace Technologies. www.polyspace.com, 2002.

[8]   S. Schulz. "System Abstract: E 0.3". *Proc. 16th CADE, LNAI* 1421, pp. 297–301. 1999.

[9]   G. Stenz and A. Wolf. "E-SETHEO: Design Configuration and Use of a Parallel Theorem Prover". *Proc. 12th Australian Joint Conf. Artificial Intelligence, LNAI* 1747, pp. 231–243. 1999.

[10] C. Weidenbach, B. Gaede, and G. Rock. "Spass and Flotter version 0.42". *Proc. 13th CADE, LNAI* 1104, pp. 141–145. 1996.

The Quest for Efficient Boolean Satisfiability Solvers

Lintao Zhang and Sharad Malik

Department of Electrical Engineering, Princeton University, Princeton, NJ 08544
{lintaoz,sharad}@ee.Princeton.edu

Abstract. The classical NP-complete problem of Boolean Satisfiability (SAT) has seen much interest in not just the theoretical computer science community, but also in areas where practical solutions to this problem enable significant practical applications. Since the first development of the basic search based algorithm proposed by Davis, Putnam, Logemann and Loveland (DPLL) about forty years ago, this area has seen active research effort with many interesting contributions that have culminated in state-of-the-art SAT solvers today being able to handle problem instances with thousands, and in same cases even millions, of variables. In this paper we examine some of the main ideas along this passage that have led to our current capabilities. Given the depth of the literature in this field, it is impossible to do this in any comprehensive way; rather we focus on techniques with consistent demonstrated efficiency in available solvers. For the most part, we focus on techniques within the basic DPLL search framework, but also briefly describe other approaches and look at some possible future research directions.

1. Introduction

Given a propositional formula, determining whether there exists a variable assignment such that the formula evaluates to true is called the Boolean Satisfiability Problem, commonly abbreviated as SAT. SAT has seen much theoretical interest as the canonical NP-complete problem [1]. Given its NP-Completeness, it is very unlikely that there exists any polynomial algorithm for SAT. However, NP-Completeness does not exclude the possibility of finding algorithms that are efficient enough for solving many interesting SAT instances. These instances arise from many diverse areas - many practical problems in AI planning [2], circuit testing [3], software verification [4] can be formulated as SAT instances. This has motivated the research in practically efficient SAT solvers.

This research has resulted in the development of several SAT algorithms that have seen practical success. These algorithms are based on various principles such as resolution [5], search [6], local search and random walk [7], Binary Decision Diagrams [8], Stålmarck's algorithm [9], and others. Gu *et al.* [10] provide an excellent review of many of the algorithms developed thus far. Some of these algorithms are **complete**, while others are **stochastic** methods. For a given SAT instance, complete SAT solvers can either find a solution (i.e. a satisfying variable assignment) or prove that no solution exists. Stochastic methods, on the other hand, cannot prove the instance to be unsatisfiable even though they may be able to find a solution for certain kinds of satisfiable instances quickly. Stochastic methods have

A. Voronkov (Ed.): CADE-18, LNAI 2392, pp. 295–313, 2002.

applications in domains such as AI planning [2] and FPGA routing [11], where instances are likely to be satisfiable and proving unsatisfiability is not required. However, for many other domains (especially verification problems e.g. [4, 12]), the primary task is to prove unsatisfiability of the instances. For these, complete SAT solvers are a requirement.

In recent years search-based algorithms based on the well-known Davis-Logemann-Loveland algorithm [6] (sometimes called the DPLL algorithm for historical reasons) are emerging as some of the most efficient methods for complete SAT solvers. Researchers have been working on DPLL-based SAT solvers for about forty years. In the last ten years we have seen significant growth and success in SAT solver research based on the DPLL framework. Earlier SAT solvers based on DPLL include Tableau (NTAB) [13], POSIT [14], 2cl [15] and CSAT [16] among others. They are still appearing occasionally in the literature for performance comparison reasons. In the mid 1990's, Silva and Sakallah [17], and Bayardo and Schrag [18] proposed to augment the original DPLL algorithm with non-chronological backtracking and conflict-driven learning. These techniques greatly improved the efficiency of the DPLL algorithm for structured (in contrast to randomly generated) SAT instances. Many practical applications emerged (e.g. [4, 11, 12]), which pushed these solvers to their limits and provided strong motivation for finding even more efficient algorithms. This led to a new generation of solvers such as SATO [19], Chaff [20], and BerkMin [21] which pay a lot of attention to optimizing various aspects of the DPLL algorithm. The results are some very efficient SAT solvers that can often solve SAT instances generated from industrial applications with tens of thousands or even millions of variables. On another front, solvers such as satz [22] and cnfs [23] keep pushing the ability to tackle hard random 3-SAT instances. These solvers, though very efficient on random instances, are typically not competitive on structured instances generated from real applications.

A DPLL-based SAT solver is a relatively small piece of software. Many of the solvers mentioned above have only a few thousand lines of code (these solvers are mostly written in C or C++, for efficiency reasons). However, the algorithms involved are quite complex and a lot of attention is focused on various aspects of the solver such as coding, data structures, choosing algorithms and heuristics, and parameter tuning. Even though the overall framework is well understood and people have been working on it for years, it may appear that we have reached a plateau in terms of what can be achieved in practice – however we feel that many open questions still exist and present many research opportunities.

In this paper we chart the journey from the original basic DPLL framework through the introduction of efficient techniques within this framework culminating at current state-of-the-art solvers. Given the depth of literature in this field, it is impossible to do this in any comprehensive way; rather, we focus on techniques with consistent demonstrated efficiency in available solvers. While for the most part, we focus on techniques within the basic DPLL search framework, we will also briefly describe other approaches and look at some possible future research directions.

2. The Basic DPLL Framework

Even though there were many developments pre-dating them, the original algorithm for solving SAT is often attributed to Davis and Putnam for proposing a resolution-based algorithm for Boolean SAT in 1960 [5]. The original algorithm proposed suffers from the problem of memory explosion. Therefore, Davis, Logemann and Loveland [6] proposed a modified version that used search instead of resolution to limit the memory required for the solver. This algorithm is often referred to as the DPLL algorithm. It can be argued that intrinsically these two algorithms are tightly related because search (i.e. branching on variables) can be regarded as a special type of resolution. However, in the future discussion we will regard search-based algorithms as their own class and distinguish them from explicit resolution algorithms.

For the efficiency of the solver, the propositional formula instance is usually presented in a Product of Sum form, usually called a **Conjunctive Normal Form (CNF)**. It is not a limitation to require the instance to be presented in CNF. There exist polynomial algorithms (e.g. [24]) to transform any propositional formula into a CNF formula that has the same satisfiability as the original one. In the discussions that follow, we will assume that the problem is presented in CNF. A SAT instance in CNF is a logical **and** of one or more **clauses**, where each clause is a logical **or** of one or more **literals**. A literal is either the positive or the negative occurrence of a **variable**.

A propositional formula in CNF has some nice properties that can help prune the search space and speed up the search process. To satisfy a CNF formula, each clause must be satisfied individually. If there exists a clause in the formula that has all its literals assigned value 0, then the current variable assignment or any variable assignment that contains this will not be able to satisfy the formula. A clause that has all its literals assigned to value 0 is called a **conflicting clause**.

```
DPLL(formula, assignment) {
  necessary = deduction(formula, assignment);
  new_asgnmnt = union(necessary, assignment);
  if (is_satisfied(formula, new_asgnmnt))
    return SATISFIABLE;
  else if (is_conflicting(formula, new_asgnmnt))
    return CONFLICT;
  var = choose_free_variable(formula, new_asgnmnt);
  asgn1 = union(new_asgnmnt, assign(var, 1));
  if (DPLL(formula, asgn1)==SATISFIABLE)
    return SATISFIABLE;
  else {
    asgn2 = union (new_asgnmnt, assign(var, 0));
    return DPLL(formula, asgn2);
  }
}
```

Fig. 1. The recursive description of DPLL algorithm

Traditionally the DPLL algorithm is written in a recursive manner as shown in Fig. 1. Function `DPLL()` is called with a formula and a set of variable assignments. Function `deduction()` will return with a set of the necessary variable assignments that can be deduced from the existing variable assignments. The recursion will end if the formula is either satisfied (i.e. evaluates to 1 or **true**) or unsatisfied (i.e. evaluates to 0 or **false**) under the current variable assignment. Otherwise, the algorithm will choose an unassigned variable from the formula and branch on it for both phases. The solution process begins with calling the function `DPLL()` with an empty set of variable assignments.

In [25], the authors generalized many of the actual implementations of various solvers based on DPLL and rewrote it in an iterative manner as shown in Fig. 2. The algorithm described in Fig. 2 is an improvement of algorithm in Fig. 1 as it allows the solver to backtrack non-chronologically, as we will see in the following sections. Different solvers based on DPLL differ mainly in the detailed implementation of each of the functions shown in Fig. 2. We will use the framework of Fig. 2 as the foundation for our discussions that follow.

The algorithm described in Fig. 2 is a branch and search algorithm. Initially, none of the variables is assigned a value. We call unassigned variables **free** variables. First the solver will do some preprocessing on the instance to be solved, done by function `preprocess()` in Fig. 2. If preprocessing cannot determine the outcome, the main loop begins with a branch on a free variable by assigning it a value. We call this operation a **decision** on a variable, and the variable will have a **decision level** associated with it, starting from 1 and incremented with subsequent decisions. This is done by function `decide_next_branch()` in Fig. 2. After the branch, the problem is simplified as a result of this decision and its consequences. The function `deduce()` performs some reasoning to determine variable assignments that are needed for the problem to be satisfiable given the current set of decisions. Variables that are assigned as a consequence of this deduction after a branch will assume the same decision level as the decision variable. After the deduction, if all the clauses are satisfied, then the instance is satisfiable; if there exists a conflicting clause, then the

```
status = preprocess();
if (status!=UNKNOWN) return status;
while(1) {
  decide_next_branch();
  while (true) {
    status = deduce();
    if (status == CONFLICT) {
      blevel = analyze_conflict();
      if (blevel == 0)
        return UNSATISFIABLE;
      else backtrack(blevel);
    }
    else if (status == SATISFIABLE)
      return SATISFIABLE;
    else break;
  }
}
```

Fig. 2. The iterative description of DPLL algorithm

current branch chosen cannot lead to a satisfying assignment, so the solver will backtrack (i.e. undo certain branches). Which decision level to backtrack to is determined by the function `analyze_conflict()`. Backtrack to level 0 indicates that even without any branching, the instance is still unsatisfiable. In that case, the solver will declare that the instance is unsatisfiable. Within the function `analyze_conflict()`, the solver may do some analysis and record some information from the current conflict in order to prune the search space for the future. This process is called **conflict-driven learning**. If the instance is neither satisfied nor conflicting under the current variable assignments, the solver will choose another variable to branch and repeat the process.

3. The Components of a DPLL SAT Solver

In this section of the paper, we discuss each of the components of a DPLL SAT solver. Each of these components has been the subject of much scrutiny over the years. This section focuses on the main lessons learnt in this process.

3.1 The Branching Heuristics

Branching occurs in the function `decide_next_branch()` in Fig. 2. When no more deduction is possible, the function will choose one variable from all the free variables and assign it to a value. The importance of choosing good branching variables is well known - different branching heuristics may produce drastically different sized search trees for the same basic algorithm, thus significantly affect the efficiency of the solver. Over the years many different branching heuristics have been proposed by different researchers. Not surprisingly, comparative experimental evaluations have also been done (e.g. [26, 27]).

Early branching heuristics such as Bohm's Heuristic (reported in [28]), Maximum Occurrences on Minimum sized clauses (MOM) (e.g. [14]), and Jeroslow-Wang [29] can be regarded as greedy algorithms that try to make the next branch generate the largest number of implications or satisfy most clauses. All these heuristics use some functions to estimate the effect of branching on each free variable, and choose the variable that has the maximum function value. These heuristics work well for certain classes of instances. However, all of the functions are based on the statistics of the clause database such as clause length etc. These statistics, though useful for random SAT instances, usually do not capture relevant information about structured problems.

In [26], the author proposed the use of literal count heuristics. Literal count heuristics count the number of unresolved (i.e. unsatisfied) clauses in which a given variable appears in either phase. In particular, the author found that the heuristic that chooses the variable with dynamic largest combined sum (DLIS) of literal counts in both phases gives quite good results for the benchmarks tested. Notice that the counts are state-dependent in the sense that different variable assignments will give different counts. The reason is because whether a clause is unresolved (unsatisfied) depends on the current variable assignment. Because the count is state-dependent, each time the function `decide_next_branch()` is called, the counts for all the free variables need to be recalculated.

As the solvers become more and more efficient, calculating counts for branching dominates the run time. Therefore, more efficient and effective branching heuristics are needed. In [20], the authors proposed the heuristic called Variable State Independent Decaying Sum (VSIDS). VSIDS keeps a score for each phase of a variable. Initially, the scores are the number of occurrences of a literal in the initial problem. Because modern SAT solvers have a learning mechanism, clauses are added to the clause database as the search progresses. VSIDS increases the score of a variable by a constant whenever an added clause contains the variable. Moreover, as the search progresses, periodically all the scores are divided by a constant number. In effect, the VSIDS score is a literal occurrence count with higher weight on the more recently added clauses. VSIDS will choose the free variable with the highest combined score to branch. Experiments show that VSIDS is quite competitive compared with other branching heuristics on the number of branches needed to solve a problem. Because VSIDS is state independent (i.e. scores are not dependent on the variable assignments), it is cheap to maintain. Experiments show that the decision procedure using VSIDS takes a very small percentage of the total run time even for problems with millions of variables.

More recently, [21] proposed another decision scheme that pushes the idea of VSIDS further. Like VSIDS, the decision strategy is trying to decide on the variables that are "active recently". In VSIDS, the activity of a variable is captured by the score that is related to the literal's occurrence. In [21], the authors propose to capture the activity by conflicts. More precisely, when a conflict occurs, all the literals in the clauses that are responsible for the conflict will have their score increased. A clause is responsible for a conflict if it is involved in the resolution process of generating the learned clauses (described in the following sections). In VSIDS, the focus on "recent" is captured by decaying the score periodically. In [21], the scores are also decayed periodically. Moreover, the decision heuristic will limit the decision variable to be among the literals that occur in the last added clause that is unresolved. The experiments seem to indicate that the new decision scheme is more robust compared with VSIDS on the benchmarks tested.

In other efforts, satz [22] proposed the use of look-ahead heuristics for branching; and cnfs [23] proposed the use of backbone-directed heuristics for branching. They share the common feature that they both seem to be quite effective on difficult random problems. However, they are also quite expensive compared with VSIDS. Random SAT problems are usually much harder than structured problems of the same size. Current solvers can only attack hard random 3-SAT problems with several hundred variables. Therefore, the instances regarded as hard for random SAT is generally much smaller in size than the instances considered hard for structured problems. Thus, while it may be practical to apply these expensive heuristics to the smaller random problems, their overhead tends to be unacceptable for the larger well-structured problems.

3.2 The Deduction Algorithm

Function deduce() serves the purpose of pruning the search space by "look ahead". When a branch variable is assigned a value, the entire clause database is simplified. Function deduce() needs to determine the consequences of the last decision to make the instance satisfiable, and may return three status values. If the instance is satisfied under the current variable assignment, it will return SATISFIABLE; if the instance contains a conflicting clause, it will return CONFLICT; otherwise, it will return UNKNOWN and the solver will continue to branch. There are various mechanisms with different deduction power and run time costs for the deduce function. The correctness of the algorithm will not be affected as long as the deduction rules incorporated are valid (e.g. it will not return SATISFIABLE when the instance contains a conflicting clause under the assignment). However, different deduction rules, or even different implementations of the same rule, can significantly affect the efficiency of the solver.

Over the years several different deduction mechanisms have been proposed. However, it seems that the **unit clause rule** [6] is the most efficient one because it requires relatively little computational power but can prune large search spaces. The unit clause rule states that for a certain clause, if all but one of its literals has been assigned the value 0, then the remaining (unassigned) literal must be assigned the value 1 for this clause to be satisfied, which is essential for the formula to be satisfied. Such clauses are called **unit clauses**, and the unassigned literal in a unit clause is called a **unit literal**. The process of assigning the value 1 to all unit literals is called **unit propagation,** or sometimes called **Boolean Constraint Propagation (BCP)**. Almost all modern SAT solvers incorporate this rule in the deduction process. In a SAT solver, BCP usually takes the most significant part of the run time. Therefore, its efficiency is directly related to the implementation of the BCP engine.

3.2.1 BCP Mechanisms

In a SAT solver, the BCP engine's function is to detect unit clauses and conflicting clauses after a variable assignment. The BCP engine is the most important part of a SAT solver and usually dictates the data structure and organization of the solver.

A simple and intuitive implementation for BCP is to keep counters for each clause. This scheme is attributed to Crawford and Auton [13] by [30]. Similar schemes are subsequently employed in many solvers such as GRASP [25], rel_sat [18], satz [22] etc. For example, in GRASP [25], each clause keeps two counters, one for the number of value 1 literals in the clause and the other for the number of value 0 literals in the clause. Each variable has two lists that contain all the clauses where that variable appears as a positive and negative literal, respectively. When a variable is assigned a value, all the clauses that contain this literal will have their counters updated. If a clause's value 0 count becomes equal to the total number of literals in the clause, then it is a conflicting clause. If a clause's value 0 count is one less than the total number of literals in the clause and the value 1 count is 0, then the clause is a unit clause. A counter-based BCP engine is easy to understand and implement, but this scheme is not the most efficient one. If the instance has m clauses and n variables, and on average each clause has l literals, then whenever a variable gets assigned, on the average $l\,m\,/\,n$ counters need to be updated. On backtracking from a conflict, we need to undo the counter assignments for the variables unassigned during the backtracking. Each undo for a variable assignment will also update $l\,m\,/\,n$ counters on average. Modern solvers usually incorporate learning mechanisms in the search process (described in the next sections), and learned clauses often have many literals. Therefore, the average clause length l is quite large, thus making a counter-based BCP engine relatively slow.

In [30], the authors of the solver SATO proposed the use of another mechanism for BCP using head/tail lists. In this mechanism, each clause has two pointers associated with it, called the head and tail pointer respectively. A clause stores all its literals in an array. Initially, the head pointer points to the first literal of the clause (i.e. beginning of the array), and the tail pointer points to the last literal of the clause (i.e. end of the array). Each variable keeps four linked lists that contain pointer to clauses. The linked lists for the variable v are clause_of_pos_head(v), clause_of_neg_head(v), clause_of_pos_tail(v) and clause_of_neg_tail(v). Each of these lists contains the pointers to the clauses that have their head/tail literal in positive/negative phases of variable v. If v is assigned with the value 1, clause_of_pos_head(v) and clause_of_pos_tail(v) will be ignored. For each clause C in clause_of_neg_head(v), the solver will search for a literal that does not evaluate to 1 from the position of the head literal of C to the position of the tail literal of C. Notice the head literal of C must be a literal corresponding to v in negative phase. During the search process, four cases may occur:

1)   If during the search we first encounter a literal that evaluates to 1, then the clause is satisfied, we need to do nothing.

2)   If during the search we first encounter a literal l that is free and l is not the tail literal, then we remove C from clause_of_neg_head(v) and add C to head list of the variable corresponding to l. We refer to this operation as moving the head literal, because in essence the head pointer is moved from its original position to the position of l.

3)   If all literals in between these two pointers are assigned value 0, but the tail literal is unassigned, then the clause is a unit clause, and the tail literal is the unit literal for this clause.

4)   If all literals in between these two pointers and the tail literal are assigned value 0, then the clause is a conflicting clause.

Similar actions are performed for clause_of_neg_tail(v), only the search is in the reverse direction (i.e. from tail to head).

Head/tail list method is faster than the counter-based scheme because when the variable is assigned value 1, the clauses that contain the positive literals of this clause will not be visited at all and vice-versa. As each clause has only two pointers, whenever a variable is assigned a value, the status of only m/n clauses needs to be updated on the average, if we assume head/tail literals are distributed evenly in either phase. Even though the work needed to be done for each update is different from the counter-based mechanism, in general head/tail mechanism is still much faster.

For both the counter-based algorithm and the head/tail list-based algorithm, undoing a variable's assignment during backtrack has about the same computational complexity as assigning the variable. In [20], the authors of the solver Chaff proposed another BCP algorithm called 2-literal watching. Similar to the head/tail list algorithm, 2-literal watching also has two special literals for each clause called *watched literals*. Each variable has two lists containing pointers to all the watched literals corresponding to it in either phase. We denote the lists for variable v as pos_watched(v) and neg_watched(v). In contrast to the head/tail list scheme in SATO, there is no imposed order on the two pointers within a clause, and each of the pointers can move in either direction. Initially the watched literals are free. When a variable v is assigned value 1, for each literal p pointed to by a pointer in the list of neg_watched(v) (notice p must be a literal of v with negative phase), the solver will search for a literal l in the clause containing p that is not set to 0. There are four cases that may occur during the search:

1) If there exists such a literal l and it is not the other watched literal, then we remove pointer to p from neg_watched(v), and add pointer to l to the watched list of the variable corresponding to l. We refer to this operation as moving the watched literal, because in essence one of the watched pointers is moved from its original position to the position of l.

2) If the only such l is the other watched literal and it is free, then the clause is a unit clause, with the other watched literal being the unit literal.

3) If the only such l is the other watched literal and it evaluates to 1, then we need to do nothing.

4) If all literals in the clause is assigned value 0 and no such l exists, then the clause is a conflicting clause.

2-literal watching has the same advantage as the head/tail list mechanism compared with the literal counting scheme. Moreover, unlike the other two mechanisms, undoing a variable assignment during backtrack in the 2-literal watching scheme takes constant time. This is because the two watched literals are the last to be assigned to 0, so as a result, any backtracking will make sure that the literals being watched are either unassigned, or assigned to one. Thus, no action is required to update the pointers for the literals being watched. Therefore, it is significantly faster than both counter-based and head/tail mechanisms for BCP. In Fig. 3, we show a comparison of 2-literal watching and head/tail list mechanism.

In [31], the authors examined the mechanisms mentioned above and introduced some new deduction data structures and mechanisms. In particular, the experiments suggest that the mechanism called Head/Tail list with Literal Sifting actually outperforms the 2-literal watching mechanism for BCP. However, the experiments are carried out in a framework implemented in Java. The authors admit that it may not represent the actual performance if implemented in C/C++.

3.2.2 Other Deduction Mechanisms

Besides the unit clause rule, there are other rules that can be incorporated into a deduction engine. In this section, we briefly discuss some of them. We want to point out that though many of the deduction mechanisms have been shown to work on certain classes of SAT instances, unlike the unit clause rule, none of them seems to work without deteriorating the overall performance of the SAT solver for general SAT instances.

One of the most widely known rules for deduction is the **pure literal rule** [6]. The pure literal rule states that if a variable only occurs in a single phase in all the unresolved clauses, then it can be assigned with a value such that the literal of the variable in that phase evaluates to 1. Whether a variable satisfies the pure literal rule is expensive to detect during the actual solving process, and the consensus seems to be that incorporating the pure literal rule will generally slow down the solving process for most of the benchmarks encountered.

Another explored deduction mechanism is equivalence reasoning. In particular, eqsatz [32] incorporated equivalence reasoning into the satz [22] solver and found that it is effective on some particular classes of benchmarks. In that work, the

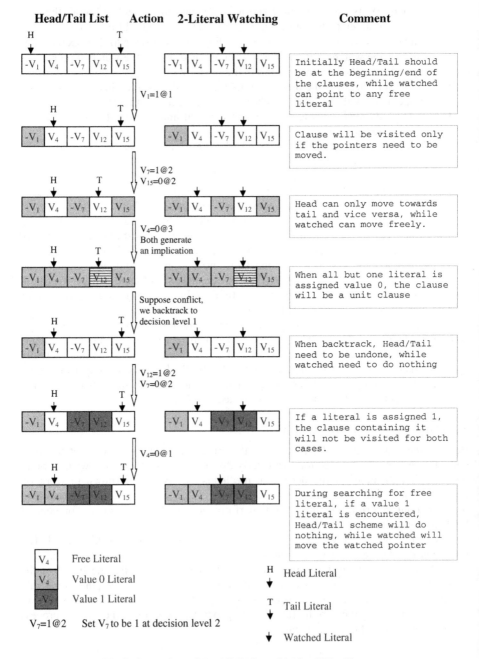

Fig. 3. Comparison of Head/Tail List and 2-Literal Watching

equivalence reasoning is accomplished by a pattern-matching scheme for equivalence clauses. A related deduction mechanism was proposed in [33]. There, the authors propose to include more patterns in the matching process for simplification purpose in deduction.

The unit literal rule basically guarantees that all the unit clauses are consistent with each other. We can also require that all the 2 literal clauses be consistent with each other and so on. Researchers have been exploring this idea in the deduction process in works such as [34, 35]. In particular, these approaches maintain a transitive closure of all the 2 literal clauses. However, the overhead of maintaining this information seems to far outweigh any benefit gained from them on the average.

Recursive Learning [36] is another reasoning technique originally proposed in the context of learning with a logic circuit representation of a formula. Subsequent research [37] has proposed to incorporate this technique in SAT solvers and found that it works quite well for some benchmarks generated from combinational circuit equivalence checking problems.

3.3 Conflict Analysis and Learning

When a conflicting clause is encountered, the solver needs to backtrack and undo the decisions. Conflict analysis is the procedure that finds the reason for a conflict and tries to resolve it. It tells the SAT solver that there exists no solution for the problem in a certain search space, and indicates a new search space to continue the search.

The original DPLL algorithm proposed the simplest conflict analysis method. For each decision variable, the solver keeps a flag indicating whether it has been tried in both phases (i.e. flipped) or not. When a conflict occurs, the conflict analysis procedure looks for the decision variable with the highest decision level that has not been flipped, marks it flipped, undoes all the assignments between that decision level and current decision level, and then tries the other phase for the decision variable. This method is called **chronological backtracking** because it always tries to undo the last decision that is not flipped. Chronological backtracking works well for random generate SAT instances and is employed in some SAT solvers (e.g satz [22]).

For structured problems (which is usually the case for problems generated from real world applications), chronological backtracking is generally not efficient in pruning the search space. More advanced conflict analysis engines will analyze the conflicting clauses encountered and figure out the direct reason for the conflict. This method will usually backtrack to an earlier decision level than the last unflipped decision. Therefore, it is called **non-chronological backtracking**. During the conflict analysis process, information about the current conflict may be recorded as clauses and added to the original database. The added clauses, though redundant in the sense that they will not change the satisfiability of the original problem, can often help to prune search space in the future. This mechanism is called **conflict-directed learning**. Such learned clauses are called **conflict clauses** as opposed to **conflicting clauses**, which refer to clauses that generate conflicts.

Non-chronological backtracking, sometimes referred to as **conflict-directed backjumping**, was proposed first in the Constraint Satisfaction Problem (CSP) domain (e.g. [38]). This, together with conflict-directed learning, were first incorporated into a SAT solver by Silva and Sakallah in GRASP [25], and by Bayardo and Schrag in rel_sat [18]. These techniques are essential for efficient solving of structured problems. Many solvers such as SATO [19] and Chaff [20] have incorporated similar technique in the solving process.

Previously, learning and non-chronological backtracking have been discussed by analyzing implication graphs (e.g. [17, 39]). Here we will formulate learning as an alternate but equivalent resolution process and discuss different schemes in this framework.

Researchers have adapted the conflict analysis engine to some deduction rules other than the unit clause rule in previous work (e.g. [33, 37]). However, because the unit clause rule is usually the only rule that is incorporated in most SAT solvers, we will describe the learning algorithm that works with such a deduction engine. In such a solver, when a variable is implied by a unit clause, the clause is called the **antecedent** of the variable. Because the unit clause rule is the only rule in the deduction engine, every implied variable will have an antecedent. Decision variables, on the other case, have no antecedents.

In conflict driven learning, the learned clauses are generated by resolution. Resolution is a process to generate a clause from two clauses analogous to the process of **consensus** in the logic optimization domain (e.g. [40]). Resolution is given by

$$(x + y)(y' + z) \bullet (x + y)(y' + z)(x + z)$$

The term $(x + z)$ is called the **resolvent** of clause $(x + y)$ and $(y' + z)$. Because of this, we have

$$(x + y)(y' + z) \bullet (x+z)$$

Similar to the well-known consensus law (e.g. [40]), the resulting clause of resolution between two clauses is redundant with respect to the original clauses. Therefore, we can always generate clauses from original clause database by resolution and add the generated clause back to the clause database without changing the satisfiability of the original formula. However, randomly choosing two clauses and adding the resolvent to the clause database will not generally help the solving process. Conflict-driven learning is a way to generate learned clauses with some direction in the resolution process.

The pseudo-code for conflict analysis is shown in Fig. 4. Whenever a conflicting clause is encountered, `analyze_conflict()` will be called. Function `choose_literal()` will choose a literal from the clause. Function `resolve(cl1, cl2, var)` will return a clause that contains all the literals in cl1 and cl2 except for the literals that corresponds to variable var. Note that one of the input clauses to `resolve()` is a conflicting clause (i.e. all literals evaluate to 0), and the other is the antecedent of the variable *var* (i.e. all but one literal evaluate to 0). Therefore, the resulting clause will have all literals evaluating to 0, i.e. it will still be a conflicting clause.

The clause generation process will stop when some predefined stop criterion is met. In modern SAT solvers, the stop criterion is that the resulting clause be an **asserting clause**. A clause is asserting if the clause contains all value 0 literals; and among them only one is assigned at current decision level. After backtracking, this clause will become a unit clause and force the literal to assume another value (i.e. evaluate to 1), thus bringing the search to a new space. We will call the decision level of the literal with the second highest decision level in an asserting clause the **asserting level** of that clause. The asserting clause is a unit clause at its asserting decision level.

```
analyze_conflict(){
    cl = find_conflicting_clause();
    while (!stop_criterion_met(cl)) {
        lit = choose_literal(cl);
        var = variable_of_literal( lit );
        ante = antecedent( var );
        cl = resolve(cl, ante, var);
    }
    add_clause_to_database(cl);
    back_dl = clause_asserting_level(cl);
    return back_dl;
}
```

Fig. 4. Generating Learned Clause by Resolution

In addition to the above asserting clause requirement, different learning schemes may have some additional requirements. Different learning schemes differ in their stop criterion and the way to choose literals. Notice the stop criterion can always be met if function choose_literal() always chooses the literal that is assigned last in the clause. If that is the case, the resolution process will always resolve the conflicting clause with the antecedent of the variable that is assigned last in the clause. After a certain number of calls to resolve(), there will always be a time when the variable that is assigned last in the clause is the decision variable of the current decision level. At this time, the resulting clause is guaranteed to be an asserting clause. The SAT solver rel_sat [18] actually uses this stop criterion, i.e. it requires that the variable that has the highest decision level in the resulting clause be a decision variable. The literal corresponding to this variable will be a unit literal after backtracking, resulting in essentially flipping the decision variable.

In [39], the authors discussed a scheme called the FirstUIP scheme. The FirstUIP scheme is quite similar to the rel_sat scheme but the stop criterion is that it will stop when the *first* asserting clause is encountered. In [17], the authors of GRASP use a similar scheme as the FirstUIP, but add extra clauses other than the asserting clause into the database. If function choose_literal() does not choose literals in reversed chronological order, then extra mechanisms are needed to guarantee that the stop criterion can be met. Some of the schemes discussed in [39] may need function choose_literal() to choose literals that are not in the current decision level.

Different learning schemes affect the SAT solver's efficiency greatly. Experiments in [39] show that among all the discussed schemes, FirstUIP seems to be the best on the benchmarks tested. Therefore, recent SAT solvers (e.g. Chaff [20]) often employ this scheme as the default conflict-driven learning scheme.

Conflict-driven learning will add clauses to the clause database during the search process. Because added clauses are redundant, deleting some or all of them will not affect the correctness of the algorithm. In fact, the added clauses will slow down the deduction engine, and keeping all added clauses may need more memory for storage than the available memory. Therefore, it is often required for the solver to delete some of the less useful learned clauses and learned clauses that have too many literals. There are many heuristics to measure the usefulness of a learned clause. For example, rel_sat [18] proposes to use relevance to measure a clause's usefulness, while BerkMin [21] use the number of conflicts that involve this clause in the history to measure a clause's usefulness. These measures seem to work reasonably well.

3.4 Data Structure for Storing Clause Database

Current state-of-the-art SAT solvers often need to solve instances that are quite large in size. Some instances generated from circuit verification problems may contain millions of variables and several million clauses. Moreover, during the SAT solving process, learned clauses are generated for each conflict encountered and may further increase the dataset size. Therefore, efficient data structures for storing the clauses are needed.

Most commonly, clauses are stored in a linear way (sometimes called **sparse matrix representation**), i.e. each clause occupies its own space and no overlap exists between clauses. Therefore, the dataset size is linear in the number of literals in the clause database. Early SAT solvers (e.g. GRASP [25], rel_sat [18]) use pointer heavy data structures such as linked lists and array of pointers pointing to structures to store the clause database. Pointer heavy data structures, though convenient for manipulating the clause database (i.e. adding/deleting clauses), are not memory efficient and usually cause a lot of cache misses during the solving process because of lack of access locality. Chaff [20] uses a data structure that stores clause data in a large array. Because arrays are not as flexible as linked lists, some additional garbage collection code is needed when clauses are deleted. The advantage of the array data structure is that it is very efficient in memory utilization. Moreover, because an array occupies contiguous memory space, access locality is increased. Experiments shows that the array data structure has a big advantage compared with linked lists in terms of cache misses that translates to substantial speed-up in the solving process.

Researchers have proposed schemes other than sparse matrix representation for storing clauses. In [41], the authors of the solver SATO proposed the use of a data structure called **trie** to store clauses. A trie is a ternary tree. Each internal node in the trie structure is a variable index, and its three children edges are labeled Pos, Neg, and DC, for positive, negative, and don't care, respectively. A leaf node in a trie is either True or False. Each path from root of the trie to a True leaf represents a clause. A trie is said to be ordered if for every internal node V, Parent(V) has a smaller variable index than the index of variable V. The ordered trie structure has the nice property of being able to detect duplicate and tail subsumed clauses of a database quickly. A clause is said to be tail subsumed by another clause if its first portion of the literals (a prefix) is also a clause in the clause database. For example, (a + b + c) is tail subsumed by (a + b). Fig. 5 shows a simple clause database represented in a trie structure.

An ordered trie has obvious similarities with Binary Decision Diagrams. This has naturally led to the exploration of decision diagram style set representations. In [42] and [43], the authors have experimented with using Zero-suppressed Binary Decision Diagrams (ZBDDs) [44] to represent the clause database. A ZBDD representation of the clause database can detect not only tail subsumption but also head subsumption. Both authors report significant compression of the clause database for certain classes of problems.

Based on current experimental data it does not seem that the data compression advantages of the trie and ZBDD data structures are sufficient to justify the additional maintenance overhead of these data structures compared to the sparse matrix representation.

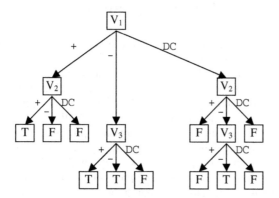

Fig. 5. A trie data structure representing clauses (V_1+V_2) $(V_1'+V_3)$ $(V_1'+V_3')(V_2'+V_3')$

3.5 Preprocess, Restart, and Other Techniques

Preprocess aims at simplifying the instances before the regular solving begins in order to speed up the solving process. Usually the preprocessor of a SAT solver is just an extra deduction mechanism applied at the beginning of the search. Because the preprocessor will only be applied once in the solving process, it is usually possible to incorporate some deduction rules that are too expensive to be applied at every node of the search tree. The preprocessor can be applied on-line (within the solver) or off-line (it produces an equivalent instance to be fed to a solver). In [45], the authors give an overview of some of the existing preprocessing techniques and find that the result of applying simplification techniques before the regular search is actually mixed.

The time required for solving similar SAT instances often varies greatly for complete algorithms. Two problems that are exactly the same except for the variable order may require totally different times to solve by a certain SAT solver (e.g. one can be solved in seconds while the other takes days). In [46], the authors proposed to use **random restart** to cope with this phenomenon. Random restart randomly throws away the already searched space and starts from scratch. This technique is applied in modern SAT solvers such as Chaff [20] and BerkMin [21]. In these cases, when restart is invoked, even though the current search tree is abandoned, because the solver still keeps some of the learned clauses, the previous search effort is not totally lost. Experiments show that random restarts can increase the robustness of certain SAT solvers.

Researchers have been extending the randomization idea of random restart to other aspects of the SAT solving process as well. For example, portfolio design [47] aims at using different solving strategies during one solving process in order to make the solver robust. Some researchers [48] also propose to randomize backtracking. All in all, it seems that randomization is quite important because of the heavy tail [49] nature of SAT solving process.

4. Other Techniques Used in SAT Solvers

In this section, we briefly discuss some of the other techniques used to solve SAT problems besides the basic DPLL search.

The original Davis Putnam algorithm [5] was based on resolution. A well-known problem of the resolution-based algorithm is that the solver tends to blow up in memory. Because of this, resolution based algorithm is seldom employed in modern SAT solvers. In [42], the authors propose the use of ZBDDs to represent clauses in a resolution-based solver and utilize the compression power of decision diagrams to control the memory blowup. Their experiment shows that for certain classes of SAT problems, the resolution-based approach shows very good results.

Stalmärck's algorithm [9] is a patented proprietary algorithm for solving SAT. Stalmärck's algorithm use breath-first search in contrast to the depth-first search employed by DPLL. There are commercial implementations of SAT solvers based on this algorithm [50]. HeerHugo [51] is a publicly available solver that claims to be using an algorithm similar to the Stalmärk's algorithm.

Another approach is to use stochastic algorithms. Stochastic algorithms cannot prove a SAT instance to be unsatisfiable. However, for some hard satisfiable instances, stochastic methods may find solutions very quickly. Currently, two of the more successful approaches to the stochastic method are random walk based algorithms such as walksat [7] and Discrete Lagrangian-Based global search methods such as DLM [52].

For more about other SAT solving techniques, we refer the readers to a survey[10].

5. Conclusions and Future Works

In this paper, we briefly discussed some of the techniques employed in modern Boolean Satisfiability solvers. In particular, we concentrated on the procedure based on the DPLL search algorithm. In recent years, SAT solvers based on DPLL search have made phenomenal progress. Efficient SAT solvers such as Chaff [20] are deployed in industrial strength applications for hardware verification and debugging. In these environments, the SAT solver routinely encounters instances with thousands or even millions of variables. Therefore, it is of great importance to increase the capacity and efficiency of the SAT solver.

Even though researchers have been working on SAT engines for quite a long time, there is still a lot of work that remains to be done. First of all, the overall understanding of SAT instances is still quite limited. For example, though there exist some rough ideas about the difficulty of SAT problems (e.g. [53, 54]), it is still not clear how can we estimate the hardness of a given problem without actually solving it. Experimental evaluation of different SAT solving algorithms is more like an art than a science because it is easy to tune a solver to a given set of benchmarks, but the parameters may not work for the same benchmarks with some simple permutation (e.g.[55]). On the application side, currently most of the applications use SAT solvers as blackboxes and no interaction is possible between the applications and the SAT solvers. Application specific knowledge can help a lot in the solving process as demonstrated in [56]. For a particular application, custom implementation of a SAT solver may also be helpful (e.g. [57]). All in all, we believe there are still many research topics to be explored. As more and more applications utilize SAT solvers as deduction and reasoning engine, we believe many new algorithms will emerge and push the envelope for efficient implementations even further.

Acknowledgments. The authors would like to thank Dr. Aarti Gupta for suggestions and help in improving the paper.

References

[1]   S. A. Cook, "The complexity of theorem-proving procedures," presented at Third Annual ACM Symposium on Theory of Computing, 1971.

[2]   H. Kautz and B. Selman, "Planning as Satisfiability," presented at European Conference on Artificial Intelligence(ECAI-92), 1992.

[3]   P. Stephan, R. Brayton, and A. Sangiovanni-Vencentelli, "Combinational Test Generation Using Satisfiability," *IEEE Transactions on Computer-Aided Design of Integrated Circuits and Systems*, vol. 15, pp. 1167–1176, 1996.

[4]   D. Jackson and M. Vaziri, "Finding Bugs with a Constraint Solver," presented at International Symposium on Software Testing and Analysis, Portland, OR, 2000.

[5]   M. Davis and H. Putnam, "A computing procedure for quantification theory," *Journal of ACM*, vol. 7, pp. 201-215, 1960.

[6]   M. Davis, G. Logemann, and D. Loveland, "A machine program for theorem proving," *Communications of the ACM*, vol. 5, pp. 394-397, 1962.

[7]   B. Selman, H. Kautz, and B. Cohen, "Local Search Strategies for Satisfiability Testing," in *Cliques, Coloring, and Satisfiability: Second DIMACS Implementation Challenge, DIMACS Series in Discrete Mathematics and Theoretical Computer Science*, vol. 26, D. S. Johnson and M. A. Trick, Eds.: American Methematical Society, 1996.

[8]   R. E. Bryant, "Graph-Based Algorithms for Boolean Function Manipulation," *IEEE Transactions on Computers*, vol. C-35, pp. 677–691, 1986.

[9]   G. Stålmarck, "A system for determining prepositional logic theorems by applying values and rules to triplets that are generated from a formula." US Patent N 5 27689, 1995.

[10]   J. Gu, P. W. Purdom, J. Franco, and B. W. Wah, "Algorithms for the Satisfiability (SAT) Problem: A Survey," in *DIMACS Series in Discrete Mathematics and Theoretical Computer Science*: American Mathematical Society, 1997.

[11]   G.-J. Nam, K. A. Sakallah, and R. A. Rutenbar, "Satisfiability-Based Layout Revisited: Detailed Routing of Complex FPGAs Via Search-Based Boolean SAT," presented at ACM/SIGDA International Symposium on Field-Programmable Gate Arrays (FPGA'99), Monterey, California, 1999.

[12]   A. Biere, A. Cimatti, E. M. Clarke, and Y. Zhu, "Symbolic Model Checking without BDDs," presented at Tools and Algorithms for the Analysis and Construction of Systems (TACAS'99), 1999.

[13]   J. Crawford and L. Auton, "Experimental results on the cross-over point in satisfiability problems," presented at National Conference on Artificial Intelligence (AAAI), 1993.

[14]   J. W. Freeman, "Improvements to Propositional Satisfiability Search Algorithms," in *Ph.D. Thesis, Department of Computer and Information Science*: University of Pennsylvania, 1995.

[15]   A. V. Gelder and Y. K. Tsuji, "Satisfiability Testing with more Reasoning and Less guessing," in *Cliques, Coloring and Satisfiability: Second DIMACS Implementation Challenge, DIMACS Series in Discrete Mathematics and Theoretical Computer Science*, M. Trick, Ed.: American Mathematical Society, 1995.

[16]   O. Dubois, P. Andre, Y. Boufkhad, and J. Carlier, "SAT v.s. UNSAT," in *Cliques, Coloring and Satisfiability: Second DIMACS Implementation Challenge, DIMACS Series in Discrete Mathematics and Theoretical Computer Science*, D. S. Johnson and M. Trick, Eds., 1993.

[17]   J. P. Marques-Silva and K. A. Sakallah, "Conflict Analysis in Search Algorithms for Propositional Satisfiability," presented at IEEE International Conference on Tools with Artificial Intelligence, 1996.

[18]   R. Bayardo and R. Schrag, "Using CSP look-back techniques to solve real-world SAT instances," presented at National Conference on Artificial Intelligence (AAAI), 1997.

[19]   H. Zhang, "SATO: An efficient propositional prover," presented at International Conference on Automated Deduction (CADE), 1997.

[20]   M. Moskewicz, C. Madigan, Y. Zhao, L. Zhang, and S. Malik, "Chaff: Engineering an Efficient SAT Solver," presented at 39th Design Automation Conference, 2001.

[21]   E. Goldberg and Y. Novikov, "BerkMin: a Fast and Robust SAT-Solver," presented at Design Automation & Test in Europe (DATE 2002), 2002.

[22]   C. M. Li and Anbulagan, "Heuristics based on unit propagation for satisfiability problems," presented at the fifteenth International Joint Conference on Artificial Intelligence (IJCAI'97), Nagayo, Japan, 1997.

[23]   O. Dubois and G. Dequen, "A backbone-search heuristic for efficient solving of hard 3-SAT formulae," presented at International Joint Conference on Artificial Intelligence (IJCAI), 2001.

[24]   D. A. Plaisted and S. Greenbaum, "A Stucture-preserving Clause Form Translation," *Journal of Symbolic Computation*, vol. 2, pp. 293–304, 1986.

[25]   J. P. Marques-Silva and K. A. Sakallah, "GRASP – A New Search Algorithm for Satisfiability," presented at IEEE International Conference on Tools with Artificial Intelligence, 1996.

[26]   J. P. Marques-Silva, "The Impact of Branching Heuristics in Propositional Satisfiability Algorithms," presented at the 9th Portuguese Conference on Artificial Intelligence (EPIA), 1999.

[27]   J. N. Hooker and V. Vinay, "Branching rules for satisfiability," *Journal of Automated Reasoning*, vol. 15, pp. 359-383, 1995.

[28]   M. Buro and H. Kleine-Buning, "Report on a SAT competition," Technical Report, University of Paderborn 1992.

[29]   R. G. Jeroslow and J. Wang, "Solving propositional satisfiability problems," *Annals of Mathematics and Artificial Intelligence*, vol. 1, pp. 167–187, 1990.

[30]   H. Zhang and M. Stickel, "An efficient algorithm for unit-propagation," presented at International Symposium on Artificial Intelligence and Mathematics, Ft. Lauderdale, Florida, 1996.

[31]   I. Lynce and J. P. Marques-Silva, "Efficient data structures for backtrack search SAT solvers," presented at Fifth International Symposium on the Theory and Applications of Satisfiability Testing, 2002.

[32]   C. M. Li, "Integrating equivalency reasoning into Davis-Putnam Procedure," presented at National Conference on Artificial Intelligence (AAAI), 2000.

[33]   I. Lynce and J. P. Marques-Silva, "Integrating Simplification Techniques in SAT Algorithms," presented at Logic in Computer Science Short Paper Session (LICS-SP), 2001.

[34]   A. V. Gelder and Y. K. Tsuji, "Satisfiability Testing with more Reasoning and Less guessing," in *Cliques, Coloring and Satisfiability: Second DIMACS Implementation Challenge, DIMACS Series in Discrete Mathematics and Theoretical Computer Science*, D. S. Johnson and M. Trick, Eds.: American Mathematical Society, 1993.

[35]   S. T. Chakradhar and V. D. Agrawal, "A Transitive Closure Based Algorithm for Test Generation," presented at Design Automation Conference (DAC), 1991.

[36] W. Kunz and D. K. Pradhan, "Recursive Learning: A New Implication Technique for Efficient Solutions to CAD-problems: Test, Verification and Optimization," *IEEE Transactions on Computer-Aided Design of Integrated Circuits and Systems*, vol. 13, pp. 1143–1158, 1994.

[37] J. P. Marques-Silva, "Improving Satisfiability Algorithms by Using Recursive Learning," presented at International Workshop on Boolean Problems (IWBP), 1998.

[38] P. Prosser, "Hybrid algorithms for the constraint satisfaction problem," *Computational Intelligence*, vol. 9, pp. 268–299, 1993.

[39] L. Zhang, C. Madigan, M. Moskewicz, and S. Malik, "Efficient Conflict Driven Learning in a Boolean Satisfiability Solver," presented at International Conference on Computer Aided Design (ICCAD), San Jose, CA, 2001.

[40] G. Hachtel and F. Somenzi, *Logic Sysntheiss and Verification Algorithms*: Kluwer Academic Publishers, 1996.

[41] H. Zhang and M. Stickel, "Implementing Davis-Putnam's method," Technical Report, University of Iowa 1994.

[42] P. Chatalic and L. Simon, "Multi-Resolution on Compressed Sets of Clauses," presented at International Conference on Tools with Artificial Intelligence, 2000.

[43] F. Aloul, M. Mneimneh, and K. Sakallah, "Backtrack Search Using ZBDDs," presented at International Workshop on Logic Synthesis (IWLS), 2001.

[44] S. I. Minato, "Zero-Suppressed BDDs for Set Manipulation in Combinatorial Problems," presented at 30th Design Automation Conference (DAC), 1993.

[45] I. Lynce and J. P. Marques-Silva, "The Puzzling Role of Simplification in Propositional Satisfiability," presented at EPIA'01 Workshop on Constraint Satisfaction and Operational Research Techniques for Problem Solving (EPIA-CSOR), 2001.

[46] C. P. Gomes, B. Selman, and H. Kautz, "Boosting Combinatorial Search Through Randomization," presented at National Conference on Artificial Intelligence (AAAI), Madison, WI, 1998.

[47] B. A. Huberman, R. M. Lukose, and T. Hogg, "An Economics approach to hard computational problems," *Science*, vol. 275, pp. 51–54, 1997.

[48] I. Lynce and J. P. Marques-Silva, "Complete unrestricted backtracking algorithms for Satisfiability," presented at Fifth International Symposium on the Theory and Applications of Satisfiability Testing, 2002.

[49] C. P. Gomes, B. Selman, N. Crator, and H. Kautz, "Heavy-tailed phenomena in satisfiability and constraint satisfaction problems," *Journal of Automated Reasoning*, vol. 24(1/2), pp. 67–100, 1999.

[50] "Prover Proof Engine," Prover Technology.

[51] J. F. Groote and J. P. Warners, "The propositional formula checker HeerHugo," *Journal of Automated Reasoning*, vol. 24, 2000.

[52] Y. Shang and B. W. Wah, "A Discrete Lagrangian-Based Global-Search Method for Solving Satisfiability Problems," *Journal of Global Optimization*, vol. 12, pp. 61–99, 1998.

[53] I. Gent and T. Walsh, "The SAT Phase Transition," presented at European Conference on Artificial Intelligence (ECAI-94), 1994.

[54] M. Prasad, P. Chong, and K. Keutzer, "Why is ATPG easy?," presented at Design Automation Conference (DAC99), 1999.

[55] F. Brglez, X. Li, and M. Stallmann, "The role of a skeptic agent in testing and benchmarking of SAT algorithms," presented at Fifth International Symposium on theTheory and Applications of Satisfiability Testing, 2002.

[56] O. Strichman, "Pruning techniques for the SAT-based Bounded Model Checking Problem," presented at 11th Advanced Research Working Conference on Correct Hardware Design and Verification Methods (CHARM'01), 2001.

[57] M. Ganai, L. Zhang, P. Ashar, A. Gupta, and S. Malik, "Combining Strengths of Circuit-based and CNF-based Algorithms for a High-Performance SAT Solver," presented at Design Automation Conference (DAC'02), 2002.

Recursive Path Orderings Can Be Context-Sensitive

Cristina Borralleras[1], Salvador Lucas[2], and Albert Rubio[3]*

[1] Dept. Informàtica i Matemàtica, E.P.S. Universitat de Vic,
C/ de la Laura, 13. 08500 Vic Spain
cristina.borralleras@uvic.es
[2] D.S.I.C. Universidad Politécnica de Valencia
C/ Camino de Vera, s/n. 46022 Valencia Spain
slucas@dsic.upv.es
[3] Dept. L.S.I. Universitat Politècnica de Catalunya,
C/Jordi Girona, 1-3. 08034 Barcelona, Spain
rubio@lsi.upc.es

Abstract. Context-sensitive rewriting (CSR) is a simple restriction of rewriting which can be used e.g. for modelling non-eager evaluation in programming languages. Many times *termination* is a crucial property for program verification. Hence, developing tools for automatically proving termination of CSR is necessary.

All known methods for proving termination of (CSR) systems are based on transforming the CSR system $\mathcal{R}$ into a (standard) rewrite system $\mathcal{R}'$ whose termination implies the termination of the CSR system $\mathcal{R}$.

In this paper first several negative results on the applicability of existing transformation methods are provided. Second, as a general-purpose way to overcome these problems, we develop the first (up to our knowledge) method for proving directly termination of context-sensitive rewrite systems: the *context sensitive recursive path ordering* (CSRPO).

Many interesting (realistic) examples that cannot be proved or are hard to prove with the known transformation methods are easily handled using CSRPO. Moreover, CSRPO is very suitable for automation.

1 Introduction

One of the main applications of automated deduction is (e.g. program) verification. Many correctness proofs include termination as an essential property. Therefore automatic tools for termination analysis may be crucial in verification.

Obviously, automatically proving termination of arbitrary programs written in languages like C is extremely hard. Hence, one focuses on more abstract computation formalisms like term rewrite systems (TRSs). Termination proofs

* C. Borralleras and A. Rubio are supported by the CICYT TIC2001-2476-C03-01, A. Rubio also by the DURSI group 2001SGR 00254 and S. Lucas by CICYT TIC2001-2705-C03-01, Acciones Integradas HI 2000-0161, HA 2001-0059, HU 2001-0019, and Generalitat ValencianaGV01-424.

A. Voronkov (Ed.): CADE-18, LNAI 2392, pp. 314–331, 2002.
© Springer-Verlag Berlin Heidelberg 2002

for other (e.g. logic or functional) programs can be obtained by translating them into a TRS (see e.g. [GW93,AZ96]).

Context-sensitive (CS) rewriting (*CSR* [Luc98]) is a simple generalization of rewriting which is formalized by imposing fixed syntactic restrictions on replacements: a *replacement map* μ discriminates, for each symbol of the signature, the argument positions on which replacements are allowed. E.g., with $\mu(\text{if-then-else}) = \{1\}$, reductions are permitted *only* on the first argument of calls to if-then-else. Many *eager* programming languages (e.g., Lisp, OBJ2, OBJ3, CafeOBJ, or Maude) provide a special (non-eager) semantics for this operator which can be modeled with a replacement map [Luc01]. Note that in the particular case where μ includes all argument positions CSR becomes standard rewriting.

Any terminating TRS is also μ-*terminating*, i.e., no term initiates an infinite sequence of *CSR* under μ. However, *CSR* can *enforce* termination, by pruning (all) infinite rewrite sequences. Therefore, particular methods for proving μ-termination have been developed. All currently known such methods are transformation methods [Luc96,Zan97,SX98,FR99,GM99,GM01]: one proves the termination of a CS-TRS $\mathcal{R}$ by building a (standard) TRS $\mathcal{R}'$ whose termination implies the μ-termination of $\mathcal{R}$. Then one can use standard techniques for proving the termination of $\mathcal{R}'$.

Example 1. The following term rewrite system (given in [GM01]) defines some operations on lists and, in particular, allow us to generate an infinite list of zeros (from *zeros*) and the list of all natural numbers (from *nats*).

$$
\begin{array}{ll}
incr(nil) \to nil & nats \to adx(zeros) \\
incr(cons(x,l)) \to cons(s(x), incr(l)) & zeros \to cons(0, zeros) \\
adx(nil) \to nil & head(cons(x,l)) \to x \\
adx(cons(x,l)) \to incr(cons(x, adx(l))) & tail(cons(x,l)) \to l
\end{array}
$$

This non-terminating TRS becomes μ-terminating with the replacement map $\mu(cons) = \mu(incr) = \mu(adx) = \mu(s) = \mu(head) = \mu(tail) = \{1\}$. Note that, since *cons* has its second argument blocked (not active) we cannot produce an infinite rewriting sequence starting from *zeros*.

All these transformation methods (except the one in [Luc96]) use new symbols and rules, often introducing a loss of structure and intuition due to the encoding of the CS-control by such new elements.

In [GM99] a complete transformation (i.e., a transformation that never turns CS-terminating $\mathcal{R}$ into non-terminating $\mathcal{R}'$) was given. The completeness of their method motivated the claim in [GM99] (pg. 272) that "it appears that from a termination point of view there is no reason to study context-sensitive rewriting further". However, such claims are based on the (mis)understanding that whenever the transformed system $\mathcal{R}'$ terminates it will be easily provable, obviating the fact that termination of a TRS is an undecidable property[1].

---

[1] Moreover, the existence of such complete transformations is no surprise: it can be directly extracted from the Turing completeness proof of TRS: simulate the CS-TRS

In this paper we give good reasons for believing that in many cases it may be more feasible to directly prove the CS-termination of the original system. For instance, with the complete method proposed in [GM99] (and also the incomplete one given there), even when the termination of the initial context-sensitive system is quite trivial, the termination of the transformed system can be hard (this is the case for the CS-TRS of Example 1 above): in Section 3 we prove that with the methods given in [GM99] the transformed TRS can be proved terminating with the *recursive path ordering* (RPO) [Der82] only if the original CS-TRS was already RPO-terminating *without the CS restrictions*. It can even be the case that the original system is RPO-terminating and the transformed one is not. Similar negative results are obtained for the *Knuth-Bendix ordering* (KBO) [KB70], the other main general-purpose termination proof method.

For all these reasons, here we focus on specific methods for directly proving the termination of *CSR*, and give evidence for the fact that simple but powerful automated termination methods for *CSR* can be obtained in this way.

Due to its simplicity and its success in the (standard) term rewriting setting, our aim has been to obtain a recursive path ordering which is context-sensitive, i.e., terms are ordered differently depending on the context they are in. In Section 4 we define such a context-sensitive RPO (CSRPO) and state its main properties (all proofs can be found in [BLR02]).

In sections 5 and 6 evidence for the power of CSRPO is given, by means of several realistic examples where CSRPO easily proves the termination of context-sensitive term rewrite systems which are not terminating without the context-sensitivity restrictions. For most of these examples the known transformation methods cannot work or do not work in practice.

Moreover, the ideas of the CSRPO, especially the ones concerning the treatment of variables, carry over to other more powerful ordering-based methods, obtaining its corresponding context-sensitive version. This may produce proper extensions of the most powerful existing methods for direct termination proofs of context-sensitive rewriting in many cases.

2   Preliminaries

Given a binary relation R on A, we say that R is *terminating* (*strongly normalizing*) iff there is no infinite sequence $a_1 \ R \ a_2 \ R \ a_3 \cdots$. Throughout the paper, $\mathcal{X}$ denotes a countable set of variables and $\mathcal{F}$ denotes the set of function symbols $\{f, g, \dots\}$, each having a fixed arity given by a mapping $ar : \mathcal{F} \to \mathbb{N}$. The set of terms built from $\mathcal{F}$ and $\mathcal{X}$ is $\mathcal{T}(\mathcal{F}, \mathcal{X})$ and the set of ground terms built from $\mathcal{F}$ is $\mathcal{T}(\mathcal{F})$. Terms are viewed as labeled trees in the usual way. The set of positions of a term t is $\mathcal{P}os(t)$. The subterm at position p of t is denoted as $t|_p$ and $t[s]_p$ is the term t with the subterm at position p replaced by s. The symbol labeling the root of t is denoted as $root(t)$.

---

by a C-program (easy), which is simulated by a Turing machine (well-known as well), which is finally encoded by a (even single-rule) TRS as in [Dau92].

A rewrite rule is an ordered pair of terms, written $l \to r$, with $l \notin \mathcal{X}$ and $Var(r) \subseteq Var(l)$. A TRS is a pair $\mathcal{R} = (\mathcal{F}, R)$ where R is a set of rewrite rules. An instance $\sigma(l)$ of a *lhs* l of a rule is a redex. A term $t \in \mathcal{T}(\mathcal{F}, \mathcal{X})$ rewrites to s (at position p), written $t \xrightarrow{p}_{\mathcal{R}} s$ (or just $t \to s$), if $t|_p = \sigma(l)$ and $s = t[\sigma(r)]_p$, for some rule $l \to r \in R$, $p \in \mathcal{P}os(t)$ and substitution σ. A TRS is terminating if $\to$ is terminating.

2.1   Orderings

A (strict partial) ordering is a transitive and irreflexive relation. An ordering $\succ$ is compatible with an equality (or a congruence) relation $\sim$ if for all terms s, s', t, t' we have that $s' \sim s \succ t \sim t'$ implies $s' \succ t'$. An ordering $\succ$ is stable under substitutions if $s \succ t$ implies $s\sigma \succ t\sigma$ for all terms s and t and substitution σ, and it is said to be stable under ground substitutions if $s \succ t$ implies $s\sigma \succ t\sigma$ for all ground substitution σ. An ordering $\succ$ is well-founded if there exists no infinite sequence $t_1 \succ t_2 \succ \dots$.

Given an ordering $\succ$ and a compatible equality relation $\sim$, the multiset extension of $\succ$ with respect to $\sim$, denoted by $\succ\!\!\succ$, is defined as the smallest transitive relation containing

$$X \cup \{s\} \;\succ\!\!\succ\; Y \cup \{t_1, \dots, t_n\} \qquad \text{if } X \sim Y \text{ and } s \succ t_i \text{ for all } i \in \{1 \dots n\}$$

If $\succ$ is a well-founded ordering on terms then $\succ\!\!\succ$ is a well-founded ordering on finite multisets of terms.

Let $\sim$ be an equality relation compatible with a given ordering $\succ$. Then the lexicographic extension of $\succ$ with respect to $\sim$, denoted by $\succ^{lex}$, is defined as $\langle s_1, \dots, s_m \rangle \succ^{lex} \langle t_1, \dots, t_n \rangle$ if and only if $m \geq n$ and there is some $i \in \{1 \dots n\}$ such that $s_i \succ t_i$ and $s_k \sim t_k$ for all $k \in \{1 \dots i-1\}$. If $\succ$ is a well-founded ordering on terms then $\succ^{lex}$ is a well-founded ordering on finite sequences of terms.

For standard rewriting one of the most successful general methods applied to prove termination is the *recursive path ordering* (RPO) [Der82]. Given a precedence $\succeq_{\mathcal{F}}$ on the set of function symbols, which is the union of a well-founded ordering $\succ_{\mathcal{F}}$ and a compatible equality $=_{\mathcal{F}}$, and a status function $stat(f) \in \{lex, mul\}$ s.t. if $f =_{\mathcal{F}} g$ then $stat(f) = stat(g)$, RPO is defined recursively as follows:

$s = f(s_1, \dots, s_n) \succ_{rpo} t$ iff

1. $s_i \succeq_{rpo} t$,   for some $i = 1, \dots, n$ or
2. $t = g(t_1, \dots, t_m)$ with $f \succ_{\mathcal{F}} g$ and $s \succ_{rpo} t_i$ for all $i = 1 \dots n$ or
3. $t = g(t_1, \dots, t_m)$ with $f =_{\mathcal{F}} g$, $stat(f) = mul$ and
   $\{s_1, \dots, s_n\} \succ\!\!\succ_{rpo} \{t_1, \dots, t_m\}$ or
4. $t = g(t_1, \dots, t_m)$ with $f =_{\mathcal{F}} g$, $stat(f) = lex$, $\langle s_1, \dots, s_n \rangle \succ^{lex}_{rpo} \langle t_1, \dots, t_m \rangle$
   and $s \succ_{rpo} t_i$ for all $i \in \{1 \dots m\}$.

where $\succeq_{rpo}$ is the union of $\succ_{rpo}$ and syntactic equality.

2.2   Context-Sensitive Rewriting

A mapping $\mu : \mathcal{F} \to \mathcal{P}(\mathbb{N})$ is a *replacement map* (or $\mathcal{F}$-map) if $\forall f \in \mathcal{F}$, $\mu(f) \subseteq \{1, \ldots, ar(f)\}$ [Luc98]. A replacement map μ specifies the *argument* positions which can be reduced for each *symbol* in $\mathcal{F}$. Accordingly, the set of μ-*replacing* or *active* positions $\mathcal{P}os^\mu(t)$ of $t \in \mathcal{T}(\mathcal{F}, \mathcal{X})$ is: $\mathcal{P}os^\mu(t) = \{\Lambda\}$, if $t \in \mathcal{X}$ and $\mathcal{P}os^\mu(t) = \{\Lambda\} \cup \bigcup_{i \in \mu(root(t))} i.\mathcal{P}os^\mu(t|_i)$, if $t \notin \mathcal{X}$.

In *context-sensitive rewriting* (*CSR* [Luc98]), we (only) contract *replacing* redexes: t μ-rewrites to s, written $t \hookrightarrow_\mu s$, if $t \xrightarrow{p}_\mathcal{R} s$ and $p \in \mathcal{P}os^\mu(t)$.

Example 2. Consider $\mathcal{R}$ and μ as in Example 1. Then, we have: $adx(zeros) \hookrightarrow_\mu adx(cons(0, zeros)) \hookrightarrow_\mu incr(cons(0, adx(zeros))) \hookrightarrow_\mu cons(s(0), incr(adx(zeros)))$. Since $2.1.1 \notin \mathcal{P}os^\mu(cons(s(0), incr(adx(zeros))))$, redex $zeros$ cannot be μ-rewritten.

A TRS $\mathcal{R}$ is μ-*terminating* if $\hookrightarrow_\mu$ is terminating.

2.3 μ-Reduction Orderings

Here we adapt the reduction orderings framework to the context sensitive case. In order to obtain an appropriate notion of reduction orderings we only have to modify the definition of monotonicity. In context-sensitive rewriting the redexes are always in active positions, therefore, we only need to ensure monotonicity for these positions (this notion was already considered in [Zan97]).

Definition 1. *An ordering $\succ$ is μ-monotonic iff $s \succ t$ implies $C[s]_p \succ C[t]_p$ for all context C and for all active position p.*

Definition 2. $\succ$ *is a μ-reduction ordering if it is a μ-monotonic, stable under substitutions, well-founded ordering.*

Then we have that μ-reduction orderings characterize μ-termination.

Theorem 1. *Let $\mathcal{R}$ be a TRS and μ be a replacement map. Then $\mathcal{R}$ is μ-terminating if and only if there exists a μ-reduction ordering $\succ$ such that $l \succ r$ for every rule $l \to r$ in $\mathcal{R}$.*

In fact, stability under substitutions can be relaxed by considering only ground substitutions. Then we speak about *ground stable μ-reduction orderings*.

Definition 3. $\succ$ *is a ground stable μ-reduction ordering if it is a μ-monotonic, stable under ground substitutions, well-founded ordering.*

Ground stable μ-reduction orderings characterize μ-termination as well, provided there is at least one constant symbol in the signature, since any infinite sequence of rewriting can be instantiated to obtain a ground infinite sequence.

Theorem 2. *Let $\mathcal{R}$ be a TRS and μ be a replacement map. Then $\mathcal{R}$ is μ-terminating if and only if there exists a ground stable μ-reduction ordering $\succ$ such that $l \succ r$ for every rule $l \to r$ in $\mathcal{R}$.*

To simplify the proof of μ-monotonicity we can equivalently state the property in a different way.

Property 1. An ordering $\succ$ is μ-monotonic iff $s \succ t$ implies $f(\dots [s]_i \dots) \succ f(\dots [t]_i \dots)$ for all function symbol $f \in \mathcal{F}$ and for all $i \in \mu(f)$.

3   Transformation Methods

In this section we analyze the transformation methods presented in [GM99] from a practical point of view. In particular, we provide some results showing that general purpose methods like RPO or KBO (see the appendix) cannot be used for proving termination of the transformed system. This result shows that only very powerful termination techniques can be used to prove the termination of the transformed TRS even when the μ-termination of the original CS-TRS looks quite trivial. All proofs can be found in [BLR02].

In the first presented transformation method, denoted by $\mathcal{R}_{GM}^{\mu}$, the basic idea is to explicitly *mark* the replacing positions of a term (by using a new symbol active), since these positions are the only ones where *CSR* may take place. Given a TRS $\mathcal{R} = (\mathcal{F}, R)$ and μ a replacement map, the TRS $\mathcal{R}_{GM}^{\mu} = (\mathcal{F} \cup \{\texttt{active}, \texttt{mark}\}, R_{GM}^{\mu})$ consists of the following rules (for all $l \to r \in R$ and $f \in \mathcal{F}$):

$$\texttt{active}(l) \to \texttt{mark}(r)$$
$$\texttt{mark}(f(x_1, \dots, x_k)) \to \texttt{active}(f([x_1]_f, \dots, [x_k]_f))$$
$$\texttt{active}(x) \to x$$

where $[x_i]_f = \texttt{mark}(x_i)$ if $i \in \mu(f)$ and $[x_i]_f = x_i$ otherwise. The second (confluent and terminating) collection of rules is labeled $\mathcal{M}$ in [GM99].

Example 3. Consider $\mathcal{R}$ and μ as in Example 1. Then, $\mathcal{R}_{GM}^{\mu}$ is

$$\texttt{active}(incr(nil)) \to \texttt{mark}(nil)$$
$$\texttt{active}(incr(cons(x,l))) \to \texttt{mark}(cons(s(x), incr(l)))$$
$$\texttt{active}(adx(nil)) \to \texttt{mark}(nil)$$
$$\texttt{active}(adx(cons(x,l))) \to \texttt{mark}(incr(cons(x, adx(l))))$$
$$\texttt{active}(nats) \to \texttt{mark}(adx(zeros))$$
$$\texttt{active}(zeros) \to \texttt{mark}(cons(0, zeros))$$
$$\texttt{active}(head(cons(x,l))) \to \texttt{mark}(x)$$
$$\texttt{active}(tail(cons(x,l))) \to \texttt{mark}(l)$$

$$\texttt{mark}(incr(x)) \to \texttt{active}(incr(\texttt{mark}(x)))$$
$$\texttt{mark}(nil) \to \texttt{active}(nil)$$
$$\texttt{mark}(cons(x,y)) \to \texttt{active}(cons(\texttt{mark}(x), y))$$
$$\texttt{mark}(s(x)) \to \texttt{active}(s(\texttt{mark}(x)))$$
$$\texttt{mark}(adx(x)) \to \texttt{active}(adx(\texttt{mark}(x)))$$
$$\texttt{mark}(nats) \to \texttt{active}(nats)$$
$$\texttt{mark}(zeros) \to \texttt{active}(zeros)$$
$$\texttt{mark}(0) \to \texttt{active}(0)$$
$$\texttt{mark}(head(x)) \to \texttt{active}(head(\texttt{mark}(x)))$$
$$\texttt{mark}(tail(x)) \to \texttt{active}(tail(\texttt{mark}(x)))$$
$$\texttt{active}(x) \to x$$

Although it is not complete (see Example 1 of [GM99]), this transformation preserves termination for strictly more CS-TRSs than Lucas' contractive transformation [Luc96], denoted by $\mathcal{R}_L^\mu$, and Zantema's transformation [Zan97], denoted by $\mathcal{R}_Z^\mu$. For instance, μ-termination of $\mathcal{R}$ in the introduction cannot be proved by using either $\mathcal{R}_L^\mu$ or $\mathcal{R}_Z^\mu$, while $\mathcal{R}_{GM}^\mu$ of example 3 can be proved terminating using the dependency pairs technique [AG00] with a lexicographic combination of polynomial interpretations.

However in practice, many times $\mathcal{R}_L^\mu$ and $\mathcal{R}_Z^\mu$ can more easily be proved terminating automatically. In fact, although it is terminating, we do not know about any available automatic termination proof system able to prove the termination of $\mathcal{R}_{GM}^\mu$ in Example 3. In the Section 6 we will provide a very simple proof of termination using our method.

Here we show that RPO can only be used to prove termination of the transformed system when the original system is already provable terminating by RPO (i.e. the system is terminating without any restriction). Note that in such a case there is no reason for proving μ-termination.

Theorem 3. *Let $\mathcal{R} = (\mathcal{F}, R)$ be a TRS and μ a replacement map. If $\mathcal{R}$ is not* rpo-*terminating, then $\mathcal{R}_{GM}^\mu$ is not* rpo-*terminating.*

Proof. For the second group of rules, any proof of *rpo*-termination of $\mathcal{R}_{GM}^\mu$ would need mark $\succ_\mathcal{F}$ active in the precedence. Therefore, for the first group of rules we also need $l \succeq_{rpo} \text{mark}(r)$ for all rule $l \to r \in R$, which implies $l \succ_{rpo} r$.

Moreover note that even when $\mathcal{R}$ is *rpo*-terminating, it can still happen that $\mathcal{R}_{GM}^\mu$ is not *rpo*-terminating. This is showed in the following example.

Example 4. Consider the following *rpo*-terminating TRS $\mathcal{R}$ (consider $f \succ_\mathcal{F} b$):

$$f(b(x)) \to b(f(x))$$

Let $\mu(b) = \mu(f) = \{1\}$. Then, $\mathcal{R}_{GM}^\mu$:

$$\begin{array}{ll}
\texttt{active}(f(b(x))) \to \texttt{mark}(b(f(x))) & \texttt{mark}(b(x)) \to \texttt{active}(b(\texttt{mark}(x))) \\
\texttt{mark}(f(x)) \quad\;\; \to \texttt{active}(f(\texttt{mark}(x))) & \texttt{active}(x) \to x
\end{array}$$

is not *rpo*-terminating: the rule $\texttt{mark}(f(x)) \to \texttt{active}(f(\texttt{mark}(x)))$ requires mark $\succ_\mathcal{F}$ active, f; in that case, the rule $\texttt{active}(f(b(x))) \to \texttt{mark}(b(f(x)))$ cannot be satisfied by any RPO.

Using Knuth-Bendix orderings is even worse, since only when the original system is already kbo-terminating and we are considering the minimum replacement map $\mu_\perp$ (defined as $\mu_\perp(f) = \emptyset$ for all symbols f) the termination of $\mathcal{R}_{GM}^\mu$ may be provable by KBO.

Theorem 4. *Let $\mathcal{R} = (\mathcal{F}, R)$ be a TRS and μ a replacement map. If $\mu \neq \mu_\perp$ or $\mathcal{R}$ is not* kbo-*terminating, then $\mathcal{R}_{GM}^\mu$ is not* kbo-*terminating.*

Proof. (sketch) First it is shown that if $\mu \neq \mu_\perp$ then for any admissible weight function there is at least one rule in the second group rules that cannot be proved. Second, if $\mu = \mu_\perp$ then using the fact that $\mathcal{R}$ is not *kbo*-terminating then for any admissible weight function either we cannot prove the rules of the first group or we cannot prove the rules of the second one.

Giesl and Middeldorp proposed a second transformation method, denoted by $\mathcal{R}_C^\mu$, which is correct and complete. The idea is to permit *a single* (context-sensitive) reduction step each time. They achieve this by using new symbols f' for each (non-constant) symbol $f \in \mathcal{F}$ and shifting a single symbol active to (non-deterministically) reach the replacing position where the redex is placed. The application of a rewrite rule changes active into mark which is propagated upwards through the term, in order to be replaced by a new symbol active that enables new reduction steps. After checking that no 'strange' symbols remain uncontrolled (using a symbol proper such that proper(t) reduces to ok(t) if and only if t is a ground term of the original signature), a rule top(ok(x)) $\rightarrow$ top(active(x)) enables a new reduction step (see [GM99] for a detailed explanation). Given a TRS $\mathcal{R} = (\mathcal{F}, R)$ and a replacement map μ, the TRS $\mathcal{R}_C^\mu = (\mathcal{F} \cup \{f' \mid f \in \mathcal{F} \wedge ar(f) > 0\} \cup \{\text{active}, \text{mark}, \text{ok}, \text{proper}, \text{top}\}, R_C^\mu)$ consists of the following rules: for all $l \rightarrow r \in R$, $f \in \mathcal{F}$ such that $k = ar(f) > 0$, $i \in \mu(f)$, and constants $c \in \mathcal{F}$,

$$\text{active}(l) \rightarrow \text{mark}(r)$$
$$\text{active}(f(x_1, \ldots, x_i, \ldots, x_k)) \rightarrow f'(x_1, \ldots, \text{active}(x_i), \ldots, x_k)$$
$$f'(x_1, \ldots, \text{mark}(x_i), \ldots, x_k) \rightarrow \text{mark}(f(x_1, \ldots, x_i, \ldots, x_k))$$
$$\text{proper}(c) \rightarrow \text{ok}(c)$$
$$\text{proper}(f(x_1, \ldots, x_k)) \rightarrow f(\text{proper}(x_1), \ldots, \text{proper}(x_k))$$
$$f(\text{ok}(x_1), \ldots, \text{ok}(x_k)) \rightarrow \text{ok}(f(x_1, \ldots, x_k))$$
$$\text{top}(\text{mark}(x)) \rightarrow \text{top}(\text{proper}(x))$$
$$\text{top}(\text{ok}(x)) \rightarrow \text{top}(\text{active}(x))$$

Regarding *rpo*-termination this new transformation is even less powerful than the previous one since *rpo*-termination of $\mathcal{R}_C^\mu$ implies *rpo*-termination of $\mathcal{R}_{GM}^\mu$. Therefore only in a few (useless) cases RPO can be applied.

Theorem 5. *Let $\mathcal{R} = (\mathcal{F}, R)$ be a TRS and μ a replacement map. If $\mu \neq \mu_\perp$ or $\mathcal{R}$ is not rpo-terminating, then $\mathcal{R}_C^\mu$ is not rpo-terminating.*

Finally regarding *kbo*-termination we have the following result, which states that if there is a constant symbol (which is always the case) and a non-unary function symbol then KBO cannot be applied.

Theorem 6. *Let $\mathcal{R} = (\mathcal{F}, R)$ be a TRS and μ a replacement map. If there exist $c, f \in \mathcal{F}$ such that $ar(c) = 0$ and $ar(f) \geq 2$, then $\mathcal{R}_C^\mu$ is not kbo-terminating.*

4   The Context-Sensitive Recursive Path Ordering

First we provide some intuition behind the definition of the ordering we are going to present. Following the example of the introduction we consider a replacement map satisfying $\mu(cons) = 1$ (i.e. blocking the second argument).

A first attempt to define an RPO for context-sensitive rewriting (which closely relates to the ideas behind the transformation method given in [Luc96]) is to simply consider that the second argument of *cons* does not exist, i.e. it should not be considered when *cons* is heading the right hand side term and it cannot be used when *cons* is heading the left hand side term. This ordering is a very simple μ-reduction ordering, but unfortunately, it will fail in many cases due to the variables occurring in an active position in the right hand side which are in a blocked position in the left hand side.

Therefore, since removing blocked subterms does not work, the reasonable alternative would be to mark the symbols which are in blocked positions and consider them smaller than the active ones. Therefore terms in blocked positions become smaller.

However, if we simply apply RPO to the terms after marking the symbols in blocked positions the resulting ordering is not stable under substitutions. The problem comes from the treatment of variables, since variables in blocked positions are somehow smaller than variables in active positions, which is not taken into account in RPO. For instance, following the example above, when comparing the terms $cons(x, l)$ and l, the variable l in the first term is in a blocked position while in the second one it is not.

If we solve this problem by simply marking the variables in blocked positions then the resulting ordering would be too weak. For instance, a term t like $tail(cons(x, l))$ could not be greater than l, since the l in t would be marked.

The key idea for obtaining a powerful ordering is using not only the variable l in $tail(cons(x, l))$ but the whole term to take care of the l, since if $tail$ is the greatest symbol in the precedence for any substitution σ we have that $tail(cons(x, l))\sigma$ is greater than $l\sigma$, since $tail$ is "taking care" of the head symbol of $l\sigma$ which is the one that is not marked.

However, this idea is not enough if we mark all symbols below blocked positions. The alternative is to mark only the necessary symbols. Therefore, an additional ingredient to our ordering is a *marking map*, denoted by $\mathfrak{m}$, which defines for every symbol and every blocked position the set of symbols that should be marked. For instance, in our example, we may have $\mathfrak{m}(cons, 2) = \{zeros, incr\}$, which means that if either the constant symbol *zeros* or the function symbol *incr* are heading the second argument of *cons* they will become the marked symbols <u>zeros</u> and <u>incr</u> respectively. For any other symbol no marking is applied. With such a marking, taking $tail \succ_{\mathcal{F}} zeros$ and $tail \succ_{\mathcal{F}} incr$ is enough to ensure that $tail(cons(x, l))$ is greater than l for all substitutions.

Finally, many times it is necessary to propagate the marking to the arguments of marked symbols. This can easily be expressed using the same marking map $\mathfrak{m}$ but defined on the arguments of the marked symbols. For instance, if we want to propagate the marking of <u>incr</u> to the symbol *cons* we take $\mathfrak{m}(\underline{incr}, 1) = \{cons\}$ and again we can decide whether we want to propagate through <u>cons</u> or not. Note that we can mark any symbol under a marked symbol since they are all blocked positions.

This notion of marking map generalizes the replacement map if we consider that positions headed by a marked symbol are blocked. Hence marking maps may be seen as a more flexible way to define blocked positions. As a consequence of our work, it turns out that many times considering a smaller set of blocked positions can simplify the termination proof.

To conclude this first look at our method, let us mention that we will not apply the marking map to the whole term but only to the top symbol of the arguments in the recursive calls of the definition of our recursive path ordering. Therefore the only one symbol that can be marked in the terms is the head symbol.

4.1 Marked Symbols and Marking Maps

Let μ be a replacement map and $\mathcal{F}$ be a signature. By $\underline{\mathcal{F}}$ we denote the set of marked symbols corresponding to $\mathcal{F}$ and by $\underline{\mathcal{X}}$ we denote the set of labeled variables corresponding to $\mathcal{X}$. The variables in $\underline{\mathcal{X}}$ are labeled by subsets of $\mathcal{F}$, for instance $x_{\{f,g,h\}}$, and we will ambiguously use the variables of $\mathcal{X}$ to denote variables labeled by the empty set.

Given a symbol f in $\mathcal{F} \cup \underline{\mathcal{F}}$ and a positive integer i in $\{1...ar(f)\}$, a marking map $\mathfrak{m}$ provides the subset of symbols in $\mathcal{F}$ that should be marked, i.e. $\mathfrak{m}(f,i) \subseteq \mathcal{F}$.

For instance, given the symbols $f, g, h \in \mathcal{F}$, $\mathfrak{m}(f,2) = \{g, h\}$ means that if the top of the second component of a term headed by f is g or h, when we obtain this subterm, its top symbol (g or h) will be marked, and $\mathfrak{m}(\underline{g},1) = \{h\}$ means that if the top of the first component of a term headed by $\underline{g}$ is h, when we reach the subterm this symbol h will be marked.

The precedence $\succeq_{\mathcal{F}}$ and the marking map $\mathfrak{m}$ has to satisfy some conditions. On the one hand, to preserve μ-monotonicity we need to ensure that $\mathfrak{m}$ never marks an active position, i.e. it must mark only blocked positions, and on the other hand, to be able to have a powerful treatment of variables, any symbol in $\mathcal{F}$ has to be greater than or equal to in the precedence than its marked version and it cannot mark more than its marked version. If these conditions are fulfilled, we say that $(\succeq_{\mathcal{F}}, \mathfrak{m})$ is a *valid* marking pair.

Definition 4. *Let $\succeq_{\mathcal{F}}$ be a precedence, μ a replacement map and $\mathfrak{m}$ a marking map. Then $(\succeq_{\mathcal{F}}, \mathfrak{m})$ is a valid marking pair if*

1. $\mathfrak{m}(f,i) = \emptyset \quad \forall f \in \mathcal{F}, \quad \forall i \in \mu(f)$
2. $f \succeq_{\mathcal{F}} \underline{f} \quad \forall f \in \mathcal{F}$
3. $\mathfrak{m}(f,i) \subseteq \mathfrak{m}(\underline{f},i) \quad \forall f \in \mathcal{F}, \quad \forall i \in \{1...ar(f)\}$

When using the ordering, the marking map tell us whether we have to mark the top symbol every time we go to an argument. Therefore, if we have a term $f(s_1...s_k)$, we will access to the arguments using $mt(s_i, \mathfrak{m}(f,i))$, which represents the result of marking the top symbol when required, and it is defined as:

$$mt(f(s_1...s_n), W) = \underline{f}(s_1...s_n) \ if \ f \in W$$
$$f(s_1...s_n) \ otherwise$$

$$mt(x, W) = x_W \quad \textit{where } x \textit{ is a variable}$$

We say that a term $s \in \underline{\mathcal{T}}(\mathcal{F}, \mathcal{X})$ if $s \in \underline{\mathcal{X}}$, or $s = f(s_1...s_n)$, with $f \in \mathcal{F} \cup \underline{\mathcal{F}}$ and $s_i \in \mathcal{T}(\mathcal{F}, \mathcal{X})$ for all $i \in \{1...n\}$. Note that, as said, marked symbols can only appear at the top of a term. A ground term s is in $\underline{\mathcal{T}}(\mathcal{F})$ if it is in $\underline{\mathcal{T}}(\mathcal{F}, \mathcal{X})$ and contains no variable.

4.2   Dealing with Labeled Variables

In this section we will present the way we are going to deal with the labeled variables. Roughly speaking, given a term s, we will provide the set of labeled variables that can be considered smaller than (or equal to) s without risk of losing stability under substitutions.

The basic idea is the following. As seen, we label the variables with the symbols that should be marked in case of applying a substitution. To ensure that some labeled variable x_W is in the set of safe (wrt. stability) labeled variables of a term s, we need x to occur in s and to be sure that for any substitution σ we have that $mt(x\sigma, W)$ is smaller than $s\sigma$. Therefore, assuming that x occurs in s, the important point is what happens with the function symbols heading $x\sigma$. Due to this we analyze which function symbols are harmless as head symbols. In all cases the symbols which are included in the label W of x. Additionally, all function symbols which do not appear in the label when we reach some occurrence of x in s are safe. Finally, and more importantly, the symbols g that can be proved to be safe because the head symbol of s (or recursively using some subterm of s containing x) is greater than or equal to g (and in the latter case they have multiset status), and $\underline{g}$ and g have the same marking.

Definition 5. *Let s be a non-variable term in $\underline{\mathcal{T}}(\mathcal{F}, \mathcal{X})$ and x_W a labeled variable. Then $x_W \in Stable(s)$ if and only if $x \in Var(s)$ and $f \in Safe(s, x)$ for all $f \in \mathcal{F} \setminus W$.*

The set $Safe(s, x)$ for some variable x s.t. $x \in Var(s)$ or $s = x_V$ (for some label V) is defined as the smallest subset of $\mathcal{F}$ containing

1. *if $s = x_V$ then all symbols in $\mathcal{F} \setminus V$.*
2. *if $s = f(s_1, \ldots, s_n)$ then*
   a) *the union of all $Safe(mt(s_i, \mathrm{m}(f, i)), x)$ with $i \in \{1 \ldots n\}$ and $x \in Var(s_i)$, and*
   b) *all $g \in \mathcal{F}$ such that $f =_{\mathcal{F}} g$ and $stat(f) = stat(g) = mul$, and $(\mathrm{m}(\underline{g}, i) = \mathrm{m}(g, i))$ for all $i \in \{1...ar(g)\}$.*
   c) *all $g \in \mathcal{F}$ such that $f \succ_{\mathcal{F}} g$ and $(\mathrm{m}(\underline{g}, i) = \mathrm{m}(g, i))$ for all $i \in \{1...ar(g)\}$.*

For instance, given the term $tail(cons(x, l))$, the marking map $\mathrm{m}(cons, 2) = \{zeros, incr\}$ and the precedence $tail \succ_{\mathcal{F}} zeros$ and $tail \succ_{\mathcal{F}} incr$, we have that $l_\emptyset \in Stable(tail(cons(x, l)))$ as $l \in Var(tail(cons(x, l)))$ and for all $f \in \mathcal{F} \setminus \emptyset$, $f \in Safe(tail(cons(x, l)), x)$. Since $\mathrm{m}(cons, 2) = \{zeros, incr\}$ then for all $f \in \mathcal{F} \setminus \{zeros, incr\}$ we have that $f \in Safe(tail(cons(x, l)), x)$ by applying first case 2a twice and then case 1. Finally, we have that $zeros, incr \in Safe(tail(cons(x, l)), x)$ by case 2c twice since $tail \succ_{\mathcal{F}} zeros$ and $tail \succ_{\mathcal{F}} incr$ and $\mathrm{m}(incr, 1) = \mathrm{m}(\underline{incr}, 1) = \emptyset$.

4.3 The Ordering

First we give the definition of the equality relation, induced by the equality on function symbols, that we will use.

Definition 6. *Given two terms in $\underline{T}(\mathcal{F}, \mathcal{X})$, we define $=_\mathcal{S}$ as follows:*

- $f(s_1...s_k) =_\mathcal{S} g(t_1...t_k)$ *iff* $f =_\mathcal{F} g$ *and* $mt(s_i, \mathfrak{m}(f, i)) =_\mathcal{S} mt(t_i, \mathfrak{m}(g, i))$ *for every* $i \in \{1, \ldots, k\}$.
- $x_W =_\mathcal{S} x_{W'}$ *iff* $W = W'$

We can enlarge the equality relation by considering permutations of arguments of symbols with multiset status.

Now we can give the definition of our context-sensitive recursive path ordering.

Definition 7. *Let $s, t \in \underline{T}(\mathcal{F}, \mathcal{X})$*
$s = f(s_1...s_n) \succ_\mathcal{S} t$ *with* $t \in \underline{\mathcal{X}}$ *or* $t = g(t_1...t_m)$ *iff*

1. $t = x_W \in Stable(s)$
2. *or* $mt(s_i, \mathfrak{m}(f, i)) \succeq_\mathcal{S} t$, *for some* $i \in \{1...n\}$
3. *or* $t = g(t_1...t_m)$ *with* $f \succ_\mathcal{F} g$ *and* $s \succ_\mathcal{S} mt(t_i, \mathfrak{m}(g, i))$ *for all* $i \in \{1...m\}$
4. *or* $t = g(t_1...t_m)$ *with* $f =_\mathcal{F} g$, *stat*$(f) = mul$ *and*
   $\{mt(s_1, \mathfrak{m}(f, 1)), ..., mt(s_n, \mathfrak{m}(f, n))\} \succ\!\!\succ_\mathcal{S} \{mt(t_1, \mathfrak{m}(g, 1)), ..., mt(t_m, \mathfrak{m}(g, m))\}$
5. *or* $t = g(t_1...t_m)$, $f =_\mathcal{F} g$, *stat*$(f) = lex$, $\langle mt(s_1, \mathfrak{m}(f, 1)), ..., mt(s_n, \mathfrak{m}(f, n)) \rangle$
   $\succ_\mathcal{S}^{lex} \langle mt(t_1, \mathfrak{m}(g, 1)), ..., mt(t_m, \mathfrak{m}(g, m)) \rangle$ *and* $s \succ_\mathcal{S} mt(t_i, \mathfrak{m}(g, i))$ *for all* $i \in \{1...m\}$.

where $s \succeq_\mathcal{S} t$ denotes $s \succ_\mathcal{S} t$ or $s =_\mathcal{S} t$, and $\succ\!\!\succ_\mathcal{S}$ and $\succ_\mathcal{S}^{lex}$ are respectively the multiset and lexicographic extension of $\succ_\mathcal{S}$ wrt. $=_\mathcal{S}$.

The ordering satisfies the following properties:

Lemma 1.

1. $=_\mathcal{S}$ *and* $\succ_\mathcal{S}$ *are transitive.*
2. $\succ_\mathcal{S}$ *is compatible with* $=_\mathcal{S}$.
3. $f(t_1...t_k) \succeq_\mathcal{S} \underline{f}(t_1...t_k)$ *for all* $f \in \mathcal{F}$ *and* $\forall t_i \in \mathcal{T}(\mathcal{F})$.

Theorem 7. $\succ_\mathcal{S}$ *over terms in* $\mathcal{T}(\mathcal{F}, \mathcal{X})$ *is a ground stable μ-reduction ordering.*

μ-monotonicity easily follows, and well-foundedness is shown directly by contradiction on the existence of a minimal (in the sense of e.g. Nash-Williams' proof of Kruskal's theorem [NW63]) infinite decreasing sequence with $\succ_\mathcal{S}$. It can also be proved using the general method described in [Gou01].

For stability we first proof that $\succ_\mathcal{S}$ is stable under ground μ-substitutions, which are substitution satisfying that $x_W \sigma = mt(x\sigma, W)$ for all variables in the domain of σ. This is the most difficult part, an requires to prove that if $x_W \in Stable(s)$ then $s\sigma \succ_\mathcal{S} x_W \sigma$ for all ground μ-substitutions σ. Finally, for terms in $\mathcal{T}(\mathcal{F}, \mathcal{X})$, i.e. without marked symbols, we can show stability under ground substitutions.

Note that the ordering can be adapted to be stable under substitutions (not only ground). We have not included this definition since it is a bit more complex and there is no gain in practice.

5   Examples

First, two simple "training" examples are presented. Although none of them can be proved by $\mathcal{R}_Z^\mu$, only the second one holds with $\mathcal{R}_L^\mu$ and e.g. dependency pairs technique is needed for $\mathcal{R}_{GM}^\mu$, they both have a very easy proof using CSRPO.

Example 5. (taken from [GM99]).

$$g(x) \rightarrow h(x)$$
$$c \;\; \rightarrow \;\; d$$
$$h(d) \rightarrow g(c)$$

with $\mu(g) = \mu(h) = \emptyset$.

Termination is proved using CSRPO with the marking $\mathrm{m}(g, 1) = \mathrm{m}(\underline{g}, 1) = \mathrm{m}(h, 1) = \mathrm{m}(\underline{h}, 1) = \{c\}$ and the precedence $c \succ_\mathcal{F} d \succ_\mathcal{F} g \succ_\mathcal{F} h$ and $d \succ_\mathcal{F} \underline{c}$.

Example 6. (taken from [Zan97]).

$$f(x) \rightarrow g(h(f(x)))$$

with $\mu(f) = \mu(h) = \{1\}$ and $\mu(g) = \emptyset$.

We can prove that this rule is included in $\succ_\mathcal{S}$ with the marking $\mathrm{m}(g, 1) = \mathrm{m}(\underline{g}, 1) = \{h\}$, $\mathrm{m}(\underline{h}, 1) = \{f\}$ and the precedence $f \succ_\mathcal{F} g, \underline{h}, \underline{f}$.

The following example present the definition of some functions that can handle infinite lists.

Example 7. Lists.

$$
\begin{aligned}
from(x) &\rightarrow cons(x, from(s(x))) \\
head(cons(x, xs)) &\rightarrow x \\
2nd(cons(x, xs)) &\rightarrow head(xs) \\
take(0, xs) &\rightarrow nil \\
take(s(n), cons(x, xs)) &\rightarrow cons(x, take(n, xs)) \\
sel(0, cons(x, xs)) &\rightarrow x \\
sel(s(n), cons(x, xs)) &\rightarrow sel(n, xs)
\end{aligned}
$$

with $\mu(cons) = \mu(2nd) = \mu(from) = \mu(head) = \mu(s) = \{1\}$ and $\mu(take) = \mu(sel) = \{1, 2\}$.

This CS-TRS is included in $\succ_\mathcal{S}$ with the marking $\mathrm{m}(cons, 2) = \mathrm{m}(\underline{cons}, 2) = \{from\}$; the precedence $2nd \succ_\mathcal{F} \{head, from\}$, $take \succ_\mathcal{F} \{from, nil, cons\}$ and $sel \succ_\mathcal{F} from \succ_\mathcal{F} \{cons, s, \underline{from}\}$; and the status $stat(take) = stat(sel) = lex$ and *mul* for all others. Note that *take* and *sel* must be greater than *from*, because it is marked by *cons*.

In the next example, the function fib produces (in an efficient way) the infinite sequence of Fibonacci numbers. This example can also be proved using $\mathcal{R}_Z^\mu$ and RPO.

Example 8. Fibonacci.

$$
\begin{aligned}
fib(n) &\rightarrow sel(n, fib1(s(0), s(0))) \\
fib1(x, y) &\rightarrow cons(x, fib1(y, add(x, y))) \\
add(0, x) &\rightarrow x \\
add(s(x), y) &\rightarrow s(add(x, y)) \\
sel(0, cons(x, xs)) &\rightarrow x \\
sel(s(n), cons(x, xs)) &\rightarrow sel(n, xs)
\end{aligned}
$$

with $\mu(cons) = \mu(fib) = \mu(s) = \{1\}$ and $\mu(fib1) = \mu(add) = \mu(sel) = \{1, 2\}$.

We can prove it with $\succ_S$ using the marking $\mathsf{m}(cons, 2) = \mathsf{m}(\underline{cons}, 2) = \{fib1\}$; the precedence $fib \succ_{\mathcal{F}} \{sel, fib1, s, 0\}$, $sel \succ_{\mathcal{F}} fib1 \succ_{\mathcal{F}} \{cons, add, \underline{fib1}\}$ and $add \succ_{\mathcal{F}} s$; and the status $stat(sel) = lex$ and mul for all others.

The last example of this section defines a function which produces the infinite list of prime numbers, with some zeros inserted. In fact, the list coincides with the list of natural numbers (from 2 on), where every non-prime number has been replaced by zero, e.g. $2, 3, 0, 5, 0, 7, 0, 0, 0, 11, \ldots$ This example is a slight modification of a definition given in [KdV02]. This example can also be proved with $\mathcal{R}_L^\mu$ and RPO, but not with $\mathcal{R}_Z^\mu$ and RPO.

Example 9. Primes.

$$
\begin{aligned}
filter(cons(x, y), 0, m) &\rightarrow cons(0, filter(y, m, m)) \\
filter(cons(x, y), s(n), m) &\rightarrow cons(x, filter(y, n, m)) \\
sieve(cons(0, y)) &\rightarrow cons(0, sieve(y)) \\
sieve(cons(s(n), y)) &\rightarrow cons(s(n), sieve(filter(y, n, n))) \\
nats(n) &\rightarrow cons(n, nats(s(n))) \\
zprimes &\rightarrow sieve(nats(s(s(0))))
\end{aligned}
$$

with $\mu(cons) = \mu(nats) = \mu(sieve) = \mu(s) = \{1\}$ and $\mu(filter) = \{1, 2, 3\}$.

We can prove it with $\succ_S$ using the marking $\mathsf{m}(cons, 2) = \mathsf{m}(\underline{cons}, 2) = \mathsf{m}(\underline{filter}, 1) = \mathsf{m}(\underline{sieve}, 1) = \{filter, sieve, nats\}$; the precedence $zprimes \succ_{\mathcal{F}} \{sieve, nats, s, 0\}$, $nats \succ_{\mathcal{F}} \{cons, \underline{nats}, s\}$ and $sieve \succ_{\mathcal{F}} \{cons, \underline{sieve}, filter\}$ $filter \succ_{\mathcal{F}} \{cons, \underline{filter}\}$; and the status mul for all symbols.

Note that the list of prime numbers can be obtained by removing the zeroes from the list, but then proving termination of this example would be much harder (maybe impossible automatically) since termination follows from the fact that there are no infinitely many consecutive zeros in the list (which holds since there are infinitely many prime numbers).

6 Improvements

The presented ordering, although it is quite powerful, cannot prove examples like the one in the introduction. This is due to the fact that conditions we have imposed in the definition of *Safe* in order to ensure stability under substitution are too strong. In particular, in case 2c, when we say that g is a safe symbol for a term s headed by f with $f \succ_{\mathcal{F}} g$, the condition $\mathrm{m}(g, i) = \mathrm{m}(\underline{g}, i)$ is added to avoid problems with the propagated marks by $\underline{g}$. By a deeper analysis, we can see that if f is greater than all symbols that are marked by propagation from $\underline{g}$ then g is also safe. In fact we only have to be careful with the symbols that are marked by propagation from $\underline{g}$ and not from g.

The following definition describes this set of "dangerous" symbols with respect to propagation of marks for a given symbol g.

Definition 8. *Given a mapping m and a function symbol g in $\mathcal{F}$, the set $prop(g)$ is defined as the smallest set satisfying that $h \in prop(g)$ if*

- $h \in \mathrm{m}(\underline{g}, i) \setminus \mathrm{m}(g, i)$ *for some $i \in \{1...ar(f)\}$*
- $h \in prop(f)$ *and $f \in prop(g)$*

Note that we can actually compute $prop(g)$ as a closure, starting from the symbols satisfying the first condition and computing their propagation until no new symbol is added to the set.

Let us give the new definition of $Safe$. Note that the definition of $Stable$ and the definition of the ordering remain unchanged.

Definition 9. *Let s be a non-variable term in $\underline{T}(\mathcal{F}, \mathcal{X})$. The set $Safe(s, x)$ for some variable x s.t. $x \in Var(s)$ or $s = x_V$ (for some label V) is defined as the smallest subset of $\mathcal{F}$ containing*

1. *if $s = x_V$ then all symbols in $\mathcal{F} \setminus V$.*
2. *if $s = f(s_1, \ldots, s_n)$ then*
   a) *the union of all $Safe(mt(s_i, \mathrm{m}(f, i)), x)$ with $i \in \{1 \ldots n\}$ and $x \in Var(s_i)$, and*
   b) *all $g \in \mathcal{F}$ such that $f =_{\mathcal{F}} g$ and $stat(f) = stat(g) = mul$, and, $(\mathrm{m}(\underline{g}, i) = \mathrm{m}(g, i))$ for all $i \in \{1...ar(g)\}$.*
   c) *all $g \in \mathcal{F}$ such that $f \succ_{\mathcal{F}} g$ and $f \succ_{\mathcal{F}} h$ for all $h \in prop(g)$.*

With this new definition of $Safe$ the ordering keeps the same properties (and the modification only affects to the proof of stability under ground substitutions).

Theorem 8. $\succ_S$ *over terms in $\mathcal{T}(\mathcal{F}, \mathcal{X})$ is a ground stable μ-reduction ordering.*

Now we can easily prove the termination of the example in the introduction.

Example 10. Proof of example 1.

For this example we just need the marking map $\mathrm{m}(cons, 2) = \mathrm{m}(\underline{cons}, 2) = \mathrm{m}(\underline{adx}, 1) = \mathrm{m}(\underline{incr}, 1) = \{zeros, adx, incr\}$, (for all other symbol and argument positions it is the empty set); the precedence $tail \succ_{\mathcal{F}} \{zeros, adx, incr\}$, $zeros \succ_{\mathcal{F}} \{cons, \underline{zeros}, 0\}$, $nats \succ_{\mathcal{F}} \{adx, zeros\}$, $adx \succ_{\mathcal{F}} incr \succ_{\mathcal{F}} \{cons, s\}$, $adx \succeq_{\mathcal{F}} \underline{adx}$, $incr \succeq_{\mathcal{F}} \underline{incr}$; and multiset status for all symbols. Note that to prove the last rule we need to use case 2c of the definition of $Safe$.

Finally let us mention that using this notion of propagation but defined on marked symbols as well, we can relax one of the conditions for having a valid marking pair (see Definition 4), but by now we have not seen any interesting example in which this improvement is necessary.

7 Conclusions

In this paper we have presented the first method for directly proving termination of context-sensitive rewriting. Our method, called the context-sensitive recursive path ordering, is the first alternative to transformation methods. We have presented some negative results on the practical applicability of Giesl's and Middeldorp transformation methods. Our results show that these transformations are not useful combined with general-purpose termination proof methods like RPO or KBO.

In fact, we have also made some experiments using the CiME 2.0 system (available at `http://cime.lri.fr`), which includes an implementation of the dependency pairs technique with polynomial interpretations, for proving the termination of the transformed system (with the different methods) for all examples given in this paper. The results have been quite poor: with $\mathcal{R}_L^\mu$ only examples 6 and 9 can be proved; with $\mathcal{R}_Z^\mu$ no example could be proved; with $\mathcal{R}_{GM}^\mu$ only examples 6 and 9 hold (and example 5 holds as well if we use an improved version of $\mathcal{R}_{GM}^\mu$ which consists of normalizing the right-hand sides of the transformed system); and with the complete transformation $\mathcal{R}_C^\mu$ only example 6 was proved.

As we have seen, using CSRPO we can easily prove termination of all these examples, including the ones where the transformation methods cannot work or do not work in practice. Moreover, CSRPO is very suitable for automation. The main difficulty for obtaining a fully automatic system based on CSRPO is to automatically generate in a clever way, not only the precedence (as in the implementations of standard RPO) but also the marking map. Note that a naive implementation, which exhaustively checks all possible precedences and markings, may be inefficient (for examples involving many function symbols with large arities), but, in practice, only a few well-chosen markings would have to be tried.

As future developments, apart from the implementation of the method, we want to extend the ideas behind CSRPO, especially the ones concerning the treatment of variables, to more powerful ordering-based methods in order to obtain for context-sensitive rewriting the same kind of automatic tools that can be used for standard rewriting.

Acknowledgements. We would like to thank Robert Nieuwenhuis for his helpful comments on this work.

References

[AG00]   T. Arts and J. Giesl. Termination of term rewriting using dependency pairs. *Theoretical Computer Science*, 236:133–178, 2000.

[AZ96]   Thomas Arts and Hans Zantema. Termination of logic programs using semantic unification. *Fifth International Workshop on Logic Program Synthesis and Transformation*, LNCS 1048:219–233. Springer, 1996.

[BN98]   F. Baader and T. Nipkow. *Term Rewriting and all that*. Cambridge University Press, 1998.

[BLR02]   C. Borralleras, S. Lucas and A. Rubio. Recursive Path Orderings can be Context-Sensitive. Available at www.lsi.upc.es/~albert/papers.html, 2002. Long version.

[Dau92]   Max Dauchet. Simulation of turing machines by a regular rewrite rule. *Theoretical Computer Science*, 103(2):409–420, 1992.

[Der82]   Nachum Dershowitz. Orderings for term-rewriting systems. *Theoretical Computer Science*, 17(3):279–301, 1982.

[FR99]   M.C.F. Ferreira and A.L. Ribeiro. Context-Sensitive AC-Rewriting. *Proc. of 10th International Conference on Rewriting Techniques and Applications*, LNCS 1631:286-300, Springer, 1999.

[GM99]   J. Giesl and A. Middeldorp. Transforming Context-Sensitive Rewrite Systems. *Proc. of 10th International Conference on Rewriting Techniques and Applications*, LNCS 1631:271–285, Springer, 1999.

[GM01]   J. Giesl and A. Middeldorp. Transforming Context-Sensitive Rewrite Systems. *Proc. of 1th International Workshop on Rewriting Proof and Computation, RPC'01*, pages 14-33, RIEC, Tohoku University, 2001.

[Gou01]   Jean Goubault-Larrecq. Well-Founded Recursive Relations. *Proc. 15th Int. Workshop Computer Science Logic*, LNCS 2142:484–497, Springer, 2001.

[GW93]   Harald Ganzinger and Uwe Waldmann. Termination proofs of well-moded logic programs via conditional rewrite systems. *Proc. of 3rd International Workshop on Conditional Term Rewriting Systems*, LNCS 656:113–127, Springer, 1993.

[KB70]   D.E. Knuth and P.B. Bendix. Simple word problems in universal algebras. In *Computational Problems in Abstract Algebra*, pages 263–297. Pergamon Press, 1970.

[KdV02]   J. Kennaway and F.J. de Vries. Infinitary rewriting. In *Term Rewriting Systems*. Cambridge University Press, 2002. To appear.

[Luc96]   S. Lucas. Termination of context-sensitive rewriting by rewriting. *Proc. of 23rd. International Colloquium on Automata, Languages and Programming, ICALP'96*, LNCS 1099:122-133, Springer, 1996.

[Luc98]   S. Lucas. Context-sensitive computations in functional and functional logic programs. *Journal of Functional and Logic Programming*, 1998(1):1-61, 1998.

[Luc01]   S. Lucas. Termination of Rewriting With Strategy Annotations. *Proc. of 8th International Conference on Logic for Programming, Artificial Intelligence and Reasoning*, LNAI 2250:669-684, Springer, 2001.

[NW63]   C. St. J. A. Nash-Williams. On well-quasi-ordering finite trees. *Proceedings of the Cambridge Philosophical Society*, 59(4):833–835, 1963.

[SX98]   J. Steinbach and H. Xi. Freezing – Termination Proofs for Classical, Context-Sensitive and Innermost Rewriting. Institut für Informatik, T.U. München, 1998.

[Zan97]   H. Zantema. Termination of Context-Sensitive Rewriting. *Proc. of 8th International Conference on Rewriting Techniques and Applications, RTA'97*, LNCS 1232:172-186, Springer, 1997.

Appendix

Given a finite signature $\mathcal{F}$, a Knuth-Bendix ordering on $\mathcal{T}(\mathcal{F}, \mathcal{X})$ is determined by [BN98]:

1. A strict ordering $\succ_{\mathcal{F}}$ on $\mathcal{F}$,
2. A weight function

$$w : \mathcal{F} \cup \mathcal{X} \to \mathbb{R}_0^+$$

where $\mathbb{R}_0^+$ are the non-negative real numbers.

The weight function w is admissible if

1. There exists $w_0 \in \mathbb{R}_0^+ - \{0\}$ such that $w(x) = w_0$ for all variables $x \in \mathcal{X}$ and $w(c) > w_0$ for all constants $c \in \mathcal{F}$.
2. If $f \in \mathcal{F}$ is a unary symbol of weight $w(f) = 0$, then f is the greatest element in $\mathcal{F}$, i.e., $f \geq g$ for all $g \in \mathcal{F}$.

The weight function extends to $\mathcal{T}(\mathcal{F}, \mathcal{X})$ as follows: for $t \in \mathcal{T}(\mathcal{F}, \mathcal{X})$,

$$w(t) = \sum_{x \in Var(t)} w(x) \cdot |t|_x + \sum_{f \in \mathcal{F}} w(f) \cdot |t|_f$$

According to this, the Knuth-Bendix ordering $>_{kbo}$ on $\mathcal{T}(\mathcal{F}, \mathcal{X})$ induced by $>$ and w is as follows: for $t, s \in \mathcal{T}(\mathcal{F}, \mathcal{X})$,

$$t >_{kbo} s$$

if and only if $|t|_x \geq |s|_x$ for every $x \in \mathcal{X}$ and either

KBO1 $w(t) > w(s)$, or
KBO2 $w(t) = w(s)$, and one of the following properties holds
    KBO2a There are a unary function symbol f, a variable x and a positive integer n such that $t = f^n(x)$ and $s = x$.
    KBO2b There exist function symbols $f, g \in \mathcal{F}$ such that $f \succ_{\mathcal{F}} g$ and $t = f(t_1, \dots, t_{ar(f)})$, $s = g(s_1, \dots, s_{ar(g)})$.
    KBO2c There exist a function symbol $f \in \mathcal{F}$ and an index i, $1 \leq i \leq ar(f)$ such that $t = f(t_1, \dots, t_{ar(f)})$, $s = f(s_1, \dots, s_{ar(f)})$, $t_j = s_j$ for $1 \leq j < i$ and $t_i >_{kbo} s_i$.

Shostak Light

Harald Ganzinger

MPI Informatik, D-66123 Saarbrücken, Germany, hg@mpi-sb.mpg.de

Abstract. We represent the essential ingredients of Shostak's procedure at a high level of abstraction, and as a refinement of the Nelson-Oppen procedure. We analyze completeness issues of the method based on a general notion of theories. We also formalize a notion of σ-models and show that on the basis of Shostak's procedure we cannot distinguish a theory from its approximation represented by the class of its σ-models.

1 Introduction

Shostak (1984) introduced a procedure that decides the universal fragment of the theory of equality. This congruence closure procedure can be combined with decision procedures for other theories, provided they are what Shostak called "canonizable" and "solvable". Shostak's procedure is at the core of several theorem proving systems, including PVS (Owre, Rushby & Shankar 1992), STeP (Manna et al. 1995) and SVC (Barrett, Dill & Levitt 1996). Previous papers have often suffered from a too technical description of the procedure. Consequently completeness of those formulations of Shostak's procedure has always been difficult to prove. Kapur (2002) compiles a list of technical problems with some of these papers.

More recently several papers have helped in advancing the status of this matter. Tiwari (2000) described Shostak's procedure at an abstract level of inference rules extending the inference system for congruence closure given by Bachmair & Tiwari (2000) (also see Kapur 1997). In Tiwari's presentation Shostak's method appears as a special case of the Nelson/Oppen method (Nelson & Oppen 1979) and is proved complete for equational theories. Rueß & Shankar (2001) presented a more implementation-oriented version of Shostak's procedure eliminating certain sources of incompleteness in Shostak's original formulation. However because of the lack of a more abstract specification, the proofs in the latter paper are somewhat hard to verify. Also, Rueß & Shankar (2001) only treat the validity problem for Horn clauses, and their completeness proof involves a specific notion of σ-models. Barrett, Dill & Stump (2002) describe a procedure without treating free function symbols, concentrating on the relation between convexity, a prerequisite for the completeness of Shostak's method, and stable infiniteness. They observe that convexity implies stable infiniteness for first-order theories without trivial models so that solvers for different theories can be combined with the Nelson-Oppen approach.

The present paper attempts at achieving two goals. One goal is to provide a formal presentation of Shostak's procedure intended to be useful as an abstract

A. Voronkov (Ed.): CADE-18, LNAI 2392, pp. 332–346, 2002.

layer with respect to which more concrete implementations can be verified and variations of the procedure can be developed. Secondly we want to adopt a semantic view where built-in theories are arbitrary classes of structures, not necessarily first-order, and then investigate completeness issues from that general point of view.

As in (Tiwari 2000) and in (Bjørner 1998) we shall present Shostak's procedure (modeled by an inference system $\mathcal{S}$) as a refinement of an inference system $\mathcal{NO}$ modeling a non-branching variant of the Nelson-Oppen procedure. Our view is similar to the one adopted by Bjørner (1998) in that we relate both Shostak's and the Nelson-Oppen method to the general framework of constraint programming and constraint theorem proving: The solvers assumed for Shostak's procedure transform constraints into solved form which in turn can be used to simplify other constraints by eliminating variables. In the Nelson-Oppen procedure constraints are only tested for satisfiability but never solved. So the main difference is that of satisfiability checking for constraints vs. actually computing their solutions. In refutational theorem proving constraint solving is not needed for completeness, and for theories where complete sets of unifiers are large (or infinite) constraint solving is not advisable anyway (Huet 1972, Nieuwenhuis & Rubio 1995). To keep matters simple, in our presentation we do not model any specific efficient version of congruence closure computation. For these issues the reader is referred to (Bachmair, Tiwari & Vigneron 2002) and (Kapur 1997).

As theories in this paper are not restricted a priori we will be able to derive precise characterizations for completeness. Our completeness proofs are semantic and do not require any reasoning about the combinatorics of congruences and canonical term algebras. We show that convexity of a theory is necessary and sufficient for the completeness of $\mathcal{NO}$ and, hence, of $\mathcal{S}$. That convexity is necessary is immediate when one wants to apply Shostak's procedure to the validity problem of equational clauses with more than one positive literal. What we prove here is that even if, as in (Rueß & Shankar 2001), the procedure is only applied to Horn clauses, in the presence of additional free function symbols convexity is indispensable for completeness.

In Section 5, we shall relate convexity to the concept of σ-models. Shostak's (1984) definition of σ-models is somewhat loose. The notion defined in (Rueß & Shankar 2001) turns out to be too restrictive. For the more liberal definition that we shall provide the class of σ-models of a solvable theory represents a convex theory, and hence either Shostak's procedure is incomplete, or else we cannot distinguish between the theory and its σ-models by deciding clausal validity problems.

In Section 6 we briefly take a closer look at the special case of the Nelson-Oppen procedure for a single built-in theory plus free function symbols. In this case the procedure turns out to be complete for any, not necessarily stably infinite, theory. That is we show that if clausal validity is decidable for a theory it remains decidable upon adding free function symbols. Refining that procedure by employing a solver would give one a version of Shostak's procedure complete also for non-convex theories.

2 Basic Concepts

We employ the usual logical notions and notation. Specifically we consider first-order signatures of function symbols and assume that $\approx$ denotes formal equality, a logical symbol present implicitly in any signature. If Σ is a signature, a Σ-term [Σ-formula] is built from function symbols in Σ and from variables. When we write $\forall X F$, we assume that X is some superset of the set of free variables appearing in F. We consider equality $\approx$ as syntactically symmetric so that $u \approx v$ also matches $v \approx u$. Negated equations $\neg(s \approx t)$ are also written as $s \not\approx t$. We shall sometimes use oriented equations as rewrite rules $s \Rightarrow t$. The semantics of a rewrite rule is that of an equation, but rewrite rules are oriented, that is, not considered symmetric syntactically. Sets of equations and disequations are semantically viewed as the conjunction of their elements.

For us a Σ-theory $\mathcal{M}$ is simply a class of Σ-structures, the *models* of the theory, not necessarily first-order. We are interested in deciding the validity problem for clauses for such theories. The *word problem* for $\mathcal{M}$ is to decide whether or not $\mathcal{M} \models \forall X(s \approx t)$ for Σ-equations $s \approx t$. If $\mathcal{M} \models \forall X(s \approx t)$ we call s and t *equal modulo* $\mathcal{M}$, and call them *different* modulo $\mathcal{M}$, otherwise. The *uniform word problem*, also called the *validity problem for Horn clauses*, is the problem of deciding implications $\mathcal{M} \models \forall X(\Gamma \to A)$ for finite sets of Σ-equations Γ and for $A = \bot$ or $A = s \approx t$ a Σ-equation. The *clausal validity problem* in $\mathcal{M}$ is the problem of deciding $\mathcal{M} \models \forall X(A_1 \wedge \ldots \wedge A_n \to B_1 \vee \ldots \vee B_m)$ for arbitrary clauses over Σ-equations A_i and B_j.

A theory $\mathcal{M}$ is called *convex* if for any finite set Γ of Σ-equations and for Σ-equations A_i, $1 \le i \le n$, whenever $\mathcal{M} \models \forall X(\Gamma \to A_1 \vee \ldots \vee A_n)$, then there exists an index j such that $\mathcal{M} \models \forall X(\Gamma \to A_j)$. For convex theories, any clausal validity problem can be reduced to a linear number of validity problems for Horn clauses. Clausal validity problems are often presented as unsatisfiability problems for sets of equational literals since $\mathcal{M} \models \forall X(\Gamma \to A_1 \vee \ldots \vee A_n)$ if, and only if, $\exists X(\Gamma \wedge \neg A_1 \wedge \ldots \wedge \neg A_n)$ is unsatisfiable in $\mathcal{M}$.

In the simple case, both the Nelson/Oppen and Shostak's method deal with two disjoint signatures Δ and Φ of *defined function symbols* and of *free function symbols*, respectively, where the semantics of the defined symbols are given by a Δ-theory $\mathcal{T}$.[1] The theory models are considered in contexts where additional free functions from Φ exist. To that end, by $\mathcal{T}^{\Phi}$ we denote the class of $\Delta \cup \Phi$-structures I such that the restriction of I to Δ (one simply ignores the interpretations of the function symbols from Φ) is in $\mathcal{T}$. Both the Nelson/Oppen method and Shostak's method are designed to extend given decision procedures for the clausal validity problem in the theory $\mathcal{T}$ to a decision procedure for the validity of clauses in $\mathcal{T}^{\Phi}$.

---

[1] In the general case of the Nelson-Oppen method we may have more than one theory over disjoint signatures, possibly including a theory of free functions. The original definition of Shostak's procedure in (Shostak 1984) was given for a single built-in theory, and since then several authors including Bjørner (1998), Kapur (2002), Barrett et al. (2002), and Shankar & Rueß (2002) have described variants to be applied to the combination of solvable theories.

Contradiction

$$\frac{E \parallel D}{\bot}$$

if $\mathcal{T} \models \forall X(E \to \bot)$.

Compose

$$\frac{E \parallel D \cup \{f(s_1, \dots, s_n) \approx s, \; f(s_1', \dots, s_n') \approx s'\}}{E \cup \{s \approx s'\} \parallel D \cup \{f(s_1, \dots, s_n) \approx s\}}$$

if $\mathcal{T} \models \forall X(E \to s_i \approx s_i')$, for $1 \le i \le n$.

Fig. 1. Inference system $\mathcal{NO}$ modeling a non-branching Nelson-Oppen procedure

3   A Non-branching Nelson/Oppen Procedure

Let us assume that we have a theory $\mathcal{T}$ for which the clausal validity problem is decidable and that we want to decide the clausal validity problem in $\mathcal{T}^\Phi$. One possibility is to employ a non-branching version of the the Nelson/Oppen method. When a theory clause $A_1 \wedge \dots \wedge A_n \to B_1 \vee \dots \vee B_m$ is valid without $A_1 \wedge \dots \wedge A_n$ entailing one of the disjuncts B_i we are not going to non-deterministically backtrack over the m disjuncts. Also we do not consider the free theory of Φ as another built-in theory, but rather deal with it explicitly using a specific rule for congruence closure. The system $\mathcal{NO}$ given in Figure 1, where rules may be applied in any order, models that particular version of the Nelson/Oppen procedure.

The inference rules manipulate configurations of the form $E \parallel D$ and are intended to decide the satisfiability of $\exists X(E \wedge D)$ in $\mathcal{T}^\Phi$, with X the set of variables appearing in E or D. Our format is such that E contains equations and disequations over Δ, the *constraints*. (We use the letters s, t, u, v, and w to denote Δ-terms.) D is a set of *function definitions* $F \approx u$ for free function symbols. Here, F denotes terms of the form $f(s_1, \dots, s_n)$, with f in Φ and with Δ-terms s_i as arguments. Since $\mathcal{NO}$ only deals with this restricted ("purified") syntactic format of constraints and function definitions, we have to assume that the initially given problem is presented in this form. This is no essential restriction as the satisfiability problems arising from clausal validity problems over $\Delta \cup \Phi$ can be purified with the help of auxiliary variables in linear time.

The rule Contradiction derives $\bot$ if the set of constraints is unsatisfiable in $\mathcal{T}$. Compose computes overlaps between two function definitions, provided their arguments (which are Δ-terms) are equal for every solution of the constraints in E. Note that the formulas $E \to \bot$ and $E \to s_i \approx s_i'$ are equivalent to clauses and hence their validity is decided by the theory module.

We shall write $E \parallel D \vdash_{\mathcal{NO}} E' \parallel D'$ whenever the first configuration can be transformed into the second by application of a rule in $\mathcal{NO}$. An $\mathcal{NO}$-derivation is a sequence of configurations $\kappa_0 \vdash_{\mathcal{NO}} \kappa_1 \vdash_{\mathcal{NO}} \dots$. A configuration to which no inference rule applies is called *terminal* in $\mathcal{NO}$ or *irreducible* by $\mathcal{NO}$.

Proposition 1. *The inference system is sound. More specifically, (i) whenever* $E \parallel D \vdash E' \parallel D'$ *then* $\mathcal{T}^{\varPhi} \models \forall X (E \wedge D \leftrightarrow E' \wedge D')$; *and (ii) if* $E \parallel D \vdash \perp$ *then* $E \cup D$ *is unsatisfiable in* $\mathcal{T}^{\varPhi}$

Proposition 2. *The derivation relation* $\vdash_{\mathcal{N}\mathcal{O}}$ *is well-founded.*

Theorem 1. $\mathcal{N}\mathcal{O}$ *is complete for a theory* $\mathcal{T}$ *if* $\mathcal{T}$ *is convex.*

Proof. We assume that $\mathcal{T}$ is convex and show that whenever the procedure terminates with final state $E \parallel D$ then $E \wedge D$ is satisfiable in $\mathcal{T}^{\varPhi}$. For this we need to identify a suitable $\mathcal{T}$-model I satisfying E and extend it by definitions for the free function symbols so that D is also satisfied. Consider the set M of Δ-terms that appear either in a disequation in E, or as an argument of a free function symbol on the left side of a function definition in D. Call two terms s and t in M equivalent if $\mathcal{T} \models \forall X (E \rightarrow s \approx t)$. Define N such that it contains exactly one representative of each equivalence class of M. Suppose $N = \{u_1, \ldots, u_m\}$. If $E \cup \{u_i \not\approx u_j \mid i \neq j\}$ were unsatisfiable in $\mathcal{T}$ then either $m \leq 1$ and E is unsatisfiable, or else $m > 1$ and $\mathcal{T} \models \forall X (E \rightarrow \bigvee_{i \neq j} u_i \approx u_j)$. In the first case Contradiction would have derived $\perp$ which it did not. In the second case, by the convexity of $\mathcal{T}$, again either E is unsatisfiable which it is not, or else $\mathcal{T} \models \forall X (E_+ \rightarrow u_i \approx u_j)$ for some pair $i \neq j$, where E_+ is the subset of positive equations in E. The latter situation would contradict the way N was constructed. We have shown that there exists a structure I in $\mathcal{T}$ and a variable assignment $\alpha : X \rightarrow I$ satisfying E and where the terms u_i denote pairwise different values in I.

Now extend I by interpretations for the free function symbols as follows: If f is a free function symbol and $f(s_1, \ldots, s_n) \approx u$ is a function definition in D, evaluate the s_i as well as u in I, α, yielding values a_i and c, respectively, and define $f_I(a_1, \ldots, a_n)$ to be c. Define f_I arbitrarily at all other argument tuples of the domain of I. We have to show that f is well-defined. A potential ambiguity may arise from the presence of two definitions $f(s_1, \ldots, s_n) \approx s$ and $f(s'_1, \ldots, s'_n) \approx s'$ in D, should it be the case that $I, \alpha \models s_i \approx s'_i$, for $1 \leq i \leq n$. However, if these two function definitions were present then there would exist an index j such that $\mathcal{T} \not\models \forall X (E \rightarrow s_j \approx s'_j)$, for otherwise Compose would have eliminated one of the two definitions. By construction N contains different terms u and u' equivalent to s_j and s'_j, respectively. Since we picked I and α such that different terms in N denote different values in I, it cannot be possible that $I, \alpha \models s_j \approx s'_j$. $\square$

In the general branching version of the Nelson-Oppen procedure with an arbitrary number of theory components a property weaker than convexity, called stable infiniteness, suffices to obtain completeness. For a detailed proof of this fact the reader is referred to (Tinelli & Harandi 1996). For theories having only non-trivial models—these are structures with more than one element—convexity is sufficient for the completeness also of the general version of the Nelson-Oppen procedure. This is a consequence of the results in (Barrett et al. 2002). Above we gave a direct and simple model construction proof that neither relies on the general completeness result nor on the relation between convexity and stable infiniteness.

If a theory has non-trivial models only, convexity is also necessary for $\mathcal{NO}$ to be complete even for merely deciding the validity of Horn clauses.

Theorem 2. *If $\mathcal{T}$ is a non-convex theory of non-trivial structures then there exists a Horn clause of the form $E, D \to s \approx t$ valid in $\mathcal{T}^\Phi$ such that $E \cup \{s \napprox t\} \parallel D$ is irreducible by $\mathcal{NO}$.*

Proof. Suppose $\mathcal{T}$ is not convex. Then there exists a set of Δ-equations E and a set of $n \geq 2$ Δ-equations $s_i \approx t_i$, $1 \leq i \leq n$, such that the clause $C = \forall X(E \to \bigvee_i s_i \approx t_i)$ is valid in $\mathcal{T}$ but $\mathcal{T} \not\models \forall X(E \to s_i \approx t_i)$, for any i. Let Φ contain n different monadic function symbols f_i, and define D to be the set of function definitions containing the equations $f_i(s_i) \approx x$, and $f_i(t_i) \approx y$, with x and y two different variables not occurring in E, s_i, and t_i. We show that $\mathcal{T} \models \forall X(E \wedge D \to x \approx y)$. Suppose that I is in $\mathcal{T}$ and α a variable assigment such that $I, \alpha \models E \wedge D$. As C is valid in I there exists an index i such that $I, \alpha \models s_i \approx t_i$. Moreover, as the function definitions are satisfied in I, α we infer that $I, \alpha \models f_i(t_i) \approx y$ and $I, \alpha \models f_i(s_i) \approx x$ and, hence, $I, \alpha \models x \approx y$. On the other hand no inference in $\mathcal{NO}$ applies to the configuration $E \cup \{x \napprox y\} \parallel D$. Compose cannot be applied as $\mathcal{T} \not\models \forall X(E \to s_i \approx t_i)$, for every i. For the same reason E must be satisfiable in $\mathcal{T}$. As $\mathcal{T}$ has only non-trivial models, Contradiction does not apply to $E \cup \{x \napprox y\}$. $\square$

The system $\mathcal{NO}$ only formalizes the bare bones of a variant of the Nelson/Oppen procedure. In practice one may want to add additional (sound) inference rules to increase the efficiency of the method. There is a uniform method of doing this in a way such that completeness is maintained. Call a set of additional inference rules on configurations *admissible* if they are sound and if termination is maintained. Completeness can not be lost by adding additional inference rules. However one can also safely delete instances of inference rules as long as it is guaranteed that configurations reducible by deleted inference rules can also be reduced by some other inference rules. In the next section we are going to model Shostak's method as a refinement in this sense of the inference system $\mathcal{NO}$.

4   Shostak Light

Shostak's procedure assumes the presence of a (unitary) unification algorithm for $\mathcal{T}$. More specifically it is assumed that there exists an effectively computable function solve such that, for any $\mathcal{T}$-equation $s \approx t$:

(A) solve$(s \approx t) = \bot$ if, and only if, $\mathcal{T} \models \forall X(s \napprox t)$;
(B) solve$(s \approx t) = \emptyset$ if, and only if, $\mathcal{T} \models \forall X(s \approx t)$; and otherwise
(C) solve$(s \approx t) = \{x_1 \Rightarrow u_1, \ldots, x_n \Rightarrow u_n\}$ is a finite set of rewrite rules over Δ such that

(i)   the x_i are pairwise different variables occurring in $s \approx t$;

(ii) the x_i do not occur in the u_j; and

(iii) $\mathcal{T} \models \forall X[(s \approx t) \leftrightarrow \exists Y(x_1 \approx u_1 \wedge \ldots \wedge x_n \approx u_n)]$, where Y is the set of variables occurring in one of the u_j but not in $s \approx t$, and $X \cap Y = \emptyset$.

If a function solve with these properties exists we call the theory *solvable*. solve$(s \approx t)$, if different from $\bot$, may be viewed as a (possibly empty) substitution $\sigma = [u_1/x_1, \ldots, u_n/x_n]$, written as a set of rewrite rules $\{x_1 \Rightarrow u_1, \ldots, x_n \Rightarrow u_n\}$, that solves the $\mathcal{T}$-equation $s \approx t$.

Solutions can be parameterized by new variables, those in Y. It is assumed that in each calling context for solve, the variables in Y are fresh. Where this needs to be formalized we shall write solve$_Z(s \approx t) = S$, assuming that then the extra variables appearing in S are not in Z.

Example 1. Let $\mathbb{Q}$ be the single-model theory consisting of the rational numbers with linear arithmetic. In the signature of $\mathbb{Q}$ we have all rational numbers as constants, the binary addition operator $+$, and, for each rational number q, a unary operator $q \cdot \_$ multiplying its argument by q. Equations over $\mathbb{Q}$ can be solved by Gaussian elimination, and it is well-known that the theory is convex.

Example 2. Let $\mathbb{Z}/(3)$ be the one-model theory of the three-element field obtained by considering the remainders from division by 3. Let the signature consist of the constants 0 and 1, and the binary addition $+$. Clearly, $\mathbb{Z}/(3)$ is solvable. For example, $a + a + 1 = b + b$ is solved by $a \Rightarrow 1 + b$. However $\mathbb{Z}/(3)$ is not convex as witnessed by the disjunction $\forall x(x \approx 0 \vee x \approx 1 \vee x \approx 1 + 1)$.

Due to (B), solvers effectively decide the word problem for $\mathcal{T}$.[2] Further, if a theory is solvable we can also effectively decide the *uniform* word problem for $\mathcal{T}$. In fact, for deciding $\mathcal{T} \models \forall X(\Gamma \rightarrow A)$ we iteratively apply solve to the equations in Γ. If this yields $\bot$, the implication is valid in $\mathcal{T}$. Otherwise for the implication to be valid A has to be an equation $s \approx t$, and we obtain a substitution σ that is equivalent to Γ such that $\mathcal{T} \models \forall X(\Gamma \rightarrow s \approx t)$ if, and only if, $\mathcal{T} \models \forall X, Y(s \approx t)\sigma$ (with Y the extra variables in the codomain of σ), if and only if, solve$((s \approx t)\sigma) = \emptyset$.

The Nelson/Oppen method is based on being able to decide the [un-]solvability of certain theory constraints. When one has a solver available one can do more and additionally replace constraints by their solved forms (the unifiers). Since solvable theories are required to have unique most general solutions

---

[2] Most presentations of Shostak's method do not require property (B) for solve, but assume the presence of a canonizer so that the word problem can be decided by comparing canonical forms. We present Shostak's procedure without a canonizer. The word problem is all we need to be able to decide, and we may leave it to the implementation of the solver as to whether solutions computed will always be in canonical form. For increasing the efficiency of an actual implementation, the presence of a canonizer might be helpful, but keeping terms always canonical may not be the most efficient strategy. Formalizing normalization strategies involving a canonizer only requires to add more reduction inference rules to our inference system below. We shall discuss this in more detail at the end of this section.

Contradiction

$$\frac{U \cup \{s \approx t\}, R \parallel D}{\bot} \qquad \text{if solve}(s \approx t) = \bot$$

$$\frac{U \cup \{s \not\approx t\}, R \parallel D}{\bot} \qquad \text{if solve}(s \approx t) = \emptyset$$

Solve

$$\frac{U \cup \{s \approx t\}, R \parallel D}{U, R \cup S \parallel D}$$

where
(i) $S = \text{solve}_X(s \approx t) \neq \bot$, with X the set of variables appearing in the antecedent,
(ii) both s and t are irreducible by R.

Reduce

$$\frac{U, R \cup \{x \Rightarrow t\} \parallel D \cup \{F[x] \approx s\}}{U, R \cup \{x \Rightarrow t\} \parallel D \cup \{F[t] \approx s\}}$$

$$\frac{U \cup \{L[x]\}, R \cup \{x \Rightarrow t\} \parallel D}{U \cup \{L[t]\}, R \cup \{x \Rightarrow t\} \parallel D}$$

Compose

$$\frac{U, R \parallel D \cup \{f(s_1, \dots, s_n) \approx s, \ f(s_1', \dots, s_n') \approx s'\}}{U \cup \{s \approx s'\}, R \parallel D \cup \{f(s_1, \dots, s_n) \approx s\}}$$

if $\text{solve}(s_i \approx s_i') = \emptyset$, for $1 \leq i \leq n$.

Fig. 2. Inference system $\mathcal{S}$ modeling Shostak's procedure

for solvable constraints, no backtracking occurs. Also, applying solutions to unsolved constraints and to function definitions effectively eliminates some of the variables and in this sense simplifies the satisfiability problem. So Shostak is to Nelson/Oppen what theorem proving and CLP with computation of unifiers for built-in theories is to constraint theorem proving and CLP with constraint propagation and constraint satisfiability checking.

The figure 2 presents the inference system $\mathcal{S}$ where again rules may be applied in any order. $\mathcal{S}$ refines $\mathcal{NO}$ in that the constraints E in $\mathcal{NO}$ are now represented by the union of two constraints U and R. In other words, $\mathcal{S}$-configurations $U, R \parallel D$ correspond to $\mathcal{NO}$-configurations $U \cup R \parallel D$. In the refined format, U is the subset of disequations and of "unsolved" positive equations, whereas R is a positive constraint in *solved form*, a substitution derived from previous constraint solving steps. The Contradiction and Compose rules are instances of the Contradiction and Compose rules, respectively, of $\mathcal{NO}$. Configurations reducible by instances of Contradiction and Compose in $\mathcal{NO}$ that are not dealt with by Contradiction and Compose in $\mathcal{S}$ can be reduced by instances of Solve or Reduce (cf. Proposition 8).

Solve solves Δ-equations $s \approx t$. Soundness of this rule is a consequence of the soundness of the solver, cf. Proposition 4 below. More precisely, we only solve normalized equations in which both s and t are irreducible by R. The reduce inferences are designed to compute those normal forms. The solved equation is deleted from U and its solution S is added to the solved form R. The rules added to R upon Solve are all of the form $x \Rightarrow w$, and are called *variable definitions*. By Propositions 3 and 5 R always contains at most one definition for a variable and is terminating. Sets of constraints R with these properties we call *solved forms*.

Reduce expands variables in the F-terms in D as well as in the Δ-terms in U by their definitions. In most presentations of Shostak's method one would apply both the Contradiction and the Compose rules only to irreducible terms s, t, s_i and s'_i, respectively. Since our results will be applicable to all fair (that is, maximal) strategies of inference rule application, soundness and completeness also follows for any more refined strategy of substitution application.

We shall write $U, R \parallel D \vdash_S U', R' \parallel D'$ whenever the first configuration can be transformed into the second by application of a rule in S. An S-derivation is a sequence of configurations $\kappa_0 \vdash_S \kappa_1 \vdash_S \ldots$ with κ_0 a configuration of the form $U, \emptyset \parallel D$. A configuration to which no inference rule applies is called *terminal* in S or *irreducible* by S. A derivation is called *maximal* if its end configuration is terminal.

Proposition 3. *Any rule set R appearing in an S-derivation contains at most one definition for any variable.*

Proof. The property is trivially true initially. When adding a rule set S to R in Solve, if R contains a definition $x' \Rightarrow t'$, S cannot contain a rule for x'. Otherwise x' would have to occur in $s \approx t$, and the equation being solved at this step would not be irreducible with respect to R. $\square$

Proposition 4. *The inference system is sound. More specifically, (i) whenever $U, R \parallel D \vdash_S U', R' \parallel D'$ then $\mathcal{T}^\Phi \models \exists X(U \wedge R \wedge D) \rightarrow \exists X, Y(U' \wedge R' \wedge D')$ and $\mathcal{T}^\Phi \models \forall X, Y(U' \wedge R' \wedge D' \rightarrow U \wedge R \wedge D)$, with Y the variables in $U', R' \parallel D'$ but not in $U, R \parallel D$; and (ii) if $U, R \parallel D \vdash_S \bot$ then $U \cup R \cup D$ is unsatisfiable in $\mathcal{T}^\Phi$.*

In the rewrite systems R, variables are considered as constants which can not be substituted by other terms. In this sense the systems R induce terminating rewrite relations.

Proposition 5. *If $U, R \parallel D \vdash_S U', R' \parallel D'$ and if R is terminating then R' is terminating.*

Proof. Let us, for a configuration $U, R \parallel D$ with variables in X, define $x \succ^X y$ if, and only if, y occurs on the right side of a definition for x in R. R is terminating if, and only if, $\succ^X$ is a well-founded partial ordering on X. (For the "if" part, use a lexicographic path ordering over some precedence $>^X$ for which $\Phi >^X X >^X \Delta$, and which coincides with $\succ^X$ on X to show termination of R.)

We now show that if $\succ^X$ is a well-founded partial ordering on X and if $U, R \parallel D \vdash_S U', R' \parallel D'$ then $\succ^{X'}$ is a well-founded partial ordering on X', the set of variables in the new configuration. The only non-trivial case is when the derivation is by Solve where the new variable definitions S are added to R. However only equations $s \approx t$ irreducible by R are solved, so that no variable appearing in s or t is reducible by R. Therefore any variable occurring on the right side of a rule in S is irreducible by R. Also, according to the definition of a solver, right sides of rules in S are irreducible by S. Consequently, $\succ^{X'}$ is well-founded. $\square$

Proposition 6. *The inference system S is terminating.*

Proof. We need to describe a well-founded ordering $\succ$ on configurations with terminating rewrite systems R for which all inference rules are strictly monotone. Define $\succ$ such that $\bot$ is minimal. Moreover if $\kappa = U, R \parallel D$ and $\kappa' = U', R' \parallel D'$ are two configurations with X and X', respectively, the set of variables occurring in κ and κ', let $\kappa \succ \kappa'$ whenever

(i) $|D| > |D'|$; or else
(ii) $|D| = |D'|$, and $U \supset U'$; or else
(iii) $|D| = |D'|$, $R = R'$, and $U \Rightarrow_R U'$; or else
(iv) $|D| = |D'|$, $R = R'$, $U = U'$, and $D \Rightarrow_R D'$.

This ordering is well-founded. For if in a sequence $\kappa_0 \succ \kappa_1 \succ \ldots$ the number of function definitions does not decrease and no equations are deleted from U no new rules can be introduced, and therefore $R_i = R_{i+1}$. As the rewrite relations in configurations are all terminating any such sequence must be terminating. Clearly, the rules in S are strictly decreasing with respect to $\succ$. $\square$

The proposition in particular shows that the number of new variables introduced during a derivation must be finite, irrespective of the way a solver introduces them.

Proposition 7. *(i) If R is a solved form and if s and t are irreducible by R then $\mathcal{T} \models \forall X(R \to s \approx t)$ if, and only if, $\mathcal{T} \models \forall X(s \approx t)$.*
(ii) Let $\mathcal{T}$ be convex. If R is a solved form, U a set of Δ-disequations satisfiable in $\mathcal{T}$ and irreducible by R, and if s and t are irreducible by R then $\mathcal{T} \models \forall X(U, R \to s \approx t)$ if, and only if, $\mathcal{T} \models \forall X(s \approx t)$.

Proposition 8. *Let $\mathcal{T}$ be a convex theory. If $U, R \parallel D$ is a terminal configuration of S then $U \cup R \parallel D$ is a terminal configuration of $\mathcal{NO}$.*

Proof. If no inference in S can be applied to $U, R \parallel D$ then U contains only negative equations and is satisfiable in $\mathcal{T}$, R is a solved form (cf. propositions 3 and 5), and any term appearing in U or in an F-term in D is irreducible by R. We first show that Compose in $\mathcal{NO}$ cannot be applied to $U \cup R \parallel D$. Otherwise, there would be two definitions $f(s_1, \ldots, s_n) \approx s$ and $f(s'_1, \ldots, s'_n) \approx s'$ in D such that $\mathcal{T} \models \forall X(U, R \to s_i \approx s'_i)$, for $1 \leq i \leq n$. From (ii) in Proposition 7 we conclude that $\mathcal{T} \models \forall X(s_i \approx s'_i)$, for $1 \leq i \leq n$. Therefore, $\mathsf{solve}(s_i \approx s'_i) = \emptyset$ and Compose would also be applicable in S, which is a contradiction.

Showing that also the Contradiction inference in $\mathcal{NO}$ is not applicable to $U \cup R \parallel D$ is essentially similar. $\square$

To summarize, we have shown that for convex theories $\mathcal{S}$ is a refinement of $\mathcal{NO}$:

(i)   All new instances of inference rules are sound. (Proposition 4)

(ii) There is a well-founded refinement of the ordering on $\mathcal{NO}$-configurations such that the new inference rules are strictly monotone (Proposition 6).

(iii) If $U, R \parallel D$ is a terminal configuration for $\mathcal{S}$ then $U \cup R \parallel D$ is a terminal configuration for $\mathcal{NO}$ so that configurations reduced by $\mathcal{NO}$-rules not present anymore in $\mathcal{S}$ can be reduced by other rules in $\mathcal{S}$.

Convexity of $\mathcal{T}$ was required for showing (iii). As a consequence we obtain completeness of $\mathcal{S}$ for convex, solvable theories.

Theorem 3. *$\mathcal{S}$ is complete for any solvable convex theory $\mathcal{T}$.*

For theories without trivial models, convexity is also a necessary requirement for the completeness of Shostak's procedure. The proof can be given essentially as for Theorem 2. Another possibility is to exploit one more correspondence between derivations in $\mathcal{NO}$ and $\mathcal{S}$.

Lemma 1. *If $E \parallel D$ is a terminal configuration for $\mathcal{NO}$ then all maximal derivations in $\mathcal{S}$ from configurations $U, R \parallel D$, where $E = U \cup R$, end in a configuration different from $\bot$.*

Proof. If $E \parallel D$ is irreducible by $\mathcal{NO}$, Contradiction is not applicable to $U, R \parallel D$. Also Compose is not applicable in $U, R \parallel D$ as otherwise Compose in $\mathcal{NO}$ would be applicable to $E \parallel D$. Therefore only Solve and Reduce can be applied to $U, R \parallel D$. Observe that $\mathcal{T} \models \forall X (U \wedge R \leftrightarrow \exists Y (U' \wedge R'))$ with Y the new variables in the configuration obtained from any such inference. Moreover, if $F \approx s$ is a function definition for a free symbol f in D' then there exists a corresponding definition $G \approx t$ in D for f such that $\mathcal{T} \models \forall X (R \rightarrow s \approx t)$, and $\mathcal{T} \models \forall X (R \rightarrow u \approx v)$ for any two terms u and v appearing at corresponding argument positions in F and G, respectively. Therefore Contradiction and Compose can also not be applied in $U', R' \parallel D'$ as otherwise the respective rule in $\mathcal{NO}$ would be applicable to $E \parallel D$. The Lemma now follows by induction. $\square$

Theorem 4. *If $\mathcal{T}$ is a solvable non-convex theory of non-trivial structures then there exists a Horn clause valid in $\mathcal{T}^{\Phi}$ such that $\mathcal{S}$ fails to derive $\bot$ on the corresponding unsatisfiability problem.*

Proof. We apply Theorem 2 to obtain a Horn clause $E, D \rightarrow s \approx t$ that is valid in $\mathcal{T}^{\Phi}$ and for which $E \cup \{s \not\approx t\} \parallel D$ is irreducible by $\mathcal{NO}$. Now apply the previous Lemma. $\square$

So far we have not modeled the concept of canonizers. We briefly sketch how to accommodate canonizers in $\mathcal{S}$. A *canonizer* for a theory $\mathcal{T}$ is a ground[3] rewrite system C on $T_{\Delta}(X)$ where the right side of every rule is irreducible by C and does not contain any variable that does not already appear on the left side.

---

[3] The rules may contain variables from X but they are considered as constants.

Moreover, each rule in C must be universally valid in $\mathcal{T}$. (Usually canonizers are assumed to have further properties of which we, however, do not make any use here.) Since right sides of rules are reduced, canonizers are terminating rewrite systems. However, $C \cup R$, where R is a solved form appearing in an $\mathcal{S}$-deduction, in general will not be terminating. Therefore, when extending the Reduce rules to a canonizer one needs to decide upon a terminating strategy for interleaving C-steps and R-steps. One example of a terminating reduction relation would be $\Rightarrow_R^{||} \cup \Rightarrow_C$, if $\Rightarrow_R^{||}$ denotes one step of parallel replacement of all R-redexes in a term. Then the termination proof (Proposition 6) remains the same with $\Rightarrow_R$ replaced by $\Rightarrow_R^{||} \cup \Rightarrow_C$.

5 σ-Models

Shostak's original paper as well as (Rueß & Shankar 2001) employ a notion of σ-models relative to which they state completeness. Shostak's definition is somewhat imprecise. According to (Rueß & Shankar 2001), a σ-model is a Δ-structure satisfying all equations $\forall X (s \approx t)$ for which s and t are equal modulo $\mathcal{T}$, and all disequations $s \not\approx t$ such that s and t are ground terms that are different modulo $\mathcal{T}$. They call a theory solvable if the class of these σ-models is solvable. This definition of σ-models and solvable theories appears to be too restrictive as it does not capture many intuitively solvable theories. As an example, consider the theory of lists over car, cdr and $cons$ satisfying the rules $\forall x, y (car(cons(x,y)) \Rightarrow x)$, $\forall x, y (cdr(cons(x,y)) \Rightarrow y)$, and $\forall x (cons(car(x), cdr(x)) \Rightarrow x)$ and also the disequations $\forall X (x \not\approx t)$, whenever t is irreducible by the list rules and contains an occurrence of x as an argument of an occurrence of $cons$ in t. Shostak (1984) shows that these lists form a solvable theory. The σ-models of lists, however, contain (non-trivial) structures L in which $l = cdr(l)$ for some element l in L. Therefore, for any solver, $\mathsf{solve}(x \approx cdr(x)) \neq \bot$, and as a consequence of this fact no solver can exist for the theory of σ-models of lists. In fact, $\mathsf{solve}(x \approx cdr(x))$ would have to be a rule $x \Rightarrow t$, with x not in t, and thus $\forall Y (t \approx cdr(t))$ would have to be a consequence of the list rules which it is not. (To see this assume, wolog, that t is irreducible by the list rules. If t does not start with a $cons$, also $cdr(t)$ is irreducible. Otherwise $t = cons(t_1, t_2)$ and t_2 is the canonical form of $cdr(t)$ and different from t.)

The definition of σ-models in (Rueß & Shankar 2001) is solely based on the properties of the canonizer σ (hence the name). Our subsequent definition will be based on the solver (so we should rather speak of solve-models), and as a consequence of this we can avoid the shortcomings illustrated by the list example. Given $\mathcal{T}$, we define $\sigma(\mathcal{T})$, the class of σ-models of $\mathcal{T}$ (with respect to solve), to be the class of Δ-structures for which solve is sound. This is the class of structures satisfying (i) $\sigma(\mathcal{T}) \models \forall X (s \not\approx t)$, whenever $\mathsf{solve}(s \approx t) = \bot$, and (ii) $\sigma(\mathcal{T}) \models \forall X [(s \approx t) \leftrightarrow \exists Y (x_1 \approx u_1 \wedge \ldots \wedge x_n \approx u_n)]$, whenever $\mathsf{solve}(s \approx t) = \{x_1 \Rightarrow u_1, \ldots, x_n \Rightarrow u_n\}$, where X is the set of parameters in $s \approx t$ and Y is the set of new parameters in the solution. Hence if solve is a solver for $\mathcal{T}$ then it is also a solver for $\sigma(\mathcal{T})$. It is easy to see that $\mathcal{T} \subseteq \sigma(\mathcal{T})$. Therefore, any solver for $\sigma(\mathcal{T})$ is also a solver for $\mathcal{T}$. Also, $\sigma(\sigma(\mathcal{T})) = \sigma(\mathcal{T})$.

Proposition 9. $\mathcal{S}$ *is sound with respect to* $\sigma(\mathcal{T})$.

As equational theories, the σ-theories of (Rueß & Shankar 2001) are closed under products and, therefore, are convex. Our σ-theories are also convex.

Proposition 10. *If* $\mathcal{T}$ *is a solvable theory then* $\sigma(\mathcal{T})$ *is convex.*

Proof. σ-models are axiomatized by the first-order conditions (i) and (ii) above. It is not difficult to see that theories axiomatized by formulas of this kind are closed under products, and hence are convex. $\square$

This proves the completeness of the method with respect to σ-models and, thus, extends the results in (Rueß & Shankar 2001) on a more abstract level to a more liberal notion of σ-models. In general $\mathcal{T}$ is a proper subset of $\sigma(\mathcal{T})$. Examples are $\mathcal{T} = \{\mathbb{Q}\}$ or $\mathcal{T} = \{\mathbb{Z}/(3)\}$ as defined above. Yet, if $\mathcal{T}$ is convex then we cannot distinguish $\mathcal{T}$ from $\sigma(\mathcal{T})$ with respect to clausal tautology problems.

Theorem 5. *If* $\mathcal{T}$ *is convex and solvable and if* E *is a finite set of equations and disequations over* $\Delta \cup \Phi$, *then* E *is satisfiable in* $\mathcal{T}^{\Phi}$ *if, and only if,* E *is satisfiable in* $\sigma(\mathcal{T})^{\Phi}$.

Proof. We have shown that $\mathcal{S}$ is sound with respect to both $\mathcal{T}$ and $\sigma(\mathcal{T})$. Since both $\mathcal{T}$ and $\sigma(\mathcal{T})$ are convex, $\mathcal{S}$ is also complete with respect to both $\mathcal{T}$ and $\sigma(\mathcal{T})$. The result of running $\mathcal{S}$ on E will, therefore, establish [un-]satisfiability of E both with respect to $\mathcal{T}$ and $\sigma(\mathcal{T})$. $\square$

This result can be viewed as a justification for the semantic concept of σ-models as defined here. Deciding satisfiability with respect to its σ-models is all one can get for a solvable theory.

6   Branching Nelson-Oppen

From the model construction in the proof of Theorem 1 one sees what is lacking for making $\mathcal{NO}$ complete also for non-convex theories. One needs to non-deterministically branch on all possible ways two function definitions rules might be inconsistent with the constraints. Hence, a branching version of the procedure can be defined by adding this inference rule to $\mathcal{NO}$

$$\frac{E \parallel D}{E \cup \{s \approx t\} \parallel D[s/t] \quad | \quad E \cup \{s \not\approx t\} \parallel D}$$

whenever there are two definitions $f(s_1, \ldots, s_n) \approx s$ and $f(s_1', \ldots, s_n') \approx s'$ in D such that $s = s_i \neq s_i' = t$, for some index i, and for no index j the disequation $s_j \not\approx s_j'$ is in E. (By $D[s/t]$ we denote the result of substituting all occurrences of t as an argument of a free function symbol in D by s.)

In the extended system derivations are trees of inference rule applications with the new rule introducing a branching into two sub-derivations. Clearly, the system remains terminating. Terminal configurations in a derivation are either

$\perp$ or are such that if $f(s_1, \ldots, s_n) \approx s$ and $f(s'_1, \ldots, s'_n) \approx s'$ are two different function definitions in D for the same f then there exists an index i such that $s_i \not\approx s'_i$ is in E. Configurations of the first kind are unsatisfiable whereas those of the second kind are satisfiable. In fact since the configuration is terminal, E is satisfiable in $\mathcal{T}$, and extending any model I of E by definitions for the free f satisfying D is no problem as the argument tuples for any two definition rules for any f are different in I. As a consequence we obtain soundness and completeness of the branching version of the Nelson-Oppen procedure. We assume that a run producing a derivation returns "valid" if all leaves in the tree are $\perp$, and "not valid", otherwise.

Theorem 6. *Branching $\mathcal{NO}$ is sound and complete for the clausal validity problem in $\mathcal{T}^\Phi$, for any theory $\mathcal{T}$ where clausal validity is decidable.*

This result is not in contradiction with previous results in the literature. For one we only have a single theory built-in and the free function symbols are explicitly dealt with by the Compose rule. Only when combining more than one built-in theory stable infiniteness of the theories is needed. Secondly, the example 2.2 in (Baader & Tinelli 1997) which appears like a counterexample to our theorem allows negative equations to also contain free function symbols. Our preprocessing of satisfiability problems purifies such disequations by introducing new variables the disequality of which might lead to a contradiction in $\mathcal{T}$ that the procedure in (Baader & Tinelli 1997) might fail to infer.

7   Conclusion

We have modeled a version of Shostak's procedure at a high-level of abstraction and as a refinement of a similarly high-level model of a Nelson-Oppen-like procedure. On the semantic side theories were arbitrary sets of structures. Among others we have show that completeness for Horn clause validity problems is equivalent with the convexity of the theory. We have given a definition of σ-models based on the properties of solvers and have shown that these σ-models represent a tight approximation of solvable theories. Hence one may argue that the concept of a solver is more fundamental in Shostak's procedure than the concept of a canonizer (that we have not formalized here). Our completeness result for branching $\mathcal{NO}$ indicates how to obtain a Shostak procedure for non-convex solvable theories. We expect that we can extend our modeling and proof techniques also to the interesting and natural combination procedure for Shostak theories presented in (Shankar & Rueß 2002).

Acknowledgments. I am grateful to Viorica Sofronie-Stokkermans, Uwe Waldmann, Natarajan Shankar, Harald Rueß, and Franz Baader for fruitful discussions on the subject of this paper. I also thank the referees for their detailed and constructive criticism on a much different initial version of this paper.

References

Baader, F. & Tinelli, C. (1997), A new approach for combining decision procedures for the word problem, and its connection to the nelson-oppen combination method, *in* W. McCune, ed., 'Automated Deduction – CADE-14, 14th International Conference on Automated Deduction', LNAI 1249, Springer-Verlag, Townsville, North Queensland, Australia, pp. 19–33.

Bachmair, L. & Tiwari, A. (2000), Abstract congruence closure and specializations, *in* D. McAllester, ed., 'Automated Deduction – CADE-17, 17th International Conference on Automated Deduction', LNAI 1831, Springer-Verlag, Pittsburgh, PA, USA, pp. 64–78.

Bachmair, L., Tiwari, A. & Vigneron, L. (2002), 'Abstract congruence closure', *J. Automated Reasoning* . To appear.

Barrett, C., Dill, D. & Levitt, J. (1996), Validity checking for combinations of theories with equality, *in* M. Srivas & A. Camilleri, eds, 'Formal Methods In Computer-Aided Design, Palo Alto/CA, USA', Vol. 1166, Springer-Verlag, pp. 187–201. citeseer.nj.nec.com/barrett96validity.html

Barrett, C., Dill, D. & Stump, A. (2002), A generalization of Shostak's method for combining decision procedures, *in* 'Proc. FroCos 2002', Springer-Verlag. to appear.

Bjørner, N. (1998), Integrating decision procedures for temporal verification, PhD thesis, Stanford University.

Huet, G. (1972), Constrained Resolution: A Complete Method for Higher Order Logic, PhD thesis, Case Western Reserve University.

Kapur, D. (1997), Shostak's congruence closure as completion, *in* H. Comon, ed., 'Rewriting Techniques and Applications', Lecture Notes in Computer Science, Springer, Sitges, Spain, pp. 23–37.

Kapur, D. (2002), A rewrite rule based framework for combining decision procedures, *in* 'Proc. FroCos 2002', Springer-Verlag. to appear.

Manna, Z., Anuchitanulu, A., Bjørner, N., Browne, A., Chang, E. S., Colón, M., de Alfaro, L., Devarajan, H., Kapur, A., Lee, J., Sipma, H. & Uribe, T. E. (1995), STeP: The Stanford Temporal Prover, *in* 'TAPSOFT', Vol. 915 of *Lecture Notes in Computer Science*, Springer-Verlag, pp. 793–794.

Nelson, G. & Oppen, D. C. (1979), 'Simplification by cooperating decision procedures', *ACM Transactions on Programming Languages and Systems* **2**(2), 245–257.

Nieuwenhuis, R. & Rubio, A. (1995), 'Theorem proving with ordering and equality constrained clauses', *J. Symbolic Computation* **19**(4), 321–352.

Owre, S., Rushby, J. M. & Shankar, N. (1992), PVS: A prototype verification system, *in* D. Kapur, ed., '11th International Conference on Automated Deduction', LNAI 607, Springer-Verlag, Saratoga Springs, New York, USA, pp. 748–752.

Rueß, H. & Shankar, N. (2001), Deconstructing Shostak, *in* 'Proceedings of the Sixteenth IEEE Symposium On Logic In Computer Science (LICS'01)', IEEE Computer Society Press, pp. 19–28.

Shankar, N. & Rueß, H. (2002), Combining Shostak theories, *in* 'Proc. RTA 2002', Lecture Notes in Computer Science, Springer-Verlag. to appear.

Shostak, R. E. (1984), 'Deciding combinations of theories', *J. Association for Computing Machinery* **31**(1), 1–12.

Tinelli, C. & Harandi, M. (1996), A new correctness proof of the Nelson-Oppen combination procedure, *in* '1st Int'l Workshop on Frontiers of Combining Systems (FroCoS'96)', Vol. 3 of *Applied Logic Series*, Kluwer Academic Publishers.

Tiwari, A. (2000), Decision procedures in automated deduction, PhD thesis, SUNY at Stony Brook.

Formal Verification of a Combination Decision Procedure*

Jonathan Ford and Natarajan Shankar

Computer Science Laboratory
SRI International, Menlo Park CA 94025 USA
{ford, shankar}@csl.sri.com
Phone: (650)859-5272

Abstract. Decision procedures for combinations of theories are at the core of many modern theorem provers such as ACL2, EHDM, PVS, SIM-PLIFY, the Stanford Pascal Verifier, STeP, SVC, and Z/Eves. Shostak, in 1984, published a decision procedure for the combination of canonizable and solvable theories. Recently, Ruess and Shankar showed Shostak's method to be incomplete and nonterminating, and presented a correct version of Shostak's algorithm along with informal proofs of termination, soundness, and completeness. We describe a formalization and mechanical verification of these proofs using the PVS verification system. The formalization itself posed significant challenges and the verification revealed some gaps in the informal argument.

1 Introduction

Decision procedures play an important rôle in a number of areas such as automated deduction, computer-aided verification, and constraint solving. Since bugs in decision procedures can lead to unsound inferences, it is natural to ask if such verification tools can themselves be verified. We present here the first instance of a verified decision procedure for a combination of theories based on Shostak's ideas. Shostak's algorithm [Sho84] for building decision procedures for the union of canonizable and solvable equational theories has been widely used despite the lack of a convincing correctness proof. Recently, Ruess and Shankar [RS01] showed that this algorithm (even with minor flaws corrected [CLS96]) was both nonterminating and incomplete. They gave a corrected version of the algorithm along with informal proofs for termination, soundness, and completeness. We undertook the challenge of formalizing and verifying these informal arguments using the PVS verification system [ORS92]. The results of our verification are presented here along with observations regarding the challenges that we encountered in the formalization and verification process.

* This work was funded by NSF Grant CCR-0082560, DARPA/AFRL Contract F33615-00-C-3043, and NASA Contract NAS1-00079. Sam Owre, Harald Rueß, and John Rushby of SRI provided insightful comments on earlier drafts. We thank the anonymous referees for their constructive criticism.

A. Voronkov (Ed.): CADE-18, LNAI 2392, pp. 347–362, 2002.
© Springer-Verlag Berlin Heidelberg 2002

The correctness of decision procedures has been an important theme in automated reasoning. Several approaches have been developed for using decision procedures to gain efficiency in proof construction without compromising soundness. The LCF approach [GMW79] admits only those decision procedures that can be introduced as *tactics*, which are metalanguage operations for reducing proof goals to subgoals in a way that is justifiable in terms of the primitive inferences of the object logic. Tactics can be hard to define (since they have to mimic proof steps) and inefficient (since they have to generate low-level inference steps). The generation of *proof objects* from finished proofs is another way of ensuring that each proof can be constructed using only the primitive inference steps. The construction of proof objects even from finished proofs can be inefficient in both time and space.

In order to avoid the inefficiency of fully expansive proof generation, a number of researchers have advocated the verification of decision procedures. Boyer and Moore [BM81] introduce a notion of metafunctions, i.e., function definitions in the object logic that could be applied to object logic expressions. They use computational reflection to capture the meanings of these expressions in the object logic and verify the soundness of some simple derived inference rules in this manner. Boyer and Moore [BM79] also verified the semantic correctness of a tautology checker for conditional expressions. Shankar [Sha85] verified both the semantic and proof-theoretic correctness of a tautology checker for propositional logic. Some recent examples of verified decision procedures include a Coq verification of a Gröbner basis algorithm for membership in polynomial ideals by Théry [Thé98], the verification of ordered binary decision diagram (OBDD) operations using PVS by von Henke, Pfab, Pfeifer, and Ruess [vHPPR98], and a similar Coq verification of OBDD operations by Verma and Goubault [VGL00]. Both the algorithm and the theory underlying the combination decision procedure considered here are significantly more complex than these previously verified decision procedures.

The primary contribution of our work is in demonstrating the feasibility of formally verifying complex decision procedures. The variant of Shostak's algorithm we have verified is quite recent and its foundations are not widely understood. Our verification closely follows the published informal proof [RS01] so that we could directly assess its validity. We also used details from an unpublished report that included proofs of some of the lemmas that were given without proof in the published paper. The verification exposed some gaps in the informal argument. We found a monotonicity claim in the informal argument to be false without qualification, but only the qualified form was actually used. A step that is hinted at as being routine, turned out to not be all that obvious. In the algorithm, any solution returned by the solver must contain variables that are either from the given equality or are "fresh". Making the notion of freshness precise, and working with this constraint proved to be one of the major challenges in the formal verification. The verification makes very heavy use of the PVS type system. Our use of PVS types exposed some of the weaknesses in a type propagation feature of the language called *typing judgements*.

Since PVS itself employs Shostak's method (with the incompleteness and nontermination bugs), the validity of this verification might be called into question. However, the Shostak procedure used in PVS is not known to be unsound. Future versions of PVS will employ the ICS decision procedures [FORS01] that are based on the theory verified here. Despite the circularity between the verifier and the verified program, this kind of verification is still quite useful. An unsuccessful proof attempt might reveal significant bugs. A successful verification of the decision procedures could be certified through proof-object generation but subsequently used without the supporting proof objects.

The decision procedure as verified here is not executable, but it is possible to derive a verified, executable version that can be turned into efficient Common Lisp code [Sha99]. The code generated from the verified decision procedure is unlikely to be as efficient as the highly optimized ICS implementation, but it could still be used as a reference procedure that can be invoked when certified results are needed.

We verify both soundness and completeness. The completeness property is crucial. Higher-level simplification routines might diverge or behave erroneously if they incorrectly assume completeness. Due to its complexity and popularity, the verification of Shostak's algorithm is a good case-study for assessing the feasibility of certifying decision procedures.

2 Shostak's Algorithm

We focus here on the verification of a decision procedure for equational theories where terms are constructed from a combination of interpreted and uninterpreted function symbols. There are two basic methods for building decision procedures for combinations of disjoint theories. Nelson and Oppen's method [NO79] combines decision procedures for the individual theories by allowing them to share specific kinds of equality information. Shostak's method [Sho84] extends congruence closure to equational theories that are canonizable and solvable. Nelson and Oppen's method is more generally applicable, but Shostak's method has certain advantages. It is an online algorithm, i.e., processes inputs incrementally, so that the term universe for the input is not known in advance. It also yields a useful function for computing a canonical form respecting the given input equalities.

All formulas are equalities between terms which are constructed from variables by means of n-ary function application for $n \geq 0$. Sequents of the form $T \vdash a = b$ assert the implication between the antecedent equalities in the set T and the consequent equality $a = b$. The basic theory of equality with all function symbols uninterpreted, i.e., without any fixed interpretation, is decidable by means of *congruence closure*. Shostak's algorithm extends the congruence closure decision procedure to handle interpreted operations from a *canonizable* and *solvable* theory. Informally, a theory is canonizable if there is a canonizer operation σ such that $\sigma(a) \equiv \sigma(b)$ exactly when $a = b$ is valid in the theory. It is solvable if there is an operation *solve* such that *solve*$(a = b)$ either returns $\perp$ when $a = b$ is unsatisfiable, or a solved form S that is equivalent to $a = b$.

Shostak's procedure takes as parameters, a solver *solve* and canonizer σ for a theory such as linear arithmetic. The algorithm verifies a sequent $T \vdash a = b$ by processing the equalities in T to build a solution set S of equalities in solved form, or to return $\bot$ indicating that a contradiction was found in T. If a solution set S is returned, then one can use S and σ to define a canonizer *can* such that $can(S)(f(e))$ returns $\sigma(f(can(S)(e)))$ if f is interpreted. If f is uninterpreted, $can(S)(f(e))$ returns c' for some c equivalent to $f(can(S)(e))$ where $c = c'$ is in S. The conclusion equality $a = b$ can be tested for validity by checking if $can(S)(a) \equiv can(S)(b)$. The operation $can(S)$ is also used for preprocessing the input equalities from T. The preprocessed input equalities are solved and the solution (if any) is composed with the existing value of S. The solution set S is maintained in congruence-closed form so that the right-hand sides of congruent left-hand side terms are merged by solving the equality between them and merging the results into S.

The theory of linear arithmetic is a typical example of a canonizable and solvable theory. A canonizer can be given by means of a function that returns an ordered sum-of-products representation for a given linear polynomial by merging monomials over the same variable into a single monomial. A solver can be given by using algebraic manipulations to isolate a variable on the left-hand side. The Shostak procedure of Ruess and Shankar [RS01] can be illustrated on the sequent

$$f(x-1) - 1 = f(y) + 1, \ y - x + 1 = 0 \vdash false,$$

where $+$, $-$, and the numerals are from the theory of linear arithmetic, *false* is an abbreviation for $0 = 1$, and f is an uninterpreted function symbol. Starting with $S \equiv \emptyset$ in the base case, the preprocessing of $f(x-1) - 1 = f(y) + 1$ causes the equality to be placed into canonical form as $-1 + f(-1 + x) = 1 + f(y)$. The solution set S is initialized to contain reflexivity statements for the non-interpreted subterms in the canonicalized input equality as $\{x = x, y = y, f(-1 + x) = f(-1 + x), f(y) = f(y)\}$. Solving $-1 + f(-1 + x) = 1 + f(y)$ yields $f(-1+x) = 2 + f(y)$, and S is set to $\{x = x, y = y, f(-1+x) = 2+f(y), f(y) = f(y)\}$. No unmerged congruences are detected in S. Next, $y - x + 1 = 0$ is canonized as $1 - x + y = 0$, and solved as $x = 1 + y$. This solution is composed with S to yield $\{x = y + 1, y = y, f(-1 + x) = 2 + f(y), f(y) = f(y)\}$. The congruence between $f(-1 + x)$ and $f(y)$ is detected since the canonical form of $-1 + x$ is y when the solution for x is inserted and the result is canonized by σ. The procedure then tries to merge the respective solutions of $f(-1+x)$ and $f(y)$ by solving $2 + f(y) = f(y)$. The solver returns $\bot$ so that the original sequent is asserted to be valid.

As a second example, one can check that the sequent $f(x-1) - 1 = f(y) + 1 \vdash g(f(x-1)-2) = g(f(y))$ is valid by computing S to be $\{x = x, y = y, f(-1+x) = 2+f(y), f(y) = f(y)\}$, and verifying $can(S)(g(f(x-1)-2)) \equiv can(S)(g(f(y)))$.

3 Formalizing Shostak's Algorithm in PVS

A brief introduction to PVS is given in Appendix A. The formalization exploits several advanced features of the PVS language including recursive datatypes, predicate subtypes, dependent types, Hilbert's choice operator, and inductive relations. We describe the formalization in sufficient detail so that it can be checked for conformity with the informal arguments [RS01] (abbreviated below as **RS**) and reproduced using some other automated proof checker.[1]

Syntax. Terms are built from a given signature consisting of a set of variables X and function symbols F. A *term* is either a variable x for $x \in X$ or of the form $f(a_1, \ldots, a_n)$, where $f \in F$. A term of the form $f(a_1, \ldots, a_n)$ is *interpreted* (respectively, *uninterpreted*) if f is interpreted (respectively, uninterpreted). Terms are formalized by means of a recursive datatype `syntax` consisting of a constructor v for variables with a natural number index field `index`, and an application constructor `app` with a function symbol field `func` and an arguments field `args` which is formalized as a *dependent* type `[below(arity(func)) -> syntax]` which represents an *array* of `syntax` in the arity of the function symbol of the term. The type `below(num)` for a natural number `num` is the (possibly empty) subrange $0, \ldots, num - 1$.[2] The function symbol type `funsymbs` is also a datatype consisting of constructors `ifn` and `ufn` for interpreted and uninterpreted function symbols, respectively, each with an `index` field and an `arity` field, and a `thry` (theory) field for interpreted function symbols.

```
funsymbs: DATATYPE                                              1
  BEGIN
    IMPORTING theories
    ifn(index: nat, arity: nat, thry: TH): ifn?
    ufn(index: nat, arity: nat): ufn?
  END funsymbs

syntax: DATATYPE
  BEGIN
    IMPORTING funsymbs, max_lemmas
    v(index: nat): v?
    app(func: funsymbs,
        args: [below(arity(func)) -> syntax]): app?
  END syntax
```

Since we are admitting just one interpreted theory, we fix a theory `th`. The predicate `thry_func` checks that its argument is an interpreted function symbol

---

[1] The complete PVS 2.4.1 dump file is available at
    `ftp://ftp.csl.sri.com/pub/users/shankar/shostak-verification-dump`.

[2] An application could also be formalized in terms of a *list* of arguments whose length is the arity of the function symbol. The array-based formalization has some important advantages. Terms are well-formed by construction thus avoiding the need for cumbersome proof obligations. Operations on terms can be defined by a simple structural recursion without the use of mutual recursion on terms and lists of terms.

from theory th. The type thry_func is the predicate subtype corresponding to the predicate thry_func.

```
thry_func(ff:funsymbs): bool =                                    2
   ifn?(ff) AND thry(ff) = th
```

The type of equalities is defined as a record type with fields lhs and rhs.

```
equality: TYPE = [# lhs, rhs: syntax #]                           3
```

The variables a, b, and c are declared to range over terms, aa, bb, and cc range over equalities, and R, S, and T range over lists of equalities.

The set of variables in a term a is defined using datatype recursion as vars(a). Sets are just predicates in the higher-order logic so that a variable x is in the set vars(a) iff vars(a)(x) holds. The set vars(a) can be shown to be finite by structural induction. A term a is well-typed in n for a natural number n, if the index of any variable in a is below n. This is represented by the predicate well_typed?(n)(a) and the corresponding type typed(n). The operation of collecting the set of subterms of a given term is represented by subterm(a). The definitions of these operations are omitted.

Pure Terms. The canonizer and solver are defined for *pure* terms, i.e., terms without uninterpreted function symbols, but then applied to arbitrary terms by treating the uninterpreted subterms as variables. We formalize pure terms by means of a datatype pure that has two classes of variables: v(i) for the ordinary variables indexed by i, and u(a) corresponding to the uninterpreted term a. Function applications for pure terms are typed to contain only interpreted function symbols. It is easy to define an operation abs that converts a term to the corresponding pure term, and its inverse gamma.

```
pure[(IMPORTING theories) th: TH]: DATATYPE WITH SUBTYPES var?, func?  4
BEGIN
   IMPORTING syntax_ops[th]
   v(index: nat): v?  : var?
   u(a: uninterpreted): u? :var?
   app(func: thry_func,
        args: [below(arity(func)) -> pure]): app? : func?
END pure
```

Semantics. The semantics for a term a is given by $M[\![a]\!]\rho$ for an *interpretation* M over a domain D such that $M(f)$ yields a mapping from D^n to D for function symbol f of arity n, and an *assignment* ρ mapping variables to values in D. For variables, $M[\![x]\!]\rho = \rho(x)$, and $M[\![f(a_1,\ldots,a_n)]\!]\rho = M(f)(M[\![a_1]\!]\rho,\ldots,M[\![a_n]\!]\rho)$. We say that $M, \rho \models a = b$ iff $M[\![a]\!]\rho = M[\![b]\!]\rho$, and $M \models a = b$ iff $M, \rho \models a = b$ for all assignments ρ over $vars(a = b)$. An equality is *valid* if for all D, M: $M \models a = b$.

The concept of a valid equality requires quantification over all domains D and interpretations M over D. In PVS, such a domain would have to be introduced as the type parameter of a theory. Since PVS does not admit quantification over types, the domain must be given as a subset or a subtype of a fixed type. We take this fixed type to be the set of all terms.[3] This type can be informally shown to be adequate for representating any domain set D for the purposes of equality. The assignment ρ is formalized as a mapping from the set of all variables to the domain D.

In the semantics for pure terms, the domain type D is the type of pure terms and a model is a dependent record type consisting of a domain field mdom that is a subset of D, and a function interpretation field f that is a dependent type mapping a function ff and an array of argument valuations to a valuation for the application. The type arity(ff) is an abbreviation for below(arity(ff)).

```
D: TYPE+ = pure                                              5

model: TYPE = [# mdom : setof[D],
               f: [ff: thry_func ->
                  [[arity(ff) -> (mdom)] -> (mdom)]] #]
```

Solutions. The "state" of the algorithm is maintained in a solution set S that is just a list of equalities of a special form. The operation apply(S)(a) (informally, $S(a)$) is defined recursively to look up the solution for a (if any) in S.[4]

```
apply(S)(a): RECURSIVE syntax =                             6
  CASES S OF
    null: a,
    cons(aa, R): IF lhs(aa) = a
                 THEN rhs(aa)
                 ELSE apply(R)(a)
                 ENDIF
  ENDCASES
MEASURE length(S)
```

The operation replace_vars(S)(d) (informally, $S[d]$) returns the result of replacing all occurrences of any left-hand side variable from S in a pure term d, by the corresponding right-hand side. The replace_vars operation is extended from pure terms to arbitrary terms as replace_solvables. The operation subst(rho)(d) (used in [7]) is similar to replace_vars(S)(d) but rho here is a substitution mapping variables to terms.

Canonizers. A canonizer σ for pure terms from a theory τ is a parameter to the combination decision procedure. A valid canonizer is required to verify validities, i.e., $\models_\tau a = b$ implies $\sigma(a) \equiv \sigma(b)$, and additionally preserve variables, $\sigma(x) = x$ and $vars(\sigma(a)) \subseteq vars(a)$, be idempotent, $\sigma(\sigma(a)) = \sigma(a)$, and leave

---

[3] The type of closed terms, when nonempty, is also a valid candidate for the domain.

[4] The termination of the recursive definition is justified by the measure length(S) which causes the typechecker to generate proof obligations verifying that the measure decreases with each recursive call.

subterms canonical, $\sigma(b) = b$ for any subterm b of $\sigma(a)$. These conditions on a valid canonizer are captured by the predicate `canonizer?(sigma)`. The validity condition is awkward since it uses an oracle $\models_\tau$ for τ-validity. We found a way to replace this condition by the sufficient pair of conditions on σ:

1. σ-substitutivity: $\sigma(\rho[a]) \equiv \sigma(\rho[\sigma(a)])$, for any substitution ρ, and
2. σ-distributivity: $\sigma(f(\sigma(a_1), \ldots, \sigma(a_n))) \equiv \sigma(f(a_1, \ldots, a_n))$.

`canonical?(sigma)(a)` is defined to hold when `sigma(a) = a`.

```
canonizer?(sigma): bool =                                           7
(    (FORALL d, rho: sigma(subst(rho)(d)) = sigma(subst(rho)(sigma(d))))
 AND (FORALL d: app?(d) IMPLIES
         sigma(app(func(d), LAMBDA (i:arity(func(d))): sigma(args(d)(i))))
         = sigma(d))
 AND (FORALL u   : sigma(u) = u)
 AND (FORALL d, u: vars(sigma(d))(u) IMPLIES vars(d)(u))
 AND (FORALL d   : sigma(sigma(d)) = sigma(d))
 AND (FORALL d, f: sigma(d) = f IMPLIES
         (FORALL (i:arity(func(f))): canonical?(sigma)(args(f)(i)))))
```

The adaptation of the canonizer from pure terms to terms is done through **gamma** and **abs**. The canonizer for arbitrary terms, `sig(a)` (used in $\boxed{9}$ and $\boxed{10}$), is defined as `gamma(sigma(abs(a)))`, where **sigma** is the given canonizer for pure terms. Model M is a σ-model if $M \models \sigma(a) = a$ for all a, and $a = b$ is σ-unsatisfiable (formalized as the PVS predicate `unsatisfiable`) if $M, \rho \not\models a = b$ for all M and ρ.

Solver.   A solver *solve* is another parameter to the algorithm. A valid solver must be such that $solve(a = b)$ either returns $\bot$ when $a = b$ is σ-unsatisfiable, or returns a (possibly empty) list S of n equalities of the form $x_i = t_i$ for $1 \le i \le n$, where $x_i \in vars(a = b)$ $x_i \not\equiv x_j$ for $i \ne j$, $x_i \not\in vars(t_j)$, t_i is canonical $(\sigma(t_i) = t_i)$, for $1 \le x, y \le n$, and $a = b$ and S are σ-equivalent: for all σ-models M and assignments ρ over the variables in a and b, $M, \rho \models a = b$ iff there is an assignment ρ' extending ρ, over the variables in S, a, and b, such that $M, \rho' \models S$.

The notion of a *solution* for pure term equalities is formalized as the predicate `solve(n, dd, S)` for an index `n`, an equality `dd`, and a solution list `S`. The predicate checks that `dd` is satisfiable, the solution list of equalities `S` is a well-formed solution that is σ-equivalent (formalized as the PVS predicate `sig_equivalent?`) to `dd`. Any variables in `S` not in `dd` must be of index above `n`.

```
solve(n, dd, S): bool =                                             8
  IF unsatisfiable(dd) THEN
    FALSE
  ELSE
    new_vars_above(n, dd)(S) AND
    check_solution(dd)(S) AND
    sig_equivalent?(dd, S)
  ENDIF
```

A pure term solver is easily extended to one that works on terms. A given solver `solv` is typed so that `solv(m, dd)` returns a dependent record `r` with fields `n` and `s`, where `r'n` is an index that is at least `m` and `r's` is either `bottom` or of the form `up(S)` for a solution list of equalities `S` that is well-typed in `r'n`.

Canonical Forms. The operation $norm(S)(a)$ (represented as `norm(S)(a)`) for a canonizer `sig`, is informally defined as $\sigma(S[a])$. The definition of `norm` is used to show that if `solve(m, aa, S)` holds, then `norm(S)(lhs(aa)) = norm(S)(rhs(aa))`, and to define the composition of two equality lists `R` and `S` as `R o S`.

```
norm(S)(a): syntax = sig(replace_solvables(S)(a))                      9

o(R, S): RECURSIVE eqlist =
  CASES R OF
    null: S,
    cons(aa, T): cons(eq(lhs(aa), norm(S)(rhs(aa))), T o S)
  ENDCASES
  MEASURE length(R)
```

Since composition is defined recursively, its definition includes a termination measure `length(R)` that is used to generate termination proof obligations. The definitions above are used to prove the associativity of composition and the claim: `norm(R o S)(a) = norm(S)(norm(R)(a))`.

The operation `lookup(S)(a)` is defined so that if `a` is a variable, then it returns `apply(S)(a)` which is the formalization of $S(a)$. When a is an application, then `lookup` is defined to scan S till it finds an equality whose left-hand side is of the form $f(a_1, \ldots, a_n)$, where $f(norm(S)(a_1), \ldots, norm(S)(a_n)) \equiv a$.[5]

The canonizer `can(S)(a)` is then defined in terms of the `lookup` operation.

```
can(S)(a): RECURSIVE syntax =                                         10
  CASES a OF
    v(i): apply(S)(a),
    app(ff, args):
      IF intheory?(a) THEN
        sig(app(ff, LAMBDA (i:arity(ff)): can(S)(args(i))))
      ELSE
        lookup(S)(app(ff, LAMBDA (i:arity(ff)): can(S)(args(i))))
      ENDIF
  ENDCASES
  MEASURE rank(a)
```

Congruence. Congruence with respect to a solution set S, $f(a_1, \ldots, a_n) \overset{S}{\sim} f(b_1, \ldots, b_n)$, is defined to hold exactly when $norm(S)(a_i) \equiv norm(S)(b_i)$ for $1 \leq i \leq n$. This is captured formally by the predicate `congruent(S)(a, b)`.

---

[5] This definition of `lookup` is slightly different from that of **RS** which uses $S(a_i)$ instead of $norm(S)(a_i)$. The **RS** definition requires keeping $dom(S)$ subterm-closed, whereas we only require closure under the uninterpreted subterms. Our definition is executable in contrast to the **RS** definition which uses Hilbert's epsilon operator.

```
congruent(S)(a, b): bool =                                          11
  app?(a) AND
  app?(b) AND
  func(a) = func(b) AND
  (FORALL (i:arity(func(a))):
    norm(S)(args(a)(i)) = norm(S)(args(b)(i)))
```

A solution set is *congruence-closed* when the right-hand sides corresponding to any pair of congruent left-hand sides are identical.

```
congruence_closed(S): bool =                                        12
  (FORALL (a,b:(dom(S))): congruent(S)(a, b) IMPLIES
                          apply(S)(a) = apply(S)(b))
```

The solution set that forms the "state" of the algorithm is typed to satisfy the invariants given by the predicate invariants(S). These invariants assert that the left-hand sides of equalities in the solution set S must be variables or uninterpreted terms, the uninterpreted subterms of any equality S must in the domain of S, and any right-hand side term must be canonical, and $S(a)$ and $norm(S)(a)$ must coincide for any $a \in dom(S)$, among other conditions. The predicate invariant(S) is used to define a type above_tinvariants(n) which ensures that the state is a record r consisting of an index r'n and a solution set r's which is either bottom or up(S), where S is well-typed in r'n and satisfies invariants(S).

The Main Procedure. The congruence closure operation cc(r) successively merges the right-hand sides corresponding to *chosen* congruent pairs of left-hand side terms in the solution set r's. The operation merge(m, aa, S) (used in 13 and 14) computes solv(m, aa) as a record r, returning bottom if r's is bottom, and the record (# n := r'n, s := S o down(r's)#), otherwise, where down(up(R)) is R. The return type of cc ensures that cc(r)'s is bottom when r's is bottom and the cc(r)'s satisfies the invariants spelled out above when it is different from bottom. The termination of cc, a significant step in the proof, is established by showing that the number of equivalence classes of uninterpreted terms in the domain of r's decreases with each recursive call. The invariants on the solution set play a crucial role in proving termination.

```
cc(r): RECURSIVE {s : above_tinvariants(r'n) | bottom?(r's)        13
                                     IMPLIES bottom?(s's)} =
  CASES r's OF
    bottom: tbottom,
    up(T) : IF (NOT congruence_closed(T))
              THEN cc(merge(r'n, apply(T)(choose(congruent_pair?(T))), T))
              ELSE r
            ENDIF
  ENDCASES
  MEASURE cc_rank(r)
```

The assert(r, aa) operation places aa in canonical form as aa', then expands r's (if r's is up(T)) with dummy identities for the new subterms in aa' as expand(T, aa'). It then merges aa' into this expanded solution set and applies congruence-closure cc to the result.

```
assert((r:{r:tinvariants | up?(r's) IMPLIES                      14
                      congruence_closed(down(r's))}),
       (aa:typed_equality(r'n))):
   {s:above_tinvariants(r'n) | up?(s's) IMPLIES
                             congruence_closed(down(s's))} =
CASES r's OF
   bottom: tbottom,
   up(T): cc(merge(r'n, can(T)(aa), expand(T, can(T)(aa))))
ENDCASES
```

Finally, process(m, S) returns a record consisting of a number n and a well-typed solution in n which may be bottom. The type of process(m, S) ensures that any solution returned is congruence-closed.

```
process(m, (S:typed_eqlist(m))): RECURSIVE                       15
   {r:above_tinvariants(m) | up?(r's) IMPLIES
                          congruence_closed(down(r's))} =
CASES S OF
   null      : (# n := m, s := up(null)#),
   cons(aa, T): IF up?(process(m, T)'s)
                THEN assert(process(m, T), aa)
                ELSE tbottom
                ENDIF
ENDCASES
MEASURE length(S)
```

The type and termination proof obligations generated by the PVS type-checker corresponding to the subtype constraints and measures given with the definitions of process, cc, and other related definitions, ensure the well-typedness and termination of process.

4   Verifying Shostak's Algorithm in PVS

The algorithm verifies a sequent $T \vdash a = b$ by computing $S = process(T)$. The sequent is considered valid if either $S = \bot$ or $can(S)(a) \equiv can(S)(b)$. For the soundness of the procedure is established relative to a proof system whose inference rules characterize when a sequent $T \vdash a = b$ is derivable. We prove that the following are equivalent:

1. If $process(T) = S$, then $S = \bot$ or $can(S)(a) \equiv can(S)(b)$.
2. $T \vdash a = b$ is derivable.
3. $T \vdash a = b$ is σ-valid, i.e., valid in all σ-models.

The implication from (1) to (2) is the soundness argument. The implication from (2) to (3) validates the soundness of the proof system with respect to

σ-models. The implication from (3) to (1) establishes the completeness of the decision procedure.

For verifying soundness, we first formally define the class of provable sequents by means of an inductive definition of a predicate has_proof?(m, T, aa) for an index m, a list of equalities T, and an equality aa.

```
has_proof?(m,                                                  16
          (T:typed_eqlist(m)),
          (aa:typed_equality(m))): INDUCTIVE bool =
  member(aa, T) OR                                    % Axiom
  lhs(aa) = rhs(aa) OR                                % Reflexivity
  has_proof?(m, T, eq(rhs(aa), lhs(aa))) OR           % Symmetry
  (EXISTS (a:typed(m)):                               % Transitivity
    has_proof?(m, T, eq(lhs(aa), a)) AND
    has_proof?(m, T, eq(a, rhs(aa)))) OR
  (LET a = lhs(aa), b = rhs(aa) IN                    % Congruency
    app?(a) AND app?(b) AND
    func(a) = func(b) AND
    (FORALL (i:arity(func(a))):
      has_proof?(m, T, eq(args(a)(i), args(b)(i))))) OR
  (rhs(aa) = sig(lhs(aa))) OR                         % Canonization
  (EXISTS (bb:typed_equality(m)),                     % Solve
          (n:upfrom(m)), (S:typed_eqlist(n))):
    solve(m, bb, S) AND
    has_proof?(m, T, bb) AND
    has_proof?(n, append(T, S), aa)) OR
  (EXISTS (bb:typed_equality(m)):                     % Contradiction
    unsatisfiable(bb) AND
    has_proof?(m, T, bb))
```

The proof soundness theorem below captures the implication from (2) to (3) above. It asserts that any provable sequent is σ-valid since the variable M is declared to range over σ-models. It can be proved by the induction scheme generated by the inductive definition of has_proof?.

```
proof_soundness: LEMMA                                         17
  (FORALL m, (T:typed_eqlist(m)), (aa:typed_equality(m)):
    has_proof?(m, T, aa) IMPLIES
      (FORALL M, (rho:assign(M)): satisfies(M, rho)(T, aa)))
```

The following two theorems correspond to the implication between (1) and (2) above. These theorems capture the respective cases of soundness when process(m, S) returns a valid solution or a bottom value.

```
soundness_1: THEOREM                                          18
  (FORALL m, (S:typed_eqlist(m)), (a, b:typed(m)):
    up?(process(m, S)'s) AND
    can(down(process(m, S)'s))(a) = can(down(process(m, S)'s))(b)
    IMPLIES has_proof?(m, S, eq(a, b)))
```

```
soundness_2: THEOREM                                           19
  (FORALL m, (S:typed_eqlist(m)), (aa:typed_equality(m)):
    bottom?(process(m, S)'s) IMPLIES
      has_proof?(m, S, aa))
```

Completeness is proved by constructing a canonical σ-model M_R and assignment ρ_R, where $R = process(T) \neq \bot$. The bulk of the proof involves showing that this construction does in fact yield a σ-model satisfying the equalities in T. A crucial property for demonstrating this is confluence which asserts that `can(S)(a) = norm(S)(a)` when `S` is congruence-closed and the uninterpreted terms of `a` are included in `dom(S)`.

```
confluence: LEMMA                                              20
  invariants(S) AND
  congruence_closed(S) AND
  subset?(U(subterm(a)), dom(S)) IMPLIES
    can(S)(a) = norm(S)(a)
```

Completeness is then proved as the theorem below which formalizes the implication from (2) to (1) above, but it is verified via proof soundness and (3). The theorem states that when the sequent $S \vdash a = b$ is derivable, then either $process(S) = \bot$ or $process(S) = T$ and $can(T)(a) = can(T)(b)$.

```
completeness: LEMMA                                            21
  (FORALL m, (S:typed_eqlist(m)), T, (aa:typed_equality(m)):
    up?(process(m, S)'s) AND
    down(process(m, S)'s) = T AND
    has_proof?(m, S, aa) IMPLIES
      can(T)(lhs(aa)) = can(T)(rhs(aa)))
```

5 Concluding Observations

Both the formalization and the verification closely follow the informal presentation **RS** [RS01]. There were some areas where **RS** was found to be inadequate or incorrect and where PVS itself was deficient.[6]

RS is terse about the introduction of fresh variables by the *solve* operation. These variables must be fresh with respect to the entire execution of the algorithm or the construction of a proof. Proof transformations like weakening and cut require the variables generated by *solve* to be invariant with respect to a certain kind of renaming.[7] The bookkeeping involved in tracking the well-

---

[6] One minor problem was already noticed prior to this verification attempt. Several of the lemmas in the informal proof regarding the composition of solutions were qualified with the condition that $R \cup S$ be functional, where the appropriate condition is that $R \circ S$ must be functional. This was immaterial for the verification since the definition of composition is in terms of lists and not sets.

[7] A similar renaming problem arises with alpha-renaming in the lambda-calculus and *eigenvariables* in sequent proofs, but the renaming issue is far more complicated here. The variable indices affect the type and the well-typedness of equalities and proofs so that renaming is not a local operation.

formedness of terms and equalities up to a given index, occupy a substantial fraction of the effort in both the formalization and proof. PVS has a judgement mechanism that records certain typing relations for use in the typechecker, but we were unable to use it for demonstrating that an expression well-typed in n is also well-typed in any index above n.

Quantification over types, needed to define semantic validity, is not expressible in PVS. We instead restricted the semantic domains to subtypes of the type of terms since any model for terms and equalities is essentially characterized by a partition of the term universe into equivalence classes.

A monotonicity lemma is stated in the informal proof (Lemma 3.12) as: *If $R \cup S$ is functional, then if $R(a) \equiv R(b)$, then $(R \circ S)(a) \equiv (R \circ S)(b)$, for any a and b.* In addition to the above-mentioned correction to the antecedent, this lemma only holds when a and b are in $dom(R)$. Fortunately, only the weak form of this lemma is actually used.

In the **RS** proof of Lemma 5.11, it is claimed that *it can also be shown that* $can(S'^{+})(a) \equiv can(S')(a)$, *and similarly for b.* This claim asserts that padding the solution set S' with reflexivity equalities on the subterms from $can(S')(a)$, does not affect the value of $can(S')(a)$. The claim is in fact valid, but the proof is not all that obvious.

Despite the flaws identified above, the **RS** proofs held up quite well to the rigors of formal scrutiny. We were actually operating from a draft document that contained proofs of lemmas that were given without proof in the published version. Once the formalization challenges were overcome, it was possible to make steady progress in the mechanical verification of the proofs. The procedure as we have defined it is not executable since it uses a choice operator. Further work is needed to derive efficiently executable versions of the verified algorithm while preserving its correctness.

The formalization and proof occupied four months of work with PVS carried out entirely by the first author.[8] The proof involves 68 theories, 120 definitions, 192 TCCs (typing and termination proof obligations), 594 lemmas, and the proof checking time is 2,265 seconds on a 1-Gigahertz Pentium 3. There are roughly 6,200 tokens in the detailed informal presentation as measured by a word count of the text file generated from the LaTeX input. There are approximately 13,000 tokens in the PVS specification, and over 25,000 tokens in the PVS proofs. The proof is highly interactive. We are currently working on improving the degree of mechanization in various ways. The level of effort indicates that the certification of complex decision procedures remains a tough challenge.

References

[BM79]   R. S. Boyer and J. S. Moore. *A Computational Logic*. Academic Press, New York, NY, 1979.

---

[8] The first author already had prior experience with PVS having used it for two substantial proof developments[FM01b,FM01a].

[BM81]   R. S. Boyer and J. S. Moore. Metafunctions: Proving them correct and
             using them efficiently as new proof procedures. In R. S. Boyer and J. S.
             Moore, editors, *The Correctness Problem in Computer Science*. Academic
             Press, London, 1981.
[CLS96]   David Cyrluk, Patrick Lincoln, and N. Shankar. On Shostak's decision
             procedure for combinations of theories. In M. A. McRobbie and J. K.
             Slaney, editors, *Automated Deduction—CADE-13*, volume 1104 of *Lec-
             ture Notes in Artificial Intelligence*, pages 463–477, New Brunswick, NJ,
             July/August 1996. Springer-Verlag.
[FM01a]   J. Ford and I. A. Mason. Establishing a General Context Lemma in
             PVS. In *Proceedings of the 2nd Australasian Workshop on Computational
             Logic, AWCL'01* , 2001. submitted.
[FM01b]   J. Ford and I. A. Mason. Operational techniques in PVS—a preliminary
             evaluation. In *Proceedings of the Australasian Theory Symposium, CATS
             '01*, Gold Coast, Queensland, Australia, January–February 2001.
[FORS01]   J.-C. Filliâtre, S. Owre, H. Rueß, and N. Shankar. ICS: Integrated Can-
             onization and Solving. In G. Berry, H. Comon, and A. Finkel, editors,
             Computer-Aided Verification, CAV '2001, volume 2102 of *Lecture Notes
             in Computer Science*, pages 246–249, Paris, France, July 2001. Springer-
             Verlag.
[GMW79]   M. Gordon, R. Milner, and C. Wadsworth. *Edinburgh LCF: A Mechanized
             Logic of Computation*, volume 78 of *Lecture Notes in Computer Science*.
             Springer-Verlag, 1979.
[NO79]   G. Nelson and D. C. Oppen. Simplification by cooperating decision pro-
             cedures. *ACM Transactions on Programming Languages and Systems*,
             1(2):245–257, 1979.
[ORS92]   S. Owre, J. M. Rushby, and N. Shankar. PVS: A prototype verification
             system. In Deepak Kapur, editor, *11th International Conference on Au-
             tomated Deduction (CADE)*, volume 607 of *Lecture Notes in Artificial
             Intelligence*, pages 748–752, Saratoga, NY, June 1992. Springer-Verlag.
[RS01]   Harald Rueß and Natarajan Shankar. Deconstructing Shostak. In *16th
             Annual IEEE Symposium on Logic in Computer Science*, pages 19–28,
             Boston, MA, July 2001. IEEE Computer Society.
[Sha85]   N. Shankar. Towards mechanical metamathematics. *Journal of Auto-
             mated Reasoning*, 1(4):407–434, 1985.
[Sha99]   N. Shankar. Efficiently executing PVS. Project report, Computer Sci-
             ence Laboratory, SRI International, Menlo Park, CA, November 1999.
             Available at http://www.csl.sri.com/shankar/PVSeval.ps.gz.
[Sho84]   Robert E. Shostak. Deciding combinations of theories. *Journal of the
             ACM*, 31(1):1–12, January 1984.
[Thé98]   Laurent Théry. A certified version of Buchberger's algorithm. In H. Kirch-
             ner and C. Kirchner, editors, *Proceedings of CADE-15*, number 1421 in
             Lecture Notes in Artificial Intelligence, pages 349–364, Berlin, Germany,
             July 1998. Springer-Verlag.
[VGL00]   K.N. Verma and J. Goubault-Larrecq. Reflecting BDDs in Coq. Technical
             Report 3859, INRIA, Rocquencourt, France, January 2000.
[vHPPR98]   F. W. von Henke, S. Pfab, H. Pfeifer, and H. Rueß. Case studies in meta-
             level theorem proving. In Jim Grundy and Malcolm Newey, editors, *Proc.
             Intl. Conf. on Theorem Proving in Higher Order Logics*, number 1479
             in Lecture Notes in Computer Science, pages 461–478. Springer-Verlag,
             September 1998.

A   Introduction to PVS

We give a very brief introduction to the PVS language and proof checker. PVS specifications are a collection of theories. A theory can have type or individual parameters that are instantiated when the theory is imported within another theory. A parameterized theory can include constraining assumptions on the parameters. The instances of these assumptions corresponding to the actual parameters are generated as proof obligations when a theory instance is imported.

A theory is a list of declarations of types, constants, and formulas. The expression language of PVS is based on simply typed higher-order logic extended with predicate subtypes, dependent types, and recursive datatypes. PVS types consist of the *base* types bool and real, and *compound* types constructed as tuples, as in $[\text{bool}, \text{real}]$, records, as in $[\#\text{flag} : \text{bool}, \text{length} : \text{real}\#]$, or function types of the form $[A{\rightarrow}B]$. Predicates over a type A are of type $[A{\rightarrow}\text{bool}]$.

Predicate subtypes are a distinctive feature of the PVS higher-order logic. Given a predicate p over A, $\{x : A \,|\, p(x)\}$ (or, (p)) is a predicate subtype of A consisting of those elements of A satisfying p. The type nzreal of nonzero real can be defined as $\{x : \text{real} \,|\, x \mathrel{/=} 0\}$. The type nat of natural numbers is a predicate subtype of the type int of integers, which in turn is a subtype of the subtype rat (of real) of rational numbers. Subranges can also be defined as predicate subtypes, and arrays can be typed as functions with subranges as domains, e.g., $[\text{below}(N){\rightarrow}A]$. The PVS typechecker generates proof obligations (called TCCs) corresponding to predicate subtype constraints. Out-of-bounds array accesses generate unprovable TCCs.

Dependent versions of tuple, record, and function types can be constructed by introducing dependencies between different components of the type through predicates. Dependent typing can be used to define a finite sequence (of arbitrary length) as a dependent record consisting of a length and an array of the given length $[\#\text{length} : \text{nat}, \text{seq} : [\text{below}(\text{length}){\rightarrow}T]\#]$.

PVS expressions include variables x, constants c, applications $f(a)$, and abstractions LAMBDA $(x : T) : a$, conditionals IF a_1 THEN a_2 ELSE a_3 ENDIF, tuple expressions $(a_1, \ldots, a_n)$, tuple projections $a\text{'}i$, record expressions $(\#l_1\text{:=}a_1, \ldots \#)$, record projections $a\text{'}l$, and (tuple, record, and function) updates $e[a := v]$.

The definition of a recursive datatype can be illustrated with the list type built from the constructors cons and null. Theories containing the relevant axioms, induction schemes, and useful datatype operations are generated from the datatype declaration.

```
list [T: TYPE]: DATATYPE                                    1
 BEGIN
  null: null?
  cons (car: T, cdr:list):cons?
 END list
```

Combining Multisets with Integers

Calogero G. Zarba

Stanford University and University of Catania

Abstract. We present a decision procedure for a constraint language combining multisets of ur-elements, the integers, and an arbitrary first-order theory T of the ur-elements. Our decision procedure is an extension of the Nelson-Oppen combination method specifically tailored to the combination domain of multisets, integers, and ur-elements.

1 Introduction

Sets obey the extensionality principle according to which two sets are equal if and only if they contain the same elements, regardless of their multiplicity. In contrast, multisets (also known as bags) are collections of elements in which multiplicity is relevant. Two multisets are equal if and only if they contain the same elements *and* all elements have the same multiplicity in each multiset. Thus, for instance, while the set $\{a, a, b\}$ is considered to be equal to the set $\{a, b\}$, the multiset $[\![a, a, b]\!]$, in which a occurs twice, is different from the multiset $[\![a, b]\!]$, in which a occurs only once.

Multisets appear frequently in mathematics and computer science, and their applications range to combinatorial counting arguments, database query languages, termination proofs, etc.

In this paper we introduce the constraint language **BUI** for expressing constraints over *B*ags, *U*r-elements, and *I*ntegers. Beside a first-order signature Σ_{ur} for expressing constraints over the ur-elements, the language contains:

- the symbols 0, 1, $+$, $-$, max, min and $\leq$ for expressing constraints over integers;
- the empty multiset constant $[\![\,]\!]$, a multiset constructor $[\![\cdot]\!]^{(\cdot)}$, and the multiset operators union ($\cup$), sum ($\uplus$) and intersection ($\cap$) for expressing constraints over multisets;
- a 'count' operator which returns, for each element a and multiset x, the number of occurrences of a in x.

Given an arbitrary theory T modeling the ur-elements, we use a decision procedure that decides the quantifier-free consequences of T and a decision procedure for integer linear arithmetic as black boxes to provide in a modular fashion a decision procedure for the satisfiability of any quantifier-free formula in the language **BUI**.

In addition, we prove that if the decision procedure for the theory T runs in nondeterministic polynomial time, then the satisfiability problem for quantifier-free formulae in the language **BUI** is $\mathcal{NP}$-complete.

A. Voronkov (Ed.): CADE-18, LNAI 2392, pp. 363–376, 2002.

Our decision procedure is an extension of the Nelson-Oppen combination method specifically tailored to the combination domain of integers, ur-elements, and multisets. The Nelson-Oppen combination method [1,3] combines decision procedures for stably infinite[1] first-order theories over disjoint signatures into a single decision procedure for the union theory by means of propagating equalities. It should be noted, however, that our decision procedure for the language **BUI** remains correct even if the underlying theory T of the ur-elements is not stably infinite.

The decision procedure in this paper is inspired by our previous work on the combination of lists with integers [4], and of sets with integers [5].

The paper is organized as follows. In Section 2 we introduce some preliminary notions which will be needed in what follows. In Section 3 we describes our decision procedure, and in Section 4 we prove its correctness. In Section 5 we prove that the satisfiability problem for quantifier-free formulae in the language **BUI** is $\mathcal{NP}$-complete. In Section 6 we discuss some efficiency issues. Finally, in Section 7 we draw conclusions from our work.

2   Preliminaries

In this section we give some basic definitions which will be used in the rest of the paper, and we define the syntax and semantics of the language **BUI**.

2.1   Multisets

Multisets are collections that may contain duplicate elements. Formally, a multiset x is a function $x : A \to \mathbb{N}^+$, for some set A.[2] Given a multiset x and an element a, the number of occurrences of a in x is denoted by $\mathrm{count}(a, x)$, that is:

$$\mathrm{count}(a, x) = \begin{cases} x(a), & \text{if } a \in \mathrm{domain}(x), \\ 0, & \text{otherwise.} \end{cases}$$

Equality between two multisets x, y can then be expressed in terms of the count operator:

$$x = y \quad \text{iff} \quad (\forall a)(\mathrm{count}(a, x) = \mathrm{count}(a, y)).$$

---

[1] A first-order theory T is stably infinite if every quantifier-free formula which is satisfiable in T is also satisfiable in an infinite model of T.

[2] Note that according to this definition a multiset $x : A \to \mathbb{N}^+$ can be infinite only if it contains an infinite number of elements, that is, if A is infinite.

Several memberships constructs over multisets can be expressed in terms of the count operator:

$$a \in x \ : \ \operatorname{count}(a,x) \geq 1 \qquad (a \text{ is a member of } x)$$
$$a \notin x \ : \ \operatorname{count}(a,x) = 0 \qquad (a \text{ is not a member of } x)$$
$$a \in^{(n)} x \ : \ \operatorname{count}(a,x) \geq n \qquad (a \text{ occurs in } x \text{ at least } n \text{ times})$$
$$a \in!^{(n)} x \ : \ \operatorname{count}(a,x) = n \qquad (a \text{ occurs in } x \text{ exactly } n \text{ times}).$$

We use the symbol $[\![\,]\!]$ to denote the empty multiset, whereas we write $[\![a]\!]^{(n)}$ to denote the multiset containing exactly n occurrences of a and nothing else. Let x, y be two multisets. Then:

- their *union* is the multiset $x \cup y$ such that, for each element a, the equality $\operatorname{count}(a, x \cup y) = \max(\operatorname{count}(a,x), \operatorname{count}(a,y))$ holds;
- their *sum* is the multiset $x \uplus y$ such that, for each element a, the equality $\operatorname{count}(a, x \uplus y) = \operatorname{count}(a,x) + \operatorname{count}(a,y)$ holds;
- their *intersection* is the multiset $x \cap y$ such that, for each element a, the equality $\operatorname{count}(a, x \cap y) = \min(\operatorname{count}(a,x), \operatorname{count}(a,y))$ holds.

2.2   The Language BUI: Syntax

The language **BUI** is essentially a many-sorted language with three basic sorts bag, ur, and int.

To express constraints over the ur-elements, we are given a first-order signature Σ_{ur}, which we write as $\Sigma_{\mathsf{ur}}^{\mathrm{C}} \cup \Sigma_{\mathsf{ur}}^{\mathrm{F}} \cup \Sigma_{\mathsf{ur}}^{\mathrm{P}}$ where $\Sigma_{\mathsf{ur}}^{\mathrm{C}}$, $\Sigma_{\mathsf{ur}}^{\mathrm{F}}$, $\Sigma_{\mathsf{ur}}^{\mathrm{P}}$ are the collections of constants, function symbols and predicate symbols in Σ_{ur}. In other words, each element of $\Sigma_{\mathsf{ur}}^{\mathrm{C}}$ has sort ur, each element of $\Sigma_{\mathsf{ur}}^{\mathrm{F}}$ of arity n has sort $\underbrace{\mathsf{ur} \times \cdots \times \mathsf{ur}}_{n} \to \mathsf{ur}$, and each element of $\Sigma_{\mathsf{ur}}^{\mathrm{P}}$ of arity n has sort $\underbrace{\mathsf{ur} \times \cdots \times \mathsf{ur}}_{n}$.

To express constraints over the integers, the language **BUI** contains the following symbols:

- the constants 0 (*zero*) and 1 (*one*), both of sort int;
- the operators $+$ (*addition*), $-$ (*subtraction*), max (*maximum*), min (*minimum*), all of them having sort int $\times$ int $\to$ int;
- the predicate symbol $\leq$, of sort int $\times$ int;

To express constraints over multisets, the language **BUI** contains the following symbols:

- the constant $[\![\,]\!]$ (*empty multiset*), of sort bag;
- the operator $[\![\cdot]\!]^{(\cdot)}$ (*multiset construction*), of sort ur $\times$ int $\to$ bag;
- the operators $\cup$ (*union*), $\uplus$ (*sum*), and $\cap$ (*intersection*), all of them having sort bag $\times$ bag $\to$ bag;
- the operator $\operatorname{count}(\cdot, \cdot)$, of sort ur $\times$ bag $\to$ int;

Finally, for each sort $\tau \in \{\mathsf{bag}, \mathsf{ur}, \mathsf{int}\}$, the language **BUI** contains an enumerable quantity of variables of sort τ and an equality symbol $=_\tau$ of sort $\tau \times \tau$.[3]

Definition 1. *BUI-terms (resp.* **BUI**-*formulae) are well-sorted terms (resp. formulae) constructed using the symbols of the language* **BUI**.

Definition 2. *A* bag-*term*[4] *is* PURE *if all symbols in it are either variables or one of* $[\![\,]\!], [\![\cdot]\!]^{(\cdot)}, \cup, \uplus, \cap$. *Pure* ur-*terms and pure* int-*terms are defined similarly.*

A pure bag-*atom is an atom of the form* $s = t$, *where* s, t *are pure* bag-*terms. Similarly one can define pure* ur-*atom, pure* int-*atoms, and, in general, pure* τ-*formulae, for* $\tau \in \{\mathsf{bag}, \mathsf{ur}, \mathsf{int}\}$.

Unless otherwise specified, in the rest of the paper x, y, z will denote bag-variables, u, v, w will denote int-variables, and a, b, c will denote ur-variables.

2.3   The Language BUI: Semantics

Definition 3. *An* INTERPRETATION $\mathcal{A}$ *of* **BUI** *is a many-sorted interpretation of the sorts, variables and symbols in the language* **BUI** *satisfying the following conditions:*

- *each sort* $\tau \in \{\mathsf{bag}, \mathsf{ur}, \mathsf{int}\}$ *is mapped to a non-empty set* A_τ *such that:*
  - A_{ur} *is a non-empty set;*
  - A_{int} *is the set of all integers* $\mathbb{Z} = \{0, \pm 1, \pm 2, \dots\}$;
  - A_{bag} *is the collection of all multisets whose elements are in* A_{ur};
- *for each sort* τ, *each variable* x *of sort* τ *is mapped to an element* $x^{\mathcal{A}}$ *in* A_τ;
- *the symbols* $[\![\,]\!], [\![\cdot]\!]^{(\cdot)}, \cup, \uplus, \cap$, count, $0, 1, +, -$, max, min, $\leq$, *are interpreted according to their standard interpretation;*
- $=_\tau$ *is interpreted as the identity in* A_τ, *for* $\tau \in \{\mathsf{bag}, \mathsf{ur}, \mathsf{int}\}$.

In the rest of the paper the calligraphic letters $\mathcal{A}, \mathcal{B}, \dots$ will denote interpretations, and the corresponding Roman letters, properly subscripted, will denote the domains of the interpretations.

Definition 4. *A* **BUI**-*formula* φ *is*

- VALID, *if it evaluates to true in all interpretations;*
- SATISFIABLE, *if it evaluates to true in some interpretation;*
- UNSATISFIABLE, *if it evaluates to false in all interpretations.*

---

[3] We will write $=$ in place of $=_\tau$ when τ is clear from the context. In addition, we will use the notation $s \neq t$ as an abbreviation of $\neg(s = t)$.

[4] For a sort τ, a τ-term is a term of sort τ.

2.4   Theories

We use ur-*theories* in order to model the elements of sort ur.

Definition 5. *An* ur-THEORY *is any set of pure* ur-*formulae.*

Given an ur-theory T, a T-interpretation is an interpretation in which all formulae in T evaluate to true.

Definition 6. *Given an* ur-*theory* T, *a* **BUI**-*formula* φ *is*

- T-VALID, *if it evaluates to true in all T-interpretations;*
- T-SATISFIABLE, *if it evaluates to true in some T-interpretation;*
- T-UNSATISFIABLE, *if it evaluates to false in all T-interpretations.*

3   The Decision Procedure

Let T be an ur-theory for which a decision procedure for the T-satisfiability of quantifier-free pure ur-formulae is available. We now describe a decision procedure for checking the T-satisfiability of any quantifier-free **BUI**-formula φ. Note that, by converting φ into a disjunctive normal form, without loss of generality we may restrict ourselves to consider only conjunctions of **BUI**-literals.

The decision procedure consists of five phases, which we systematically describe in the next five subsections.

3.1   First Phase: Variable Abstraction

The first phase of our decision procedure takes as input a conjunction φ of mixed **BUI**-literals, and converts it into a conjunction of pure **BUI**-literals. More specifically, the output of the variable abstraction phase is a pair $\langle \varphi', \varphi'' \rangle$ of conjunctions of **BUI**-literals with the following properties:

(a) $\varphi' \cup \varphi''$ is T-satisfiable if and only if so is φ;
(b) each literal in φ' is pure;
(c) each pure bag-literal in φ' is of the form

$$
\begin{array}{cccc}
x = y, & x \neq y, & x = [\![\,]\!], & x = [\![a]\!]^{(u)}, \\
x = y \cup z, & x = y \uplus z, & x = y \cap z, &
\end{array} \tag{1}
$$

(d) each literal in φ'' is of the form $u = \mathrm{count}(a, x)$.

Note that all properties can be effectively enforced with the help of new auxiliary variables.

3.2   Second Phase: Partition

In the second phase we partition $\varphi' \cup \varphi''$ into four disjoint sets of literals φ_{ur}, φ_{int}, φ_{bag} and φ_{count} where

- φ_{ur} contains all pure ur-literals in φ';
- φ_{int} contains all pure int-literals in φ';
- φ_{bag} contains all pure bag-literals in φ';
- $\varphi_{\mathsf{count}} = \varphi''$.

We call $\varphi_{\mathsf{ur}} \cup \varphi_{\mathsf{int}} \cup \varphi_{\mathsf{bag}} \cup \varphi_{\mathsf{count}}$ a conjunction of **BUI**-literals in *separate* form.

3.3   Third Phase: Variable Generation

Let $\varphi = \varphi_{\mathsf{ur}} \cup \varphi_{\mathsf{int}} \cup \varphi_{\mathsf{bag}} \cup \varphi_{\mathsf{count}}$ be a conjunction of **BUI**-literals in separate form. The third phase of our decision procedure does not change φ, but instead generates new ur-variables and new int-variables which will be used in the later phases.

More specifically, the variable generation phase consists of two steps:

Step 1: generate ur-variables. For each literal of the form $x \neq y$ in φ_{bag}, generate a new ur-variable $a_{x,y}$.

Step 2: generate int-variables. For each ur-variable a either generated in Step 1 or occurring in φ, and for each bag-variable x occurring in φ_{bag}, generate a new int-variable $w_{a,x}$.

Note that:

- the intuition behind Step 1 is that if two bags x, y are different then there must exist some element a such that $\mathrm{count}(a, x) \neq \mathrm{count}(a, y)$;
- the intuitive meaning of the variables generated in the second step is to represent, for each ur-element a and for each bag x, the value of $\mathrm{count}(a, x)$.

We denote with V_τ, for $\tau \in \{\mathsf{bag}, \mathsf{ur}, \mathsf{int}\}$, the collection of τ-variables that either occur in φ or are generated in the variable generation phase. We also denote with $wax(\varphi)$ the collection of literals $\{0 \leq w_{a,x} : a \in V_{\mathsf{ur}} \text{ and } x \in V_{\mathsf{bag}}\}$.

3.4   Fourth Phase: Decomposition

Let $\varphi = \varphi_{\mathsf{ur}} \cup \varphi_{\mathsf{int}} \cup \varphi_{\mathsf{bag}} \cup \varphi_{\mathsf{count}}$ be a conjunction of **BUI**-literals in separate form. In the fourth phase of our decision procedure we nondeterministically guess an *arrangement* of φ.

Definition 7. *Let* $\varphi = \varphi_{\mathsf{ur}} \cup \varphi_{\mathsf{int}} \cup \varphi_{\mathsf{bag}} \cup \varphi_{\mathsf{count}}$ *be a conjunction of* **BUI**-*literals in separate form. An* ARRANGEMENT *of* φ *is any equivalence relation* R *on* V_{ur}.

For an arrangement R of φ, we define $res_{ur}(\varphi, R)$ to be the following collection of literals

$$res_{ur}(\varphi, R) = \{a = b : a, b \in V_{ur} \text{ and } aRb\} \cup$$
$$\{a \neq b : a, b \in V_{ur} \text{ and not } aRb\},$$

and we also define $res_{int}(\varphi, R)$ to be the collection of literals obtained by replacing all literals in $\varphi_{bag} \cup \varphi_{count} \cup res_{ur}(\varphi, R)$ with the following formulae:[5]

$x = y$	$\Longrightarrow$	$\bigwedge_{a \in V_{ur}} (w_{a,x} = w_{a,y})$
$x \neq y$	$\Longrightarrow$	$w_{a_{x,y},x} \neq w_{a_{x,y},y}$
$x = [\![\,]\!]$	$\Longrightarrow$	$\bigwedge_{a \in V_{ur}} (w_{a,x} = 0)$
$x = [\![a]\!]^{(u)}$	$\Longrightarrow$	$(w_{a,x} = u) \wedge \bigwedge_{\neg(bRa)} (w_{b,x} = 0)$
$x = y \cup z$	$\Longrightarrow$	$\bigwedge_{a \in V_{ur}} (w_{a,x} = \max(w_{a,y}, w_{a,z}))$
$x = y \uplus z$	$\Longrightarrow$	$\bigwedge_{a \in V_{ur}} (w_{a,x} = w_{a,y} + w_{a,z})$
$x = y \cap z$	$\Longrightarrow$	$\bigwedge_{a \in V_{ur}} (w_{a,x} = \min(w_{a,y}, w_{a,z}))$
$u = \text{count}(a, x)$	$\Longrightarrow$	$u = w_{a,x}$
$a = b$	$\Longrightarrow$	$\bigwedge_{x \in V_{bag}} (w_{a,x} = w_{b,x})$
$a \neq b$	$\Longrightarrow$	$true.$

All replacements are fairly intuitive, except maybe the last two ones. Indeed, for any multiset x, if $a = b$ then $\text{count}(a, x) = \text{count}(b, x)$. On the other hand, if $a \neq b$ then nothing can be said about $\text{count}(a, x)$ and $\text{count}(b, x)$.

Note also that the only replacement that needs to take into account nonequivalent ur-variables is the one dealing with the operator $[\![\cdot]\!]^{(\cdot)}$.

3.5 Fifth Phase: Check

Let $\varphi = \varphi_{ur} \cup \varphi_{int} \cup \varphi_{bag} \cup \varphi_{count}$ be a conjunction of **BUI**-literals in separate form, and let R be the arrangement guessed in the decomposition phase.

The fifth and last phase of our decision procedure consists in:

1. checking $\varphi_{ur} \cup res_{ur}(\varphi, R)$ for T-satisfiability;
2. checking $\varphi_{int} \cup wax(\varphi) \cup res_{int}(\varphi, R)$ for satisfiability in $\mathbb{Z}$.

If both checks 1 and 2 succeed, we declare φ to be T-satisfiable.

---

[5] Where $true$ is an abbreviation of $0 = 0$.

Note that check 1 can be performed by using the decision procedure for the ur-theory T, whereas check 2 can be performed by using any decision procedure for integer linear arithmetic.[6]

3.6   An Example

As an example of how our decision procedure works, let us consider the counting law for multisets:

$$x \uplus y = (x \cup y) \uplus (x \cap y). \tag{2}$$

We want to show that (2) is T-valid, where T is the empty ur-theory. To do so, it is sufficient to prove that its negation

$$x \uplus y \neq (x \cup y) \uplus (x \cap y) \tag{3}$$

is T-unsatisfiable. After applying the variable abstraction and partition phases, we obtain the following conjunction $\varphi = \varphi_{ur} \cup \varphi_{int} \cup \varphi_{bag} \cup \varphi_{count}$ in separate form:

$$\varphi_{ur} = \emptyset, \qquad\qquad\qquad \varphi_{int} = \emptyset,$$

$$\varphi_{bag} = \begin{cases} z_0 = x \uplus y, \\ z_1 = x \cup y, \\ z_2 = x \cap y, \\ z_3 = z_1 \uplus z_2, \\ z_0 \neq z_3 \end{cases}, \qquad \varphi_{count} = \emptyset.$$

Since φ_{bag} contains only one disequality, in the variable generation phase we generate one new ur-variable a and six new int-variables $w_{a,x}$, $w_{a,y}$, w_{a,z_0}, w_{a,z_1}, w_{a,z_2}, w_{a,z_3}, obtaining the following conjunction $wax(\varphi)$:

$$wax(\varphi) = \{0 \leq w_{a,z} : z \in \{x, y, z_0, z_1, z_2, z_3, z_4\}\}.$$

In the decomposition phase, since $V_{ur} = \{a\}$, the only permitted arrangement is $R = \{(a, a)\}$. We then have $res_{ur}(\varphi, R) = \{a = a\}$ and

$$res_{int}(\varphi, R) = \begin{cases} w_{a,z_0} = w_{a,x} + w_{a,y} \\ w_{a,z_1} = \max(w_{a,x}, w_{a,y}) \\ w_{a,z_2} = \min(w_{a,x}, w_{a,y}) \\ w_{a,z_3} = w_{a,z_1} + w_{a,z_2} \\ w_{a,z_0} \neq w_{a,z_3} \end{cases}.$$

Clearly, $\varphi_{ur} \cup res_{ur}(\varphi, R)$ is T-satisfiable. However, $\varphi_{int} \cup wax(\varphi) \cup res_{int}(\varphi, R)$ has no solution in $\mathbb{Z}$, and therefore we conclude that (3) is T-unsatisfiable, hence (2) is T-valid.

---

[6] Since integer linear arithmetic is a decidable and complete theory.

4   Soundness, Completeness, and Decidability

In this section we prove that our decision procedure is sound and complete for the T-satisfiability of conjunctions of **BUI**-literals. Let us start with soundness.

Theorem 1 (soundness). *Let* $\varphi = \varphi_{\mathsf{ur}} \cup \varphi_{\mathsf{int}} \cup \varphi_{\mathsf{bag}} \cup \varphi_{\mathsf{count}}$ *be a conjunction of* **BUI**-*literals in separate form, and let* T *be an* ur-*theory. Assume that there exists an arrangement* R *of* φ *such that:*

(i) $\varphi_{\mathsf{ur}} \cup res_{\mathsf{ur}}(\varphi, R)$ *is* T-*satisfiable;*
(ii) $\varphi_{\mathsf{int}} \cup wax(\varphi) \cup res_{\mathsf{int}}(\varphi, R)$ *is satisfiable in* $\mathbb{Z}$.

Then φ *is* T-*satisfiable.*

Proof. Let $\mathcal{A}$ be a T-interpretation satisfying $\varphi_{\mathsf{ur}} \cup res_{\mathsf{ur}}(\varphi, R)$ and let $\mathcal{B}$ be an interpretation satisfying $\varphi_{\mathsf{int}} \cup wax(\varphi) \cup res_{\mathsf{int}}(\varphi, R)$.

We now define an interpretation $\mathcal{M}$. First, we specify the domains by letting $M_{\mathsf{ur}} = A_{\mathsf{ur}}$, $M_{\mathsf{int}} = \mathbb{Z}$ and $M_{\mathsf{bag}} = \{x : x$ is a multiset and $\mathrm{domain}(x) \subseteq A_{\mathsf{ur}}\}$. Then:

- for each ur-variable $a \in V_{\mathsf{ur}}$, we let $a^{\mathcal{M}} = a^{\mathcal{A}}$
- for each int-variable $u \in V_{\mathsf{int}}$, we let $u^{\mathcal{M}} = u^{\mathcal{B}}$.
- for each bag-variable $x \in V_{\mathsf{bag}}$, we let $x^{\mathcal{M}}$ be the unique multiset such that

$$\mathrm{domain}(x^{\mathcal{M}}) = \{a^{\mathcal{A}} : a \in V_{\mathsf{ur}} \text{ and } w^{\mathcal{B}}_{a,x} > 0\},$$

and

$$\mathrm{count}(a^{\mathcal{A}}, x^{\mathcal{M}}) = w^{\mathcal{B}}_{a,x}, \qquad \text{for each } a \in V_{\mathsf{ur}}.$$

Note that in order for the above definition to be sound, we must ensure that for every two ur-variables a, b and for every bag-variable x, if $a^{\mathcal{A}} = b^{\mathcal{A}}$ then $w^{\mathcal{B}}_{a,x} = w^{\mathcal{B}}_{b,x}$. To see that this is the case, assume that $a^{\mathcal{A}} = b^{\mathcal{A}}$. But then the literal $a = b$ must occur in $res_{\mathsf{ur}}(\varphi, R)$, and therefore the literal $w_{a,x} = w_{b,x}$ is in $res_{\mathsf{int}}(\varphi, R)$. It follows $w^{\mathcal{B}}_{a,x} = w^{\mathcal{B}}_{b,x}$.

We claim that $\mathcal{M}$ is a T-interpretation satisfying φ. Clearly, $\mathcal{M}$ satisfies $T \cup \varphi_{\mathsf{ur}} \cup \varphi_{\mathsf{int}}$. Moreover, by inspecting the replacements in Subsection 3.4, it is easy to verify that $\mathcal{M}$ also satisfies all literals in $\varphi_{\mathsf{bag}} \cup \varphi_{\mathsf{count}}$. $\square$

Our decision procedure is also complete, as proved by the following theorem.

Theorem 2 (completeness). *Let* $\varphi = \varphi_{\mathsf{ur}} \cup \varphi_{\mathsf{int}} \cup \varphi_{\mathsf{bag}} \cup \varphi_{\mathsf{count}}$ *be a* T-*satisfiable conjunction of* **BUI**-*literals in separate form, where* T *is an* ur-*theory.*
Then there exists an arrangement R *of* φ *such that:*

(a) $\varphi_{\mathsf{ur}} \cup res_{\mathsf{ur}}(\varphi, R)$ *is* T-*satisfiable;*
(b) $\varphi_{\mathsf{int}} \cup wax(\varphi) \cup res_{\mathsf{int}}(\varphi, R)$ *is satisfiable in* $\mathbb{Z}$.

Proof. Let $\mathcal{M}$ be a T-interpretation satisfying φ. Let us define an arrangement R by putting:

$$u R v \quad \text{if and only if} \quad u^{\mathcal{M}} = v^{\mathcal{M}}, \qquad \text{for each } u, v \in V_{\mathsf{ur}}.$$

Clearly, property (a) holds since $\mathcal{M}$ satisfies $T \cup \varphi_{\mathsf{ur}}$ and, by construction, $\mathcal{M}$ also satisfies $res_{\mathsf{ur}}(\varphi, R)$.

Next, in order to verify property (b), notice that by assumption $\mathcal{M}$ satisfies φ_{int}. In addition, since the variables $w_{a,x}$'s do not occur in φ, we can safely modify $\mathcal{M}$ by letting $w_{a,x}^{\mathcal{M}} = \mathrm{count}(a^{\mathcal{M}}, x^{\mathcal{M}})$, for each $a \in V_{\mathsf{ur}}$ and $x \in V_{\mathsf{bag}}$. Clearly, by construction the modified $\mathcal{M}$ satisfies $wax(\varphi)$. Moreover, by inspecting the replacements in Subsection 3.4 it is easy to verify that the modified $\mathcal{M}$ also satisfies all literals in $res_{\mathsf{int}}(\varphi, R)$. $\qquad\square$

Combining Theorems 1 and 2 with the observation that there is only a finite number of arrangements of any collection φ of **BUI**-literals in separate form, we obtain the following decidability result.

Theorem 3 (decidability). *Let T be an ur-theory for which a decision procedure for the T-satisfiability of quantifier-free pure ur-formulae is available. Then the T-satisfiability problem for quantifier-free formulae in the language **BUI** is decidable.*

5   NP-Completeness

In this section we show that the T-satisfiability problem for quantifier-free **BUI**-formulae is $\mathcal{NP}$-complete, provided that the T-satisfiability problem for quantifier-free pure ur-formulae is in $\mathcal{NP}$.

Clearly, $\mathcal{NP}$-hardness follows by the fact that the propositional calculus is embedded into the language **BUI**. Thus, we obtain $\mathcal{NP}$-completeness if we show that the procedure described in Section 3 takes nondeterministic polynomial time, since guessing one of the disjuncts of a disjunctive normal form of any **BUI**-formula takes nondeterministic polynomial time.

Clearly, the variable abstraction and partition phases can be done in deterministic linear time in the size of the input formula.

Concerning the other phases, let $\varphi = \varphi_{\mathsf{ur}} \cup \varphi_{\mathsf{int}} \cup \varphi_{\mathsf{bag}} \cup \varphi_{\mathsf{count}}$ be a conjunction of **BUI**-literals in separate form. As usual, denote with V_τ, for $\tau \in \{\mathsf{bag}, \mathsf{ur}, \mathsf{int}\}$, the collection of τ-variables that either occur in φ or are generated in the variable generation phase.

Note that:

- the variable generation phase takes deterministic time $\mathcal{O}(t^2 + (s + t^2) \cdot t)$, where s is the number of ur-variables occurring in φ and t is the number of bag-variables occurring in φ;
- guessing an arrangement takes nondeterministic time $\mathcal{O}(|V_{\mathsf{ur}}|^2)$;
- computing $res_{\mathsf{ur}}(\varphi, R)$ takes deterministic time $\mathcal{O}(|V_{\mathsf{ur}}|^2)$.

- computing $res_{\mathsf{int}}(\varphi, R)$ takes deterministic time $\mathcal{O}(m \times (|V_{\mathsf{ur}}| + |V_{\mathsf{bag}}|))$, where m is the number of literals in $\varphi_{\mathsf{bag}} \cup \varphi_{\mathsf{count}} \cup res_{\mathsf{ur}}(\varphi, R)$
- computing $wax(\varphi)$ takes deterministic time $\mathcal{O}(|V_{\mathsf{ur}}| \cdot |V_{\mathsf{bag}}|)$
- by assumption, checking the T-satisfiability of $\varphi_{\mathsf{ur}} \cup res_{\mathsf{ur}}(\varphi, R)$ take nondeterministic polynomial time.
- checking $\varphi_{\mathsf{int}} \cup wax(\varphi) \cup res_{\mathsf{int}}(\varphi, R)$ for satisfiability in $\mathbb{Z}$ takes nondeterministic polynomial time (cf. [2]).

Thus, we obtain the following $\mathcal{NP}$-completeness result.

Theorem 4 ($\mathcal{NP}$-completeness). *Let T be an ur-theory such that the T-satisfiability problem for quantifier-free pure ur-formulae is in $\mathcal{NP}$.*

Then the T-satisfiability problem for quantifier-free formulae in the language **BUI** *is $\mathcal{NP}$-complete.*

6   Efficiency Issues

Since the language **BUI** properly extends both the propositional calculus and integer linear arithmetic, the $\mathcal{NP}$-completeness result proved in the previous section is the best complexity result one could expect from a theoretical point of view. From a pragmatic point of view, however, the decision procedure described in Section 3 is not susceptible of a practical and efficient implementation because of a very expensive nondeterministic decomposition phase. Nevertheless, in this section we show that, under some additional assumptions, the nondeterminism induced by the decomposition phase can be avoided by appealing to the simple idea of *convexity*.

The notion of convexity was introduced in [1] in order to avoid case splitting and make efficient the deterministic version of the Nelson-Oppen combination method. The following is a formal definition.

Definition 8. *An ur-theory T is* CONVEX *if for every collection φ of pure ur-literals and for every disjunction of pure ur-equalities $\bigvee_{i=1}^{n} s_i = t_i$, if $T \cup \varphi \models \bigvee_{i=1}^{n} s_i = t_i$ then $T \cup \varphi \models s_i = t_i$, for some $i \in \{1, \ldots, n\}$.*

Unfortunately, the language **BUI** is not convex. In fact:

- the theory of integer linear arithmetic is not convex. As an example, the conjunction $1 \leq u \leq 2 \wedge v = 1 \wedge w = 2$ entails the disjunction $u = v \vee u = w$ but does not entail neither $u = v$ nor $u = w$;
- the underlying theory T of the ur-elements is arbitrary, and therefore it may not be convex;
- the operator $[\![\cdot]\!]^{(\cdot)}$ is also a source of non-convexity. For example, the literal $a \in [\![b]\!]^{(1)} \uplus [\![c]\!]^{(1)}$ entails $a = b \vee a = c$ but does not entail neither $a = b$ nor $a = c$.

The non convexity of integer linear arithmetic is not a problem since the decomposition phase involves only ur-variables and not int-variables. Thus, in order to obtain an efficient deterministic version of our decision procedure for

BUI, all is needed is to assume that T is convex and that there is no occurrence of the operator $[\![\cdot]\!]^{(\cdot)}$ in the formula to be checked for T-satisfiability.

In this deterministic procedure, the variable abstraction, partition, and variable generation phases are exactly as the ones described in Section 3. The decomposition phase is, however, replaced by the following equality propagation phase.

> **Equality propagation.** Let $\varphi = \varphi_{ur} \cup \varphi_{int} \cup \varphi_{bag} \cup \varphi_{count}$ be the conjunction of **BUI**-literals in separate form obtained in the partition phase. If φ_{ur} is T-unsatisfiable, declare φ to be T-unsatisfiable. Otherwise, compute the collection of literals $det\text{-}res_{ur}(\varphi)$ and $det\text{-}res_{int}(\varphi)$ defined as follows:
>
> – $det\text{-}res_{ur}(\varphi) = \{a = b : a, b \in V_{ur} \text{ and } T \cup \varphi_{ur} \models a = b\}$;[7]
> – $det\text{-}res_{int}(\varphi)$ is the collection of literals obtained by applying the replacements in Subsection 3.4 to $\varphi_{bag} \cup \varphi_{count} \cup det\text{-}res_{ur}(\varphi)$.

After applying the equality propagation phase, we check whether $\varphi_{int} \cup wax(\varphi) \cup det\text{-}res_{int}(\varphi)$ is satisfiable in $\mathbb{Z}$. If this is the case, we declare φ to be T-satisfiable, otherwise we declare φ to be T-unsatisfiable.

Note that the deterministic procedure just described is much more efficient than the one described in Section 3. Efficiency mainly stems from the fact that equalities are propagated only in one direction, with the effect that only *one* integer linear system needs to be solved, whereas in the procedure described in Section 3 we solve a linear system for each guessed arrangement.

Before proving that the deterministic procedure presented in this section is correct, we need the following technical lemma.

Lemma 1. *Let V be a collection of* ur-*variables, and let φ be a T-satisfiable conjunction of* ur-*literals. Then there exists a T-interpretation $\mathcal{A}$ satisfying φ such that $a^{\mathcal{A}} \neq b^{\mathcal{A}}$, for all* ur-*variables $a, b \in V$ for which $T \cup \varphi \not\models a = b$.*

Proof. Let $S = \{(a, b) : a, b \in V \text{ and } T \cup \varphi \not\models a = b\}$, and consider the disjunction

$$\psi : \bigvee_{(a,b) \in S} a = b.$$

If $T \cup \varphi \not\models \psi$ then the lemma is proved. If instead $T \cup \varphi \models \psi$ then, by the convexity of T, there exists a pair $(a, b) \in S$ such that $T \cup \varphi \models a = b$, a contradiction.   □

The following two theorems show the correctness of the deterministic procedure presented in this section.

Theorem 5 (soundness). *Let T be a convex* ur-*theory and let $\varphi = \varphi_{ur} \cup \varphi_{int} \cup \varphi_{bag} \cup \varphi_{count}$ be a conjunction of* **BUI**-*literals in separate form not involving the operator $[\![\cdot]\!]^{(\cdot)}$. Assume that:*

---

[7] Note that $det\text{-}res_{ur}(\varphi)$ can be effectively computed due to our decidability assumptions on T.

(i) φ_{ur} *is* T*-satisfiable;*

(ii) $\varphi_{\mathsf{int}} \cup wax(\varphi) \cup det\text{-}res_{\mathsf{int}}(\varphi)$ *is satisfiable in* $\mathbb{Z}$*.*

Then φ *is* T*-satisfiable*

Proof. Since T is convex, by Lemma 1 there exists a T-interpretation $\mathcal{A}$ satisfying φ_{ur} such that $a^{\mathcal{A}} \neq b^{\mathcal{A}}$, for all ur-variables $a, b \in V_{\mathsf{ur}}$ for which $T \cup \varphi_{\mathsf{ur}} \not\models a = b$. Let also $\mathcal{B}$ be an interpretation satisfying $\varphi_{\mathsf{int}} \cup wax(\varphi) \cup det\text{-}res_{\mathsf{int}}(\varphi)$.

We now define an interpretation $\mathcal{M}$ exactly as it was done in the proof of Theorem 1. As before, in order to ensure that $\mathcal{M}$ is well-defined, we need to ensure that for every two ur-variables a, b and for every bag-variable x, if $a^{\mathcal{A}} = b^{\mathcal{A}}$ then $w_{a,x}^{\mathcal{B}} = w_{b,x}^{\mathcal{B}}$.

Thus, assume that $a^{\mathcal{A}} = b^{\mathcal{A}}$. Then $T \cup \varphi_{\mathsf{ur}} \models a = b$ and therefore the literal $a = b$ must occur in $res_{\mathsf{ur}}(R)$. Thus, the literal $w_{a,x} = w_{b,x}$ is in $res_{\mathsf{int}}(\varphi, R)$, which implies that $w_{a,x}^{\mathcal{B}} = w_{b,x}^{\mathcal{B}}$.

The proof can now continue smoothly by verifying, exactly as done in the proof of Theorem 1, that $\mathcal{M}$ is a T-interpretation satisfying φ. $\square$

Theorem 6 (completeness). *Let* T *be an* ur-*theory, and let* $\varphi = \varphi_{\mathsf{ur}} \cup \varphi_{\mathsf{int}} \cup \varphi_{\mathsf{bag}} \cup \varphi_{\mathsf{count}}$ *be a* T*-satisfiable conjunction of* **BUI***-literals in separate form not involving the operator* $[\![\cdot]\!]^{(\cdot)}$*.*

Then the following holds:

(a) φ_{ur} *is* T*-satisfiable;*

(b) $\varphi_{\mathsf{int}} \cup wax(\varphi) \cup det\text{-}res_{\mathsf{int}}(\varphi)$ *is satisfiable in* $\mathbb{Z}$*.*

Proof. Obviously φ_{ur} is T-satisfiable. In addition, since the variables $w_{a,x}$'s do not occur in φ, we can safely modify $\mathcal{M}$ by letting $w_{a,x}^{\mathcal{M}} = \mathrm{count}(a^{\mathcal{M}}, x^{\mathcal{M}})$, for each $a \in V_{\mathsf{ur}}$ and $x \in V_{\mathsf{bag}}$. Clearly, by construction the modified $\mathcal{M}$ satisfies $wax(\varphi)$. Moreover, by inspecting the replacements in Subsection 3.4 it is easy to verify that the modified $\mathcal{M}$ also satisfies all literals in $det\text{-}res_{\mathsf{int}}(\varphi)$. $\square$

7   Conclusion

We defined the constraint language **BUI** for combining multisets, integers, and ur-elements. We then presented a decision procedure for **BUI** and we proved its correctness. In particular, we showed that our decision procedure remains correct even if the underlying theory T of the ur-elements is not stably infinite.

We also addressed the problem of efficiency by presenting a second procedure which avoids the expensive nondeterminism of the decomposition phase. The second procedure is correct provided that T is convex and that the formula to be checked for T-satisfiability does not involve the operator $[\![\cdot]\!]^{(\cdot)}$.

Finally, we proved that if the T-satisfiability problem for quantifier-free pure ur-formulae is in $\mathcal{NP}$ then the T-satisfiability problem for quantifier-free **BUI**-formulae is $\mathcal{NP}$-complete.

Although not shown in this paper, it is easy to verify that the results of Sections 4 and 5 generalize to the case of multisets of integers, thus allowing the expression of constraints such as $count(count(a, x), x) = 1$, which are forbidden by the syntax of **BUI**. However, due to the non convexity of integer linear arithmetic, it is not clear to us whether the same generalization can be done for the results of Section 6.

Acknowledgments. We thank Cesare Tinelli and the anonymous reviewers for useful comments.

This research was supported in part by NSF(ITR) grant CCR-01-21403, by NSF grant CCR-99-00984-001, by ARO grant DAAD19-01-1-0723, and by ARPA/AF contracts F33615-00-C-1693 and F33615-99-C-3014.

References

1. Greg Nelson and Derek C. Oppen. Simplification by cooperating decision procedures. *ACM Transactions on Programming Languages and Systems*, 1(2):245–257, 1979.
2. Christos H. Papadimitriou. On the complexity of integer programming. *Journal of the Association for Computing Machinery*, 28(4):765–768, 1981.
3. Cesare Tinelli and Mehdi T. Harandi. A new correctness proof of the Nelson-Oppen combination procedure. In Franz Baader and Klaus U. Schulz, editors, *Frontiers of Combining Systems*, volume 3 of *Applied Logic Series*, pages 103–120. Kluwer Academic Publishers, 1996.
4. Calogero G. Zarba. Combining lists with integers. In Rajeev Goré, Alexander Leitsch, and Tobias Nipkow, editors, *International Joint Conference on Automated Reasoning (Short Papers)*, Technical Report DII 11/01, pages 170–179. University of Siena, Italy, 2001.
5. Calogero G. Zarba. Combining sets with integers. In Alessandro Armando, editor, *Frontiers of Combining Systems*, volume 2309 of *Lecture Notes in Artificial Intelligence*, pages 103–116. Springer, 2002.

The Reflection Theorem: A Study in Meta-theoretic Reasoning

Lawrence C. Paulson

University of Cambridge, Computer Laboratory, JJ Thomson Avenue,
Cambridge CB3 0FD, UK, lcp@cl.cam.ac.uk

Abstract. The reflection theorem has been proved using Isabelle/ZF. This theorem cannot be expressed in ZF, and its proof requires reasoning at the meta-level. There is a particularly elegant proof that reduces the meta-level reasoning to a single induction over formulas. Each case of the induction has been proved with Isabelle/ZF, whose built-in tools can prove specific instances of the reflection theorem upon demand.

1 Introduction

A vast amount of mathematics has been verified using proof tools. The Mizar Mathematical Library[1] is probably the largest single repository, but others exist, built using a variety of theorem-provers. An optimist might conclude that any theorem can be verified given enough effort. A sufficiently large and talented team could enter the whole of Wiles's proof of Fermat's Last Theorem [17] and its mathematical prerequisites into a theorem prover, which would duly assert the formula $\forall nxyz \, (n > 2 \rightarrow x^n + y^n \neq z^n)$.

The flaw in this point of view is that mathematicians sometimes reason in ways that are hard to formalize. Typical is Gödel's proof [5] of the relative consistency of the axiom of choice (AC). Gödel begins with a complicated set-theoretic construction. At a crucial stage, he introduces operations on syntax. He defines *absoluteness* in terms of the *relativization* $\phi^{\mathbf{M}}$ of a first-order formula ϕ with respect to a class $\mathbf{M}$. He proceeds to apply absoluteness to his entire construction. His proof is of course correct, but it mixes reasoning about sets with reasoning about the language of sets.

Relativization [8, p. 112] replaces each subformula $\exists x \, \phi$ by $\exists x \, (x \in \mathbf{M} \wedge \phi)$ and dually $\forall x \, \phi$ by $\forall x \, (x \in \mathbf{M} \rightarrow \phi)$, bounding all quantifiers by $\mathbf{M}$. In Zermelo-Fraenkel (ZF) set theory, a class is simply a formula and $x \in \mathbf{M}$ denotes $\mathbf{M}(x)$. So relativization combines the two formulas, ϕ and $\mathbf{M}$, to yield a third, $\phi^{\mathbf{M}}$. This suggests that we recursively define the set F of first-order formulas within ZF. Relativization for elements of F is trivial to formalize, but it is useless—we cannot relate the "formulas" in F to real formulas. More precisely, no formula χ expresses the truth of elements of F. If for each formula ϕ we write $\ulcorner \phi \urcorner$ for the corresponding element of F, then some formula ψ is handled incorrectly:

---

[1] Available via http://mizar.org

A. Voronkov (Ed.): CADE-18, LNAI 2392, pp. 377–391, 2002.
© Springer-Verlag Berlin Heidelberg 2002

$\psi \leftrightarrow \neg\chi(\ulcorner\psi\urcorner)$ can be proved in ZF. This fact is Tarski's theorem on the non-definability of truth [8, p. 41].

Gödel introduced meta-level reasoning in order to make his consistency proof effective. He could have worked entirely with sets and demonstrated how to transform a model of set theory into a model of set theory that also satisfied AC. In the latter approach, if we found a contradiction from the axioms of set theory and AC, then we would know that there existed a contradiction in set theory, but we would have no idea how to find the contradiction. Gödel's methods let us transform the contradiction involving AC into a contradiction involving the axioms of set theory alone.

One way to handle meta-level reasoning is to throw away our set theory provers and work formalistically. We could work in a weak logic, such as PRA, which has been proposed for the QED project for mechanizing mathematics [13]. In this logic, we would define the set of formulas (the set F), an internalized inference system, and the ZF axioms. Instead of proving the theorem ϕ in a ZF prover, we would prove the theorem ZF $\vdash \ulcorner\phi\urcorner$ in PRA. Then we could easily express syntactic operations on formulas.

However, the formalist approach is not easy. The formal language of set theory has no function symbols and its only relation symbols are $=$ and $\in$. An assertion such as $\langle x, y\rangle \in A \cup B$ has to be expressed in purely relational form, say $\exists p\, C\, [\mathsf{isPair}(x, y, p) \wedge \mathsf{isUnion}(A, B, C) \wedge p \in C]$. Expressions such as $\{x \in A \mid \phi(x)\}$ and $\bigcup_{x\in A} B(x)$ require a treatment of variable binding. Theorems would be hard even to state, and their proofs would require reasoning about syntax when we would rather reason about sets. My earlier work with Grąbczewski [12] using Isabelle/ZF [10,11] demonstrates that large amounts of set theory can be formalized without taking such an extreme measure. It is worth trying to see what can be accomplished using a set theory prover, recognizing that we can never formalize arguments performed at the meta-level. As it happens, our result can be proved as a collection of separate theorems that Isabelle can use automatically to prove any desired instance of the reflection theorem.

Overview. The paper introduces the reflection theorem (§2) and the proof eventually formalized (§3). Excerpts from the two Isabelle/ZF theories are presented, concerning normal functions (§4) and the reflection theorem (§5). An interactive Isabelle session demonstrates the reflection theorem being applied (§6), and the paper concludes (§7).

2   The Reflection Theorem

The *reflection theorem* is a simple result that illustrates the issues mentioned above. Let **ON** denote the class of ordinals. Suppose that $\{M_\alpha\}_{\alpha\in\mathbf{ON}}$ is a family of sets that is *increasing* (which means $\alpha < \beta$ implies $M_\alpha \subseteq M_\beta$) and *continuous* (which means $M_\alpha = \bigcup_{\xi\in\alpha} M_\xi$ when α is a limit ordinal). Define the class **M** by $\mathbf{M} = \bigcup_{\alpha\in\mathbf{ON}} M_\alpha$, Then the reflection theorem states that if $\phi(x_1, \ldots, x_n)$ is a formula in n variables and α is an ordinal, then for some $\beta > \alpha$ and all $x_1, \ldots,$ $x_n \in M_\beta$ we have (intuitively)

$$\mathbf{M} \models \phi(x_1, \dots, x_n) \leftrightarrow M_\beta \models \phi(x_1, \dots, x_n).$$

I say intuitively, because $\mathbf{M}$ could be $\mathbf{V}$, the universal class; as remarked above, truth in ZF is not definable by a formula. A precise statement of the conclusion requires relativization:

$$\phi^{\mathbf{M}}(x_1, \dots, x_n) \leftrightarrow \phi^{M_\beta}(x_1, \dots, x_n).$$

The reflection theorem reduces truth in the class $\mathbf{M}$ to truth in the set M_β, where β can be made arbitrarily large. It is valuable because classes do not exist in ZF; they are merely notation. The theorem can be applied by letting $\mathbf{M}$ be $\mathbf{V}$ and letting M_α be V_α, the cumulative hierarchy defined by $V_0 = 0$, $V_{\alpha+1} = \mathcal{P}(V_\alpha)$ and $V_\alpha = \bigcup_{\xi \in \alpha} V_\xi$ when α is limit. The reflection theorem is also applied to $\mathbf{L}$, the constructible universe [8, p. 169]; it is an essential part of modern treatments of Gödel's consistency proof that are based on ZF set theory.

Proving the reflection theorem is not difficult, if only we can formalize it. Bancerek [1] proved it in Mizar. Mizar's native Tarski-Grothendieck properly extends ZF: classes really do exist, and we can define $\mathbf{M} \models \ulcorner \phi(x_1, \dots, x_n) \urcorner$ when $\mathbf{M}$ is a class. This solves the problem concerning the definability of truth. It is ironic that the formalization problems can be solved by working either in the weaker logic PRA or in a stronger logic.

The approach taken below is more in the spirit of set theory: a *theorem* follows from the axioms, while a *meta-theorem* is a mechanical procedure for yielding theorems. Most authors do not formalize the meta-theory. Results such as the following are not meta-theorems, but merely *theorem schemes*:

$$a \in \{x \in A \mid \phi(x)\} \leftrightarrow a \in A \wedge \phi(a)$$

$$a \in \bigcup_{x \in A} B(x) \leftrightarrow \exists x \, (x \in A \wedge a \in B(x))$$

Their proofs depend not at all on the structure of the formula ϕ or the expression B. Thanks to Isabelle's higher-order syntax, each is a single Isabelle/ZF theorem, with a trivial proof. The reflection theorem is different: it is proved by reasoning about a formula's structure.

3   Proof Overview

The first task in formalizing the reflection theorem is to find a proof with the least amount of meta-level reasoning. Kunen's proof [8, p. 136] needs a lemma, also proved at the meta-level, about a subformula-closed list of formulas. The proof idea is related to Skolemization and involves finding all existentially quantified subformulas. Drake's proof [4, p. 99] requires the formula to be presented in prenex form and involves a simultaneous construction for the whole quantifier string. In both proofs, the meta-level component is substantial.

Mostowski's proof [9, p. 23], fortunately, is a simple structural induction. Reflection for atomic formulas is trivial. Reflection for $\neg\phi(x)$ and $\phi(x) \wedge \phi'(x)$ follows trivially from induction hypotheses for $\phi(x)$ and $\phi'(x)$. Reflection for $\exists y\, \phi(x,y)$ follows from an induction hypothesis for $\phi(x,y)$. The main complication is that the case for $\exists y\, \phi(x,y)$ adds a variable to the induction hypothesis; we do not want the theorem statement to depend upon the number of free variables in the formula. By assuming that the class $\mathbf{M}$ is closed (in a suitable way) under ordered pairing, it suffices to derive reflection for $\exists y\, \phi(\langle x,y\rangle)$ from reflection for $\phi(\langle x,y\rangle)$, which trivially follows from reflection for $\phi(z)$. The proofs are nontrivial, but they take place entirely within ZF. The only meta-level reasoning is the structural induction itself: noting that it suffices to prove the cases for atomic formulas, $\neg$, $\wedge$ and $\exists$. The simple structure of these lemmas makes it easy to apply reflection to individual formulas and yields an expression for the class of ordinals that reflect the formula. At the end of this paper, we shall see Isabelle doing this automatically.

Mostowski's proof owes its simplicity to the classic technique of strengthening the induction hypothesis. The required conclusion has the form $\forall \alpha\, \exists \beta > \alpha\, \dots$; in other words, the possible values of β form an unbounded class. In Mostowski's proof, this class is closed as well as unbounded. A class $\mathbf{X}$ of ordinals is *closed* provided for every nonempty set Y, if $Y \subseteq \mathbf{X}$ then $\bigcup Y \in \mathbf{X}$. (The union $\bigcup Y$ is the supremum, or limit, of the set Y.) It turns out that if $\mathbf{X}$ and $\mathbf{X}'$ are closed and unbounded, then so is $\mathbf{X} \cap \mathbf{X}'$. This fact is crucial; in particular, it gives an immediate proof for the conjunctive case of the reflection theorem: if $\mathbf{X}$ is the class of ordinals for $\phi(x)$ and $\mathbf{X}'$ is the class of ordinals for $\phi'(x)$ then $\mathbf{X} \cap \mathbf{X}'$ is a closed, unbounded class of ordinals for $\phi(x) \wedge \phi'(x)$.

The function $F : \mathbf{ON} \to \mathbf{ON}$ is *normal* provided it is increasing and continuous:

$$F(\alpha) < F(\beta) \quad \text{if } \alpha < \beta$$
$$F(\alpha) = \bigcup_{\xi < \alpha} F(\xi) \quad \text{if } \alpha \text{ is a limit ordinal}$$

Every normal function enjoys a key property: the class of fixedpoints $\{\alpha \mid F(\alpha) = \alpha\}$ is closed and unbounded. This fact has surprising consequences. Consider the enumeration of the cardinals, $\{\aleph_\alpha\}_{\alpha \in \mathbf{ON}}$. Given that even $\aleph_0$ is infinite, one might expect $\alpha < \aleph_\alpha$ to be a trivial theorem, but in fact $\aleph$ is a normal function and the solutions of $\aleph_\alpha = \alpha$ form a closed and unbounded class.

Normal functions are used in the critical case of the reflection theorem, when we have an existential quantifier. Here is a sketch of the argument. At a key stage in the proof, we seek an ordinal β such that for all $x \in M_\beta$ we have

$$\exists y \in \mathbf{M}\ \phi(x,y) \to \exists y \in M_\beta\ \phi(x,y). \tag{1}$$

Let α be an ordinal. If $x \in M_\alpha$ and $y \in \mathbf{M}$ then (since $\mathbf{M} = \bigcup_{\alpha \in \mathbf{ON}} M_\alpha$) we can choose the least $\xi(x)$ such that $y' \in M_\xi$ and $\phi(x,y')$. This ordinal is a function of x, and we can apply the replacement axiom over the set M_α to find the least upper bound of the set $\{\xi(x)\}_{x \in M_\alpha}$. This map from α to $\bigcup_{x \in M_\alpha} \xi(x)$ can be used to define a normal function, F. Let β be a fixedpoint of F. Then, by construction, if $x \in M_\beta$ and $y \in \mathbf{M}$ then there exists $y' \in M_{F(\beta)}$ such that $\phi(x, y')$. Since $F(\beta) = \beta$ we conclude $y' \in M_\beta$, which establishes (1).

Two points remain before we can proceed to the Isabelle/ZF proofs. First, recall that we can restrict attention to unary formulas, deriving reflection for $\exists y\, \phi(\langle x, y \rangle)$ rather than for $\exists y\, \phi(x, y)$. This requires assuming that the class $\mathbf{M}$ is closed under ordered pairing *in a suitable way*. The natural way is to assume that M_α is closed under ordered pairing whenever α is a limit ordinal. The class of limit ordinals is closed and unbounded, so we can intersect this class with the class found by the proof sketched above and the resulting class will still be closed and unbounded.

For the second point, recall that the conclusion of the reflection theorem is

$$\phi^{\mathbf{M}}(z) \leftrightarrow \phi^{M_\beta}(z).$$

Working with real formulas makes it impossible to formalize the relativizations $\phi^{\mathbf{M}}$ and ϕ^{M_β}. It turns out that we can abstract $\phi^{\mathbf{M}}(z)$ to $\phi(z)$ and $\phi^{M_\beta}(z)$ to $\psi(\beta, z)$ in the crucial case of the existential quantifier, proving

$$\exists y \in \mathbf{M}\ \phi(\langle x, y \rangle) \leftrightarrow \exists y \in M_\beta\ \psi(\beta, \langle x, y \rangle).$$

For the induction hypothesis, we merely need a closed unbounded class of ordinals α such that $\phi(x) \leftrightarrow \psi(\alpha, x)$ for $x \in M_\alpha$. The proof does not require $\psi(\alpha, x)$ to behave like $\phi^{M_\alpha}(x)$. The resulting theorems inductively generate (at the meta-level!) pairs of formulas of the form $\phi^{\mathbf{M}}$ and ϕ^{M_β}.

4   Normal Functions in Isabelle/ZF

Two Isabelle/ZF theories define the concepts covered in this paper: one for normal functions and closed and unbounded classes, the other for the reflection theorem itself. The files (available from the author) prove about 90 lemmas and theorems using about 210 proof commands. The next two sections present highlights, omitting most proofs and many technical lemmas. The formal material presented below was generated automatically from the Isabelle theories. It is similar to what the user sees on the screen when using Proof General.[2] These proofs were not written in ML, as in traditional Isabelle, but as tactic scripts in the Isar language [16].

Iteration of the function `F`, written `iterates(F,x,n)`, corresponds to $F^n(x)$. The following concept is the limit of all such iterations, corresponding to $F^\omega(x)$.

constdefs
```
iterates_omega :: "[i⇒i,i] ⇒ i"
    "iterates_omega(F,x) ≡ ⋃n∈nat. iterates(F,x,n)"
```

The ordinal ω is written nat in Isabelle/ZF because it is the set of natural numbers.

---

[2] http://www.proofgeneral.org/

4.1   Closed and Unbounded Classes of Ordinals

Classes have no special status in Isabelle/ZF. Although Isabelle's overloading mechanism [15] makes it possible to extend operations such as $\in$, $\cup$, $\cap$ and $\subseteq$ to classes, the theories adopt the traditional approach. A class $\mathbf{M}$ is really a formula ϕ. Membership in a class, $a \in \mathbf{M}$, means $\phi(a)$. Intersection of two classes, $\mathbf{M} \cap \mathbf{N}$, denotes the conjunction of the predicates, $\lambda x.\, \phi(x) \wedge \psi(x)$. A family of classes, $\{\mathbf{M}_z\}_{z \in \mathbf{N}}$, denotes a 2-argument predicate; for example, $a \in \bigcup_{z \in \mathbf{N}} \mathbf{M}_z$ stands for $\exists z\, \psi(z) \wedge \phi(z, a)$. These examples illustrate the extent to which we can reason about classes in ZF.

The theory defines closed and unbounded (c.u.) classes of ordinals. A class has type $i \Rightarrow o$, which is the type of functions from sets to truth values.

constdefs
```
Closed :: "(i⇒o) ⇒ o"
    "Closed(P) ≡ ∀I. I≠0⟶ (∀i∈I. Ord(i) ∧ P(i)) ⟶ P(⋃(I))"

Unbounded :: "(i⇒o) ⇒ o"
    "Unbounded(P) ≡ ∀i. Ord(i) ⟶ (∃j. i<j ∧ P(j))"

Closed_Unbounded :: "(i⇒o) ⇒ o"
    "Closed_Unbounded(P) ≡ Closed(P) ∧ Unbounded(P)"
```

The predicate `Ord` recognizes the class of ordinal numbers, which is traditionally written **ON**, while `Limit` recognizes the limit ordinals. The predicate `Card` recognizes the class of cardinals, which is traditionally written **CARD**. All three classes are easily proved to be closed and unbounded.

```
theorem Closed_Unbounded_Ord   [simp]: "Closed_Unbounded(Ord)"
theorem Closed_Unbounded_Limit [simp]: "Closed_Unbounded(Limit)"
theorem Closed_Unbounded_Card  [simp]: "Closed_Unbounded(Card)"
```

4.2   The Intersection of a Family of Closed Unbounded Classes

A key lemma for the reflection theorem is that the intersection of a family of closed unbounded (c.u.) classes is c.u. (The family must be indexed by a set, not a class, for $\bigcap_{\alpha \in \mathbf{ON}} \{\beta \mid \beta > \alpha\}$ is empty.) The constructions below come from Kunen [8, p. 78].

A *locale* [7] lets us fix the class P and the index set A. It states assumptions that hold for the whole development, namely that P is closed and unbounded and that A is nonempty. It also contains definitions of functions `next_greater` and `sup_greater`, which are local to the proof.

```
locale cub_family =
    fixes P and A
    fixes next_greater   — the next ordinal satisfying class A
    fixes sup_greater    — sup of those ordinals over all A
```

assumes *closed:*   "a∈A ⟹ Closed(P(a))"
   and *unbounded:* "a∈A ⟹ Unbounded(P(a))"
   and *A_non0:* "A≠0"
defines "next_greater(a,x) ≡ μy. x<y ∧ P(a,y)"
   and "sup_greater(x) ≡ ⋃a∈A. next_greater(a,x)"

Our result is the culmination of a series of lemmas proved in the scope of this locale. We begin by proving that the intersection is closed.

lemma (**in** cub_family) Closed_INT: "Closed(λx. ∀i∈A. P(i,x))"

The proof (omitted) is a one-liner. The difficulty is showing that the intersection is unbounded. For a∈A, by the unboundedness of P(a), it contains an ordinal next_greater(a,x) greater than x. By reasoning about the μ-operator, which denotes the least ordinal satisfying a formula, these claims are easily verified:

   "⟦Ord(x); a∈A⟧ ⟹ P(a, next_greater(a,x))"
   "⟦Ord(x); a∈A⟧ ⟹ x < next_greater(a,x)"

I have omitted the **lemma** commands, for brevity.

   Now sup_greater(x) is the supremum of next_greater(a,x) for a∈A. We can iterate this step to reach sup_greater$^\omega$(x). The point is that sup_greater$^\omega$(x) belongs to all of the classes, and thus to the intersection. First, a number of trivial facts have to be verified, such as these:

   "Ord(x) ⟹ x < iterates_omega(sup_greater,x)"
   "a∈A ⟹ next_greater(a,x) ≤ sup_greater(x)"

This is a key stage in the argument. Fixing a∈A, we find that sup_greater$^\omega$(x) can be written as the supremum of values of the form next_greater(a,−), that is, as the supremum of members of P(a).

   "⟦Ord(x); a∈A⟧
   ⟹ iterates_omega(sup_greater,x) =
      (⋃n∈nat. next_greater(a, iterates(sup_greater,x,n)))"

Since this class is closed, it must contain sup_greater$^\omega$(x).

   "⟦Ord(x); a∈A⟧ ⟹ P(a, iterates_omega(sup_greater,x))"

The desired result follows immediately. Note that the intersection of a family of classes is expressed as a universally-quantified formula:

theorem Closed_Unbounded_INT:
   "(⋀a. a∈A ⟹ Closed_Unbounded(P(a)))
   ⟹ Closed_Unbounded(λx. ∀a∈A. P(a, x))"

Since 2 = {0,1} in set theory, the intersection of two classes can be reduced to the general case by using 2 for the index set:

   "P(x) ∧ Q(x) ⟷ (∀i∈2. (i=0 ⟶ P(x)) ∧ (i=1 ⟶ Q(x)))"

Thus we obtain the corollary for binary intersections, which is the version used in the reflection theorem:

theorem Closed_Unbounded_Int:
   "⟦Closed_Unbounded(P); Closed_Unbounded(Q)⟧
   ⟹ Closed_Unbounded(λx. P(x) ∧ Q(x))"

4.3   Fixedpoints of Normal Functions

Our proof of the reflection theorem uses the lemma that the class of fixedpoints of a normal function is closed and unbounded. The Isabelle/ZF proof follows Drake [4, pp. 113–114]. It begins by defining normal functions as those that are monotonic and continuous over the ordinals:

constdefs
```
mono_Ord :: "(i⇒i) ⇒ o"
  "mono_Ord(F) ≡ ∀i j. i<j ⟶ F(i) < F(j)"

cont_Ord :: "(i⇒i) ⇒ o"
  "cont_Ord(F) ≡ ∀l. Limit(l) ⟶ F(l) = (⋃i<l. F(i))"

Normal :: "(i⇒i) ⇒ o"
  "Normal(F) ≡ mono_Ord(F) ∧ cont_Ord(F)"
```

Among the consequences of these definitions is an equation expressing continuity of normal functions over unions. It follows (with a little effort) from their continuity over limit ordinals.

```
"⟦X≠0; ∀x∈X. Ord(x); Normal(F)⟧
  ⟹ F(Union(X)) = (⋃y∈X. F(y))"
```

From this lemma, it is easy to prove that the class of fixedpoints is closed:

```
"Closed(λi. F(i) = i)"
```

As with the intersection theorem, the work goes into showing that the class is unbounded, by reasoning about suprema. If F is a normal function, then consider $F^\omega(\alpha) = \bigcup_{\alpha \in \omega} F^n(\alpha)$. It is easy to show that $F^\omega(\alpha)$ is a fixedpoint of F.

```
"⟦Normal(F); Ord(a)⟧
  ⟹ F(iterates_omega(F,a)) = iterates_omega(F,a)"
```

Since $\alpha \le F^\omega(\alpha)$, there are arbitrarily large fixedpoints, which yields the desired result.

theorem `Normal_imp_fp_Closed_Unbounded:`
```
  "Normal(F) ⟹ Closed_Unbounded(λi. F(i) = i)"
```

4.4   Function `normalize`

The key construction of the reflection theorem maps an ordinal α to another ordinal, $F(\alpha)$, but F might not be monotonic, so it is not necessarily normal. The usual proof complicates the construction in order to force F to be monotonic. However, we can define a separate operator for this purpose.

Function `normalize` maps a continuous function $F : \mathbf{ON} \to \mathbf{ON}$ to a normal function F' that bounds it above. Continuity of F is needed to show that $F(\alpha) \le F'(\alpha)$. For a counterexample, consider the successor function $S : \mathbf{ON} \to \mathbf{ON}$, which is not continuous. If S' is normal, then let α be one of its fixedpoints. Then $S'(\alpha) = \alpha < S(\alpha)$.

constdefs
```
normalize :: "[i⇒i, i] ⇒ i"
  "normalize(F,a) ≡ ..."
```

The definition is omitted because it is too technical. It defines `normalize(F,a)` to be the function $F'(\alpha)$ satisfying the transfinite recursion

$$F'(0) = F(0)$$
$$F'(\alpha + 1) = \max\{F'(\alpha) + 1, F(\alpha + 1)\}$$
$$F'(\alpha) = \bigcup_{\xi < \alpha} F'(\xi) \qquad \text{if } \alpha \text{ is a limit ordinal}$$

Monotonicity follows directly, since by the definition $F'(\alpha + 1) > F'(\alpha)$. The essential properties of `normalize` are easily shown:

theorem `Normal_normalize`:
```
  "(⋀x. Ord(x) ⟹ Ord(F(x))) ⟹ Normal(normalize(F))"
```

theorem `le_normalize`:
```
  "⟦Ord(i); cont_Ord(F); ⋀x. Ord(x) ⟹ Ord(F(x))⟧
   ⟹ F(i) ≤ normalize(F,i)"
```

5   The Reflection Theorem in Isabelle/ZF

Recall that the reflection theorem concerns a class $\mathbf{M} = \bigcup_{\alpha \in \mathbf{ON}} M_\alpha$, where the $\{M_\alpha\}_{\alpha \in \mathbf{ON}}$ are an increasing and continuous family of sets indexed by the ordinals. The constant `mono_le_subset` expresses the notion of *increasing*:

constdefs
```
mono_le_subset :: "(i⇒i) ⇒ o"
  "mono_le_subset(M) ≡ ∀i j. i≤j ⟶ M(i) ⊆ M(j)"
```

A locale (Fig. 1) fixes `Mset`, which stands for the family $\{M_\alpha\}_{\alpha \in \mathbf{ON}}$. It states the assumptions that `Mset` is increasing, continuous and (at limit stages) closed under ordered pairing. Its definition of the class `M` uses an existential quantifier to express $\bigcup_{\alpha \in \mathbf{ON}} M_\alpha$. It defines reflection as the ternary relation `Reflects(Cl,P,Q)` joining a closed, unbounded class `Cl` with a predicate `P` (supposed to be relativized to $\mathbf{M}$) and a predicate `Q` (supposed to be relativized to M_α).

The locale also defines some items that are needed only to prove the existential case. The ordinal-valued functions mentioned in §3 are formalized as `FO` and `FF`. The class `ClEx(P)` consists of all limit ordinals that are fixedpoints of the normal function `normalize(FF(P))`. This class will be closed and unbounded because it is the intersection of two other c.u. classes, and the restriction to limit ordinals lets us use the assumption that `Mset` is closed under pairing at limit stages.

Now we find ourselves reasoning at the meta-level. Formulas have not been defined within set theory; rather they are part of the language of set theory. Therefore, the induction on the structure of formulas cannot be formalized. We simply state and prove the separate cases of this induction.

```
locale reflection =
  fixes Mset and M and Reflects
  assumes Mset_mono_le : "mono_le_subset(Mset)"
    and Mset_cont    : "cont_Ord(Mset)"
    and Pair_in_Mset : "⟦x ∈ Mset(a); y ∈ Mset(a); Limit(a)⟧
                         ⟹ <x,y> ∈ Mset(a)"
  defines "M(x) ≡ ∃a. Ord(a) ∧ x ∈ Mset(a)"
    and "Reflects(Cl,P,Q) ≡
                 Closed_Unbounded(Cl) ∧
                 (∀a. Cl(a) ⟶ (∀x∈Mset(a). P(x) ⟷ Q(a,x)))"
  fixes F0 — ordinal for a specific value y
  fixes FF — sup over the whole level, y ∈ Mset(a)
  fixes ClEx — Reflecting ordinals for the formula ∃z. P
  defines "F0(P,y) ≡ μb. (∃z. M(z) ∧ P(<y,z>)) ⟶
                                  (∃z∈Mset(b). P(<y,z>))"
    and "FF(P)   ≡ λa. ⋃y∈Mset(a). F0(P,y)"
    and "ClEx(P) ≡ λa. Limit(a) ∧ normalize(FF(P),a) = a"
```

Fig. 1. The locale reflection

5.1 Proving Easy Cases of the Reflection Theorem

The base case is when the two formulas are identical, which in practice means
that they contain no quantifiers. All ordinals belong to the reflecting class. The
proof, **by** (simp ...), is shown to emphasize that the proof is immediate by
definition.

theorem (**in** reflection) Triv_reflection [intro]:
    "Reflects(Ord, λx. P(x), λa x. P(x))"
by (simp add: Reflects_def)

The reflecting class for a negation equals that for its operand. This proof is also
trivial.

theorem (**in** reflection) Not_reflection [intro]:
    "Reflects(Cl,P,Q) ⟹ Reflects(Cl, λx. ~P(x), λa x. ~Q(a,x))"
by (simp add: Reflects_def)

The reflecting class for a conjunction is the intersection of those for the two
conjuncts. This proof uses Closed_Unbounded_Int, our lemma that the intersection
of two c.u. classes is c.u. Not shown are the theorems for ∨, → and ↔, whose
proofs are equally trivial.

theorem (**in** reflection) And_reflection [intro]:
    "⟦Reflects(Cl,P,Q); Reflects(C',P',Q')⟧
       ⟹ Reflects(λa. Cl(a) ∧ C'(a), λx. P(x) ∧ P'(x),
                                    λa x. Q(a,x) ∧ Q'(a,x))"
by (simp add: Reflects_def Closed_Unbounded_Int, blast)

The attribute *[intro]*, which appears in each of the theorems above, labels them as *introduction rules* for Isabelle's classical reasoner. This will enable Isabelle to perform reflection automatically.

5.2   Reflection for Existential Quantifiers

This is the most important part of the development. A key lemma is that the function *FO* works as it should: if $y \in$ *Mset(a)* then *FO(P,y)* is a large enough ordinal for $\exists z \in$ *Mset(FO(P,y))*. *P(<y,z>)* to hold. The proof is four lines long, using simple reasoning about the μ-operator.

```
"[[y∈Mset(a); Ord(a); M(z); P(<y,z>)]]
 ⟹ ∃z∈Mset(FO(P,y)). P(<y,z>)"
```

Similarly, the function *FF* works as it should: if *a* is an ordinal then *FF(P,a)* is large enough for the desired conclusion to hold.

```
"[[M(z); y∈Mset(a); P(<y,z>); Ord(a)]]
 ⟹ ∃z∈Mset(FF(P,a)). P(<y,z>)"
```

Similarly again, the normal function derived from *FF* returns an ordinal large enough for the conclusion to hold.

```
"[[M(z); y∈Mset(a); P(<y,z>); Ord(a)]]
 ⟹ ∃z∈Mset(normalize(FF(P),a)). P(<y,z>)"
```

To complete the proof, a further locale declares the induction hypothesis. More precisely, it declares half of it: namely that *Cl* consists of ordinals that correctly relate *P* and *Q*. At this point, there is no need to assume that *Cl* is closed and unbounded.

```
locale ex_reflection = reflection +
   fixes P   — the original formula
   fixes Q   — the reflected formula
   fixes Cl  — the class of reflecting ordinals
   assumes Cl_reflects:
          "[[Cl(a); Ord(a)]] ⟹ ∀x∈Mset(a). P(x) ⟷ Q(a,x)"
```

Now we can reap the benefits of the previous work, such as the lemmas about *FF*. Translated into mathematical language, the next result states that if $z \in \mathbf{M}$ and $y \in M_\alpha$, where α is an ordinal belonging to the class we have constructed, and $P(\langle y,z \rangle)$ holds, then $Q_\alpha(\langle y,z \rangle)$ holds for some $z \in M_\alpha$.

```
"[[M(z); y∈Mset(a); P(<y,z>); Cl(a); ClEx(P,a)]]
 ⟹ ∃z∈Mset(a). Q(a,<y,z>)"
```

This lemma is the opposite and easy direction, for if $z \in M_\alpha$ then obviously $z \in \mathbf{M}$.

```
"[[z∈Mset(a); y∈Mset(a); Q(a,<y,z>); Cl(a); ClEx(P,a)]]
 ⟹ ∃z. M(z) ∧ P(<y,z>)"
```

Combining these results, we find that *ClEx* indeed expresses closed and unbounded classes of ordinals for reflection:

```
"Closed_Unbounded(ClEx(P))"
```

```
"[y∈Mset(a); Cl(a); ClEx(P,a)]
    ==> (∃z. M(z) ∧ P(<y,z>)) <--> (∃z∈Mset(a). Q(a,<y,z>))"
```

It only remains to package up the existential case using the *Reflects* symbol:

```
"Reflects(Cl,P0,Q0)
    ==> Reflects(λa. Cl(a) ∧ ClEx(P0,a),
                 λx. ∃z. M(z) ∧ P0(<x,z>),
                 λa x. ∃z∈Mset(a). Q0(a,<x,z>))"
```

The previous version applies only to formulas that involve ordered pairs. To correct that problem, we can use the projection functions *fst* and *snd*, which return the first and second components of a pair:

theorem (in *reflection*) *Ex_reflection* [*intro*]:
```
    "Reflects(Cl, λx. P(fst(x),snd(x)),
                  λa x. Q(a,fst(x),snd(x)))
    ==> Reflects(λa. Cl(a) ∧ ClEx(λx. P(fst(x),snd(x)), a),
                 λx. ∃z. M(z) ∧ P(x,z),
                 λa x. ∃z∈Mset(a). Q(a,x,z))"
```

The dual rule for the universal quantifier is trivial, since $\forall x \, \phi(x)$ is $\neg \exists x \, \neg \phi(x)$.

6   Invoking the Reflection Theorem

We have no formal statement of the reflection theorem in Isabelle/ZF. However, we have a mechanical procedure for applying it in specific cases, which is one interpretation of a meta-theorem. That procedure is simply Isabelle's classical reasoner, *fast*. No modifications are necessary. Declaring each case of the reflection theorem with the [*intro*] attribute flags them as introduction rules, suitable for backward chaining. The many λ-bound variables in these rules pose no problems for *fast*: it searches for proofs using Isabelle's inbuilt inference mechanisms, which employ higher-order unification [6].

Here the reflection theorem is applied to $\phi(x) \equiv \exists y \, \forall z \, (z \subseteq x \rightarrow z \in y)$. I have explicitly written the relativitized formulas, namely $\phi^{\mathbf{M}}$ and $\phi^{M\alpha}$, though this can be automated using ML if necessary. We have no idea what the reflecting class will be, but we can write it as the variable *?Cl* and let Isabelle work it out.

lemma (in *reflection*)
```
    "Reflects(?Cl,
              λx. ∃y. M(y) ∧ (∀z. M(z) --> z ⊆ x --> z ∈ y),
              λa x. ∃y∈Mset(a). ∀z∈Mset(a). z ⊆ x --> z ∈ y)"
```
by *fast*

Here, reflection is applied to a more complicated formula. Despite the three quantifiers, the call to *fast* takes only 90 milliseconds.

lemma (in reflection**)**
```
"Reflects(?C1,
    λx. ∃y. M(y) ∧ (∀z. M(z) ⟶
                        (∀w. M(w) ⟶ w∈z ⟶ w∈x) ⟶ z∈y),
    λa x. ∃y∈Mset(a). ∀z∈Mset(a).
                        (∀w∈Mset(a). w∈z ⟶ w∈x) ⟶ z∈y)"
```
by fast

Conducting a single-step proof shows how easy these theorems are to prove and also illustrates how the reflecting class is determined incrementally. For this, let us return to the first example:

lemma (in reflection**)**
```
    "Reflects(?C1,
            λx. ∃y. M(y) ∧ (∀z. M(z) ⟶ z ⊆ x ⟶ z ∈ y),
            λa x. ∃y∈Mset(a). ∀z∈Mset(a). z ⊆ x ⟶ z ∈ y)"
```

The outermost connective is ∃, so we apply the corresponding instance of the reflection theorem. Observe how the variable ?C1 in the main goal is replaced by an expression involving an invocation of ClEx and a new variable, ?C11. This variable must be replaced by some class ?C11 that reflects the remaining subformulas:

apply (rule Ex_reflection**)**
```
Reflects
(λa. ?C11(a) ∧
    ClEx(λx. ∀z. M(z) ⟶ z ⊆ fst(x) ⟶ z ∈ snd(x), a),
  λx. ∃y. M(y) ∧ (∀z. M(z) ⟶ z ⊆ x ⟶ z ∈ y),
  λa x. ∃y∈Mset(a). ∀z∈Mset(a). z ⊆ x ⟶ z ∈ y)
 1. Reflects
      (?C11, λx. ∀z. M(z) ⟶ z ⊆ fst(x) ⟶ z ∈ snd(x),
       λa x. ∀z∈Mset(a). z ⊆ fst(x) ⟶ z ∈ snd(x))
```

Now the outermost connective is ∀, so we apply All_reflection. The variable ?C11 is in its turn replaced by another invocation of ClEx and another new variable, ?C12:

apply (rule All_reflection**)**
```
Reflects
(λa. (?C12(a) ∧
    ClEx(λx. ¬ (snd(x) ⊆ fst(fst(x)) ⟶
                snd(x) ∈ snd(fst(x))),
        a)) ∧
    ClEx(λx. ∀z. M(z) ⟶ z ⊆ fst(x) ⟶ z ∈ snd(x), a),
  λx. ∃y. M(y) ∧ (∀z. M(z) ⟶ z ⊆ x ⟶ z ∈ y),
  λa x. ∃y∈Mset(a). ∀z∈Mset(a). z ⊆ x ⟶ z ∈ y)
 1. Reflects
      (?C12,
       λx. snd(x) ⊆ fst(fst(x)) ⟶ snd(x) ∈ snd(fst(x)),
       λa x. snd(x) ⊆ fst(fst(x)) ⟶ snd(x) ∈ snd(fst(x)))
```

The two formulas are now identical, so `Triv_reflection` completes the proof. It replaces `?C12` by `Ord`, the class of all ordinals.

```
apply (rule Triv_reflection)
Reflects
 (λa. (Ord(a) ∧
        ClEx(λx. ¬ (snd(x) ⊆ fst(fst(x)) ⟶
                    snd(x) ∈ snd(fst(x))),
             a)) ∧
       ClEx(λx. ∀z. M(z) ⟶ z ⊆ fst(x) ⟶ z ∈ snd(x), a),
  λx. ∃y. M(y) ∧ (∀z. M(z) ⟶ z ⊆ x ⟶ z ∈ y),
  λa x. ∃y∈Mset(a). ∀z∈Mset(a). z ⊆ x ⟶ z ∈ y)
No subgoals!
```

We should not use defined predicates such as `Ord` in the formula being reflected. The resulting theorems, although valid, would not be instances of the reflection theorem: `Ord` is itself defined in terms of quantifiers, which need to be relativized. I have defined relativized versions of many set-theoretic concepts, such as order-isomorphism, and proved their equivalence to the originals. These relativized concepts form a vocabulary for specific invocations of the reflection theorem.

7 Conclusions

Gödel worked in von Neumann-Bernays-Gödel (NBG) set theory. Modern versions of his proof are typically expressed in ZF set theory. Either way, the base set theory is proved to be relatively consistent with AC. Bancerek [1] proved the reflection theorem years ago, in Mizar, also following Mostowski [9]. However, Bancerek's proof does not address the issue of meta-level reasoning. It instead uses Tarski-Grothendieck set theory to reason about ZF, a weaker system. It does not suggest how to prove the consistency of the axiom of choice with respect to Tarski-Grothendieck set theory, which is a natural question for users of that theory.

My aim is not simply to mechanize the reflection theorem but to capture the spirit of Gödel's consistency proof. I have not given a general way of eliminating meta-reasoning, but I have shown how to treat one specific case. A number of researchers [2,14] have done mechanical proofs using NBG set theory. Gödel's original proof [5] does not require the reflection theorem, but perhaps other parts of his proof could be mechanized in NBG.

Acknowledgements. Alexander S. Kechris and Ken Kunen gave valuable advice by electronic mail. I learned that there was a suitable proof of the reflection theorem in Kechris's unpublished 1976 lecture notes. Markus Wenzel added his Isar language and proof presentation tools to Isabelle/ZF.

References

1. Grzegorz Bancerek. The reflection theorem. *Journal of Formalized Mathematics*, 2, 1990. http://megrez.mizar.org/mirror/JFM/Vol2/zf_refle.html.
2. Johan G. F. Belinfante. Computer proofs in Gödel's class theory with equational definitions for composite and cross. *Journal of Automated Reasoning*, 22(3):311–339, March 1999.
3. Yves Bertot, Gilles Dowek, André Hirschowitz, Christine Paulin, and Laurent Théry, editors. *Theorem Proving in Higher Order Logics: TPHOLs '99*, LNCS 1690. Springer, 1999.
4. Frank R. Drake. *Set Theory: An Introduction to Large Cardinals*. North-Holland, 1974.
5. Kurt Gödel. The consistency of the axiom of choice and of the generalized continuum hypothesis with the axioms of set theory. In S. Feferman et al., editors, *Kurt Gödel: Collected Works*, volume II. Oxford University Press, 1990. First published in 1940.
6. G. P. Huet. A unification algorithm for typed λ-calculus. *Theoretical Computer Science*, 1:27–57, 1975.
7. Florian Kammüller, Markus Wenzel, and Lawrence C. Paulson. Locales: A sectioning concept for Isabelle. In Bertot et al. [3], pages 149–165.
8. Kenneth Kunen. *Set Theory: An Introduction to Independence Proofs*. North-Holland, 1980.
9. Andrzej Mostowski. *Constructible Sets with Applications*. North-Holland, 1969.
10. Lawrence C. Paulson. Set theory for verification: I. From foundations to functions. *Journal of Automated Reasoning*, 11(3):353–389, 1993.
11. Lawrence C. Paulson. Set theory for verification: II. Induction and recursion. *Journal of Automated Reasoning*, 15(2):167–215, 1995.
12. Lawrence C. Paulson and Krzysztof Grąbczewski. Mechanizing set theory: Cardinal arithmetic and the axiom of choice. *Journal of Automated Reasoning*, 17(3):291–323, December 1996.
13. The QED manifesto. http://www-unix.mcs.anl.gov/qed/, 1995.
14. Art Quaife. Automated deduction in von Neumann-Bernays-Gödel set theory. *Journal of Automated Reasoning*, 8(1):91–147, 1992.
15. Markus Wenzel. Type classes and overloading in higher-order logic. In Elsa L. Gunter and Amy Felty, editors, *Theorem Proving in Higher Order Logics: TPHOLs '97*, LNCS 1275, pages 307–322. Springer, 1997.
16. Markus Wenzel. Isar: A generic interpretative approach to readable formal proof documents. In Bertot et al. [3], pages 167–183.
17. Andrew J. Wiles. Modular elliptic curves and Fermat's Last Theorem. *Annals of Mathematics*, 141(3):443–551, 1995.

Faster Proof Checking in the Edinburgh Logical Framework

Aaron Stump and David L. Dill

Computer Systems Laboratory
Stanford University, Stanford, CA 94305, USA
{stump,dill}@cs.stanford.edu
http://verify.stanford.edu

Abstract. This paper describes optimizations for checking proofs represented in the Edinburgh Logical Framework (LF). The optimizations allow large proofs to be checked efficiently which cannot feasibly be checked using the standard algorithm for LF. The crucial optimization is a form of result caching. To formalize this optimization, a path calculus for LF is developed and shown equivalent to a standard calculus.

1   Introduction

The ability for automated reasoning systems to produce easily verifiable proofs has been widely recognized as valuable (e.g., [23,4]). Recently, applications like proof-carrying code and proof-carrying authentication have created a new need for proofs that can be efficiently verified by a simple proof checker [15,2]. The Edinburgh Logical Framework (LF) [10] is a widely used meta-language for representing proof systems for these applications. The representation is such that proof checking is reduced to LF type checking.

The CVC ("a Cooperating Validity Checker") [21] system has the capability to produce proofs in a variant of LF for valid formulas in a quantifier-free fragment of first-order logic with background theories. During validity checking, CVC computes values like a normal form n for a first-order term t. The computation produces a proof p that $t = n$. The normal form and the proof are both cached with t, and they can then both be reused later without repeating the computation. Internally, CVC represents proofs as a directed acyclic graph (DAG) with maximal sharing of common subexpressions. Reusing the cached normal form n for t results in a proof where the subproof p has more than one incoming edge in the DAG.

The problem then arises, how are proofs represented as DAGs to be checked? Since the DAG form for an expression can be exponentially smaller than the tree form, it would be disastrous to unfold the DAG to a tree by duplicating shared subexpressions wherever they occur. Proofs produced for large formulas by CVC can be megabytes long as a DAG, and at least gigabytes long as trees. Clearly, the proof checker must itself use some form of result caching if it is to check a proof represented as a DAG. The result that should be cached is the theorem (if any) that a subproof proves.

A. Voronkov (Ed.): CADE-18, LNAI 2392, pp. 392–407, 2002.

A naive approach to caching would have the proof checker cache the theorem which a subproof proves and reuse that result whenever that subproof is encountered subsequently. This approach is unsound, because syntactically identical subproofs may prove different theorems, depending on where they appear in a proof. This is because proofs introduce (named) local assumptions. For example, a proof (*modus-ponens assumption$_1$ assumption$_2$*) might prove B in a part of the proof where *assumption$_1$* is an assumption that $A \to B$ holds and *assumption$_2$* is an assumption that A holds; and it might prove C in a part of the proof where *assumption$_1$* is an assumption that $A \to C$ holds. Proofs produced by CVC have this kind of dependency of subproofs on local assumptions. So some form of caching is required that respects the scope of local assumptions.

One approach that is sound but turns out to be inefficient is to maintain a table H mapping subproofs to the theorems they prove, and simply clear H during proof checking whenever the set of active assumptions changes. This approach is sound because multiple occurrences of the same subproof do indeed prove the same theorem under the same set of assumptions. It is inefficient because a subproof may depend on only a subset of the set of active assumptions, and so clearing all results may cause the theorem proved by that subproof to be computed again unnecessarily. A prototype proof checker using this approach was unable to check the proofs produced by CVC in a reasonable amount of time and space.

A natural alternative to clearing all cached results whenever an assumption a changes is to clear cached results only for those subproofs that depend on a. Also, there is no need to clear cached results eagerly, as soon as a changes. Results may be cleared lazily; whenever an attempt is made to reuse the theorem cached for some subproof, a check can be performed to see if the assumptions that the subproof depends on have changed. This is better than eager clearing of cached results, because not all subproofs will occur multiple times, and so not all cached results will need to be cleared. This lazy approach to caching has been implemented in a proof checker called flea, which is able to check example proofs produced by CVC in a modest amount of time and space that could not be checked at all previously.

The first contribution of this paper is to formalize a generalization of this approach to context-dependent caching in the setting of LF, and prove it correct with respect to a standard algorithm for LF type-checking (Sections 2, 3, and 4). To improve the performance of type checking further, two other optimizations are developed: variable-sensitive safe substitution (Section 5) and incremental classifier computation for left-nested applications (Section 6). Experimental results using flea are given for proofs produced by CVC (Section 7). The paper assumes some familiarity with type theory.

2   The Edinburgh Logical Framework

In this section, we briefly describe a standard calculus for LF. This is done in technical detail to enable the precise statement of subsequent theorems. Let *Sym* be an infinite set of symbols. A *binding* of a symbol $a \in Sym$ is an expression of the form $a : \tau$. If a list L of bindings contains a binding $x : \tau$, we say that L binds x. The addition of a binding $x : \tau$ to the end of a list of bindings Γ is denoted $\Gamma, x : \tau$.

Definition 1 (*lookup*). *If Γ is a list of bindings of symbols , then $lookup(v, \Gamma)$ is defined inductively as follows. If Γ is of the form $\Gamma', x : \tau$, then $lookup(v, \Gamma)$ equals τ if $v \equiv x$, and $lookup(v, \Gamma')$ otherwise. If Γ is the empty list, then $lookup(v, \Gamma)$ is undefined.*

Figure 1 presents a standard calculus for LF (cf. [17], Chapter 5 of [3]). The primary derivable objects are sequents of the form $\Gamma \vdash X : Y$. It is required in all rules that $\vdash \Gamma$ *Ctx* is derivable. Symbols may be bound more than once by Γ in sequents; the *lookup* function is used to find the most recently added binding in Γ for a symbol. Bound variables may not be tacitly renamed. The notation $A[x := N]$ is used for the result of safely substituting expression N for symbol x in expression A. A formal definition of safe substitution is delayed till Section 5 below. The rule (app) requires the domain type A of the operator M and the type A' of the argument N to be equivalent ($A \cong A'$). This is different from other presentations, which usually require those types to be syntactically identical, not just equivalent; they then use a separate rule of conversion to reclassify N with type A, if indeed $A \cong A'$. The test used for equivalence is the term-directed, context-independent one of [7], whose description is omitted here. It should be possible to extend the results to a context-dependent test like that of [11].

3   An Annotation Calculus for LF

This section presents a new calculus for LF, which is used to present the context-dependent caching optimization in Section 4 below. It is clear that some technical machinery beyond the standard calculus of Section 2 is required to describe caching. The technical device used here is that of typing annotations. The new calculus for LF derives an entire typing annotation of an expression e and all its subexpressions, as opposed to the type of a single expression only. Caching may then be formalized in a rule that says when typing information may be copied from one occurrence of a subterm of e to annotate another occurrence. An alternative technical device for formalizing caching, but one which we do not pursue here, might be some kind of explicit definition or abbreviation.

3.1   Preliminaries

The standard set-theoretic notion of partial function is assumed, together with related set-theoretic operations such as union, which will be performed on functions (cf. [9]). For a unary partial function e, we use the notation $e(x) \downarrow$ to mean e is defined at x and $e(x) \uparrow$ to mean it is not. The domain of definition of e is denoted *Def*(e). Expressions are formalized as unary partial functions

I. Classifications:

(ax) $\dfrac{}{\Gamma \vdash v : A}$ $A = lookup(v,\, \Gamma)$ (type) $\dfrac{}{\Gamma \vdash type : kind}$

(lam) $\dfrac{\Gamma, x : A \vdash M : B \qquad \Gamma \vdash \Pi\, x : A.\, B : \alpha}{\Gamma \vdash \lambda x : A.\, M : \Pi\, x : A.\, B}$ $\alpha \in \{type, kind\}$

(app) $\dfrac{\Gamma \vdash M : \Pi\, x : A.\, B \qquad \Gamma \vdash N : A'}{\Gamma \vdash (M\ N) : B[x := N]}$ $A \cong A'$

(pi) $\dfrac{\Gamma \vdash A : type \qquad \Gamma, x : A \vdash B : \alpha}{\Gamma \vdash \Pi\, x : A.\, B : \alpha}$ $\alpha \in \{type, kind\}$

II. Contexts:

(ctxemp) $\dfrac{}{\vdash \cdot\ Ctx}$ (ctxadd) $\dfrac{\Gamma \vdash A : \alpha}{\vdash \Gamma, c : A\ Ctx}$ $\alpha \in \{type, kind\}$

Fig. 1. A standard presentation of LF

from the set of positions (Definition 2) to a set of symbols (as in, e.g., [6]). This approach allows expressions and annotations of expressions to be treated uniformly. We assume a countably infinite set *Sym* of symbols (disjoint from $\{type, kind, \lambda, \Pi, @\}$.)

Definition 2 (*Pos* : the set of positions). *Let Nat be the set of natural numbers. The inductive set Pos of positions is defined by the following constructors:*

$\epsilon : Pos$
$. : Pos \rightarrow Nat \rightarrow Pos$ (applications of "." written infix)

If $n \in Nat$, n will often be used ambiguously to denote $\epsilon.n$.

We now define operations $\gg$ and $\ll$. The first right-shifts a position by prepending another position as a prefix, and the second left-shifts a position to remove a prefix. The notation is chosen to recall standard right and left bit-shifting operations. In meta-theoretic expressions, $\ll$ and $\gg$ will bind more loosely than the "." constructor.

Definition 3 ($\ll$ and $\gg$: shifting positions). *If $\pi, \psi \in Pos$ and $n \in Nat$, then the operation $\gg$ of prepending ψ to π is defined inductively by: $\epsilon \gg \psi = \psi$ and $\pi.n \gg \psi = (\pi \gg \psi).n$. Now suppose $\pi = (\pi' \gg \psi)$. Then $\pi \ll \psi$ is defined to be π'. Otherwise, it is undefined.*

Definition 4 (*Exp* : the set of LF expressions). *The set Exp of LF expressions is the set of all partial functions e from Pos to $Sym \cup \{type, kind, \lambda, \Pi, @\}$ satisfying the following requirements:*

- *e is undefined on all but a finite non-empty subset of Pos .*
- *Def(e) is prefix-closed: if $e(\pi.n) \downarrow$, then $e(\pi) \downarrow$.*
- *If $e(\pi) \in Sym \cup \{type, kind\}$, then $\{i \mid e(\pi.i) \downarrow\} = \emptyset$.*
- *If $e(\pi) = @$, then $\{i \mid e(\pi.i) \downarrow\} = \{0,1\}$.*
- *If $e(\pi) \in \{\lambda, \Pi\}$, then $e(\pi.0) \in Sym$ and $\{i \mid e(\pi.i) \downarrow\} = \{0,1,2\}$.*

We will use the customary notation for LF expressions. The inductive definition of this notation is omitted, as is the justification for the principle of structural induction on LF expressions, which we will also use.

We now extend $\gg$ and $\ll$ to expressions. The intention is that if e is an expression with $e(\pi) \downarrow$, then $(e \ll \pi)$ is the subexpression at position π in e (usually written $e|_\pi$).

Definition 5 ($\gg$ and $\ll$ extended). *The extensions of $\gg$ and $\ll$ which shift a function whose domain is Pos by a position are also denoted $\gg$ and $\ll$. For input $\pi' \in Pos$, $(f \gg \pi)$ and $(f \ll \pi)$ are defined by*

$$(f \gg \pi)(\pi') = f(\pi' \ll \pi)$$
$$(f \ll \pi)(\pi') = f(\pi' \gg \pi)$$

Equivalently, viewing f as a set of pairs, $(\_ \gg \pi)$ and $(\_ \ll \pi)$ are applied to f by applying them to the first component of each pair. We also extend $\gg$ and $\ll$ to shift sets of positions by a position. The definition for $S \subseteq Pos$ is

$$(S \gg \pi) = \{\psi \gg \pi | \psi \in S\}$$
$$(S \ll \pi) = \{\psi \ll \pi | \psi \in S\}$$

Example 1. Consider the following expression e:

$$\{\epsilon \mapsto @, \ 0 \mapsto @, \ 0.0 \mapsto f, \ 0.1 \mapsto a, \ 1 \mapsto b\}$$

In customary notation, this is denoted $((f\ a)\ b)$, and $(e \ll 0)$ is $(f\ a)$, since, e.g., $(e \ll 0)(0) = e(0.0) = f$.

Definition 6 (annotations). *Suppose $e \in Exp$. An annotation of e is a partial function from Def(e) to Exp .*

An annotation of $e \in Exp$ labels some subexpressions of e with other expressions.

3.2   A Calculus of Annotations

In this section, a new calculus for LF is presented. Derivable objects are essentially annotations of LF expressions. For a given $e \in Exp$, the idea is to derive an annotation a of e such that for all $\pi \in Def(e)$, $a(\pi) = \tau$ iff $\Gamma \vdash e(\pi) : \tau$ is derivable in the standard calculus, where Γ is a context determined by the bindings occurring at prefixes of π in e. By deriving such annotations, we make all computed classifiers available at every point in the derivation. This sets the stage for reusing computed classifiers in Section 4. Similar technical machinery is used in [8]. There is also some resemblance to the marked calculus for LF of [22].

Notation 1 (annotations) *Suppose a is an annotation of $e \in Exp$ with $Def(a) = \{\pi_1, \ldots, \pi_n\}$. Then a may be denoted $\{\pi_1 : a(\pi_1), \ldots, \pi_n : a(\pi_n)\}$.*

Figure 2 presents the calculus. The primary derivable objects are sequents $\Sigma \mid e \vdash a$, where a is an annotation and $e \in Exp$. It is required in all rules that $\vdash \Sigma$ *Sig* is derivable. The list Σ is called a signature instead of a context because it never changes during a derivation (after it has been proved well-formed using (sigemp) and (sigadd)). The (ax) rule specifies an expression's initial annotation, which is defined in the last part of Figure 2 by structural induction. The classificational rules (lam), (app), and (pi) just show how an annotation is extended to a new position. For the premises of those rules, the notation $\Sigma \mid e \vdash a \supseteq X$ means that $\Sigma \mid e \vdash a$ is derivable, where $a \supseteq X$.

A few further remarks on the calculus are needed. Meta-theoretic expressions like $(e \ll \pi.1)$ in the conclusion of (lam) denote the expression resulting from performing the shift. Second, the standard calculus is used computationally by applying the rules bottom-up to analyze a goal classification into subgoals. In contrast, the annotation calculus is used by applying the rules top-down to saturate the initial annotation specified by (ax). Finally, it is not obvious that the annotation calculus of Figure 2 is well-defined, since it is not obvious that the derived objects are always functional and not sometimes merely relational. Functionality up to equivalence will be a consequence of the equivalence of the annotation calculus with the standard presentation of LF, since LF enjoys unicity of classifiers up to equivalence (theorem 2.4 of [10]).

Notation 2 (derivable sequents) *In addition to denoting sequents (theoretical objects), expressions like $\Sigma \mid e \vdash a$ will be used to denote the meta-theoretic proposition that the corresponding sequent is derivable in the annotation calculus.*

3.3   Equivalence with the Standard Calculus

This section states the equivalence of the annotation calculus and the standard calculus of Section 2. This result may be proved from three lemmas about the annotation calculus, which are stated first. Omitted proofs may be found in [20].

Lemma 1 (monotonicity). *Suppose $\Sigma \mid e \vdash a$ is derivable starting from a sequent $\Sigma \mid e \vdash a'$ (used as an assumption to which the inference rules are then applied). Then $\Sigma \mid e \vdash a \cup X$ is derivable starting from sequent $\Sigma \mid e \vdash a' \cup X$. Furthermore, $\Sigma \mid e \vdash a$ implies $a \supseteq I_\Sigma(e)$.*

Proof: Both claims follow by induction on the assumed derivation: every rule only extends annotations (starting from the initial annotation $I_\Sigma(e)$), and no rule is prevented from being applied by definedness of an annotation at a position. $\square$

I. Classifications:

$$\text{(ax)} \ \frac{}{\Sigma \,|\, e \vdash I_\Sigma(e)}$$

$$\text{(lam)} \ \frac{\Sigma \,|\, e \vdash a \supseteq \{\pi.2 : \tau\} \quad \Sigma \,|\, \Pi\, x : \sigma.\tau \vdash a' \supseteq \{\epsilon : \alpha\}}{\Sigma \,|\, e \vdash a \cup \{\pi : \Pi\, x : \sigma.\tau\}} \quad \begin{array}{l} e(\pi) = \lambda \text{ and} \\ \alpha \in \{type, kind\}, \\ x = (e \ll \pi.0) \text{ and} \\ \sigma = (e \ll \pi.1) \end{array}$$

$$\text{(app)} \ \frac{\Sigma \,|\, e \vdash a \supseteq \{\pi.0 : \Pi\, x : \sigma.\tau, \ \pi.1 : \sigma'\}}{\Sigma \,|\, e \vdash a \cup \{\pi : \tau[x := (e \ll \pi.1)]\}} \quad e(\pi) = @ \text{ and } \sigma \cong \sigma'$$

$$\text{(pi)} \ \frac{\Sigma \,|\, e \vdash a \supseteq \{\pi.1 : type, \ \pi.2 : \alpha\}}{\Sigma \,|\, e \vdash a \cup \{\pi : \alpha\}} \quad e(\pi) = \Pi \text{ and } \alpha \in \{type, kind\}$$

II. Signatures:

$$\text{(sigemp)} \ \frac{}{\vdash \cdot Sig} \qquad \text{(sigadd)} \ \frac{\Sigma \,|\, e \vdash a}{\vdash \Sigma, c : e \ Sig} \quad a(\epsilon) \in \{type, kind\}$$

III. Initial annotation:

$$
\begin{aligned}
&& I_\Sigma(type) &= \{\epsilon : kind\} \\
&& I_\Sigma(kind) &= \emptyset \\
&& I_\Sigma(M_0\, M_1) &= (I_\Sigma(M_0) \gg 0) \cup (I_\Sigma(M_1) \gg 1) \\
\text{for } \Xi \in \{\lambda, \Pi\}, && I_\Sigma(\Xi\, x : \sigma.M) &= (I_\Sigma(\sigma) \gg 1) \cup (I_{\Sigma, x:\sigma}(M) \gg 2) \\
\text{for } v \in Sym, && I_\Sigma(v) &= \begin{cases} \{\epsilon : lookup(v, \Sigma)\} & \text{if } lookup(v, \Sigma) \downarrow, \\ \emptyset & \text{otherwise} \end{cases}
\end{aligned}
$$

Fig. 2. Annotation calculus for LF

Lemma 2 ($\gg$-shifting sequents). *Let $\Xi \in \{\lambda, \Pi\}$ be arbitrary.*

i. $\Sigma \,|\, M_i \vdash a$ implies $\Sigma \,|\, (M_0\, M_1) \vdash \ (a \gg i) \cup I_\Sigma(M_0\, M_1)$,
          for $i \in \{0, 1\}$

ii. $\Sigma \,|\, \sigma \vdash a$ implies $\Sigma \,|\, \Xi\, x : \sigma.M \vdash (a \gg 1) \cup I_\Sigma(\Xi\, x : \sigma.M)$

iii. $\Sigma, x : \sigma \,|\, M \vdash a$ implies $\Sigma \,|\, \Xi\, x : \sigma.M \vdash (a \gg 2) \cup I_\Sigma(\Xi\, x : \sigma.M)$

Lemma 3 ($\ll$-shifting sequents). *Let $\Xi \in \{\lambda, \Pi\}$ be arbitrary.*

i. $\Sigma \,|\, (M_0\, M_1) \vdash a$ implies $\Sigma \,|\, M_i \vdash \quad (a \ll i)$, for $i \in \{0, 1\}$

ii. $\Sigma \,|\, \Xi\, x : \sigma.M \vdash a$ implies $\Sigma \,|\, \sigma \vdash \quad (a \ll 1)$

iii. $\Sigma \,|\, \Xi\, x : \sigma.M \vdash a$ implies $\Sigma, x : \sigma \,|\, M \vdash (a \ll 2)$

Theorem 1 (correctness of annotation calculus). *Let $e, \tau \in Exp$ be arbitrary, and let Δ be an arbitrary list of bindings. Then the following are equivalent:*

1. *$\vdash \Delta$ Ctx and $\Delta \vdash e : \tau$ are both derivable in the standard calculus for LF.*
2. *There is an annotation a of e with $a(\epsilon) = \tau$ such that $\vdash \Delta$ Sig and $\Delta | e \vdash a$ are both derivable in the annotation calculus.*

4   Context-Dependent Classifier Caching

This section presents the formalization of the approach to caching and reusing computed classifiers described in Section 1, and proves it sound. Some preliminary definitions are needed.

Definition 7 ($FS(e)$: free symbols of e). *The function FS computing the set of symbols occurring freely in $e \in Exp$ is defined by:*

$$FS(type) = FS(kind) = \emptyset$$
$$FS(M\ N) = FS(M) \cup FS(N)$$
$$\text{for } \varXi \in \{\lambda, \varPi\}, FS(\varXi\, x : \sigma.\, M) = FS(\sigma) \cup (FS(M) \setminus \{x\})$$
$$\text{for } v \in Sym, FS(v) = \{v\}$$

Definition 8 ($Ctx_e(\pi)$: context at π in e). *Let $e \in Exp$, $\pi \in Def(e)$, and $n \in Nat$. $Ctx_e(\pi)$ is the list of bindings at proper prefixes of π in e:*

$$Ctx_e(\epsilon) = \cdot$$
$$Ctx_e(\pi.n) = \begin{cases} Ctx_e(\pi), (e \ll \pi.0) : (e \ll \pi.1) & \text{if } e(\pi) \in \{\lambda, \varPi\} \text{ and } n = 2 \\ Ctx_e(\pi) & \text{otherwise} \end{cases}$$

Example 2. Let e be $\lambda x : \sigma.\, \lambda y : \sigma.\, \lambda x : \tau.\, x$. Then

$$Ctx_e(2) = x : \sigma \qquad Ctx_e(2.2.2) = x : \sigma,\, y : \sigma,\, x : \tau$$

Definition 9 ($Dep_e(\pi)$: dependencies at π in e). *Let $e \in Exp$ and $\pi \in Def(e)$. $Dep_e(\pi) = \{x : lookup(x, Ctx_e(\pi)) \mid x \in FS(e \ll \pi)\}$.*

Intuitively, the intention is that $Dep_e(\pi)$ be the set of all those bindings in $Ctx_e(\pi)$ that the classification of $(e \ll \pi)$ depends on.

Example 3. Let e be as in Example 2. Then $Dep_e(2.2.2) = \{x : \tau\}$.

Now consider the extension of the annotation calculus of Figure 2 by the following new rule:

$$(\text{copy}) \ \frac{\varSigma \,|\, e \vdash a}{\varSigma \,|\, e \vdash a \cup ((a \ll \pi) \gg \pi')} \ (e \ll \pi) = (e \ll \pi') \text{ and } Dep_e(\pi) = Dep_e(\pi')$$

Suppose subexpression $(e \ll \pi)$ of e occurs at position $\pi' \neq \pi$ (as well as at position π). Then informally, the (copy) rule says that if the annotation for the subexpression at the first position has been computed, then it can be simply copied in a single step to annotate that subexpression at the second position (π'), as long as the dependencies of the subexpression are the same at the two positions.

Example 4 (derivation using (copy)). Let Σ be a signature

$$\tau : type, \; f : \tau \to (\tau \to \tau), \; g : \tau \to \tau, \; \ldots$$

Let e be $\lambda x : \tau.\,(f \; (g \; (g \; x)))\,(g \; (g \; x))$. The following derivation uses (copy) to avoid recomputing the annotation for the second occurrence of $(g \; (g \; x))$. Note that the position of the first occurrence of that expression is 2.0.1 and the position of the second occurrence is 2.1. We abbreviate the derivation by showing just how annotations are extended. The rules used are, from top to bottom, (ax), (app), (app), and (copy). In the instance of (copy), $\pi = 2.0.1$ and $\pi' = 2.1$. Note that (copy) extends the annotation at several positions, because (copy) copies the entire annotation of one subexpression to another. So a single application of (copy) annotates at the second occurrence of $(g \; (g \; x))$ all those subterms which are annotated at the first occurrence.

$$\frac{\dfrac{\Sigma \,|\, e \vdash \{\ldots, \; 2.0.1.0 : \tau \to \tau, \; 2.0.1.1.0 : \tau \to \tau, \; 2.0.1.1.1 : \tau\}}{2.0.1.1 : \tau}}{\dfrac{2.0.1 : \tau}{2.1.1 : \tau, \; 2.1 : \tau}}$$

Theorem 2 (conservativity of (copy)). *A sequent is derivable in the calculus with (copy) iff it is derivable in the original calculus without (copy).*

Proof: The "if" direction of the proof is obvious. For the "only if" direction, the proof is by induction on the assumed derivation with (copy). All cases follow easily using the induction hypothesis, except the case for (copy). In that case, by the induction hypothesis, we have a derivation without (copy) of $\Sigma \,|\, e \vdash a$. We must show that $\Sigma \,|\, e \vdash a \cup ((a \ll \pi) \gg \pi')$ is derivable without (copy), where $(e \ll \pi) = (e \ll \pi')$ and $Dep_e(\pi) = Dep_e(\pi')$.

Let $C = Ctx_e(\pi)$ and $C' = Ctx_e(\pi')$. Observe first that

$$\Sigma \,|\, e \vdash a \quad \text{implies} \quad \Sigma, C \,|\, (e \ll \pi) \vdash (a \ll \pi).$$

This follows readily by induction on π using Lemma 3 (shifting). Then we can show that $\Sigma, C' \,|\, (e \ll \pi') \vdash (a \ll \pi)$ is derivable. This is proved by showing that $I_{\Sigma,C}(e \ll \pi) = I_{\Sigma,C'}(e \ll \pi')$, which is done readily by induction on the structure of $(e \ll \pi)$: all cases go through easily using the induction hypothesis, except for the case when $(e \ll \pi)$ is a symbol, where the fact that $Dep_e(\pi) = Dep_e(\pi')$ is used. Finally, it can then be proved by induction on π' using Lemma 2 (shifting) that

$$\Sigma, C' \,|\, (e \ll \pi') \vdash (a \ll \pi) \quad \text{implies} \quad \Sigma \,|\, e \vdash ((a \ll \pi) \gg \pi') \cup I_\Sigma(e)$$

The result now follows using Lemma 1 (monotonicity). $\square$

4.1 Implementation

The (copy) rule forms the theoretical basis for context-dependent caching. One way to implement (copy) would be to maintain a hash table H mapping a pair of the form $\langle (e \ll \pi), Dep_e(\pi) \rangle$ to the classifier computed for $(e \ll \pi)$ at a position with dependencies $Dep_e(\pi)$. This would result in the maximum reusing of computed classifiers allowed by (copy). The table H, however, could become very large, with no guarantee that cached results would be reused frequently. The flea proof checker implements a more memory-efficient approximation to this scheme; the approximation seems to work well in practice, although there are cases where it achieves less reuse than the full caching scheme. We approximate $Dep_e(\pi)$ by the position of e's deepest relevant binding. More precisely, we approximate $Dep_e(\pi)$ by the longest prefix ψ of π in e such that the binding $(e \ll \psi.0) : (e \ll \psi.1)$ is in $Dep_e(\pi)$. This position ψ is called the *context id* of the occurrence of $(e \ll \pi)$ at π. Now H is taken to be a hash table from subexpressions $(e \ll \pi)$ to pairs $\langle \tau, id \rangle$, where τ is a classifier and id is the context identifier of the occurrence of $(e \ll \pi)$ for which τ was computed. Before trying to compute the classifier for a subexpression s, H is consulted to see whether or not there is a cached classifier τ for s which has the same context identifier as this occurrence of s. If so, τ is used for this occurrence. If not, the classifier τ' for s at this occurrence is computed, and H is modified to map s to $\langle \tau', id \rangle$, where id is the context id for s at this occurrence. See Section 7 for empirical results.

4.2 Proof Compression

We briefly sketch an approach based on context-dependent caching to proof compression. An expression e is compressed as follows. With each subexpression $(e \ll \pi)$ at position π, we cache in a context-dependent way an abbreviation

$$a := \lambda\, x_1 : \tau_1. \ldots \lambda\, x_n : \tau_n.\, (e \ll \pi)$$

where $Dep_e(\pi) = \{x_1 : \tau_1,\ \ldots,\ x_n : \tau_n\}$ and a is some new symbol. We then transform the subexpression $(e \ll \pi)$ by replacing it with $(\ldots (a\, x_1) \ldots x_n)$. If the type checker permits, the abbreviation can be inserted at the position in the transformed expression corresponding to the context id of this subexpression at this position π. More work is required to pull the abbreviation all the way to the front of the transformed expression. This is because the types $\tau_1, \ldots, \tau_n$ may contain free variables besides the ones $x_1, \ldots, x_n$ accounted for in the body of the abbreviation. To pull the abbreviation upward in the expression across a λ- or Π-binding of a variable v, if the body of the abbreviation as it currently stands contains v free, then that body will have to be augmented by a λ-abstraction of v. Applications of the new constant a will then have to take in v as another argument.

5   Variable-Sensitive Safe Substitution

Profiling runs of flea checking proofs produced by CVC typically show that a large fraction of the time (around 30% on the dlx-pc example of Section 7) is spent performing safe substitutions. In this section, we describe some improvements to safe substitution. We define a substitution to be a function $\sigma : Sym \to Exp$ with a finite domain of definition $\{v_1, \ldots, v_n\}$. It may be denoted $\{v_1 := \sigma(v_1), \ldots, v_n := \sigma(v_n)\}$, possibly without the curly brackets. Let $\Xi \in \{\lambda, \Pi\}$ be arbitrary. Then the safe application $e[\sigma]$ of such a substitution σ to $e \in Exp$ is defined by induction on the structure of e. In the second case for λ-abstractions, $\hat{x}$ is a symbol not occurring in M or the range of σ.

$$\alpha[\sigma] = \alpha, \text{ for } \alpha \in \{type, kind\}$$
$$(M\ N)[\sigma] = (M[\sigma]\ N[\sigma])$$
$$(\Xi x : A.\ M)[\sigma] = \begin{cases} (\Xi x : A[\sigma].\ M[\sigma']) & \text{if } \sigma = (\sigma' \cup \{x := t\}) \\ & \text{for some } t \\ \Xi \hat{x} : A[\sigma].\ M[\sigma \cup \{x := \hat{x}\}] & \text{if } x \in FS(\sigma(v)) \text{ for some } v, \\ \Xi x : A[\sigma].\ M[\sigma] & \text{otherwise} \end{cases}$$
$$\text{for } v \in Sym, v[\sigma] = \begin{cases} \sigma(v) & \text{if } \sigma(v) \downarrow \\ v & \text{otherwise} \end{cases}$$

Safe substitution requires sets of free symbols of expressions to be computed. If the symbols bound by signature Σ are disjoint from the symbols bound by all Π- and λ-abstractions, then instead of $FS(e)$ it can easily be shown that we can use the set of free variables of e (relative to Σ), defined by

$$FV_\Sigma(e) = \{v \in FS(e) \mid \Sigma \text{ does not bind } v\}.$$

Furthermore, $FV_\Sigma(e)$ can be cached with e, so it need not be recomputed. Also, it is to be expected that many expressions will have the same set of free variables. A set S of the sets of free variables is maintained, and memory is allocated for a new set of free variables only if a set storing exactly those variables is not already in S. Finally, if $FV_\Sigma(e) \cap Def(\sigma) = \emptyset$, then an easy inductive proof shows that $e[\sigma] = e$. So there is no need to compute $e[\sigma]$ if this intersection is empty.

5.1   de Bruijn Indices

The optimizations of safe substitution are described for the version of LF that uses named variables; this is what is implemented in flea. An alternative is to use de Bruijn indices for variables (see, e.g., [13]). The optimization of returning e for $e[\sigma]$ without actually applying the substitution in the case where $FV_\Sigma(e) \cap Def(\sigma) = \emptyset$ is still relevant with de Bruijn indices. The definition of $FS(\Xi x : \sigma.\ M)$ for $\Xi \in \{\lambda, \Pi\}$ is changed to be the following:

$$FS(\Xi x : \sigma.\ M) = FS(\sigma) \cup \{v - 1 | v \in FS(M)\}$$

The optimization is performed by checking the intersection of $FS(e)$ and $Def(\sigma)$ for emptiness. It would then make sense to share sets of free variables, as proposed in the case of named variables. We might expect many fewer different sets of de Bruijn indices, and so the optimization of using a set of sets of free variables could be even more effective. Furthermore, sets of de Bruijn indices can be compactly represented as bitvectors.

5.2   Explicit Substitutions

A further improvement, which was also not implemented in flea, would be to use explicit substitutions and cache the result of computing $e[\sigma]$. This could be done by maintaining a hash table mapping expressions $e[\sigma]$ to the results of carrying out the substitutions. Using such a caching scheme could help improve performance, although it might be necessary to use a cache of fixed maximum size and implement some cache replacement policy to keep from using too much memory.

6   Classifier Computation for Left-Nested Applications

A left-nested application is an application like $(((c\,a_1)\,a_2)\,a_3)$. Suppose the classifier for a classifiable left-nested application $(\ldots(c\,a_1)\ldots a_n)$ is to be computed. Assuming that classifiers $\tau_1',\ldots,\tau_n'$ for $a_1,\ldots,a_n$ and $\Pi\,x_1:\tau_1.\ldots\Pi\,x_n:\tau_n.\tau$ (call this *optype*) for c have already been computed, the derivation in the annotation calculus (with positions written in bold for readability) would be

$$
\cdots
$$

$$
\frac{\mathbf{0^{n-1}.0}:\Pi\,x_1:\tau_1.\ldots\Pi\,x_n:\tau_n.\tau,\quad \mathbf{0^{n-1}.1}:\tau_1'}{\mathbf{0^{n-2}.0}:\Pi\,x_2:\tau_2[x_1:=a_1].\ldots\Pi\,x_n:\tau_n[x_1:=a_1].\tau[x_1:=a_1],\quad \mathbf{0^{n-2}.1}:\tau_2}
$$

$$
\vdots
$$

$$
\frac{\mathbf{0}:\Pi\,x_n:\tau_n[x_1:=a_1]\ldots[x_{n-1}:=a_{n-1}].\tau[x_1:=a_1]\ldots[x_{n-1}:=a_{n-1}],\quad \mathbf{1}:\tau_n}{\epsilon:\tau[x_1:=a_1]\ldots[x_n:=a_n]}
$$

where the following definition has been used:

Definition 10 (iterated "."). *For $n,m \in Nat$, n^m is defined inductively by* $n^0 = \epsilon$ *and* $n^{m+1} = (n^m).n$.

Several things may be observed about how substitutions are carried out in this derivation. First, $\Omega(n^2)$ time is spent doing substitutions, since in the i'th step of the derivation, a substitution is performed on $(optype \ll 2^i)[x_1 := a_1]\ldots[x_{i-1} := a_{i-1}]$. This last expression is at least as big as $(optype \ll 2^i)$, which is of size at least $n - i$. There are n steps in the derivation, so the total time is at least quadratic. Second, consider what happens in, for example, step 3 of such a derivation. If τ_3 has an occurrence of x_1 in it, then computing $\tau_3[x_1 := a_1][x_2 := a_2]$ will require computing $a_1[x_2 := a_2]$, even though a_1 cannot possibly contain x_2 free. Variable-sensitive substitution would keep the second observation from leading to inefficiency, but not the first; the following solution prevents both problems. The annotation calculus's (app) rule is replaced by the rule (app') below. For notational simplicity, we give just the instance of the rule that extends the annotation at position ϵ, instead of at an arbitrary position. For $i \in \{1, \ldots, n\}$, let a_i abbreviate $(e \ll 0^{n-i}.1)$, which is the i'th innermost argument in the nested application.

$$(\text{app'}) \ \frac{0^{n-1}.0 : \Pi\, x_1 : \tau_1. \ldots .\Pi\, x_n : \tau_n. \tau, \quad 0^{n-1}.1 : \tau_1', \ \ldots, \ 1 : \tau_n'}{\epsilon : \tau[x_1 := a_1, \ldots, x_n := a_n]} \ \phi$$

The side condition ϕ on the rule is the conjunction of the following:

- $e(0^i) = @$, for all $i \in \{0, \ldots, n-1\}$
- $\tau_1 \cong \tau_1'$
- for $i \in \{2, \ldots, n-1\}$, $\tau_i[x_1 := a_1, \ldots, x_{i-1} := a_{i-1}] \cong \tau_i'$

In the case where for some $1 \le i < j \le n$, $x_i \equiv x_j$, we stipulate that the binding of x_i occurring further to the left in the substitution is dropped from the substitution. If the types $\tau_1, \ldots, \tau_n$ are each of constant size, then this rule (whose proof of correctness we omit to save space) requires only $O(n)$ time to be spent performing substitutions. This is because the side condition applies a substitution (of size $O(i)$) n times to something of constant size.

7 Empirical Results

This section gives some empirical results on proofs produced by CVC for formulas generated from verification problems. The proofs use some extensions to LF for dealing with lists more directly. In order to compare with two other systems implementing LF type-checking, a large piece of one example was hand-translated to remove the extensions, and common subexpressions were pulled out using abbreviations (see Section 4.2); dlx-pc.pure is the result. This example could then be run through Twelf [18] and, with a minor translation, LEGO [14].[1]

Figure 3 gives the results. Entries in the table show time and peak memory usage on a 850MHz Pentium III with 256M of main memory. "all optimizations" is the flea proof checker with all the optimizations described above. "-distinct vars" is "all" except without the optimization allowed by keeping bound variables distinct from constants declared in the signature (Section 5). "-intersection check" is "all" without the check on the intersection of domain of definition of substitution and set of free variables of expression (Section 5). "-fv sets" is "all" except that memory for a set of free variables is allocated without consulting a set of sets of free variables (Section 5). "-left nest" is "all" except without the modification to allow efficient computation of the classifier of left-nested applications (Section 6). Example size is the size in ASCII text with maximal sharing

---

[1] The example in pure LF is available on the web in Twelf and LEGO formats at http://verify.stanford.edu/~stump/dlx-pc.pure/. Also, the flea proof checker ships with CVC, which is freely available at http://verify.stanford.edu/CVC/.

of common subexpressions. No results are given in the table for checking without context-dependent caching, because as mentioned earlier, checking is not feasible without this optimization. As one example of this, a small subproof of dlx-pc of size 90K takes 1.3s to check with context-dependent caching and over 1 minute to check without. This is because as a tree, the subproof is 3.5M long.

	dlx-pc.pure	dlx-pc	satyaki5	pp-invariant
all optimizations	4.4s, 31M	24.7s, 49M	21.6 s, 36M	68s, 68M
-distinct vars	8.9s, 42M	46.7s, 65M	47.6s, 39M	97s, 95M
-intersection check	4.0s, 31M	>1000s, >256M	720s, 167M	127s, 72M
-fv sets	4.1s, 32M	22.3s, 60M	19.9s, 42M	84s, 90M
-left nest	6.4s, 60M	21.3s, 72M	24.5s, 48M	53.5s, 94M
Twelf	26.8s, 84M	[examples not in pure LF format]		
LEGO	930s, 51M	[examples not in pure LF format]		
example size	2.4M	2.2M	0.9M	4.6M

Fig. 3. Empirical results comparing optimizations

Without "intersection check", checking time varies rather widely, possibly because the intersection check ameliorates some of the inefficiency of performing substitution over a DAG without caching. The results of substituting cannot be easily cached, because the substitution being applied changes; as explained in Section 5 above, using explicit substitutions would help with this problem. The asymptotically better classifier computation for left-nested applications is slower on half the benchmarks, possibly because the average depth of immediate nesting of Π-abstractions (less than 10 in these examples) is not great enough for the linear algorithm to overcome its constant overhead.

8   Conclusion

Several optimizations for LF type-checking have been presented. To formalize context-dependent caching, a path calculus for LF has been developed and proven equivalent to a standard calculus. Optimizations related to safe substitution and classifier computation for left-nested applications have also been presented. Further empirical work is needed to see which optimizations are most important for particular classes of represented proofs. The results of the paper should generalize to Pure Type Systems (PTSs), although it is not obvious how to extend caching to PTSs that are not singly sorted, since unicity of classifiers can fail (see Lemma 5.2.21 of [3]). For similar reasons, it is not clear to what extent context-dependent caching can be used in type-checking implicit LF [16] or systems of the Rho Cube [5].

Acknowledgements. This work was supported under ARPA/Air Force contract F33615-00-C-1693 and NSF contract CCR-9806889. We thank Nikolaj

Bjørner and Iliano Cervesato for valuable discussion and criticism of this paper, and the anonymous reviewers for their helpful suggestions.

References

1. S. Abramsky, D. Gabbay, and T. Maibaum, editors. *Handbook of Logic in Computer Science*. Oxford University Press, 1992.
2. A. Appel and E. Felten. Proof-carrying authentication. In *6th ACM Conference on Computer and Communication Security*, 1999.
3. H. Barendregt. *Lambda Calculi with Types*, pages 117–309. Volume 2 of Abramsky et al. [1], 1992.
4. S. Berghofer and T. Nipkow. Proof terms for simply typed higher order logic . In *Theorem Proving in Higher Order Logics, 13th International Conference*, volume 1869 of *LNCS*, 2000.
5. H. Cirstea, C. Kirchner, and L. Liquori. The Rho Cube. In F. Honsell, editor, *Foundations of Software Science and Computation Structures (FOSSACS)*, 2001.
6. H. Comon, M. Dauchet, R. Gilleron, F. Jacquemard, D. Lugiez, S. Tison, and M. Tommasi. Tree automata techniques and applications. Available at http://www.grappa.univ-lille3.fr/tata, 1997.
7. T. Coquand. *An algorithm for testing conversion in Type Theory*, pages 255–79. In Huet and Plotkin [12], 1991.
8. A. Degtyarev and A. Voronkov. *The Inverse Method*, chapter IV. In Robinson and Voronkov [19], 2001.
9. W. Farmer and J. Guttman. A Set Theory with Support for Partial Functions. *Logica Studia*, 66(1):59–78, 2000.
10. R. Harper, F. Honsell, and G. Plotkin. A Framework for Defining Logics. *Journal of the Association for Computing Machinery*, 40(1):143–184, January 1993.
11. R. Harper and F. Pfenning. On Equivalence and Canonical Forms in the LF Type Theory. Technical Report CMU-CS-00-148, Carnegie Mellon University, July 2000.
12. G. Huet and G. Plotkin, editors. *Logical Frameworks*. Cambridge University Press, 1991.
13. F. Kamareddine. Reviewing the classical and the de Bruijn notation for λ-calculus and pure type systems. *Logic and Computation*, 11(3):363–394.
14. Z. Luo and R. Pollack. LEGO Proof Development System: User's Manual. Technical Report ECS-LFCS-92-211, Edinburgh LFCS, 1992.
15. G. Necula. Proof-Carrying Code. In *24th ACM SIGPLAN-SIGACT Symposium on Principles of Programming Languages*, pages 106–119, January 1997.
16. G. Necula and P. Lee. Efficient representation and validation of proofs. In *13th Annual IEEE Symposium on Logic in Computer Science*, pages 93–104, 1998.
17. F. Pfenning. *Logical Frameworks*, chapter XXI. In Robinson and Voronkov [19], 2001.
18. F. Pfenning and Carsten Schürmann. System Description: Twelf — A Meta-Logical Framework for Deductive Systems. In *16th International Conference on Automated Deduction*, 1999.
19. A. Robinson and A. Voronkov, editors. *Handbook of Automated Reasoning*. Elsevier and MIT Press, 2001.
20. A. Stump. *Checking Validities and Proofs with CVC and flea*. PhD thesis, Stanford University, 2002. In preparation: check http://verify.stanford.edu/~stump/ for a draft.

21. A. Stump, C. Barrett, and D. Dill. CVC: a Cooperating Validity Checker. In *14th International Conference on Computer-Aided Verification*, 2002.
22. R. Virga. *Higher-Order Rewriting with Dependent Types*. PhD thesis, Carnegie Mellon University, October 1999.
23. W. Wong. Validation of HOL Proofs by Proof Checking. *Formal Methods in System Design*, 14(2):193–212, 1999.

Solving for Set Variables in Higher-Order Theorem Proving

Chad E. Brown*

Department of Mathematical Sciences, Carnegie Mellon University,
Pittsburgh, PA 15213, USA. cebrown@andrew.cmu.edu

Abstract. In higher-order logic, we must consider literals with flexible (set variable) heads. Set variables may be instantiated with logical formulas of arbitrary complexity. An alternative to guessing the logical structures of instantiations for set variables is to solve for sets satisfying constraints. Using the Knaster-Tarski Fixed Point Theorem [15], constraints whose solutions require recursive definitions can be solved as fixed points of monotone set functions. In this paper, we consider an approach to higher-order theorem proving which intertwines conventional theorem proving in the form of mating search with generating and solving set constraints.

1 Introduction

Church's simple type theory [10] allows quantification over set variables. This expressive power allows one to express mathematical statements and represent mathematical objects in a natural way. For example, one can express a statement asserting the existence of a least set containing a base element 0 and closed under a function S (intuitively the natural numbers, unless some iterate of S has a fixed point). To prove the existence of such a set, we must use a higher-order formula involving logical quantifiers and connectives. In this paper, we present a method for discovering sets (including such recursively defined sets) during the process of theorem proving.

The higher-order theorem provers Tps [3] and LEO [6] ensure completeness using primitive (and general) substitutions to enumerate terms with a certain logical structure. A *primitive substitution* (primsub) for a set variable v is a term introducing a single logical constant or quantifier, or projecting an argument to the head. A simple theorem requiring a primsub is the theorem expressing the existence of the union v of two sets X and Y. An appropriate primsub for the set variable v would introduce a disjunction (corresponding to the disjunction in the definition of union). A *general substitution* (gensub) for a set variable v is a term introducing several logical constants, quantifiers, and projections. A gensub can be thought of as a composition of several primsubs. Primitive and general substitutions in Tps are discussed in [3] on page 331.

---

* This material is based upon work supported by the National Science Foundation under grants CCR-9732312 and CCR-0097179.

A. Voronkov (Ed.): CADE-18, LNAI 2392, pp. 408–422, 2002.

In this paper, we present a conceptual alternative to this kind of enumeration and its implementation in TPS[1]. The approach presented here combines mating search [1] (also called the connection method [7]) already used by TPS with generating and solving set constraints. Just as one can use unification to delay the instantiation of first-order (and some higher-order) variables, one can use set constraints to delay the instantiation of set variables. The approach described here extends TPS in the following ways:

- Instead of instantiating set variables in a preprocessing step, the instantiations can be delayed by intertwining search with the process of instantiating set variables.
- Instead of guessing instantiations, we can solve for sets satisfying properties.
- Instead of using large terms naming sets with certain properties, we can introduce lemmas asserting the existence of such sets.

Bledsoe [8; 9] used a method of finding maximal and minimal solutions for predicates to reduce higher-order problems to first-order problems when this is possible. Bledsoe's method applies to certain classes of set constraints. The problem of instantiating set variables also occurs in the Calculus of Constructions, and Felty [11; 12] extended Bledsoe's maximal method to this setting. The Calculus of Constructions includes (but is stronger than) intuitionistic higher-order logic via a Curry-Howard correspondence [13]. The present work clarifies Bledsoe's method by placing it into the larger context of searching with set constraints and solving set constraints. The present work also extends Bledsoe's method in the following ways:

- Since we work in full higher-order logic, we need not reduce to a first-order problem.
- Using full higher-order logic we can solve for sets with inductive (and coinductive) definitions.
- Instead of combining solutions, we combine constraints and solve them simultaneously. This is necessary in the recursive case where the constraints cannot be solved independently.

Z-match [4] provides a method for instantiating set variables in the context of the first-order set theory theorem prover &. The & theorem prover searches in a sequent calculus with rules for (partially) instantiating set variables. Applying the Z-match rules is similar to solving certain kinds of set constraints. Incremental elaboration allows Z-match to establish a collection of sequents. This corresponds to solving a collection of constraints. Also, some of the extensions to Z-match proposed in [4] correspond to aspects of instantiating set variables using set constraints. In particular, in the present work, we find solutions by quantifying over "bad" variables (as defined in [4]), and we allow multiple "matching formulae" (as defined in [4]) by allowing set constraints to contain several literals.

---

[1] The TPS web site is http://gtps.math.cmu.edu/tps.html

$$\left[\begin{array}{c} \left[\boxed{1}\, A \vee \boxed{2}\, B \right] \\ \boxed{3} \sim B \\ \boxed{4} \sim A \end{array} \right]$$

Fig. 1. A Simple Propositional Jform

A very different approach is used by the SCAN algorithm [18]. This algorithm reduces some second-order formulas to equivalent first-order formulas, avoiding the need to instantiate the set variables.

This paper is organized as follows. In Section 2, the framework of higher-order theorem proving and the set variable problem are presented. In Section 3, the notion of set constraints is introduced. In Section 4, generalized solutions to set constraints are defined. In Section 5, a general search algorithm intertwining mating search with solving set constraints is described. In Section 6, we consider examples proven by TPS using this new approach.

2   Preliminaries

In this section we sketch some of the ideas underlying this work. Additional information may be found in the cited references. Church's simple type theory [10] is a simply typed λ-calculus with types generated from a base type o of propositions and a base type ι of individuals. The type of functions from β to α is written $(\alpha\beta)$, which could alternatively be written as $(\beta \to \alpha)$. The type of a term is written as a subscript to the term, so that A_α represents a term A of type α. (We will often omit writing types.) Included in the signature are logical constants (such as $\sim_{oo}$ and $\wedge_{ooo}$). We also include $\forall$ and $\exists$ quantifiers at each type α as binders. (We often use Church's dot convention. A dot stands for a left bracket whose mate is as far to the right as possible without changing the pairing of existing brackets.) Elementary type theory is Church's simple type theory without axioms of extensionality, description, choice, or infinity. Proofs in elementary type theory can be represented as *expansion proofs* as described in [16; 3; 2]. An expansion proof consists of an expansion tree and a complete mating.

Convention: We use lower case letters to stand for *expansion variables* (variables that can be instantiated) and bound variables which correspond to expansion variables. We use upper case letters to stand for constants, *selected variables* (variables that cannot be instantiated), and bound variables which correspond to selected variables.

The simple propositional example $[A \vee B] \supset [B \vee A]$ gives the flavor of mating search. In order to describe a complete mating, we must first pass to the negation normal form of the negation of the formula. This can be viewed as a matrix called the *jform* (junctive-form) of the expansion tree as shown in Figure 1.

A *connection* (see [1]) is a pair of literals sharing a vertical (conjunctive) path. In this example, two possible connections are $(\boxed{1}.\boxed{4})$ and $(\boxed{2}.\boxed{3})$. A

$$\left[\left[\begin{array}{c} \boxed{1}\,v\,Z \\ \boxed{2}\sim X\,Z \\ \boxed{3}\sim Y\,Z \end{array}\right] \vee \left[\begin{array}{c} \boxed{4}\,X\,Z \\ \boxed{5}\sim v\,Z \end{array}\right] \vee \left[\begin{array}{c} \boxed{6}\,Y\,Z \\ \boxed{7}\sim v\,Z \end{array}\right]\right]$$

Fig. 2. A Jform with a Set Variable

mating is a set of such connections. A connection *spans* any vertical path containing both of the literals in the connection. In this example, there are two vertical paths. The connection ($\boxed{1}$.$\boxed{4}$) spans the left vertical path, and the connection ($\boxed{2}$.$\boxed{3}$) spans the right vertical path. A *complete mating* is a set of connections that spans every vertical path. In this example, the two connections combined form a complete mating. A complete mating is *acceptable* if there is a substitution making connected literals complementary. An acceptable complete mating corresponds to a refutation of the negation of the theorem. This can be translated by TPS into a natural deduction proof of the theorem.

To illustrate proof search with a set variable, consider this simple theorem expressing the existence of the union of two sets $X_{o\iota}$ and $Y_{o\iota}$:

$$\exists v_{o\iota}\,\forall Z_\iota\,.\,[v\,Z \supset [[X\,Z] \vee [Y\,Z]]] \wedge [X\,Z \supset v\,Z] \wedge [Y\,Z \supset v\,Z]$$

We construct an expansion tree with this formula as its *shallow formula*. The *deep formula* of the expansion tree will be

$$[v\,Z \supset [[X\,Z] \vee [Y\,Z]]] \wedge [X\,Z \supset v\,Z] \wedge [Y\,Z \supset v\,Z]$$

where v is an expansion variable that can be instantiated and Z is a selected variable on which v cannot depend. A *set variable* is an expansion variable of type $o\alpha_n \cdots \alpha_1$ for some $n \geq 1$ and types $\alpha_1, \ldots, \alpha_n$. We will be particularly interested in set variables that occur at the heads of literals. The v in the union example above is an example of a set variable. The jform for this example is shown in Figure 2.

In this simple example, there is no acceptable complete mating of the jform. To see this, we consider the leftmost path $\boxed{1}$-$\boxed{2}$-$\boxed{3}$. We cannot connect $\boxed{2}$ and $\boxed{3}$ since they are both negative. If we connect $\boxed{1}$ with $\boxed{2}$, unification forces us to instantiate v with X. But then the path $\boxed{6}$-$\boxed{7}$ cannot be spanned. Similarly, connecting $\boxed{1}$ with $\boxed{3}$ does not lead to a solution.

We can solve this example by instantiating v with the primitive substitution $\lambda z_\iota\,.\,v^1\,z \vee v^2\,z$ where $v^1_{o\iota}$ and $v^2_{o\iota}$ are new expansion variables. The new jform is shown in Figure 3.

This jform has the complete mating $\boxed{1^1\text{-}2}$, $\boxed{1^2\text{-}3}$, $\boxed{4\text{-}5^1}$, $\boxed{6\text{-}7^2}$.

An alternative to using a primitive substitution in this example is to view the vertical paths of the jform in Figure 2 as constraints on the set variable v.

$$\left[\left[\left[\boxed{1^1}v^1\,Z \vee \boxed{1^2}v^2\,Z\right] \atop {\boxed{2}\sim X\,Z \atop \boxed{3}\sim Y\,Z}\right] \vee \left[{\boxed{4}X\,Z \atop {\boxed{5^1}\sim v^1\,Z \atop \boxed{5^2}\sim v^2\,Z}}\right] \vee \left[{\boxed{6}Y\,Z \atop {\boxed{7^1}\sim v^1\,Z \atop \boxed{7^2}\sim v^2\,Z}}\right]\right]$$

Fig. 3. Jform after a Primitive Substitution

3   Set Constraints

Consider the vertical path $\boxed{\text{1-2-3}}$ in the jform in Figure 2. We can represent this path as a sequent

$$v\,Z \to X\,Z, Y\,Z$$

with the positive literal $\boxed{1}$ on the left and the negative literals $\boxed{2}$ and $\boxed{3}$ on the right. Semantically, this means that if Z is in v, then we want Z to be in X or Z to be in Y. Since the quantifier structure of the theorem does not allow the definition of v to depend on the variable Z, we read this sequent as saying that *any* Z in v must be in X or Y. We can make this independence of v on Z explicit in the notation by including it in a prefix to the sequent as

$$\forall Z \langle v\,Z \to X\,Z, Y\,Z \rangle.$$

Semantically, the constraint is equivalent to the formula

$$\forall Z [v\,Z \supset X\,Z \vee Y\,Z].$$

A solution to the constraint is any instantiation for v for which this formula is provable. This sequent is an example of a upper bound set constraint for v. Intuitively, the constraint means that v must be contained in the union of X and Y.

Other set constraints for v can be extracted from the jform in Figure 2. Set constraints correspond to subpaths of vertical paths containing a literal with a flexible head. There is one positive literal $\boxed{1}$ with v at the head, and there are two negative literals $\boxed{5}$ and $\boxed{7}$ with v at the head. These literals and the subpaths of the vertical paths containing them give the following upper and lower bound constraints:

	Upper Bound Constraints		Lower Bound Constraints
$\boxed{1}$	$\forall Z \langle v\,Z \to \cdot \rangle$	$\boxed{5}$	$\forall Z \langle \cdot \to v\,Z \rangle$
$\boxed{\text{1-2}}$	$\forall Z \langle v\,Z \to X\,Z \rangle$	$\boxed{\text{4-5}}$	$\forall Z \langle X\,Z \to v\,Z \rangle$
$\boxed{\text{1-3}}$	$\forall Z \langle v\,Z \to Y\,Z \rangle$	$\boxed{7}$	$\forall Z \langle \cdot \to v\,Z \rangle$
$\boxed{\text{1-2-3}}$	$\forall Z \langle v\,Z \to X\,Z, Y\,Z \rangle$	$\boxed{\text{6-7}}$	$\forall Z \langle Y\,Z \to v\,Z \rangle$

(where $\cdot$ indicates an empty list of formulas). Either the upper bound constraint $\boxed{\text{1-2-3}}$ or the two lower bound constraints $\boxed{\text{4-5}}$ and $\boxed{\text{6-7}}$ will lead to a solution.

We now describe the general case. Let v be a set variable. A *set constraint* for v is of the form

$$\forall \Psi \langle \Gamma(v) \rightarrow \Delta(v) \rangle \tag{1}$$

where Ψ is a list of variables on which v cannot depend and $\Gamma(v)$ and $\Delta(v)$ are finite sets of formulas. Intuitively, this set constraint has the same meaning as the formula

$$\forall Z^1 \ldots \forall Z^n . A^1(v) \wedge \cdots \wedge A^m(v) \supset . B^1(v) \vee \cdots \vee B^k(v)$$

where Ψ is $Z^1, \cdots, Z^n$, $\Gamma(v)$ is $A^1(v), \cdots, A^m(v)$, and $\Delta(v)$ is $B^1(v), \cdots, B^k(v)$. A term V is a *solution* to the set constraint (1) if the formula

$$\forall Z^1 \ldots \forall Z^n . A^1(V) \wedge \cdots \wedge A^m(V) \supset . B^1(V) \vee \cdots \vee B^k(V)$$

is provable. A term V is a *solution* to a collection of set constraints if it is a solution to each of the set constraints in the collection.

A *lower bound* constraint for v is of the form

$$\forall \Psi \langle \Gamma(v) \rightarrow [v\,\bar{t}] \rangle$$

where $[v\,\bar{t}]$ is $[v\,t^1 \cdots t^n]$, $\Gamma(v)$ is a collection of literals, and Ψ is a list of variables that occur in the sequent but cannot occur in the instantiation for v. An *upper bound* constraint for v is of the form

$$\forall \Psi \langle [v\,\bar{t}] \rightarrow \Gamma(v) \rangle.$$

In Bledsoe's case, the Γ is not allowed to depend on the set variable v, as this corresponds to making a recursive definition. In Z-match [4], Γ must be a single formula (the "matching formula") not depending on v or any of the variables in Ψ (the "bad" variables).

In terms of jforms, an upper or lower bound constraint can be obtained from any pair $< L, \Gamma' >$ where L is a literal whose atom has the form $v\,\bar{t}$ and Γ' is a collection of literals whose formulas correspond to Γ. L and all members of Γ' must share some vertical path. A vertical path containing all the literals of the constraint is said to be *spanned* by the constraint. Recall that a connection between two literals spans any vertical path containing the two literals. The relationship is that once a constraint is solved, the solution induces a set of connections spanning (in the sense of connections) every vertical path spanned by the constraint. The constraint is an upper bound or lower bound constraint depending on whether the literal L is positive or negative.

Any collection of lower bound constraints (or upper bound constraints) can be easily simultaneously solved, as $v = \lambda \bar{z} \top$ ($v = \lambda \bar{z} \bot$) is a solution. However, these trivial solutions are usually not the ones we want. Usually, we want solutions to constraints that satisfy additional properties as well. In particular, we are interested in minimal solutions (with respect to set inclusion) to lower bound constraints and maximal solutions to upper bound constraints.

First, consider the case in which the lower bound constraint is of the form

$$\forall w^1 \cdots w^m \langle A^1, \ldots, A^l \to [v\, t^1 \cdots t^n] \rangle$$

where v does not occur in any A^i. As in Bledsoe and Feng [9], we can directly define the minimal solution as follows. We start by choosing new variables x^i of the same type as t^i for $i = 1, \ldots, n$. The minimal solution V can be defined by

$$\lambda x^1 \cdots \lambda x^n \exists w^1 \cdots \exists w^m [x^1 = t^1 \wedge \cdots \wedge x^n = t^n \wedge A^1 \wedge \cdots \wedge A^l]. \qquad (2)$$

To show this is a solution, we substitute V for v in the formula

$$\forall w^1 \cdots \forall w^m.[A^1 \wedge \cdots \wedge A^l] \supset v\, t^1 \cdots t^n$$

to obtain

$$\forall w^1 \cdots \forall w^m . [A^1 \wedge \cdots \wedge A^l] \supset$$
$$[\lambda x^1 \cdots \lambda x^n\, [\exists w^1 \cdots \exists w^m.x^1 = t^1 \wedge \cdots \wedge x^n = t^n \wedge A^1 \wedge \cdots \wedge A^l]]\, t^1 \cdots t^n.$$

Although the w^j variables may occur in the terms t^i, this formula is easily derivable from

$$\forall w^1 \cdots \forall w^m . [A^1 \wedge \cdots \wedge A^l] \supset [t^1 = t^1 \wedge \cdots \wedge t^n = t^n \wedge A^1 \wedge \cdots \wedge A^l].$$

When some members of Ψ occur as the t^j's, we can simplify this solution. Consider the lower bound constraint

$$\forall z_\iota\, w_\iota \langle R_{o\iota\iota}\, z\, w \to v\, z\, z\, [f_{\iota\iota\iota}\, z\, w] \rangle$$

for the set variable $v_{o\iota\iota\iota}$. The solution above is

$$\lambda x_\iota^1\, \lambda x_\iota^2\, \lambda x_\iota^3 . \exists z_\iota\, \exists w_\iota\, [[x^1 = z] \wedge [x^2 = z] \wedge [x^3 = [f\, z\, w]] \wedge R\, z\, w].$$

Since the variable z occurs as an argument in the main literal $v\, z\, z\, [f_{\iota\iota\iota}\, z\, w]$, we have the simpler solution

$$\lambda z_\iota\, \lambda x_\iota^2\, \lambda x_\iota^3 . \exists w_\iota\, [[x^2 = z] \wedge [x^3 = [f\, z\, w]] \wedge R\, z\, w].$$

In general, we need to solve sets of constraints including the case where v occurs on both sides of some constraints. This may require making a recursive definition of v. This is best illustrated by the simple example of a set (N) of two constraints

$$(N) \begin{cases} \qquad\qquad\cdot \to [v\, 0] \\ \forall w \langle [v\, w] \to [v\, [S\, w]] \rangle \end{cases}$$

Intuitively, the minimal solution to this is the least set containing 0 and closed under the function S. Using the expressive power of higher-order logic, a solution can be defined by

$$\lambda x \forall p . [[p\, 0] \wedge [\forall z . [p\, z] \supset [p\, [S\, z]]]] \supset p\, x. \qquad (3)$$

4   Generalized Solutions and Set Existence Lemmas

Making instantiations with large terms can be prohibitive in higher-order automated theorem proving since TPS may need to perform higher-order matching with the solution in some other part of the problem. This suggests that to prove the main theorem, it may be simpler to use lemmas asserting the existence of required sets without using explicit definitions of these sets. When using these lemmas, the sets are represented by selected variables (*very* small terms). Another motivation for using such lemmas is that we gain more control over what properties of the sets are included in the lemmas. Using lemmas in this way corresponds to allowing special instances of cut in the proof. (Once a proof is found, TPS can perform cut elimination to produce a proof without lemmas where the definitions of the sets used in the proof are explicit.)

To use these lemmas to prove the main theorem, we need a new notion of a solution to set constraints. A *generalized solution* to the constraint (1) is a formula $\phi(v)$ where both

$$\phi(v) \supset \forall Z^1 \ldots \forall Z^n . A^1(v) \wedge \cdots \wedge A^m(v) \supset . B^1(v) \vee \cdots \vee B^k(v)$$

and $\exists v \, \phi(v)$ are provable. Note that if a term V is a solution to (1), then the formula $[v = V]$ is a generalized solution. A formula $\phi(v)$ is a *generalized solution* to a collection of constraints if it is a generalized solution to each constraint in the collection. The *set existence lemma* of a generalized solution $\phi(v)$ is a theorem of the form $\forall \overline{y} \, \exists v \, \phi(v)$ where $\overline{y}$ are the free variables occurring in $\phi(v)$ other than v.

To construct generalized solutions to set constraints, we first need to consider what properties minimal and maximal solutions satisfy. Let $\mathcal{N}$ be the minimal solution (3) to the constraint set (N). The most important property $\mathcal{N}$ has is that it satisfies the constraints. That is, $\mathcal{N}$ contains 0 and is closed under S. An inversion property also follows from the definition of $\mathcal{N}$. In particular, every element of $\mathcal{N}$ is either 0 or $S\,y$ for some $y \in \mathcal{N}$. Finally, $\mathcal{N}$ satisfies an induction principle which characterizes it as minimal. In general, a minimal solution V to a collection of lower bound constraints satisfies three basic properties:

- *Constraint Satisfaction:* The set V satisfies all of the constraints.
- *Inversion Principle:* The only members of the set V are those forced to be a member by the constraints.
- *Induction Principle:* Any other set satisfying all of the constraints should contain V.

Identifying these properties as basic, we can create generalized solutions to lower bound constraints by conjoining the properties of a set v into a single formula $\phi(v)$. Strictly speaking, only the property of Constraint Satisfaction is necessary to make $\phi(v)$ a generalized solution. Other properties are explicitly included in the generalized solution to help prove the rest of the theorem. One may wonder why the Inversion Principle is included. It is, in fact, the case that the Inversion Principle follows from the Induction Principle. However, the *proof* of this fact involves a nontrivial instantiation of the set variable in the Induction Principle. So, when trying to use these properties to prove a theorem, it is useful to have the Inversion Principle explicitly given.

A maximal solution to a collection of upper bound constraints should satisfy dual properties, and generalized solutions to upper bound constraints are constructed by conjoining these dual properties. (A typical example would be the existence of a set of streams.)

For the constraint set (N), Tps finds the generalized solution $\phi(v)$:

$$v\,0 \,\wedge\, \forall w\,[v\,w \,\supset\, v.\,S\,w]$$
$$\wedge \forall x\,[v\,x \,\supset\, .\,x \,=\, 0 \,\vee\, \exists w[x \,=\, S\,w \,\wedge\, v\,w]]$$
$$\wedge \forall p.\,[p\,0 \,\wedge\, \forall W\,[p\,W \,\supset\, p.\,S\,W]] \,\supset\, \forall x.\,[v\,x] \,\supset\, [p\,x].$$

The set existence lemma in this case is $\exists v\,\phi(v)$.

4.1   Proving Set Existence Lemmas

Along with any generalized solution $\phi(v)$, Tps must also generate a proof of the corresponding set existence lemma. Fortunately, proving these lemmas does not require arbitrary theorem proving. Instead, the lemmas are generated along with their expansion proofs. The precise nature of the generated proofs depends on the nature of the constraints. If v only occurs once in each constraint (at the head of the main literal of each constraint), then the proof of the set existence lemma can be constructed in a fairly straightforward way. The definition of the set can be constructed directly as was the solution (2). In the general case, a proof of the set existence lemma may use the Knaster-Tarski Fixed Point Theorem. The Knaster-Tarski Theorem must be applied to a monotone set function. The monotone function of interest can be constructed from the Inversion Principle.

4.2   The Knaster-Tarski Fixed Point Theorem

The Knaster-Tarski Fixed Point Theorem states that monotone set functions have fixed points. There are more specific versions showing the least pre-fixed point is a fixed point and the greatest post-fixed point is a fixed point. (Other examples of using the Knaster-Tarski Theorem in higher-order logic can be found in [19; 20; 21; 5].)

Definitions: Suppose $K : \mathcal{P}(A) \to \mathcal{P}(A)$, where $\mathcal{P}(A)$ is the power set of A. A *pre-fixed point* of K is a set v such that $K(v) \subseteq v$. A *post-fixed point* of K is a set v such that $v \subseteq K(v)$. A *fixed point* of K is a set v satisfying $K(v) = v$. The function K is *monotone* if $K(v) \subseteq K(w)$ whenever $v \subseteq w \subseteq A$.

When the Induction Principle is not included in the generalized solution, it is enough to use the following version of the Knaster-Tarski fixed point theorem:

Knaster-Tarski Fixed Point Theorem: Every monotone function K has a fixed point.

When the induction principle is included, more specific versions of the theorem are needed that show the least pre-fixed point and the greatest post-fixed point of a monotone set function K are fixed points. These statements and proofs have a straightforward representation in type theory. The same proof idea works regardless of the arity of the set type of v. In the process of proving set existence lemmas where the set must be defined recursively, the appropriate version of the Knaster-Tarski Theorem is generated along with an expansion proof. The expansion proof is generated algorithmically, not by using automatic search.

When the Knaster-Tarski Theorem is used to prove a set existence lemma, the set function K must be chosen and shown to be monotone. Monotonicity can be guaranteed by restricting K to be of a certain syntactic form.[2]

5 Combining Mating Search with Set Constraints

In first-order theorem proving, one could in principle guess the instantiations for free variables and reduce the problem to propositional theorem proving. However, using unification to delay the instantiation of variables has been far more successful. In higher-order theorem proving, TPS does delay some parts of the instantiation of free variables for (higher-order) unification, but TPS has traditionally performed set instantiations (using general substitutions) in a preprocessing step before mating search begins. If mating search fails, TPS may start over with a different collection of general substitutions. Using set constraints to handle set variables allows us to intertwine mating search with solving for sets.

Definition: The *rigid part* of a jform is the result of replacing flexible literals by empty disjunctions (essentially removing every vertical path passing through flexible literals).

The basic idea of the search procedure is to perform mating search on the rigid part of the jform, generate set constraints for the leftover part of the jform, solve a collection of constraints, then return to mating search on the new jform. In the implementation, the nondeterminism is handled by a simple queue giving a breadth first search. The basic search procedure using set constraints is outlined below.

1: Given a jform J, perform ordinary mating search on J. If this succeeds, halt. If this fails, more complex set substitutions may be needed. Compute the rigid part J^r of J. If J^r is the empty jform with no vertical paths, proceed directly to generating set constraints from J in step 3. Otherwise, go to step 2 with J and its rigid part J^r.

2: Given a jform J and its rigid part J^r, perform mating search on J^r. Record any complete matings found along with substitutions given by (partially) unifying the connections. Nondeterministically pick a complete mating M for J^r and the corresponding substitution θ. Dissolve the connections in M from the jform $\theta(J)$ to obtain a jform J_1. (The dissolution operation is described in [17; 14] and is implemented as part of TPS.) Even though we have spanned every path in the rigid part J^r of J, J_1 may still have a

---

[2] Due to space restrictions, details will be given later in the author's Ph.D. thesis.

nontrivial rigid part since θ may instantiate a set variable. So, return to step 1 with the jform J_1 for J.

3: Given a jform J where every vertical path has a literal with a flexible head, generate set constraints for the set variables occurring at the heads of literals in J. Nondeterministically choose one of these set variables v and a collection $\mathcal{S}$ of upper or lower bound constraints for v. Since J depends on v, write J as $J(v)$. Go to step 4 with the set variable v, jform $J(v)$, and set of constraints $\mathcal{S}$.

4: Given a set variable v, jform $J(v)$, and set $\mathcal{S}$ of upper or lower bound constraints for v generated from $J(v)$, create a generalized solution $\phi(v)$ for the constraints by conjoining the statements that v satisfies each constraint in $\mathcal{S}$ with an appropriate Inversion Principle and possibly an Induction (or Co-Induction) Principle. Use the generalized solution to instantiate the set variable v and eliminate the constraints in $\mathcal{S}$ from $J(v)$ as described below.

(a) Create an expansion tree for the set existence lemma $\forall \overline{y} \, \exists v \, \phi(v)$ using a selected variable V in the selected node corresponding to the $\exists v$ quantifier occurrence. Construct a jform $J^\phi(V)$ from this expansion tree.

(b) Instantiate the set variable v with selected variable V in $J(v)$ to obtain a jform $J(V)$.

(c) Create a new jform $J_2 = \begin{bmatrix} J^\phi(V) \\ J(V) \end{bmatrix}$ by conjoining the jforms $J^\phi(V)$ and $J(V)$.

(d) Since each constraint in $\mathcal{S}$ corresponds to a conjunct in the generalized solution $\phi(v)$, there are acceptable connections between literals in $J^\phi(V)$ and the literals in $J(V)$ from which the constraints were generated. These connections span each vertical path in J_2 which (when restricted to a vertical path in $J(V)$) was spanned by a constraint in $\mathcal{S}$. Dissolve these connections from J_2 to obtain a jform J_3. The constraints from $\mathcal{S}$ have been eliminated from J_3 in the sense that there is no vertical path passing through all the literals of a constraint in $\mathcal{S}$.

Since the set variable v has been instantiated during the construction of J_3, return to step 1 with the jform J_3 for J.

6 Examples

We now consider examples of theorems that can be proven in the new implementation of TPS using set constraints, including examples too difficult to prove using general substitutions.

6.1 A Topology Example

Our first example is a simple topology example which could already be proven by the SET-VAR theorem prover [9]. TPS can now prove the theorem in 9 seconds[3] using set constraints; TPS proved the theorem in 2.7 minutes using general substitutions.

BLEDSOE-FENG-SV-10

$$\forall d_{o\iota} \forall g_{o(o\iota)} [g \subseteq OPEN_{o(o\iota)} \wedge d = \bigcup g \supset OPEN\, d]$$
$$\supset \forall B_{o\iota}.\forall x_{\iota}[B\, x \supset \exists D.OPEN\, D \wedge D\, x \wedge D \subseteq B] \supset OPEN\, B$$

This theorem states that if the collection $OPEN$ of "open" sets is closed under arbitrary unions, and B satisfies the neighborhood property (for each $x \in B$ there is an open $D \subseteq B$ with $x \in D$), then B is open.

The search procedure starts by building a jform and isolating its rigid part. Mating search on the rigid part allows unification to determine the set variable d should be instantiated with B. Two of the upper bound constraints generated are $\forall X \langle g\, X \rightarrow OPEN\, X \rangle$ and $\forall S, X \langle g\, S \rightarrow \sim [S\, X], [B\, X] \rangle$. From these constraints, TPS creates a generalized solution whose lemma asserts the existence of a set G solving the constraints and furthermore satisfying the Inversion Principle $\forall S\, [OPEN\, S \wedge \forall X\, [\sim [S\, X] \vee [B\, X]] \supset .G\, S]$. Since g does not occur on the right sides of these upper bound constraints, the set existence lemma follows by comprehension. The definition of the set is

$$\lambda S.OPEN\, S \wedge \forall X.\sim [S\, X] \vee [B\, X]$$

which can be extracted directly from the Inversion Principle.

Once the set existence lemma is added to the hypothesis of the theorem, TPS eliminates the constraints, leaving a jform corresponding to the goal $B \subseteq \bigcup G$. This goal follows from the Inversion Principle and the neighborhood property. Mating search on the jform succeeds within seconds.

6.2 A Transitive Closure Example

The technique of solving set variable constraints can also be used to prove theorems in which one must discover a set with a *recursive* definition. Consider **THM575** which states that every relation R has a least transitive superrelation s. This is a theorem TPS could not prove with general substitutions since the required substitution is too large. Using set constraints, this example can be proven by TPS in 20 seconds.

THM575 $\forall R_{o\iota\iota} \exists s_{o\iota\iota}. R \subseteq s \wedge \text{TRANSITIVE } s$
$$\wedge \forall T_{o\iota\iota}. R \subseteq T \wedge \text{TRANSITIVE } T \supset s \subseteq T$$

Here, TRANSITIVE is an abbreviation for the formula

$$\lambda p_{o\iota\iota} \forall X \forall Y \forall Z .p\, X\, Y \wedge p\, Y\, Z \supset p\, X\, Z.$$

THM575 follows from considering the two lower bound constraints for s

$$\begin{cases} \forall A, B \langle R\, A\, B \rightarrow s\, A\, B \rangle \\ \forall X, Y, Z \langle s\, X\, Y, s\, Y\, Z \rightarrow s\, X\, Z \rangle \end{cases}$$

---

[3] All examples in this paper were proved using a computer with a 500 MHz Pentium 3 processor.

simultaneously.[4] The set existence lemma for the generalized solution to these constraints asserts the existence of a relation S satisfying the two constraints, the Inversion Principle $S\,X\,Z \supset [\,[R\,X\,Z] \vee \exists Y\,.\,S\,X\,Y \wedge S\,Y\,Z]$, and the Induction Principle

$$\forall p_{o\iota\iota}\,.\,[\text{TRANSITIVE } p] \wedge [\text{RSUB } p] \supset \forall X\,\forall Y\,.\,S\,X\,Y \supset p\,X\,Y$$

where RSUB is the formula $\lambda p\,\forall A\,\forall B\,.\,R\,A\,B \supset p\,A\,B$.

Once this set existence lemma is included in the hypothesis of the theorem and the constraints are eliminated, the remaining problem corresponds to showing the relation S is really the least such relation. This is precisely the Induction Principle part of the generalized solution.

This is an example which is virtually solved once the right set of constraints are generated. So, we should take a closer look at how these constraints are discovered. In this example, TPS starts with the jform shown in Figure 4.

$$\left[\begin{array}{c}\boxed{1}RAB \\ \boxed{2}\sim sAB\end{array} \vee \begin{array}{c}\boxed{3}sXY \\ \boxed{4}sYZ \\ \boxed{5}\sim sXZ\end{array} \vee \left[\begin{array}{c}\left[\boxed{6}\sim Rab \vee \boxed{7}Tab\right] \\ \left[\boxed{8}\sim TX^1Y^1 \vee \boxed{9}\sim TY^1Z^1 \vee \boxed{10}TX^1Z^1\right] \\ \boxed{11}sA^1B^1 \\ \boxed{12}\sim TA^1B^1\end{array}\right]\right]$$

Fig. 4. JForm for **THM575**

Every vertical path has a flexible literal with head s (i.e., there is no vertical path through the rigid part of the jform), so TPS proceeds directly to generating and solving set constraints. In order to create lower bound constraints, TPS finds every negative literal with head s. These are $\boxed{2}$ and $\boxed{5}$. For upper bound constraints, TPS finds the positive literals with head s. These are $\boxed{3}$, $\boxed{4}$ and $\boxed{11}$. For each of these literals, TPS finds collections of conjunctively related literals and uses these to form constraints.

Let us consider the lower bound constraints since these lead to the solution. First, consider $\boxed{2}$. $\boxed{1}$ is the only conjunctively related literal. As a result, there are exactly two lower bound constraints generated by $\boxed{2}$:

$-\ \boxed{2_1}\ \forall A, B\,\langle\,\cdot\,\rightarrow\,s\,A\,B\,\rangle$
$-\ \boxed{2_2}\ \forall A, B\,\langle\,R\,A\,B\,\rightarrow\,s\,A\,B\,\rangle$

The other literal giving lower bound constraints is $\boxed{5}$. There are only two conjunctively related literals $\boxed{3}$ and $\boxed{4}$, giving four lower bound constraints:

---

[4] Note that the minimal solutions for the two constraints considered independently are R and the empty relation. These two solutions do not combine in any way to give a solution to the two constraints. So, the two constraints must be solved simultaneously.

- $\boxed{5_1}$ $\forall\,X,\,Z\,\langle\,\cdot\;\rightarrow\;s\,X\,Z\,\rangle$
- $\boxed{5_2}$ $\forall\,X,\,Y,\,Z\,\langle\,s\,X\,Y\;\rightarrow\;s\,X\,Z\,\rangle$
- $\boxed{5_3}$ $\forall\,X,\,Y,\,Z\,\langle\,s\,Y\,Z\;\rightarrow\;s\,X\,Z\,\rangle$
- $\boxed{5_4}$ $\forall\,X,\,Y,\,Z\,\langle\,s\,X\,Y,\,s\,Y\,Z\;\rightarrow\;s\,X\,Z\,\rangle$

The constraints $\boxed{2_1}$ and $\boxed{5_1}$ are special since only the universal binary relation on type ι (represented by $\lambda X\,\lambda Y\,\top$) can satisfy the constraints. The remaining constraints $\boxed{2_2}$, $\boxed{5_2}$, $\boxed{5_3}$, and $\boxed{5_4}$ can be combined to give sets of lower bound constraints which can be simultaneously solved. In this case, it is easy to see that $\boxed{2_2}$ and $\boxed{5_4}$ combine to give the two constraints which solve the problem.

6.3 Other Examples

Other examples TPS can prove automatically include **THM595** (asserting the existence of a set of v streams over a set P with destructor constants FST and RST) and **THM596** (a variation of the Knaster-Tarski Fixed Point Theorem stating that if K is order reversing then $K \circ K$ has a fixed point).

THM595 $\qquad \exists\,v_{o\beta}.\forall\,x_\beta[\,v\,x\;\supset\;P_{o\alpha}.\,FST_{\alpha\beta}\,x]\wedge$
$$\forall\,x[\,v\,x\;\supset\;v.\,RST_{\beta\beta}\,x]\wedge$$
$$\forall\,u_{o\beta}.\forall\,x[\,u\,x\;\supset\;P.\,FST\,x]\wedge\forall\,x[\,u\,x\;\supset\;u.\,RST\,x]$$
$$\supset\;u\subseteq v \qquad\qquad (197\;\mathrm{sec})$$

THM596 $\qquad \forall\,K_{o\iota(o\iota)}.\forall\,u_{o\iota}\forall\,v_{o\iota}[\,u\subseteq v\;\supset\;K\,v\subseteq K\,u]$
$$\supset\;\exists\,w_{o\iota}.K[\,K\,w]\;=\;w \qquad\qquad (21\;\mathrm{sec})$$

7 Conclusion

The procedure described in this paper only generates and solves upper and lower bound constraints. This is not a complete procedure, but a heuristic which can solve certain problems. It remains for future work to investigate what would need to be added to obtain completeness. Also, while some proposed extensions of Z-match [4] are built into the search procedure described here, the idea of "abstracting" the "matching formula" could correspond to making use of higher-order unification while solving set constraints and remains a goal of future work.

Acknowledgements. The author would like to thank his advisor Peter Andrews and colleagues Brigitte Pientka and Hongwei Xi for valuable discussions and comments.

References

1. Peter B. Andrews. On connections and higher-order logic. *Journal of Automated Reasoning*, 5:257–291, 1989.
2. Peter B. Andrews. Classical type theory. In Alan Robinson and Andrei Voronkov, editors, *Handbook of Automated Reasoning*, volume 2, chapter 15, pages 965–1007. Elsevier Science, 2001.

3. Peter B. Andrews, Matthew Bishop, Sunil Issar, Dan Nesmith, Frank Pfenning, and Hongwei Xi. TPS: A theorem proving system for classical type theory. *Journal of Automated Reasoning*, 16:321–353, 1996.

4. Sidney C. Bailin and Dave Barker-Plummer. Z-match: An inference rule for incrementally elaborating set instantiations. *Journal of Automated Reasoning*, 11:391–428, 1993. Errata: JAR 12 (1994), 411–412.

5. F. Bartels, A. Dold, F. W. v. Henke, H. Pfeifer, and H. Rueß. Formalizing Fixed-Point Theory in PVS. Ulmer Informatik-Berichte 96-10, Universität Ulm, Fakultät für Informatik, 1996.

6. Christoph Benzmüller and Michael Kohlhase. System description: LEO — a higher-order theorem prover. In Claude Kirchner and Hélène Kirchner, editors, *Proceedings of the 15th International Conference on Automated Deduction*, volume 1421 of *Lecture Notes in Artificial Intelligence*, pages 139–143, Lindau, Germany, 1998. Springer-Verlag.

7. Wolfgang Bibel. Matings in matrices. *Communications of the ACM*, 26:844–852, 1983.

8. W. W. Bledsoe. A maximal method for set variables in automatic theorem proving. In J. E. Hayes, Donald Michie, and L. I. Mikulich, editors, *Machine Intelligence 9*, pages 53–100. Ellis Harwood Ltd., Chichester, and John Wiley & Sons, 1979.

9. W. W. Bledsoe and Guohui Feng. Set-Var. *Journal of Automated Reasoning*, 11:293–314, 1993.

10. Alonzo Church. A formulation of the simple theory of types. *Journal of Symbolic Logic*, 5:56–68, 1940.

11. Amy Felty. Proof search with set variable instantiation in the calculus of constructions. In M. A. McRobbie and J. K. Slaney, editors, *Automated Deduction: CADE-13*, volume 1104 of *Lecture Notes in Artificial Intelligence*, pages 658–672. Springer, 1996.

12. Amy Felty. The calculus of constructions as a framework for proof search with set variable instantiation. *Theoretical Computer Science*, 232:187–229, 2000.

13. J. H. Geuvers. The calculus of constructions and higher order logic. In Ph. de Groote, editor, *The Curry-Howard Isomorphism*, pages 139–191. Academia, Louvain-la-Neuve (Belgium), 1995.

14. Sunil Issar. *Operational Issues in Automated Theorem Proving Using Matings*. PhD thesis, Carnegie Mellon University, 1991. 147 pp.

15. B. Knaster. Une théorème sur les fonctions d'ensembles. *Annales Soc. Polonaise Math.*, 6:133–134, 1927.

16. Dale A. Miller. A compact representation of proofs. *Studia Logica*, 46(4):347–370, 1987.

17. Neil V. Murray and Erik Rosenthal. Dissolution: Making paths vanish. *Journal of the ACM*, 40(3):504–535, July 1993.

18. H. J. Ohlbach. SCAN—elimination of predicate quantifiers. In M. A. McRobbie and J. K. Slaney, editors, *Automated Deduction: CADE-13*, volume 1104 of *Lecture Notes in Artificial Intelligence*, pages 161–165. Springer, 1996.

19. Lawrence C. Paulson. A fixedpoint approach to implementing (co)inductive definitions. In Alan Bundy, editor, *Proceedings of the 12th International Conference on Automated Deduction*, pages 148–161, Nancy, France, June 1994. Springer-Verlag LNAI 814.

20. Lawrence C. Paulson. Set theory for verification: II. Induction and recursion. *Journal of Automated Reasoning*, 15(2):167–215, 1995.

21. Lawrence C. Paulson. Mechanizing coinduction and corecursion in higher-order logic. *Journal of Logic and Computation*, 7(2):175–204, March 1997.

The Complexity of the Graded μ-Calculus

Orna Kupferman[1], Ulrike Sattler[2], and Moshe Y. Vardi[3*]

[1] School of Computer Science and Engineering, Hebrew University, Jerusalem, Israel
orna@cs.huji.ac.il
[2] Institut für Theoretische Informatik, TU Dresden, Germany
sattler@tcs.inf.tu-dresden.de
[3] Department of Computer Science, Rice University, Houston, TX 77251-1892, U.S.A.
vardi@cs.rice.edu

Abstract. In classical logic, existential and universal quantifiers express that there exists at least one individual satisfying a formula, or that all individuals satisfy a formula. In many logics, these quantifiers have been generalized to express that, for a non-negative integer n, at least n individuals or all but n individuals satisfy a formula. In modal logics, *graded modalities* generalize standard existential and universal modalities in that they express, e.g., that there exist at least n accessible worlds satisfying a certain formula. Graded modalities are useful expressive means in knowledge representation; they are present in a variety of other knowledge representation formalisms closely related to modal logic. A natural question that arises is how the generalization of the existential and universal modalities affects the satisfiability problem for the logic and its computational complexity, especially when the numbers in the graded modalities are coded in binary. In this paper we study the *graded μ-calculus*, which extends graded modal logic with fixed-point operators, or, equivalently, extends classical μ-calculus with graded modalities. We prove that the satisfiability problem for graded μ-calculus is EXPTIME-complete – not harder than the satisfiability problem for μ-calculus, even when the numbers in the graded modalities are coded in binary.

1 Introduction

In classical logic, existential and universal quantifiers express that there exists *at least one* individual satisfying a formula, or that *all* individuals satisfy a formula. In many logics, these quantifiers have been generalized to express that, for a non-negative integer n, *at least n* individuals or *all but n* individuals satisfy a formula. For example, predicate logic has been extended with so-called *counting quantifiers* $\exists^{\geq n}$ and $\exists^{\leq n}$ [GOR97,PST00]. In modal logics, *graded modalities* [Fin72,vD95,Tob01] generalize standard existential and universal modalities in that they express, e.g., that there exist at least n accessible worlds satisfying a certain formula. In description logics, *number restrictions* have always played a central role; e.g., they are present in almost all knowledge-representation systems based on description logic [PSMB+91,BFH+94], [Hor98,HM01]. Indeed, in a typical such system, one can describe cars as those vehicles having at least four wheels, and bicycles as those vehicles having exactly two wheels.

---

* Supported in Part by NSF grants CCR-9988322, IIS-9908435, IIS-9978135, and EIA-0086264, and by BSF grant 9800096.

A. Voronkov (Ed.): CADE-18, LNAI 2392, pp. 423–437, 2002.
© Springer-Verlag Berlin Heidelberg 2002

A natural question that arises is how the generalization of the existential and universal quantifiers affects the satisfiability problem for the logic and its computational complexity. The complexity of a variety of description logics with different forms of number restrictions has been investigated; see, e.g. [DLNdN91,HB91,DL94b,BS99]. It turned out that, in many cases, one can extend a logic with these forms of counting quantifiers without increasing its computational complexity. On the other hand, in some cases the extension makes the logic much more complex. A prominent example is the guarded fragment of first order logic, which becomes undecidable when extended with a very weak form of counting quantifiers (global functionality conditions on binary relations) [Grä99].

When investigating the complexity of a logic with a form of counting quantifiers, one must decide how the numbers in these quantifiers contribute to the length of a formula, i.e., to the input of a decision procedure. Assuming that these numbers are coded in unary (i.e., $|\exists^{\geq n}x.\varphi(x)| = n + |\varphi(x)|$) might seem odd, but is an assumption often made, for example in description and predicate logics. It reflects the way in which many decision procedures for these logic work: they explicitly generate n individuals for $\exists^{\geq n}$. In contrast, the assumption that the numbers are coded in binary (i.e., $|\exists^{\geq n}x.\varphi(x)| = \lceil \log n \rceil + |\varphi(x)|$) corresponds more closely to our intuition on the length of a formula, but it is not clear whether and how decision procedures can avoid the exponential blow up that a translation from the binary to the unary coding involves.

It is an interesting question whether the complexity of a logic is sensitive to the coding of numbers in counting quantifiers. It seems as if many logics are insensitive to the coding, i.e., both complexities coincide, even though one has to "work harder" for binary coding. For many logics with counting quantifiers, the complexity of the satisfiability problem is known for unary coding only, and is unknown for binary coding. For example, C^2 (two-variable first-order logic with counting) is known to be NExpTime-complete if numbers in counting quantifiers are coded in unary [PST00]. While this coincides with the complexity of first-order two-variable logic without counting [GKV97], the complexity of C^2 with binary coding is, to the best of our knowledge, unknown so far. Similarly, all the above mentioned complexity results for description and modal logics, with the exception of [Tob00,Tob01], assume unary coding of numbers.

In [Tob00,Tob01], Tobies studies *graded modal logic*, the extension of modal logic with graded modalities. He proves that the satisfiability problem for this logic is PSPACE-complete — not harder than the satisfiability problem for classical modal logic [Lad77], even when the numbers in the graded modalities are coded in binary. The binary coding requires additional technical machinery. Indeed, since the number of individuals that satisfy a graded modality is exponential in the length of the modality, one cannot simply generate the individuals, but use some form of book keeping to keep track and count the individuals required by counting quantifiers.

The *μ-calculus* [Koz83] extends modal logic with least and greatest fixpoint operators. The extension makes μ-calculus a highly expressive logic, of great theoretical and practical interest (cf. [Eme97]). In this paper, we study the graded μ-calculus, i.e., μ-calculus with graded modalities. We show that the satisfiability problem for graded μ-calculus is ExpTime-complete — not harder than the satisfiability problem for classical μ-calculus [FL79], even if the numbers are coded in binary. Our result substantiates the above hypothesis that most logics are insensitive to the coding of numbers, and is interesting for two additional reasons. Firstly, many relevant description, modal, and dynamic logics are fragments of the graded μ-calculus; see, e.g., [Sch94,DL94b,DL94a]. Hence we obtain corresponding ExpTime upper bounds for these fragments for free. Secondly, other relevant description, modal, and dynamic logics such as $\mathcal{DLR}_\mu$, $\mathcal{SHIQ}$, graded modal logics, and $\mathcal{DN}$ [CDL99,HST00,Fin72,De 95] are close "relatives" of the graded μ-calculus. Thus we could use the techniques developed here to prove ExpTime upper bounds and develop optimal reasoning algorithms for these relatives using similar techniques.

Our techniques are based on the automata-theoretic approach [VW86,SE89,Var97]: to develop a decision procedure for a logic with the tree-model property, one first develops an appropriate notion of tree automata and studies their emptiness problem. The satisfiability problem for the logic is then reduced to the automata emptiness problem. We show here that the appropriate notion of automata is that of *graded alternating tree automata*, which generalize standard alternating tree automata by having the ability to count the number of successors that satisfy a certain condition[1] We show that graded μ-calculus has a tree model property and that, given a formula φ, we can construct a graded alternating automaton $\mathcal{A}_\varphi$ that accepts exactly the (tree abstractions of) models of φ. The size of $\mathcal{A}_\varphi$ is linear in $|\varphi|$, even if numbers in graded modalities are coded in binary. We then present an ExpTime decision procedure for the emptiness of graded alternating automaton by an appropriate translation into *graded non-deterministic automata* (with an exponential blow-up in the size of the automaton), and show that emptiness of graded non-deterministic automata can be decided in polynomial time. Like other automata-based decision procedures, the techniques developed here can be re-used: once a suitable class of automata for a certain class of logics is designed (together with the corresponding emptiness test), these automata can be easily re-used for similar logics. In particular, our technique can be easily extended to handle in ExpTime μ-calculus with *fractional modalities*, where we can express, e.g., that at least half of the accessible worlds satisfy some predicate, as well as all modalities that involve polynomially-checkable conditions on the number of accessible words that satisfy a formula.

2   The Graded μ-Calculus

The *graded μ-calculus* is a propositional modal logic augmented with least and greatest fixpoint operators [Koz83]. Specifically, we consider a μ-calculus where formulas are constructed from atomic propositions with Boolean connectives, the *graded modalities* $\langle n, \alpha \rangle$ ("exist at least n α-successors") and $[n, \alpha]$ ("all but at most n α-successors"), as well as least (μ) and greatest (ν) fixpoint operators. We assume that μ-calculus formulas are written in positive normal form (negation is applied only to atomic propositions). Formally, given a set AP of atomic propositions, a set Var of propositional variables,

---

[1] Some variants of alternating automata that support counting are studied in the literature (c.f., [Wal96]). Unlike these variants, where counting is done in the transition function of the automaton, our graded automata count by maintaining binary counters that should satisfy counting constraints. This is essential for the efficient treatment of constraints coded in binary.

and a set Prog of (atomic) programs, the set of formulas of the graded μ-calculus is the smallest set such that the following holds.

- true, false, p and $\neg p$, for $p \in$ AP, are formulas,
- $x \in$ Var is a formula, and
- if φ_1 and φ_2 are formulas, α is a program, n is a non-negative integer, and x is a propositional variable, then $\varphi_1 \wedge \varphi_2$, $\varphi_1 \vee \varphi_2$, $\langle n, \alpha \rangle \varphi_1$, $[n, \alpha] \varphi_1$, $\mu y.\varphi_1(y)$, and $\nu y.\varphi_1(y)$ are formulas.

A propositional variable x occurs *free* in a formula if it is not in the scope of a fixpoint operator. Note that x may occur both bound and free in a formula. A *sentence* is formula that contains no free variables. We use λ to denote a fixpoint operator μ or ν. For a λ-formula $\lambda x.\varphi(x)$, we write $\varphi(\lambda x.\varphi(x))$ to denote the formula that is obtained by replacing each free occurrence of x in φ with $\lambda x.\varphi(x)$. We refer to formulas of the form $\langle n, \alpha \rangle \varphi_1$ and $[n, \alpha] \varphi_1$ as *atleast* and *allbut* formulas, respectively.

We say that a formula φ *counts up to* b if the maximal integer occurring in graded modalities in φ is $b - 1$. We refer to b as the *counting bound* of φ. We assume that the integers in graded modalities are given in binary. The *length* of φ, denoted $|\varphi|$, reflects this fact. Formally, $|\varphi|$ is defined by induction on the structure of φ in a standard way, with $|\langle n, \alpha \rangle \varphi_1| = \lceil \log n \rceil + 1 + |\varphi_1|$, and similarly for $|[n, \alpha] \varphi_1|$.

We define the semantics of graded μ-calculus with respect to *Kripke structures*. The semantics is similar to the one for standard μ-calculus (see [Koz83]), with the exception of the graded modalities: a state w of a Kripke structure K satisfies the atleast formula $\langle n, \alpha \rangle \varphi$ iff at least $n + 1$ successors of w in α satisfy φ. Dually, w satisfies the allbut formula $[n, \alpha] \varphi$ iff all but at most n successors of w in α satisfy φ. Note that $\neg \langle n, \alpha \rangle \varphi$ is equivalent to $[n, \alpha] \neg \varphi$. Indeed, $\neg \langle n, \alpha \rangle \varphi$ means that less than $n + 1$ successors of w satisfy φ, that is, at most n successors do not satisfy $\neg \varphi$. The least and greatest fixpoint operators are interpreted as in μ-calculus; thus, for example, $\mu y.p \vee \langle 1, \alpha \rangle y$ is satisfied in a point w if either w satisfies p or w has two different α-successors each of which either satisfies p or has two different α-successors etc., or equivalently, w is a root of a binary tree embedded in the transition relation of α in which each path eventually reaches a point that satisfies p. Note that the interpretation of a sentence is independent of valuations. A sentence ψ is called *satisfiable* iff there is a Kripke structure K and a state u of K such that u satisfies ψ.

The modalities $\langle n, \alpha \rangle \varphi$ and $[n, \alpha] \varphi$ are natural generalizations of the standard existential and universal next modalities. In particular, $\langle \alpha \rangle \varphi$ and $[\alpha] \varphi$ of modal logic are equivalent to $\langle 0, \alpha \rangle \varphi$ and $[0, \alpha] \varphi$, respectively, and the *number restrictions* $(\geq n \, r \, \varphi)$ and $(\leq n \, r \, \varphi)$ for a role r in description logics [HB91] are equivalent to $\langle n - 1, r \rangle \varphi$ and $[n, r] \neg \varphi$, respectively (note that $(\geq 0 \, r \, \varphi)$ is equivalent to true).

For technical convenience, we restrict our attention to formulas and Kripke structures in which only one program occurs. By adding atomic propositions associated with programs, one can reduce formulas and structures with several programs to our setting. Note that we can also add new atomic propositions that would take care of the counting done in graded modalities. Formally, if φ counts up to b, we add propositions $c_1, \ldots, c_b$, conjoin φ with a requirement that exactly one c_i holds in each point, that successors that are labeled by the same c_i agree on their label with respect to all the subformulas of φ, and replace an atleast modality $\langle n, \psi \rangle$ by a $\bigvee_{\{j_1, \ldots, j_{n+1}\} \subseteq \{1, \ldots, b\}} \bigwedge_{1 \leq i \leq n+1} \Diamond(\psi \wedge c_{j_i})$, and dually for allbut modalities. The μ-calculus formula we get is satisfiable iff φ is satisfiable, yet the length of each disjunct that replaces a graded modality is exponential in b. Since the bounds in the graded modalities are written in binary, the length of the formula we get is doubly exponential in the length of φ.

A *tree* is a set $T \subseteq \mathbb{N}^*$ such that if $x \cdot c \in T$ where $x \in \mathbb{N}^*$ and $c \in \mathbb{N}$, then also $x \in T$. The elements of T are called *nodes*, and the empty word ε is the *root* of T. For every $x \in T$, the nodes $x \cdot c$ where $c \in \mathbb{N}$ are the *children* of x. The number of children of x is called the *degree* of x, and is denoted $deg(x)$. The *degree* of a tree is the maximum degree of a node in the tree. A node is a *leaf* if it has no children. A *path* π of a tree T is a set $\pi \subseteq T$ such that $\varepsilon \in \pi$ and for every $x \in \pi$, either x is a leaf or there exists a unique $c \in \mathbb{N}$ such that $x \cdot c \in \pi$. Given an alphabet Σ, a Σ-*labeled tree* is a pair $\langle T, V \rangle$ where T is a tree and $V : T \to \Sigma$ maps each node of T to a letter in Σ.

In the full version, we show that the graded μ-calculus has the tree model property. Thus, if a formula φ is satisfiable, it is also satisfiable in a tree. Moreover, the number of atleast formulas in φ and its counting bound induce a sufficient degree for the tree. Formally, we have the following.

Theorem 1. *Consider a sentence ψ such that ψ has l atleast subsentences, each counting to at most b. If ψ is satisfiable, then ψ is satisfied in a tree whose degree is at most $l \cdot (b+1)$.*

3   Graded Automata

Automata over infinite trees (tree automata) run over Σ-labeled trees that have no leaves [Tho90]. *Alternating automata* generalize nondeterministic tree automata and were first introduced in [MS87]. Intuitively, while a nondeterministic automaton that visits a node x of the input tree send one copy of itself to each of the successors of x, an alternating automata can several copies of itself to the same successor.

3.1   Graded Alternating Parity Tree Automata

For a given set Y, let $\mathcal{B}^+(Y)$ be the set of positive Boolean formulas over Y (i.e., Boolean formulas built from elements in Y using $\wedge$ and $\vee$), where we also allow the formulas **true** and **false** and, as usual, $\wedge$ has precedence over $\vee$. For a set $X \subseteq Y$ and a formula $\theta \in \mathcal{B}^+(Y)$, we say that X *satisfies* θ iff assigning **true** to elements in X and assigning **false** to elements in $Y \setminus X$ makes θ true.

For $b \geq 0$, let $\langle [b] \rangle = \{\langle 0 \rangle, \langle 1 \rangle, \ldots, \langle b \rangle\}$ and $[[b]] = \{[0], [1], \ldots, [b]\}$, and let $D_b = \{\varepsilon\} \cup \langle [b] \rangle \cup [[b]]$. A *graded alternating tree automaton* is an automaton in which the transition function δ maps a state q and a letter σ to a formula in $\mathcal{B}^+(D_b \times Q)$. Intuitively, an atom (ε, q) means that the automaton sends a copy of itself in state q to the current node, an atom $(\langle n \rangle, q)$ means that the automaton sends copies in states q to $n + 1$ different children of the current node, and $([n], q)$ means that the automaton sends copies in state q to all but n children of the current node. When, for instance, the automaton is in state q, reads a node x and $\delta(q, V(x)) = (\langle 3 \rangle, q_1) \wedge (\varepsilon, q_2) \vee ([2], q_3)$, it can either send four copies in state q_1 to four different children of x and send a copy in state q_2 to x, or send copies in state q_3 to $deg(x) - 2$ children of x. So, while nondeterministic tree automata send exactly one copy to each child, graded automata can send several copies to the same child, they have ε transitions, and extend *symmetric automata* [JW95,Wil99] by specifying the number of children that need to satisfy an existential requirement or are exempt from satisfying a universal one.

Formally, a graded automaton is a tuple $\mathcal{A} = \langle \Sigma, b, Q, \delta, q_0, \alpha \rangle$, where Σ, Q, q_0, and α are as in alternating automata, b is a *counting bound*, and $\delta : Q \times \Sigma \rightarrow \mathcal{B}^+(D_b \times Q)$ is a transition function. A *run* of $\mathcal{A}$ on an input Σ-labeled tree $\langle T, V \rangle$ is a tree $\langle T_r, r \rangle$ (to be formally defined shortly) in which each node corresponds to a node of T and is labeled by an element of $\mathbb{N}^* \times Q$. A node in T_r, labeled by (x, q), describes a copy of the automaton that reads the node x of T and visits the state q. Note that many nodes of T_r can correspond to the same node of T; in contrast, in a run of a nondeterministic automaton on $\langle T, V \rangle$ there is a one-to-one correspondence between the nodes of the run and the nodes of the tree. The labels of a node and its children have to satisfy the transition function. Formally, the run $\langle T_r, r \rangle$ is an $(\mathbb{N}^* \times Q)$-labeled $\mathbb{N}$-tree such that $\varepsilon \in T_r$ and $r(\varepsilon) = (\varepsilon, q_0)$, and for all $y \in T_r$ with $r(y) = (x, q)$ and $\delta(q, V(x)) = \theta$, there is a (possibly empty) set $S \subseteq D_b \times Q$, such that S satisfies θ, and for all $(c, s) \in S$, the following holds:

- If $c = \varepsilon$, then there is $j \in \mathbb{N}$ such that $y \cdot j \in T_r$ and $r(y \cdot j) = (x, s)$.
- If $c = \langle n \rangle$, then there are distinct $i_1, \ldots, i_{n+1} \in \mathbb{N}$ such that for all $1 \leq j \leq n+1$, there is $j' \in \mathbb{N}$ such that $y \cdot j' \in T_r$ and $r(y \cdot j') = (x \cdot i_j, s)$.
- If $c = [n]$, then there are distinct $i_1, \ldots, i_{deg(x)-n} \in \mathbb{N}$ such that for all $1 \leq j \leq deg(x) - n$, there is $j' \in \mathbb{N}$ such that $y \cdot j' \in T_r$ and $r(y \cdot j') = (x \cdot i_j, s)$.

Note that if $\theta = \textbf{true}$, then y need not have children. This is the reason why T_r may have leaves. Also, since there exists no set S as required for $\theta = \textbf{false}$, we cannot have a run that takes a transition with $\theta = \textbf{false}$.

A run $\langle T_r, r \rangle$ is *accepting* if all its infinite paths satisfy the acceptance condition. We consider here the *parity acceptance condition*, where $\alpha = \{F_1, F_2, \ldots, F_k\}$ is such that $F_1 \subseteq F_2 \subseteq \cdots \subseteq F_k = Q$. The number k of sets in α is called the *index* of the automaton. Given a run $\langle T_r, r \rangle$ and an infinite path $\pi \subseteq T_r$, let $inf(\pi) \subseteq Q$ be such that $q \in inf(\pi)$ if and only if there are infinitely many $y \in \pi$ for which $r(y) \in \mathbb{N}^* \times \{q\}$. That is, $inf(\pi)$ contains exactly all the states that appear infinitely often in π. A path π satisfies a parity acceptance condition $\alpha = \{F_1, F_2, \ldots, F_k\}$ iff the minimal index i for which $inf(\pi) \cap F_i \neq \emptyset$ is even. An automaton accepts a tree if and only if there exists a run that accepts it. We denote by $\mathcal{L}(\mathcal{A})$ the set of all Σ-labeled trees that $\mathcal{A}$ accepts.

Theorem 2. *Given a sentence ψ of the graded μ-calculus[2] that counts up to b, we can construct a graded alternating parity automaton $\mathcal{A}_\psi$ such that*

---

[2] A graded μ-calculus sentence is *guarded* if for all $y \in \textsf{Var}$, all the occurrences of y that are in a scope of a fixpoint modality λ are also in a scope of a graded modality that is itself in the scope of λ. Thus, a μ-calculus sentence is guarded if for all $y \in \textsf{Var}$, all the occurrences of y are in the scope of a graded modality. For example, the formula $\mu y.(p \vee \langle 0 \rangle y)$ is guarded and the formula $\langle 0 \rangle \mu y.(p \vee y)$ is not guarded. Given a graded μ-calculus formula, we can construct, in linear time, an equivalent guarded formula (see [BB87,KVW00] for a proof for μ-calculus, which is easily extendible to graded μ-calculus). Accordingly, we assume that all formulas are guarded. This is essential for the correctness of the construction in the proof.

1. $\mathcal{A}_\psi$ accepts exactly all trees that satisfy ψ.
2. $\mathcal{A}_\psi$ has $|\psi|$ states, index $|\psi|$, and counting bound b.

Proof. The construction generalizes the one for μ-calculus sentences and parity automata [KVW00]. Given ψ, we define $\mathcal{A}_\psi = \langle 2^{AP}, b, \mathrm{cl}(\psi), \delta, \psi, \alpha \rangle$, where for all $\sigma \in 2^{AP}$, we define:

$$\delta(p, \sigma) = \textbf{true} \text{ if } p \in \sigma, \qquad\qquad \delta(p, \sigma) = \textbf{false} \text{ if } p \notin \sigma,$$
$$\delta(\neg p, \sigma) = \textbf{true} \text{ if } p \notin \sigma, \qquad\qquad \delta(\neg p, \sigma) = \textbf{false} \text{ if } p \in \sigma,$$
$$\delta(\varphi_1 \wedge \varphi_2, \sigma) = (\varepsilon, \varphi_1) \wedge (\varepsilon, \varphi_2), \qquad \delta(\varphi_1 \vee \varphi_2, \sigma) = (\varepsilon, \varphi_1) \vee (\varepsilon, \varphi_2),$$
$$\delta(\langle n \rangle \varphi, \sigma) = (\langle n \rangle, \varphi), \qquad\qquad \delta([n]\varphi, \sigma) = ([n], \varphi),$$
$$\delta(\mu y.f(y), \sigma) = \delta(f(\mu y.f(y)), \sigma), \qquad \delta(\nu y.f(y), \sigma) = \delta(f(\nu y.f(y)), \sigma)).$$

The acceptance condition α is defined as in the automata for standard μ-calculus, according to the *alternation level* of the formulas in $\mathrm{cl}(\psi)$. For details, see [BC96, KVW00].

3.2 Graded Nondeterministic Parity Tree Automata

For an integer b, a *b-bound* is pair in $B_b = \{(>, 0), (\leq, 0), (>, 1), (\leq, 1), \ldots, (>, b), (\leq, b)\}$. For a set X, a subset $P \subseteq X$, an $m > 0$, and a tuple $t = \langle x_1, \ldots, x_m \rangle \in X^m$, the *weight* of P in t, denoted $weight(P, t)$, is the number of elements in t that are members of P. That is, $weight(P, t) = |\{i : x_i \in P\}|$. For example, $weight(\{1, 2, 3\}, \langle 1, 2, 2, 4, 2 \rangle) = 4$. We say that t satisfies a b-bound $(>, n)$ with respect to P if $weight(P, t) > n$, and t satisfies a b-bound $(\leq, n)$ with respect to P if $weight(P, t) \leq n$.

For a set Y, we use $\mathcal{B}(Y)$ to denote the set of all Boolean formulas over atoms in Y. Each formula $\theta \in \mathcal{B}(Y)$ induces a set $sat(\theta) \subseteq 2^Y$ such that $x \in sat(\theta)$ iff x satisfies θ. For an integer $b \geq 0$, a *b-counting constraint* for 2^Y is a relation $C \subseteq \mathcal{B}(Y) \times B_b$. For example, if $Y = \{y_1, y_2, y_3\}$, then we can have $C = \{\langle y_1 \vee \neg y_2, (\leq, 3) \rangle, \langle y_3, (\leq, 2) \rangle, \langle y_1 \wedge y_3, (>, 1) \rangle\}$. A tuple $t = \langle x_1, \ldots, x_m \rangle \in (2^Y)^m$ satisfies the b-counting constraint C if for all $\langle \theta, \xi \rangle \in C$, the tuple t satisfies ξ with respect to $sat(\theta)$. Thus, when $\theta \in \mathcal{B}(Y)$ is paired with $(>, n)$, at least $n + 1$ elements of t should satisfy θ, and when θ is paired with $(\leq, n)$, at most n elements in the tuple satisfy θ.

For a constraint C, the *width* of C is the number of $\theta \in \mathcal{B}(Y)$ for which there is a b-bound ξ such that $\langle \theta, \xi \rangle \in C$. Note that θ may be paired with several b-bounds. Still, it is easy to replace C by an equivalent constraint C' (that is, a tuple t satisfies C iff t satisfies C') in which θ is paired with at most one constraint of the form $(>, n)$ and at most one constraint of the form $(\leq, n)$. We assume that we work with such *minimized* constraints. For two b-counting constraints C_1 and C_2, we denote by $C_1 \oplus C_2$ the minimization of $C_1 \cup C_2$. That is, if $\langle \theta, (>, n_1) \rangle \in C_1$ and $\langle \theta, (>, n_2) \rangle \in C_2$, then $C_1 \oplus C_2$ contains only $\langle \theta, (>, \max\{n_1, n_2\}) \rangle$, and dually for constraints of the form $(\leq, n)$.[3]

We say that a constraint C is *short* if all the formulas θ that appear in C are of size linear in $|Y|$ and the width of C is at most $|Y|$. We use $\mathcal{C}(Y, b)$ to denote the set of all

---

[3] To keep the $\oplus$ operator efficient, we do not care for redundancies and contradictions that originate from the relation between the formulas in the constraints. For example, a minimized C may contain both $\langle \theta_1, (>, n) \rangle$ and $\langle \theta_2, (>, n) \rangle$ for θ_1 that implies θ_2, and it may contain both $\langle \theta, (>, n) \rangle$ and $\langle \theta, (\leq, n) \rangle$

short b-counting constraints for 2^Y. We assume that the integers in the constraints are coded in binary. Thus, the size of $C \in \mathcal{C}(Y, b)$ is $O(|Y|^2 \lceil \log b \rceil)$.

Lemma 1. *Given a constraint $C \in \mathcal{C}(Y, b)$ and a set $S \subseteq 2^Y$, deciding whether there is a tuple $t \in (2^Y)^*$ such that t satisfies C can be done in space $(1 + \lceil \log(b + 1) \rceil)|Y|$ or time $(2b + 2)^{|Y|}$.*

Proof. Since the width of C is at most $|Y|$, an algorithm that guesses t (element by element) and updates a counter for each θ that participate in C requires space for storing the guess for the current element in 2^Y, and for storing the values of the counters. The algorithm terminates with a positive decision when the values of the counters are such that all the b-bounds in C are satisfied. There are at most $|Y|$ counters, each may count up to at most $b + 1$. Thus, the space required is $|Y| + |Y|\lceil \log(b + 1) \rceil$. In addition, since the length of each formula θ that participate in C is linear in $|Y|$, its valuation with respect to each element of the tuple can be done in space $\log |Y|$ [Lyn77].

A *graded nondeterministic parity tree automaton* (GNPT, for short) is a tuple $\mathcal{A} = \langle \Sigma, b, Q, \delta, q_0, \alpha \rangle$, where Σ and b, q_0, and α are as in GAPT, and the other components are as follows.

- The state space Q is encoded by a finite set Y of variables; that is, $Q \subseteq 2^Y$.
- The function $\delta : Q \times \Sigma \to \mathcal{C}(Y, b)$ maps a state and a letter to a b-counting constraint for 2^Y.

Note that, like GAPT, a GNPT is symmetric, in the sense it cannot distinguish between the different children of a node.

A *run* of the graded nondeterministic automaton $\mathcal{A}$ on a Σ-labeled tree $\langle T, V \rangle$ is a Q-labeled tree $\langle T, r \rangle$ such that $r(\varepsilon) = q_0$ and for every $x \in T$, the tuple $\langle r(x \cdot 1), r(x \cdot 2), \ldots, r(x \cdot deg(x)) \rangle$ satisfies $\delta(r(x), V(x))$. The run $\langle T, r \rangle$ is accepting if all its paths satisfy the parity acceptance condition.

We consider two special cases of GNPT.

- In *forall* automata, for each $q \in Q$ and $\sigma \in \Sigma$ there is $s \in Q$ such that $\delta(q, \sigma) = \{\langle (\neg \theta_s), (\leq, 0) \rangle\}$, where $\theta_s \in \mathcal{B}(Y)$ is such that $sat(\theta_s) = \{s\}$. Thus, a forall automaton is a notational invariant of a deterministic tree automaton, where the transition function maps q and σ to $\langle s, \ldots, s \rangle$.
- In *safety* automata, there is no acceptance condition, and all runs are accepting. Note that this does not mean that safety automata accept all trees, as it may be that on some trees the automaton does not have a run.

Lemma 2. *Given a forall GNPT $\mathcal{A}_1$ with n_1 states and index k, and a safety GNPT $\mathcal{A}_2$ with n_2 states and counting bound b, we can define a GNPT $\mathcal{A}$ such that $\mathcal{L}(\mathcal{A}) = \mathcal{L}(\mathcal{A}_1) \cap \mathcal{L}(\mathcal{A}_2)$. Moreover, $\mathcal{A}$ has $n_1 n_2$ states, index k, and counting bound b.*

4   The Nonemptiness Problem for GAPT

In this section we solve the nonemptiness problem for GAPT and conclude that the satisfiability problem for graded μ-calculus can be solved in EXPTIME. We first translate GAPT to GNPT, and then solve the nonemptiness problem for GNPT. In the case of standard μ-calculus, the solution to the satisfiability problem follows the same plan: we translate the formula to an alternating automaton $\mathcal{A}$, and then check the nonemptiness of $\mathcal{A}$ by first translating it to an equivalent nondeterministic automaton [MS95]. In our case, the automaton $\mathcal{A}$ is graded, so its translation into a nondeterministic automaton and the nonemptiness problem for the latter are more involved.

4.1   From GAPT to GNPT

Consider a GAPT $\mathcal{A} = \langle \Sigma, b, Q, \delta, q_0, \alpha \rangle$. Let $D_b = (\{\varepsilon\} \cup \langle [b] \rangle \cup [[b]])$. Recall that the transition function $\delta : Q \times \Sigma \to \mathcal{B}^+(D_b \times Q)$ maps a state and a letter to a formula in $\mathcal{B}^+(D_b \times Q)$. A *restriction* of δ is a partial function $\eta : Q \to 2^{D_b \times Q}$. For a letter $\sigma \in \Sigma$, we say that a restriction η is *relevant* to σ if for all $q \in Q$ for which $\delta(q, \sigma)$ is satisfiable (i.e., $\delta(q, \sigma)$ is not **false**), the set $\eta(q)$ satisfies $\delta(q, \sigma)$. If $\delta(q, \sigma)$ is not satisfiable, then $\eta(q)$ is undefined. Intuitively, by choosing the atoms that are going to be satisfied, η removes the nondeterminism in δ. Let F be the set of restrictions of δ. A *running strategy* of $\mathcal{A}$ for a Σ-labeled tree $\langle T, V \rangle$ is an F-labeled tree $\langle T, f \rangle$. We say that $\langle T, f \rangle$ is relevant with respect to $\langle T, V \rangle$ if for all $x \in T$, the restriction $f(x)$ is relevant to $V(x)$.

Consider a restriction η relevant to σ. For $q \in Q$, we say that a finite sequence $s = s_0, s_1, \ldots, s_{l+1}$ is a *step of η with q and σ* if $s_0 = q$, for all $0 \leq i < l$, we have $(\varepsilon, s_{i+1}) \in \eta(s_i)$, and $(\lambda, s_{l+1}) \in \eta(s_l)$, for $\lambda \in \langle b \rangle \cup [b]$. Thus, s is a step of η with q and σ if by following the restriction η at a node x labeled σ, a run that visits q can continue by first taking l subsequent ε-transitions and visiting $s_0, \ldots, s_l$, and then moving to a child of x in state s_{l+1}. We refer to (λ, s_{l+1}) as the last atom taken in the step. Note that l may be 0. We define the *value* of s, denoted $val(s)$, as the minimal i such that there is $0 < j \leq l + 1$ with $s_j \in F_i$. Note that when s contains only two states, its value is induced by s_1.

We say that a finite sequence $s = s_0, s_1, \ldots, s_l$ is an *ε-lasso of η with q and σ* if $s_0 = q$, for all $0 \leq i \leq l - 1$, we have $(\varepsilon, s_{i+1}) \in \eta(s_i)$, and there is $0 \leq c \leq l$ such that $(\varepsilon, s_c) \in \eta(s_l)$ Thus, s is an ε-lasso of η with q and σ if by following the restriction η at a node x labeled σ, there is $0 \leq c \leq l$ such that a run that visits q can eventually loop forever in $s_c, \ldots, s_l$ by taking subsequent ε-transitions. The value of s with a loop starting at c, denoted $val(s, c)$, is the minimal i such that there is $c \leq j \leq l$ with $s_j \in F_i$. We say that s is rejecting if there is $0 \leq c \leq l$ such that $val(s)$ is odd.

A *local promise* for the automaton $\mathcal{A}$ is a function $\rho : Q \to 2^Q$. We extend ρ to sets of states, thus for $P \subseteq Q$, we have $\rho(P) = \bigcup_{q \in P} \rho(q)$. Let G be the set of all local promises. A *promise* of $\mathcal{A}$ for a Σ-labeled tree $\langle T, V \rangle$ is a G-labeled tree $\langle T, g \rangle$. Intuitively, in a run that proceeds according to $\langle T, g \rangle$, if a node $y \cdot j$ has $s \in g(y \cdot j)(q)$ and the run visits its parent y in state q and proceeds by choosing an atom $\langle n \rangle s$ or $[n]s$, for some $0 \leq n \leq b$, then $y \cdot j$ is among the children of y that inherit s.

Consider a Σ-labeled tree $\langle T, V \rangle$, a running strategy $\langle T, f \rangle$ relevant to $\langle T, V \rangle$, and a promise $\langle T, g \rangle$. A $(T \times Q)$-labeled tree $\langle T_r, r \rangle$ is *consistent* with f and g if $\langle T_r, r \rangle$ suggests a possible run of $\mathcal{A}$ on $\langle T, V \rangle$ such that whenever the run $\langle T_r, r \rangle$ is in state q as it reads a node $x \in T$, the restriction $f(x)(q)$ is defined, the run proceeds according to $f(x)(q)$, and it delivers requirements to each child $x \cdot j$ according to $g(x \cdot j)(q)$. Note that since the counting constraints in $f(x)(q)$ may not be satisfied, $\langle T_r, r \rangle$ may not be a legal run. Formally, $\langle T_r, r \rangle$ is consistent with f and g iff the following hold.

1. $\varepsilon \in T_r$ and $r(\varepsilon) = (\varepsilon, q_0)$.
2. Consider a node $y \in T_r$ with $r(y) = (x, q)$. Then, $f(x)(q)$ is defined, and for all $(c, s) \in f(x)(q)$, the following hold:
   - If $c = \varepsilon$, then there is $j \in \mathbb{N}$ such that $y \cdot j \in T_r$ and $r(y \cdot j) = (x, s)$.
   - If $c = \langle n \rangle$ or $c = [n]$, then for each $j \in \mathbb{N}$ with $s \in g(x \cdot j)(q)$, there is $j' \in \mathbb{N}$ such that $y \cdot j' \in T_r$ and $r(y \cdot j') = (x \cdot j, s)$.

For a node $x \in T$ and a state $q \in Q$, we say that x is *obliged to q* by f, g, and V if x is visited by q in some labeled tree $\langle T_r, r \rangle$ consistent with f and g.

Let $\Sigma' \subseteq \Sigma \times F \times G$ be such that for all $\langle \sigma, \eta, \rho \rangle \in \Sigma'$, we have that η is relevant to σ. For an infinite sequence $\langle \sigma_0, \eta_0, \rho_0 \rangle, \langle \sigma_1, \eta_1, \rho_1 \rangle, \ldots$ of triples in Σ' and a sequence (either finite or infinite) $q_0, q_1, \ldots$ of states, we say that $q_0, q_1, \ldots$ is a *trace* induced by $\langle \sigma_0, \eta_0, \rho_0 \rangle, \langle \sigma_1, \eta_1, \rho_1 \rangle, \ldots$ if q_0 is the initial state of $\mathcal{A}$ and there is a function $pos : \mathbb{N} \to \mathbb{N}$ such that $pos(0) = 0$ and for every $i \geq 0$, one of the following holds.

1. $\eta_{pos(i)}(q_i)$ is empty, in which case q_i is the last state in the trace,
2. there is $(\varepsilon, q_{i+1}) \in \eta_{pos(i)}(q_i)$ and $pos(i + 1) = pos(i)$, or
3. $\eta_{pos(i)}(q_i)$ contains $(\langle n \rangle, q_{i+1})$ or $([n], q_{i+1})$, $q_{i+1} \in \rho_{pos(i)+1}(q_i)$, and $pos(i+1) = pos(i) + 1$.

Intuitively, $q_0, q_1, \ldots$ is a trace induced by $\langle \sigma_0, \eta_0, \rho_0 \rangle, \langle \sigma_1, \eta_1, \rho_1 \rangle, \ldots$, if for every path $\pi \subseteq T$ and for every run $\langle T_r, r \rangle$ on a Σ-labeled tree in which π is labeled by $\sigma_0, \sigma_1, \ldots$, if $\langle T_r, r \rangle$ is consistent with a running strategy in which π is labeled $\eta_0, \eta_1, \ldots$ and a promise in which π is labeled $\rho_0, \rho_1, \ldots$, then $\langle T_r, r \rangle$ contains a path that visits the states $q_0, q_1, \ldots$.

Recall that $\Sigma' \subseteq \Sigma \times F \times G$. We refer to a Σ'-labeled tree as $\langle T, (V, f, g) \rangle$, where V, f, and g are the projections of the tree on Σ, F, and G, respectively. We say that a running strategy $\langle T, f \rangle$ and a promise $\langle T, g \rangle$ are *good* for $\langle T, V \rangle$ if all the infinite traces induced by paths in $\langle T, (V, f, g) \rangle$ satisfy the acceptance condition α.

Consider a Σ-labeled tree $\langle T, V \rangle$, a running strategy $\langle T, f \rangle$, and a promise $\langle T, g \rangle$. We say that *g fulfills f* for V if the states promised to be visited by g satisfy the obligations induced by f as it runs on V. Formally, g fulfills f for V if for every node $x \in T$, and state q such that x is obliged to q by f, g, and V, the following hold:

1. For every atom $\langle n \rangle s \in f(x)(q)$, at least $n + 1$ children $x \cdot j$ of x have $s \in g(x \cdot j)(q)$.
2. For every atom $[n]s \in f(x)(q)$, at least $deg(x) - n$ children $x \cdot j$ of x have $s \in g(x \cdot j)(q)$.

Theorem 3. *A GAPT $\mathcal{A}$ accepts $\langle T, V \rangle$ iff there exist a running strategy $\langle T, f \rangle$ and a promise $\langle T, g \rangle$ such that f is relevant for V, f and g are good for $\langle T, V \rangle$, and g fulfills f for V.*

Intuitively, if f and g as above exist, the $(T \times Q)$-labeled trees that are consistent with f and g suggest legal accepting runs of $\mathcal{A}$ on $\langle T, V \rangle$.

Annotating input trees with restrictions and local promises enables us to transform GAPT to GNPT, with an exponential blow up:

Theorem 4. *Consider a GAPT $\mathcal{A}$ such that $\mathcal{A}$ runs on Σ-labeled trees. There is a GNPT $\mathcal{A}'$ such that $\mathcal{A}'$ runs on Σ'-labeled trees and the following hold:*

1. *$\mathcal{A}'$ accepts a tree iff $\mathcal{A}$ accepts its projection on Σ.*
2. *If $\mathcal{A}$ has n states, index k, and counting bound b, then $\mathcal{A}'$ has $2^{n(2+k \log nk)}$ states, index nk, and b-counting constraints.*

Proof. Let $\mathcal{A} = \langle \Sigma, b, Q, \delta, q_0, \alpha \rangle$ with $\alpha = \{F_1, \ldots, F_k\}$. The automaton $\mathcal{A}'$ is the intersection of two automata $\mathcal{A}_1'$ and $\mathcal{A}_2'$. The automaton $\mathcal{A}_1'$ is a forall GNPT and it accepts a tree $\langle T, (V, f, g) \rangle$ iff f and g are good for V. The automaton $\mathcal{A}_2'$ is a safety GNPT, and it accepts a tree $\langle T, (V, f, g) \rangle$ iff g fulfills f for V. Note that, since Σ' contains only triplets $\langle \sigma, \eta, \rho \rangle$ for which η is relevant to σ, it must be that f is relevant to V. Thus, by Theorem 3, it follows that $\mathcal{A}'$ accepts $\langle T, (V, f, g) \rangle$ iff $\mathcal{A}$ accepts $\langle T, V \rangle$.

In order to define $\mathcal{A}_1'$, we first define a nondeterministic co-parity word automaton $\mathcal{U}$ over Σ' such that $\mathcal{U}$ accepts a word if some trace it induces is infinite and violates the acceptance condition α. We define $\mathcal{U} = \langle \Sigma', S, M, s_0, F' \rangle$, where

- $S = (Q \times Q \times \{1, \ldots, k\}) \cup \{q_{acc}\}$. Intuitively, a state $\langle q, q_{prev}, v \rangle$ indicates that the current state of the trace is q, that it was reached by following a step whose last transition is from the state q_{prev}, and the value of the step is v (note that values are calculated with respect to α). Thus, q corresponds to states q_{i+1} in traces for which $pos(i + 1) = pos(i) + 1$. The number v is used for the acceptance condition. In addition, q_{prev} is used for checking the obligation of the current position, given a local promise in the input word.
- For every $\langle q, q_{prev}, v \rangle \in S$ and $\langle \sigma, \eta, \rho \rangle \in \Sigma'$, we distinguish between two cases. If $q \notin \rho(q_{prev})$, then the current position is not obliged to q and $M(\langle q, q_{prev}, v \rangle, \langle \sigma, \eta, \rho \rangle) = \emptyset$. Otherwise, we again distinguish between two cases: if there is a rejecting ε-lasso of η with q and σ, then $M(\langle q, q_{prev}, v \rangle, \langle \sigma, \eta, \rho \rangle) = \{q_{acc}\}$. Otherwise, $\langle q', q_{prev}', v' \rangle \in M(\langle q, q_{prev}, v \rangle, \langle \sigma, \eta, \rho \rangle)$ iff there is a step $q, \ldots, q_{prev}', q'$ of η with q and σ such that the value of the step is v'. In addition, $M(q_{acc}, \langle \sigma, \eta, \rho \rangle) = \{q_{acc}\}$ for all $\langle \sigma, \eta, \rho \rangle \in \Sigma'$. Intuitively, $\mathcal{U}$ checks whether a possible step of η with q and σ can participate in a rejecting trace. If the current position is not obliged to the current state, no step of η can participate in a trace, so $\mathcal{U}$ gets stuck. Otherwise, if there is a rejecting ε-lasso of η with q and σ, a rejecting trace is found and $\mathcal{U}$ moves to an accepting sink. Otherwise, $\mathcal{U}$ guesses other possible steps of η with q and σ, and moves to a state which remembers the last two states visited in the step (possibly $q_{prev}' = q$), and the value of the step.
- $s_0' = \langle q_0, q_0, l \rangle$, where l is such that $q_0 \in F_l$. Note that the choice of the second element is arbitrary, as the local promise at the root of the input tree is irrelevant.
- The co-parity condition is $F' = \{F_1', F_2', \ldots, F_k'\}$, where for $l \geq 2$, we have $F_l' = Q \times Q \times \{l\}$, and $F_1' = (Q \times Q \times \{1\}) \cup \{q_{acc}\}$. That is, acceptance is determined with respect to the values of the steps taken along the trace. Also, since F' is a co-parity condition, the accepting sink q_{acc} is in F_1'.

In order to get $\mathcal{A}'_1$, we co-determinize $\mathcal{U}$ (note that $\mathcal{U}$ does not have ε-transitions) and expand it to a tree automaton on Σ'. That is, we first construct a deterministic parity word automaton $\tilde{\mathcal{U}}$ that complements $\mathcal{U}$, and then replace a transition $\tilde{M}(s, \tau) = s'$ in $\tilde{\mathcal{U}}$ by a transition $\tilde{M}_t(s, \tau) = \{\langle \neg \theta_{s'}, (\leq, 0) \rangle\}$ in $\mathcal{A}'_1$, where the states of $\tilde{\mathcal{U}}$ are encoded by some set Y_1 of variables and for every state s', the formula $\theta_{s'} \in \mathcal{B}(Y_1)$ holds only in the subset of Y_1 that encodes s'. By [Saf89,Tho97], the automaton $\tilde{\mathcal{U}}$ has $(nk)^{nk}$ states and index nk, thus so does $\mathcal{A}'_1$. Hence $|Y_1| = nk \log nk$.

It is left to define the safety GNPT $\mathcal{A}'_2$. Let $Q_{prev} = \{q_{prev} : q \in Q\}$ be a copy of Q in which each state is tagged with $prev$. The state space of $\mathcal{A}'_2$ is $Q' = 2^{Q \cup Q_{prev}}$. Intuitively, each state q' of $\mathcal{A}'_2$ corresponds to a pair $\langle P, P_{prev} \rangle \in Q \times Q$, with $P = q' \cap Q$ and P_{prev} is obtained from $q' \cap Q_{prev}$ by removing the $prev$ tags. The element P of q' is a set of "commitments" that the current node should satisfy. The element P_{prev} is used for remembering the state of $\mathcal{A}$ that is visited in the parent node. When $\mathcal{A}'_2$ is in state $\langle P, P_{prev} \rangle$ and reads the letter $\langle \sigma, \eta, \rho \rangle$, it checks that all the commitments in P are covered by the local promise $\rho(P_{prev})$ in the input, and it delivers, for each $q \in P$, the requirements on the children as specified in $\eta(q)$.

Consider a state $\langle P, P_{prev} \rangle \in Q'$ and a letter $\langle \sigma, \eta, \rho \rangle \in \Sigma'$. For every $q \in P$, let $C^q_{\sigma, \eta}$ be the b-counting restriction in $\mathcal{C}(Q, b)$ imposed by $\eta(q)$. (If $\eta(q)$ is undefined, we do not care about $C^q_{\sigma, \eta}$, since, as we see shortly, in that case $\mathcal{A}'_2$ simply gets stuck.) Thus, $C^q_{\sigma, \eta} = \{\langle s, (>, n) \rangle : \langle n \rangle s \in \eta(q)\} \cup \{\langle \neg s, (\leq, n) \rangle : [n]s \in \eta(q)\}$. Intuitively, $C^q_{\sigma, \eta}$ restricts the tuple of the states that visit the children of the current node, which is visited by $\langle P, P_{prev} \rangle$, so that $\eta(q)$ is satisfied by the first elements of the states. In addition, the second element of the states in the tuple should be the encoding of P tagged with $prev$. This is done by the counting constraint $\{\langle \neg \theta^{prev}_P, (\leq, 0) \rangle\}$, where $\theta^{prev}_P \in \mathcal{B}(Q_{prev})$ is such that the only set that satisfies θ^{prev}_P is the encoding of P tagged with $prev$. Finally, for every $P \in 2^Q$, let $C^P_{\sigma, \eta} = (\oplus_{q \in P} C^q_{\sigma, \eta}) \cup \{\langle \neg \theta^{prev}_P, (\leq, 0) \rangle\}$. Then, $\mathcal{A}'_2 = \langle \Sigma', Q', \delta', \{q_0, q_0\} \rangle$, where for every $\langle P, P_{prev} \rangle \in Q'$ and $\langle \sigma, \eta, \rho \rangle \in \Sigma'$, we have that $\delta'(\langle P, P_{prev} \rangle, \langle \sigma, \eta, \rho \rangle)$ is empty if $\rho(P_{prev}) \not\subseteq P$ or there is $q \in P$ for which $\eta(q)$ is undefined, and is $C^P_{\sigma, \eta}$ otherwise. Note that Q' is defined with respect to the $2n$ variables $Q \cup Q_{prev}$. Also, all the formulas θ that are paired to constraints in $C^P_{\sigma, \eta}$ are either s or $\neg s$, for $s \in Q$, or $\neg \theta^{prev}_P$. Hence, the counting constraints in $\mathcal{A}'_2$ are in $\mathcal{C}(Q \cup Q_{prev}, b)$.

Now, by Lemma 2, we can define the the intersection $\mathcal{A}'$ of $\mathcal{A}'_1$ and $\mathcal{A}'_2$ as a GNPT with $2^{n(2+k \log nk)}$ states, index nk, and b-counting constraints.

4.2   The Nonemptiness Problem for GNPT

In a nondeterministic parity tree automaton $\mathcal{U} = \langle \Sigma, Q, M, q_0, \alpha \rangle$, the transition function $M : Q \times \Sigma \to 2^{Q^*}$ maps a state and a letter to a set of possible tuples for the children states. Thus, a run of nondeterministic tree automaton on a tree $\langle T, V \rangle$ is a Q-labeled tree $\langle T, r \rangle$ in which $r(\varepsilon) = q_0$ and for all $x \in T$, the tuple $\langle r(x \cdot 1), r(x \cdot 2), \ldots, r(x \cdot deg(x)) \rangle \in M(r(x), V(x))$. The nonemptiness test for parity tree automata then uses the local test $is\_mother : 2^Q \times Q \to \{\textbf{true}, \textbf{false}\}$ that given a set $S \subseteq Q$ and a state q, returns $\textbf{true}$ iff there is a tuple $t \in S^*$ and $\sigma \in \Sigma$ such that $t \in M(q, \sigma)$. It is easy to see how the is_mother test is used in a bottom-up nonemptiness algorithm for automata on finite trees, where in order to find the set S of states from which the automaton accepts some tree, one starts with the set S_0 of accepting states then define S_{i+1} as the set of states q such that either q is in S_i or $is_mother(t, q) = $ **true**. In parity automata, the algorithm is more complicated, as one has to also keep track of the acceptance condition, but the same local test is used. Several nonemptiness algorithms for nondeterministic parity tree automata are known. In particular, the algorithms in [EJS93,KV98] use $O(n^k)$ calls to is_mother, where n is the size of Q and k is the index of the automaton.

Recall that in GNPT, a run $\langle T, r \rangle$ should satisfy $r(\varepsilon) = q_0$ and for all $x \in T$, the tuple $\langle r(x \cdot 1), r(x \cdot 2), \ldots, r(x \cdot deg(x)) \rangle$ satisfies $\delta(r(x), V(x))$, which is a b-counting constraint. Thus, the nonemptiness test is similar, only that the local test $is\_mother : 2^Q \times Q \to \{\mathbf{true}, \mathbf{false}\}$ now returns **true** for a set $S \subseteq Q$ and a state q, iff there is $t \in S^*$ and $\sigma \in \Sigma$ such that t satisfies $\delta(q, \sigma)$. As with nondeterministic automata, the nonemptiness algorithm can do $O(n^k)$ calls to is_mother. Unlike the case for nondeterministic automata, however, here there is no simple transition function to consult when we perform the local test. In addition, we should take into an account the fact that the GNPT whose emptiness we check have larger alphabets than the GAPT we have started with.

Consider a GAPT $\mathcal{A} = \langle \Sigma, b, Q, \delta, q_0, \alpha \rangle$ with n states, index k, and counting bound b. Let us analyse carefully the complexity of the local is_mother test in the GNPT $\mathcal{A}'$ we constructed from $\mathcal{A}$ in Theorem 4. First, $\mathcal{A}'$ has counting constraints in $\mathcal{C}(Y', b)$, for Y' of size $n(2 + k \log nk)$. Hence, by Lemma 1, given S, the check whether there is a tuple $t \in S^*$ such that t satisfies $\delta(q, \sigma')$, for a particular $\sigma' \in \Sigma'$, can be done in time $O((2b + 2)^{n(2+k \log nk)})$. Now, $\Sigma' \subseteq \Sigma \times F \times G$, where F is the set of restrictions for δ and G is the set of all local promises. Let $|\Sigma| = l$. Recall that a restriction relevant to a letter $\sigma \in \Sigma$ maps a state $q \in Q$ to a subset of $D_b \times Q$ that satisfies $\delta(q, \sigma)$. We can restrict our attention to restrictions in which each state is paired with at most one element of $\langle\langle b \rangle\rangle$, one element of $[\langle b \rangle]$, and ε. Thus, $|F|$ is bounded by $(2b + 4)^{n^2}$ and $|G|$ is bounded by 2^{n^2}. It follows that $|\Sigma'| \leq l(2b + 4)^{n^2} 2^{n^2}$, thus is_mother can be checked in time $l(b + 2)^{O(n(n+2+k \log nk))}$. Since, as in [EJS93,KV98], the nonemptiness problem can be solved by $O(n^k)$ applications of is_mother, we have the following.

Theorem 5. *The nonemptiness problem for $\mathcal{A}'$ can be solved in time* $n^k l(b + 2)^{O(n(n+2+k \log nk))}$.

For a graded μ-calculus formula ψ, we get, by Theorem 2, a GAPT $\mathcal{A}$ with n and k bounded by $|\psi|$, and the same counting bound b as ψ. While b and l may be exponential in $|\psi|$, only n and k appear in the exponents in the expression in Theorem 5. This implies the upper bound in the theorem below. The lower bound is due to the fact that the μ-calculus is known to be EXPTIME-hard [FL79].

Corollary 1. *The satisfiability problem for graded μ-calculus is EXPTIME-complete even if the numbers in the graded modalities are coded in binary.*

Note that the space and time bounds in Lemma 1 stay valid for counting constraints that involve richer bounds than $(>, n)$ and $(\leq, n)$. For example, we can handle bounds of the form $(>, \frac{1}{2})$ or $(\leq, \frac{1}{2})$, bounding the fraction of elements in the tuple that satisfy a predicate (of course, this is applicable only to structures where all points have only finitely many successors). In general, Lemma 1 can handle arbitrary polynomial predicates $\alpha \subseteq$

$\mathbb{N}^2$, where a tuple $t \in (2^Y)^m$ satisfies such a constraint $\langle \theta, \alpha \rangle$ if $\alpha(weight(sat(\theta), t), m)$ holds. By defining the corresponding types of alternating automata, we can thus handle μ-calculus formulas with richer types of modalities.

References

[BB87]   B. Banieqbal and H. Barringer. Temporal logic with fixed points. In *Temporal Logic in Specification*, volume 398 of *LNCS*, pages 62–74. Springer-Verlag, 1987.

[BC96]   G. Bhat and R. Cleaveland. Efficient local model-checking for fragments of the modal μ-calculus. In *Proc. of TACAS-96, LNCS* 1055. Springer-Verlag, 1996.

[BFH⁺94]   F. Baader, E. Franconi, B. Hollunder, B. Nebel, and H.J. Profitlich. An empirical analysis of optimization techniques for terminological representation systems, or: Making KRIS get a move on. *Applied Artificial Intelligence*, 4:109–132, 1994.

[BS99]   F. Baader and U. Sattler. Expressive number restrictions in description logics. *Journal of Logic and Computation*, 9(3):319–350, 1999.

[CDL99]   D. Calvanese, G. De Giacomo, and M. Lenzerini. Reasoning in expressive description logics with fixpoints based on automata on infinite trees. In *IJCAI'99*, 1999.

[De 95]   G. De Giacomo. *Decidability of Class-Based Knowledge Representation Formalisms*. PhD thesis, Università degli Studi di Roma "La Sapienza", 1995.

[DL94a]   G. De Giacomo and M. Lenzerini. Boosting the correspondence between description logics and propositional dynamic logics. In *Proc. of AAAI-94*, 1994.

[DL94b]   G. De Giacomo and M. Lenzerini. Concept language with number restrictions and fixpoints, and its relationship with mu-calculus. In *Proc. of ECAI-94*, 1994.

[DLNdN91]   F. Donini, M. Lenzerini, D. Nardi, and W. Nutt. The complexity of concept languages. In *Proc. of KR-91*, 1991.

[EJS93]   E.A. Emerson, C. Jutla, and A.P. Sistla. On model-checking for fragments of μ-calculus. In *Proc. 4th CAV*, LNCS 697, pages 385–396. Springer-Verlag, 1993.

[Eme97]   E.A. Emerson. Model checking and the μ-calculus. In *Descriptive Complexity and Finite Models*, pages 185–214. American Mathematical Society, 1997.

[Fin72]   K. Fine. In so many possible worlds. *Notre Dame Journal of Formal Logics*, 13:516–520, 1972.

[FL79]   M.J. Fischer and R.E. Ladner. Propositional dynamic logic of regular programs. *Journal of Computer and Systems Sciences*, 18:194–211, 1979.

[GKV97]   E. Grädel, Ph. G. Kolaitis, and M. Y. Vardi. The decision problem for 2-variable first-order logic. *Bulletin of Symbolic Logic*, 3:53–69, 1997.

[GOR97]   E. Grädel, M. Otto, and E. Rosen. Two-variable logic with counting is decidable. In *Proc. of LICS-97*, 1997.

[Grä99]   E. Grädel. On the restraining power of guards. *Journal of Symbolic Logic*, 64, 1999.

[HB91]   B. Hollunder and F. Baader. Qualifying number restrictions in concept languages. In *Proc. of KR-91*, pages 335–346, 1991.

[HM01]   V. Haarslev and R. Möller. RACER system description. In *Proc. of IJCAR-01*, volume 2083 of *LNAI*. Springer-Verlag, 2001.

[Hor98]   I. Horrocks. Using an Expressive Description Logic: FaCT or Fiction? In *Proc. of KR-98*, 1998.

[HST00]   I. Horrocks, U. Sattler, and S. Tobies. Reasoning with individuals for the description logic shiq. In *Proc. of CADE-17*, LNCS 1831, Germany, 2000. Springer-Verlag.

[JW95]   D. Janin and I. Walukiewicz. Automata for the modal μ-calculus and related results. In *Proc. of MFCS-95*, LNCS, pages 552–562. Springer-Verlag, 1995.

[Koz83]   D. Kozen. Results on the propositional μ-calculus. *Theoretical Computer Science*, 27:333–354, 1983.

[KV98]   O. Kupferman and M.Y. Vardi. Weak alternating automata and tree automata emptiness. In *Proc. STOC-98*, pages 224–233, 1998.

[KVW00]   O. Kupferman, M.Y. Vardi, and P. Wolper. An automata-theoretic approach to branching-time model checking. *Journal of the ACM*, 47(2):312–360, March 2000.

[Lad77]   R. E. Ladner. The computational complexity of provability in systems of modal propositional logic. *SIAM Journal of Control and Optimization*, 6(3):467–480, 1977.

[Lyn77]   N. Lynch. Log space recognition and translation of parenthesis languages. *Journal of the ACM*, 24:583–590, 1977.

[MS87]   D.E. Muller and P.E. Schupp. Alternating automata on infinite trees. *Theoretical Computer Science*, 54:267–276, 1987.

[MS95]   D.E. Muller and P.E. Schupp. Simulating alternating tree automata by nondeterministic automata: New results and new proofs of theorems of Rabin, McNaughton and Safra. *Theoretical Computer Science*, 141:69–107, 1995.

[PSMB+91]   P. Patel-Schneider, D. McGuinness, R. Brachman, L. Resnick, and A. Borgida. The CLASSIC knowledge representation system: Guiding principles and implementation rationale. *SIGART Bulletin*, 2(3):108–113, 1991.

[PST00]   L. Pacholski, W. Szwast, and L. Tendera. Complexity results for first-order two-variable logic with counting. *SIAM Journal of Computing*, 29(4):1083–1117, 2000.

[Saf89]   S. Safra. *Complexity of automata on infinite objects*. PhD thesis, Weizmann Institute of Science, Rehovot, Israel, 1989.

[Sch94]   K. Schild. Terminological cycles and the propositional μ-calculus. In *Proc. of KR-94*, pages 509–520. Morgan Kaufmann, 1994.

[SE89]   R.S. Streett and E.A. Emerson. An automata theoretic decision procedure for the propositional μ-calculus. *Information and Computation*, 81(3):249–264, 1989.

[Tho90]   W. Thomas. Automata on infinite objects. In J. Van Leeuwen, editor, *Handbook of Theoretical Computer Science*, pages 165–191. North Holland, 1990.

[Tho97]   W. Thomas. Languages, automata, and logic. In G. Rozenberg and A. Salomaa, editors, *Handbook of Formal Language Theory*, volume III, pages 389–455, 1997.

[Tob00]   S. Tobies. The complexity of reasoning with cardinality restrictions and nominals in expressive description logics. *Journal of Artificial Intelligence Research*, 12:199–217, 2000.

[Tob01]   S. Tobies. PSPACE reasoning for graded modal logics. *Journal of Logic and Computation*, 11(1):85–106, 2001.

[Var97]   M.Y. Vardi. What makes modal logic so robustly decidable? In *Descriptive Complexity and Finite Models*, pages 149–183. American Mathematical Society, 1997.

[vD95]   W. van der Hoek and M. De Rijke. Counting objects. *Journal of Logic and Computation*, 5(3):325–345, 1995.

[VW86]   M.Y. Vardi and P. Wolper. Automata-theoretic techniques for modal logics of programs. *Journal of Computer and System Science*, 32(2):182–221, 1986.

[Wal96]   I. Walukiewicz. Monadic second order logic on tree-like structures. In *Proc. of STACS-96*, LNCS, pages 401–413. Springer-Verlag, 1996.

[Wil99]   T. Wilke. CTL^+ is exponentially more succinct than CTL. In *Proc. of FSTTCS-99*, volume 1738 of *LNCS*, pages 110–121. Springer-Verlag, 1999.

Lazy Theorem Proving for Bounded Model Checking over Infinite Domains*

Leonardo de Moura, Harald Rueß, and Maria Sorea**

SRI International
Computer Science Laboratory
333 Ravenswood Avenue
Menlo Park, CA 94025, USA
{demoura, ruess, sorea}@csl.sri.com
http://www.csl.sri.com/

Abstract. We investigate the combination of propositional SAT checkers with domain-specific theorem provers as a foundation for bounded model checking over infinite domains. Given a program M over an infinite state type, a linear temporal logic formula φ with domain-specific constraints over program states, and an upper bound k, our procedure determines if there is a falsifying path of length k to the hypothesis that M satisfies the specification φ. This problem can be reduced to the satisfiability of Boolean constraint formulas. Our verification engine for these kinds of formulas is *lazy* in that propositional abstractions of Boolean constraint formulas are incrementally refined by generating lemmas on demand from an automated analysis of spurious counterexamples using theorem proving. We exemplify bounded model checking for timed automata and for RTL level descriptions, and investigate the lazy integration of SAT solving and theorem proving.

1 Introduction

Model checking decides the problem of whether a system satisfies a temporal logic property by exploring the underlying state space. It applies primarily to finite-state systems but also to certain infinite-state systems, and the state space can be represented in symbolic or explicit form. Symbolic model checking has traditionally employed a boolean representation of state sets using binary decision diagrams (BDD) [4] as a way of checking temporal properties, whereas explicit-state model checkers enumerate the set of reachable states of the system.

Recently, the use of Boolean satisfiability (SAT) solvers for linear-time temporal logic (LTL) properties has been explored through a technique known as *bounded model checking* (BMC) [7]. As with symbolic model checking, the state

---

* This research was supported by SRI International internal research and development, the DARPA NEST program through Contract F33615-01-C-1908 with AFRL, and the National Science Foundation under grants CCR-00-86096 and CCR-0082560.
** Also affiliated with University of Ulm, Germany.

is encoded in terms of booleans. The program is unrolled a bounded number of steps for some bound k, and an LTL property is checked for counterexamples over computations of length k. For example, to check whether a program with initial state I and next-state relation T violates the invariant Inv in the first k steps, one checks, using a SAT solver:

$$I(s_0) \land T(s_0, s_1) \land T(s_1, s_2) \land \ \ldots \ \land T(s_{k-1}, s_k) \land (\neg Inv(s_0) \lor \ \ldots \ \lor \neg Inv(s_k)).$$

This formula is satisfiable if and only if there exists a path of length at most k from the initial state s_0 which violates the invariant Inv. For finite state systems, BMC can be seen as a complete procedure since the size of counterexamples is essentially bounded by the diameter of the system [3]. It has been demonstrated that BMC can be more effective in falsifying hypotheses than traditional model checking [7,8].

It is possible to extend the range of BMC to infinite-state systems by encoding the search for a counterexample as a satisfiability problem for the logic of Boolean constraint formulas. For example, the BMC problem for timed automata can be captured in terms of a Boolean formula with linear arithmetic constraints. But the method presented here scales well beyond such simple arithmetic clauses, since the main requirement on any given constraint theory is the decidability of the satisfiability problem on conjunctions of atomic constraints. Possible constraint theories include, for example, linear arithmetic, bitvectors, arrays, regular expressions, equalities over terms with uninterpreted function symbols, and combinations thereof [20,24].

Whereas BMC over finite-state systems deals with finding satisfying Boolean assignments, its generalization to infinite-state systems is concerned with satisfiability of Boolean constraint formulas. In initial experiments with PVS [21] strategies, based on a combination of BDDs for propositional reasoning and a variant of loop residue [27] for arithmetic, we were usually only able to construct counterexamples of small depths (≤ 5). Clearly, more specialized verification techniques are needed. Since BMC problems are often propositionally intensive, it seems to be more effective to augment SAT solvers with theorem proving capabilities, such as ICS [10], than add propositional search capabilities to theorem provers.

Here, we look at the specific combination of SAT solvers with decision procedures, and we propose a method that we call *lemmas on demand*, which invokes the theorem prover *lazily* in order to efficiently prune out spurious counterexamples, namely, counterexamples that are generated by the SAT solver but discarded by the theorem prover by interpreting the propositional atoms. For example, the SAT solver might yield the satisfying assignment p, $\neg q$, where the propositional variable p represents the atom $x = y$, and q represents $f(x) = f(y)$. A decision procedure can easily detect the inconsistency in this assignment. More importantly, it can be used to generate a set of conflicting assignments that can be used to construct a lemma that further constrains the search. In the above example, the lemma $\neg p \lor q$ can be added as a new clause in the input to the SAT solver. This process of refining Boolean formulas is similar in spirit to the refinement of abstractions based on the analysis of spurious counterexamples or failed proof attempts [26,25,6,16,9,14,17].

From a set of inconsistent constraints in a spurious counterexample we obtain an *explanation* as an overapproximation of the minimal, inconsistent subset of these constraints. The smaller the explanation that is generated from a spurious counterexample, the greater the pruning in the subsequent search. In this way, the computation of explanations accelerates the convergence of our procedure.

Altogether, we present a method for bounded model checking over infinite-state systems that consists of:

- A reduction to the satisfiability problem for Boolean constraint formulas.
- A lazy combination of SAT solving and theorem proving.
- An efficient method for constructing small explanations.

In general, BMC over infinite-state systems is not complete, but we obtain a completeness result for BMC problems with invariant properties. The main condition on constraints is that the satisfiability of the conjunction of constraints is decidable. Thus, our BMC procedure can be applied to infinite-state systems even when the (more) general model-checking problem is undecidable.

The paper is structured as follows. In Section 2 we provide some background material on Boolean constraints. Section 3 lays the foundation of a refinement-based satisfiability procedure for Boolean constraint logic. Next, Section 4 presents the details of BMC over domain-specific constraints, and Section 5 discusses some simple examples for BMC over clock constraints and the theory of bitvectors. In Section 6 we experimentally investigate various design choices in lazy integrations of SAT solvers with theorem proving. Finally, in Sections 7 and 8 we compare with related work and we draw conclusions.

2   Background

A set of variables $V := \{x_1, \ldots, x_n\}$ is said to be typed if there are nonempty sets D_1 through D_n and a *type assignment* τ such that $\tau(x_i) = D_i$. For a set of typed variables V, a *variable assignment* is a function ν from variables $x \in V$ to an element of $\tau(x)$.

Let V be a set of typed variables and L be an associated logical language. A set of constraints in L is called a *constraint theory* $\mathcal{C}$ if it includes constants *true*, *false* and if it is closed under negation; a subset of $\mathcal{C}$ of constraints with free variables in $V' \subseteq V$ is denoted by $\mathcal{C}(V')$. For $c \in \mathcal{C}$ and ν an assignment for the free variables in c, the value of the predicate $[\![c]\!]_\nu$ is called the *interpretation* of c w.r.t. ν. Hereby, $[\![true]\!]_\nu$ ($[\![false]\!]_\nu$) is assumed to hold for all (for no) ν, and $[\![\neg c]\!]_\nu$ holds iff $[\![c]\!]_\nu$ does not hold. A set of constraints $C \subseteq \mathcal{C}$ is said to be *satisfiable* if there exists a variable assignment ν such that $[\![c]\!]_\nu$ holds for every c in C; otherwise, C is said to be *unsatisfiable*. Furthermore, a function $\mathcal{C}\text{-}sat(C)$ is called a $\mathcal{C}$-satisfiability solver if it returns $\bot$ if the set of constraints C is unsatisfiable and a satisfying assignment for C otherwise.

For a given theory $\mathcal{C}$, the set of *boolean constraints* $\mathsf{Bool}(\mathcal{C})$ includes all constraints in $\mathcal{C}$ and it is closed under conjunction $\wedge$, disjunction $\vee$, and negation $\neg$. The notions of satisfiability, inconsistency, satisfying assignment, and satisfiability solver are homomorphically lifted to the set of boolean constraints in the usual way. If $V = \{p_1, \ldots, p_n\}$ and the corresponding type assignment $\tau(p_i)$ is either true or false, then $\mathsf{Bool}(\{true, false\} \cup V)$ reduces to the usual notion of Boolean logic with propositional variables $\{p_1, \ldots, p_n\}$. We call a Boolean satisfiability solver also a SAT solver. N-ary disjunctions of constraints are also referred to as *clauses*, and a formula $\varphi \in \mathsf{Bool}(\mathcal{C}(V))$ is in *conjunctive normal form* (CNF) if it is an n-ary conjunction of clauses. There is a linear-time satisfiability-preserving transformation into CNF [22].

3   Lazy Theorem Proving

Satisfiability solvers for propositional constraint formulas can be obtained from the combination of a propositional SAT solver with decision procedures simply by converting the problem into disjunctive normal form, but the result is prohibitively expensive. Here, we lay out the foundation of a lazy combination of SAT solvers with constraint solvers based on an incremental refinement of Boolean formulas. We restrict our analysis to formulas in CNF, since most modern SAT solvers expect their input to be in this format.

Translation schemes between propositional formulas and Boolean constraint formulas are needed. Given a formula φ such a correspondence is easily obtained by abstracting constraints in φ with (fresh) propositional variables. More formally, for a formula $\varphi \in \mathsf{Bool}(\mathcal{C})$ with atoms $C = \{c_1, \ldots, c_n\} \in \mathcal{C}$ and a set of propositional variables $P = \{p_1, \ldots, p_n\}$ not occurring in φ, the mapping α from Boolean formulas over $\{c_1, \ldots, c_n\}$ to Boolean formulas over P is defined as the homomorphism induced by $\alpha(c_i) = p_i$. The inverse γ of such an abstraction mapping α simply replaces propositional variables p_i with their associated constraints c_i. For example, the formula $\varphi \equiv f(x) \neq x \wedge f(f(x)) = x$ over equalities of terms with uninterpreted function symbols determines the function α with, say, $\alpha(f(x) \neq x) = p_1$ and $\alpha(f(f(x)) = x) = p_2$; thus $\alpha(\varphi) = p_1 \wedge p_2$. Moreover, a Boolean assignment $\nu : P \to \{true, false\}$ induces a set of constraints

$$\gamma(\nu) \equiv \{c \in \mathcal{C} \mid \exists i. \text{ if } \nu(p_i) = true \text{ then } c = \gamma(p_i) \text{ else } c = \neg\gamma(p_i)\} \ .$$

Now, given a Boolean variable assignment ν such that $\nu(p_1) = false$ and $\nu(p_2) = true$, $\gamma(\nu)$ is the set of constraints $\{f(x) = x, f(f(x)) = x\}$. A consistent set of constraints C determines a set of assignments. For choosing an arbitrary, but fixed assignment from this set, we assume as given a function $choose(C)$.

Theorem 1. Let $\varphi \in \mathsf{Bool}(\mathcal{C})$ be a formula in CNF, $\mathcal{L}$ be the literals in $\alpha(\varphi)$, and $I(\varphi) := \{L \subseteq \mathcal{L} \mid \gamma(L) \text{ is } \mathcal{C}\text{-inconsistent}\}$ be the set of $\mathcal{C}$-inconsistencies for φ; then: φ is $\mathcal{C}$-satisfiable iff the following Boolean formula is satisfiable:

$$\alpha(\varphi) \wedge \left(\bigwedge_{\{l_1, \ldots, l_n\} \in I(\varphi)} (\neg l_1 \vee \ldots \vee \neg l_n) \right).$$

$$\mathbf{sat}(\varphi)$$

$$p := \alpha(\varphi);$$

loop

$$\nu := \mathcal{B}\text{-}sat(p);$$

if $\nu = \bot$ then return $\bot$;

if $\mathcal{C}\text{-}sat(\gamma(\nu)) \neq \bot$ then return $choose(\gamma(\nu))$;

$$I := \bigvee_{c \in \gamma(\nu)} \neg\alpha(c); \ p := p \wedge I$$

endloop

Fig. 1. Lazy theorem proving for $\mathsf{Bool}(\mathcal{C})$.

Thus, every $\mathsf{Bool}(\mathcal{C})$ formula can be transformed into an equisatisfiable Boolean formula as long as the consistency problem for sets of constraints in $\mathcal{C}$ is decidable. This transformation enables one to use off-the-shelf satisfiability checkers to determine the satisfiability of Boolean constraint formulas. On the other hand, the set of literals is exponential in the number of variables and, therefore, an exponential number of $\mathcal{C}$-*inconsistency* checks is required in the worst case. It has been observed, however, that in many cases only small fragments of the set of $\mathcal{C}$-*inconsistencies* are needed.

Starting with $p = \alpha(\varphi)$, the procedure $\mathbf{sat}(\varphi)$ in Figure 1 realizes a guided enumeration of the set of $\mathcal{C}$-*inconsistencies*. In each loop, the SAT solver $\mathcal{B}$-*sat* suggests a candidate assignment ν for the Boolean formula p, and the satisfiability solver $\mathcal{C}$-*sat* for $\mathcal{C}$ checks whether the corresponding set of constraints $\gamma(\nu)$ is consistent. Whenever this consistency check fails, p is refined by adding a Boolean analogue I of this inconsistency, and $\mathcal{B}$-*sat* is applied to suggest a new candidate assignment for the refined formula $p \wedge I$. This procedure terminates, since, in every loop, I is not subsumed by p, and there are only a finite number of such strengthenings.

Corollary 1. $\mathbf{sat}(\varphi)$ in Figure 1 is a satisfiability solver for $\mathsf{Bool}(\mathcal{C})$ formulas in CNF.

We list some essential optimizations. If the variable assignments returned by the SAT solver are partial in that they include *don't care* values, then the number of argument constraints to $\mathcal{C}$-*sat* can usually be reduced considerably. The use of don't care values also speeds up convergence, since more general lemmas are generated. Now, assume a function $explain(C)$, which, for an inconsistent set of constraints C, returns a minimal number of inconsistent constraints in C or a "good" overapproximation thereof. The use of $explain(C)$ instead of the stronger C obviously accelerates the procedure. We experimentally analyze these efficiency issues in Section 6.

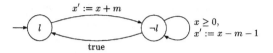

Fig. 2. The *simple* example.

4   Infinite-State BMC

Given a BMC problem for an infinite-state program, an LTL formula with constraints, and a bound on the length of counterexamples to be searched for, we describe a sound reduction to the satisfiability problem of Boolean constraint formulas and we show completeness for invariant properties. The encoding of transition relations follows the now-standard approach already taken in [13]. Whereas in [7] LTL formulas are translated directly into propositional formulas, we use Büchi automata for this encoding. This simplifies substantially the notations and the proofs, but a direct translation can sometimes be more succinct in the number of variables needed. We use the common notions for finite automata over finite and infinite words, and we assume as given a constraint theory $\mathcal{C}$ with a satisfiability solver.

Typed variables in $V := \{x_1, \ldots, x_n\}$ are also called *state variables*, and a *program state* is a variable assignment over V. A pair $\langle I, T \rangle$ is a $\mathcal{C}$-program over V if $I \in \mathsf{Bool}(\mathcal{C}(V))$ and $T \in \mathsf{Bool}(\mathcal{C}(V \cup V'))$, where V' is a primed, disjoint copy of V. I is used to restrict the set of initial program states, and T specifies the transition relation between states and their successor states. The set of $\mathcal{C}$-programs over V is denoted by $\mathsf{Prg}(\mathcal{C}(V))$. The semantics of a program P is given in terms of a *transition system* M in the usual way, and, by a slight abuse of notation, we sometimes write M for both the program and its associated transition system. The system depicted in Figure 2, for example, is expressed in terms of the program $\langle I, T \rangle$ over $\{x, l\}$, where the counter x is interpreted over the integers and the variable l for encoding locations is interpreted over the Booleans (the n-ary connective $\otimes$ holds iff exactly one of its arguments holds).

$$
\begin{aligned}
I(x, l) \quad &:= \quad x \geq 0 \wedge l \\
T(x, l, x', l') \quad &:= \quad (l \wedge x' = x + m \wedge \neg l') \otimes \\
&\qquad (\neg l \wedge x \geq 0 \wedge x' = x - m - 1 \wedge \neg l') \otimes (\neg l \wedge x' = x \wedge l')
\end{aligned}
$$

Initially, the program is in location l and x is greater than or equal to 0, and the transitions in Figure 2 are encoded by a conjunction of constraints over the current state variables x, l and the next state variables x', l'.

The formulas of the *constraint linear temporal logic* $\mathsf{LTL}(\mathcal{C})$ (in negation normal form) are linear-time temporal logic formulas with the usual "next", "until", and "release" operators, and constraints $c \in \mathcal{C}$ as atoms.

$$
\varphi ::= \mathit{true} \mid \mathit{false} \mid c \mid \varphi_1 \wedge \varphi_2 \mid \varphi_1 \vee \varphi_2 \mid \mathbf{X}\,\varphi \mid \varphi_1 \,\mathbf{U}\, \varphi_2 \mid \varphi_1 \,\mathbf{R}\, \varphi_2
$$

The formula $\mathbf{X}\,\varphi$ holds on some path π iff φ holds in the second state of π. $\varphi_1 \,\mathbf{U}\, \varphi_2$ holds on π if there is a state on the path where φ_2 holds, and at every preceding state on the path φ_1 holds. The release operator $\mathbf{R}$ is the logical dual of $\mathbf{U}$. It requires that φ_2 holds along the path up to and including the first state, where φ_1 holds. However, φ_1 is not required to hold eventually. The derived operators $\mathbf{F}\,\varphi = true\,\mathbf{U}\,\varphi$ and $\mathbf{G}\,\varphi = false\,\mathbf{R}\,\varphi$ denote "eventually φ" and "globally φ". Given a program $M \in \mathsf{Prg}(\mathcal{C})$ and a path π in M, the satisfiability relation $M, \pi \models \varphi$ for an $\mathsf{LTL}(\mathcal{C})$ formula φ is given in the usual way with the notable exception of the case of constraint formulas c. In this case, $M, \pi \models c$ if and only if c holds in the start state of π. Assuming the notation above, the $\mathcal{C}$-model checking problem $M \models \varphi$ holds iff for all paths $\pi = s_0, s_1, \ldots$ in M with $s_0 \in I$ it is the case that $M, \pi \models \varphi$. Given a bound k, a program $M \in \mathsf{Prg}(\mathcal{C})$ and a formula $\varphi \in \mathsf{LTL}(\mathcal{C})$ we now consider the problem of constructing a formula $[\![M, \varphi]\!]_k \in \mathsf{Bool}(\mathcal{C})$, which is satisfiable if and only if there is a counterexample of length k for the $\mathcal{C}$-model checking problem $M \models \varphi$. This construction proceeds as follows.

1. Definition of $[\![M]\!]_k$ as the unfolding of the program M up to step k from initial states (this requires k disjoint copies of V).
2. Translation of $\neg\varphi$ into a corresponding Büchi automaton $\mathcal{B}_{\neg\varphi}$ whose language of accepting words consists of the satisfying paths of $\neg\varphi$.
3. Encoding of the transition system for $\mathcal{B}_{\neg\varphi}$ and the Büchi acceptance condition as a Boolean formula, say $[\![\mathcal{B}]\!]_k$.
4. Forming the conjunction $[\![M, \varphi]\!]_k := [\![\mathcal{B}]\!]_k \wedge [\![M]\!]_k$.
5. A satisfying assignment for the formula $[\![M, \varphi]\!]_k$ induces a counterexample of length k for the model checking problem $M \models \varphi$.

Definition 1 (Encoding of $\mathcal{C}$-Programs). The encoding $[\![M]\!]_k$ of the kth unfolding of a $\mathcal{C}$-program $M = \langle I, T \rangle$ in $\mathsf{Prg}(\mathcal{C}(\{x_1, \ldots, x_n\}))$ is given by the $\mathsf{Bool}(\mathcal{C})$ formula $[\![M]\!]_k$.

$$I_0(x[0]) := I\langle\{x_i \mapsto x_i[0] \mid x_i \in V\}\rangle$$
$$T_j(x[j], x[j+1]) := T\langle\{x_i \mapsto x_i[j] \mid x_i \in V\} \cup \{x'_i \mapsto x_i[j+1] \mid x_i \in V\}\rangle$$
$$[\![M]\!]_k := I_0(x[0]) \wedge \bigwedge_{j=0}^{k-1} T_j(x[j], x[j+1])$$

where $\{x_i[j] \mid 0 \leq j \leq k\}$ is a family of typed variables for encoding the state of variable x_i in the jth step, $x[j]$ is used as an abbreviation for $x_1[j], \ldots, x_n[j]$, and $T\langle x_i \mapsto x_i[j]\rangle$ denotes simultaneous substitution of x_i by $x_i[j]$ in formula T.

A two-step unfolding of the *simple* program in Figure 2 is encoded by $[\![simple]\!]_2 := I_0 \wedge T_0 \wedge T_1$ $(*)$.

$$I_0 := x[0] \geq 0 \wedge l[0]$$
$$T_0 := (\, l[0] \wedge (x[1] = x[0] + m) \wedge \neg l[1]\,) \otimes$$
$$(\neg l[0] \wedge (x[0] \geq 0) \wedge (x[1] = x[0] - m - 1) \wedge \neg l[1]\,) \otimes$$
$$(\neg l[0] \wedge (x[1] = x[0]) \wedge l[1]\,)$$

$$\begin{aligned}
T_1 \quad := \quad & (\, l[1] \,\wedge\, (x[2] = x[1] + m) \,\wedge\, \neg l[2]\,) \otimes \\
& (\, \neg l[1] \,\wedge\, (x[1] \geq 0) \,\wedge\, (x[2] = x[1] - m - 1) \,\wedge\, \neg l[2]\,) \otimes \\
& (\, \neg l[1] \,\wedge\, (x[2] = x[1]) \,\wedge\, l[2]\,)
\end{aligned}$$

The translation of linear temporal logic formulas into a corresponding Büchi automaton is well-studied in the literature [11] and does not require additional explanation. Notice, however, that the translation of LTL($\mathcal{C}$) formulas yields Büchi automata with $\mathcal{C}$-*constraints* as labels. Both the resulting transition system and the bounded acceptance test based on the detection of reachable cycles with at least one final state can easily be encoded as Bool($\mathcal{C}$) formulas.

Definition 2 (Encoding of Büchi Automata). Let $V = \{x_1, \ldots, x_n\}$ be a set of typed variables, $\mathcal{B} = \langle \Sigma, Q, \Delta, Q^0, F \rangle$ be a Büchi automaton with labels Σ in Bool($\mathcal{C}$), and pc be a variable (not in V), which is interpreted over the finite set of locations Q of the Büchi automaton. For a given integer k, we obtain, as in Definition 1, families of variables $x_i[j]$, $pc[j]$ ($1 \leq i \leq n$, $0 \leq j \leq k$) for representing the jth state of $\mathcal{B}$ in a run of length k. Furthermore, the transition relation of $\mathcal{B}$ is encoded in terms of the $\mathcal{C}$-*program* $\mathcal{B}_M$ over the set of variables $\{pc\} \cup V$, and $[\![\mathcal{B}_M]\!]_k$ denotes the encoding of this program as in Definition 1. Now, given an encoding of the acceptance condition

$$acc(\mathcal{B})_k \;:=\; \bigvee_{j=0}^{k-1} \left(pc[k] = pc[j] \,\wedge\, \bigwedge_{v=1}^{n} x_v[k] = x_v[j] \,\wedge\, \Big(\bigvee_{l=j+1}^{k} \bigvee_{f \in F} pc[l] = f \Big) \right)$$

the k-th unfolding of $\mathcal{B}$ is defined by $[\![\mathcal{B}]\!]_k := [\![\mathcal{B}_M]\!]_k \wedge acc(\mathcal{B})_k$.

An LTL($\mathcal{C}$) formula is said to be **R-free** (**U-free**) iff there is an equivalent formula (in negation normal form) not containing the operator **R** (**U**). Note that **U**-free formulas correspond to the notion of *syntactic safety formulas* [28, 15]. Now, it can be directly observed from the semantics of LTL($\mathcal{C}$) formulas that every **R**-free formula can be translated into an automaton over finite words that accepts a prefix of all infinite paths satisfying the given formula.

Definition 3. Given an automaton $\mathcal{B}$ over finite words and the notation as in Definition 2, the encoding of the k-ary unfolding of $\mathcal{B}$ is given by $[\![\mathcal{B}_M]\!]_k \wedge acc(\mathcal{B})_k$ with the acceptance condition

$$acc(\mathcal{B})_k \;:=\; \bigvee_{j=0}^{k} \bigvee_{f \in F} pc[j] = f \;.$$

Consider the problem of finding a counterexample of length $k = 2$ to the hypothesis that our running example in Figure 2 satisfies $\mathbf{G}\,(x \geq 0)$. The negated property $\mathbf{F}\,(x < 0)$ is an **R**-free formula, and the corresponding automaton $\mathcal{B}$ over finite words is displayed in Figure 3 (l_1 is an accepting state.).

This automaton is translated, according to Definition 3, into the formula

$$[\![\mathcal{B}]\!]_2 \;:=\; I(\mathcal{B}) \wedge T_0(\mathcal{B}) \wedge T_1(\mathcal{B}) \wedge acc(\mathcal{B})_2 \;. \qquad (**)$$

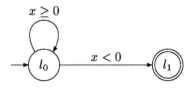

Fig. 3. Automaton for $\mathbf{F}\,(x < 0)$.

The variables $pc[j]$ and $x[j]$ $(j = 0, 1, 2)$ are used to represent the first three states in a run.

$$I(\mathcal{B}) := pc[0] = l_0$$
$$T_0(\mathcal{B}) := (pc[0] = l_0 \wedge x[0] \geq 0 \wedge pc[1] = l_0) \otimes (pc[0] = l_0 \wedge x[0] < 0 \wedge pc[1] = l_1)$$
$$T_1(\mathcal{B}) := (pc[1] = l_0 \wedge x[1] \geq 0 \wedge pc[2] = l_0) \otimes (pc[1] = l_0 \wedge x[1] < 0 \wedge pc[2] = l_1)$$
$$acc(\mathcal{B})_2 := pc[0] = l_1 \vee pc[1] = l_1 \vee pc[2] = l_1$$

The bounded model checking problem $[\![simple]\!]_2 \wedge [\![\mathcal{B}]\!]_2$ for the *simple* program is obtained by conjoining the formulas $(*)$ and $(**)$. Altogether, we obtain the counterexample $(0, l) \to (m, \neg l) \to (-1, l)$ of length 2 for the property $\mathbf{G}\,(x \geq 0)$.

Theorem 2 (Soundness). Let $M \in \mathsf{Prg}(\mathcal{C})$ and $\varphi \in \mathsf{LTL}(\mathcal{C})$. If there exists a natural number k such that $[\![M, \varphi]\!]_k$ is satisfiable, then $M \not\models \varphi$.
Proof sketch. If $[\![M, \varphi]\!]_k$ is satisfiable, then so are $[\![\mathcal{B}]\!]_k$ and $[\![M]\!]_k$. From the satisfiability of $[\![\mathcal{B}]\!]_k$ it follows that there exists a path in the Büchi automaton $\mathcal{B}$ that accepts the negation of the formula φ.

In general, BMC over infinite-state systems is not complete. Consider, for example, the model checking problem $M \models \varphi$ for the program $M = \langle I, T \rangle$ over the variable $V = \{x\}$ with $I = (x = 0)$ and $T = (x' = x + 1)$ and the formula $\varphi = \mathbf{F}\,(x < 0)$. M can be seen as a one-counter automaton, where initially the value of the counter x is 0, and in every transition the value of x is incremented by 1. Obviously, it is the case that $M \not\models \varphi$, but there exists no $k \in \mathbb{N}$ such that the formula $[\![M, \varphi]\!]_k$ is satisfiable. Since $\neg\varphi$ is not an $\mathbf{R}$-free formula, the encoding of the Büchi automaton $\mathcal{B}_k$ must contain, by Definition 2, a finite accepting cycle, described by $pc[k] = pc[0] \wedge x[k] = x[0]$ or $pc[k] = pc[1] \wedge x[k] = x[1]$ etc. Such a cycle, however, does not exist, since the program M contains only one noncycling, infinite path, where the value of x increases in every step, that is $x[i + 1] = x[i] + 1$, forall $i \geq 0$.

Theorem 3 (Completeness for Finite States). Let M be a $\mathcal{C}$-*program* with a finite set of reachable states, φ be an $\mathsf{LTL}(\mathcal{C})$ formula φ, and k be a given bound; then: $M \not\models \varphi$ implies $\exists k \in \mathbb{N}.\ [\![M, \varphi]\!]_k$ is satisfiable.
Proof sketch. If $M \not\models \varphi$, then there is a path in M that falsifies the formula. Since the set of reachable states is finite, there is a finite k such that $[\![M, \varphi]\!]_k$ is satisfiable by construction.

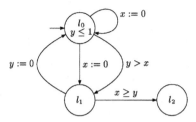

Fig. 4. Timed automata example.

For a **U**-free formula φ, the negation $\neg\varphi$ is **R**-free and can be encoded in terms of an automaton over finite words. Therefore, by considering only **U**-free properties one gets completeness also for programs with an infinite set of reachable states. A particularly interesting class of **U**-free formulas are invariant properties.

Theorem 4 (Completeness for Syntactic Safety Formulas). Let M be a $\mathcal{C}$-program, $\varphi \in \mathsf{LTL}(\mathcal{C})$ be a **U**-free property, and k be some given integer bound. Then $M \not\models \varphi$ implies $\exists k \in I\!N. [\![M, \varphi]\!]_k$ is satisfiable.
Proof sketch. If $M \not\models \varphi$ and φ is **U**-free then there is a finite prefix of a path of M that falsifies φ. Thus, by construction of $[\![M, \varphi]\!]_k$, there is a finite k such that $[\![M, \varphi]\!]_k$ is satisfiable.

This completeness result can easily be generalized to all safety properties [15] by observing that the prefixes violated by these properties can also be accepted by an automaton on finite words.

5 Examples

We demonstrate BMC over clock constraints and the theory of bitvectors by means of some simple but, we think, illustrative examples.

The timed automaton [1] in Figure 4 has two real-valued clocks x, y, the transitions are decorated with clock constraints and clock resets, and the invariant $y \leq 1$ in location l_0 specifies that the system may stay in l_0 only as long as the value of y does not exceed 1. The transitions can easily be described in terms of a program with linear arithmetic constraints over states (pc, x, y), where pc is interpreted over the set of locations $\{l_0, l_1, l_2\}$ and the clock variables x, y are interpreted over $I\!R_0^+$. Here we show only the encoding of the time *delay* steps.

$$delay(pc, x, y, pc', x', y') :=$$
$$\exists \delta \geq 0. ((pc = l_0 \Rightarrow y' \leq 1) \wedge (x' = x + \delta) \wedge (y' = y + \delta) \wedge (pc' = pc)).$$

This relation can easily be transformed into an equivalent quantifier-free formula. Now, assume the goal of falsifying the hypothesis that the timed automaton in Figure 4 satisfies the LTL($\mathcal{C}$) property $\varphi = (\mathbf{G} \neg l_2)$, that is, the automaton never reaches location l_2. Using the BMC procedure over linear arithmetic constraints one finds the counterexample

$$(l_0, x = 0, y = 0) \rightarrow (l_1, x = 0, y = 0) \rightarrow (l_2, x = 0, y = 0)$$

of length 2. By using Skolemization of the delay step δ instead of quantifier elimination, explicit constraints are synthesized for the corresponding delay steps in countertraces.

Now, we examine BMC over a theory $\mathcal{B}$ of bitvectors by encoding the shift register example in [3] as follows.

$$I_{BS}(x_n) := true \qquad T_{BS}(x_n, y_n) := (y_n = x_n[1 : n - 1] \star 1_1)$$

The variables x_n and y_n are interpreted over bitvectors of length n, $x_n[1 : n - 1]$ denotes extraction of bits 1 through $n - 1$, $\star$ denotes concatenation, and 0_n (1_n) is the constant bitvector of length n with all bits set to zero (one). In the initial state the content of the register x_n is arbitrary. Given the LTL($\mathcal{B}$) property $\varphi = \mathbf{F}(x_n = 0_n)$ and $k = 2$ the corresponding BMC problem reduces to showing satisfiability of the Bool($\mathcal{B}$) formula

$$(x_1 = x_0[1 : n - 1] \star 1_1) \wedge (x_2 = x_1[1 : n - 1] \star 1_1) \wedge$$
$$(x_0 \neq 0_n \vee x_1 \neq 0_n \vee x_2 \neq 0_n) \wedge (x_0 = x_2 \vee x_1 = x_2).$$

The variables x_0, x_1, x_2 are interpreted over bitvectors of size n, since they are used to represent the first three states in a run of the shift register. The satisfiability of this formula is established by choosing all unit literals to be true. Using theory-specific canonization (rewrite) steps for the bitvector theory $\mathcal{B}$ [18], we obtain an equation between variables x_2 and x_0.

$$x_2 = x_1[1 : n - 1] \star 1_1 = (x_0[1 : n - 1] \star 1_1)[1 : n - 1] \star 1_1 = x_0[2 : n - 1] \star 1_2$$

This canonization step corresponds to a symbolic simulation of depth 2 of the synchronous circuit. Now, in case the SAT solver decides the equation $x_0 = x_2$ to be true, the bitvector decision procedures are confronted with solving the equality $x_0 = x_0[2 : n - 1] \star 1_2$. The most general solution for x_0 is obtained using the solver in [18] and, by simple backsubstitution, one gets a satisfying assignment for x_0, x_1, x_2, which serves as a counterexample for the assertion that the shift register eventually is zero. The number of case splits is linear in the bound k, and, by leaving the word size uninterpreted, our procedure invalidates a family of shift registers without runtime penalties.

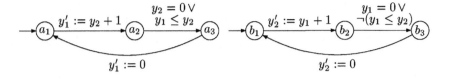

Fig. 5. Bakery Mutual Exclusion Protocol.

6 Efficiency Issues

The purpose of the experiments in this section is to identify useful concepts and techniques for obtaining efficient implementations of the lazy theorem proving approach. For these experiments we implemented several refinements of the basic lazy theorem proving algorithm from Section 3, using SAT solvers such as Chaff [19] and ICS [10] for deciding linear arithmetic constraints. These programs either returns $\bot$ in case the input Boolean constraint problem is unsatisfiable or an assignment for the variables. We describe some of our experiments using the Bakery mutual exclusion protocol (see Figure 5). Usually, the y_i counters are initialized with 0, but here we simultaneously consider a family of Bakery algorithms by relaxing the condition on initial values of the counters to $y_1 \geq 0 \wedge y_2 \geq 0$. Our experiments represent worst-case scenarios in that the corresponding BMC problems are all unsatisfiable. Thus, unsatisfiability of the BMC formula for a given k corresponds to a verification of the mutual exclusion property for paths of length $\leq k$.

Initial experiments with a direct implementation of the refinement algorithm in Figure 1 clearly show that this approach quickly becomes impractical. We identified two main reasons for this inefficiency.

First, for the interleaving semantics of the Bakery processes, usually only a small subset of assignments is needed for establishing satisfiability. This can already be demonstrated using the *simple* example in Figure 2. Suppose a satisfying assignment ν (counterexample) corresponding to executing the transition $l \longrightarrow \neg l$ with $x' = x + m$ in the first step; that is, $[\![l[0]]\!]_\nu$, $[\![x[1] = x[0] + m]\!]_\nu$ and $[\![\neg l[1]]\!]_\nu$ hold. Clearly, the value of the literals $x[0] \geq 0$, $x[1] = x[0] - m - 1$, and $x[1] = x[0]$ are *don't cares*, since they are associated with some other transition. Overly eager assignment of truth values to these constraints results in useless search. For example, if $[\![x[1] = x[0]]\!]_\nu$ holds, then an inconsistency is detected, since $m > 0$, and $x[1] = x[0] + m \neq x[0]$. Consequently, the assignment ν is discarded and the search continues. To remedy the situation we analyze the structure of the formula before converting it to CNF, and use this information to assign *don't care* values to literals corresponding to unfired transitions in each step.

Second, the convergence of the refinement process must be accelerated by finding concise overapproximations $explain(C)$ of the minimal set of inconsistent constraints C corresponding to a given Boolean assignment. There is an obvious trade-off between the conciseness of this approximation and the cost for computing it. We are proposing an algorithm for finding such an overapproxi-

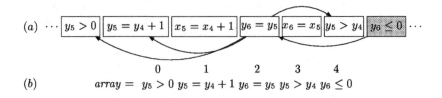

Fig. 6. Trace for linear time *explain* function.

mation based on rerunning the decision procedures $O(m \times n)$ times, where m is some given upper bound on the number of iterations (see below) and n is the number of given constraints.

The run in Figure 6 illustrates this procedure. The constraints in Figure 6.(a) are asserted to ICS from left-to-right. Since ICS detects a conflict when asserting $y_6 \leq 0$, this constraint is in the minimal inconsistent set. Now, an overapproximation of the minimal inconsistent sets is produced by connecting constraints with common variables (Figure 6.(a)). This overapproximation is iteratively refined by collecting the constraints in an array as illustrated in Figure 6.(b). Configurations consist of triples (C, l, h), where C is a set of constraints guaranteed to be in the minimal inconsistent set, and the integers l, h are the lower and upper bounds of constraint indices still under consideration. The initial configuration in our example is $(\{y_6 \leq 0\}, 0, 3)$. In each refinement step, we maintain the invariant that $C \cup \{array[i] \mid l \leq i \leq h\}$ is inconsistent. Given a configuration (C, l, h), individual constraints of index between l and h are added to C until an inconsistency is detected. In the first iteration of our running example, we process constraints from right-to-left, and an inconsistency is only detected when processing $y_5 > 0$. The new configuration $(\{y_6 \leq 0, y_5 > 0\}, 1, 3)$ is obtained by adding this constraint to the set of constraints already known to be in a minimal inconsistent set, by leaving h unchanged, and by setting l to the increment of the index of the new constraint. The order in which constraints are asserted is inverted after each iteration. Thus, in the next step in our example, we successively add constraints between 1 and 3 from left-to-right to the set $\{y_6 \leq 0, y_5 > 0\}$. An inconsistency is first detected when asserting $y_6 = y_5$ to this set, and the new configuration is obtained as $(\{y_6 \leq 0, y_5 > 0, y_6 = y_5\}, 1, 1)$, since the lower bound l is now left unchanged and the upper bound is set to the decrement of the index of the constraint for which the inconsistency has been detected. The procedure terminates if C in the current configuration is inconsistent or after m refinements. In our example, two refinement steps yield the minimal inconsistent set $\{y_5 > 0, y_6 = y_5, y_6 \leq 0\}$. In general, the number of assertions is linear in the number of constraints, and the algorithm returns the exact minimal set if its cardinality is less than or equal to the upper bound m of iterations.

Given these refinements to the satisfiability algorithm in Figure 1, we implemented an *offline* integration of Chaff with ICS, in which the SAT solver and the decision procedures are treated as black boxes, and both procedures are restarted in each lazy refinement step. Table 1 includes some statistics for three different configurations depending on whether *don't care* processing or the linear *explain* are enabled. For each configuration, we list the total time (in seconds) and the number of conflicts detected by the decision procedure. This table indicates that

Table 1. Offline lazy theorem proving ('-' is time $\geq$ 1800 secs).

depth	don't cares, no explain		no don't cares, explain		don't cares, explain	
	time	conflicts	time	conflicts	time	conflicts
5	0.71	66	45.23	577	0.31	16
6	2.36	132	83.32	855	0.32	18
7	12.03	340	286.81	1405	1.75	58
8	56.65	710	627.90	1942	2.90	73
9	230.88	1297	1321.57	2566	8.00	105
10	985.12	2296	-	-	15.28	185
15	-	-	-	-	511.12	646

the effort of assigning don't care values depending on the asynchronous nature of the program and the use of explain functions significantly improves performance.

Recall that the experiments so far represent worst-case scenarios in that the given formulas are unsatisfiable. For BMC problems with counterexamples, however, our procedure usually converges much faster. Consider, for example the mutual exclusion problem of the Bakery protocol with a guard $y_1 \geq y_2 - 1$ instead of $\neg(y_1 \leq y_2)$. The corresponding counterexample for $k = 5$ is produced in a fraction of a second after eight refinements.

$$(a_1, k_1, b_1, k_2) \qquad \rightarrow (a_2, 1 + k_2, b_1, k_2) \qquad \rightarrow (a_3, 1 + k_2, b_1, k_2) \rightarrow$$
$$(a_3, 1 + k_2, b_2, 2 + k_2) \rightarrow (a_3, 1 + k_2, b_3, 2 + k_2)$$

This counterexample actually represents a family of traces, since it is parameterized by the constants k_1 and k_2, with $k_1, k_2 \geq 0$, which have been introduced by the ICS decision procedures.

In the case of lazy theorem proving, the *offline* integration is particular expensive, since restarts implies the reconstruction of ICS logical contexts repetitively. Memoization of the decision procedure calls does not improve the situation significantly, since the assignments produced by Chaff in subsequent calls usually do not have long enough common prefixes. This observation, however, might not be generalizable, since it depends on the specific, randomized heuristics of Chaff for choosing variable assignments.

In an *online* integration, choices for propositional variable assignments are synchronized with extending the logical context of the decision procedures with the corresponding atoms. Detection of inconsistencies in the logical context of the decision procedures triggers backtracking in the search for variable assignments. Furthermore, detected inconsistencies are propagated to the propositional search engine by adding the corresponding inconsistency clause (or, using an explanation function, a good overapproximation of the minimally inconsistent set

Table 2. Online lazy theorem proving.

	no explain			explain		
depth	time	conflicts	calls to ICS	time	conflicts	calls to ICS
5	0.03	24	162	0.01	7	71
6	0.08	48	348	0.01	7	83
7	0.19	96	744	0.02	7	94
8	0.98	420	3426	0.05	29	461
9	2.78	936	7936	0.19	70	1205
10	8.60	2008	17567	0.26	85	1543
15	-	-	-	4.07	530	13468

of atoms in the logical context). Since state-of-the-art SAT solvers such as Chaff are missing the necessary API for realizing such an online integration, we developed a homegrown SAT solver which has most of the features of modern SAT solvers and integrated it with ICS. The results of using this online integration for the Bakery example can be found in Table 2 for two different configurations.[1] For each configuration, we list the total time (in seconds), the number of conflicts detected by ICS, and the total number of calls to ICS. Altogether, using an explanation facility clearly pays off in that the number of refinement iterations (conflicts) is reduced considerable.

7   Related Work

There has been much recent work in reducing the satisfiability problem of Boolean formulas over the theory of equality with uninterpreted function symbols to a SAT problem [5,12,23] using *eager* encodings of possible instances of equality axioms. In contrast, lazy theorem proving introduces the semantics of the formula constraints *on demand* by analyzing spurious counterexamples. Also, our procedure works uniformly for much richer sets of constraint theories. It would be interesting experimentally to compare the eager and the lazy approach, but benchmark suites (e.g. www.ece.cmu.edu/~mvelev) are currently only available as encodings of Boolean satisfiability problems.

In research that is most closely related to ours, Barrett, Dill, and Stump [2] describe an integration of Chaff with CVC by abstracting the Boolean constraint formula to a propositional approximation, then incrementally refining the approximation based on diagnosing conflicts using theorem proving, and finally adding the appropriate conflict clause to the propositional approximation. This integration corresponds directly to an online integration in the lazy theorem paradigm. Their approach to generate good explanations is different from ours in that they extend CVC with a capability of abstract proofs for overapproximating minimal sets of inconsistencies. Also, optimizations based on *don't cares* are not considered in [2]. The experimental results in [2] coincide with ours in

---

[1] The differences in the number of conflicts compared to Table 1 are due to the different heuristics of the SAT solvers used.

that they suggest that lazy theorem proving without explanations (there called the *naive* approach) and offline integration quickly become impractical. Using equivalence checking for pipelined microprocessors, speedups of several orders of magnitude over their earlier SVC system are obtained.

8 Conclusion

We developed a bounded model checking (BMC) procedure for infinite-state systems and linear temporal logic formulas with constraints based on a reduction to the satisfiability problem of Boolean constraint logic. This procedure is shown to be sound, and although incomplete in general, we establish completeness for invariant formulas. Since BMC problems are propositionally intensive, we propose a verification technique based on a *lazy* combination of a SAT solver with a constraint solver, which introduces only the portion of the semantics of constraints that is relevant for constructing a BMC counterexample.

We identified a number of concepts necessary for obtaining efficient implementations of lazy theorem proving. The first one is specialized to BMC for asynchronous systems in that we generate partial Boolean assignments based on the structure of program for restricting the search space of the SAT solver. Second, good approximations of minimal inconsistent sets of constraints at reasonable cost are essential. The proposed any-time algorithm uses a mixture of structural dependencies between constraints and a linear number of reruns of the decision procedure for refining overapproximations. Third, offline integration and restarting the SAT solver results in repetitive work for the decision procedures. Based on these observations we realized a lazy, online integration in which the construction of partial assignments in the Boolean domain is synchronized with the construction of a corresponding logical context for the constraint solver, and inconsistencies detected by the constraint solver are immediately propagated to the Boolean domain. First experimental results are very promising, and many standard engineering can be applied to significantly improve running times.

We barely scratched the surface of possible applications. Given the rich set of possible constraints, including constraints over uninterpreted function symbols, for example, our extended BMC methods seems to be suitable for model checking open systems, where environments are only partially specified. Also, it remains to be seen if BMC based on lazy theorem proving is a viable alternative to specialized model checking algorithms such as the ones for timed automata and extensions thereof for finding bugs, or even to AI planners dealing with resource constraints and domain-specific modeling.

Acknowledgements. We would like to thank the referees for their invaluable comments for improving this paper. S. Owre, J. Rushby, and N. Shankar provided many useful inputs.

References

1. R. Alur, C. Courcoubetis, and D. Dill. Model-checking for real-time systems. *5th Symp. on Logic in Computer Science (LICS 90)*, pages 414–425, 1990.
2. C. W. Barrett, D. L. Dill, and A. Stump. Checking Satisfiability of First-Order Formulas by Incremental Translation to SAT, 2002. To be presented at CAV 2002.
3. A. Biere, A. Cimatti, E. M. Clarke, and Y. Zh. Symbolic model checking without BDDs. *LNCS*, 1579, 1999.
4. R. E. Bryant. Graph-based algorithms for Boolean function manipulation. *IEEE Transactions on Computers*, C-35(8):677–691, August 1986.
5. R. E. Bryant, S. German, and M. N. Velev. Exploiting positive equality in a logic of equality with uninterpreted functions. *LNCS*, 1633:470–482, 1999.
6. Edmund M. Clarke, Orna Grumberg, Somesh Jha, Yuan Lu, and Helmut Veith. Counterexample-guided abstraction refinement. *LNCS*, 1855:154–169, 2000.
7. E.M. Clarke, A. Biere, R. Raimi, and Y. Zhu. Bounded model checking using satisfiability solving. *Formal Methods in System Design*, 19(1):7–34, 2001.
8. F. Copty, L. Fix, R. Fraer, E. Giunchiglia, G. Kamhi, A. Tacchella, and M.Y. Vardi. Benefits of bounded model checking in an industrial setting. *LNCS*, 2101:436–453, 2001.
9. Satyaki Das and David L. Dill. Successive approximation of abstract transition relations. In *Symposium on Logic in Computer Science*, pages 51–60. IEEE, 2001.
10. J.-C. Filliâtre, S. Owre, H. Rueß, and N. Shankar. ICS: Integrated Canonizer and Solver. *LNCS*, 2102:246–249, 2001.
11. Rob Gerth, Doron Peled, Moshe Vardi, and Pierre Wolper. Simple on-the-fly automatic verification of linear temporal logic. In *Protocol Specification Testing and Verification*, pages 3–18, Warsaw, Poland, 1995. Chapman & Hall.
12. A. Goel, K. Sajid, H. Zhou, and A. Aziz. BDD based procedures for a theory of equality with uninterpreted functions. *LNCS*, 1427:244–255, 1998.
13. T. A. Henzinger, X. Nicollin, J. Sifakis, and S. Yovine. Symbolic model checking for real-time systems. *Information and Computation*, 111(2):193–244, June 1994.
14. Thomas A. Henzinger, Ranjit Jhala, Rupak Majumdar, and Grégoire Sutre. Lazy abstraction. *ACM SIGPLAN Notices*, 31(1):58–70, 2002.
15. Orna Kupferman and Moshe Y. Vardi. Model checking of safety properties. *Formal Methods in System Design*, 19(3):291–314, 2001.
16. Yassine Lachnech, Saddek Bensalem, Sergey Berezin, and Sam Owre. Incremental verification by abstraction. *LNCS*, 2031:98–112, 2001.
17. M.O. Möller, H. Rueß, and M. Sorea. Predicate abstraction for dense real-time systems. *Electronic Notes in Theoretical Computer Science*, 65(6), 2002.
18. O. Möller and H. Rueß. Solving bit-vector equations. *LNCS*, 1522:36–48, 1998.
19. Matthew W. Moskewicz, Conor F. Madigan, Ying Zhao, Lintao Zhang, and Sharad Malik. Chaff: Engineering an Efficient SAT Solver. In *Proceedings of the 38th Design Automation Conference (DAC'01)*, June 2001.
20. G. Nelson and D. C. Oppen. Simplification by cooperating decision procedures. *ACM Transactions on Programming Languages and Systems*, 1(2):245–257, 1979.
21. S. Owre, J. M. Rushby, and N. Shankar. PVS: A prototype verification system. In *11th International Conference on Automated Deduction (CADE)*, volume 607 of *Lecture Notes in Artificial Intelligence*, pages 748–752. Springer-Verlag, 1992.
22. David A. Plaisted and Steven Greenbaum. A structure preserving clause form translation. *Journal of Symbolic Computation*, 2(3):293–304, September 1986.

23. A. Pnueli, Y. Rodeh, O. Shtrichman, and M. Siegel. Deciding equality formulas by small domains instantiations. *LNCS*, 1633:455–469, 1999.
24. H. Rueß and N. Shankar. Deconstructing Shostak. In *16th Symposium on Logic in Computer Science (LICS 2001)*. IEEE Press, June 2001.
25. Vlad Rusu and Eli Singerman. On proving safety properties by integrating static analysis, theorem proving and abstraction. *LNCS*, 1579:178–192, 1999.
26. H. Saïdi. Modular and incremental analysis of concurrent software systems. In *14th IEEE International Conference on Automated Software Engineering*, pages 92–101. IEEE Computer Society Press, 1999.
27. Robert Shostak. Deciding linear inequalities by computing loop residues. *Journal of the ACM*, 28(4):769–779, October 1981.
28. A. P. Sistla. Safety, liveness and fairness in temporal logic. *Formal Aspects of Computing*, 6(5):495–512, 1994.

Well-Foundedness Is Sufficient for Completeness of Ordered Paramodulation

Miquel Bofill[1] and Albert Rubio[2]*

[1] Universitat de Girona, Dept. IMA,
Lluís Santaló s/n, 17071 Girona, Spain
miquel.bofill@ima.udg.es
[2] Technical University of Catalonia, Dept. LSI,
Jordi Girona 1, 08034 Barcelona, Spain
rubio@lsi.upc.es

Abstract. For many years all known completeness results for Knuth-Bendix completion and ordered paramodulation required the term ordering $\succ$ to be well-founded, monotonic and total(izable) on ground terms. Then, it was shown that well-foundedness and the subterm property were enough for ensuring completeness of ordered paramodulation.

Here we show that the subterm property is not necessary either. By using a new restricted form of rewriting we obtain a completeness proof of ordered paramodulation for Horn clauses with equality where well-foundedness of the ordering suffices. Apart from the fundamental interest of this result, some potential applications motivating the interest of dropping the subterm property are given.

1 Introduction

Knuth-Bendix-like completion techniques and their extensions to ordered paramodulation for first-order clauses are among the most successful methods for automated deduction with equality [BG98,NR01]. For many years all known completeness results for Knuth-Bendix completion and ordered paramodulation required the term ordering $\succ$ to be well-founded, monotonic and total (or extendable to a total ordering) on ground terms [HR91,BDH86,BD94,BG94], until in [BGNR99], the monotonicity requirement was dropped and well-foundedness and the subterm property were shown to be sufficient (note that any such ordering can be totalized without loosing these two properties).

After this, the fundamental question arises whether more requirements can be dropped. In this paper we prove that for ordered paramodulation on Horn clauses with equality the subterm property can be dropped as well. Therefore only well-foundedness is required. These results are a new important step in the theory

---

* Both authors partially supported by the spanish CICYT project MAVERISH ref. TIC2001-2476-C03-01, M. Bofill is also supported by the spanish CICYT project CADVIAL ref. TIC2001-2392-C03-01 and A. Rubio is also supported by the spanish DURSI group 2001SGR 00254.

A. Voronkov (Ed.): CADE-18, LNAI 2392, pp. 456–470, 2002.

of paramodulation, which somehow shows the power of ordered paramodulation regardless of the properties of the ordering which is used and leaves as the last question whether even well-foundedness is necessary.

Apart from its theoretical value, there are at least two other potential applications of these results. The first one is in deduction modulo built-in equational theories E, since for many E, finding E-*compatible* orderings fulfilling the required properties is extremely complex (for example for the associative and commutative (AC) case) or even impossible (for instance in presence of idempotence axioms [BGNR99]). Requiring only well-foundedness allows us to consider any theory E, since there is always a well-founded E-compatible ordering (note that, as any set, the set of E-congruence classes admits a well-founded ordering).

The second potential application comes from the fact that, sometimes, a goal-oriented (ordered) paramodulation proof can only be obtained if the ordering contradicts the subterm property. Let us illustrate it with a simple example.

Example 1. Consider the following set of equations:

$$y^{log_y x} \simeq x$$
$$log_y y^x \simeq x$$
$$x^{y+z} \simeq x^y \cdot x^z$$

and the goal $\qquad log_a b + log_a c \simeq log_a(b \cdot c).$

With the following well-founded ordering

$$y^{log_y x} \succ x$$
$$x \succ log_y y^x \text{ if } x \text{ is not headed by } log$$
$$log_y y^x \succ x \qquad \text{if } x \text{ is headed by } log$$
$$x^{y+z} \succ x^y \cdot x^z$$

which contradicts the subterm property, we have a goal-oriented proof by ordered paramodulation (note that some variable renamings have been applied).

$$\boxed{x} \simeq log_y y^x \qquad \boxed{log_a b + log_a c} \not\simeq log_a(b \cdot c)$$

$$\boxed{x_1^{y_1+z_1}} \simeq x_1^{y_1} \cdot x_1^{z_1} \qquad log_y \boxed{y^{log_a b + log_a c}} \not\simeq log_a(b \cdot c)$$

$$\boxed{y_1^{log_{y_1} x_1}} \simeq x_1 \qquad log_y(\boxed{y^{log_a b}} \cdot y^{log_a c}) \not\simeq log_a(b \cdot c)$$

$$\boxed{y_1^{log_{y_1} x_1}} \simeq x_1 \qquad log_a(b \cdot \boxed{a^{log_a c}}) \not\simeq log_a(b \cdot c)$$

$$log_a(b \cdot c) \not\simeq log_a(b \cdot c)$$

□

Note that there is no such fully goal-oriented proof with respect to a well-founded ordering including the subterm relation, because no paramodulation step could be applied on the goal: for the first two equations, due to the subterm property, only the term on the left can be used and it does not unify with any subterm of the goal; for the last equation neither side overlaps with the goal.   □

In this paper we introduce techniques for dropping the subterm (as well as the monotonicity) requirement. Our technique (given in Sections 4 and 5) is a new variant of the model generation technique, where, surprisingly, the ground rewrite system R that defines the model may not be terminating. For this reason, we define a *new* restricted form of rewriting, called *blocked rewriting* ($\mathcal{B}$-rewriting for short), which is terminating by definition.

$\mathcal{B}$-rewriting works on *abstracted terms*, denoted by $t \cdot \gamma$, which are terms split into two parts: the *abstraction (or term) part* t and the *substitution part* γ, such that $t\gamma$ is a term (this formalism corresponds to the *closures* defined for clauses in [BGLS95]). No rewrite steps can be applied to the γ part and when we rewrite $t \cdot \gamma$ with a rule $l \to r$ at a non-variable position p in t we obtain $t[x]_p \cdot (\gamma \cup \{x \mapsto r\})$ for some fresh variable x. It is obvious that this rewrite relation terminates since each step strictly reduces the size of the non-variable part t.

Example 2. Consider the set of equations E containing only

$$g(a) \simeq a$$

and an ordering such that $a \succ g(a)$ and $g^k(a) \succ g^j(a)$ with $k \geq 2$ and $k > j \geq 0$. In this ordering the minimal term is $g(a)$.

If we close this set E with respect to the ordered paramodulation rule, we obtain a set of equations of the form

$$g^k(a) \simeq g^j(a) \text{ with } k > j \geq 0.$$

which are oriented as

$$a \to g(a)$$
$$g^k(a) \to g^j(a) \quad \text{for all } k \geq 2 \text{ and } k > j \geq 0$$

Then the following set R containing the two rules

$$a \to g(a)$$
$$g(g(a)) \to g(a)$$

is a confluent (although overlapping) rewrite system for $\mathcal{B}$-rewriting, and furthermore all equations in the closure can be proved by $\mathcal{B}$-rewriting using R. In particular, all $g^k(a) \simeq g^j(a)$ can be proved by joining both sides into the same abstracted term $x \cdot \{x \mapsto g(a)\}$. Therefore, for every consequence of E there is a $\mathcal{B}$-rewrite proof using R.   □

In our completeness proof a (possibly infinite) rewrite system like the R above is generated. Proving confluence of R is essential but, since the system may be overlapping, this property does not follow easily. Once we have proved it, we can show that there is a $\mathcal{B}$-rewrite proof with R for every consequence of the unit positive equations. Finally, this is used to prove the completeness of ordered paramodulation for first-order Horn clauses with eager *selection* of negative literals.

Besides the proof of confluence (which is the hardest and more technical part), the core of the proof is rather simple and similar to the one in [BGNR99], since it still uses induction on the $\mathcal{B}$-rewrite relation with R (which is well-founded) for the completeness result.

The paper is structured as follows. The next section provides the basic definitions. In Section 3 $\mathcal{B}$-rewriting is introduced and its main properties stated. Section 4 is devoted to the equational case. There, the original part of our proof technique is presented and the difficulties of proving the confluence of the generated rewrite system that defines the model are outlined. In section 5, completeness for Horn clauses is proved using the results obtained for the equational case. Finally in section 6 conclusions and future developments are discussed. All proofs can be found in [BR02].

2   Basic Notions

We use the standard definitions of [DJ90]. $T(\mathcal{F}, \mathcal{X})$ $(T(\mathcal{F}))$ is the set of (ground) terms over a set of symbols $\mathcal{F}$ and a denumerable set of variables $\mathcal{X}$ (over $\mathcal{F}$). By $vars(t)$ we denote the set of variables occurring in a term t. The size of a term t is denoted by $|t|$ and its size without counting the variables by $|t|_v$.

The subterm of t at *position* p is denoted by $t|_p$, the result of replacing $t|_p$ by s in t is denoted $t[s]_p$, and syntactic equality of terms is denoted by $\equiv$. Let t be a term in $T(\mathcal{F}, \mathcal{X})$ and M a set of terms in $T(\mathcal{F}, \mathcal{X})$. We denote by $P_M(t)$ the set of positions p of t s.t. there is some prefix p' of p s.t. $t|_{p'} \in M$, i.e. if $t|_p \in M$ then $P_M(t)$ includes p and all positions below p. By $P_\mathcal{X}(t)$ we denote the set of variable positions of t, i.e. $P_{vars(t)}(t)$.

If $\to$ is a binary relation, then $\leftarrow$ is its inverse, $\leftrightarrow$ is its symmetric closure, $\overset{+}{\to}$ is its transitive closure and $\overset{*}{\to}$ is its reflexive-transitive closure. We write $s \overset{!}{\to} t$ if $s \overset{*}{\to} t$ and there is no t' such that $t \to t'$. Then t is called *irreducible* and a *normal form* of s (wrt. $\to$). If a term s has exactly one normal form then it is denoted by $s!_\to$. The relation $\to$ is *well-founded* or *terminating* if there exists no infinite sequence $s_1 \to s_2 \to \ldots$ and it is *confluent* or *Church-Rosser* if the relation $\leftarrow^* \circ \to^*$ is contained in $\to^* \circ \leftarrow^*$. It is *locally confluent* if $\leftarrow \circ \to \subseteq \to^* \circ \leftarrow^*$. By Newman's lemma, terminating locally-confluent relations are confluent. A relation $\to$ on terms is *monotonic* if $s \to t$ implies $u[s]_p \to u[t]_p$ for all terms s, t and u and positions p. A *congruence* is a reflexive, symmetric, transitive and monotonic relation on terms.

An *equation* is a multiset of terms $\{s, t\}$, denoted $s \simeq t$ or, equivalently, $t \simeq s$. By $gnd(s \simeq t)$ we denote the set of ground instances of $s \simeq t$. Let E be a set of equations. By $gnd(E)$ we denote the set of ground instances of all equations in E.

A first-order clause is a pair of finite multisets of equations Γ (the *antecedent*) and Δ (the *succedent*), denoted by $\Gamma \to \Delta$. Equations in Γ are called *negative literals* and equations in Δ are called *positive literals*. A Horn clause is a clause with at most one positive literal. The empty clause $\square$ is a clause where both Γ and Δ are empty.

A *rewrite rule* is an ordered pair of terms (s, t), written $s \to t$, and a set of rewrite rules R is a *term rewrite system* (TRS). By $Left(R)$ and $Right(R)$ we denote, respectively, the set of left-hand sides of rules in R and the set of right-hand sides of rules in R. The rewrite relation with R on $T(\mathcal{F}, \mathcal{X})$, denoted $\to_R$, is the smallest monotonic relation such that $l\sigma \to_R r\sigma$ for all $l \to r \in R$ and all substitutions σ, and if $s \to_R t$ then we say that s *rewrites into* t with R. R is called terminating, confluent, etc. if $\to_R$ is.

A (strict partial) *ordering* on $T(\mathcal{F}, \mathcal{X})$ is an irreflexive transitive relation $\succ$. It fulfils the *subterm property* if $\succ \supseteq \rhd$, where $\rhd$ denotes the strict subterm ordering.

Definition 1. *A* west-ordering *is a well-founded ordering on $T(\mathcal{F})$ that fulfils the subterm property and that is total on $T(\mathcal{F})$ (it is called* west *after well-founded, subterm and total).*

Every well-founded ordering can be totalized [Wec91], and hence every well-founded ordering satisfying the subterm property can be extended to a west-ordering.

3 $\mathcal{B}$-Rewriting

Now we define a special kind of rewrite relation, called *blocked rewriting* ($\mathcal{B}$-rewriting for short), which is always terminating. This relation restricts standard rewriting by mainly forbidding rewrite steps on right-hand sides introduced by previous rewrite steps. Roughly speaking, after every rewrite step the introduced right-hand side becomes blocked.

In order to express this blocking we use *abstracted terms* which have variables in the blocked positions. The blocked part of the term is stored in a substitution.

In what follows we only consider ground term rewrite systems, which is the only case we need. However, all definitions can easily be extended to deal with a non-ground TRS.

Definition 2. *Let R be a TRS. Let γ be a ground substitution and s a linear term with $vars(s) \subseteq Dom(\gamma)$ and $Im(\gamma) \subseteq Right(R)$. Then $s \cdot \gamma$ is called an abstracted term wrt. R, and an* abstraction *of $s\gamma$ wrt. R.*

In the following, we write s instead of $s \cdot \gamma$ whenever γ denotes the empty substitution.

Two abstracted terms $s \cdot \gamma$ and $t \cdot \delta$ are equivalent, denoted by $s \cdot \gamma \equiv t \cdot \delta$, if s and t are equal up to renaming of variables and $s\gamma \equiv t\delta$.

An abstracted term $t' \cdot \delta$ is called an argument abstraction wrt. R of a term $t = f(t_1, \ldots, t_n)$ if $t' = f(t'_1, \ldots, t'_n)$ and every $t'_i \cdot \delta$ is an abstraction of t_i which cannot be further abstracted. We (ambiguously) write $arg\_abs(t, R)$ to denote any argument abstraction of t wrt. R, since all argument abstractions of t wrt. R are equivalent.

Given an abstracted term $s \cdot \gamma$ wrt. R, the set of *blocked positions* is the set of positions q in $s\gamma$ such that q is below or equal to a variable position p in s (i.e. $p \in P_\mathcal{X}(s)$).

Now, we can define $\mathcal{B}$-rewriting as a rewrite relation on abstracted terms.

Definition 3. *Let R be a TRS and $s \cdot \gamma$ an abstracted term wrt. R. Then $s \cdot \gamma \curvearrowright_R s[x]_p \cdot (\gamma \cup \{x \mapsto r\})$ if $s|_p \notin \mathcal{X}$, $x \in \mathcal{X} \setminus vars(s)$, and either $s\gamma|_p \to r \in R$ or $s\gamma|_p \equiv r \in Right(R)$.*

If $s\gamma|_p \equiv r \in Right(R)$ we refer to the rewrite step as an abstraction step.

We will ambiguosly write $s \cdot \gamma \curvearrowright_S t \cdot \delta$ to denote a non-abstraction step using a rule of a subset S of R.

$\mathcal{B}$-rewriting fulfils the following properties:

Lemma 1. *Let R be a TRS. Then $\overset{+}{\curvearrowright}_R$ is a well-founded ordering.*

Lemma 2. *Let R be a TRS. Then $\overset{+}{\curvearrowright}_R$ is compatible with the equivalence on abstracted terms, i.e., if $s' \cdot \gamma' \equiv s \cdot \gamma \overset{+}{\curvearrowright}_R t \cdot \delta \equiv t' \cdot \delta'$ then $s' \cdot \gamma' \overset{+}{\curvearrowright}_R t' \cdot \delta'$.*

Lemma 3. *Let R be a TRS. Then $\overset{+}{\curvearrowright}_R$ is a monotonic relation, in the sense that $s \cdot \gamma \overset{+}{\curvearrowright}_R t \cdot \delta$ implies $C[s]_p \cdot (\rho \cup \gamma) \overset{+}{\curvearrowright}_R C[t]_p \cdot (\rho \cup \delta)$, where $C \cdot \rho$ is an abstracted context (i.e. an abstracted term with a hole, also denoted by $C[\ ]_p \cdot \rho$).*

We must note that what identifies a rewrite step is the rule which is applied and the position where it is applied, regardless of the context. Similarly, a derivation is identified by a sequence of steps. However, we usually refer (ambiguously) to a derivation making the context where it is applied explicit. Then, given a TRS R, we refer to $s \cdot \gamma \overset{*}{\curvearrowright}_R t \cdot \delta$ as a derivation with $\curvearrowright_R$ of $t \cdot \delta$ from $s \cdot \gamma$.

Now we define two restricted versions of $\curvearrowright_R$, denoted by $\curvearrowright_{\underline{R}}$ and $\curvearrowright_{\overline{R}}$, which respectively consist of rewriting (by non-abstraction steps) only above blocked positions and only above non-blocked positions. Recall that the only forbidden steps for $\curvearrowright_R$ are the ones at or under blocked positions. For instance in the abstracted term $f(a, x) \cdot \{x \mapsto g(a)\}$, we can rewrite with $\curvearrowright_{\underline{R}}$ only at position λ and with $\curvearrowright_{\overline{R}}$ only at position 1.

Definition 4. *Let R be a TRS and $s \cdot \gamma$ an abstracted term wrt. R.*

We write $s \cdot \gamma \curvearrowright_{\underline{R}} s[x]_p \cdot (\gamma \cup \{x \mapsto r\})$ if $s \cdot \gamma \curvearrowright_R s[x]_p \cdot (\gamma \cup \{x \mapsto r\})$, $s\gamma|_p \to r \in R$ and $vars(s|_p) \neq \emptyset$.

We write $s \cdot \gamma \curvearrowright_{\overline{R}} s[x]_p \cdot (\gamma \cup \{x \mapsto r\})$ if $s \cdot \gamma \curvearrowright_R s[x]_p \cdot (\gamma \cup \{x \mapsto r\})$, $s\gamma|_p \to r \in R$ and $vars(s|_p) = \emptyset$.

Note that one relation is the complement of the other one if we restrict to non-abstraction steps.

4   Paramodulation with Equations

In the following, let $\succ$ be a given well-founded ordering (total) on ground terms.

Definition 5. *The inference rule of (equational) ordered paramodulation with respect to $\succ$ is:*

$$\frac{l \simeq r \qquad s \simeq t}{(s[r]_p \simeq t)\sigma}$$

where $\sigma = mgu(s|_p, l)$ is the most general unifier of $s|_p$ and l, where l is maximal in its premise (that is, for some ground substitution θ, it holds that $l\sigma\theta \succ r\sigma\theta$) and $s|_p$ is not a variable or, if $s|_p$ is a variable x, then $x \in vars(t)$, $p = \lambda$ and l is also a variable.

Note that this last condition implies that in very restrictive cases we have to perform an inference on a variable position. However, these potential inferences on variable positions are not prolific at all, since both s and l should be variables (with s occurring in t, which may happen since the ordering does not need to satisfy the subterm property). Hence the only possible inference has $r\sigma \simeq t$ as conclusion where σ is the variable renaming of l by s.

We associate a ground TRS $\vec{E}$ to a set of equations E.

Definition 6. *Let E be a set of equations. We define $\vec{E}$ as the ground TRS obtained by orienting wrt. $\succ$ the ground instances of all equations in E. That is,*

$$\vec{E} = \{s \to t \mid s \simeq t \in gnd(E) \wedge s \succ t\}.$$

Example 3. Following Example 2 in the introduction, as said, the closure by ordered paramodulation of the equation $a \simeq g(a)$, consists of all equations of the form $g^k(a) \simeq g^j(a)$ with $k > j \geq 0$. Then, with the considered well-founded ordering, $\vec{E}$ consists of the rules

$$a \to g(a)$$
$$g^k(a) \to g^j(a) \quad \text{for all } k \geq 2 \text{ and } k > j \geq 0$$

□

In the following we assume E to be a set of equations closed under ordered paramodulation with respect to a well-founded ordering $\succ$. We also assume that the variables of every equation are disjoint (we rename, with fresh variables, the variables occurring in the conclusion of every inference).

Definition 7. *Let $\succ_{\rhd}$ be an arbitrary west-ordering on $T(\mathcal{F})$, and $\succ$ the well-founded ordering used in the paramodulation rule. We define the ordering $\succ_E$ on $\vec{E}$ as follows: given two rules $l \to r$ and $l' \to r'$ in $\vec{E}$, we have $l \to r \succ_E l' \to r'$ if and only if $l \succ_{\rhd} l'$, or $l \equiv l'$ and $r \succ r'$.*

Since $\succ_E$ is well-founded, we can now define, by induction on $\succ_E$, a ground TRS $\mathcal{R}$ *generated* by $\vec{E}$, and such that $\mathcal{R} \subseteq \vec{E}$. The *blockable-terms*, or simply $\mathcal{B}$-*terms*, are all terms that are right-hand sides of rules in $\mathcal{R}$.

Definition 8. *A rule e of the form $s \to t$ in $\vec{E}$ generates the rule $s \to t$ if*

1. *s is irreducible by $\mathcal{R}^e$ at positions not in $P_{\mathcal{B}^e}(s)$ and*
2. *t is irreducible by $\mathcal{R}^e$ at positions not in $P_{\mathcal{B}^e}(t)$.*

where $\mathcal{R}^e$ is the set of rules generated by all rules e' in $\vec{E}$ such that $e \succ_E e'$, and $\mathcal{B}^e = Right(\mathcal{R}^e)$. We denote by $\mathcal{R}$ the set of rules generated by all rules in $\vec{E}$, and we define $\mathcal{B} = Right(\mathcal{R})$ as the set of $\mathcal{B}$-terms.

We define the $\mathcal{B}$-positions of t as all positions in $P_{\mathcal{B}}(t)$ and the non-$\mathcal{B}$-positions of t as all other positions of t.

We denote by $\mathcal{B}^{\lhd s}$ the set of terms t in $\mathcal{B}$ s.t. $s \rhd t$.

Using a west-ordering (which includes the subterm relation) for comparing the left-hand sides of the rules is crucial in order to ensure that a rule in $\vec{E}$ is included in $\mathcal{R}$ if and only if it is irreducible at non-$\mathcal{B}$-positions by the other rules in $\mathcal{R}$.

The way we define $\mathcal{R}$ is quite similar to the definition in [BG94] and especially the one in [BGNR99]. The main difference is that only non-$\mathcal{B}$-positions are required to be irreducible. As a consequence $\mathcal{R}$ can be non-terminating and overlapping. However, if the ordering $\succ$ is a west-ordering, i.e. it fulfils the subterm property as well, taking $\succ_{\rhd}$ as $\succ$, the generated $\mathcal{R}$ coincides with the rewrite system generated in [BGNR99]. Note that in this case the right-hand sides of $\mathcal{R}$ are irreducible, which makes the fact that we only consider non-$\mathcal{B}$-positions irrelevant.

Example 4. For the closed set of equations in Example 3, $\mathcal{R}$ consists of the following two rules:

$$a \to g(a)$$
$$g(g(a)) \to g(a)$$

Definition 9. *By $\vec{E}_{\mathcal{B}}$ we denote the subset of rules $l \to r$ in $\vec{E}$ s.t. $r \in \mathcal{B}$.*

Again following the example, $\vec{E}_{\mathcal{B}}$ includes the rules

$$a \to g(a)$$
$$g^k(a) \to g(a) \quad \text{for all } k \geq 2$$

The following lemmas state several relevant properties of $\mathcal{R}$, $\vec{E}_{\mathcal{B}}$ and $\mathcal{B}$, which will be used in the confluence proof, and in particular to show the so-called *return property*.

Lemma 4 roughly states that if a term is reducible (at non-$\mathcal{B}$-positions) at some point of the construction of $\mathcal{R}$ then it will stay irreducible from this point on. As a consequence all rules that have not been included in $\mathcal{R}$ are reducible at some non-$\mathcal{B}$-position by $\mathcal{R}$. In particular it happens for the left-hand sides of rules in $\vec{E}_{\mathcal{B}} \setminus \mathcal{R}$ (Lemma 5).

Lemma 4. *Let t be a term in $T(\mathcal{F})$ which is reducible by a rule $l \to r \in \mathcal{R}^e$ at positions not in $P_{\mathcal{B}^e}(t)$, for some rule e in $\vec{E}$. Then t is reducible by $l \to r$ at positions not in $P_{\mathcal{B}^d}(t)$ for all $d \succ_E e$ in $\vec{E}$.*

Lemma 5. *If $l \to r$ is a rule in $\vec{E}_{\mathcal{B}} \setminus \mathcal{R}$ then l is reducible by $\mathcal{R}$ at some non-$\mathcal{B}$-position.*

From these two previous lemmas we can infer the following property on $\mathcal{B}$-terms.

Lemma 6. *Let t be a term in $\mathcal{B}$. Then $t \notin Left(\vec{E}_{\mathcal{B}})$.*

Therefore it follows that there are no two different rules in $\vec{E}_{\mathcal{B}}$ with the same left-hand side (by showing contradiction with the previous lemma after applying a paramodulation step between the left-hand sides of both rules).

Finally all these previous properties let us prove the following property, which precisely[1] characterizes $\mathcal{R}$ in terms of $\vec{E}_{\mathcal{B}}$ and $\mathcal{B}$.

Lemma 7. *Let $l \to r$ be a rule in $\vec{E}_{\mathcal{B}}$. Then $l \to r \in \mathcal{R}$ if and only if l is irreducible by $\vec{E}_{\mathcal{B}}$ at every non-$\mathcal{B}$-position different from λ.*

This property generalizes the notion in [BGNR99] of irreducibility of rules of the ground TRS that defines the model. Here irreducibility amounts to irreducibility at non-$\mathcal{B}$-positions of the left and right-hand sides. Note that, in particular, if the right-hand sides of rules in $\mathcal{R}$ are irreducible by $\mathcal{R}$, then left-hand sides are irreducible as well, and both notions of irreducibility coincide.

4.1   The Return Property

In this section we prove the so-called *return property* which roughly states that if we reduce a $\mathcal{B}$-term t into a term u then there is a rewrite sequence from u to t again (without reducing any $\mathcal{B}$-subterm). This property is crucial to prove that $\mathcal{R}$ is confluent.

The intuition behind this property (at the ground level) comes from the fact that t is minimal wrt. $\succ$, and that moreover ordered paramodulation gives us $t_1 \simeq t_n$ for any chain $t_1 \overset{\succ}{\simeq} t_2 \cdots \overset{\succ}{\simeq} t_n$ of equations. Then, if t_n is minimal wrt. $\succ$ and it is reducible by some rule, for instance $t_1 \to t_n$ itself, at some position $p \neq \lambda$ (which may happen since $\succ$ can contradict the subterm property), we can obtain $t_1 \simeq t_n[t_n]_p$ by an ordered paramodulation step, which gives us that $t_n[t_n]_p$ is in the same chain of equations and, hence, $t_n[t_n]_p \overset{\succ}{\simeq} t_n$ is in the closure as well. In the example, since we have $a \overset{\succ}{\simeq} g(a)$ with $g(a)$ minimal and $g(a)$ reducible by $a \to g(a)$, we obtain $a \simeq g(g(a))$ and hence $g(g(a)) \overset{\succ}{\simeq} g(a)$. Thus if we reduce $g(a)$ with $a \to g(a)$, we can return to $g(a)$ using $g(g(a)) \to g(a)$.

Thanks to this return property, t_n can be chosen as a representative (not a normal form, since it can be reducible) of all $t_1, \ldots, t_n$. Moreover for every one

---

[1] Note that, by definition of $\mathcal{R}$ and $\vec{E}_{\mathcal{B}}$, we have $\mathcal{R} \subseteq \vec{E}_{\mathcal{B}}$.

of these terms t_i the representative can be obtained by an innermost rewrite sequence consisting in replacing every reducible subterm by its representative. These representatives are the $\mathcal{B}$-terms.

As usual, the proof becomes rather technical due to the reductions applied at positions that are below a variable in the equation in E which has generated the rule $l \rightarrow t_n$ in $\mathcal{R}$ (recall that the $\mathcal{B}$-terms are the right-hand sides of rules in $\mathcal{R}$). For this reason, many times we have to reduce in one shot all redexes involving the same subterm. This is denoted by a kind of parallel rewriting.

Now, we will give the main definitions and lemmas which allow us to prove the return property (all proofs can be found in [BR02]). First we define the set of reducible positions with respect to a given reduction relation.

Definition 10. *Let R be a TRS. Let $\curvearrowright$ denote a binary relation on abstracted terms wrt. R. And let $s \cdot \gamma$ be an abstracted term wrt. R. Then $red\_pos(s \cdot \gamma, \curvearrowright)$ denotes the set of positions $\bigcup_{t \cdot \delta} P_{\mathcal{X}}(t) \setminus P_{\mathcal{X}}(s)$ for all $t \cdot \delta$ such that $s \cdot \gamma \curvearrowright t \cdot \delta$.*

Definition 12 establishes a kind of innermost rewrite notion, which fairly mimics the aforementioned process for obtaining the representative of a given term. Since this special rewriting strategy is intended to be used in the proof of the return property, we are obliged to define it not only as an innermost, but also as a kind of parallel rewrite notion (Definition 11) in order to express substitution replacements at the non-ground level. Fortunately, due to the parallel rewriting strategy, every *illegal* subderivation (that is, a subderivation at or below a $\mathcal{B}$-position) can be omitted by applying the return property by induction on smaller $\mathcal{B}$-subterms (this is mainly what Lemma 9 states).

Definition 11. *Let R be a TRS with non-overlapped left-hand sides. Let $\curvearrowright$ denote a binary relation on abstracted terms wrt. R, such that $\curvearrowright \subseteq \curvearrowright_R$. We write $s \cdot \gamma \overset{\parallel}{\curvearrowright} t \cdot \delta$ if there is a derivation D of the form $s \cdot \gamma \overset{+}{\curvearrowright} t \cdot \delta$ and $t|_p \in \mathcal{X}$ for all $p \in red\_pos(s \cdot \gamma, \curvearrowright)$.*
Note that requiring $t|_p \in \mathcal{X}$ implies p to be a valid position in t and hence the rewrite steps not being overlapped.

By definition, every rewrite step with $\overset{\parallel}{\curvearrowright}$ represents a rewrite sequence with $\curvearrowright$.

Definition 12. *Let R be a TRS. Let $u \cdot \gamma$ be an abstracted term wrt. R. We write $u \cdot \gamma \leadsto_R v \cdot \delta$ if $u \cdot \gamma \overset{\parallel}{\curvearrowright}_{\{l \rightarrow r\}} v \cdot \delta$ with $l \rightarrow r \in R$, $v \notin \mathcal{X}$, and there is no rule $s \rightarrow t \in R$ with $l \rhd s$ such that $u \cdot \gamma \curvearrowright_{\{s \rightarrow t\}} w \cdot \rho$.*
In this case we say that $l \rightarrow r$ reduces $u \cdot \gamma$ wrt. $\leadsto_R$, and we refer to any derivation $u \cdot \gamma \overset{+}{\curvearrowright}_{\{l \rightarrow r\}} v \cdot \delta$ which is equivalent to $u \cdot \gamma \overset{\parallel}{\curvearrowright}_{\{l \rightarrow r\}} v \cdot \delta$ as a derivation with $\curvearrowright_R$ equivalent to $s \cdot \gamma \leadsto_R v \cdot \delta$.

Again, by definition, every non-empty rewrite sequence with $\leadsto_R$ (i.e. $u \cdot \gamma \overset{+}{\leadsto}_R w \cdot \rho$) represents a rewrite sequence with $\curvearrowright_R$ (i.e. $u \cdot \gamma \overset{+}{\curvearrowright}_R w \cdot \rho$). If D is a rewrite sequence which includes steps with $\curvearrowright_R$ and $\leadsto_R$ for some TRS R, we will write $D(\curvearrowright_R)$ to denote the corresponding rewrite sequence with only $\curvearrowright_R$ steps.

Lemma 8 is a rather simple but useful lemma, since it allows us to guarantee that during the transformation of a $\mathcal{B}$-term t towards itself in the proof of the return property, no tautology of the form $t \simeq t$ is obtained at the equational level till the last step. It is very important to show that we get back to t at the last step, since then all *illegal* steps on smaller $\mathcal{B}$-subterms are guaranteed to be already *repaired* and hence they can be omitted, as Lemma 9 states. Recall that $arg\_abs(t, R)$ is the result of abstracting as much as possible the arguments of t wrt. R (Definition 2), which implies that all proper $\mathcal{B}$-subterms of t are in the substitution part and, hence, blocked.

Lemma 8. *Let t be a term in $T(\mathcal{F})$ and p a position not in $P_{\mathcal{B}^{\triangleleft t}}(t)$. If $t \curvearrowright_{\vec{E}_{\mathcal{B}}} t[x]_p \cdot \delta \overset{*}{\curvearrowright}_{\vec{E}_{\mathcal{B}}} t' \cdot \gamma$ and $t' \notin \mathcal{X}$ then $t'\gamma \not\equiv t$.*

Lemma 9. *Let t be a term in $\mathcal{B}$. Let $\mathcal{S}$ be a subset of $\vec{E}_{\mathcal{B}}$ with non-overlapped left-hand sides. Let D be a rewrite sequence of the form $t \overset{!}{\curvearrowright_{\mathcal{S}}} t_1 \cdot \rho \overset{!}{\leadsto}_{\vec{E}_{\mathcal{B}}} t_m \cdot \beta$. Then there is a rewrite sequence D' of the form $arg\_abs(t, \mathcal{R}) \overset{*}{\curvearrowright}_{\vec{E}_{\mathcal{B}}} t'_m \cdot \beta'$ with $t'_m\beta' \equiv t_m\beta$ consisting of the steps in $D(\curvearrowright_{\vec{E}_{\mathcal{B}}})$ which are applied at positions not in $P_{\mathcal{B}^{\triangleleft t}}(t)$.*

The following lemma establishes the return property of $\mathcal{B}$-terms for rewrite sequences using $\vec{E}_{\mathcal{B}}$. Its proof, although based on the relatively simple intuition given at the beginning of this subsection, is quite long and technical, due mainly to the parallel rewriting issue combined with the need of explicity constructing a fair and complete return path to the initial term while avoiding tautologies.

We must point out that, although our aim is to prove the return property for rewrite sequences using $\mathcal{R}$ (Theorem 1), this weaker lemma is necessary since sometimes illegal steps can only be repaired by using rules in $\vec{E}_{\mathcal{B}} \setminus \mathcal{R}$.

Lemma 10. *Let t be a term in $\mathcal{B}$. Let $\mathcal{S}$ be a non-empty subset of $\vec{E}_{\mathcal{B}}$ with non-overlapped left-hand sides. If $t \overset{!}{\curvearrowright_{\mathcal{S}}} t_1 \cdot \rho \overset{!}{\leadsto}_{\vec{E}_{\mathcal{B}}} t_m \cdot \beta$ then $t_m\beta \equiv t$ or $t_m\beta \to t \in \vec{E}_{\mathcal{B}}$.*

Now, roughly we have to go from the return property with $\vec{E}_{\mathcal{B}}$ to the return property with $\mathcal{R}$. To this end we show that for some particular abstracted terms, the so-called *innermost reduced terms*, innermost rewrite sequences with $\curvearrowright_{\vec{E}_{\mathcal{B}}}$ are in fact rewrite sequences with $\curvearrowright_{\mathcal{R}}$ and preserve the innermost reduction property of the terms (Lemma 11). The proof of this lemma is based on Lemma 7.

Definition 13. *Let $s \cdot \gamma$ be an abstracted term wrt. $\mathcal{R}$. We say that $s \cdot \gamma$ is innermost reduced if there is no position $p \in red\_pos(s \cdot \gamma, \curvearrowright_{\vec{E}_{\mathcal{B}}})$ (i.e. redex in $s \cdot \gamma$) with $vars(s|_p) = \emptyset$ (i.e. which has never been reduced inside).*

Lemma 11. *Let $s \cdot \gamma$ be an abstracted term wrt. $\mathcal{R}$ which is innermost reduced and let D an innermost rewrite sequence of the form $s \cdot \gamma \overset{+}{\curvearrowright}_{\vec{E}_{\mathcal{B}}} t \cdot \delta$. Then D is a rewrite sequence with $\curvearrowright_{\mathcal{R}}$ and $t \cdot \delta$ is innermost reduced.*

Finally we obtain the return property of $\mathcal{B}$-terms for rewrite sequences using $\mathcal{R}$ by combining Lemmas 9 and 10: by carefully choosing the subset $\mathcal{S}$ of $\vec{E}_\mathcal{B}$ (and, in fact, of $\mathcal{R}$) for these lemmas, we obtain an abstracted term $t_1 \cdot \rho$ which is innermost reduced, and then we can show, by Lemma 11, that we have a return rewrite sequence using only $\mathcal{R}$. Finally, we can remove some steps of the resulting sequence showing that we have the sequence with $\mathcal{R}$ from $arg\_abs(t, \mathcal{R})$ (with the required initial step) to an abstraction of t again.

Theorem 1. *(return property) Let t be a term in $\mathcal{B}$. If $arg\_abs(t, \mathcal{R}) \curvearrowright_\mathcal{R} u \cdot \gamma$ then $u \cdot \gamma \overset{!}{\curvearrowright}_\mathcal{R} v \cdot \rho$ with $v\rho \equiv t$.*

4.2   Rewrite Proofs for the Equational Case

First we prove the confluence of the rewrite relation $\overset{*}{\curvearrowright}_\mathcal{R}$, which is essential for showing that we have $\mathcal{B}$-rewrite proofs for all consequences of the set of equations.

Using the return property we can show that if we reduce an abstraction of a left-hand side in $\mathcal{R}$ (not at top position) then there is a $\mathcal{B}$-rewrite sequence going back to (another abstraction of) the left-hand side again. The proof is based on the fact that left-hand sides can only be reducible by the other rules at $\mathcal{B}$-positions.

Lemma 12. *Let $s \cdot \gamma$ be an abstracted term such that $s\gamma \in Left(\mathcal{R})$. If there is a position $p \neq \lambda$, such that $s|_p\gamma \equiv l$ for some rule $l \rightarrow r$ in $\mathcal{R}$, then $s[x]_p \cdot (\gamma \cup \{x \mapsto r\} \overset{+}{\curvearrowright}_\mathcal{R} s' \cdot \gamma'$, where s' is not a variable and $s\gamma \equiv s'\gamma'$.*

From the previous lemma we know that we can close the only potential "picks" that we may have with $\curvearrowright_\mathcal{R}$. Therefore, local confluence follows.

Lemma 13. *(Local confluence) Let $s \cdot \gamma$ be an abstracted term. If $t \cdot \gamma_1 \curvearrowright_\mathcal{R} s \cdot \gamma \curvearrowright_\mathcal{R} u \cdot \gamma_2$ then $t \cdot \gamma_1 \overset{*}{\curvearrowright}_\mathcal{R} v \cdot \delta \overset{*}{\curvearrowright}_\mathcal{R} u \cdot \gamma_2$ for some abstracted term $v \cdot \delta$.*

Since $\curvearrowright_\mathcal{R}$ is terminating and locally confluent, it is confluent.

Theorem 2. *(Confluence) $\curvearrowright_\mathcal{R}$ is confluent.*

Now we prove that all equations in E have a $\mathcal{B}$-rewrite proof using $\mathcal{R}$, which also implies that $\mathcal{R}^*$ is a model for E.

First, we show that there is a $\mathcal{B}$-rewrite proof for all instances which are irreducible (at non-$\mathcal{B}$-positions) in the substitution part. A substitution σ is irreducible by $\mathcal{R}$ at non-$\mathcal{B}$-positions in a term t if, for all variables $x \in Dom(\sigma)$, $x\sigma$ is irreducible by $\mathcal{R}$ at non-$\mathcal{B}$-positions or x occurs in t only at $\mathcal{B}$-positions of $t\sigma$. A substitution σ is irreducible by $\mathcal{R}$ at non-$\mathcal{B}$-positions in an equation $s \simeq t$ if σ is irreducible by $\mathcal{R}$ at non-$\mathcal{B}$-positions in s and t. This irreducibility property is roughly inherited by the conclusion in paramodulation inferences with rules in $\mathcal{R}$.

Lemma 14. *Let $s \simeq t$ be an equation in E and σ a substitution irreducible at non-$\mathcal{B}$-positions in $s \simeq t$. If $u_1 \cdot \gamma_1$ is an abstraction of $s\sigma$ wrt. $\mathcal{R}$ and $u_2 \cdot \gamma_2$ is an abstraction of $t\sigma$ wrt. $\mathcal{R}$ then $u_1 \cdot \gamma_1 \overset{*}{\curvearrowright}_\mathcal{R} u \cdot \gamma \overset{*}{\curvearrowright}_\mathcal{R} u_2 \cdot \gamma_2$ for some abstracted term $u \cdot \gamma$.*

Second, by first normalizing the substitution wrt. $\overset{*}{\curvearrowright}_{\mathcal{R}}$, which gives us an irreducible instance, we have that there are $\mathcal{B}$-rewrite proofs for all instances.

Lemma 15. *Let $s \simeq t$ be an equation in $gnd(E)$. Then $s \overset{*}{\curvearrowright}_{\mathcal{R}} u \cdot \gamma \overset{*}{\curvearrowleft}_{\mathcal{R}} t$ for some abstracted term $u \cdot \gamma$.*

The following theorem follows directly from the previous lemma. Note that rewriting with $\curvearrowright_{\mathcal{R}}$ provides also a rewrite sequence with $\rightarrow_{\mathcal{R}}$.

Theorem 3. $\mathcal{R}^* \models E$.

Now, together with confluence of $\overset{*}{\curvearrowright}_{\mathcal{R}}$, we can show that all consequences of E have a $\mathcal{B}$-rewrite proof.

Lemma 16. $E \models s \simeq t$ *implies* $s \overset{*}{\curvearrowright}_{\mathcal{R}} u \cdot \gamma \overset{*}{\curvearrowleft}_{\mathcal{R}} t$ *for some abstracted term $u \cdot \gamma$.*

This result implies that we have produced a Knuth-Bendix completion procedure for $\mathcal{B}$-rewriting, i.e. for ordered rewriting with well-founded orderings.

5   The Horn Case

In this section we generalise the results of the previous section to Horn clauses. In the following inference system it is assumed that in each clause with a non-empty antecedent one of the negative equations, the one that is written underlined, has been *selected* (see, e.g., [BG98]). In the Horn case this leads to positive unit strategies: left premises of paramodulations are unit clauses, and the only inferences involving non-unit clauses are equality resolution or paramodulation left on its selected equation.

Definition 14. *The inference system $\mathcal{H}$ for Horn clauses with respect to the well-founded ordering $\succ$ is defined as follows:*

paramodulation right:
$$\frac{\rightarrow l \simeq r \qquad \rightarrow s \simeq t}{\rightarrow (s[r]_p \simeq t)\sigma} \qquad \text{where } \sigma = mgu(l, s|_p)$$

paramodulation left:
$$\frac{\rightarrow l \simeq r \qquad \Gamma, \underline{s \simeq t} \rightarrow \Delta}{(\Gamma, s[r]_p \simeq t \rightarrow \Delta)\sigma} \qquad \text{where } \sigma = mgu(l, s|_p)$$

equality resolution:
$$\frac{\Gamma, \underline{s \simeq t} \rightarrow \Delta}{(\Gamma \rightarrow \Delta)\sigma} \qquad \text{where } \sigma = mgu(s, t)$$

where moreover in both paramodulation rules l is maximal in its premise (that is, for some ground substitution θ, it holds that $l\sigma\theta \succ r\sigma\theta$), and $s|_p$ is not a variable except in the paramodulation right inference when $s|_p = x \in vars(t)$, $p = \lambda$ and l is also a variable (as it happens in the equational case).

Definition 15. *Let S be a set of Horn clauses. We denote by E_S the subset of all positive unit clauses in S, that is, $E_S = \{ s \simeq t \mid \rightarrow s \simeq t \in S \}$, and we denote by $\mathcal{R}_S$ the set of rules generated by E_S as in Definition 8.*

First, it is shown that if S does not contain the empty clause then $\mathcal{R}_S^*$ is a model for all irreducible (at non-$\mathcal{B}$-positions) instances of clauses in S.

A substitution σ is irreducible by $\mathcal{R}_S$ at non-$\mathcal{B}$-positions in a clause $\Gamma \rightarrow \Delta$ if σ is irreducible at non-$\mathcal{B}$-positions in all equation $s \simeq t$ occurring in Γ or Δ.

Lemma 17. *Let S be a set of Horn clauses closed under $\mathcal{H}$. Then $\mathcal{R}_S^* \models C\sigma$ for all clauses C in S and substitutions σ that are irreducible by $\mathcal{R}_S$ at non-$\mathcal{B}$-positions in C.*

Now, as in the equational case, by first normalizing the substitution, we can prove the main theorem.

Theorem 4. *(refutation completeness of $\mathcal{H}$ for Horn clauses)*
Let S be a set of Horn clauses closed under $\mathcal{H}$. Then $\square \in S$ if, and only if, S is unsatisfiable.

6   Conclusion

In this paper we have proved that well-foundedness of the term ordering is sufficient for the completeness of ordered paramodulation on Horn clauses with equality.

Our completeness proof is based on the use of $\mathcal{B}$-rewriting, a new restricted form of rewriting which forbids further rewriting in the right-hand sides introduced in the rewrite steps. Interestingly, a by-product of our results is a Knuth-Bendix completion procedure for $\mathcal{B}$-rewriting, and its completeness.

$\mathcal{B}$-rewriting is closely related to the use of *basic* strategies [BGLS95,NR95], which we believe can be compatible with our results (the only part of the proof that may have some problems is the so called return property). In fact, we plan to work out the basicness results using the notion of *closures* defined for clauses in [BGLS95], since it coincides, at the level of clauses, with our abstracted terms (which, for now, we only use in the proofs).

We also have to carefully explore to what extent redundancy notions are applicable in our framework for ordered paramodulation. Note that from our proof only tautology deletion is clearly possible. Subsumption seems to be possible but it may interfere with the proof of the return property. Other redundancy notions like demodulation may only be applicable in very restricted cases.

Finally we have to study how to extend our results to full first-order clauses. Here the problem comes from the fact that, within the model generation proof technique, the completeness for general clauses is usually based on the fact that, at most one positive equation is satisfied in the generated (rewrite) model. Since, in our case, the ordering can contradict the subterm relation, we do not know how to obtain such a minimal model.

Acknowledgements. We would like to thank Robert Nieuwenhuis for his help in the development and the presentation of this work.

References

[BD94]   Leo Bachmair and Nachum Dershowitz. Equational inference, canonical proofs, and proof orderings. *J. of the Association for Computing Machinery*, 41(2):236–276, February 1994.

[BDH86]   Leo Bachmair, Nachum Dershowitz, and Jieh Hsiang. Orderings for equational proofs. In *First IEEE Symposium on Logic in Computer Science (LICS)*, pages 346–357, Cambridge, Massachusetts, USA, June 16–18, 1986. IEEE Computer Society Press.

[BG94]   Leo Bachmair and Harald Ganzinger. Rewrite-based equational theorem proving with selection and simplification. *Journal of Logic and Computation*, 4(3):217–247, 1994.

[BG98]   Leo Bachmair and Harald Ganzinger. Equational reasoning in saturation-based theorem proving. In W. Bibel and P. Schmitt, editors, *Automated Deduction: A Basis for Applications*. Kluwer, 1998.

[BGLS95] L. Bachmair, H. Ganzinger, Chr. Lynch, and W. Snyder. Basic paramodulation. *Information and Computation*, 121(2):172–192, 1995.

[BGNR99] Miquel Bofill, Guillem Godoy, Robert Nieuwenhuis, and Albert Rubio. Paramodulation with non-monotonic orderings. In *14th IEEE Symposium on Logic in Computer Science (LICS)*, pages 225–233, Trento, Italy, July 2–5, 1999.

[BR02]   Miquel Bofill and Albert Rubio. Well-foundedness is sufficient for completeness of Ordered Paramodulation. Long version, 2002. Available at www.lsi.upc.es/~albert/papers.html.

[DJ90]   Nachum Dershowitz and Jean-Pierre Jouannaud. Rewrite systems. In Jan van Leeuwen, editor, *Handbook of Theoretical Computer Science*, volume B: Formal Models and Semantics, chapter 6, pages 244–320. Elsevier Science Publishers B.V., Amsterdam, New York, Oxford, Tokyo, 1990.

[HR91]   J. Hsiang and M Rusinowitch. Proving refutational completeness of theorem proving strategies: the transfinite semantic tree method. *Journal of the ACM*, 38(3):559–587, July 1991.

[NR95]   Robert Nieuwenhuis and Albert Rubio. Theorem Proving with Ordering and Equality Constrained Clauses. *Journal of Symbolic Computation*, 19(4):321–351, April 1995.

[NR01]   Robert Nieuwenhuis and Albert Rubio. Paramodulation-based theorem proving. In J.A. Robinson and A. Voronkov, editors, *Handbook of Automated Reasoning*. Elsevier Science Publishers and MIT Press, 2001.

[Wec91]   W. Wechler. *Universal Algebra for Computer Scientists*, volume 25 of *EATCS Monographs on Theoretical Computer Science*. Springer-Verlag, Berlin, 1991.

Basic Syntactic Mutation*

Christopher Lynch and Barbara Morawska

Department of Mathematics and Computer Science Box 5815, Clarkson University,
Potsdam, NY 13699-5815, USA, {clynch,morawskb}@clarkson.edu

Abstract. We give a set of inference rules for E-unification, similar to
the inference rules for Syntactic Mutation. If the E is finitely saturated by
paramodulation, then we can block certain terms from further inferences.
Therefore, E-unification is decidable in NP, as is also the case for Basic
Narrowing. However, if we further restrict E, then our algorithm runs in
quadratic time, whereas Basic Narrowing does not become polynomial,
since it is still nondeterministic.

1 Introduction

E-unification is the problem of deciding if there are substitutions for variables
which make two terms equal modulo an equational theory E. E-unification occurs in many applications. Unfortunately, it is an undecidable problem in general.
We are interested in finding classes of equational theories where the E-unification
problem is decidable and tractable.

One method of attacking this problem is to examine equational theories which
are finitely saturated under a given set of inference rules. For example, if an
equational theory E is saturated under the Critical Pair rule of Knuth-Bendix
Completion[11], then the word problem is decidable for E, i.e., the problem of
deciding if two terms are equal modulo E. However, the E-unification problem
can still be undecidable for such theories.

The Critical Pair rule allows inferences only into a subterm of the larger side
of an equation. It can be extended to an inference rule called Paramodulation[3],
which allows inferences also into the smaller side of an equation. In [14], it is
shown that if E is saturated by Paramodulation then the E-unification problem
is decidable, and furthermore the decision procedure is in NP. In the Narrowing
procedure used in that paper, whenever Narrowing is performed, the smaller side
of the equation from E is marked in the conclusion and future inferences are not
allowed into the marked positions. Each inference "consumes" a position of the
goal, and therefore each Narrowing sequence halts in a linear number of steps.
Therefore, the procedure is in NP, since it is a non-deterministic procedure.

Here, we also consider equational theories E saturated under Paramodulation. The inference system we use is not Narrowing, but a variant of the Syntactic
Mutation inference rules of [10]. However, our inference rules are Basic, in the

---

* This work was supported by NSF grant number CCR-0098270 and ONR grant number N00014-01-1-0435.

A. Voronkov (Ed.): CADE-18, LNAI 2392, pp. 471–485, 2002.
© Springer-Verlag Berlin Heidelberg 2002

sense that we can mark terms from the equation from E, and not allow any more inferences into these terms. Therefore, just like in [14] we get an NP algorithm.

The important part of our paper is what comes next. We show that if E is further restricted (see section 6), then the algorithm is no longer nondeterministic. In fact, the algorithm runs in a linear number of steps, in $O(n^2)$ time. This is in contrast to Basic Narrowing, where these restrictions do not allow the procedure to become deterministic, so it does not become polynomial.[1]

We show an interesting connection to Syntactic Theories[10]. If E' is saturated by Paramodulation, then we can always quickly perform a few extra inference rules to E', yielding E. Then E is a resolvent presentation of a syntactic theory. Our results basically follow from the fact that E is resolvent, and there is an equivalent subset of E such that all proper subterms in E are reduced by E.

Most of this paper deals with the set of inference rules yielding the NP algorithm. The inference rules have been designed so that when we present the definition of restricted equations, the polynomial time result is almost immediate.

Our full proofs are given in [13].

2   Preliminaries

We assume standard definitions of term rewriting[1].

We assume we are given a set of variables and a set of uninterpreted function symbols of various arities. *Terms* are defined recursively in the following way: each variable is a term, and if $t_1, \cdots, t_n$ are terms, and f is of arity $n \geq 0$, then $f(t_1, \cdots, t_n)$ is a term, and f is the symbol at the *root* of $f(t_1, \cdots, t_n)$. A term (or any object) without variables is called *ground*. We consider equations of the form $s \approx t$, where s and t are terms. Let E be a set of equations, and $u \approx v$ be an equation, then we write $E \models u \approx v$ (or $u =_E v$) if $u \approx v$ is true in any model of E. If G is a set of equations, then $E \models G$ if and only if $E \models e$ for all e in G.

A *substitution* is a mapping from the set of variables to the set of terms, such that it is almost everywhere the identity. We identify a substitution with its homomorphic extension. If θ is a substitution then $Dom(\theta) = \{x \mid x\theta \neq x\}$ and $Range(\theta) = \{x\theta \mid x \in Dom(\theta)\}$. If R_E is a set of rewrite rules, then a substitution θ is R_E-reduced if all terms in $Range(\theta)$ are R_E-reduced.

A substitution θ is an *E-unifier* of an equation $u \approx v$ if $E \models u\theta \approx v\theta$. θ is an *E-unifier* of a set of equations G if θ is an E-unifier of all equations in G.

If σ and θ are substitutions, then we write $\sigma \leq_E \theta[Var(G)]$ if there is a substitution ρ such that $E \models x\sigma\rho \approx x\theta$ for all x appearing in G. If G is a set of equations, then a substitution θ is a *most general E-unifier of G*, written $\theta = mgu(G)$ if θ is an E-unifier of G, and for all E-unifiers σ of G, $\theta \leq_E \sigma[Var(G)]$. A complete set of E-unifiers of G, is a set of E-unifiers Θ of G such that for all E-unifiers σ of G, there is a θ in Θ such that $\theta \leq_E \sigma[Var(G)]$.

Given a unification problem we can either solve the unification problem or decide the unification problem. Given a goal G and a set of equations E, to

---

[1] See the example in Section 7.

solve the unification problem means to find a complete set of E-unifiers of G. To *decide* the unification problem simply means to answer true or false as to whether G has an E-unifier.

If E is a set of equations, then define $Gr(E)$ as the set of all ground instances of equations in E. We assume a reduction ordering $\prec$ on E, which is total on ground terms. In order to extend the ordering to equations, we treat equations as multisets of terms, i.e. $(s \approx t) \prec (u \approx v)$ iff $\{s, t\} \prec_{mul} \{u, v\}$.

3 Saturation

We will show that if E is a finite set of equations *saturated* by *Paramodulation*, then the E-unification problem is in NP. Paramodulation and saturation are defined below.

Paramodulation

$$\frac{u[s'] \approx v \quad s \approx t}{u[t]\sigma \approx v\sigma}$$

where $\sigma = mgu_\emptyset(s, s')$, $s\sigma \not\prec t\sigma$, and s' is not a variable.

This inference rule is an extension of the Critical Pair rule, which also allows inferences into the smaller side of an equation.

In a set E of ground equations, an inference is *redundant* if its conclusion follows from equations of E smaller than its largest premise. In a general set of equations E, an inference is *redundant* if it is redundant in $Gr(E)$. A set of equations is *saturated* if all of the inferences among equations in E are redundant. Automated theorem provers generally saturate a set of equations by some inference rule.

In this section we will inductively define a set R_E of rewrite rules from an equational theory E. This construction is originally from [2]. R_E will be used in the completeness proof of the inference system we give in the next section. A rule $s \to t$ is *reducible* by some set of rules T (T-*reducible*), if there is a rule $u \to v \in T$ different from $s \to t$ such that u is a subterm of s or t.

Definition 1. *For each $s \approx t \in Gr(E)$ such that $s \succ t$,*

- $I^{s \approx t} = \begin{cases} \emptyset, & \text{if } s \text{ or } t \text{ is reducible by } R^{\prec s \approx t} \\ \{s \to t\}, & \text{otherwise.} \end{cases}$
- $R^{\prec s \approx t} = \bigcup_{(u \approx v) \prec (s \approx t)} I^{u \approx v}$
- $R_E = \bigcup_{s \approx t \in Gr(E)} I^{s \approx t}$

Proposition 1. *The term rewriting system R_E is confluent and terminating.*

Lemma 1. *If $s \approx t$ is in $Gr(E)$ and $s \to t$ is R_E-reducible, then $s \to t$ is $R^{\prec s \approx t}$-reducible.*

Corollary 1. *If $s \to t$ is R_E-reducible and $s \approx t \in Gr(E)$, then $s \to t \notin R_E$.*

The corollary follows, because if $s \to t$ is R_E-reducible, then it is $R^{\prec s \approx t}$-reducible, and hence $I^{s \approx t} = \emptyset$. Therefore $s \to t \notin R_E$.

R_E^* denotes a congruence induced by R_E.

Theorem 1. *If E is saturated under Paramodulation, $s \approx t \in E$ and σ is a ground substitution, then $R_E^* \models s\sigma \approx t\sigma$.*

4   The *BSM* Algorithm

In this section we give an algorithm for E-unification. It is based on a set of inference rules and a selection rule. The algorithm is "don't know" non-deterministic, i.e. sometimes more than one inference rule has to be checked. Because we assume that all applicable equations will be used in inference rules, and since R_E is logically equivalent to E, we can assume in our completeness proof in the ground case that equations used are from R_E. Therefore, the proper subterms will be reduced by R_E, hence we can argue that no inferences will need to take place in those terms. Therefore, we will forbid inferences into them. This will restrict the search space, and allow us to show that the algorithm will halt. The terms of which we assume that their ground instances are reduced will be marked with boxes.

We define the Right-Hand-Side Critical Pair rule:

Right-Hand-Side Critical Pair (at the root)

$$\frac{s \approx t \quad u \approx v}{s\sigma \approx u\sigma}$$

where $s\sigma \not\prec t\sigma$, $u\sigma \not\prec v\sigma$, $\sigma \approx mgu_\emptyset(v,t)$ and $s\sigma \neq u\sigma$.

Define $RHS(E) = \{e \mid e$ is the conclusion of a Right-Hand-Side Critical Pair inference of two members of $E\} \cup E$. This is not a saturation, because conclusions of these inferences cannot be used in further inferences with Right-Hand-Side Critical Pair rule . Therefore, $RHS(E)$ can be computed in quadratic time and only adds a quadratic number of equations to E.

Note that, if $s\sigma\gamma \to t\sigma\gamma$ and $u\sigma\gamma \to v\sigma\gamma$, for some ground substitution γ, are in R_E, then all proper subterms in the equation $s\sigma\gamma \approx u\sigma\gamma$ are R_E-reduced. We will show that if E is saturated under Paramodulation, then $RHS(E)$ is a Syntactic Theory. This allow us to design a decision procedure for E-unification.

Theorem 2. *Let $E = RHS(E')$, where E' is finite and saturated by Paramodulation. Then, for each ground R_E-reduced equation $u \approx v$, such that $E \models u \approx v$ one of the following is true:*

1. $u = f(u_1, \dots, u_n)$, $v = f(v_1, \dots, v_n)$ and $E \models \bigcup_i^n u_i \approx v_i$
2. $u = f(u_1, \dots, u_n)$, $v = g(v_1, \dots, v_m)$ and there is $f(s_1, \dots, s_n) \approx t \in E$ and an R_E-reduced substitution σ, such that $E \models \bigcup_i^n u_i \approx s_i\sigma$ and $E \models g(v_1, \dots, v_m) \approx t\sigma$, and if $t = g(t_1, \dots, t_m)$, then $E \models \bigcup_j^m v_j \approx t_j\sigma$. All $s_i\sigma$, $t_j\sigma$ are R_E-reduced.

Proof. $E \models u \approx v$ and $u \approx v$ is a ground equation, hence also $R_E^* \models u \approx v$ (by Theorem 1). Consider the rewrite proof in R_E of $u \approx v$. All RHS of the rules in R_E are R_E-reduced, so in a rewrite proof of $t \xrightarrow{*} t'$ in R_E, for ground terms t and t', where t' is the normal form of t, there may be some steps reducing subterms of t and then at most one step at the root at the end, reducing the whole term to t'.

$$t = f(t_1, \dots, t_n) \xrightarrow{*} f(t'_1, \dots, t'_n) \xrightarrow{\text{root-step}} t'$$

Hence we have 3 cases here:

i. No step at the root of either side in the proof of $u \approx v$:

$$u = f(u_1, \dots, u_n) \xrightarrow{*} f(u'_1, \dots, u'_n) \xleftarrow{*} f(v_1, \dots, v_n) = v$$

Then $R_E \models u_i \xrightarrow{*} u'_i$ for all $i = 1, \dots, n$. Hence also $E \models u_i \approx u'_i$. $v_j \xrightarrow{*} u'_j \in R$ for all $j = 1, \dots, n$. Hence also $E \models v_j \approx u'_j$. Hence $E \models u_j \approx v_j$, for all $j = 1, \dots, n$ and the first statement of the theorem is true.

ii. One step at the root in the proof of $u \approx v$. Then $u = f(u_1, \dots, u_n)$ and $v = g(v_1, \dots, v_m)$. Suppose that there is a step at the root in the proof:

$$f(u_1, \dots, u_n) \xrightarrow{*} f(u'_1, \dots, u'_n) \xrightarrow{\text{root-step}} u'$$

where u' is an R_E-normal form of u, and there is no step at the root in the proof:

$$g(v_1, \dots, v_m) \xrightarrow{*} u'$$

Hence $u' = g(v'_1, \dots, v'_m)$ and the step at the root has the form: $f(u'_1, \dots, u'_n) \rightarrow g(v'_1, \dots, v'_m)$. Hence this must be a rule in R_E. Therefore there are two possibilities:

a) $f(s_1, \dots, s_n) \approx g(t_1, \dots, t_m) \in E$ and there is a R_E-reduced substitution σ, such that $s_i\sigma = u'_i$, for all $i = 1, \dots, n$, and $t_j\sigma = v'_j$, for all $j = 1, \dots, m$. Since $u_i \xrightarrow{*} u'_i$, for all $i = 1, \dots, n$, $E \models \bigcup_i^n u_i \approx s_i\sigma$.
Since $R_E \models g(v_1, \dots, v_m) \xrightarrow{*} g(v'_1, \dots, v'_m)$, then $E \models g(v_1, \dots, v_m) \approx g(t_1, \dots, t_m)\sigma$ and since $v_j \xrightarrow{*} v'_j$ for all $j = 1, \dots, m$, $E \models \bigcup_j^m v_j \approx t_j\sigma$,

b) $f(s_1, \dots, s_n) \approx x \in E$, and there is a R_E-reduced substitution σ, such that $s_i\sigma = u'_i$, for all $i = 1, \dots, n$, and $x\sigma = g(v'_1, \dots, v'_m)$.
Since $u_i \xrightarrow{*} u'_i$, for all $i = 1, \dots, n$, $E \models \bigcup_i^n u_i \approx s_i\sigma$. Since $R_E \models g(v_1, \dots, v_m) \xrightarrow{*} g(v'_1, \dots, v'_m)$, then $E \models g(v_1, \dots, v_m) \approx x\sigma$.

Since $f(u'_1, \ldots, u'_n) \to g(v'_1, \ldots, v'_m)$ is in R_E, all subterms u'_i and v'_j are R_E-reduced. Hence the second statement of the theorem is true.

iii. Two steps at the root in the proof of $u \approx v$. Then $u = f(u_1, \ldots, u_n)$ and $v = g(v_1, \ldots, v_m)$. The rewrite proof has the following form:

$$f(u_1, \ldots, u_n) \overset{*}{\to} f(u'_1, \ldots, u'_n) \overset{\text{root-step}}{\to} w \overset{\text{root-step}}{\leftarrow} g(v'_1, \ldots, v'_m) \overset{*}{\leftarrow} g(v_1, \ldots, v_m)$$

where w is a normal form for both terms and $f(u'_1, \ldots, u'_n) \neq g(v'_1, \ldots, v'_m)$. (The case where $f(u'_1, \ldots, u'_n) = g(v'_1, \ldots, v'_m)$ reduces to the first case, since there is a proof of $u \approx v$ with no step at the root on either side.) Since $R_E \models u_i \overset{*}{\to} u'_i$ for each $i = 1, \ldots, n$, $E \models \bigcup_i^n u_i \approx u'_i$ and since $R_E \models g(v_1, \ldots, v_m) \overset{*}{\to} g(v'_1, \ldots, v'_m)$, $E \models g(v_1, \ldots, v_m) \approx g(v'_1, \ldots, v'_m)$. The subterms u'_i and v'_j are all R_E-reduced.

Since $f(u'_1, \ldots, u'_n) \to w$ and $g(v'_1, \ldots, v'_m) \to w$ are in R_E, hence there must be an equation $f(s_1, \ldots, s_n) \approx t$ in E and also $g(t_1, \ldots, t_m) \approx t'$ in E, and an R_E-reduced substitution σ, such that $s_i\sigma = u'_i$, for all $i = 1, \ldots, n$, and also $t_j\sigma = v'_j$, for all $j = 1, \ldots, m$, and $t\sigma = w$ and $t'\sigma = w$. By the saturation with the Right-Hand-Side Critical Pair rule, also $f(s_1, \ldots, s_n)\theta \approx g(t_1, \ldots, t_m)\theta$ is in E, where $\theta = mgu_\emptyset(t, t')$. Obviously, $\theta \leq \sigma$, and hence for some τ, $s_i\theta\tau = s_i\sigma$ for any $i = 1, \ldots, n$ and $t_j\theta\tau = t_j\sigma$ for each $j = 1, \ldots, m$. The second statement of the theorem is therefore true.

Our inference rules are presented in Figures 1 and 2. They use a *selection rule* which is defined after the inference rules. We call the set of inference rules *BSM* (Basic Syntactic Mutation). We also define a procedure called *BSM*, which is the result of closing a set of equations under the inference rules *BSM*.

We treat the equations in the inference rules as symmetric, i.e., an equation $s \approx t$ can also be viewed as $t \approx s$.

The boxed elements in the assumptions of the rules are boxed also in the conclusion. The subterms of boxed terms are treated as also boxed. In the inference rules, if we do not box a term then it can be either boxed or unboxed, unless we explicitly say that it is not boxed.

The rule Imitation is allowed only when there are multiple equations with variable x on one side and terms with the same function symbol on the other side, as in the example:

$$\frac{\{x \approx f(a), x \approx f(b), x \approx f(c)\} \cup G}{\{x \approx \boxed{f(y)}, y \approx a, y \approx b, y \approx c\} \cup G}$$

In the case where all function symbols are different, Imitation is not applicable, instead we must use Mutate&Imitate in a successful proof, as in the example:

$$\frac{\{x \approx f(a), x \approx g(b)\} \cup G}{\{x \approx g(y), \boxed{b} \approx b, y \approx \boxed{b}, \boxed{a} \approx a\} \cup G}$$

where $f(a) \approx g(b)$ is in E.

Decomposition:

$$\frac{\{f(u_1,\cdots,u_n) \approx f(v_1,\cdots,v_n)\} \cup G}{\{u_1 \approx v_1,\cdots,u_n \approx v_n\} \cup G}$$

where $f(u_1,\cdots,u_n) \approx f(v_1,\cdots,v_n)$ is selected. **Mutate:**

$$\frac{\{f(u_1,\cdots,u_n) \approx g(v_1,\cdots,v_m)\} \cup G}{\bigcup_i \{u_i \approx \boxed{s_i}\} \cup \bigcup_i \{\boxed{t_i} \approx v_i\} \cup G}$$

where $f(u_1,\cdots,u_n) \approx g(v_1,\cdots,v_m)$ is selected, $f(u_1,\cdots,u_n)$ is not boxed and $f(s_1,\cdots,s_n) \approx g(t_1,\cdots,t_m) \in E$. **Imitation:**

$$\frac{\bigcup_i \{x \approx f(v_{i_1},\cdots,v_{i_n})\} \cup G}{\{x \approx \boxed{f(y_1,\cdots,y_n)}, \bigcup_i \{y_1 \approx v_{i_1}\},\cdots,\bigcup_i \{y_n \approx v_{i_n}\}\} \cup G}$$

where $i > 1$ and at least two of $\bigcup_i \{x \approx f(v_{i_1},\cdots,v_{i_n})\}$ are selected, and there are no more equations of the form $x \approx f(u_1,\cdots,u_n)$ in G. **Mutate&Imitate:**

$$\frac{\{x \approx f(u_1,\cdots,u_n), x \approx g(v_1,\cdots,v_m)\} \cup G}{\{x \approx f(y_1,\cdots,y_m), y_1 \approx \boxed{s_1},\ldots,y_n \approx \boxed{s_n}, \boxed{s_1} \approx u_1,\cdots,\boxed{s_n} \approx u_n, \boxed{t_1} \approx v_1,\cdots,\boxed{t_m} \approx v_m\} \cup G}$$

where $f(s_1,\cdots,s_n) \approx g(t_1,\cdots,t_m)$ is in E, $x \approx f(u_1,\cdots,u_n)$ and $x \approx g(v_1,\cdots,v_m)$ are selected in the goal and

1. $f(u_1,\cdots,u_n)$ is boxed , $g(v_1,\cdots,v_m)$ is unboxed in the premise and $f(y_1,\cdots,y_m)$ is boxed in the conclusion, or
2. both $f(u_1,\cdots,u_n)$ and $g(v_1,\cdots,v_m)$ are not boxed in the premise and $f(y_1,\cdots,y_m)$ is not boxed in the conclusion.

Variable Elimination:

if $x \not\approx y$:

$$\frac{x \approx y, \quad G}{x \approx y, \quad G[x \mapsto y]}$$

where both x and y appear in G.

otherwise:

$$\frac{x \approx x \cup G}{G}$$

Fig. 1. The BSM inference rules

VariableMutate:

$$\frac{\{f(u_1, \cdots, u_n) \approx v\} \cup G}{\{u_1 \approx \boxed{s_1}, \cdots, u_n \approx \boxed{s_n}, \quad x \approx v\} \cup G}$$

where $f(u_1, \cdots, u_n) \approx v$ is selected, $f(u_1, \cdots, u_n)$ is not boxed and there is an equation of the form $f(s_1, \cdots, s_n) \approx x \in E$.
Mutate&Imitate-cycle:

$$\frac{\{x \approx f(v_1, \ldots, v_n)\} \cup G}{\{x \approx \boxed{g(t_1, \ldots, t_k)}, \bigcup_i^n \boxed{s_i} \approx v_i\} \cup G}$$

where $g(t_1, \ldots, t_k) \approx f(s_1, \ldots, s_n) \in E$, $x \approx f(v_1, \ldots, v_n)$ only is selected. **Imitation-cycle:**

$$\frac{\{x \approx f(v_1, \cdots, v_n)\} \cup G}{\{x \approx \boxed{f(y_1, \cdots, y_n)}, y_1 \approx v_1, \cdots, y_n \approx v_n\} \cup G}$$

where $x \approx f(v_1, \cdots, v_n)$ only is selected.

Fig. 2. BSM inference rules continued

Definition 2. *We recursively define an equation $x \approx t$ in G to be* solved *if the variable x does not appear in $G \backslash \{x \approx t\}$ or the variable x does not appear in an unsolved equation in G. The variable x is then called* solved.

We use a notion of cycle in the definition of our selection rule. By *cycle*, we understand a set of equations of the type $x \approx t$, where x is a variable, t is a term, that can be ordered as $\{x_1 = t_1, \ldots, x_n = t_n\}$, in such a way that $\{x_{i+1}\} \cap Var(t_i) \neq \emptyset$, where at least one t_i is not variable and $x_1 \in Var(t_n)$.

The following selection rule is used in the inference rules. Conditions imposed by the definition deal with "don't care" nondeterminism in the procedure.

Definition 3. *A selection rule* is a function from a multiset of equations S to a nonempty subset T of S, such that if $x \approx t_1 \in T$, $x \in Vars$ and $t_1 \notin Vars$, then either there is another member of T, $x \approx t_2$, or $x \approx t_1$ is in a cycle and t_1 is not boxed. Every equation in T is considered selected.

Notice that if $x \approx t$ is in a solved form, it cannot be selected.

We will prove that BSM always halts on a goal G, and if G is E-unifiable then a normal form will be found.

Definition 4. *A goal G is in* normal form *if the equations of G are all solved and they can be arranged in the form $\{x_1 \approx t_1, \cdots, x_n \approx t_n\}$ such that for all $i \leq j$, x_i is not in t_j.*

Then we define θ_G to be the substitution $[x_1 \mapsto t_1][x_2 \mapsto t_2] \cdots [x_n \mapsto t_n]$. θ_G is a most general E-unifier of G.

One application of any inference rule to the goal G with the resulting goal G', is denoted by $G \rightarrow G'$.

5 Completeness and Termination

In this section we prove that if $E = RHS(E')$ where E' is finite and saturated under Paramodulation, then the BSM procedure always terminates in nondeterministic polynomial time, and it finds a normal form if the goal is E-unifiable.

Definition 5. *Let G be a goal and σ be a ground substitution. Then (G, σ) is reduced if $x\sigma$ is reduced wrt R_E for all variables $x \in G$, and $t\sigma$ is reduced wrt R_E whenver t is boxed.*

Lemma 2. *Let $E = RHS(E')$, where E' is finite and saturated by Paramodulation. If (G, σ) is reduced, $E \models G\sigma$, G is not in normal form, then there is G' and σ' such that $G \rightarrow G'$, (G', σ') is reduced, $E \models G'\sigma'$ and $\sigma' \leq_E \sigma[Var(G)]$.*

Proof. If G is not in a normal form, some equation or equations will be selected and we have several cases to consider. We give the proof of one case, and the others can be found in [13].

1. $u \approx v$ **is selected and u and v are variables**
2. $u \approx v$ **is selected and u, v are not variables**

   Since $E \models u\sigma \approx v\sigma$, there are two possibilities according to Theorem 2:

   a) **Th.2(1) holds for $u\sigma \approx v\sigma$**

   $u = f(u_1, \cdots, u_n)$, $v = f(v_1, \cdots, v_n)$, and $E \models \bigcup_{i=1}^{n} u_i\sigma \approx v_i\sigma$. Thus $G \rightarrow G'$ by Decomposition and $E \models G'\sigma$. (G', σ) is reduced with respect to the variables (we have not changed anything about the variables in this case).

   As for the other terms in G', if $f(u_1, \cdots, u_n)$ was boxed in G, then we assume that $f(u_1, \cdots, u_n)\sigma$ is R_E-reduced. Hence the same can be said about all subterms of $f(u_1, \cdots, u_n)\sigma$. Hence $u_1, \ldots, u_n$, which will be boxed in the result of Decomposition, preserve the property: each $u_i\sigma$, which will be boxed in the conclusion, will also be R_E-reduced.

   b) **Th.2(2) holds for $u\sigma \approx v\sigma$**

   $u = f(u_1, \ldots, u_n)$ and $v = g(v_1, \ldots, v_m)$, $f(s_1, \ldots, s_n) \approx t \in E$, $E \models \bigcup_{i=1}^{n} u_i\sigma \approx s_i\sigma'$ and $E \models g(v_1, \ldots, v_m)\sigma \approx t\sigma'$, where σ' is an extension of σ for new variables in the terms from E.

   There are two possibilities depending on the form of t:

   i. If $t = g(t_1, \ldots, t_m)$, $E \models \bigcup_{j=1}^{m} v_j\sigma \approx t_j\sigma'$, where $\sigma = \sigma'[Var(G)]$. Hence Mutate is applicable. Either the first case applies, where e.g. $f(u_1, \ldots, u_n)$ is boxed, i.e. $f(u_1, \ldots, u_n)\sigma$ is R_E-reduced, and this allows to box $f(y_1, \ldots, y_n)$ in the conclusion of the rule, or the second case applies, where both $f(u_1, \ldots, u_n)$ and $g(v_1, \ldots, v_m)$ are unboxed, hence their ground instances are not necessarily R_E-reduced, and $f(y_1, \ldots, y_n)$ cannot be boxed in the conclusion of the rule. Therefore $G \to G'$ and $E \models G'\sigma'$. New terms in G' introduced from E are boxed, because by theorem 2, they are R_E-reduced. Hence (G', σ') is reduced.

ii. If $t = x$, where x is a variable. Then $f(s_1, \ldots, s_n) \approx x \in E$ and $E \models \bigcup_{i=1}^{n} u_i\sigma \approx s_i\sigma'$ and $E \models x\sigma \approx g(v_1, \ldots, v_m)\sigma$. The rule VariableMutate is then applicable, and $G \to G'$ by this rule, $E \models G'\sigma'$. By Theorem 2, all $s_i\sigma$ are R_E-reduced, hence all s_i can be boxed in the conclusion of the rule. (G', σ') is reduced, where $\sigma = \sigma'[Var(G)]$, because of the only new variable x, by theorem 2, we know that $x\sigma$ is R_E-reduced.

3. $x \approx v$ **is selected, where** x **is a variable,** v **is not a variable and** $x \approx v$ **is part of a cycle**

4. $x \approx v_1$ **and** $x \approx v_2$ **are selected, where** x **is a variable, and** v_1 **and** v_2 **are not variables**

In order to prove that BSM always halts, we define a measure:

Definition 6. *Let M be a measure function from a unification problem G to a triple (m, n, p) of natural numbers, where m is the number of unboxed, non-variable symbols in G, n is the number of non-variable symbols in G, and p is the number of unsolved variables in G.*

Theorem 3. *Let $E = RHS(E')$ where E' is finite and saturated by Paramodulation. Then BSM solves the E-unification problem G in nondeterministic polynomial time.*

Proof. The following table shows how $M(G)$ decreases with the application of each rule, and hence can be compared wrt lexicographic order. For example, Decomposition preserves or decreases the number m of unboxed, non-variable symbols in G, but always decreases the number n of non-variable symbols in G.

	m	n	p
Decomposition	≥	>	
Mutate	>		
Imitation	≥	>	
Mutate&Imitate	>		
Variable Elimination	=	=	>
VariableMutate	>		
Mutate&Imitate-cycle	>		
Imitation-cycle	>		

Let a be the greatest arity in the signature of $E \cup G$. To prove the claim, we show that the number, $\mu(G) = (a + 2)|E| * m + (a + 1)n + p$ is decreased with the application of every rule. Hence the run of the algorithm will take no longer than $O(|G|)$, since a and $|E|$ are constant, and m, n and p are bounded by $|G|$.

In the following, G' is the goal obtained by an application of one inference rule, $G \to G'$, $M(G) = (m, n, p)$, and $M(G') = (m', n', p')$. Missing cases are in [13].

- **Decomposition:** $m' \le m$, $n' = n - 2$ and $p' \le p$.
  $\mu(G') \le (a+2)|E| * m + (a+1)(n-2) + p < (a+2)|E| * m + (a+1)n + p$.
- **Mutate:** $m' \le m - 1$, $n' \le n + |E| - 2$, $p' \le p + |E|$.
  $\mu(G') \le (a+2)|E| * (m-1) + (a+1)(n+|E|-2) + p + |E| = (a+2)|E| * m + (a+1)n + p - 2a - 2 < (a+2)|E| * m + (a+1)n + p$.
- **Imitation:** $m' \le m$, $n' \le n - 1$, $p' \le p + a$.
  $\mu(G') \le (a+2)|E|*m+(a+1)(n-1)+p+a = (a+2)|E|*m+(a+1)n+p-1 < (a+2)|E| * m + (a+1)n + p$.
- **Mutate&Imitate:** $m' = m - 1$, $n' \le n + |E| - 1$, $p' \le p + |E|$.
  $\mu(G') \le (a+2)|E| * (m-1) + (a+1)(n+|E|-1) + p + |E| = (a+2)|E| * m + (a+1)n + p - a - 1 < (a+2)|E| * m + (a+1)n + p$.
- **Variable Elimination:** $m' = m$, $n' = n$, $p' = p - 1$.
  $\mu(G') = (a+2)|E| * m + (a+1)n + p - 1 < (a+2)|E| * m + (a+1)n + p$.
- **Imitation-cycle:** $m' = m - 1$, $n' = n$, $p' = p$.
  $\mu(G') = (a+2)|E| * (m-1) + (a+1)n + p = (a+2)|E| * m + (a+1)n + p - (a+2)|E| < (a+2)|E| * m + (a+1)n + p$.

By Lemma 2, the algorithm must halt with a normal form if the goal is E-unifiable, therefore the algorithm runs in nondeterministic polynomial time.

There are several sources of "don't know" non-determinism here:

1. We don't know which equation from E to use for a given form of Mutate rule (Mutate, Mutate&Imitate, VariableMutate or Mutate&Imitate-cycle each taken alone), if several equations are applicable.
2. There may be conflicts between VariableMutate and any of the following Mutate rules: Mutate, Mutate&Imitate, Mutate&Imitate-cycle.
3. Decomposition may be in conflict with Mutate or with VariableMutate.
4. Imitation-cycle may conflict with Mutate&Imitate-cycle or VariableMutate.

6 Achieving Determinism

There are 4 sources of non-determinism in the BSM procedure, as explained above. Here further restrictions will be put on E in order to make the algorithm deterministic. The first of these restrictions will address the problem of the choice of equations to use with a form of Mutate, and the second and third will deal with the choice of the inference rules that could be applied to a unification problem.

A set of equations E is *subterm-collapsing* if there are terms t and u such that, t is a proper subterm of u and $t =_E u$.

Definition 7. *We call E deterministic if E is not subterm-collapsing and:*

1. No two equations in E have the same root symbols at their sides. For example, we can't have both $f(a) \approx g(b)$ and $f(c) \approx g(d)$ in E.

2. *If $s \approx t \in E$, then neither t nor s is a variable*
3. *If $s \approx t \in E$, then $root(s) \neq root(t)$.*

We will show that if $E = RHS(E')$ where E' is saturated under Paramodulation and E is deterministic, then BSM can be turned into a deterministic algorithm, which will mean that the algorithm halts deterministically in a linear number of inference steps. Each step takes no more than linear time, so the algorithm is $O(n^2)$. It will also show that the theory is unitary[1], because we get a most general unifier from the algorithm.

Lemma 3. *Let $E = RHS(E')$, such that E' is finite and saturated by Paramodulation, and E is deterministic. Then in the BSM algorithm for theory E, the rule VariableMutate is not applicable.*

Notice that the elimination of VariableMutate rule removes source 2 and part of source 1 and 3 of non-determinism in the BSM algorithm.

Lemma 4. *Let $E = RHS(E')$, where E' is finite and saturated by Paramodulation, and E is deterministic. Then in the BSM algorithm for the theory E, if Imitation-cycle or Mutate&Imitate-cycle is applicable to a goal G, then G has no solution.*

We define algorithm $BSMd$ the same as algorithm BSM, only without rules VariableMutate, Imitation-cycle and Mutate&Imitate-cycle. Notice that the elimination of cycle-rules completely removes the 4th source and partially the 1st and 2nd source of non-determinism in the BSM algorithm.

Theorem 4. *Let $E = RHS(E')$, where E' is finite and saturated under Paramodulation, and E is deterministic. Then the algorithm $BSMd$ for the theory E solves the E-unification problem G deterministically in $O(|G|)$ inference steps, so in time $O(|G|^2)$. Also, E is unitary.*

Proof. By the completeness argument, the algorithm BSM solves the E-unification problem. By Lemmas 3 and 4, the algorithm $BSMd$ also solves the problem. But there are no sources of non-determinism in the algorithm $BSMd$. Recall the possible sources of non-determinism given at the end of the last section. After the removal of the VariableMutate rule and cycle-rules, we have to consider the following, remaining cases:

1. As for the first source of non-determinism, we are left with a possible conflict of various equations from E used with Mutate or Mutate&Imitate. But Restriction 1 on E in an obvious way rules out these cases. Hence this source of non-determinism disappears. The conflicts with VariableMutate or Mutate&Imitate cycle are no longer there, because the inference rules are no longer there.
2. We got rid of the second source of non-determinism by removing VariableMutate from the $BSMd$ algorithm.
3. As for the third source of non-determinism, we are left with a possible conflict between Decomposition and Mutate. But notice that Restriction 3 on E precludes any such conflict, since Decomposition is used only when an equation in the goal has both sides with the same root symbol.

4. The fourth source of non-determinism disappeared with the removal of the cycle-rules from the $BSMd$ algorithm.

There are no other sources of possible non-determinism in $BSMd$. Hence the algorithm $BSMd$ is deterministic and will only take $O(|G|)$ inference steps. Each step can be done in linear time, so the algorithm is $O(|G|^2)$. Since it is deterministic, it computes a most general unifier.

For subterm-collapsing theories, it is possible to show that all those properties are necessary. For example, [14] exhibits a ground theory that satisfies the second and third properties, but whose unification problem is NP-complete. The theory $E = \{f(x,x) \approx x\}$ satisfies the first and third property, but its unification problem is NP-complete[9]. Also, consider the theory $E' = \{f(x,x) \approx 0\}$. In this case $E = RHS(E') = \{f(x,x) \approx 0, f(x,x) \approx f(x',x')\}$, which satisfies the first two properties, but its unification problem is NP-complete[5]. All of those are subterm-collapsing theories, and we don't know if it is possible to show that a subterm-collapsing theory with the above three properties always has a polynomial time procedure to decide the unification problem. However, we know that it cannot be solved in polynomial time. Consider the theory $E = \{fa \approx a, fb \approx b\}$. This is subterm-collapsing and it satisfies all three properties above, but the goal $fx_1 \approx x_1, \cdots, fx_n \approx x_n$ has a complete set of unifiers of size 2^n.

7   Comparison with Basic Narrowing

We will show some advantages of $BSMd$ over Basic Narrowing, which is defined in Figure 7. The Basic Narrowing rules[6] are presented here in the formalism of constraints. To the right of the bar, we put constraints in the form of substitutions, that composed together give the possible solution. Substitutions from the constraints part are never applied to the goal, hence we prevent any inferences into the substituted terms. This is exactly the same as boxing the terms in $BSMd$. Also, any term into which an inference is made, cannot be a variable, and in $BSMd$ we treat variables as boxed.

As an example, we take $E = \{fa \approx b\}$ and the goal $g(fx_1,\ldots,fx_n) \approx g(fy_1,\ldots,fy_n)\}$.

In this case, $BSMd$ gives us the most general unifier our algorithm in a deterministic way, in polynomial time gives us the most general unifier $[x_1 \mapsto y_1,\ldots,x_n \mapsto y_n]$. The only possible rule to apply is Decomposition.

Basic Narrowing is non-deterministic in this case and will search for the solution in exponential time, applying the Narrowing rule to each fx_i and fy_i. It will find all solutions of the form $\{x_i \mapsto a, y_i \mapsto a \mid i \in N\} \cup \{x_i \mapsto y_i \mid i \in N\}$. for all $N \subseteq \{1, \cdots, n\}$. Therefore, it will find 2^n different unifiers, all of which are subsumed by the one unifier generated by $BSMd$.

On the other hand, if we change E to contain $fa \approx fb$ instead of $fa \approx b$, we need to use BSM. There will be exponentially many solutions, but E is not deterministic in this case.

Basic Narrowing:

$$\frac{s[u] \approx t, G \mid \tau}{s[x] \approx t, G \mid \tau[x \mapsto r]\sigma}$$

where $l \approx r$ is in E, $l \not\leq r$, $s \not\leq t$, $\sigma = mgu_\emptyset(l, u\tau)$ and u is not a variable.

Equality Resolution:

$$\frac{u \approx v, G \mid \tau}{G \mid \tau\sigma}$$

where $\sigma = mgu_\emptyset(u\tau, v\tau)$.

8 Conclusion

This paper gives an algorithm which solves E-unification for a certain class of equational theories in NP, and for a more restricted class of theories in quadratic time. There have been other decidability and complexity results shown for classes of equational theories such as [4,7,14,8,12]. The classes defined in those other papers are not related to ours, except that [14] shows NP-completeness for theories saturated under Paramodulation.

We have defined an inference system for E-unification called Basic Syntactic Mutation (BSM). We apply BSM to solve E-unification for sets of equations finitely saturated by Paramodulation. BSM resembles the Syntactic Mutation inference rules of [10], but after an inference, the terms introduced by the inference are blocked from further inferences, as in Basic Paramodulation[3, 15]. Therefore, our inference rules will halt on equational theories saturated by Paramodulation in nondeterministic polynomial time, as in [14], giving a decision procedure for E-unification in such theories.

A main interest of our inference system was to find equational theories where E-unification can be solved in polynomial time, and our inference rules were designed with that in mind. We give further restrictions on the equational theory, and we show that with those restrictions, our algorithm will halt in deterministic quadratic time, with a linear number of inference steps, and that such theories are unitary. We call such theories *deterministic*. This means unification in these theories is not much harder than in the empty theory. We conjecture that the complexity of our procedure could be reduced to $O(nlg(n))$ or $O(n)$, as in syntactic unification.

The idea behind our reults on deterministic theories is to deal with equational theories which express non-recursive definitions. For example, the definition of adding elements to a list looks like this:

$$add(x, cons(y, z)) = cons(x, cons(y, z))$$

This theory is deterministic, as would be similar theories consisting of adds and inserts. Many natural theories contain axioms such as these. They may contain other axioms, which destroy the deterministic property, however they may still meet many of the conditions for a deterministic theory. Therefore, it is still possible to use the results in this paper to analyze the determinism in the BSM E-unification algorithm and understand how efficient the algorithm will be.

References

1. F. Baader and T. Nipkow. *Term Rewriting and All That.* Cambridge, 1998.
2. L. Bachmair and H. Ganzinger. Rewrite-based equational theorem proving with selection and simplification. In *Journal of Logic and Computation* 4(3), 1-31, 1994.
3. L. Bachmair, H. Ganzinger, C. Lynch, and W. Snyder. Basic Paramodulation. *Information and Computation Vol. 121, No. 2* (1995) pp. 172–192.
4. H. Comon, M. Haberstrau and J.-P. Jouannaud. Syntacticness, Cycle-Syntacticness and shallow theories. In *Information and Computation* 111(1), 154-191, 1994.
5. Q. Guo, P. Narendran and D. Wolfram. Unification and Matching modulo Nilpotence. In *Proceedings 13th International Conference on Automated Deduction,* Rutgers University, NJ, 1996.
6. J.-M. Hullot. Canonical forms and unification. In *Proc. 5th Int. Conf. on Automated Deduction,* LNCS, vol. 87, pp. 318–334, Berlin, 1980. Springer-Verlag.
7. F. Jacquemard. Decidable approximations of term rewriting systems. In H. Ganzinger, ed., *Rewriting Techniques and Applications, 7th International Conference, RTA-96,* LNCS, vol. 1103, Springer, 362-376, 1996.
8. F. Jacquemard, Ch. Meyer, Ch. Weidenbach. Unification in Extensions of Shallow Equational Theories. In T. Nipkow, ed., *Rewriting Techniques and Applications, 9th International Conference, RTA-98,* LNCS, vol. 1379, Springer, 76-90, 1998.
9. D. Kapur and P. Narendran. Matching, Unification, and Complexity. In SIGSAM Bulletin, 1987.
10. C. Kirchner. Computing unification algorithms. In *Proceedings of the Fourth Symposium on Logic in Computer Science,* Boston, 200-216, 1990.
11. D. E. Knuth and P. B. Bendix. Simple word problems in universal algebra. In *Computational Problems in Abstract Algebra,* ed. J. Leech, 263-297, Pergamon Press, 1970.
12. S. Limet and P. Réty. *E*-unification by Means of Tree Tuple Synchronized Grammars. In *Discrete Mathematics and Theoretical Computer Science,* volume 1, pp. 69–98, 1997.
13. C. Lynch and B. Morawska. http://www.clarkson.edu/~clynch/papers/bsm_full.ps/, 2002.
14. R. Nieuwenhuis. Basic paramodulation and decidable theories. (Extended abstract), In *Proceedings 11th IEEE Symposium on Logic in Computer Science, LICS'96,* IEEE Computer Society Press, 473-482, 1996.
15. R. Nieuwenhuis and A. Rubio. Basic Superposition is Complete. In *Proc. European Symposium on Programming,* Rennes, France (1992).

The Next Waldmeister Loop

Thomas Hillenbrand[1] and Bernd Löchner[2]

[1] Max-Planck-Institut für Informatik, Saarbrücken, Germany,
hillen@mpi-sb.mpg.de
[2] FB Informatik, Universität Kaiserslautern, Kaiserslautern, Germany,
loechner@informatik.uni-kl.de

Abstract. In saturation-based theorem provers, the reasoning process consists in constructing the closure of an axiom set under inferences. As is well-known, this process tends to quickly fill the memory available unless preventive measures are employed. For implementations based on the DISCOUNT loop, the passive facts are responsible for most of the memory consumption. We present a refinement of that loop allowing such a compression that the space needed for the passive facts is linearly bound by the number of active facts. In practice, this will reduce memory consumption in the WALDMEISTER system by more than one order of magnitude as compared to previous compression schemes.

1 Introduction

Theorem proving procedures are refutationally complete under the idealized assumption of unlimited resources. But implementations thereof are run on finite machines and so can only analyze a finite part of the infinite search space. For provers based on saturation procedures, this resource restriction shows up as sky-high growing memory consumption if, in order to solve a difficult problem, they need to be run not for a few minutes only, but for say hours to days; and a bundle of preventive measures thereagainst has been suggested.

The WALDMEISTER system is an example of such an implementation. Since the very beginning, ad-hoc compression techniques have been employed, condensing the individual conclusions derived into a more compact representation. Spurred by the renewed discussion of how to organize the proof search within saturation-based theorem provers – OTTER or DISCOUNT loop [Vor01, pp. 15–17] – we reconsider our system's proof procedure in this paper (Sect. 2) and show that the latter loop variant in an elegant way allows the compression of coarse-grained sets of conclusions (Sect. 3.1). Our technique requires for completeness reasons that the successive normal form functions developed during completion remain accessible. We present a simple and efficient realization of this requirement in Sect. 3.2. Since we avoid to discard non-redundant critical pairs, the prover delivers a decision procedure in case the saturation process terminates.

The DISCOUNT loop thereby being developed into its ultimate form, memory consumption will be reduced by more than one order of magnitude with this concept, which we demonstrate by a simulation-based estimation (Sect. 4). Today's

A. Voronkov (Ed.): CADE-18, LNAI 2392, pp. 486–500, 2002.

Algorithm 1 The proof procedure of WALDMEISTER

FUNCTION WALDMEISTER$(\mathcal{E}, \mathcal{C}, >, \varphi)$: BOOLEAN
1: $(\mathcal{A}, \mathcal{P}) := (\varnothing, \mathcal{E})$
2: **WHILE** $\neg$trivial$(\mathcal{C}) \wedge \mathcal{P} \neq \varnothing$ **DO**
3:    $e := \min_\varphi(\mathcal{P})$; $\mathcal{P} := \mathcal{P} \setminus \{e\}$
4:    **IF** $\neg$orphan(e) **THEN**
5:       $e := \text{Normalize}_{\mathcal{A}}^>(e)$
6:       **IF** $\neg$redundant(e) **THEN**
7:          $(\mathcal{A}, P_1) := \text{Interred}^>(\mathcal{A}, e)$
8:          $\mathcal{A} := \mathcal{A} \cup \{\text{Orient}^>(e)\}$
9:          $P_2 := \text{CP}^>(e, \mathcal{A})$
10:        $\mathcal{P} := \mathcal{P} \cup \text{Normalize}_{\mathcal{A}}^>(P_1 \cup P_2)$
11:        $\mathcal{C} := \text{Normalize}_{\mathcal{A}}^>(\mathcal{C})$
12:       **END**
13:    **END**
14: **END**
15: **RETURN** trivial$(\mathcal{C})$

---

computer architecture rewards smaller process sizes with faster execution. More importantly, decent resource consumption is an essential prerequisite for getting provers productive in practice and for increasing acceptance by the users.

As an aside, any overhead for the construction of the detailed proof object is completely removed from the proof search (Sect. 3.3). It even becomes possible to depart from the given-clause algorithm. – This paper is a revised and extended version of [HL01]. We use standard notions and notations (cf. [DP01]).

2   An Inspection of WALDMEISTER's Proof Procedure

2.1   The Proof Procedure Itself

The procedure (cf. Alg. 1) is an instance of the *given-clause algorithm* [McC97, Chap. 5.5.1]. The input consists of an equation set $\mathcal{E}$, the *axioms*, a ground equation set $\mathcal{C}$, the *conjectures*, a reduction ordering $>$ total on ground terms, and a *weighting function* φ mapping equations to *weights*.

The saturation is performed in a cycle working on a set $\mathcal{A}$ of *active facts* that participate in inferences and a set $\mathcal{P}$ of *passive facts* waiting to become members of $\mathcal{A}$. The function φ heuristically assesses passive facts. It has to ensure that every passive fact becomes minimal at some point in time and hence selected. This guarantees the fairness of the proof procedure. We require φ to induce a total ordering on the equations that have been assessed so far. Typical examples such as $\varphi(s{=}t) = |s| + |t|$, i.e. the sum of term lengths, only induce quasi-orderings. These can be refined lexicographically with some timestamp, or with parents numbers and overlap position. Weights therefore are tuples with several components. Within limited storage, each of these components is bound, and so is the space needed to store it. In that sense, weights need constant space.

The active facts $\mathcal{A}$ induce, via their orientable instances $\mathcal{A}^>$, an ordered rewrite relation $\rightarrow_\mathcal{A}$ and thereby a normal form relation $\rightarrow_\mathcal{A}^!$. We stipulate a total *normal form function* $\text{Normalize}_{\mathcal{A}}^{>} \subseteq \to_{\mathcal{A}}^{!}$ that is deterministic for any parameter value of $\mathcal{A}$ and $>$. Furthermore, an *interreduction function* $\text{Interred}^{>}$ is needed that, given $\mathcal{A}$ and a new equation e, returns both those active facts that are e-reducible and the remainder of $\mathcal{A}$. Finally, let $\text{CP}^{>}(e, \mathcal{A})$ denote the set of all critical pairs between the equation e and all equations in $\mathcal{A}$.

We comment now on some details of the proof procedure (cf. Alg. 1). (L. 2) The saturation proceeds as long as (i) the conjectures have not become trivial, i.e. equations of the form $t=t$, and (ii) there are still passive facts. (L. 3) Select an equation e from $\mathcal{P}$ which has minimal weight with respect to φ. (L. 4) Skip if a parent equation has been reduced meanwhile. The critical pair has not participated in any inference and hence is redundant. (L. 6) Skip if e has become trivial now, or redundant in some other way, e.g. via subsumption. (L. 10) Normalize the generated critical pairs and the reduced active facts, and add the non-redundant ones to $\mathcal{P}$.

For this proof procedure, the following two invariants hold: (i) Every non-redundant one-step conclusion of $\mathcal{A}$ is contained in $\mathcal{A} \cup \mathcal{P}$. (ii) The active facts $\mathcal{A}$ are completely interreduced. Hence, in case of termination with $\mathcal{P} = \varnothing$, $\mathcal{A}$ is an interreduced rewrite system, convergent on ground terms and equivalent to $\mathcal{E}$, i.e. a decision procedure for the uniform word problem of $\mathcal{E}$. Furthermore, if φ ensures fairness, then the procedure demonstrates any valid identity on ground terms in $\mathcal{C}$ within finite time.

In the following sections we will denote by $\mathcal{A}_i$ the value of $\mathcal{A}$ after the i-th iteration of the loop core in lines 7–11; this iteration count gives an abstract notion of time. The sets $\mathcal{A}_i$ induce the rewrite relations $\to_i := \to_{\mathcal{A}_i}$ and the normal form functions $\text{Norm}_i := \text{Normalize}_{\mathcal{A}_i}^{>}$.

The passive facts are, as can be seen in the proof procedure, subject to normalization only right after their generation and in case they get selected. This variant of given-clause algorithm is called *DISCOUNT loop*. In contrast, within an *OTTER loop* the whole set of passive facts is normalized in every iteration of the cycle. Line 10 then would read "$\mathcal{P} := \text{Normalize}_{\mathcal{A}}^{>}(\mathcal{P} \cup P_1 \cup P_2)$" instead. Some OTTER loop implementations moreover use the rewrite relation generated by the union of active and passive facts, i.e. they always employ $\text{Normalize}_{\mathcal{A} \cup \mathcal{P}}^{>}$ instead of $\text{Normalize}_{\mathcal{A}}^{>}$.[1] The loop variants are named after well-known respective implementations, cf. [ADF95] and [McC94]. An early experimental comparison of both loops was done in [Küc82, p. 131], where, based on observations when completing the group axioms using the ALDES Data-Type Completion System, preference is given to the OTTER loop. The loop names have been coined in [RV00, Chap. 2 and 6], where also extensive experiments of both variants are reported. A discussion within the frame of resolution and superposition is contained in [Wei01, Sect. 3 and 5.3].

It is clear that, since nothing is done with passive facts but selection, the DISCOUNT loop leads to a simpler system design, because no term indexing

---

[1] More precisely, this involves a more subtle form of interreduction. Note also that then the orphan predicate (L. 4) requires tagging passive facts that have ever participated in reductions, and that only untagged orphans may be deleted.

is necessary on the elements of $\mathcal{P}$ as would be the case if $\mathcal{P}$ were to be kept fully normalized. Apart from relieving the system developers, this should also reduce the system run time, presuming that the search behavior of the prover is essentially the same, which admittedly is an issue still under discussion.

Interesting related work on the resource problem in theorem proving can be found in [RV00]. The setting there is to attack a proof problem *within some given time limit*. A *limited resource strategy*, LRS for short, is developed that explicitly takes this limitation into account in order to analyze a larger part of the search space in the time given. To this end, the prover keeps track of the average time spent for processing a selected passive fact. This allows to estimate the number N of facts that still can be activated before the time limit is reached. Hence $|\mathcal{P}| - N$ passive facts are not likely to be selected; and so the $|\mathcal{P}| - N$ heaviest ones of them are discarded. LRS is a refinement of the weight-limit strategy of OTTER where clauses are discarded if their weight exceeds a given, fixed bound. For the VAMPIRE system the authors observe an increase in performance with LRS. The approach pays off for systems implementing the OTTER loop, since fewer passive facts have to be kept and indexed. As to the DISCOUNT loop, space savings are to be expected there, but no speed-ups, since passive facts are not indexed. – The setting we are dealing with in this paper is a different one, namely running a prover without time limit; and the specialized compression techniques developed here will result in more memory savings.

2.2   Aspects of Space Consumption

Typically $\mathcal{P}$ contains far more equations than $\mathcal{A}$, as a rule of thumb $|\mathcal{P}| = O(|\mathcal{A}|^2)$ on the average (i.e. one can fit parabolas into the plot of these quantities). Therefore the space requirements of WALDMEISTER are dominated by the representation of the passive facts. Hence, methods to save space mainly have to tackle $\mathcal{P}$. Up to now, we have used simple *compression schemes* to minimize the space needed for single elements. Within WALDMEISTER, this can be done in three ways: (i) Not at all, i.e. flatterms are employed at the cost of 12 bytes per symbol. (ii) Stringterms: Terms are stored simply as strings of symbols, at the cost of one byte per symbol. (iii) Overlap representation: After heuristical assessment, the terms themselves are thrown away, and just minimal reconstruction information is kept, at constant cost.

The influence of these representations on the process size over abstract time can be studied in Fig. 1. For each variant, the WALDMEISTER system was run on the ROB001-1 proof task from the TPTP problem library [SS99] using an UltraSPARC-IIi workstation. The process size minus the space consumption of $\mathcal{P}$ serves as a baseline (lowest curve). Stringterms allow compression rates of about 10, which is comparable to what can be achieved with a shared term representation [LS01]. The overlap representation improves on this by another factor of nearly 10. But still here the overall space consumption, exceeding 1 GByte after some thousand activation steps, is mostly due to the data structure for $\mathcal{P}$, which mirrors the estimated quadratic relation between $|\mathcal{A}|$ and $|\mathcal{P}|$.

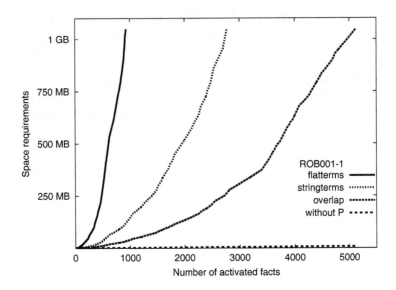

Fig. 1. Size of the process over abstract time

The above-mentioned overlap representation is apparently the best one in terms of space. But – contrary to one's expectations – it may influence the behavior of the proof search. To quantify the effect, we performed the following experiment: On the 431 unit equality proof problems in the current TPTP release [SS99] WALDMEISTER is run with six different settings, two orderings (KBO/LPO) combined with three general purpose weighting functions (addweight/mixweight/gtweight). For each of the 2586 cases we compare the prover's behavior using stringterms with that using overlap representation.

Within the resource limit of 120 seconds on a 1 GHz Pentium III system 1819 cases are solved by both versions and 699 by none. Whereas in 68 cases the run with the stringterm representation succeeds, and that with the overlap representation does not, there is no case where the opposite happens. From the 1819 cases solved by both versions, 1332 ($\approx$ 74%) show no difference. In 385 ($\approx$ 21%) cases, the stringterm version is better, in 102 ($\approx$ 6%) the overlap version. Comparing the degree of difference, the improvements of the overlap representation are rather modest. In the other direction, however, the effects are stronger, e.g. there are numerous examples which are solved in under 5 seconds by the stringterm version and encounter a time-out with the overlap version.

On the inference level, the reason for the differences is the following: When a critical pair e is generated at time i, it is normalized to $\mathrm{Norm}_i(e)$ and inserted into $\mathcal{P}$. Let e be selected at time $j \gg i$. The reconstruction process needed by overlap representation then yields $\mathrm{Norm}_j(e)$, whereas with stringterms the critical pair would enter the completion loop in the shape $\mathrm{Norm}_j(\mathrm{Norm}_i(e))$. Since confluence is missing during completion, these shapes may differ.

With a detailed analysis of individual proof runs we have identified two main causes for the changes in the search behavior. (i) One version activates an equation that is shown to be redundant by the other. This incurs the generation of additional redundant critical pairs, so that the first version performs worse. (ii) Occurring less often, the size of an activated equation recomputed from overlap representation is larger. Since the weighting function φ typically prefers small equations, this disturbs the search. Furthermore, larger equations are less useful for simplification. Here the stringterm version behaves better.

These two phenomena are are consequence of the differences between Norm_i and Norm_j. Analyzing single cases on the level of single rewrite steps, we found e. g. that newer rewrite rules, with larger right-hand sides, were favored over the ones originally used. Or, a rule was no longer available due to interreduction. Since the detailed analysis is very costly and the cases investigated show no dominant pattern, we cannot give conclusive explanations.

3   The New Approach

To reduce the memory consumption, which is mostly due to the subsystem $\mathcal{P}$, we develop further the idea of compression and reconstruction at need. The key idea of our approach is to represent *whole subsets* of $\mathcal{P}$ by *single entries*. These subsets are not arbitrary, but reflect the structure of the given-clause algorithm. The first kind of sets contains the critical pairs belonging to two *p*arent equations e_i and e_j. We therefore call them *p-sets*. The second kind of sets, called *a-sets*, consists of all the critical pairs jointly generated at the *a*ctivation of one given clause. Since these sets are structured they can be represented in the same compact way as individual entries. Especially, we will show a variant that guarantees that the size of the representation of $\mathcal{P}$ is linear in abstract time.

For intrinsic completeness reasons of our approach that will be worked out in Sect. 3.1, an important prerequisite is the availability of the *collected history* of $\mathcal{A}$, i. e. all the preceding states $\mathcal{A}_1, \mathcal{A}_2, \ldots$ of the active facts, to re-induce the corresponding normalization functions Norm_i. An elegant and efficient realization will be discussed in Sect. 3.2.

3.1   The New Design of the $\mathcal{P}$ Subsystem

The task of the subsystem $\mathcal{P}$ is to fairly enumerate all inserted equations with the help of a weighting function φ. $\mathcal{P}$ communicates with its environment via two methods: "insert" inserts all (non-redundant) critical pairs between an equation e_i and $\mathcal{A}_i$ at once. Additionally, all equations interreduced by e_i are inserted. The other method is "deleteMin". It extracts the minimal equation from $\mathcal{P}$. Concerning the abstractly formulated Alg. 1, deleteMin realizes the functionality for line 3, and insert is needed in line 10.

We require an implementation of $\mathcal{P}$ to be neutral with respect to inferences and proof search. Even if it performs internally some inferences for recomputations it shall appear from the outside like a mere container, namely as a priority queue storing the unmodified equations augmented with their weight computed by φ. Of course, this idealized *reference implementation* assumes the availability of unlimited memory. An actual implementation shall then show the same input/output (I/O)-behavior. That is, for the same sequence of insert and deleteMin operations (with the same arguments for insert), it shall return the same equations for deleteMin operations as the reference implementation.

In a first step, we only consider the use of compact representations for individual elements. Given two equations e_i and e_j, $i \geq j$, the critical pair at the overlap position p is uniquely determined. The position information can be encoded in a single integer, e. g. as number of the top symbol of the subterm identified by p when the symbols are counted from left to right. We extend p to an *extended position* xp with 3 bits. These encode the sides that are overlapped and whether p is a position of e_i or e_j. If $s=t$ is the critical pair, its weight w is calculated as $w = \varphi(\mathrm{Norm}_i(s=t))$. It can be represented within constant space via its *overlap entry* $\langle w, i, j, xp \rangle$. Equations stemming from interreduction can be encoded in a similar way: When e_i gets reduced by e_j, $j > i$, the entry is $\langle w, i, j, \dagger \rangle$, with $w = \varphi(\mathrm{Norm}_j(e_i))$ and a special symbol $\dagger$.

Since the data in the entries is sufficient for the reconstruction of the equations the following lemma is an easy consequence of the availability of the different Norm_i:

Lemma 1. *An implementation of $\mathcal{P}$ using only overlap and interreduction entries will show the same I/O-behavior as the reference implementation.* $\square$

In the second step, we define entries that represent more than one equation. *p-entries* arise from individual entries by abstracting from the extended position component and replacing it by a wildcard $*$. More formally the p-entry $\langle w, i, j, * \rangle$ represents all individual entries $\langle w', i, j, xp' \rangle$ with $w' \geq w$. Note that p-entries are a refinement of p-sets: they do not represent *all* critical pairs between the parents, but only the heavier ones. This allows to keep the "better" critical pairs individually. Abstracting again, now from the second equation, we can represent in an *a-entry* $\langle w, i, *, * \rangle$ all critical pairs $\langle w', i, j', xp' \rangle$ with $w' \geq w$ that are computed at the activation of e_i, hence $j' \leq i$. For the same reasons as above we distinguish between a-entries and a-sets analogously to p-entries and p-sets.

These new entry types allow the realization of stronger forms of compression. As building blocks for concrete algorithms we define the following conversions:

p-compression: $\mathcal{P} \cup \{\langle w', i, j, xp \rangle \mid w' \geq w\} \rightsquigarrow \mathcal{P} \cup \{\langle w, i, j, * \rangle\}$ if there is neither some p-entry for e_i and e_j nor an a-entry for e_i in $\mathcal{P}$.

a-compression: $\mathcal{P} \cup \{\langle w', i, j, xp \rangle \mid w' \geq w\} \rightsquigarrow \mathcal{P} \cup \{\langle w, i, *, * \rangle\}$ if there is neither some p-entry for e_i and some e_j nor an a-entry for e_i in $\mathcal{P}$.

p-decompression: $\mathcal{P} \cup \{\langle w, i, j, * \rangle\} \rightsquigarrow \mathcal{P} \cup \{\langle w', i, j, xp \rangle \mid$ there exists a critical pair $s=t$ between e_i and e_j at the extended position xp, $s'=t' = \mathrm{Norm}_i(s=t)$, $s' \not\equiv t'$, $w' = \varphi(s'=t')$, $w' \geq w\}$

a-decompression: $\mathcal{P} \cup \{\langle w, i, *, * \rangle\} \rightsquigarrow \mathcal{P} \cup \{\langle w', i, j, xp \rangle \mid e_j \in \mathcal{A}_i$, there exists a critical pair $s=t$ between e_i and e_j at the extended position xp, $s'=t' = \mathrm{Norm}_i(s=t)$, $s' \not\equiv t'$, $w' = \varphi(s'=t')$, $w' \geq w\}$

The side conditions imply that the intersection of two a- or p-entries is empty, which gives the important invariant that a critical pair is represented exactly once, either in an individual overlap entry or in an a- or p-entry.

Lemma 2. *p-decompression is the exact inverse of p-compression, a-decompression is the exact inverse of a-compression. The conversions preserve the property that any critical pair is represented once.* □

This lemma relies on the availability of the different Norm_i: The compression steps are parameterized by a weight limit w. Consider critical pairs descending from a pair e_i, e_j of parents (p-compression) respectively from a single parent e_i and $\mathcal{A}_i$ (a-compression). These have a weight which has been determined with respect to their normal form at generation time. We want to group only those critical pairs together that have a sufficiently heavy weight, since the smaller ones have already been selected. The problem arises in the corresponding decompression step. For every overlap between e_i and e_j respectively $\mathcal{A}_i$, we have to (i) rebuild the critical pair, (ii) normalize it, (iii) compute its weight, (iv) compare that weight to the w parameter of the group entry, and (v) add the normalized critical pair to the decompressed set in case the weight is not too small. If in (ii) we employ the normalization function of generation time, then we get the original normal form back and hence in (iii) the original weight, so that the decision in (iv) gives the correct result. However, with the current normalization function in (ii), we might obtain a different normal form, possibly with smaller weight. If that weight were smaller than w, then the critical pair erroneously would not be included in the decompressed set and hence not be considered in the completion process. – Without the previous Norm_i available, it would not be possible to discard the light-weighted critical pairs. They hence would, unless proven redundant by the current normalization, re-enter the saturation process. So the implementation of $\mathcal{P}$ would influence the behavior of the proof search, in addition to the weighting function φ. This influence will have to be studied when an implementation is at hand.

When the deleteMin operation is slightly modified, Lemma 1 carries over: Whenever a p- or a-entry becomes minimal the appropriate decompression conversion is called before deleting the minimal entry.

In a third step, we will now sketch a realization of $\mathcal{P}$ with a space usage which is linear with abstract time.

The idea is to store the light-weighted critical pairs individually in a constant-size buffer B and to compress only the heavier-weighted ones into appropriate a-sets in a buffer B' that grows linearly with abstract time. For each e_i it has either an a-entry or an interreduction entry[2]. The intention is to use B as some kind of *cache* for critical pairs with small weight. All the remaining critical pairs are represented in B'. This design reduces the need of recomputation. As a consequence of the previous lemmas we get the desired result:

---

[2] This requires to perform the orphan criterion actively, that is, as soon as an element of $\mathcal{A}$ is reduced, all accompanying orphans in $\mathcal{P}$ are deleted.

Corollary 1. *With the accumulated history of $\mathcal{A}$ available, it is possible to implement a $\mathcal{P}$-subsystem which has a space usage which is linear with abstract time and which shows the same I/O-behavior as the reference implementation.*

3.2   The Set of Active Facts $\mathcal{A}$ and Its Accumulated History

The problem we want to tackle now is how to efficiently provide the normal form function Norm_i at time $j \geq i$. Usually the normal form of a term t is computed by traversing its subterms in some fixed order (*reduction strategy*) up to the first one that is an instance of the left-hand side of some active fact. If such a subterm is not found, t is irreducible; otherwise the subterm is replaced with the instance of the right-hand side, and the traversal starts all over again.

For such normal form functions, remembering Norm_i reduces to remembering the generalization retrieval with respect to $\mathcal{A}_i$. In today's provers, this retrieval is based on some kind of indexing technique; see [Gra96] and [RSV01] for an overview. It is not necessarily unique, since more than one left-hand side may fit. For performance reasons *first-fit retrieval* is commonplace. We therefore need to remember the corresponding generalization functions Match_i.

In the WALDMEISTER system, *perfect discrimination trees* are employed to represent the active facts. That is a trie-like structure where terms are interpreted as sequences of symbols in left-to-right traversal, and every edge carries a symbol as a label. The construction principle is that, for every subtree, its term entries all have the same prefix, namely the sequence of labels on the path from the root to that very subtree. To increase the amount of this sharing of prefixes, variables of indexed terms are *normalized*, i.e. renamed to $x_1, x_2, \ldots$ in order of their left-to-right fresh appearance.

The retrieval algorithm then works in a backtracking fashion (cf. [Hil00]), on a triple of data: a pointer into the query term which is traversed in left-to-right order; a reference to the subtree to be searched through; and a partial substitution constructed so far. For every triple, there may be up to three possibilities to proceed: (i) The subterm starts with a function symbol, and the subtree has a descendant via an edge labeled with that very symbol. (ii) There is a descendant corresponding to a yet unbound variable. (iii) The same but with a variable already bound, such that its substitute is a prefix of the current query part. We stipulate that alternative possibilities are tested in that arrangement, i.e. first function symbols, and then variables by decreasing index. The algorithm succeeds in case it reaches a leaf node.

Consider as an example the search for generalizations of $f(a, a, b)$ in the index for $\mathcal{A}_3$ depicted in Fig. 2 (b); that index contains the entries $f(a, b, a)$, $f(x_1, x_2, b)$, and $f(x_1, x_1, x_2)$. The retrieval starts with the empty substitution in node ①. There is a descendant via the top function symbol f; so ② is reached with the query rest $a\,a\,b$. This node has two successors that might match: one via the constant symbol a, and another one via the variable x_1. According to the above convention, ③ is visited first, where the query rest is $a\,b$. There is no suitable successor, so backtracking is invoked to ② where the descent to ⑥

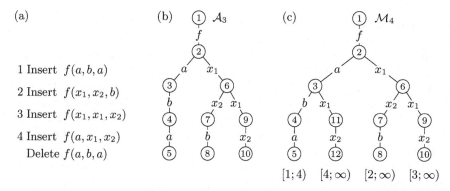

(a)

1 Insert $f(a,b,a)$

2 Insert $f(x_1,x_2,b)$

3 Insert $f(x_1,x_1,x_2)$

4 Insert $f(a,x_1,x_2)$

Delete $f(a,b,a)$

$[1;4)$ $[4;\infty)$ $[2;\infty)$ $[3;\infty)$

Fig. 2. (a) Incremental construction of $\mathcal{A}_1 \ldots \mathcal{A}_4$ (b) and (c) Indexes for $\mathcal{A}_3$ and $\mathcal{M}_4$

via the edge labeled x_1 is done, establishing a binding $\{x_1 \mapsto a\}$. The query rest is $a\,b$, and the node offers two possibilities to continue, namely with the free variable x_2 and the already bound one x_1. By convention x_2 is checked first, with binding $\{x_2 \mapsto a\}$, and thereby reaching ⑦ with query rest b. This is followed by the descent to ⑧ whereby a leaf node is reached, implying that the entry $f(x,y,b)$ matches $f(a,a,b)$ with the substitution $\{x \mapsto a, y \mapsto b\}$. Note that also the leaf node ⑩ corresponds to a successful match, namely $f(x,x,y)$ with $\{x \mapsto a, y \mapsto b\}$, but it is not the first one found.

The tree traversal induces an ordering on prefix symbol sequences in the index. This can be formalized with an appropriate total precedence $\sqsupset$ on the function symbols $\mathcal{F}$, extended to $\mathcal{F} \cup \mathcal{X}$ via $f \sqsupset x_j$ and $x_i \sqsupset x_j$ iff $i >_\mathbb{N} j$. Then the lexicographic extension $\sqsupset^*$ is a total ordering on symbol sequences, and also on terms considered as sequences of symbols. We then can formulate the following invariants for the retrieval process reaching a tree node:

1. The sequence of query term symbols considered so far equals the sequence of labels from the root to the current node under the substitution at hand; and hence every term indexed by the current subtree also has that prefix.
2. Consider a node which has a label sequence greater with respect to $\sqsupset^*$ than the current one. Then the corresponding subtree contains a match only if it contains the current node.

For the retrieval example at hand when e. g. visiting node ⑥, this means first that the entries $f(x_1,x_2,b)$ and $f(x_1,x_1,x_2)$ under the substitution $\{x_1 \mapsto a\}$ start with $f\,a$, and second that the nodes ③, ④ and ⑤ do not lead to successful matches, but ① and ② might. – These invariants guarantee not only that generalization retrieval is sound and complete, but also that the match found, if at all, is the greatest one with respect to $\sqsupset^*$. That is, the algorithm without any overhead returns a uniquely determined match. We will exploit this property for efficiently remembering $Match_i$.

Corresponding to the state sequence of the active facts $\mathcal{A} = \mathcal{A}_1, \mathcal{A}_2, \ldots$, we construct a *memory sequence* $\mathcal{M} = \mathcal{M}_1, \mathcal{M}_2, \ldots$ containing all the active facts that have ever been active so far, along with an additional activation and deactivation timestamp. The key point now will be that a single additional discrimination tree is sufficient to represent $\mathcal{M}$.

An insertion into the index for $\mathcal{A}$ is reflected by a parallel insertion into the index for $\mathcal{M}$, with an appropriate activation timestamp attached to the element. A deletion from the index for $\mathcal{A}$, however, is not mirrored by a deletion from the index for $\mathcal{M}$, but just by setting a deactivation time for the element. We need to define a generalization function $\text{Match}_{i,j}$ that, if called at a current time $j \geq i$, uses the index for $\mathcal{M}_j$ to reconstruct the operation Match_i once performed on the index for $\mathcal{A}_i$.

For doing so, we only have to impose an additional, simple condition in the above standard operation for the retrieval of generalizations: When a leaf node is reached, this implies success only if the attached activation and deactivation timestamps comply with i.

Figure 2 shows a sequence of activation and deactivation steps that results in an index for $\mathcal{M}_4$ to memorize the sequence of active fact sets $\mathcal{A}_1, \ldots, \mathcal{A}_4$. Above we have shown how a generalization for $f(a, a, b)$ is found in the index for $\mathcal{A}_3$. This can now be reconstructed with the index for $\mathcal{M}_4$: The retrieval operation successively visits the nodes ① and ② just like in the index for $\mathcal{A}_3$. In node ③, there now is an appropriate successor via x_1 that leads to ⑪ and the leaf node ⑫. That node holds the matching entry $f(a, x_1, x_2)$, but its timestamps indicate that it is not in $\mathcal{A}_3$. Therefore, backtracking to ② is invoked, and thereafter the nodes ⑥, ⑦ and ⑧ are inspected. That leaf node holds an entry with appropriate timestamps, and is hence returned. In fact, it is the one previously found in the index for $\mathcal{A}_3$.

The reason behind this can be seen in the refinement of the second invariant for the adapted retrieval operation: Any node with a label sequence greater than that of the current one leads to a *timely* match only if it leads to the current node. Therefore this retrieval returns the $\sqsupseteq^*$-greatest timely match in $\mathcal{M}_j$. By construction of the $\mathcal{M}$ sequence, the set of all timely matches is equal to the set of all matches in $\mathcal{A}_i$. The uniqueness of the greatest match now implies that both operations return the same; so we have $\text{Match}_{i,j} = \text{Match}_i$. – Note that the timestamp constraints could also be attached not only to leaves, but also to inner nodes, as union or covering of the timestamps of the descendants. In our example backtracking then would have been invoked not in node ⑫, but already in ⑪.

Let us finally remark that here a crucial prerequisite for efficiently remembering the generalization functions Match_i has been that the sets of all matches are naturally ordered such that the retrieval automatically stops with the unique greatest one. It is unclear to us how the same result can be achieved with other indexing schemes, especially if the index for a term set is not unique.

3.3 The WALDMEISTER Loop

All in all, the elaborate scheme of compression and decompression results in a proof procedure that considerably departs from the original DISCOUNT loop. From a more abstract point of view, the differences can be interpreted as follows:

The generation the critical pairs is delegated from the main loop to $\mathcal{P}$. It is then the task of the subsystem $\mathcal{P}$ to enumerate all non-redundant critical pairs in a fair way. $\mathcal{P}$ is seen as a black box here. It may perform the same normalizations as the main loop did, but these are no "real" inferences, they are for heuristical purposes only. Conceptually, the "real" inferences occur merely at the point of selection; only "good" critical pairs ever enter the completion loop.

This opens the avenue for further developments: Either one can replace the initial normalizations by some approximations. Or, one can completely depart from the given-clause algorithm and simulate e. g. the *pair algorithm* [McC97]. In this alternative a pair of activated equations e_i and e_j is selected via some heuristic ψ and then all critical pairs between them are generated. After simplification all the non-redundant ones are activated and the next pair is determined. In our framework, $\mathcal{P}$ essentially consists of p-entries of the form $\langle \psi(e_i, e_j), i, j, * \rangle$. When a p-decompression occurs, we set the weight of the individual entries to the smallest possible value to ensure that all individual entries are handled before the next p-entry is considered. If for an individual entry the values of ψ on the parents and φ on the equation are combined into one, we get hybrid versions.

Of course, the whole approach is suitable for reasoning with full clauses as well. The only requirement is that any sequence of simplification steps and redundancy tests performed on a passive fact at generation time can *identically* be reproduced at selection time. For binary resolution, the entry format simply has to be adapted such that the position information encodes the literal resolved upon. The extension to superposition or hyperresolution is an easy exercise as well. The more complex the logical objects dealt with are, the more the benefits of the approach, take for example clauses augmented with constraints.

As a final point, since the collected history of $\mathcal{A}$ is available, it is for the generation of a proof object no longer necessary to protocol the inferences of the proof search. When a proof has been found, the contributing active facts are determined. These are then reconstructed while full logging of the inferences is enabled, delivering a detailed proof object. This separates proof search and proof object construction, a further win in architectural clarity.

4   First Practical Results

Several important questions remain: What is the trade-off between space savings and recomputation effort in practice? What are typical values for the average sizes of p-sets and a-sets? Is it worthwhile to modify core parts of existing systems for the integration of the new technique? As it turns out we can answer these question by retrofitting WALDMEISTER to write run-time traces logging the equations inserted into or deleted from $\mathcal{P}$. These traces allow to gather the desired data. Furthermore, we can then simulate different compression schemes and can thus estimate the benefits of an implementation.

Table 1. Characteristic data of representative examples

problem	activated facts	critical pairs			avg. size of p-sets	avg. size of a-sets
		generated	inserted	deleted		
GRP164-1	1 089	1 460 000	963 000	80 900	1.40	486
X6	1 408	2 760 000	2 650 000	47 200	3.64	1 960
RNG027-5	1 089	3 270 000	3 170 000	310 000	6.46	3 000
LAT038-1	2 753	3 760 000	1 630 000	179 000	1.68	1 370
ROB006-1	5 588	10 300 000	10 100 000	82 800	2.45	1 850
ROB001-1	6 220	42 400 000	42 400 000	37 800	8.07	6 820

4.1   Writing and Analyzing $\mathcal{P}$-Traces

WALDMEISTER is modified to write the following information into a file: for each generated critical pair the contributing parents, a unique identifier, and whether it can be shown to be redundant or if it is inserted into $\mathcal{P}$. For each element selected from $\mathcal{P}$ the same identifier is written again. Each deletion of an element of $\mathcal{A}$ is protocoled as well to allow a proper handling of interreductions and orphans in the simulations.

The proof problems we consider are mostly taken from different domains of the TPTP library [SS99] to cover a wide range, except for problem X6 that each ring where $x^6 = x$ is commutative. For all these problems we choose parameter settings for WALDMEISTER such that they can be proved within several minutes. As a contrast, we add the problem ROB001-1 which suffers a memory overflow even with the overlap term representation (cf. Sect. 2.2 and Fig. 1).

In Table 1 we summarize relevant data extracted from the traces. Despite that all the chosen examples generate more than a million critical pairs, the average size of p-sets is rather small, with a rather homogeneous distribution. We conclude that the use of p-entries for compression purposes is rather limited. Their real potential lies in the emulation and variation of the pair algorithm. The distribution of the sizes of the a-sets is far more widespread. After a short amount of abstract time we can expect them to be at least in the range of several hundreds of equations. So their use opens the real opportunity for the drastic reduction of the space requirements.

4.2   Simulations

The complete implementation of the developed scheme requires a significant amount of developer time since core modules of a theorem prover are affected. Fortunately, it is possible to simulate the component $\mathcal{P}$ in such a degree that we can estimate the trade-offs between space usage and time consumption.

We determine the amount of computation effort as the number of critical pairs which have to be computed and normalized. Thus, the costs for additional recomputations in case of a deleteMin operation or an decompression conversion is based on the number of affected equations. We choose this notion since the

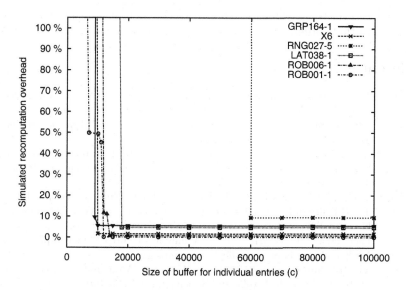

Fig. 3. Recomputation effort as function of size parameter c, for examples of Table 1

costs for each critical pair are in our experience quite evenly distributed. To get a useful measure across the different examples we set the computation effort of the simulated strategy in relation to that of the reference implementation.

From our simulations, we present the following strategy for the two-buffer approach, which shows a quite good behavior. The parameter c determines the size of buffer B for the individual entries. Buffer B' for the a-entries grows with abstract time. Furthermore, we have a *weight limit* w_B which is initially ∞. For each newly inserted clause the weight is compared with w_B. If it is smaller the overlap representation is inserted into B. Otherwise the corresponding a-entry in B' is modified and the equation is discarded. When B gets full, the heavier half of entries is discarded (the a-entries in B' are updated accordingly). Then w_B is determined as the weight of the maximal clause in B. For the selection of clauses from $\mathcal{P}$ the entry with the minimal weight within B and B' is determined. If it is in B, the critical pair is reconstructed from the overlap taken out of B. In the other case, the a-entry is expanded.

Figure 3 shows the recomputation effort as a function of the size parameter c for the examples listed in Table 1. As can be seen this straight-forward strategy performs quite well. Even with a rather small value for c of say 20 000 all but one of the examples can be handled within a small overhead of less than ten per cent. To be useful in general, the strategy has to be extended to dynamically monitor the reconstruction overhead and react accordingly.

Comparing Fig. 1 in Sect. 2.2 with the results of the simulation, we can conclude that we will gain a huge reduction of the space usage of WALDMEISTER: Instead of wasting 1 GByte of memory a new implementation will be satisfied by less than 10 MByte, an improvement of two orders of magnitude for the whole system, and three orders of magnitude considering $\mathcal{P}$ alone.

References

[ADF95]   J. Avenhaus, J. Denzinger, and M. Fuchs. DISCOUNT: a system for distributed equational deduction. In J. Hsiang, ed., *Proceedings of the 6th International Conference on Rewriting Techniques and Applications*, volume 914 of *LNCS*, pp. 397–402. Springer-Verlag, 1995.

[DP01]   N. Dershowitz and D. A. Plaisted. Rewriting. In A. Robinson and A. Voronkov, eds., *Handbook of Automated Reasoning*, volume I, chapter 9, pp. 535–610. Elsevier, 2001.

[Gra96]   P. Graf. *Term Indexing*, volume 1053 of *LNAI*. Springer-Verlag, 1996.

[Hil00]   Th. Hillenbrand. Schnelles Gleichheitsbeweisen: Vom Vervollständigungskalkül zum WALDMEISTER-System. Diplomarbeit, Universität Kaiserslautern, Fachbereich Informatik, 2000. Available via http://www.mpi-sb.mpg.de/~hillen/documents/SchnellesBeweisen.ps.gz.

[HL01]   Th. Hillenbrand and B. Löchner. The next WALDMEISTER loop (extended abstract). In H. de Nivelle and S. Schulz, eds., *Proceedings of the Second International Workshop on Implementation of Logics*, Technical Report MPI-I-2001-2-006, pp. 13–21. Max-Planck-Institut für Informatik Saarbrücken, 2001.

[Küc82]   W. Küchlin. An implementation and investigation of the Knuth-Bendix completion procedure. Interner Bericht 17/82, Universität Karlsruhe, 1982.

[LS01]   B. Löchner and S. Schulz. An evaluation of shared rewriting. In H. de Nivelle and S. Schulz, eds., *Proceedings of the Second International Workshop on Implementation of Logics*, Technical Report MPI-I-2001-2-006, pp. 33–48. Max-Planck-Institut für Informatik Saarbrücken, 2001.

[McC94]   W. McCune. OTTER 3.0 reference manual and guide. Technical Report ANL-94/6, Argonne National Laboratory, 1994.

[McC97]   W. McCune. 33 basic test problems: a practical evaluation of some paramodulation strategies. In R. Veroff, ed., *Automated Reasoning and its Applications: Essays in Honor of Larry Wos*, chapter 5, pp. 71–114. MIT Press, 1997.

[RSV01]   I. V. Ramakrishnan, R. Sekar, and A. Voronkov. Term indexing. In A. Robinson and A. Voronkov, eds., *Handbook of Automated Reasoning*, volume II, chapter 26, pp. 1853–1964. Elsevier, 2001.

[RV00]   A. Riazanov and A. Voronkov. Limited resource strategy in resolution theorem proving. Technical Report CSPP-7, University of Manchester, 2000. Accepted for publication in *Journal of Symbolic Computation*.

[SS99]   C. B. Suttner and G. Sutcliffe. The TPTP problem library (TPTP v2.2.0). Technical Report 99/02, James Cook University, Townsville, 1999.

[Vor01]   A. Voronkov. Algorithms, datastructures, and other issues in efficient automated deduction (invited talk). In R. Goré, A. Leitsch, and T. Nipkow, eds., *Proceedings of the First International Joint Conference on Automated Reasoning*, volume 2083 of *LNAI*, pp. 13–28. Springer-Verlag, 2001.

[Wei01]   Chr. Weidenbach. Combining superposition, sorts and splitting. In A. Robinson and A. Voronkov, eds., *Handbook of Automated Reasoning*, volume II, chapter 27, pp. 1965–2013. Elsevier, 2001.

Focussing Proof-Net Construction as a Middleware Paradigm

Jean Marc Andreoli

Xerox Research Centre Europe, Grenoble, France
Institut de Mathématiques de Luminy, France
Jean-Marc.Andreoli@xrce.xerox.com

Abstract. This paper introduces a new formulation of the computational paradigm based on proof-construction in terms of proof-nets. It shows the relevance of this paradigm, thus formulated, to capture some of the fundamental mechanisms of distributed computation (and in particular, transaction mechanisms), which are familiar concepts of middleware infrastructures. It therefore constitutes a first step in the direction of the definition of a steady conceptual framework in which to formalise and study various middleware notions, which, until now, have essentially been studied through ad-hoc and diverse formalisms.
Due to space constraints, the proofs of the technical results of this paper have been skipped. They were reviewed with the initially submitted version of the paper and are available from the author.

Keywords. Proof-nets, Proof search, Proof construction, Focussing, Middleware, Transactions

1 Introduction

Ever since the early days of Prolog, the computational paradigms based on proof construction have always relied on the use of sequentialised representations of proofs, be it Resolution proofs in the Horn clauses fragment of Classical Logic or Uniform proofs [1,2] in the Hereditary Harrop fragment of Intuitionistic Logic, or Focussing proofs [3] in Linear Logic [4,5]. This makes sense when proof construction aims at theorem proving, where sequentiality often reflects the behaviour of the inference engine of the prover, viewed as a centralised machine managing the entire proof being built, and executing an essentially sequential selection-application loop (though there is a possibility of concurrent expansions on different branches).

This view of proof construction adapted to theorem proving is inadequate when the goal is to model the execution of widely distributed applications. The Coordination Language Facility (CLF) [6] is a typical instance of such an approach. CLF is a middleware toolkit that aims at coordinating autonomous software components on a large area network such as the Internet. The typical applications targeted by CLF are in the domain of information- and work-flow

A. Voronkov (Ed.): CADE-18, LNAI 2392, pp. 501–516, 2002.

control for electronic commerce or document dissemination. In such applications, it is impossible to identify a central locus where the execution takes place. For example, they often include multiple legacy databases or, more generally, heterogeneous data repositories (file systems, document management systems, dedicated components etc.) which have an activity of their own and constitute autonomous components, not devoted to a single application. Furthermore, the set of such components involved in an application may not be known in advance, since the frequent use of dynamic discovery mechanisms makes it impossible to precisely identify the boundaries of the application.

In the face of this complexity, CLF adopts a very flexible, modular approach to application design, based on the paradigm of proof construction in Linear Logic, but with essential differences wrt the theorem-proving approach. First, CLF borrows from Linear Logic its powerful notion of *resource*. The state of the computational universe at any time is given by a set of abstract resources, which, in the proof construction paradigm, correspond to the formulas occurring at the open nodes of the proof being built. A state transition is given by an inference step in the proof construction. We therefore have the isomorphism: proof=state; inference=transition. Now, CLF essentially differs from the theorem proving tradition in the way this isomorphism is exploited. In CLF, there is no central locus where the state is stored and where the transitions are performed. Instead, every component in CLF is viewed as an abstract resource manager holding a bit of the proof, never the totality, and performing some of its inferences. That does not mean that all the components need be implemented as explicit resource managers contributing bits of proofs: that would not make sense with legacy applications such as databases. All it requires is that some components, called *participants* in CLF, be *encapsulated* so as to be seen from the outside world as resource managers contributing to the proof, while other components, called *coordinators* in CLF, are explicitly programmed to build pieces of proofs. Thus, all the components in CLF are modules participating in the proof construction, some of them implicitly (participants) while others explicitly (coordinators).

Unfortunately, sequent proofs are difficult to cut into composable proof-modules [7], precisely because of their artificial sequential nature. Some attempts have been made in the past to minimise the effects of arbitrary sequentialisations, using a constraint based approach [8,9] or the IO-model of resource consumption [10], but this is not sufficient for our purpose. A much more appealing solution consists in using proof-nets [11], or more precisely some form of desequentialised proof-structure, in which the composition operation is simply given by juxtaposition (with some constraints though). Hence the need to redefine the proof-construction paradigm in the context of such proof-structures.

The first problem in this program is to choose the adequate notion of proof-structure. The traditional one is oriented towards the desequentialisation of *complete* proofs, while obviously, the proof construction paradigm only deals with incomplete proofs, always under construction. Therefore, a variant of the traditional notion of proof-structure (and proof-net) is proposed here, adapted to the desequentialised representation of *incomplete* proofs, more precisely those of the focussing bipolar sequent calculus for Linear Logic, which is the adequate system in which to perform proof construction.

The second problem is then to define a correctness criterion adapted to this new notion of proof-structure. The criterion must express the ability to sequentialise a proof-structure into the focussing bipolar sequent calculus, and, since this calculus is equivalent to that of Linear Logic, the criterion could be obtained simply by adapting the traditional criterions for Linear Logic. However, the challenge here is to adapt to the context of proof construction outlined above, so that the criterion must be modular, decentralised and must be amenable to *incremental* testing. CLF offers a solution by restricting to a fragment of Linear Logic where checking the criterion is trivial. One of the goals of this paper is to extend the CLF approach to a larger fragment of Linear Logic preserving the modularity and the locality of the criterion.

2   Focussing Proof-Structures

Focussing (bipolar) proof-structures are desequentialised representations of possibly incomplete (open) proofs in the focussing bipolar sequent calculus. Working in this calculus is in no way limitative, since it has been shown in [8] that:

1. The possibly open focussing proofs of Linear Logic are strictly isomorphic to the possibly open proofs in the focussing bipolar sequent calculus, hence proof-construction is performed equivalently in the two systems;
2. Closed focussing proofs are fully representative of all the closed proofs of Linear Logic, so, as far as the final object being constructed is concerned, proof-construction in Linear Logic can as well work with focussing proofs: this restriction only excludes some intermediate steps in the construction which, anyway, are deemed to fail.

The next sections recall the definition of the focussing bipolar sequent calculus, and then introduce its desequentialised version.

2.1   The Focussing Bipolar Sequent Calculus

More formal definitions can be found in [8].

– Given a set $\mathcal{A}$ of atoms (arbitrarily assigned the negative polarity), an $\mathcal{A}$-formula is a formula built from the (negative) $\mathcal{A}$-atoms and their (positive) duals, using the connectives of Linear Logic:

	multiplicative	additive
negative	$\bot, \otimes, ?$	$\top, \&$
positive	$1, \otimes, !$	$0, \oplus$

– An $\mathcal{A}$-*monopole* is an $\mathcal{A}$-formula built from the negative $\mathcal{A}$-atoms, using only the negative connectives, with the restriction that ? should only have a (negative) atomic sub-formula.

- An $\mathcal{A}$-*bipole* is an $\mathcal{A}$-formula built from the $\mathcal{A}$-monopoles and positive $\mathcal{A}$-atoms, using only the positive connectives, with the restriction that ! should only have a monopolar subformula. Furthermore, bipoles must contain at least one positive connective or be reduced to a positive atom (so that they are always disjoint from monopoles).
- Given a set $\mathcal{F}$ of $\mathcal{A}$-bipoles, the *focussing bipolar sequent calculus* $\Sigma[\mathcal{A}, \mathcal{F}]$ is the set of inferences of the form

$$\frac{\sigma_1 \ \cdots \ \sigma_n}{\sigma}$$

where the conclusion σ is a sequent made only of negative $\mathcal{A}$-atoms, and the premisses $(\sigma_i)_{i=1,\ldots,n}$ are obtained by fully decomposing in a focussing way some bipole $F \in \mathcal{F}$ in the context σ. The bipole F can be viewed as the label of the inference. For example, in the purely multiplicative fragment, the bipole $F = a^\perp \otimes b^\perp \otimes (c \otimes d) \otimes e$, where a, b, c, d, e are negative $\mathcal{A}$-atoms, yields the inference

$$\frac{\Gamma, c, d \quad \Delta, e}{\Gamma, \Delta, a, b}[F]$$

where Γ, Δ range over multisets of negative $\mathcal{A}$-atoms. Note that, by the Focussing property, the premisses corresponding to the positive atoms $a^\perp$ and $b^\perp$ are necessarily identity axioms $a^\perp, a$ and $b^\perp, b$ (omitted here for simplicity sake), which explains why a, b appear in the conclusion: they are the share of the conclusion taken by each of the subformulas $a^\perp$ and $b^\perp$. In this way, a, b appear as the trigger, or multi-focus, of the inference F.
- More generally, the *trigger* of a bipole is the multiset of duals of the positive atoms which occur in it. The main characteristic of the focussing bipolar sequent calculus is that its inferences are triggered by multiple focus (as in Forum [2]).
- A *naming scheme* is a triple $\langle \mathcal{A}, \mathcal{A}', \eta \rangle$ where $\mathcal{A} \subset \mathcal{A}'$ are sets of negative atoms and η is a bijection from the $\mathcal{A}$-formulas into $\mathcal{A}'$ such that $\eta_a = a$ for all $a \in \mathcal{A}$.
- The *universal program* for a naming scheme $\langle \mathcal{A}, \mathcal{A}', \eta \rangle$ is the set of $\mathcal{A}'$-bipoles of the form $\nu(F)$ where F ranges over the $\mathcal{A}$-formulas not reduced to a negative atom. The mapping ν on $\mathcal{A}$-formulas is defined in three steps as follows:
  - Negative layer: mapping $\nu^\uparrow$ from $\mathcal{A}$-formulas to $\mathcal{A}'$-monopoles

  $$\left|\begin{array}{lll} \nu^\uparrow(\bot) = \bot & \nu^\uparrow(F_1 \otimes F_2) = \nu^\uparrow(F_1) \otimes \nu^\uparrow(F2) & \nu^\uparrow(?F) = ?\eta_F \\ \nu^\uparrow(\top) = \top & \nu^\uparrow(F_1 \& F_2) = \nu^\uparrow(F_1) \& \nu^\uparrow(F2) & \\ \nu^\uparrow(F) = \eta_F \text{ in all the other cases} & & \end{array}\right.$$

  - Positive-negative layer: mapping $\nu^\downarrow$ from $\mathcal{A}$-formulas to $\mathcal{A}'$-bipoles or monopoles

  $$\left|\begin{array}{lll} \nu^\downarrow(1) = 1 & \nu^\downarrow(F_1 \otimes F_2) = \nu^\downarrow(F_1) \otimes \nu^\downarrow(F_2) & \nu^\downarrow(!F) = !\nu^\uparrow(F) \\ \nu^\downarrow(0) = 0 & \nu^\downarrow(F_1 \oplus F_2) = \nu^\downarrow(F_1) \oplus \nu^\downarrow(F_2) & \\ \nu^\downarrow(a^\perp) = a^\perp \text{ if } a \text{ is a } negative \text{ atom} & & \\ \nu^\downarrow(F) = \nu^\uparrow(F) \text{ in all the other cases} & & \end{array}\right.$$

- Mapping ν from $\mathcal{A}$-formulas to $\mathcal{A}'$-bipoles:

$$\nu(F) \;=\; \eta_F^{\perp} \otimes \nu^{\downarrow}(F)$$

Thus, for example, consider the formula $F = a^{\perp} \otimes b^{\perp} \otimes ((c^{\perp} \otimes d) \,\mathbf{\otimes}\, e) \otimes f$ and its subformula $G = c^{\perp} \otimes d$, where a, b, c, d, e, f are negative $\mathcal{A}$-atoms. We have

$$\nu(F) \;=\; \eta_F^{\perp} \otimes a^{\perp} \otimes b^{\perp} \otimes (\eta_G \,\mathbf{\otimes}\, e) \otimes f$$
$$\nu(G) \;=\; \eta_G^{\perp} \otimes c^{\perp} \otimes d$$

The following main theorem has been proved in [8]:

Theorem 1. *Given a naming scheme $\langle \mathcal{A}, \mathcal{A}', \eta \rangle$, let $\mathcal{U}$ be its universal program. For any $\mathcal{A}$-formula F there is an isomorphism between the focussing proofs of F in Linear Logic and the proofs of η_F in the focussing bipolar sequent calculus $\Sigma[\mathcal{A}', \mathcal{U}]$.*

This theorem justifies why proof construction in Linear Logic and in the focussing bipolar sequent calculus are essentially equivalent. In the sequel, we assume given a naming scheme with universal program $\mathcal{U}$, and we consider the problem of proof construction in $\Sigma[\mathcal{A}', \mathcal{U}]$.

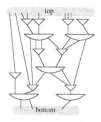

Fig. 1. Example of a focussing proof-structure

2.2 Desequentialising Proofs

Just as sequent proofs in Linear Logic contain a lot of artificial sequentialisations, so do proofs in the focussing bipolar sequent calculus. And they are amenable to the same treatment, ie. a representation as proof-structures (eventually proof-nets) which preserves only the essential sequentialisations. We consider here only the multiplicative fragment of the focussing bipolar sequent calculus, ie. proofs involving only the bipoles of $\mathcal{U}$ which are made only of connectives $1, \otimes, \perp, \mathbf{\otimes}$. The notion of *focussing* proof-structures is defined below in exactly the same way as usual proof-structures for the multiplicative fragment of Linear Logic.

  We assume given an infinite set $\mathcal{P}$ of *places*, and we define a *link* by a set of top places and a set of bottom places. The terminology top/bottom is preferred to the equivalent input/output or premiss/conclusion to better convey the orientation of proof construction (like a building: from bottom to top). The sets of top and bottom places of a link must be disjoint. Furthermore, a link has a polarity (positive or negative), and a negative link must have *exactly* one bottom place, while a positive link must have *at least* one bottom place. Graphically, links are represented as follows:

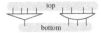

The polarities of links are distinguished by their shape: triangular for the negative links (left) and round for the positive links (right).

Definition 1. *A link L_1 is said to be* just-below *a link L_2, notation $L_1 \nearrow L_2$, if there exists a place which is both at the top of L_1 and at the bottom of L_2. The relation* just-above*, notation $\searrow$ is the converse of $\nearrow$, and can be defined in the same way inverting top and bottom. Two links are said to be* adjacent *if one is just-below (or just-above) the other.*

Using these definitions, we can now introduce the main structure for proof desequentialisation.

Definition 2. *A (multiplicative) focussing proof-structure is a set π of links satisfying the following conditions:*

1. *The sets of top (resp. bottom) places of any two links in π are disjoint.*
2. *If two links in π are adjacent, their polarities are opposite.*

A place which is at the top of a link but not at the bottom of any link in a focussing proof-structure is called a top place of the structure. The bottom places of the structure are defined similarly, by permuting top/bottom. An example of focussing proof-structure is given in Figure 1.

Definition 3. *A focussing proof-structure π is said to be* bipolar *if any place occurring at the top of some positive link in π also occurs at the bottom of some negative link in π and vice-versa. Furthermore, π is said to be* elementary *if it is bipolar and contains exactly one positive link.*

The example of Figure 1 is bipolar. Note that any bipolar focussing proof-structure is the union of disjoint elementary focussing proof-structures, and this decomposition is unique. Furthermore, each elementary focussing proof-structure corresponds to a bipole.

For any (possibly open) proof σ in the focussing bipolar sequent calculus, it is easy to build a set of links σ^* inductively defined (modulo renaming of places) as follows:

- If σ is reduced to a proper axiom, then σ^* is empty.
- Otherwise, if the last inference of σ is induced by the bipole, say, $F = a^\perp \otimes b^\perp \otimes (c \otimes d) \otimes e$, then σ^* is obtained as follows, using the representation of F as an elementary proof-structure:

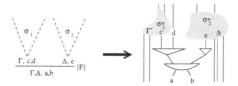

The places of σ_1^* and σ_2^* are renamed apart. The elementary proof-structure for F uses new places for its trigger a, b (bottom). For its top places c, d, e, it uses either the places at the bottom of σ_1^* and σ_2^* if they appear there (e.g. c, e), or new places if they don't (eg. d).

Note that the transformation above assumes the usual distinction, in sequent proofs, between formulas (here negative atoms) and their occurrences, and assumes that the proofs keep track of the occurrences. This is quite standard, and the occurrences thus introduced materialise as places in the links. Note also that in order for the bipole F above to correspond to an elementary focussing proof structure, there is need to introduce a dummy negative link L with just one top place for e. This slight imperfection in syntax could have been avoided by explicitly introducing a polarity inverter to prefix e, as is usually done in strictly polarised syntax [12]. Link L is the materialisation of the hidden polarity inverter.

Proposition 1. *For any proof σ in the focussing bipolar sequent calculus, σ^* is a bipolar proof-structure. The set of bottom places of σ^* is typed by a sub-multiset of the conclusion of σ. The set of top places of σ^* is typed by a sub-multiset of the union of the proper axioms of σ.*

This is shown by straightforward induction. More precisely, the bottom (resp. top) places of σ^* are the occurrences of atoms in the conclusion (resp. proper axioms) which do not also appear in the proper axioms (resp. conclusion) of σ.

Definition 4. *A focussing proof-net is a focussing proof-structure obtained by desequentialisation of a (possibly open) proof in the focussing bipolar sequent calculus.*

Note that focussing proof-nets do not correspond exactly to proof-nets in Linear Logic, since the former apply to possibly *open* proofs, ie. with proper axioms, whereas the latter are meant to represent *closed* proofs. On the other hand, there are no "identity links" in focussing proof-structures: they are implicit in the fact that positive links may have multiple bottom places. As for "cut links", they could also be introduced in focussing proof-structures, but this will not be done here since this paper is interested mainly in proof construction which, by nature, operates on cut-free proofs. Note that in essence, the normalisation of any (cut-free) proof into a focussed one, which justifies the whole approach presented here, can by itself be viewed as an internalised form of cut reduction in the presence of proper axioms: in that case, cuts cannot be completely eliminated, but they can be reduced to stacks initiated by a proper axiom, which are exactly similar to the "critical focussing sections" (see [3] for details).

In the sequel, except when explicitly mentioned otherwise, the term proof-net (or -structure) means focussing proof-net (or -structure). The simplest example of proof-net is given by:

Proposition 2. *Any elementary proof-structure is a proof-net.*

2.3   Proof-Net Construction as a Middleware Paradigm

The computational paradigm of proof construction can now be redesigned as (focussing) proof-net construction (proof-net construction is also studied in [13]). The object being constructed is a proof-net, whose places are decorated with type information (ie. a negative atom is attached to each place). Each bipole of the universal program is interpreted as an autonomous agent (or thread within an agent) which has a view of the places produced so far, and their types, and continuously attempts to contribute to the construction by adding an elementary bipolar proof-net from the places whose types match its trigger. For example, if two places have types, respectively, a and b, then the bipole $a^\perp \otimes b^\perp \otimes (c \,\mathcal{B}\, d) \otimes e$, which has trigger a, b, may attempt to add the following elementary bipolar proof-net to the construction so far:

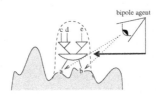

Bipoles always drive the construction bottom-up, so that in the example above, c, d, e are allocated new places. It is important to note that the bipoles of the universal program do not characterise a specific application: we are far, here, from the traditional paradigm of Logic Programming where application programs are modeled as sets of clauses. On the contrary, the universal program is, by nature, universal, ie. independent of any specific application, and the agents which execute its bipoles are typical "infrastructure" software, or, to use an over-abused but popular term, middleware. In a distributed setting, for example, the middleware typically implements the generic mechanisms that are common to all distributed applications, such as transaction [14,15] and event management, service discovery etc. The OMG [1] have established a detailed list of middleware services of that kind.

The CLF middleware, for example, has been used in many different application domains, which it would be out of purpose to detail here: the interested reader is referred to [6,16] for a starting point (or directly to the author). As with many distributed applications, their complexity does not derive from the problems they solve, which, if considered in an ideal world where everything is

---

[1] The OMG is the "Object Management Group", a consortium of major computer-industry actors, created at the beginning of the 1990's to promote and standardise Object Oriented programming in the industry.

under the control of a single programmer, would look pretty straightforward. For example, it is very easy to explain the behaviour of an electronic commerce broker, and one could think, at first glance, that implementing it is just a matter of programming skills. However, this would overlook a number of entangled issues concerning monitoring, maintenance and evolution, management of legacy software and reuse of software, management of network or node failures, etc. which are just as important as the idealised execution machinery itself. It is therefore pointless to illustrate CLF by showing the execution of a sample program, as it would only illustrate a small aspect of the whole picture. The set of needs addressed by CLF, and by middleware systems in general, is of a different nature, and concerns the definition of a computational model in a completely open and decentralised world, accounting for a number of entangled issues that come with it. The use of logic in that context is therefore very different from what it is in usual Logic Programming. In particular, it is more important to be able to model what is effectively going on in a system than what a programmer would like it to be going on. From the role of specification language, logic becomes a pure modelling tool.

Thus, in CLF, the dynamic of an application is modelled as proof-net construction and all the active entities of the application are thought-of as executing the bipoles of the universal program. This paper does not tackle the problem of how the agents which execute the bipoles are effectively notified of the available places and their types. CLF offers a solution, based on the middleware primitives for event management, to this problem which, in a distributed context, is in no way trivial. The problem considered here is rather to identify the middleware primitives underlying the coordination of the different bipole agents in order to ensure that the object being built remains a proof-net, hence could potentially always be sequentialised, even if this is never actually done. Note here the exact similarity with the philosophy behind the use of serialisability criterions for (advanced) transactions, which are used to ensure consistency of shared data, even though serialisation is never actually attempted. This suggests that the middleware primitives for transaction management should have a role here. In fact, the problem can here be decomposed in two stages: first ensure that the (shared) object being built remains a proof-structure, then that it remains a proof-net.

- To ensure that the construction remains a proof-structure, the main problem is to make sure that no two bipole agents attempt to use the same place at the same time. This obviously suggests that conflict resolution need only be based on the places used by an agent which may potentially be used by other agents, ie. the places the agent matches with its trigger. This is the solution adopted by CLF: when a bipole agent with trigger a, b attempts to expand the proof-net from two places (with types, respectively, a and b), it must first acquire these places atomically, which is achieved by a traditional two-phase commit protocol (with some subtleties to avoid deadlocks). This means in particular that the places are endowed with the infrastructure software needed to support a two-phase commit protocol, a typical requirement put on servers in transaction management. And indeed, in CLF, places and their types are managed by servers.

– One can try to use the same strategy of localising conflict resolution to deal with the second problem, that of ensuring that the construction is not only a proof-structure but a proof-net. The problem, however, is that it is not obvious in that case to identify the region of the structure which is concerned when a bipole agent attempts to make a contribution to the construction (whereas in the first problem, the places holding the trigger of the acting bipole were obvious candidates).

In this paper, we show how, in CLF, the second problem is entirely solved by a restriction on the structure of the bipoles allowed in the proof-structure, and how, with a much weaker restriction, the second problem can be considerably simplified.

3   A Correctness Criterion for Focussing Proof-Structures

A correctness criterion is a topological property that fully characterises proof-nets among the proof structures. Basically, a correctness criterion for focussing proof-structures can be derived from any one of the correctness criterions for the usual proof-structures of Linear Logic, by simple generalisation to n-ary links instead of the usual binary ones. However, the challenge here is to give a version of the criterion which is adapted to the specific context of proof-net construction outlined above. In particular, the criterion should apply to open proof-structures and not only to closed one, and should furthermore be amenable to incremental testing.

Definition 5. *A proof-structure is said to be* transitory *if all its positive links have at least one top place. Similarly, a focussing bipolar sequent proof is said to be* transitory *if the bipoles that label its inferences are transitory, ie. contain at least one monopole.*

Obviously, for any proof σ in the focussing bipolar sequent calculus, σ is transitory (as a sequent proof) if and only if σ^* is transitory (as a proof-structure). Note that a transitory sequent-proof can never be closed.

The following discussion applies only to transitory proof-structures. Indeed, handling non transitory proof-structures would complexify the criterions (as handling the multiplicative unit in traditional proof-structures), which could alternatively be avoided by the introduction of additional structural rules such as the Mix rule. In any case, from the perspective of proof construction, the restriction to transitory proofs affects only the termination of the construction process, which is ignored in the present paper.

3.1   The Basic Criterion

The aim of this section is to formulate the Danos-Regnier correctness criterion for a (transitory) proof-structure π as a property of the graph $\mathcal{f}_\pi$ (ie. the restriction to π of the relation "just-below" on links). For this purpose, and to ease the subsequent definition of transformations on this graph, it is convenient to work in a more general setting, consisting of an arbitrary set $\mathcal{L}$ (intended to be the set of all links) with an assignment of a polarity to each of its elements. For any $x \in \mathcal{L}$, the expression x^+ (resp. x^-) means that x has a positive (resp. negative) polarity. The graph $\nearrow_\pi$ thus appears as a binary graph $\mathcal{R}$ on $\mathcal{L}$, and the correctness criterion must identify a necessary and sufficient condition on $\mathcal{R}$ for π to be a proof-net. Instead of relying on Danos-Regnier's "switchings", we take here a slightly different approach and give (and prove) an alternative (albeit equivalent) formulation of the criterion.

Definition 6. *A* trip α *is a non-empty relation on* $\mathcal{L}$ *which is finite, connex and such that any element* x *in* $\mathcal{L}$ *has at most one successor (written* $\alpha^>(x)$ *when it exists) and at most one predecessor (written* $\alpha^<(x)$ *when it exists) by* α. *An element of* $\mathcal{L}$ *is called a* start-point, end-point, middle-point *of* α *if it has, respectively, a successor but no predecessor, a predecessor but no successor, both a predecessor and a successor.*

It is easy to show that for a given trip α, one and only one of the following conditions is true:

- α has no start-point nor end-point. In that case, α is called a *loop*.
- α has a unique start-point and a unique end-point, and they are distinct.

A loop is said to be *degenerated* if it has only two points. Note that a loop can never be contained in another loop.

Notations: let $\mathcal{R}$ be a binary relation over $\mathcal{L}$. Then $|\mathcal{R}|$ denotes the support set of $\mathcal{R}$, ie. the set of places $\bigcup_{x\mathcal{R}y}\{x,y\}$. Also, $\mathcal{R}^{op}$ denotes the reverse of $\mathcal{R}$ and $\mathcal{R}^*$ its transitive closure.

Definition 7. *Let* $\mathcal{R}$ *be a binary relation over* $\mathcal{L}$.

- $\mathcal{R}$ *is said to be* polarised *if adjacent elements in* $\mathcal{R}$ *are of opposite polarity:*
  $\forall x, y \in \mathcal{L} \; x\mathcal{R}y \;\Rightarrow\; (x^- \wedge y^+) \vee (x^+ \wedge y^-)$
- $\mathcal{R}$ *is said to be* bipolarised *if it is finite, polarised, and negative elements have a unique predecessor:*
  $\forall x \in |\mathcal{R}| \; (x^- \;\Rightarrow\; \exists! y \in \mathcal{L} \; y\mathcal{R}x)$
- *A trip* α *is said to be* over $\mathcal{R}$ *if* $\alpha \subset \mathcal{R} \cup \mathcal{R}^{op}$. *A* singularity *for* $\mathcal{R}$ *of a trip* α *is a negative middle-point* x *of* α *such that:*
  $\neg(\alpha^<(x)\mathcal{R}x\mathcal{R}\alpha^>(x) \vee \alpha^>(x)\mathcal{R}x\mathcal{R}\alpha^<(x))$
- $\mathcal{R}$ *is said to be* correct *if any loop over* $\mathcal{R}$ *has at least one singularity for* $\mathcal{R}$.

By definition, a trip α over $\mathcal{R}$ has a singularity for $\mathcal{R}$ if it enters a negative link and exits it by the same side (top or bottom). This is just the converse of the condition that switchings in the Danos-Regnier criterion are forced to traverse each negative link from one side to the other (no "bouncing" is permitted).

Definition 8. *A proof-structure* π *is said to be* correct *if the relation* $\nearrow_\pi$ *(the restriction to* π *of the "just-below" relation on links) is correct.*

Theorem 2. *Any proof-net is a correct, bipolar proof-structure. Any correct transitory bipolar proof-structure is a proof-net.*

The main difference with the Danos-Regnier criterion is that the connexity condition has been dropped (because we work with open, *transitory* proofs). Connexity is a global property of a graph, and that's why the notion of a (global) switching was introduced in the Danos-Regnier criterion. It disappears here precisely because we don't need connexity. What remains is just a simpler formulation of acyclicity.

3.2 Incrementality of Correctness Checking

The correctness criterion introduced in the previous section, although proved in an original way, is a direct adaptation of the Danos-Regnier criterion for usual proof-structures, with the simplification due to the restriction to transitory proof-structures (or alternatively the Mix rule), removing the problems brought by termination. However, our main purpose here is to build a procedure to check the criterion that is adapted to the context of proof-net construction. A naive procedure is given by: build all the loops of $\mathcal{R} =\!/ _\pi$ and check whether they have a singularity. However, when π (and hence $\mathcal{R}$) is built incrementally, as in the case of the proof-net construction paradigm outlined in the previous section, this is simply impossible, because it would require to entirely freeze $\mathcal{R}$ at each expansion. Of course, the minimal optimisation consists in considering, at each expansion, only the loops involving the newly introduced links, and check whether these loops have singularities. That would improve the efficiency of the method, but would still require freezing the whole structure. It is therefore crucial to find a way of testing the criterion in an incremental way.

For this, it is interesting to look at the fragment of proofs used by CLF: in this fragment, the relation $\mathcal{R}$ is characterised by the property that each positive link has only one successor by $\mathcal{R}$. And in that case, correctness checking is trivial: $\mathcal{R}$ is correct simply if it is acyclic, which is ensured, anyway, by the bottom-up way the proof-structure is built. Correctness checking in CLF is incremental, since there is nothing to check! The question is therefore to understand how much of this property of the CLF fragment can be lifted to the general case. For this, the problem of correctness checking on $\mathcal{R}$ is transformed into the same problem on a reduced graph $\mathcal{R}'$.

Definition 9. *The rewriting system denoted $\rightsquigarrow$ is defined as follows: let $\mathcal{R}, \mathcal{R}'$ be binary relations on $\mathcal{L}$; we write $\mathcal{R} \rightsquigarrow \mathcal{R}'$ if and only if one of the following conditions hold:*

- *Elimination of shortcuts: there exists distinct negative elements p, p' and a positive element q such that*

$$p\mathcal{R}^*p' \wedge p'\mathcal{R}q \wedge p\mathcal{R}q$$

and $\mathcal{R}'$ is obtained from $\mathcal{R}$ by removing the edge (p, q):

$$\mathcal{R}' = \mathcal{R} \setminus \{(p, q)\}$$

– *Contraction of forced paths: there exists distinct negative elements p, p' and a positive element q such that*

$$\forall x \in \mathcal{L} \ \begin{cases} x\mathcal{R}q \ \Leftrightarrow \ x = p \\ q\mathcal{R}x \ \Leftrightarrow \ x = p' \end{cases}$$

and $\mathcal{R}'$ is obtained from $\mathcal{R}$ by removing the vertex q and collapsing the vertex p into p':

$$\mathcal{R}' = (\mathcal{R} \setminus ((E \times \{p\}) \cup \{(p, q), (q, p')\})) \cup (E \times \{p'\})$$

where $E = \{x \mid x\mathcal{R}p\}$ is the set of $\mathcal{R}$-predecessors of p.

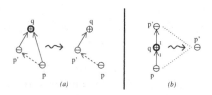

Fig. 2. Reduction of a polarised graph

Figure 2 illustrates the rewriting rules.

Theorem 3. *The rewriting system $\rightsquigarrow$ is convergent. Let $\mathcal{R}, \mathcal{R}'$ be binary relations on $\mathcal{L}$. If $\mathcal{R} \rightsquigarrow \mathcal{R}'$ then*

– *$\mathcal{R}$ is bipolarised if and only if $\mathcal{R}'$ is bipolarised.*
– *$\mathcal{R}$ is bipolarised and correct if and only if $\mathcal{R}'$ is bipolarised and correct.*

Definition 10. *Let π be a bipolar proof-structure. The normal form by $\rightsquigarrow$ of $\upharpoonright_\pi$, obtained by repeated elimination of short-cuts and contraction of forced paths, is called the* session graph *of π.*

Now, combining Theorems 3 and 2, using the fact that by construction, for any bipolar proof structure π, the relation $\upharpoonright_\pi$ is bipolarised, we get:

Proposition 3. *A transitory bipolar proof-structure is a proof-net if and only if its session graph is correct.*

3.3   Implementation

The results presented in the previous section provide an optimisation which can be applied to any algorithm checking the correctness criterion of a proof-structure. The rewriting system $\rightsquigarrow$ can be seen as a kind of compilation of the proof-structure for correctness. It can be in some cases extremely efficient: in CLF, for example, it is easy to show by induction that the session graph of π is always reduced to a single negative link (with a positive link just below it), and that is why correctness checking in CLF is trivial (hence incremental).

We now give some hints at how the use of a session graph can be incorporated into the mechanism of proof-net construction outlined above in the general case (ie. with transitory proof-structures but not necessarily in the CLF fragment). The basic idea is that the session graph can be built incrementally, just as the proof-net itself. For this, we define, for each rewrite step $\mathcal{R} \rightsquigarrow \mathcal{R}'$, a mapping θ from $\mathcal{L}$ into itself as follows: in case (a) of Figure 2, θ is the identity, and in case (b) of Figure 2, θ maps p into p' and is the identity on all the elements of $\mathcal{L}$ different from p. We write $\mathcal{R} \rightsquigarrow_\theta \mathcal{R}'$. It is easy to see that the set of negative elements of $|\mathcal{R}'|$ is exactly the image by θ of the set of negative elements of $|\mathcal{R}|$.

Proposition 4. *Let* $\mathcal{R}, \mathcal{R}', \mathcal{R}_o$ *be binary relations over* $\mathcal{L}$. *If* $\mathcal{R} \rightsquigarrow_\theta \mathcal{R}'$ *and* $|\mathcal{R}| \cap |\mathcal{R}_o|$ *contains only negative elements, then* $\mathcal{R} \cup \mathcal{R}_o \rightsquigarrow_\theta \mathcal{R}' \cup \theta\mathcal{R}_o$ *and* $|\mathcal{R}'| \cap |\theta\mathcal{R}_o|$ *contains only negative elements.*

Demonstration: Quite straightforward from the definitions. The condition that $|\mathcal{R}| \cap |\mathcal{R}_o|$ contains only negative elements ensures that in case (a) of Figure 2, $\mathcal{R}_o$ does not reassert the edge (p, q) that has been removed, and in case (b) of Figure 2, $\mathcal{R}_o$ does not interfere with the condition that q has only one predecessor and one successor. $\qquad\Box$

Now, let π be a bipolar proof-structure and $\mathcal{R}$ its session graph. Therefore, we have, for some $m \geq 0$

$$\ulcorner_\pi \rightsquigarrow_{\theta_1} \cdots \rightsquigarrow_{\theta_m} \mathcal{R} \tag{1}$$

Now let π' be obtained from π by expansion with an elementary bipolar proof-net π_o (as described in the proof-net construction paradigm above). Hence, we have

$$\ulcorner_{\pi'} = \ulcorner_\pi \cup \ulcorner_{\pi_o} \cup G \tag{2}$$

where G consists of the pairs $\{(L_i, L)\}_{i=1,\ldots,n}$ where L is the positive link of π_o and the $(L_i)_{i=1,\ldots,n}$ are the negative links in π which are just below L. Now, the intersection of $|\ulcorner_\pi|$ and $|\ulcorner_{\pi_o} \cup G|$ consists of the set $\{L_i\}_{i=1,\ldots,n}$, hence contains only negative elements. Hence, by repeated application of Proposition 4, we get

$$\ulcorner_{\pi'} \rightsquigarrow_{\theta_1} \cdots \rightsquigarrow_{\theta_m} \mathcal{R} \cup \ulcorner_{\pi_o} \cup G' $$

where $G' = \theta_m \ldots \theta_1(G)$. Hence, the session graph $\mathcal{R}'$ of the expanded proof-structure $\pi \cup \pi_o$ is the normal form of $\mathcal{R} \cup \ulcorner_{\pi_o} \cup G'$. Now, since $\mathcal{R}$ and $\ulcorner_{\pi_o}$ are already in normal form, the additional reductions can only be those involving some of the edges in G'. Hence $\mathcal{R}'$ can be obtained as follows:

- While G' contains two distinct edges $(p_i, L), (p_j, L)$ such that $p_i \mathcal{R}^* p_j$ then remove the edge (p_i, L) from G'.

- If G' is reduced to a single edge (p, L), and furthermore L has a single top place (which is the bottom place of the single negative element L' in π_o), then $\mathcal{R}' = \theta\mathcal{R}$ where θ maps p into L' and is the identity elsewhere. Otherwise, $\mathcal{R}' = \mathcal{R} \cup \lceil_{\pi_o} \cup G'$.

Thus, the session graph of the proof-structure being constructed can be computed incrementally, during the construction, and by Proposition 3, the correctness criterion need only be tested on the session graph.

However, this result does not provide an incremental way to check the correctness criterion, since it still requires freezing the entire session graph, which, in the worst case, can be identical to the original graph. But at least, the expensive cases (when the trigger of the candidate bipole is split across several sessions which are not on the same branch of the session graph) are clearly identified.

4   Conclusion

In this paper, we have reformulated the computational paradigm of proof construction in terms of proof-nets in Linear Logic. We have then shown the relevance of this exercise as a first step towards the use of logic as a universal modelling tool for distributed applications. In particular, we have shown the connexion between the correctness criterions of proof-nets and one of the most important middleware mechanisms for distributed applications, namely transactions. We have studied the problem of incrementally checking correctness and defined a method to reduce this problem based on the incremental construction of a session graph.

The framework we have set here is still extremely limited: it expands the fragment of Linear Logic used by CLF, which has already proved successful in capturing a basic model of transactions, but it does not yet deal with the full multiplicative fragment (because of the restriction to transitory proofs), and furthermore, although it simplifies the problem of incremental checking of the correctness criterion, it does not yet provide a complete solution to this problem. Several directions of research are therefore still open:

- Interpret the whole multiplicative fragment (including multiplicative units), and define an incremental method to check the correctness criterion in this fragment. This may yield a better understanding, in middleware terms, of advanced transaction models, esp. open nested transactions, as well as the issues of transaction termination in such models.
- Interpret the additive and exponential fragments. This may shed a new light on advanced transaction mechanisms.
- Interpret quantification, either first-order or higher-order. First-order quantification is already present in CLF, and is used to capture another important middleware concept, not discussed here: messaging. A further investigation of quantification may yield more elaborated models of messaging, beyond the traditional publish-subscribe based mechanisms (and towards a full negotiation mechanism).

References

1. Miller, D., Nadathur, G., Pfenning, F., Scedrov, A.: Uniform proofs as a foundation for logic programming. Annals of Pure and Applied Logic **51** (1991) 125–157
2. Miller, D.: Forum: A multiple-conclusion specification logic. Theoretical Computer Science **165** (1996) 201–232
3. Andreoli, J.M.: Logic programming with focusing proofs in linear logic. Journal of Logic and Computation **2** (1992)
4. Girard, J.Y.: Linear logic. Theoretical Computer Science **50** (1987) 1–102
5. Miller, D.: An overview of linear logic programming (2002) To appear in a book on linear logic, edited by Thomas Ehrhard, Jean-Yves Girard, Paul Ruet, and Phil Scott. Cambridge University Press.
6. Andreoli, J.M., Pagani, D., Pacull, F., Pareschi, R.: Multiparty negotiation for dynamic distributed object services. Science of Computer Programming **31** (1998) 179–203
7. Danos, V., Regnier, L.: The structure of multiplicatives. Archive for Mathematical Logic **28** (1989) 181–203
8. Andreoli, J.M.: Focussing and proof construction. Annals of Pure and Applied Logic **107** (2001) 131–163
9. Harland, J., Pym, D.: Resource-distribution via boolean constraints. ACM Transactions on Computational Logic (2002) to appear.
10. Hodas, J., Miller, D.: Logic programming in a fragment of intuitionistic linear logic. Information and Computation **110** (1994) 327–365
11. Girard, J.Y.: Proof-nets : the parallel syntax for proof-theory. In Ursini, A., Agliano, P., eds.: Logic and Algebra. Marcel Dekker (1996)
12. Laurent, O.: Polarized proof-nets: Proof-nets for lc. In: Proc. of Typed Lambda Calculi and Applications '99, L'Aquila, Italy (1999)
13. Galmiche, D., Notin, J.M.: Proof-search and proof nets in mixed linear logic. Electronic Notes in Theoretical Computer Science **37** (2000)
14. Gray, J., Reuter, A.: Transaction Processing: Concepts and Techniques. Morgan Kaufmann (1993)
15. Jajodia, S., Kerschberg, L., eds.: Advanced Transaction Models and Architectures. Kluwer Academic (1997)
16. Andreoli, J.M., Arregui, D., Pacull, F., Riviere, M., Vion-Dury, J.Y., Willamowski, J.: Clf/mekano: a framework for building virtual-enterprise applications. In: Proc. of Enterprise Distributed Object Computing Conference, Manheim, Germany, IEEE Computer Society Press (1999)

Proof Analysis by Resolution
(Extended Abstract)

Matthias Baaz

TU-Vienna,
Wiedner Haupstrasse 8-10,
1040 Vienna, AUSTRIA
baaz@logic.at
(joint work with Alexander Leitsch)

1 Introduction

Proof analysis of existing proofs is one of the main sources of scientific progress in mathematics: new concepts can be obtained e.g. by denoting explicit definitions in proof parts and axiomatizing them as new mathematical objects in their own right (The development of the concept of integral is a well known example.) All forms of proof analysis are intended to make informations implicit in a proof explicit i.e.visible. Logical proof analysis is mainly concerned with the implicit constructive content of more or less formalized proofs. The following are major examples for logical proof analysis:

Formal proofs of $(\forall x)(\exists y)P(x, y)$ in computational contexts can be unwinded to proofs of $(\forall x)P(x, \pi(x))$ for suitable programs π (see [5])

Herbrand disjunctions can be extracted from proofs of prenex formulas. Such disjunctions always exist in the case of first-order logic by Herbrand's famous theorem, but can be extracted from many proofs in other systems either (c.f.Luckhardt's analysis of the proof of Roth's theorem [7]). Suitable Herbrand disjunctions can be used to improve bounds or to reduce parametrical dependencies.

Interpolants can be constructed from proofs of $A \to B$.[1] Interpolation is the main tool to make implicit definitions explicit by Beth's theorem.[2]

In this paper, we concentrate on automatizable logical proof analysis in first-order logic by means of incooperating resolution.

2 Notation and Definitions

2.1 The Calculus LK

Gentzen's calculus **LK** is perhaps the most elegant and "semantic" calculus for classical first-order logic. **LK** does not work on formulas directly but on sequents:

---

[1] An *interpolant* for $A \to B$ is a formula I such that (a) $A \to I$ and $I \to B$ are provable and (b) I contains only predicate and function symbols common to A and B.

[2] P is defined *implicitely* by $\Sigma(P)$ iff $\Sigma(P) \cup \Sigma(P') \vdash (\forall x)(P(x) \leftrightarrow P'(x))$, P is defined explicitely by $\Sigma(P)$ iff $\Sigma(P) \vdash (\forall x)(P(x) \leftrightarrow L(x))$ for some L not containing P).

A. Voronkov (Ed.): CADE-18, LNAI 2392, pp. 517–531, 2002.

Definition 1 (sequent). *A sequent is an expression of the form* $\Gamma \vdash \Delta$ *where* Γ *and* Δ *are finite multisets of* PL-*formulas (i.e. two sequents* $\Gamma_1 \vdash \Delta_1$ *and* $\Gamma_2 \vdash \Delta_2$ *are considered equal if the multisets represented by* Γ_1 *and by* Γ_2 *are equal and those represented by* Δ_1, Δ_2 *are also equal).*   ♯

Definition 2 (the calculus LK). *The initial sequents are* $A \vdash A$ *for first-order formulas A. In the rules of* **LK** *we always mark the auxiliary formulas (i.e. the formulas in the premise(s) used for the inference) and the principal (i.e. the inferred) formula using different marking symbols. Thus, in our definition,* $\wedge$-*introduction to the right takes the form*

$$\frac{\Gamma_1 \vdash A^+, \Delta \qquad \Gamma_2 \vdash \Delta_2, B^+}{\Gamma_1, \Gamma_2 \vdash \Delta_1, A \wedge B^*, \Delta_2} \ \wedge : r$$

We usually avoid markings by putting the auxiliary formulas at the leftmost position in the antecedent of sequents and in the rightmost position in the consequent of sequents. The principal formula mostly is identifiable by the context. Thus the rule above will be written as

$$\frac{\Gamma_1 \vdash \Delta_1, A \qquad \Gamma_2 \vdash \Delta_2, B}{\Gamma_1, \Gamma_2 \vdash \Delta_1, \Delta_2, A \wedge B} \ \wedge : r$$

There are two rules for $\wedge$-*introduction to the left:*

$$\frac{A, \Gamma \vdash \Delta}{A \wedge B, \Gamma \vdash \Delta} \ \wedge : l_1$$

and

$$\frac{B, \Gamma \vdash \Delta}{A \wedge B, \Gamma \vdash \Delta} \ \wedge : l_2$$

For every logical operator there are introduction rules to the left and to the right; these rules are called logical rules. *There are also the so-called* structural rules, *namely weakening (w : l, w : r), contraction (c : l, c : r) and cut. The weakening rules add additional formulas to sequents, while the contraction rule "contracts" multiple occurrences of formulas to single ones. The most important structural rule is the cut rule:*

$$\frac{\Gamma_1 \vdash \Delta_1, A \quad A, \Gamma_2 \vdash \Delta_2}{\Gamma_1, \Gamma_2 \vdash \Delta_1, \Delta_2} \ cut$$

The version of **LK** *we are using here is that in [1] and slightly deviates from Gentzen's original version [4]. The differences however are without importance to the results presented in this paper. Readers who are interested in a detailed definition of* **LK** *are referred to [4], [8] and [1]*   ♯

The main result of Gentzen's famous paper [4] was the cut-elimination theorem. It shows that, in arbitrary **LK**-proofs, the cut rule can be *eliminated*. The result is a proof with the *subformula property*, i. e., a proof which is made of the syntactic material of the end sequent. By this property Gentzen's cut-free **LK** can be used as a basis for proof search and automated deduction when combined with the unification principle; the corresponding calculus is the *tableaux-calculus* [6]. The cut free proof of a prenex sequent can be rearranged such that all quantificational inferences are below all propositional inferences; the lowermost propositional sequent is called *mid-sequent*. (Mid-sequents are straightforward generalizations of Herbrand disjunctions.) Interpolants can be constructed from cut free proofs by use of Maehara's lemma (see [8]).

For illustration we give a simple cut-free **LK**-proof of the sequent

$$P(a), (\forall x)(P(x) \to P(f(x))) \vdash P(f^2(a))$$

which (semantically) stands for the formula

$$[P(a) \land (\forall x)(P(x) \to P(f(x)))] \to P(f^2(a)).$$

$$
\cfrac{
\cfrac{
P(a) \vdash P(a) \quad
\cfrac{
\cfrac{
P(f(a)) \vdash P(f(a)) \quad P(f^2(a)) \vdash P(f^2(a))
}{
P(f(a)), P(f(a)) \to P(f^2(a)) \vdash P(f^2(a))
} \;{\to:\, l}
}{
\cfrac{
\cfrac{
P(f(a)) \to P(f^2(a)), P(a) \to P(f(a))), P(a) \vdash P(f^2(a))
}{
(\forall x)(P(x) \to P(f(x))), P(a) \to P(f(a))), P(a) \vdash P(f^2(a))
} \;{\forall:\, l}
}{
(\forall x)(P(x) \to P(f(x))), (\forall x)(P(x) \to P(f(x))), P(a) \vdash P(f^2(a))
} \;{\forall:\, l}
}
}{
} \;{\to:\, l}
}{
(\forall x)(P(x) \to P(f(x))), P(a) \vdash P(f^2(a))
} \;{c:\, l}
$$

2.2 Resolution

We assume the reader to be familiar with the principles of most general unification and resolution. We only give some definitions of clauses and resolution based on a sequent notation.

Definition 3 (clause). *Let* Γ, Δ *be multisets of atom formulas. Then the expression* $C : \Gamma \vdash \Delta$ *is called a* clause.   ♮

Definition 4 (factor). *Let*

$$C = \Gamma \vdash \Delta_1, A_1, \ldots, \Delta_n, A_n, \Delta_{n+1}$$

$(C = \Delta_1, A_1, \ldots, \Delta_n, A_n, \Delta_{n+1} \vdash \Gamma)$ *be a clause where* $n \geq 1$ *and the* Δ_i *are (possibly empty) multisets of atoms. Moreover let* σ *be a most general unifier of* $\{A_1, \ldots, A_n\}$. *Then*

$$C' = \Gamma\sigma \vdash \Delta_1\sigma, \ldots, \Delta_n\sigma, A_n\sigma$$

$(C' = A_n\sigma, \Delta_1\sigma, \ldots, \Delta_n\sigma \vdash \Gamma\sigma)$ *is called a* factor *of* C.   ♮

Remark 1. If the clause does not contain variables then a factor is obtained just by contraction of identical atoms.   ♮

Definition 5 (binary resolvent). *Let $C_1 : \Gamma_1 \vdash \Delta_1, A$ and $C_2 : B, \Gamma_2 \vdash \Delta_2$ be two clauses which are variable disjoint and A, B be unifiable with m.g.u. σ. Then the clause*

$$\Gamma_1\sigma, \Gamma_2\sigma \vdash \Delta_1\sigma, \Delta_2\sigma$$

is called a binary resolvent of C_1 and C_2.   ♯

Definition 6 (resolution). *Let C_1, C_2 be two clauses and C_1', C_2' be variable disjoint variants of factors of C_1, C_2 and C be a binary resolvent of C_1' and C_2'. Then C is called a (general) resolvent of C_1 and C_2.*   ♯

3   The Method of Gentzen

Gentzen's proof of the famous "Hauptsatz" (i.e. the cut-elimination property of LK) is based on a double induction on rank and grade of a modified form of cut, namely the mix.

Definition 7 (mix). *Let $\Gamma \vdash \Pi$ and $\Delta \vdash \Lambda$ two sequents and A be a formula which occurs in Π and in Δ; let Π^*, Δ^* be Π, Δ without occurrences of A. Then the rule*

$$\frac{\Gamma \vdash \Pi \quad \Delta \vdash \Lambda}{\Gamma, \Delta^* \vdash \Pi^*, \Lambda} \; mix$$

is called a mix on A. Frequently we label the rule by $mix(A)$ to indicate that the mix is on A.

Definition 8. *Let ϕ be an **LK**-proof and ψ be a subderivation of the form*

$$\frac{\overset{(\psi_1)}{\Gamma_1 \vdash \Delta_1} \quad \overset{(\psi_2)}{\Gamma_2 \vdash \Delta_2}}{\Gamma_1, \Gamma_2^* \vdash \Delta_1^*, \Delta_2} \; mix(A)$$

Then we call ψ a mix-derivation in ϕ; if the mix is a cut we speak about a cut-derivation. We define the grade of ψ as $comp(A)$; the left-rank of ψ is the maximal number of nodes in a branch in ψ_1 s.t. A occurs in the consequent of a predecessor of $\Gamma_1 \vdash \Delta_1$. If A is "produced" in the last inference of ψ_1 then the left-rank of ψ is 1. The right-rank is defined in an analogous way. The rank of ψ is the sum of right-rank and left-rank.

The cut-elimination method of Gentzen can be considered as a reduction method consisting of rank- and grade reductions on **LK**-proofs. In a slight abuse of language we speak about cut-reduction, even if the cuts are actually mixes.

Definition 9 (cut-reduction). *In Gentzen's proof a mix-derivation ψ is selected in an **LK**-proof ϕ and replaced by a derivation ψ' (with the same endsequent) s.t. the corresponding mix-derivation(s) in ψ' has either lower grade or lower rank than ψ. We do not have the space to list all the reduction rules correponding the the case analysis in Gentzen's proof, but we list some typical ones. For the exhaustive list of the rules we refer to [4].*

– *grade reduction, where the rank is 2 and the mix formula is the conjunction* $A \wedge B$ *(obtained via logical rules on both sides):*
Let ψ be the mix-derivation:

$$\frac{\dfrac{(\psi_1) \qquad (\psi_2)}{\dfrac{\Pi_1 \vdash \Lambda_1, A \quad \Pi_2 \vdash \Lambda_2, B}{\Gamma_1 \vdash \Gamma_2, A \wedge B} \wedge : r} \quad \dfrac{(\psi_3)}{\dfrac{B, \Delta_1 \vdash \Delta_2}{A \wedge B, \Delta_1 \vdash \Delta_2}}}{\Gamma_1, \Delta_1 \vdash \Gamma_2, \Delta_2} \; mix$$

s.t. $\Gamma_1 = \Pi_1, \Pi_2$, $\Gamma_2 = \Lambda_1, \Lambda_2$ *and* $A \wedge B$ *does not occur in* Γ_2, Δ_1. *Then* ψ *is reduced to* ψ' *(we write* $\psi \succ \psi'$*):*

$$\frac{\dfrac{(\psi_2) \qquad (\psi_3)}{\dfrac{\Pi_2 \vdash \Lambda_2, B \quad B, \Delta_1 \vdash \Delta_2}{\Pi_2, \Delta_1 \vdash \Lambda_2, \Delta_2} \; mix}}{\Gamma_1, \Delta_1 \vdash \Gamma_2, \Delta_2} \; w :^*$$

– *mix-elimination, where the left-rank is 1 and the mix formula is the conjunction* $A \wedge B$ *(obtained via weakening). Let* ψ *be:*

$$\frac{\dfrac{\dfrac{(\psi_1)}{\Gamma_1 \vdash \Gamma_2}}{\Gamma_1 \vdash \Gamma_2, A \wedge B} \; w : r \quad \dfrac{(\psi_2)}{A \wedge B, \Delta_1 \vdash \Delta_2}}{\Gamma_1, \Delta_1^* \vdash \Gamma_2, \Delta_2} \; mix$$

Then ψ *reduces to* ψ' *(*$\psi \succ \psi'$*) for* ψ':

$$\frac{\dfrac{(\psi_1)}{\Gamma_1 \vdash \Gamma_2}}{\Gamma_1, \Delta_1^* \vdash \Gamma_2, \Delta_2} \; w :^*$$

– *rank reduction, where the left-rank is* > 1 *the right-rank is 1, the mix formula* A *occurs in* Π_2, *but not in* Π_1; *the last inference in the left tree of the mix derivation is* $\to : l$. *Let* ψ *be:*

$$\frac{\dfrac{(\psi_1) \qquad (\psi_2)}{\dfrac{\Lambda_1 \vdash \Pi_1, B \quad C, \Lambda_2 \vdash \Pi_2}{B \to C, \Lambda_1, \Lambda_2 \vdash \Pi_1, \Pi_2} \to : l} \quad \dfrac{(\psi_3)}{\Delta_1 \vdash \Delta_2}}{B \to C, \Lambda_1, \Lambda_2, \Delta_1^* \vdash \Pi_1, \Pi_2^*, \Delta_2} \; mix(A)$$

Then $\psi \succ \psi'$ *for* ψ':

$$\frac{\dfrac{(\psi_1)}{\Lambda_1 \vdash \Pi_1, B} \quad \dfrac{\dfrac{(\psi_2) \qquad (\psi_3)}{C, \Lambda_2 \vdash \Pi_2 \quad \Delta_1 \vdash \Delta_2}}{C, \Lambda_2, \Delta_1^* \vdash \Pi_2^*, \Delta_2} \; mix(A)}{B \to C, \Lambda_1, \Lambda_2, \Delta_1^* \vdash \Pi_1, \Pi_2^*, \Delta_2} \to : l$$

Let ψ be a mix-derivation in ϕ, $\psi \succ \psi'$ and ϕ' be the proof obtained from ϕ by replacing ψ by ψ'. If ψ is an "uppermost mix", i.e. the last inference is the only mix in ψ, then we speak about Gentzen reduction; *in this case we extend the reduction relation $\succ$ to the whole proofs ϕ, ϕ' and write $\phi \succ \phi'$. Cut-elimination via Gentzen is defined as a sequence $\phi_0, \ldots, \phi_n$ s.t. ϕ_0 is the original proof ϕ, $\phi_i \succ \phi_{i+1}$ for $i = 0, \ldots, n-1$, and ϕ_n is cut-free.*   ♮

4   Cut-Elimination by Resolution

The standard method of cut-elimination is that of Gentzen described in Section 3. Despite its elegance, Gentzen's method is algorithmically very costly (of course we cannot blame Gentzen, as his aim was not to define an algorithm!). The reason is that the method is largely independent of the derivations and of the *inner* structure of the cut formulas.

The availability of resolution theorem proving and the fact that resolution is in some sense a "subcalculus" of **LK** (see Subsection 2.1) makes resolution a natural candidate in the investigation of cut-elimination. In this section we will informally present an algorithmic method of *Cut-elimination by resolution*, an exact and exhaustive treatment can be found in [2]. The resolution method substantially differs from Gentzen's one. In the first step a set of clauses is generated from the derivations of the cut formulas. These sets of clauses are always unsatisfiable and thus have a resolution refutation. The construction of the resolution refutation is the second step of the procedure. Note that this step represents a direct application of automated theorem proving. The resolution refutation obtained from the theorem prover then serves as a *skeleton* of an **LK**-proof with only atomic cuts; this **LK**-proof is obtained by filling the skeleton with parts of the original **LK**-proof (actually with proof projections). The last step consists of the elimination of atomic cuts.

Although cut-elimination gave the original motivation to the development of the resolution method, the approach is far more general: indeed, the elimination of cuts appears as a special case of redundancy-elimination in **LK**-proofs. E.g. it suffices that the left cut formula logically implies the right one; they need not be syntactically equal. In fact the resolution method is largely a *semantic* one. Furthermore the method can be generalized to a method of occurrence elimination in **LK**-proofs which sheds more light on the role of redundancy in proofs.

In the first step we reduce cut-elimination to formula-elimination: that means we transform a proof φ with cuts into a cut-free proof ψ of an extended end-sequent; this transformation (unlike "real" cut-elimination) is harmless in the sense that the time complexity is linear in the size of φ.

Definition 10. *We define a mapping T_{cut} which transforms an LK-proof ψ of a sequent $S : \Gamma \vdash \Delta$ with cut formulas $A_1, \ldots A_n$ into an LK-proof ψ^* of*

$$\forall(A_1 \to A_1) \wedge \ldots \wedge \forall(A_n \to A_n), \Gamma \vdash \Delta$$

in the following way: Take an uppermost cut and its derivation χ:

$$\frac{\overset{(\chi_1)}{\Pi_1 \vdash \Lambda_1, A} \quad \overset{(\chi_2)}{A, \Pi_2 \vdash \Lambda_2}}{\Pi_1, \Pi_2 \vdash \Lambda_1, \Lambda_2} \; cut$$

occurring in ψ and replace it by χ'

$$\frac{\overset{(\chi_1)}{\Pi_1 \vdash \Lambda_1, A} \quad \overset{(\chi_2)}{A, \Pi_2 \vdash \Lambda_2}}{A \to A, \Pi_1, \Pi_2 \vdash \Lambda_1, \Lambda_2} \; \to: l$$

Afterwards apply $\forall : l$-inferences to the end-sequent of χ' on the free variables in $A \to A$ resulting in a proof χ'' of $\forall(A \to A), \Pi_1, \Pi_2 \vdash \Lambda_1, \Lambda_2$. Iterate the procedure on the next uppermost cuts till all cuts are eliminated and keep all other inferences unchanged. The result is a proof ψ' of the sequent S' :

$$\forall(A_1 \to A_1), \dots \forall(A_n \to A_n), \Gamma \vdash \Delta.$$

Finally ψ^* is obtained by contractions and $\wedge : l$.
We call the new sequent S' : the cut-extension of S w.r.t. ψ.   ♯

It is easy to see that $T_{cut}(\psi)$ is indeed a cut-free proof of the cut-extension of S w.r.t. ψ. The only nontrivial point is the preservation of the eigenvariable conditions.

After transformation of the proof ψ of S to $T_{cut}(\psi)$ of the cut-extension S' the problem of cut-elimination in ψ can be reduced to the construction of a cut-free proof of S from $T_{cut}(\psi)$. The new problem then consists in the elimination of the formula $B : \forall(A_1 \to A_1) \wedge \dots \wedge \forall(A_n \to A_n)$ on the left-hand-side of the end-sequent. For technical reasons we assume that the end sequent of S is skolemized. Note that **LK**-proofs can be skolemized by a polynomial transformation defined in [1].

The first step in the formula-elimination procedure consists in the construction of a set of clauses. This set corresponds to a left occurrence of a (valid) formula in the end-sequent of an **LK**-proof. Roughly speaking we trace the derivation of the formula B (encoding the cut formulas of the original proof) back to the initial sequents. In the initial sequents we separate the parts which are ancestors of B and obtain a set of clauses $\mathcal{C}$ where each $C \in \mathcal{C}$ is of the form $\vdash, A \vdash, \vdash A$ or $A \vdash A$. Going down in the proof we look whether the corresponding inference works on ancestors of B or not. In the first case we have to subject the sets of clauses to union, in the second one to a product. The formal definition is given below:

Definition 11. *Let ψ be a cut-free proof of S and α be an occurrence of a formula in S. We define the set of characteristic clauses $\mathrm{CL}(\psi, \alpha)$ inductively: Let η be an occurrence of a sequent S' in ψ; by $anc(\eta, \alpha)$ we denote the subsequent S'' of S' which consists exactly of the formulas with occurrences being ancestors of the occurrence α in S. Let η be the occurrence of an initial sequent $A \vdash A$ in ψ and η_1 (η_2) be the left (right) occurrence of A in $A \vdash A$. If neither η_1 nor η_2 is an ancestor of α then $\mathcal{C}_\eta = \{\vdash\}$; If both η_1 and η_2 are ancestors of α then*

$\mathcal{C}_\eta = \emptyset$. Otherwise (exactly one of η_1, η_2 is ancestor of α) $\mathcal{C}_\eta = \{anc(\eta,\alpha)\}$, i.e. $\mathcal{C}_\eta = \{A \vdash\}$ if η_1 is ancestor of α and $\mathcal{C}_\eta = \{\vdash A\}$ if η_2 is ancestor of α.

Let us assume that the clause sets $\mathcal{C}_\lambda$ are already constructed for all sequent–occurrences λ in ψ with depth(λ) $\leq k$ (where the depth of an occurrence λ is the length of the path in the proof tree from the root to λ).

Now let λ be an occurrence with depth(λ) $= k{+}1$. We distinguish the following cases:

a λ is the consequent of μ, i.e. a unary rule applied to μ gives λ. Here we simply define $\mathcal{C}_\lambda = \mathcal{C}_\mu$.

b λ is the consequent of μ_1 and μ_2, i.e. a binary rule X applied to μ_1 and μ_2 gives λ.

    b1 The auxiliary formulas of X are ancestors of α, i.e. the formulas occur in $anc(\mu_1,\alpha)$, $anc(\mu_2,\alpha)$. Then $\mathcal{C}_\lambda = \mathcal{C}_{\mu_1} \cup \mathcal{C}_{\mu_2}$.

    b2 The auxiliary formulas of X are not ancestors of α. In this case we define $\mathcal{C}_\lambda = \mathcal{C}_{\mu_1} \otimes \mathcal{C}_{\mu_2}$ where

$$\{\bar{P}_1 \vdash \bar{Q}_1, \dots \bar{P}_m \vdash \bar{Q}_m\} \otimes \{\bar{R}_1 \vdash \bar{T}_1, \dots \bar{R}_n \vdash \bar{T}_n\} =$$
$$\{\bar{P}_i, \bar{R}_j \vdash \bar{Q}_i, \bar{T}_j \mid i \leq m, j \leq n\}$$

Finally $\mathrm{CL}(\psi,\alpha)$ is set to $\mathcal{C}_\nu$ where ν is the occurrence of the end-sequent. Note that α is an occurrence in ν and its own ancestor. ♯

Example 1. Let ψ be the proof (for u,v free variables, a a constant symbol)

$$\frac{\psi_1 \qquad \psi_2}{(\forall x)(P(x) \to Q(x)) \vdash (\exists y)(P(a) \to Q(y))}\ cut$$

where ψ_1 is the **LK**-proof:

$$\frac{\dfrac{\dfrac{\dfrac{\dfrac{\dfrac{P(u)^* \vdash P(u) \quad Q(u) \vdash Q(u)^*}{P(u)^*, P(u) \to Q(u) \vdash Q(u)^*}\ {\to}{:}\,l}{P(u) \to Q(u) \vdash (P(u) \to Q(u))^*}\ {\to}{:}\,r}{P(u) \to Q(u) \vdash (\exists y)(P(u) \to Q(y))^*}\ \exists : r}{(\forall x)(P(x) \to Q(x)) \vdash (\exists y)(P(u) \to Q(y))^*}\ \forall : l}{(\forall x)(P(x) \to Q(x)) \vdash (\forall x)(\exists y)(P(x) \to Q(y))^*}\ \forall : r$$

and ψ_2 is:

$$\frac{\dfrac{\dfrac{\dfrac{\dfrac{\dfrac{P(a) \vdash P(a)^* \quad Q(v)^* \vdash Q(v)}{P(a), (P(a) \to Q(v))^* \vdash Q(v)}\ {\to}{:}\,l}{(P(a) \to Q(v))^* \vdash P(a) \to Q(v)}\ {\to}{:}\,r}{(P(a) \to Q(v))^* \vdash (\exists y)(P(a) \to Q(y))}\ \exists : r}{(\exists y)(P(a) \to Q(y))^* \vdash (\exists y)(P(a) \to Q(y))}\ \exists : l}{(\forall x)(\exists y)(P(x) \to Q(y))^* \vdash (\exists y)(P(a) \to Q(y))}\ \forall : l$$

The ancestors of the cut formula in ψ_1 and ψ_2 are marked by $*$. From ψ we construct the cut-extension ψ', where A denotes the cut formula $(\forall x)(\exists y)(P(x) \to Q(y))$ of ψ:

$$\frac{\psi_1 \qquad \psi_2}{A \to A, (\forall x)(P(x) \to Q(x)) \vdash (\exists y)(P(a) \to Q(y))} \to: l$$

Let α be the occurrence of $A \to A$ in the end sequent S' of ψ'. We compute the characteristic clauses $\mathrm{CL}(\psi', \alpha)$:

From the $*$-marks in the proofs ψ_1 and ψ_2 (which indicate the ancestors of α) we first get the sets of clauses corresponding to the initial sequents:

$$\mathcal{C}_1 = \{P(u) \vdash\}, \ \mathcal{C}_2 = \{\vdash Q(u)\}, \ \mathcal{C}_3 = \{\vdash P(a)\}, \ \mathcal{C}_4 = \{Q(v) \vdash\}.$$

The first inference in ψ_1 (it is $\to: l$) takes place on nonancestors of α – the auxiliary formulas of the inference are not marked by $*$. Consequently we apply $\otimes$ and obtain the set $\mathcal{C}_{1,2} = \{P(u) \vdash Q(u)\}$. The following inferences in ψ_1 are all unary and so we obtain

$$\mathrm{CL}(\psi_1, \alpha_1) = \{P(u) \vdash Q(u)\}$$

for α_1 being the occurrence of the ancestor of α in the end-sequent of ψ_1.

The first inference in ψ_2 takes place on ancestors of α (the auxiliary formulas are $*$-ed) and we have to apply the $\cup$ on $\mathcal{C}_3, \mathcal{C}_4$. We obtain $\mathcal{C}_{3,4} = \{\vdash P(a), \ Q(v) \vdash\}$. Like in ψ_1 all following inferences in ψ_2 are unary leaving the set of clauses unchanged. Let α_2 be the ancestor of α in the end-sequent of ψ_2. Then the corresponding set of clauses is

$$\mathrm{CL}(\psi_2, \alpha_2) = \{\vdash P(a), \ Q(v) \vdash\}.$$

The last inference $\to: l$ in ψ' takes place on ancestors of α and we have to apply $\cup$ on $\mathcal{C}_{1,2}$ and $\mathcal{C}_{3,4}$. This eventually yields

$$\mathrm{CL}(\psi', \alpha) = \{P(u) \vdash Q(u), \ \vdash P(a), \ Q(v) \vdash\}. \ \sharp$$

It is easy to verify that the set of characteristic clauses $\mathrm{CL}(\psi', \alpha)$ constructed in the example above is unsatisfiable. This is not merely a coincidence, but a general principle expressed in the next proposition.

Proposition 1. *Let ψ be a cut-free proof of the sequent S and α be a left-occurrence of a valid formula occurring in S. Then the set of clauses $\mathrm{CL}(\psi, \alpha)$ is unsatisfiable.*

Proof. in [1]. Basically it is shown that $B \vdash$, for B occurring at α, (which is an unsatisfiable sequent) is derivable in **LK** from the initial axioms $\mathrm{CL}(\psi, \alpha)$.

Remark 2. The proof of Proposition 1 might suggest that the set of clauses $\mathrm{CL}(\psi, \alpha)$ is just a clausal normal form of the formula $\neg B$ corresponding to the sequent $B \vdash$; but this is not the case! As a simple counterexample consider the following derivation ψ:

$$\frac{\dfrac{Q(b) \vdash Q(b)}{\vdash Q(b) \to Q(b)} \to : r}{P(a) \to P(a) \vdash Q(b) \to Q(b)} \; w : l$$

The only initial sequent of ψ is $Q(b) \vdash Q(b)$. Neither the left- nor the right occurrence of $Q(b)$ in this sequent is an ancestor of the occurrence α of $P(a) \to P(a)$ in the end sequent. Thus the set of clauses $\mathcal{C}$ corresponding to the node of the initial sequent is $\{\vdash\}$. As there are only unary rules in ψ we finally obtain $\mathrm{CL}(\psi, \alpha) = \mathcal{C} = \{\vdash\}$. On the other hand no traditional transformation to normal form (like standard- or structural transformation) transforms the formula $\neg(P(a) \to P(a))$ into $\{\vdash\}$. In particular the standard transformation gives the set of clauses $\mathcal{D}: \{\vdash P(a),\ P(a) \vdash\}$. The example above illustrates that the set of clauses $\mathrm{CL}(\psi, \alpha)$ strongly depends on the derivation ψ and not only on the form of the formula on position α! We will see in the following presentation of the method that the construction of $\mathrm{CL}(\psi, \alpha)$ from the proof ψ plays a central role in the so-called proof projection (which cannot be performed on the basis of ordinary clause forms).   ♯

Now let $\mathrm{CL}(\psi, \alpha)$ be the (unsatisfiable) set of clauses extracted from the **LK**-proof of the extended sequent S. By the completeness of the resolution principle there exists a resolution refutation γ (in form of a tree) of the set of clauses $\mathrm{CL}(\psi, \alpha)$. γ can be transformed into a ground refutation of $\mathrm{CL}(\psi, \alpha)$:

Proposition 2. *Let γ be a tree resolution refutation of a set of clauses $\mathcal{C}$. Then there exists a ground instance γ' of γ s.t. γ' is a tree resolution refutation of $\mathcal{C}'$ where $\mathcal{C}'$ is a set of ground instances from $\mathcal{C}$.*

Proof. Let λ be the simultaneous most general unifier of all the resolutions in γ. Then $\gamma\lambda$ is also a resolution refutation where the resolution rule reduces to atomic cut and contractions (i.e. to a mix, see [4]). Let σ be an arbitrary ground substitution of the variables of $\gamma\lambda$; then $\gamma':\gamma\lambda\sigma$ is the desired resolution refutation.

Remark 3. We call the refutation γ' defined above a ground refutation *corresponding to* γ.   ♯

Now let γ' be a ground refutation corresponding to a resolution refutation γ of $\mathrm{CL}(\psi, \alpha)$. By our definition of resolution γ' can easily transformed to an **LK**-proof of $\vdash$ from $\mathcal{C}'$ with atomic cuts. Indeed, only additional contractions are necessary to simulate factoring. The resulting **LK**-proof γ' will serve as a *skeleton* of an **LK**-proof ϕ of $\Gamma \vdash \Delta$ with atomic cuts. Recall that S may be a cut-extension $B, \Gamma \vdash \Delta$ of $\Gamma \vdash \Delta$.

Thus ϕ corresponds (modulo the transformation T_{cut}) to a reduction of a proof with cuts to a proof with atomic cuts. The construction of ϕ from γ' is based on so called *projections* replacing the proof ψ of the cut-extension S by proofs $\psi[C]$ of $\bar{P}, \Gamma \vdash \Delta, \bar{Q}$ for clauses $C : \bar{P} \vdash \bar{Q}$ in C', where C' is the set of ground instances refuted by γ'. The existence of such projections of ψ w.r.t. clauses in C', guaranteed by the lemma below, is the most important property of the cut-elimination method based on resolution.

Lemma 1. *Let ψ be a cut-free proof of a sequent $S: B, \Gamma \vdash \Delta$ s.t. $\Gamma \vdash \Delta$ is skolemized, B is valid and α is the occurrence of B in S. Let $C: \bar{P} \vdash \bar{Q}$ be clause in $\mathrm{CL}(\psi, \alpha)$. Then there exists a cut-free proof $\psi[C]$ of $\bar{P}, \Gamma \vdash \Delta, \bar{Q}$ with $l(\psi[C]) \le l(\psi)$ (where l denotes the length of the proof, i.e. the number of nodes occurring in the derivation tree).*

Proof. We only give a proof sketch; a full formal proof can be found in [2].

The proof goes by induction on the depth of inference nodes in ψ. In constructing $\psi[C]$ we skip all inferences in ψ leading to the extension formula B. In the other inferences with auxiliary formulas which are not ancestors of B we select two clauses from the corresponding set of clauses and construct the corresponding projections via the induction hypothesis. We concentrate on a binary inference rule X and the following proof χ:

$$\frac{(\mu_1)\ \Gamma_1 \vdash \Delta_1 \quad (\mu_2)\ \Gamma_2 \vdash \Delta_2}{(\lambda)\ \Gamma_1, \Gamma_2 \vdash \Delta_1, \Delta_2}\ X$$

$$\overset{(\rho_1)}{} \quad \overset{(\rho_2)}{}$$

where μ_1, μ_2, λ are the nodes in the proof tree ψ and $\bar{P} \vdash \bar{Q}$ is a clause in C_λ. We assume that the auxiliary formulas of X are not ancestors of α and that the subsequents of $\Gamma_i \vdash \Delta_i$ defined by formulas which are not ancestors of B are $\Pi_i \vdash \Lambda_i$ for $i = 1, 2$. Then, by Definition 11, we have $C_\lambda = C_{\mu_1} \otimes C_{\mu_2}$. Therefore there are clauses $\bar{P}_1 \vdash \bar{Q}_1 \in C_{\mu_1}$ and $\bar{P}_2 \vdash \bar{Q}_2 \in C_{\mu_2}$ s.t.

$$\bar{P} \vdash \bar{Q} = \bar{P}_1, \bar{P}_2 \vdash \bar{Q}_1, \bar{Q}_2.$$

By induction hypothesis we obtain proofs ρ_1' of $\bar{P}_1, \Pi_1 \vdash \Lambda_1, \bar{Q}_1$ and ρ_2' of $\bar{P}_2, \Pi_2 \vdash \Lambda_2, \bar{Q}_2$ with $l(\rho_1') \le l(\rho_1)$ and $l(\rho_2') \le l(\rho_2)$. Then the projection corresponding to the node λ is χ':

$$\frac{\bar{P}_1, \Pi_1 \vdash \Lambda_1, \bar{Q}_1 \quad \bar{P}_2, \Pi_2 \vdash \Lambda_2, \bar{Q}_2}{\bar{P}_1, \bar{P}_2 \Pi_1, \Pi_2 \vdash \Lambda_1, \Lambda_2, \bar{Q}_1, \bar{Q}_2}\ X$$

$$\overset{(\rho_1')}{} \quad \overset{(\rho_2')}{}$$

Clearly $l(\chi') \le l(\chi)$.

Remark 4. For the projections $\psi[C]$ we need the set of clause $\mathrm{CL}(\psi, \alpha)$ as defined in Definition 11. Here it is important that $C: \mathrm{CL}(\psi, \alpha)$ is constructed *from the proof ψ itself*! Thus C is not an ordinary clause form of $\neg B$ constructed from the syntax of B, but a clause form belonging to the derivation of $B \vdash$ within ψ. ♯

Once we we have constructed the projections $\psi[C]$ we can "insert" them into the resolution refutation γ. The formal procedure is defined below:

Definition 12. *Let ψ be a cut-free proof of $S : B, \Gamma \vdash \Delta$ s.t. B is valid, $\Gamma \vdash \Delta$ closed and skolemized and α the occurrence of B in S. Let γ' a ground refutation corresponding to a resolution refutation γ of $\mathrm{CL}(\psi, \alpha)$ s.t. $\gamma' = \gamma\sigma$. We define an **LK**-proof $\gamma'[\psi]$ inductively:*

Let N be a leaf node in γ labelled with a clause $C\sigma$ for $C \in \mathrm{CL}(\psi, \alpha)$ and let $C\sigma = \bar{P} \vdash \bar{Q}$. To N we assign the proof $\omega_N : \psi[C]\sigma$, where $\psi[C]$ is the projection of ψ to C as defined in Lemma 1 By definition ω_N is a cut-free proof of the sequent $\bar{P}, \Gamma\sigma \vdash \Delta\sigma, \bar{Q}$. By assumption S is closed and thus ω_N is a cut-free proof of $\bar{P}, \Gamma \vdash \Delta, \bar{Q}$.

Assume that N is a node in γ labelled with C and with parent nodes N_1 labelled with C_1 and N_2 labelled with C_2. Then, by definition of a resolution derivation, C is a (ground) resolvent of C_1 and C_2. Therefore $C_1 = \bar{P} \vdash \bar{Q}, A^r$, $C_2 = A^s, \bar{R} \vdash \bar{T}$ and $C = \bar{P}, \bar{R} \vdash \bar{Q}, \bar{T}$ for multisets of atoms $\bar{P}, \bar{Q}, \bar{R}, \bar{T}$ and an atom A occurring r-times in C_1 and s-times in C_2

*Let ω_{N_1} and ω_{N_2} be the **LK**-proofs corresponding to N_1 and N_2, respectively. Assume that ω_{N_1} is a proof of $\bar{P}, \Gamma^k \vdash \Delta^k, \bar{Q}, A^r$ and ω_{N_2} of $A^s, \bar{R}, \Gamma^l \vdash \Delta^l, \bar{T}$ for $k, l \in \mathbb{N}$. Then ω_N, the **LK**-proof corresponding to N, is defined as*

$$
\cfrac{
  \cfrac{(\omega_{N_1})}{\bar{P}, \Gamma^k \vdash \Delta^k, \bar{Q}, A^r} \quad
  \cfrac{}{\bar{P}, \Gamma^k \vdash \Delta^k, \bar{Q}, A} \; c : r^*
  \qquad
  \cfrac{(\omega_{N_2})}{A^s, \bar{R}, \Gamma^l \vdash \Delta^l, \bar{T}} \quad
  \cfrac{}{A, \bar{R}, \Gamma^l \vdash \Delta^l, \bar{T}} \; c : l^*
}{\bar{P}, \bar{R}, \Gamma^{k+l} \vdash \Delta^{k+l}, \bar{Q}, \bar{T}} \; cut
$$

Let N_r be the root node of γ'; then $\gamma'[\psi]$ is defined as ω_{N_r}.   ♯

If ψ is a cut-free proof of $B, \Gamma \vdash \Delta$ then $\gamma'[\psi]$ in Definition 12 is a proof with atomic cuts of $\Gamma, \ldots, \Gamma \vdash \Delta, \ldots, \Delta$ (note that the clause belonging to the root node of γ' is $\vdash$). Only additional contractions are necessary for getting a proof $\hat{\gamma}[\psi]$ with atomic cuts of $\Gamma \vdash \Delta$ itself. It remains only to eliminate the atomic cuts; to this aim any cut-elimination procedure (e.g. this in [4] does the job. The length of the proofs with atomic is essentially defined by the length of γ'.

Theorem 1. *Let ψ be a cut-free proof of a closed sequent $S : B, \Gamma \vdash \Delta$, where B is a valid formula occurring at α in S and $\Gamma \vdash \Delta$ is skolemized. Furthermore let γ' be a ground refutation which corresponds to a resolution refutation of $\mathrm{CL}(\psi, \alpha)$ and $\|\gamma\| = \max\{\|C\| \mid C \text{ in } \gamma\}$. Then there exists a proof $\hat{\gamma}[\psi]$ of $\Gamma \vdash \Delta$ with atomic cuts and $l(\hat{\gamma}[\psi]) \leq 2 \cdot l(\psi)l(\gamma)(2\|\gamma\| + 1)$.*

Proof. see [2]

To illustrate the whole procedure described above we continue with Example 1.

Example 2. Let ψ' be the proof of the sequent

$$S : A \to A, (\forall x)(P(x) \to Q(x)) \vdash (\exists y)(P(a) \to Q(y))$$

as defined in Example 1. We have shown that

$$\mathrm{CL}(\psi', \alpha) = \{P(u) \vdash Q(u), \ \vdash P(a), \ Q(v) \vdash\}$$

where α is the occurrence of $A \to A$ in S.

We first define the projections of ψ' w.r.t. clauses in $\mathrm{CL}(\psi', \alpha)$:

We start with $\psi'[C_1]$, the projection of ψ' to $C_1 : P(u) \vdash Q(u)$:
The problem can be reduced to the construction of $\psi_1[C_1]$ because of

$$\mathrm{CL}(\psi_1, \alpha_1) = \{P(u) \vdash Q(u)\}.$$

By definition of ψ_1 and of the projection, $\psi_1[C_1]$ is a proof of

$$P(u), (\forall x)(P(x) \to Q(x)) \vdash Q(u).$$

The last inference in ψ' applies to ancestors of α and thus $\psi'[C_1]$ is defined as

$$\frac{(\psi_1[C_1])}{\dfrac{P(u), (\forall x)(P(x) \to Q(x)) \vdash Q(u)}{P(u), (\forall x)(P(x) \to Q(x)) \vdash (\exists y)(P(a) \to Q(y)), Q(u)}} \ w : r$$

We proceed "inductively" and construct $\psi_1[C_1]$:

$$\frac{\dfrac{P(u) \vdash P(u) \quad Q(u) \vdash Q(u)}{\dfrac{P(u), P(u) \to Q(u) \vdash Q(u)}{P(u), (\forall x)(P(x) \to Q(x)) \vdash Q(u)} \ \forall : l} \ \to: l}{}$$

Putting the parts together we eventually obtain $\psi'[C_1]$:

$$\frac{\dfrac{\dfrac{P(u) \vdash P(u) \quad Q(u) \vdash Q(u)}{P(u), P(u) \to Q(u) \vdash Q(u)} \ \to: l}{\dfrac{P(u), (\forall x)(P(x) \to Q(x)) \vdash Q(u)}{P(u), (\forall x)(P(x) \to Q(x)) \vdash (\exists y)(P(a) \to Q(y)), Q(u)}} \ \forall : l}{} \ w : r$$

For $C_2 = \vdash P(a)$ we obtain the projection $\psi'[C_2]$:

$$\frac{\dfrac{\dfrac{\dfrac{P(a) \vdash P(a)}{P(a) \vdash P(a), Q(v)} \ w : r}{\vdash P(a) \to Q(v), P(a)} \ \to: r}{\vdash (\exists y)(P(a) \to Q(y)), P(a)} \ \exists : l}{(\forall x)(P(x) \to Q(x)) \vdash (\exists y)(P(a) \to Q(y)), P(a)} \ w : l$$

In the next step we take a resolution refutation γ of $\mathrm{CL}(\psi, \alpha)$, construct a ground projection $\gamma\sigma$ via a ground substitution σ and insert appropriate instances of $\psi[C]\sigma$ into $\gamma\sigma$. The result is a proof with (only) atomic cuts of a sequent S' in which the occurrence α is eliminated.

Recall that

$$\mathrm{CL}(\psi', \alpha) = \{C_1 : P(u) \vdash Q(u), \ C_2 : \vdash P(a), \ C_3 : Q(u) \vdash\}.$$

First we define a resolution refutation δ of $CL(\psi', \alpha)$:

$$\cfrac{\cfrac{\vdash P(a) \quad P(u) \vdash Q(u)}{\vdash Q(a)} \; R \qquad Q(v) \vdash}{\vdash} \; R$$

and a corresponding ground refutation γ:

$$\cfrac{\cfrac{\vdash P(a) \quad P(a) \vdash Q(a)}{\vdash Q(a)} \; R \qquad Q(a) \vdash}{\vdash} \; R$$

The ground substitution defining the ground projection is

$$\sigma = \{u \leftarrow a, v \leftarrow a\}.$$

Let $\chi_1 = \psi'[C_1]\sigma$, $\chi_2 = \psi'[C_2]\sigma$ and $\chi_3 = \psi'[C_3]\sigma$. For a more compact representation let us write B for $(\forall x)(P(x) \to Q(x))$ and C for $(\exists y)(P(a) \to Q(y))$.

Then $\hat{\gamma}[\psi']$ is of the form

$$\cfrac{\cfrac{\cfrac{\overset{(\chi_2)}{B \vdash C, P(a)} \quad \overset{(\chi_1)}{P(a), B \vdash C, Q(a)}}{B, B \vdash C, C, Q(a)} \; cut \qquad \overset{(\chi_3)}{Q(a), B \vdash C}}{\cfrac{B, B, B \vdash C, C, C}{B \vdash C} \; \text{contractions}} \; cut}{}$$

$\hat{\gamma}[\psi']$ can be considered as the result of a transformation eliminating the occurrence of $A \to A$ in S. ψ' was defined as $T_{cut}(\psi)$ where ψ is a proof of $B \vdash C$. Therefore $\hat{\gamma}[\psi']$ is a proof of the same end-sequent with only atomic cuts.   ♮

To put things together we obtain a procedure for occurrence-elimination, which can be transformed into a cut-elimination procedure via T_{cut}. We call this procedure OCERES (*OCcurence-Elimination by RESolution*) and display the main steps below:

procedure OCERES(ψ):

input: A (skolemized) proof ψ, a left-occurrence α of a valid formula in the end-sequent S of ψ.

output: A cut-free proof χ of the end-sequent S without the formula occurring at α:

1. Compute $CL(\psi, \alpha)$.
2. Compute a ground resolution refutation γ of $CL(\psi, \alpha)$.
3. Compute $\phi : \hat{\gamma}[\psi]$.
4. Eliminate the atomic cuts in ϕ.

Then the cut-elimination procedure itself is simply defined as

$$\mathrm{CERES}(\psi) = \mathrm{OCERES}(T_{cut}(\psi)).$$

Remark 5. As the worst-case complexity of cut-elimination is nonelementary (i.e. its time complexity cannot be bounded by a fixed iteration of the exponential function) we cannot expect CERES to be simply a fast algorithm. However it is shown in [2] that, for some sequences of **LK**-proofs, CERES gives a nonelementary speed-up of Gentzen's procedure. This speed-up is based on a "redundancy" at the atomic level of the proofs which can be detected in the construction of the set of clauses $\mathrm{CL}(\psi, \alpha)$, but not by Gentzen's procedure. By the availability of efficient refinements and search strategies for resolution CERES also performs quite well in experiments (see [3]).   ♯

5   Perspectives

It seems to be promising to incooperate mathematical knowledge about the imput proofs into the implementation of CERES by use of suitable resolution refinements, cf. the following simple example: We always know in a mathematical proof that a lemma (usually an occurence of a cut-formula on the right side of a sequent) is satisfiable in the intended structure, which might serve as a bases to apply semantic resoulution. On the other hand side, the usual cut-elimination procedures seem to correspond themselves to the application of certain resolution refinements to CERES. These refinements should be identified to develop criteria for the general comparison of cut-elimination strategies. Last not least the methods descibed in this extended abstract should be adapted to higher order systems as ACA_0 and beyond.

References

1. M. Baaz and A. Leitsch. Cut normal forms and proof complexity. *Annals of Pure and Applied Logic*, 97:127–177, 1999.
2. M. Baaz and A. Leitsch. Cut-elimination and redundancy-elimination by resolution. *J. Symbolic Computation*, 29:149–176, 2000.
3. M. Baaz, A. Leitsch, and G. Moser. System description: Cutres 01, cut elimination by resolution. In *Conference on automated deduction, CADE-16*, Lecture Notes in Artificial Intelligence, pages 212–216. Springer, 1999.
4. G. Gentzen. Untersuchungen über das logische schließen. *Mathematische Zeitschrift*, 39:405–431, 1934.
5. Jean-Yves Girard and Paul Taylor. *Proofs and Types*. Cambridge University Press, 1989.
6. R. Hähnle. Tableaux and related methods. In A. Robinson and A. Voronkov, editors, *Handbook of Automated Reasoning*, volume 1, pages 101–178. Elsevier, 2001.
7. H. Luckhard. Herbrand-Analysen zweier Beweise des Satzes von Roth: polynomiale Anzahlschranken. *The Journal of Symbolic Logic*, 54:234–263, 1989.
8. G. Takeuti. *Proof Theory*. North-Holland, second edition, 1987.

Author Index

Ahrendt, Wolfgang 211
Andreoli, Jean Marc 501
Areces, Carlos 156
Audemard, Gilles 195, 226

Baaz, Matthias 517
Benhamou, Belaid 226
Benzmüller, Christoph 144
Bernard, Andrew 31
Bertoli, Piergiorgio 195
Bofill, Miquel 456
Borralleras, Cristina 314
Boy de la Tour, Thierry 181
Brahm, Uwe 275
Brezhnev, Vladimir 144
Brown, Chad E. 408

Cheikhrouhou, Lassaad 144
Cimatti, Alessandro 195
Colton, Simon 285

Dill, David L. 392

Egly, Uwe 78

Fiedler, Armin 144
Fischer, Bernd 290
Ford, Jonathan 347
Franke, Andreas 144

Galmiche, Didier 111
Ganzinger, Harald 332
Georgieva, Lilia 260
Goldberg, Eugene 161
Gramlich, Bernhard 241

Heguiabehere, Juan 156
Hillenbrand, Thomas 275, 486
Horacek, Helmut 144
Horrocks, Ian 1
Hurd, Joe 134
Hustadt, Ullrich 260

Jamnik, Mateja 150

Keen, Enno 275

Kerber, Manfred 150
Kohlhase, Michael 139, 144
Korniłowicz, Artur 195
Kupferman, Orna 423

Larchey-Wendling, Dominique 94
Lassaad, Cheikhrouhou 144
Lee, Peter 31
Löchner, Bernd 486
Lucas, Salvador 314
Lynch, Christopher 471

Malik, Sharad 295
Meier, Andreas 144
Melis, Erica 144
Méry, Daniel 111
Møller, Jesper B. 129
Morawska, Barbara 471
Moschner, Markus 144
Moura, Leonardo de 438

Necula, George C. 47
Normann, Immanuel 144

Pan, Guoqiang 16
Paulson, Lawrence C. 377
Pichler, Reinhard 241
Pollet, Martin 144, 150

Rubio, Albert 314, 456
Rueß, Harald 438

Sattler, Ulrike 16, 423
Schmidt, Renate A. 260
Schneck, Robert R. 47
Schulz, Stephan 280
Schumann, Johann 290
Sebastiani, Roberto 195
Shankar, Natarajan 347
Siekmann, Jörg 144
Sorea, Maria 438
Sorge, Volker 144
Strecker, Martin 63
Stump, Aaron 392
Sutcliffe, Geoff 280

Theobald, Christian 275

Topić, Dalibor   275
Tour, Thierry Boy de la   181

Ullrich, Carsten   144

Vardi, Moshe Y.   16, 423

Weidenbach, Christoph   275

Whalen, Michael   290
Wirth, Claus-Peter   144

Zarba, Calogero G.   363
Zhang, Lintao   295
Zimmer, Jürgen   139, 144

Lecture Notes in Artificial Intelligence (LNAI)

Vol. 2174: F. Baader, G. Brewka, T. Eiter (Eds.), KI 2001: Advances in Artificial Intelligence. Proceedings, 2001. XIII, 471 pages. 2001.

Vol. 2175: F. Esposito (Ed.), AI*IA 2001: Advances in Artificial Intelligence. Proceedings, 2001. XII, 396 pages. 2001.

Vol. 2182: M. Klusch, F. Zambonelli (Eds.), Cooperative Information Agents V. Proceedings, 2001. XII, 288 pages. 2001.

Vol. 2190: A. de Antonio, R. Aylett, D. Ballin (Eds.), Intelligent Virtual Agents. Proceedings, 2001. VIII, 245 pages. 2001.

Vol. 2198: N. Zhong, Y. Yao, J. Liu, S. Ohsuga (Eds.), Web Intelligence: Research and Development. Proceedings, 2001. XVI, 615 pages. 2001.

Vol. 2203: A. Omicini, P. Petta, R. Tolksdorf (Eds.), Engineering Societies in the Agents World II. Proceedings, 2001. XI, 195 pages. 2001.

Vol. 2225: N. Abe, R. Khardon, T. Zeugmann (Eds.), Algorithmic Learning Theory. Proceedings, 2001. XI, 379 pages. 2001.

Vol. 2226: K.P. Jantke, A. Shinohara (Eds.), Discovery Science. Proceedings, 2001. XII, 494 pages. 2001.

Vol. 2246: R. Falcone, M. Singh, Y.-H. Tan (Eds.), Trust in Cyber-societies. VIII, 195 pages. 2001.

Vol. 2250: R. Nieuwenhuis, A. Voronkov (Eds.), Logic for Programming, Artificial Intelligence, and Reasoning. Proceedings, 2001. XV, 738 pages. 2001.

Vol. 2253: T. Terano, T. Nishida, A. Namatame, S. Tsumoto, Y. Ohsawa, T. Washio (Eds.), New Frontiers in Artificial Intelligence. Proceedings, 2001. XXVII, 553 pages. 2001.

Vol. 2256: M. Stumptner, D. Corbett, M. Brooks (Eds.), AI 2001: Advances in Artificial Intelligence. Proceedings, 2001. XII, 666 pages. 2001.

Vol. 2258: P. Brazdil, A. Jorge (Eds.), Progress in Artificial Intelligence. Proceedings, 2001. XII, 418 pages. 2001.

Vol. 2275: N.R. Pal, M. Sugeno (Eds.), Advances in Soft Computing – AFSS 2002. Proceedings, 2002. XVI, 536 pages. 2002.

Vol. 2281: S. Arikawa, A. Shinohara (Eds.), Progress in Discovery Science. XIV, 684 pages. 2002.

Vol. 2293: J. Renz, Qualitative Spatial Reasoning with Topological Information. XVI, 207 pages. 2002.

Vol. 2296: B. Dunin-Kęplicz, E. Nawarecki (Eds.), From Theory to Practice in Multi-Agent Systems. Proceedings, 2001. IX, 341 pages. 2002.

Vol. 2298: I. Wachsmuth, T. Sowa (Eds.), Gesture and Language in Human-Computer Interaction. Proceedings, 2001. XI, 323 pages.

Vol. 2302: C. Schulte, Programming Constraint Services. XII, 176 pages. 2002.

Vol. 2307: C. Zhang, S. Zhang, Association Rule Mining. XII, 238 pages. 2002.

Vol. 2308: I.P. Vlahavas, C.D. Spyropoulos (Eds.), Methods and Applications of Artificial Intelligence. Proceedings, 2002. XIV, 514 pages. 2002.

Vol. 2309: A. Armando (Ed.), Frontiers of Combining Systems. Proceedings, 2002. VIII, 255 pages. 2002.

Vol. 2313: C.A. Coello Coello, A. de Albornoz, L.E. Sucar, O.Cairó Battistutti (Eds.), MICAI 2002: Advances in Artificial Intelligence. Proceedings, 2002. XIII, 548 pages. 2002.

Vol. 2317: M. Hegarty, B. Meyer, N. Hari Narayanan (Eds.), Diagrammatic Representation and Inference. Proceedings, 2002. XIV, 362 pages. 2002.

Vol. 2321: P.L. Lanzi, W. Stolzmann, S.W. Wilson (Eds.), Advances in Learning Classifier Systems. Proceedings, 2002. VIII, 231 pages. 2002.

Vol. 2322: V. Mařík, O. Stěpánková, H. Krautwurmová, M. Luck (Eds.), Multi-Agent Systems and Applications II. Proceedings, 2001. XII, 377 pages. 2002.

Vol. 2333: J.-J.Ch. Meyer, M. Tambe (Eds.), Intelligent Agents VIII. Revised Papers, 2001. XI, 461 pages. 2001.

Vol. 2336: M.-S. Chen, P.S. Yu, B. Liu (Eds.), Advances in Knowledge Discovery and Data Mining. Proceedings, 2002. XIII, 568 pages. 2002.

Vol. 2338: R. Cohen, B. Spencer (Eds.), Advances in Artificial Intelligence. Proceedings, 2002. XII, 373 pages. 2002.

Vol. 2358: T. Hendtlass, M. Ali (Eds.), Developments in Applied Artificial Intelligence. Proceedings, 2002 XIII, 833 pages. 2002.

Vol. 2366: M.-S. Hacid, Z.W. Raś, D.A. Zighed, Y. Kodratoff (Eds.), Foundations of Intelligent Systems. Proceedings, 2002. XII, 614 pages. 2002.

Vol. 2375: J. Kivinen, R.H. Sloan (Eds.), Computational Learning Theory. Proceedings, 2002. XI, 397 pages. 2002.

Vol. 2385: J. Calmet, B. Benhamou, O. Caprotti, L. Henocque, V. Sorge (Eds.), Artificial Intelligence, Automated Reasoning, and Symbolic Computation. Proceedings, 2002. XI, 343 pages. 2002.

Vol. 2389: E. Ranchhod, N.J. Mamede (Eds.), Advances in Natural Language Processing. Proceedings, 2002. XII, 275 pages. 2002.

Vol. 2392: A. Voronkov (Ed.), Automated Deduction – CADE-18. Proceedings, 2002. XII, 534 pages. 2002.

Vol. 2393: U. Priss, D. Corbett, G. Angelova (Eds.), Conceptual Structures: Integration and Interfaces. Proceedings, 2002. XI, 397 pages. 2002.

Lecture Notes in Computer Science

Vol. 2349: J. Kontio, R. Conradi (Eds.), Software Quality – ECSQ 2002. Proceedings, 2002. XIV, 363 pages. 2002.

Vol. 2350: A. Heyden, G. Sparr, M. Nielsen, P. Johansen (Eds.), Computer Vision – ECCV 2002. Proceedings, Part I. XXVIII, 817 pages. 2002.

Vol. 2351: A. Heyden, G. Sparr, M. Nielsen, P. Johansen (Eds.), Computer Vision – ECCV 2002. Proceedings, Part II. XXVIII, 903 pages. 2002.

Vol. 2352: A. Heyden, G. Sparr, M. Nielsen, P. Johansen (Eds.), Computer Vision – ECCV 2002. Proceedings, Part III. XXVIII, 919 pages. 2002.

Vol. 2353: A. Heyden, G. Sparr, M. Nielsen, P. Johansen (Eds.), Computer Vision – ECCV 2002. Proceedings, Part IV. XXVIII, 841 pages. 2002.

Vol. 2355: M. Matsui (Ed.), Fast Software Encryption. Proceedings, 2001. VIII, 169 pages. 2001.

Vol. 2358: T. Hendtlass, M. Ali (Eds.), Developments in Applied Artificial Intelligence. Proceedings, 2002 XIII, 833 pages. 2002. (Subseries LNAI).

Vol. 2359: M. Tistarelli, J. Bigun, A.K. Jain (Eds.), Biometric Authentication. Proceedings, 2002. X, 197 pages. 2002.

Vol. 2360: J. Esparza, C. Lakos (Eds.), Application and Theory of Petri Nets 2002. Proceedings, 2002. X, 445 pages. 2002.

Vol. 2361: J. Blieberger, A. Strohmeier (Eds.), Reliable Software Technologies – Ada-Europe 2002. Proceedings, 2002 XIII, 367 pages. 2002.

Vol. 2363: S.A. Cerri, G. Gouardères, F. Paraguaçu (Eds.), Intelligent Tutoring Systems. Proceedings, 2002. XXVIII, 1016 pages. 2002.

Vol. 2364: F. Roli, J. Kittler (Eds.), Multiple Classifier Systems. Proceedings, 2002. XI, 337 pages. 2002.

Vol. 2366: M.-S. Hacid, Z.W. Raś, D.A. Zighed, Y. Kodratoff (Eds.), Foundations of Intelligent Systems. Proceedings, 2002. XII, 614 pages. 2002. (Subseries LNAI).

Vol. 2367: J. Fagerholm, J. Haataja, J. Järvinen, M. Lyly, P. Råback, V. Savolainen (Eds.), Applied Parallel Computing. Proceedings, 2002. XIV, 612 pages. 2002.

Vol. 2368: M. Penttonen, E. Meineche Schmidt (Eds.), Algorithm Theory – SWAT 2002. Proceedings, 2002. XIV, 450 pages. 2002.

Vol. 2369: C. Fieker, D.R. Kohel (Eds.), Algebraic Number Theory. Proceedings, 2002. IX, 517 pages. 2002.

Vol. 2370: J. Bishop (Ed.), Component Deployment. Proceedings, 2002. XII, 269 pages. 2002.

Vol. 2372: A. Pettorossi (Ed.), Logic Based Program Synthesis and Transformation. Proceedings, 2001. VIII, 267 pages. 2002.

Vol. 2373: A. Apostolico, M. Takeda (Eds.), Combinatorial Pattern Matching. Proceedings, 2002. VIII, 289 pages. 2002.

Vol. 2374: B. Magnusson (Ed.), ECOOP 2002 – Object-Oriented Programming. XI, 637 pages. 2002.

Vol. 2375: J. Kivinen, R.H. Sloan (Eds.), Computational Learning Theory. Proceedings, 2002. XI, 397 pages. 2002. (Subseries LNAI).

Vol. 2378: S. Tison (Ed.), Rewriting Techniques and Applications. Proceedings, 2002. XI, 387 pages. 2002.

Vol. 2380: P. Widmayer, F. Triguero, R. Morales, M. Hennessy, S. Eidenbenz, R. Conejo (Eds.), Automata, Languages and Programming. Proceedings, 2002. XXI, 1069 pages. 2002.

Vol. 2382: A. Halevy, A. Gal (Eds.), Next Generation Information Technologies and Systems. Proceedings, 2002. VIII, 169 pages. 2002.

Vol. 2383: M.S. Lew, N. Sebe, J.P. Eakins (Eds.), Image and Video Retrieval. Proceedings, 2002. XII, 388 pages. 2002.

Vol. 2384: L. Batten, J. Seberry (Eds.), Information Security and Privacy. Proceedings, 2002. XII, 514 pages. 2002.

Vol. 2385: J. Calmet, B. Benhamou, O. Caprotti, L. Henocque, V. Sorge (Eds.), Artificial Intelligence, Automated Reasoning, and Symbolic Computation. Proceedings, 2002. XI, 343 pages. 2002. (Subseries LNAI).

Vol. 2386: E.A. Boiten, B. Möller (Eds.), Mathematics of Program Construction. Proceedings, 2002. X, 263 pages. 2002.

Vol. 2389: E. Ranchhod, N.J. Mamede (Eds.), Advances in Natural Language Processing. Proceedings, 2002. XII, 275 pages. 2002. (Subseries LNAI).

Vol. 2391: L.-H. Eriksson, P.A. Lindsay (Eds.), FME 2002: Formal Methods – Getting IT Right. Proceedings, 2002. XI, 625 pages. 2002.

Vol. 2392: A. Voronkov (Ed.), Automated Deduction – CADE-18. Proceedings, 2002. XII, 534 pages. 2002. (Subseries LNAI).

Vol. 2393: U. Priss, D. Corbett, G. Angelova (Eds.), Conceptual Structures: Integration and Interfaces. Proceedings, 2002. XI, 397 pages. 2002. (Subseries LNAI).

Vol. 2398: K. Miesenberger, J. Klaus, W. Zagler (Eds.), Computers Helping People with Special Needs. Proceedings, 2002. XXII, 794 pages. 2002.

Vol. 2399: H. Hermanns, R. Segala (Eds.), Process Algebra and Probabilistic Methods. Proceedings, 2002. X, 215 pages. 2002.

Vol. 2405: B. Eaglestone, S. North, A. Poulovassilis (Eds.), Advances in Databases. Proceedings, 2002. XII 199 pages. 2002.